DEACCESSIONED

NATIONALISMS & *Sexualities*

EDITED BY ANDREW PARKER, MARY RUSSO,
DORIS SOMMER, AND PATRICIA YAEGER

ROUTLEDGE • NEW YORK & LONDON

Published in 1992 by

Routledge
An imprint of Routledge, Chapman and Hall, Inc.
29 West 35th Street
New York, NY 10001

Published in Great Britain by

Routledge
11 New Fetter Lane
London EC4P 4EE

Copyright © 1992 by Routledge, Chapman and Hall, Inc.

Printed in the United States of America

All rights reserved. No part of this book may be reprinted or reproduced or utilized in any form or by any electronic, mechanical or other means, now known or hereafter invented, including photocopying and recording, or in any information storage or retrieval system, without permission in writing from the publisher.

Cover Art: Emil Nolde's *Akte und Eunuch* (1912),
courtesy of the Indiana University Art Museum.
Permission to quote from *M. Butterfly* by David Henry Hwang
Copyright © 1989 by David Henry Hwang, granted by New American Library,
a division of Penguin Books USA Inc., and by Penguin Books Ltd., UK.

Library of Congress Cataloging-in-Publication Data

Nationalism and sexualities / edited by Andrew Parker . . . [et al.].
p. cm.
Includes bibliographical references.
ISBN 0-415-90432-3 (cloth).—ISBN 0-415-90433-1 (pbk.)
1. Sex Customs—Cross-cultural studies. 2. Sex differences—Cross-cultural studies. 3. National characteristics—Cross-cultural studies. I. Parker, Andrew, 1953– .
GN484.3.N37 1991
306.7—dc20 91-32531
CIP

British Library Cataloguing in Publication Data also available.

Contents

Preface

Nationalisms and Sexualities was first imagined at Eve Sedgwick's house in Amherst, Massachusetts during a pajama party attended by the editors and several members of the editorial board of the newly-launched journal *Genders*. The historic international conference that grew out of these initial discussions, held at Harvard University on June 16–18, 1989, was sponsored jointly by the Harvard Center for Literary and Cultural Studies, the Radcliffe Project on Interdependence, and Amherst College. For their unstinting efforts on behalf of this occasion we remain massively indebted to our conference coordinator Allison Pingree; to Marjorie Garber and her staff at the Harvard Center for Literary and Cultural Studies; to President Matina Horner of Radcliffe College; and to Acting Dean of the Faculty Ralph Beals of Amherst College. We especially wish to thank those who participated in the conference but whose work could not be accommodated within the confines of the present volume: Benedict Anderson, Nancy Armstrong, Homi Bhabha, John Borneman, Purnima Bose, Paul Brophy, Kathryn Burns, Richard Burt, Anna C. Chave, Rey Chow, Carla Freccero, Susan Gilman, Ellen K. Goodell, Phillip Brian Harper, C. L. Innes, Amy Kaplan, Cora Kaplan, Vera Kreilkamp, Laszlo Kurti, Joseph Litvak, Peter Lutze, Robert K. Martin, Eileen McDonagh, Anne M. Menke, George L. Mosse, Montserrat Ordóñez, Nancy L. Paxton, Ruth Perry, Vernon Rosario,

Nancy Ruttenberg, Jane Shattuc, Victoria Smith, Anita Sokolsky, Rajani Sudan, Sara Suleri, and Gauri Viswanathan.

For financial support in the production of this collection we are pleased to acknowledge the assistance of Dean Ronald Rosbottom of Amherst College and the Hyder E. Rollins Publication Fund of the Harvard University English Department. Our editor at Routledge, William P. Germano, believed in the project even when its future seemed, at times, precarious.

We are grateful to the publishers of several journals for allowing us to reproduce essays appearing first in their pages. Henry Abelove's "Some Speculations on the History of Sexual Intercourse" is reprinted from *Genders*, no. 6 (Fall 1989), by permission of the author and the University of Texas Press. A somewhat different version of Sander L. Gilman's "Plague in Germany, 1939/1989" appeared in *MLN*, vol. 104, no. 5 (December 1989); permission granted by the author and The Johns Hopkins University Press. Gayatri Chakravorty Spivak's "Woman in Difference" is reprinted from *Cultural Critique*, no. 14 (Winter 1989–90), by permission of the author and Oxford University Press.

Finally, we thank Penguin Books Ltd. and New American Library, a division of Penguin USA Inc., for their permission to reproduce passages held in copyright from the play *M. Butterfly,* Copyright 1989 by David Henry Hwang.

A.P., M.R., D.S., P.Y.
Flag Day, 1991

Note on Cover Art

In late 1913, Nolde and his wife joined a scientific expedition traveling through Russia, Siberia, China and Japan to the South Seas. Always a nationalist, Nolde judged Japan to be "the Germany of the East," but did not believe that its people had the depth and substance of the Germans. This nationalism and his lifelong belief in racial purity were contradicted, however, by his actions after the South Seas trip. "In 1914, he wrote an enraged letter to the colonial office in Berlin, condemning the rape of tribal cultures by 'civilized' powers and insisting on the aesthetic worth of tribal art" . . . Ironically, the National Socialists considered the "Nordic" Nolde, a member of the party, one of the most contemptible of the "degenerate" artists.

Dagmar Grimm, "Emil Nolde," in Stephanie Barron, et al., *"Degenerate Art": The Fate of the Avant-Garde in Nazi Germany* (Los Angeles: L.A. County Museum of Art, 1991), pp. 315, 320.

Introduction

Andrew Parker, Mary Russo, Doris Sommer, and
Patricia Yaeger

On July 28, 1990 two ostensibly unrelated articles appeared side-by-side on the Op Ed page of *The New York Times*. In one of them, "An 'Ism' That Won't Go Away," the British journalist George Brock questioned the current "fashion" for pan-European institutions like the EEC by reminding his readers that "for the past two centuries nationalism has been the mainspring of history." Dismissing as wishful Eric Hobsbawm's belief that the power of nationalism is receding across the globe,[1] Brock cited recent events in French Canada and Eastern Europe to bolster his claim that "the nation satisfied a need for love and allegiance—and still does."

Whenever the power of the nation is invoked—whether it be in the media, in scholarly texts, or in everyday conversation—we are more likely than not to find it couched as a *love of country*: an eroticized nationalism. The reverse is also true, for the article printed next to Brock's, "Homophobia at the N.E.A.," shows that this commerce between eros and nation can run in the other direction as well. Here the U.S. playwrights Holly Hughes and Richard Elovich indicted John Frohnmayer of the National Endowment for the Arts for denying fellowships previously recommended to four performance artists (Hughes among them) whose works "deal with the politics of sexuality." Arguing that the inclusion of the word "homoerotic" in the list of the Endowment's funding restrictions unjustly targeted the U.S. gay and lesbian communities, Hughes and Elovich urged lesbian and gay artists to demand an end to all government censorship: "This is a First Amendment issue that affects all Americans."

The persistence of nationalism explained as a passionate "need," the rights of sexual minorities legitimated through a national discourse of civil liberties—these are the kinds of convergences that *Nationalisms and Sexualities* seeks to explore. Bringing together the work of international scholars in the fields of feminist, gay, postcolonial and "area" studies (many of whom presented preliminary versions of their essays at a 1989 conference held at Harvard University), this volume examines two of the most powerful global discourses shaping contemporary notions of identity. How is it that the world has come to see itself divided along the seemingly natural lines of national affiliation and sexual attachment? How do these categories interact with, constitute, or otherwise illuminate each other?

Nationalisms and Sexualities addresses these questions by focusing, from a variety of disciplinary and theoretical perspectives, on a wide range of geographical regions and historical moments. Our title reflects an obvious debt to the historian George L. Mosse's pioneering study *Nationalism and Sexuality*, one of the first sustained attempts to break with prevailing academic paradigms that treat nation and sexuality as discrete and autonomous constructs.[2] Where other scholars have discussed sexuality without reference to nation and nation without reference to sexuality—where some, indeed, simply conflate the national with "public" identity, the sexual with "private" behavior[3]—Mosse sketched a double history of European nationalism and "respectable" sexuality as these emerged together at the end of the eighteenth century. Concentrating primarily on Germany but also drawing on Italian, French and English materials, Mosse described not only how the proliferation of modern nationalisms in Europe influenced the construction of middle-class norms of the body and of sexual behavior. He also demonstrated how these codes of bourgeois morality could facilitate, in turn, the rise of fascist nation-states in the twentieth century.

Though we have pluralized Mosse's title in acknowledgment of his precedent and achievement, *Nationalisms and Sexualities* does not merely seek to broaden his frame of reference with the goal of including other times, other nations and other sexualities. To simply follow Mosse's lead would have been to assume what is not in fact the case: that "nation" and "sexuality" are themselves trans-historical, supra-national, or self-identical categories. Rather, the best recent work on nationalism suggests that, in Homi Bhabha's formulation, there is no privileged narrative of the nation, no "nationalism in general" such that any single model could prove adequate to its myriad and contradictory historical forms.[4]

In her essay in this volume, for example, Eve Sedgwick asks us to consider just how "ragged and unrationalizable" have become the "definitional relations" of modern nationhood. For although the nation functions globally today as an irreducible component of identity, the problem remains that this single term is incapable of registering the multiple and incommensurable differences dividing one nation from another (or from itself). What distinguishes the "nation-ness" of the United States, Sedgwick asks, from "that of the nation-ness of Canada, the different nation-ness of Mexico, of the Philippines, of the Navajo Nation (within the U.S.), of the Six Nations (across the U.S.-Canada border), the nationalisms of the non-nation Québec, the non-nationalism of the non-nation Hawaii, the histories of African-American nationalisms, and so forth and so forth and so forth"? Piling difference upon difference, Sedgwick concludes that there exists, for the nation, no "normal" way to be or define itself:

> The "other" of the nation in a given political or historical setting may be the pre-national monarchy, the local ethnicity, the diaspora, the trans-national corporate, ideological, religious or ethnic unit, the sub-national locale or the ex-colonial, often contiguous unit; the colony may become national vis à vis the homeland, or the homeland become national vis à vis the nationalism of its colonies; the nationalism of the homeland may be coextensive with or oppositional to its imperialism; and so forth.[5]

The only constant in all this variety may be that, as R. Radhakrishnan emphasizes in his essay, "nationalism is back today with a vengeance all over the world," and "neither the deracinating multi- or inter-national spread of capitalism nor the Marxist theoretical assimilation of the national question within an internationalist Communism has been able to do away with the urgencies of the imagined communities of nationalism."

The category of the nation—in both its ubiquity and its capacity for nearly infinite self-differentiation—thus presents a project like ours with a number of interpretive obstacles in the vertiginous ways that it generates distinctions and abstractions. Yet such attention to particular if complex instances seems necessary if we are to offer any resistance to the powerfully homogenizing versions of the nation that constrain, oppress, and eviscerate. This kind of attention has also helped to define the recent history of feminism in the United States, which has seen both its theory and its practice newly challenged by a massive repudiation of all-inclusive categories. One of the gains of academic feminism has been its hard-won recognition that gender relations cannot be "understood in stable or abiding terms" either within or between the borders of nations, and that while patriarchy may be universal, its specific structures and embodied effects are certainly not.[6] Elaborated over the past twenty years in socialist-feminist, psychoanalytic and deconstructive thought and in the writings of women of color, this insight has challenged the assumption inherited from nineteenth-century bourgeois feminism that women are naturally or essentially united by their "common" subordination. A further challenge, perhaps, would be to move beyond this reverse logic of anti-essentialism, to acknowledge that, by working politically and philosophically through the implications of the particular, new kinds of solidarities might be forged.[7]

Similar realizations are taking hold in studies of sexuality. Claiming with Foucault and many others, for example, that sexuality is culturally variable rather than a timeless, immutable essence, David Halperin argues that "the distinction between homosexuality and heterosexuality, far from being a fixed and immutable form of some universal syntax of sexual desire, can be understood as a particular conceptual turn in thinking about sex and desire that occurred in certain sectors of northern and northwestern European society in the eighteenth and nineteenth centuries." Rejecting the notion that the sexual nomenclatures of the contemporary West are "purely descriptive, trans-cultural, and trans-historical terms, equally applicable to every culture and period," Halperin poses a series of rhetorical questions to highlight the fact that the *meanings* of what might look to be similar sexual practices do not travel well (if at all) from one moment or region to the next:

> Does the "paederast," the classical Greek adult, married male who periodically enjoys penetrating a male adolescent share *the same sexuality* with the "berdache," the native American (Indian) adult male who from childhood has taken on many aspects of a woman and is regularly penetrated by the adult male to whom he has been married in a public and socially sanctioned ceremony? Does the latter share *the same sexuality* with the New Guinea tribesman and warrior who from the ages of eight to fifteen has been orally inseminated on a daily basis by older youths and who, after years of orally inseminating his juniors, will be married to an adult woman and have children of his own? Does anyone of these three persons share *the same sexuality* with the modern homosexual?[8]

While appreciating these specificities of national and sexual categories, the essays in this volume nevertheless do offer a number of apt generalizations concerning the interplay between nation and sexuality. Many have done so by drawing on Benedict Anderson's provocative study *Imagined Communities*. Though this short book has relatively little to say about gender or sexuality,[9] it furnishes a series of terms that have proven exceedingly useful for us. Noting both the "universality" of the modern concept of the nation and "the irremediable particularity of its concrete manifestations," Anderson suggests that nationalism might best be conceived "not as *an* ideology" but "as if it belonged with 'kinship' or 'religion,' rather than with 'liberalism' or 'fascism'" (15). Though modestly framed, this is a major recasting of existing accounts of the nation. For where others have condemned nationalism simply as an effect of false consciousness, Anderson redescribes it as a variable cultural artifact that is neither reactionary nor progressive in itself. From this anthropological perspective, he proposes a few overarching characteristics that help define the conditions of modern nationhood. In the first place, nations are *limited* "because even the largest of [nations] . . . has finite, if elastic boundaries, beyond which lie other nations" (16). Nations are also *imagined* "because the members of even the smallest nation will never know most of their fellow-members, meet them, or even hear of them, yet in the minds of each lives the image of their communion" (15). And finally, nations present themselves as *communities* "because, regardless of the actual inequality and exploitation that may prevail in each, the nation is always conceived as a deep, horizontal comradeship" (16).

This "deep, horizontal comradeship" spills into and out of libidinal economies in ways that are at once consistent and unpredictable. Many of our contributors recognize, in fact, that nearly every aspect of Anderson's account of the nation raises issues of gender and sexuality. For example, in explaining why national space is intrinsically limited ("no nation imagines itself coterminous with mankind"), Anderson himself observes that "in the modern world everyone can, should, will 'have' a nationality, as he or she 'has' a gender" (16, 14). Though undeveloped in his analysis, Anderson's comparison enables the crucial recognition that—like gender—nationality is a relational term whose identity derives from its inherence in a system of differences. In the same way that "man" and "woman" define themselves reciprocally (though never symmetrically), national identity is determined not on the basis of its own intrinsic properties but as a function of what it (presumably) is not. Implying "some element of alterity for its definition," a nation is ineluctably "shaped by what it opposes."[10] But the very fact that such identities depend constitutively on difference means that nations are forever haunted by their various definitional others. Hence, on the one hand, the nation's insatiable need to administer difference through violent acts of segregation, censorship, economic coercion, physical torture, police brutality.[11] And hence, on the other, the nation's insatiable need for representational labor to supplement its founding ambivalence, the lack of self-presence at its origin or in its essence.

If the obsessive representation of the nation as a community forms one of the most persistent responses to this ambivalence, such "unity" has been modeled in a wide variety of national cultures on gender and sexual norms. One need only recall the title of a book that sold like hotcakes during the recent Gulf War—*The Rape of Kuwait*—to appreciate how deeply ingrained has been the depiction of the homeland as a female body whose violation by foreigners requires its citizens and allies to rush to her defense. (In a gesture both homophobic and misogynist, U.S. bombardiers obliged by inscribing the message "Bend Over, Saddam" on the ordinance they dropped on Iraq.) So utterly pervasive that it remains as available to imperialists as to insurgents—"Women embody Algeria not only for Algerians in the days since independence, but also for the French colonizers"[12]— this trope of the nation-as-woman of course depends for its representational efficacy on a particular image of woman as chaste, dutiful, daughterly or maternal. If Britannia and Germania can thus be gendered feminine, this iconography operates despite or rather *because* of the actual experiences of their female populations: "No nationalism in the world has ever granted women and men the same privileged access to the resources of the nation-state." Their claims to nationhood frequently dependent upon marriage to a male citizen, women have been "subsumed only symbolically into the national body politic," representing in this process "the limits of national difference between men."[13]

George Mosse and Benedict Anderson both second this view that nationalism favors a distinctly homosocial form of male bonding. Mosse argues that "nationalism had a special affinity for male society and together with the concept of respectability legitimized the dominance of men over women."[14] For Anderson this recognition is deeply implicit: "The nation is always conceived as a deep, horizontal comradeship. Ultimately, it is this *fraternity* [emphasis ours] that makes it possible, over the past two centuries, for so many millions of people, not so much to kill, as willingly to die for such limited imaginings" (16). Typically represented as a passionate brotherhood, the nation finds itself compelled to distinguish its "proper" homosociality from more explicitly sexualized male-male relations, a compulsion that requires the identification, isolation, and containment of male homosexuality. Lee Edelman's essay in this volume addresses the "threat" posed to a national imaginary when male anal eroticism protrudes into public view. And in his essay on colonial New England, Jonathan Goldberg similarly demonstrates how sodomy and related practices needed to be repudiated to preserve the Puritan community as a "union between men."[15] In the rhetorical system Goldberg describes, women are predictably enshrined as The Mother, a "trope of ideal femininity, a fantasmatic female that secures male-male arrangements and an all male history."

This idealization of motherhood by the virile fraternity would seem to entail the exclusion of all nonreproductively-oriented sexualities from the discourse of the nation. Indeed, certain sexual identities and practices are less represented and representable in nationalism. Until recently, for example, lesbianism has been far less visible than male homosexuality in Euro-American civic discourses: "As an expression of female sexuality, it was ignored through most of the nineteenth century. This was not merely a 'love that dare not speak its name'—it did not even have a name."[16] Many factors contributed to this absence or misrecognition of lesbianism, including most importantly the limited access of women of all classes to the public sphere. Where the heterosexual family played such a central role in the nation's public imaginings that motherhood could be viewed as a national service, female nonreproductive sexuality and female-female eroticism were constrained, as a consequence, to operate within the domestic (or at least the private) domain.[17] By the early twentieth century, new public identities for women as workers, consumers and political leaders emerged with new national and international social movements. But even in this changing historical context, the representation of lesbianism in national discourse remained largely off-stage in that space described by Teresa de Lauretis as "socio-sexual (in)difference."[18]

A significant and largely unanswered question here is the relationship between nationalism, women's political movements and the representation of sexual difference*(s)*. Historically, female solidarity emerged in the West after the first waves of nationalist fervor receded; working for such issues as suffrage, welfare and reproductive rights, women's movements challenged the inequalities concealed in the vision of a "common" nationhood. In anti-colonial struggles, on the other hand, feminist programs have been sacrificed to the cause of national liberation and, in the aftermath of independence, women have been reconsigned to their formerly "domestic" roles. It thus is difficult to say in advance whether or how different feminisms must negotiate through or around national political discourses.[19] De Lauretis nevertheless holds open the possibility of "a conceptual and erotic space" where women could recognize women concurrently "as subjects and as objects of female desire" (155). Theoretically, this space facilitates an *ironic* lesbian rewriting of the hegemonic erotic ethos and constructions of femininity that, from Plato onwards, have "had the effect of securing the heterosexual social contract by which all sexualities, all bodies, and all 'others' are bonded to an ideal/ideological hierarchy of males":

> The intimate relationship of sexual (in)difference with social (in)difference, whereby, for instance, the defense of the mother country and of (white) womanhood has served to bolster colonial conquest and racist violence throughout Western history, is nowhere more evident than in "the teaching of the ancient Greek philosophers," *pace* the Attorney General. Hence, the ironic rewriting of history in a female-only world of mothers and amazons by Monique Wittig and Sande Zeig in *Lesbian Peoples: Material for a Dictionary*.

> And hence, as well, the crucial emphasis in current feminist theory on articulating, specifying, and historicizing the position of the female social subject in the intricate experiential nexus of (often contradictory) heterogeneous differences, across discourses of race, gender, cultural and sexual identity, and the political working through of these differences toward a new, global, yet historically specific and even local, understanding of community. (161)

This, of course, is only one kind of imagining, located specifically within a Euro-American context. In her essay in this volume Gayatri Spivak appropriates and displaces de Lauretis' formulation of the space of socio-sexual (in)difference in order to describe another kind of invisible difference embodied in the figure of a female tribal bonded-labor prostitute. Spivak questions whether identity in this context has been or needs to be "motivated" by the discourses of nationalism and its sexually-marked categories: "It is possible to consider socio-sexual (in)difference philosophically prior to the reversal of the established codes, before the bestowal of *affective* value on homo- or hommo- or yet hetero-*sexuality*. To think therefore that the story is an evolutionary lament that *their* problems are not yet accessible to *our* solutions and they must simply come through into nationalism in order then to debate sexual preference is, I think, a mistake."

Whether a mistake or not, the fact remains (as Benedict Anderson recalls) that "nation-ness is the most universally legitimate value in the political life of our time" (12). That it is the nation rather than other forms of imagined collectivity that carries today this immense political freight has meant, of course, that disenfranchised groups frequently have had to appeal to national values precisely to register their claims as political. Though black nationalism in the U.S. might often better be termed black culturalism, what helps to lend this movement its identity *as* a movement is its very recourse to the rhetoric of the nation.[20] The same holds true for Queer Nation, the name recently adopted by gay and lesbian activists for their gender-transitive, militantly-antihomophobic organization. But the notion of a "Feminist Nation" (a contradiction in terms?) seems much less likely to mobilize women's gender-intransitive political work, and it is telling that Jill Johnston's *Lesbian Nation* remains anomalous in its apparently *un*ironic choice of the nation as an image of an all-female erotic community. R. Radhakrishnan wonders why this should be the case:

> Why is it that the advent of the politics of nationalism signals the subordination if not the demise of women's politics? Why does the politics of the "one" typically overwhelm the politics of the "other"? Why could the two not be coordinated within an equal and dialogic relationship of mutual accountability? What factors constitute the normative criteria by which a question or issue is deemed "political"? Why is it that nationalism achieves the ideological effect

of an inclusive and putatively macropolitical discourse, whereas the women's question—unable to achieve its own autonomous macropolitical identity—remains ghettoized within its specific and regional space?

Though these questions must remain suspended here, they will be broached repeatedly in the essays that follow. Taken as a whole, *Nationalisms and Sexualities* can only begin to chart a field of overlapping and contradictory networks. It does not of course attempt to cover this field either historically or geographically, nor have we in this introduction exhausted all of its possible interconnections.

The volume is divided into six thematic sections whose borders are far more permeable than they first may appear. Part I, "(De)Colonizing Gender," has as its general theme the ways that various colonialisms and postcolonialisms have altered consolidations of national and sexual identities. Widely divergent in both their sitings and methods of analysis, the essays in this section establish dialogues that develop throughout the collection. Julianne Burton's analysis of the Disney film *The Three Caballeros* (produced with U.S. government assistance) suggests that struggles in Latin America over political and cultural autonomy are often figured in relation to the "indigenous" female body, and that when cultural expression itself becomes feminized, cultural exchange with an imperial power takes the form of heterosexual (male) conquest. The parallels Burton draws between the cartoon's cross-species eroticism and the licentiousness it imagines "south of the border" complement the kinds of projections explored in Jonathan Goldberg's essay on sodomy in colonial New England. Goldberg reconstructs the rhetorical system underwriting the Puritans' articulation of sodomy with bestiality and other "savage" debaucheries, a system that implicates the bodies of criminalized males, women, "Indians," animals, and what centuries later will come to be termed gay men. His very use of the words "gay" and "nation" is particularly striking in this context: "While it is true that it is as anachronistic to speak of gay identity in relation to a colonial text as it is to read Bradford's *Plymouth Plantation* as a national text, the reading is justified by subsequent history"—a history culminating with recent U.S. Supreme Court decisions in which sodomy continues to function as "a question of national interest."

Rhonda Cobham's essay argues that in many recent African novels crises of post-colonial identity are typically elaborated as crises of gender and sexuality. Focusing on Nuruddin Farah's *Maps*, she describes how this novel's confusions of narrative boundaries, notably but not exclusively boundaries of sexual difference, stand indicatively for the fragile status of nationality both in the local community and in Somalia as a whole. A map of India covered with the body of a female tribal bonded-labor prostitute is the devastating image of spatial and bodily displacement evoked by Gayatri Spivak in her essay on a story by Mahasweta Devi. Whether and how this character's status can be made visible depends, in Spivak's reading, on her role within a political economy that resists reduction to prevailing accounts of decolonized space. Dealing also with postcolonial India, R. Radhakrishnan's essay disputes the contention that the nation is self-evidently *the* model of political legitimacy. Asking why nationalism should invariably entail the subordination of women's or other forms of "micropolitical" politics, he argues for a critical reappraisal of the normative criteria by which nationalism "becomes the binding and overarching umbrella that subsumes other and different political temporalities."

Part II, "Tailoring the Nation," discusses how the (ad)dress of the national subject may identify, disguise, distort or enhance the desired body politic. The volatility of attire as a marker of national and sexual status is described in these essays as part of a variable cultural nexus constructed from such elements as race, class and geography. As a visible sign of difference, dress can indicate the seams within a national culture where several of these elements are stitched together.[21] Arguing that transvestism functions in the play *M. Butterfly* as "a mark of gender undecidability and as an indication of category crisis elsewhere," Marjorie Garber shows how the cross-dresser stands at the crossroads where "racism and sexism . . . intersect with one another and with imperialist and colonialist fantasies." Transvestism is viewed here as analogous to spying and acting since all three involve "passing" for the national and sexual identities that they variously perform. Ann Rosalind Jones and Peter Stallybrass explain how the Irish mantle crystallized, for the early English colonizers, the image of Ireland as disorganized, unruly, and (hence) feminine. Ironically, English troops were eventually advised to adopt this mantle to protect themselves from the cold and damp of the Irish countryside: "If clothes make the man, what did it mean that the Englishman was now dressed like the Wild Irish?" Writing on the nineteenth-century Cuban novel *Cecilia Valdés*, Norman S. Holland concentrates on one of its seemingly marginal characters—the tailor—to reveal how a historic blend of the indigenous and the imported work together to pattern an emerging national consciousness. This stylish "miscegenation of clothes" corresponds to an idealized cross-mixing of races and classes even as it regulates the membership rolls of this newly-fashionable world.

Part III, "The Other Country," considers some of the ways that a nation can consolidate its identity by projecting beyond its own borders the sexual practices or gender behaviors it deems abhorrent.[22] Cindy Patton's essay describes one of the latest strategies of Western medicine to maintain its (racist and homophobic) distinction between a Western homosexual AIDS and an African heterosexual AIDS: the invention and promotion of "what had never truly existed before"—an African monogamous bourgeois family—"as the preferred prophylaxis in the catastrophe of 'African AIDS.'" Sander Gilman reads two German novels separated by half a century, finding a remarkable and frightening continuity in the ways that German-ness is constructed on the basis of "other" people's sexually-transmitted diseases. Where the second of Gilman's novels imagines the city of Berlin as an "AIDS-Ghetto," Aksenov's *The Island of Crimea*—the subject of Greta Slobin's essay—takes place in a fictive independent, capitalist enclave on the border of the Soviet Union. As "the 'feminine' counterpart to the Fatherland," Aksenov's Crimea reflects the misogyny and orientalism underlying a proleptically-resurgent, homosocial Russian nationalism.

This section also questions, however, the limits of the paradigm of "otherness" as an optic in the analysis of national and sexual identities. As Eve Sedgwick argues, "the topos of the creation, reification, and expulsion of the Other" can itself "fail to do justice to the complex activity, creativity, and engagement of those whom *it* figures simply as relegated objects." In describing the contradictions of Oscar Wilde's simultaneously "gay-affirming and gay-occluding orientalism," Sedgwick notes how recourse to the Other can make it difficult to "resist seeing [Wilde's] desired English body" as "simply the domestic Same." On the other hand, cultural or political features that appear indigenous and hence most worthy of patriotic (self-)celebration are often typical of other nations and even patterned after foreign models. Given our sometimes unspoken and even unacknowledged investments in nationalist feeling, we can miss the ironies of defining "us" against "them" when the "them" can be exemplars instead of enemies.[23] Missing the irony is less likely when, as in Donna Guy's analysis of Argentine "White Slavery," powerful Western nations project their own desires and deficiencies onto a non-European victim. But when, as Guy continues, Argentina ultimately becomes the internationally-recognized model for progressive citizenship legislation for women, "other countries" might respond with ambivalent identification.

Describing the moment of India's "birth," Salman Rushdie's novel *Midnight's Children* recalls graphically what it means to *imagine* a nation:

> A nation which had never previously existed was about to win its freedom, catapulting us into a world which, although it had five thousand years of history, although it had invented the game of chess and traded with Middle Kingdom Egypt, was nevertheless quite imaginary; into a mythical land, a country which would never exist except by the efforts of a phenomenal collective will—except in a dream we all agreed to dream.[24]

To say, however, that a nation is "imaginary" is not to consign it to the category of (mere) fiction; if it is a "dream" it is one possessing all the institutional force and affect of the real. "Communities are to be distinguished," writes Anderson, "not by their falsity/genuineness, but by the style in which they are imagined" (15). Anderson thus considers the roles played by print media in the production of these national styles, and we have tested and extended his insights in Part IV, "Spectacular Bodies." Newspapers, film, novels and theater all create sexed bodies as public spectacles, thereby helping to instill through representational practices an erotic investment in the national romance. But these same media can be deployed as well for other kinds of civic education, counter-narratives that reveal the dangers implicit in such castings of national history.[25]

The essays in this section consider the fates of a number of different bodies implicated in these spectacular constructions. Lee Edelman uses media reportage of a mid-1960s political scandal—the Jenkins Affair—to explore how a public restroom once "compromised" the interests of U.S. security. Finding Cold War rhetoric laden with the tropes of homophobia, he explains why male homosexuality could emerge, for "both the nuclear family and the nuclear state," as an "overriding national concern." Focusing on the films of the Hungarian director Márta Mészáros, Catherine Portuges notes some of the ways that state communism and its aftermath have influenced the representation of the female body. By seeking to produce images that are at once erotic and nonexploitative, Mészáros counters the portrayal of women in both Western cinema and in the work of her male national colleagues. Joyce Hope Scott traces connections between "insurrection and sex" in the history of U.S. black nationalism. Analyzing novels by Arna Bontemps, Sam Greenlee and Ishmael Reed, she describes how a "patriarchal vision of Black Power" relegates African-American women to "the margins of the struggle for freedom and equality." Stephen Tifft reads the public reception of Synge's *Playboy of the Western World* as a violent staging of the play's own psychodynamics. Arguing that Synge's Oedipal fantasy is so unstable as to make its audience identify with all of its structural positions, Tifft suggests that Irish nationalism suffers from a peculiar if calamitous predicament: a surfeit of Fathers to kill.

Juan Bautista Alberdi coined the slogan "To Govern is to Populate" in his 1852 *Bases* for the Argentine Constitution, and we have borrowed his words as the title for Part V. Alberdi's rival Domingo F. Sarmiento agreed at least on this point: that the interior "desert" had to be filled since without a dense and stable population, there literally could be no *res publica.* Other nations before and since have had to consider this relationship between demographic requirements and social control. Reviewing important new work on the population history of the "long eighteenth century" in England, Henry Abelove suggests that emerging standards of capitalist productivity coincided with "a remarkable increase in the *incidence* of cross-sex genital intercourse," a sudden vogue for reproductively-oriented heterosexuality that redefined other sexual practices as mere foreplay. In their essay on Singapore's "Great Marriage Debate," Geraldine Heng and Janadas Devan analyze the phobic social policies recently adopted by the state's governing Chinese elite. Attempting to counter the growing Malay and Indian populations that it figures pervasively as "feminine," the state has been promoting "a uterine nationalism" that imagines the educated female Chinese body as "a technology of defense." Exploring links between a population of working-class boys and concepts of national culture, Seth Koven charts "the homoerotic, national and imperial fantasies of male social welfare reformers in late-Victorian and Edwardian Britain." Having sought to unify the nation by transforming "rough lads" into model adult citizens, British reformers redirected their attention from settlement houses to the welfare state when, in the aftermath of the Boer War, the objects of their benevolence proved themselves to be "hooligans."

Part VI, "Women, Resistance and the State," considers the historical experience of particular feminisms in their relations with movements for national liberation. Resistance movements are of course also "imagined communities," and the essays here explain that such imaginings are regularly predicated upon constructions of women's bodies. Valentine Moghadam points out, for example, that the defense of purdah helped reinforce Mujahideen resistance to the "modernizing" Afghan regime. In describing the sexual politics implicit in Islamist movements, she notes how revolutionary change in Iran and Afghanistan forced dramatic and unpredictable rearticulations of gender rules and gender power. Similarly, in Ketu Katrak's account, Gandhi sought to utilize the myth of "the Indian woman's submissiveness, her ability to suffer silently" as an image of "the political resistance necessary for a nationalist struggle." Ironically, Gandhi's emphasis on non-violence had violent outcomes for women; his symbols of female obedience became repressive social instruments even as they helped to create new mechanisms for managing national crisis.

But if women's bodies can become ciphers in the imaginings of male resistance fighters, women—as Moghadam and Katrak go on to argue—have also been pulled onto the streets and actively involved in organized protests. Indeed, Mary Layoun's essay describes the ways that Palestinian women's participation in the *intifada* may challenge the prevailing nationalist paradigms that underwrite the Israeli/Palestinian conflict. In her analysis of a marketplace tragedy, she turns our attention away from state power toward "the everyday struggles and choices of everyday folk, their attempts to come to terms with and sometime change the shape" of these hegemonic narratives.

While *Nationalisms and Sexualities* as a whole thus seeks to confound many of the dominant categories of nationalism and sexuality, we want to stress, in concluding, that these categories remain volatile sites for condensing and displacing the ecstacies and terrors of political life. For it is the lived crises endured by national and sexual bodies that form our most urgent priorities. These crises are not simply opportunities for the state to activate its strategies of containment and to reimpose its normativities. They also offer dissenting subjects the possibility of producing contestatory practices, narratives of resistance that may reconfigure the horizons of what counts globally today as "the political."

NOTES

1. See E. J. Hobsbawm, *Nations and Nationalisms Since 1780: Programme, Myth, Reality* (Cambridge: Cambridge University Press, 1990), esp. pp. 163–183.

2. George L. Mosse, *Nationalism and Sexuality: Middle-Class Morality and Sexual Norms in Modern Europe* (Madison, WI: University of Wisconsin Press, 1985). See also the essays on Britain and Italy collected in *Formations of Nations and People* (London: Routledge, 1984).

3. As Anne McClintock observes, "Theories of nationalism have tended to ignore gender as a category constitutive of nationalism itself" ("'No Longer in a Future Heaven': Women and Nationalism in South Africa," *Transition*, 51 [1991], p. 120). A recent case in point would be the Irish Field Day pamphlets of Terry Eagleton, Fredric Jameson, and Edward Said (now collected in Seamus Deane, ed., *Nationalism, Colonialism, and Literature* [Minneapolis: University of Minnesota Press, 1990]). While Eagleton's is the only one of the three that treats the topic of "sexual politics" (24), it does so merely in passing and merely as an analogue to "nationalist struggles."

4. See Homi K. Bhabha, ed., *Nation and Narration* (New York: Routledge, 1990). Étienne Balibar argues as well that nationalisms "do not work everywhere the same way: in a sense they must work everywhere in a *different* way, this is part of the national 'identity'" ("Racism as Universalism," *New Political Science*, 16/17 [Fall/Winter 1989], p. 19).

5. In similarly stressing the "heterogeneity" of "that great rational abstraction—agency in a nation," Gayatri Spivak describes other fundamental differences between being "national in an equally-divided-religion state, national in a majority-religion state, exile from a theocratic state. . . . The migrant wants to redefine the nation, the post-colonial wants to identify the nation, the exile wants to explain and restore the nation

and be an agent in its normative and privative discourse" ("Reading *The Satanic Verses,*" *Public Culture,* 2, 1 [Fall 1989], p. 94).

6. Judith Butler, *Gender Trouble: Feminism and the Subversion of Identity* (New York: Routledge, 1989), pp. 1, 13. And yet, as Rey Chow explains in discussing the Chinese authoress Ding Ling, efforts to acknowledge the effect of national differences on gender and sexual identity can always reify—even if with the "best" of motives—the very differences in question: "The attempt to deconstruct the hegemony of *patriarchal* discourses through feminism is itself foreclosed by the emphasis on 'Chinese' as a mark of absolute difference. To my mind, it is when the West's 'other women' are prescribed their 'own' national and ethnic identity in this way that they are most excluded from having a claim to the reality of their existence" (*Woman and Chinese Modernity: The Politics of Reading between West and East* [Minneapolis: University of Minnesota Press, 1991], p. 163).

7. See Diana Fuss, *Essentially Speaking: Feminism, Nature and Difference* (New York: Routledge, 1989), and the special issue of *differences,* 1, 2 (Summer 1989) devoted to the possibilities of anti-anti-essentialism.

8. David M. Halperin, *One Hundred Years of Homosexuality* (New York: Routledge, 1990), pp. 43, 46. See in this volume the essays by Rhonda Cobham and Cindy Patton, both of which discuss the limits of using the Western term "homosexual" to describe African same-sex practices. Where, in Cobham's account, many African societies are not necessarily hostile to homoerotic behaviors but reject the notion of gay *identity* as a legacy of Western colonialism, Western scientists also deny the existence of African "homosexuality" because, as Patton argues, to do otherwise would be to admit the baselessness of their distinction between (homosexual) AIDS and (heterosexual) African AIDS.

9. Benedict Anderson, *Imagined Communities: Reflections on the Origin and Spread of Nationalism* (London: Verso, 1983); page references will be cited directly in the text above. Doris Sommer notes this omission while using Foucault and Anderson to supplement each other's absences; see "Love and Country in Latin America: An Allegorical Speculation," *Cultural Critique,* 16 (Fall 1990), pp. 109–128 (this is a shortened version of the introductory chapters of *Foundational Fictions: The National Romances of Latin America* [Berkeley: University of California Press, 1991]).

10. Perry Anderson, "Nation-States and National Identity," *London Review of Books,* May 9, 1991, p. 3, and John Breuilly, *Nationalism and the State* (Chicago: University of Chicago Press, 1982), p. 380. One need only recall, of course, the history of European anti-Semitism, the recent spate of English-only legislation in the U.S. or

current struggles over the identity of British national culture in order to recognize that such differences can as easily be internal as external: "National identification with 'our kind' is based on the fantasy of an enemy, an alien who has insinuated himself into our society and constantly threatens us with habits, discourse, and rituals which are not 'our kind'" (Renata Salecl, "National Identity and Socialist Moral Majority," *New Formations*, 12 [Winter 1990], p. 25). Similarly emphasizing the "lines of inclusion and exclusion that mark out the national community," Paul Gilroy notes sardonically that "to speak of the British or the English people is to speak of *white* people" ("One Nation under a Groove: The Cultural Politics of 'Race' and Racism in Britain," in David Theo Goldberg, *Anatomy of Racism* [Minneapolis: University of Minnesota Press, 1990], pp. 266, 268; see also Gilroy's *There Ain't No Black in the Union Jack* [London: Hutchinson, 1987]).

11. Cf. Khachig Tölölyan, "The Nation-State and Its Others," *Diaspora*, 1, 1 (Spring 1991), p. 6: "In [the nation-state], differences are assimilated, destroyed, or assigned to ghettoes, to enclaves demarcated by boundaries so sharp that they enable the nation to acknowledge the apparently singular and clearly fenced-off differences *within* itself, while simultaneously reaffirming the privileged homogeneity of the rest, as well as the difference *between* itself and what lies over its frontiers."

12. Winifred Woodhull, "Unveiling Algeria," *Genders*, 10 (Spring 1991), p. 117.

13. McClintock, "'No Longer in a Future Heaven,'" p. 105. In her influential essay on "The Traffic in Women," Gayle Rubin focused attention on ways that "marriage systems intersect with large-scale political processes such as state-making" (in Karen V. Hansen and Ilene J. Philipson, eds., *Women, Class, and the Feminist Imagination: A Socialist-Feminist Reader* [Philadelphia: Temple University Press, 1990], p. 106). Though Rubin was discussing Madagascar, her observation accords with the dynastic kinship systems of early-modern Europe where the notion of the family as the nation-in-miniature was not, as it has become in the modern nation-state, merely a common conceit.

14. Mosse, *Nationalism and Sexuality*, p. 67.

15. See also Robert Schwartzwald, "Fear of Federasty: Québec's Inverted Fictions," in Hortense J. Spillers, ed., *Comparative American Identities: Race, Sex and Nationality in the Modern Text* (New York: Routledge, 1991), pp. 175–195. While noting that Québécois society has been comparatively open to lesbians and gays, Schwartzwald indicates how the rhetoric of its anti-colonialism often discloses "the tragic resiliency of homophobic tropes."

16. Mosse, *Nationalism and Sexuality*, p. 91

17. On women and the public sphere in Western political discourse, see Jean Bethke Elshtain, *Public Man, Private Woman: Women in Social and Political Thought* (Amherst, MA: University of Massachusetts Press, 1982); Nancy Fraser, "Rethinking the Public Sphere," *Social Text*, 25/26 (1990), pp. 56–80; and Joan B. Landes, *Women in the Public Sphere in the Age of the French Revolution* (Ithaca: Cornell University Press, 1988). A cross-cultural study of public spheres would stress that what counts as privacy is historically contingent. For instance, while Cuban lesbian and gay life is marked by "the complete absence of a public sphere" of the kind characteristic of "the United States or Western European urban centers," Cuban "private space is far wider than in the United States, encompassing virtually all behavior outside the purview of official sanction or attention" (Lourdes Arguelles and B. Ruby Rich, "Homosexuality, Homophobia, and Revolution: Notes toward an Understanding of the Cuban Lesbian and Gay Experience," in Martin Duberman, Martha Vicinus, and George Chauncey, Jr., eds., *Hidden from History* [New York: New American Library, 1989], p. 452).

18. Teresa de Lauretis, "Sexual Indifference and Lesbian Representation," *Theater Journal*, 40, 2 (May 1988), pp. 151–177; subsequent page numbers will be cited directly in the text above. Here one may appreciate the contradictory constructions of Gertrude Stein's lesbian identity and expatriate hyper-Americanness as they intersected in the space, neither purely public nor private, of her Parisian salon.

19. But as McClintock underscores, "To ask women to wait until after the revolution serves merely as a strategic tactic to defer women's demands. Not only does it conceal the fact that nationalisms are from the outset constituted in gender power, but, as the lessons of international history portend, women who are not empowered to organize during the struggle will not be empowered to organize after the struggle" ("'No Longer in a Future Heaven,'" p. 122). For more on this question see Miranda Davies, ed., *Third World—Second Sex: Women's Struggles and National Liberation*, 2 vols. (London: Zed Press, 1983 and 1987); Kumari Jayawardena, *Feminism and Nationalism in the Third World* (London: Zed Press, 1986); Chandra Talpade Mohanty, Ann Russo, and Lourdes Torres, eds., *Third World Women and the Politics of Feminism* (Bloomington: Indiana University Press, 1991); Kumkum Sangari and Sudesh Vaid, *Recasting Women: Essays in Indian Colonial History* (New Brunswick, NJ: Rutgers University Press, 1990); and Nira Yuval-Davis and Floya Anthias, eds., *Women—Nation—State* (New York: St. Martin's Press, 1989).

20. Which means that, on occasion, it may find misogyny and homophobia congenial; see in this volume the essay by Joyce Hope Scott, and Essex Hemphill's "If Freud Had Been a Neurotic Colored Woman," *Out/Look*, 13 (Summer 1991), pp. 50–55.

21. Codes of dress may be regulated by institutional demands (as in the military),

by aesthetic requirements (as in kinds of transvestite theater), by custom as well as by fashion. Different ways of wearing the "same" apparel of course can drastically alter its meaning. For instance, wrapping oneself in the U.S. flag (so common now that it serves perhaps as the national costume *par excellence*) can be read as a sign of consummate patriotism, dissidence, or even irony. Madonna's recent video "Get Out the Vote" may be a simultaneous enactment of all three.

22. Cf. Rey Chow, "Violence in the Other Country: Preliminary Remarks on the 'China Crisis,' June 1989," *Radical America*, 22, 4 (1988), p. 28: "China as a spectacle becomes, in its relation to the West, 'woman' in the sense that it is the 'Other' onto which the unthinkable is projected, that which breaks the limits of civilized imagination." Chow's essay was first presented at the Nationalisms and Sexualities Conference.

23. See Breuilly, *Nationalism and the State*, p. 342. One such irony would be that "the political claims that are most urgent in decolonized space" have themselves been "coded within the legacy of imperialism: nationhood, constitutionality, citizenship, democracy, socialism, even culturalism. Within the historical frame of exploration, colonization, and decolonization, what is being *effectively* reclaimed is a series of regulative political concepts, the supposedly authoritative narrative of whose production was written elsewhere, in the social formations of Western Europe" (Gayatri Chakravorty Spivak, "The Making of Americans, the Teaching of English, and the Future of Cultural Studies," *New Literary History*, 21 [1990], p. 794).

24. Salman Rushdie, *Midnight's Children* (New York: Avon, 1980), pp. 129–130.

25. See Kobena Mercer, "Recoding Narratives of Race and Nation," *The Independent*, January/February 1989, pp. 19–26.

Part I

(De)Colonizing Gender

Chapter 1

Don (Juanito) Duck and the Imperial-Patriarchal Unconscious: Disney Studios, the Good Neighbor Policy, and the Packaging of Latin America

Julianne Burton

Title Song
"We're Three Caballeros"
(Sung to the tune of "Que Lindo es Jalisco"[1])

We're three caballeros
Three gay caballeros
They say we are birds of a feather
We're happy amigos
No matter where he goes,
Where one two and three goes,
We're always together.

We're three happy chappies
with snappy serapes
You'll find us beneath our sombreros
We're brave and we'll say so
We're bright as a peso.
"Who say so?" "We say so!"
The three caballeros.

Through fair or stormy weather
We stand close together
Like books on a shelf
Guitars here beside us
To play as we go
We sing and we samba
We shout, "Ay, caramba!"
"What means 'Ay, caramba!'?"
Oh yes, I don't know.

Like brother to brother,
We're all for each other
Like three caballeros
Together we'll stay.

Through fair or stormy weather
We stand close together
Like books on a shelf
and friends though we may be
When some Latin baby
Says yes, no or maybe,
Each man is for himself!

In the summer of 1987, with the runaway success of Luis Valdez's *La Bamba,* Hollywood suddenly opened its eyes (and its pocketbook) to the Hispanic. Robert Redford's *The Milagro Beanfield War,* Jane Fonda's *Old Gringo* and the Edward James Olmos vehicle *Stand and Deliver* were all part of what looks, in retrospect, like only a brief spark of interest, though it was hyped at the time as a veritable fireball. Numerous articles predicting the imminent Latinization of Hollywood appeared in the press.[2] In May 1988, Geraldo Rivera produced "Heyday for Hispanics in Hollywood." That August, *Newsweek* dedicated an entire issue to America's Latino population, emphasizing the arts and putting Olmos on the cover.

That transitory and transparently opportunistic fascination was not the first time that Hollywood has "looked Latin." The logistic and propagandistic exigencies of World War II prompted a similar "about face." This was the era of Dolores del Rio, Lupe Velez, Cesar Romero, Desi Arnaz, and the self-caricaturing but nonetheless emblematic Carmen Miranda, when Latin rhythms and entertainers were all the rage and hosts of Hollywood stars went "Flying Down to Rio" or "Down Argentine Way" or spent "A Weekend in Havana"—to name just a few titles from the period. Made-in-Hollywood-USA and exported en masse to Latin American screens, many of these projective constructs of a northern imaginary struck Latin Americans as distorted and demeaning. There is a long history of protests registered by country after country (Brazil over *Rio's Road to Hell* [1931], Cuba over *Cuban Love Song* [1931], Mexico over *Girl of the Rio* [1932] and *Viva Villa!* [1934]) in response to the condescending images of Latin-ness elaborated in Hollywood."[3]

This essay undertakes to examine one instance of the intricate process of appropriation and projection through which one Hollywood dream factory constructed its Other(s)—an exceptional instance that, despite the best intentions and a wealth of creative talent and effort, seems to prove the rule of cross-cultural borrowing as self-aggrandizing appropriation, of Good-Neighborliness as foil for empire-building-as-usual.

Cartoons are an unlikely vehicle for propaganda. Disney is an unlikely locus of lasciviousness. Yet in addition to predictable fun, frolic and fireworks, *The Three Caballeros* (1945) indulges its audience in scenes of cross-dressing and cross-species coupling, of blatant sexual punning and predation, in tales of conquest in which the patriarchal unconscious and the imperial unconscious insidiously overlap. What, we ask ourselves as we begin to glimpse these invested meanings coalescing beneath the film's chaotic surface exuberance, do *kids* make of this? What did the Latin Americans make of it? What did the Disney staff make of it even *while* they were making it? Why is this film so different from the prototypical Disney product? These questions, which initially lead us from the film to the history of the project which engendered it, will eventually bring us back to the film and a series of propositions about its textual operations and ideological effects.

FAR FROM INNOCENCE

Precisely because of their assumed innocence and innocuousness, their inherent ability—even obligation—to defy all conventions of realistic representation, animated cartoons offer up a fascinating zone within which to examine how a dominant culture constructs its subordinates. As a nonphotographic application of a photographic medium, they are freed from the basic cinematic expectation that they convey an "impression of reality." (The phrase belongs to the influential French critic Andre Bazin, who theorized that images from the real world press themselves upon the celluloid like a fingerprint.) The function and essence of cartoons is in fact the reverse: the impression of *ir*reality, of intangible and imaginary worlds in chaotic, disruptive, subversive collision. Animated cartoons reinforce this otherworldliness when their "subjects" are not humanoid but "animaloid," and in this category, Disney stands *über alles.*

The myth of the unassailable ideological innocence of Disney's anthropomorphic zoology was shattered in 1971 with the publication of Ariel Dorfman and Armand Mattelart's pathbreaking *How to Read Donald Duck.*[4] This intellectually ingenious and politically explosive little paperback cut to the measure of a comic book applied sophisticated interpretive methodologies derived from advanced literary and communications theory to examples of "low" or "popular" culture—in this case, Disney comic strips. Writing in Chile in the first year of Salvador Allende's Popular Unity coalition, Dorfman (a Chilean) and Mattelart (a Belgian) exposed the imperialist subtext lurking behind the façade of innocuous and "childish" entertainment, revealing all its underlying racist and chauvinist biases. One of their most intriguing arguments highlights the asexuality of sex/gender relations in this Disneyan universe of cousins and uncles, from which any acknowledgement of direct biological reproduction—not just maternity but paternity as well—has mysteriously vanished. Intriguingly, the authors argue that rather than undermining unchallenged patriarchal authority, this omission reinforces it.[5]

The Three Caballeros and the set of films of which it is the culmination are another product of the "collective unconscious" of that culture-industry-cum-empire known as Walt Disney Productions. *The Three Caballeros* was released in 1945, when Disney's reputation was at its zenith. (*Snow White and the Seven Dwarfs,* the studio's first animated feature, had been released in 1937, to be followed by *Fantasia* in 1940, *Dumbo* in 1941, and *Bambi* in 1942.) For some, *The Three Caballeros*'s principle interest lies in its technical accomplishment. It offers the first sustained mixing of live action and animation within the same frame in a color feature. The technology which Disney developed (multiplane cameras and three-color Technicolor processes) provided the basis for the 1988 tour de force *Who Framed Roger Rabbit?* and its sequels. But for others, the film's principal interest lies in an intriguing anomaly: *The Three Caballeros* does not exhibit the characteristic censorship mechanisms identified by Dorfman and Mattelart in the Disney comics and so familiar to anyone reared on a diet of Disney entertainments. Instead of Disney's trademark—"sexless sexiness" in James Agee's apt phrase[6]—*The Three Caballeros* parades rampant (masculine) desire and the explosive results of its repeated frustration. How are we to understand this temporary suspension of a virtually emblematic inhibition?

The Three Caballeros also lays claim to considerable significance because it, and the related set of documentary travelogues, animated cartoons and live-action/animation combinations which led up to it, are the product of a concerted effort to expiate the past sins of North American cultural chauvinism, to replace hollow and hackneyed stereotypes with representations of Latin Americans ostensibly rendered on their own terms. How did this self-correcting enterprise come about?

These two apparently unrelated questions are the point of departure for what follows.

THE SCOOP ON "EL GROUPO"

As World War II loomed in Europe and Asia, the United States government registered concern about the allegiances of the Latin American nations. According to the image-historian Allen Woll:

> [From 1939] with the growing threat of war with Germany, the United States appeared eager to ease any remaining tensions with South American governments in order to maintain hemispheric unity as a bulwark against foreign invasion. . . . Roosevelt explained the basis for his vigorous reassertion of the Good Neighbor Policy: "I began to visualize a wholly new attitude toward other American Republics based on an honest and sincere desire, first, to remove from their minds all fear of American aggression—territorial or financial—and, second, to take them into a kind of hemispheric partnership in which no Republic would take undue advantage."[7]

Nelson Rockefeller, director of the Office of the Coordinator of Inter-American Affairs, and his assistant John Hay Whitney, head of the Motion Picture Section, extended their functions beyond regulation and into production. According to Woll, Rockefeller and Whitney "were instrumental in the hiring of Walt Disney 'as the first Hollywood producer of motion pictures specifically intended to carry a message of democracy and friendship below the Rio Grande'" (55). Whitney claimed that Disney "would show the truth about the American Way" in a series of "direct propaganda films couched in the simplicity of the animation medium" (55). Disney's South American project was thus built upon a self-conscious disposition formulated at high levels of national government to represent Latin being, culture and experience with authenticity and respect for intra-regional as well as inter-regional variations.

Between 1941 and 1943,[8] Walt Disney, his wife, and a score of staff members made three trips south of the border in search of the "raw material" for this Good Neighbor initiative. The material they collected was eventually rendered into nearly two dozen films, both shorts and features, both educational and escapist, both—in the prevailing terminology—"direct and indirect propaganda."[9] Entertainment shorts like *El Gaucho Goofy* and *Pluto and the Armadillo* and educational films like *The Grain That Built a Hemisphere* and *Cleanliness Brings Health* are, from the present perspective, merely byproducts of a venture whose central importance revolves around a trilogy of films which convey a totalizing account of this cross-cultural journey: *South of the Border with Disney* (1941), *Saludos Amigos* (1943) and, in particular, *The Three Caballeros* (1945). As a composite, these films move progressively away from the literal to the figurative and from the experiential to the imaginary.

South of the Border With Disney is a thoroughly conventional travelogue, a "documentary diary" of the Disney group's original Latin American tour which Disney himself narrates. For lack of a more qualified cameraman, Disney also shot the images of "El Groupo" (as they syncretically dubbed themselves), their hosts, and their forays. *South of the Border* exhibits only occasional scraps of animation as it depicts the "birth" of various cartoon figures who will not be fully "embodied" until the two subsequent films. Joe Carioca, the fast-talking, cigar-smoking, umbrella-toting parrot from Rio makes his first appearance here as a series of uninked, backgroundless two-color pencil sketches, briefly and provisionally animated to perform an incipient samba.

Saludos Amigos retraces the same basic itinerary, but this time several animated characters assume a more central role. This anthology film, tied together with documentary footage of the Disney junket, is composed of four discrete shorts: Donald Duck's adventures and misadventures at Bolivia's Lake Titicaca in the company of animated llamas and real-life *cholas* (Bolivian peasant women in full skirts and derby hats); Pedro the little Chilean mail plane's intrepid voyage over the Andes; Goofy as egregious gaucho in the Argentine; and, finally and most rewardingly, "Aquarela do Brasil" ("Watercolor of Brazil") in which Joe Carioca introduces Donald Duck to samba, *cachaça* (cane liquor) and Rio nightclubs. This last seven and a half minute portion is animated to the strains of Ari Barroso's mellifluous "Brazil" and a second, more percussive samba by Zequinha de Abreu, and features an animated watercolor brush delineating the action in lush tropical colors and textures. "Aquarela do Brasil" is proto-music video at its finest.[10]

Finally, in *The Three Caballeros*, as described in detail below, live action becomes fully subordinate to animation. The balance of the first film has been reversed: here personality assumes precedence over geography and literal depictions of place give way to more mythic geographies animated by imagination and desire. Each of these three films thus (re)inscribes the process of appropriation of the "genuinely" Latin American in more elaborate and intricate ways. In each successive effort, the process of cross-cultural appropriation and refiguration is more effectively displaced and transmuted.

Judging from the evidence offered in *South of the Border with Disney*, the dominant assumption beneath El Groupo's good-neighborly enterprise was that culture *is* its material base and that these physical artifacts are transportable and translatable— subject not only to various means of pre- and post-mechanical reproduction but also subjectable to the artistic imaginations of the visiting Disneyites whose self-appointed mandate to refigure them in transculturating gestures is to be received by the locals as tribute rather than as expropriation. Countless sequences throughout this 20-minute travelogue emphasize the materiality of Latin American culture, the raw substance of exotic artifact, as the goal of the Disney expedition.

In their zeal to appropriate the "authentic exotic," distinctions between animate and inanimate, flora and fauna, human and non-human are set aside. In a typical sequence in the Argentine segment, the mandate "to gather more impressions, more music, more color" blinds Disney's minions to the difference between human and animal species. Two of Disney's staff come upon don Riberio Sosa, introduced in Disney's voice-over narration as "an eighty-five year old gaucho and a veteran of the Indian wars." The Americans begin to examine the man's footgear, and one even lifts a foot to give the camera a better view while the voice-over provides technical data. Over a low-angle closeup of a bewildered-looking don Riberio, the voice-over intones, "He had a sense of humor and was amused at the interest they took in his costume." After the gaucho has dismounted, both men flank him, their notebooks prominently in hand, while one fingers the hat and then unceremoniously removes it from the man's head. Cut to a llama-like animal in medium shot while the narrator, without missing a beat, recites in the same didactic tone of voice, "The *guanaco* is found in the foothills of the Andes . . ." Another brusque cut to a man photographing a small rodent while the narrator informs us, "At the San Martin Zoo in Mendoza, we found these Patagonian rabbits from the south of Argentina. They are a little shy but easily tamed." One is tempted to inquire, as easily as don Riberio?

This attachment to the material as the essence of the otherliness of culture is parodied—albeit rather lamely—in the closing sequences of *South of the Border*. These revolve around the visual trope of El Groupo's suitcases, beginning with a montage of pottery objects displayed in closeup against a serape background while the narrator explains, "We picked up many suggestions for picture ideas in the pottery designs of Oaxaca and Guadalajara." Over closeup holds on a series of small floral paintings, against the same serape backdrop, sequentially inserted into the frame by an unidentified hand, we hear, "In every part of Mexico, we found new picture material like these flower designs suggesting the lace headdress of Tehuantepec, the Yucateca costume of Yucatan, little Tehuanos from the Isthmus . . ." Cut back to a medium shot in which an unidentified man, only partially visible, places a large ceramic vase in the suitcase, which is already overflowing with the objects we have just been viewing, and then makes a futile attempts to close it. Fade in from a dissolve-montage of destination stickers to a U.S. Customs sign. "The Customs officials were really in for something," the narrator observes over images of officials rifling through ludicrously overstuffed luggage. The last suitcase belongs to none other than Uncle Walt himself, who continues to narrate in voice-over: "After half an hour of this, the officer was prepared for anything, and when he came across Walt's gaucho saddles, spurs and bridle, his only comment was, 'You might as well have brought the horse!'" A neighing on the soundtrack coincides with the final shot: a close-up of a live horse's head as if emerging from Walt's suitcase while, in the background, Walt and two companions enjoy a hearty laugh.

Appropriation and packaging lie at the foundation of the Disney endeavor here. ("Surprise Package" was the original working title of what eventually became *The Three Caballeros.*) Reelaborated in the metropolis of the Disney Studios, this raw material will be repackaged for export to its originary peripheral locales, but in barely recognizable forms and with the accrued semiotic value of its industrial refiguration.[11]

WHAT'S IN A SURPRISE PACKAGE?

The Three Caballeros is the end-product of this process of cross-cultural refiguration. At seventy minutes, it is the longest of the trio. Technically, it is the most ambitious by far. Artistically, it is indisputably the richest, containing some of the most brilliant animation sequences ever devised by the resident geniuses at Disney Studios.

Structurally, *The Three Caballeros* divides successively into threes: three progressively building parts which derive from three birthday gifts sent to Donald Duck from his "friends in Latin America"; three primary cartoon protagonists (Donald Duck, Joe Carioca, and Panchito the boisterous Mexican rooster); and three flesh-and-blood actresses who interact with them (Brazilian singer-dancer Aurora Miranda, Carmen's sister, and the Mexican dancer Carmen Molina and singer Dora Luz).

Gift #1 contains a movie projector and a film, "Aves Raras" (Strange Birds). Donald is the only "caballero" present in this all-animated sequence, which is didactic in a rather heavy-handed way, using three male narrators in voice-over, along with animated maps and other instructional devices, to "teach" Donald about Latin America. This is the most distanced sequence, both geographically (it deals primarily with Antarctica and Uruguay) and emotionally (Donald watches passively, without entering into the action, as he will do in the subsequent Brazilian and Mexican sequences). This first sequence is in turn divided into three parts: the travails of Pablo, the cold-blooded penguin who pines for and eventually attains a tropical isle; an "interstitial" essay on Latin American bird life; and the story of Little Gauchito who, seeking a condor, captures and trains a flying donkey instead but loses the jackpot when the donkey shows his true feathers. This last section is, rather curiously, narrated by Gauchito himself as an old man, giving rise to the anomalous tag line "And so I was never heard from again . . ."

Gift #2 smokes and pulses to a samba beat. Once opened, this pop-up book on Brazil becomes a kind of proscenium stage for the Brazilian parrot, Joe Carioca. After the two caballeros enter the book in a "through the looking glass"-like manoeuvre, Joe guides Donald on a trip to Bahia, where the first live action/animation sequences occur around the comely cookie-vendor Yaya (Aurora Miranda), the first Latin American lass to capture Donald's heart, and her horde of male admirers.

With gift #3, Panchito the Mexican rooster completes the group. The three caballeros then "tour" Mexico via a portfolio of folk paintings and tourist photographs, with the additional aid of a piñata and a magic serape. Pacing and complexity also increase here, with numerous tour de force sequences of animation and mixed action, accelerating to the final explosive crescendo.

Parts two and three, the core segments of the film, combine animation with live action footage, sharing a similar dual configuration of *demonstration* and *transportation*. The demonstration, hosted in the first part by Joe Carioca and in the second by Panchito and accomplished through the surrogacy of the visual aids mentioned above, revolves around a love song crooned in the syrupy style of the period, a love song ostensibly dedicated to the place but also clearly evoking the notions of absence, of longing, and of pairing as ideal completion: "Oh Bahia, someone that I long to see, is haunting my reverie, and this loneliness deep in my heart, calls to you, calls to you . . ."; and "Mexico, that's where I found you . . . your song of romance calls me to you . . ."

Clearly, Donald feels compelled to answer the call. In the "transportation" portions, his earlier passive contemplation gives way to direct participation. Donald is magically transported into the spectacle which is being offered him—through the square-wheeled storybook train of the Brazilian sequence which dumps him and Joe Carioca at the Bahia station, and later via the flying serape which magically enters the tourist photos displayed in the Mexican portfolio. This transport consists not only of his physical presence in "otherland" but also of his emotional transport into a state of frenzied arousal once he comes face-to-face with the Other's Other (that is, the women implicitly assumed to "belong" to the Latin American male). With typical lack of restraint, Donald falls head-over-heels in love with every Latin beauty he lays eyes on. The text is sexualized at this point, where physical entry into the space of the other becomes possible. In both the Brazilian and the Mexican sequences, these persistently frustrated pursuits "transport" Donald in a third sense—to an altered state, a hallucination within the hallucination that is the film which, dreamlike, recapitulates and condenses all that has gone before without actually *taking* him (or us) anywhere: transportation as reprise.

The Acapulco beach sequence, when Donald jumps off the flying serape to join the live action bathing beauties on the sand,[12] marks the inception of a kind of hyperkinetic hysteria that characterizes the culminating fifteen minutes of the film. At the close of the Acapulco sequence Donald, who has been playing blind man's bluff with several dozen señoritas, is abducted by his impatient buddies. Back on the magic serape, the blindfolded Donald, thinking he has caught one of the girls at last, throws his arms around Joe Carioca, kissing him noisily as Joe protests, "Oh no, Donald, don't do *that*!" Heterosexual, cross-species pursuit is confounded by same-species injunctions against homosexuality.

Finally, in the subsequent Mexico City nightlife sequence, watching Dora Luz sing "You Belong to My Heart" ("Solamente Una Vez"), Donald at last succeeds in making carnal contact with an object of his desire. Her willingness dissolves his former bravado into puerile reticence. Donald's long-sought release only releases him into nightmare. Overwhelmed by the simultaneous kisses of several pairs of disembodied female lips, Donald takes off like a rocket, loses his "mass" and is reduced to a mere outline of his former self, sprouts wings (an angel? a fairy?) and then a wreath of flower petals. Images of past experiences return transmuted. Donald turns green with surfeit. The syrupy love song is repeatedly disrupted by Donald's gun-slinging sidekicks and their raucous anthem as Donald attempts to partner first a dancing *tehuana* (woman from the traditionally matriarchal Tehuantepec) and then a phallic female *charra* (roughly, cowgirl) surrounded by syncopated cacti. The frenzy of competing rhythms and imagery continue to mount until the explosive finale.

ANIMATING PHILOSOPHIES

Whatever their explicit content, cartoons are often also *about* the film medium itself and its mechanisms of representation—about, that is, what they simultaneously are and are not; about the medium which they to some degree embody and yet also, inevitably, defy. Representationality and realist conventions are persistently invoked only to be defied. This perversely contrary self-reflexivity becomes one of the most intense (and disturbing) pleasures offered by cartoons.

Because cartoon figures inhabit a world beyond materiality, beyond mortality, beyond conventionality, cartoons can also be the site of unbridled expressions of the individual and collective unconscious, defying norms of propriety and well as physics. In philosophical terms, ontological otherliness invites axiological otherliness. Cartoons in this sense can be understood as a kind of dream's dreaming, the unconscious of the unconscious.

Cartoon figures are simultaneously, quintessentially both self and Other. Rather than dissipating, this effect is heightened to dizzying levels of intensity and confusion in those films which combine animation and live action. (Remember that *The Three Caballeros* is the first color feature to sustain this mixture within the same frame although Disney had been experimenting with this combination since his first cartoon series in the 1920s.[13]) It is this otherly (under)side of mixed animation that comes across so vividly and disconcertingly in *Who Framed Roger Rabbit,* direct heir of *The Three Caballeros* (and hard-pressed at times, despite the intervening forty years of technological evolution, to outdo its eye-popping prototype).

Such hybrid cartoons produce a metaphysical effect in both senses of the word: they literally transcend the plane of physical reality, and they situate their viewers in a disquieting zone of epistemological and ethical question marks. The metaphysics of hybrid animation is morally unsettling for a number of reasons—not least among them the persistent subordination/annihilation/resuscitation of the marginals, and the explicit allusions to acts of celluloid miscegenation.[14]

The consequent moral discomfiture may account for the outrage such films elicit. John Mason Brown, writing in the *Saturday Review* in 1945, called "the mixture of drawn and real people in . . . *The Three Caballeros* one of the most unfortunate experiments since Prohibition."[15] Barbara Deming, writing in *Partisan Review* that same year, mused, "Walt has indeed wrought something monstrous . . . [but] *The Three Caballeros* is not Disney's private monster, his personal nightmare. It is a nightmare of these times."[16] Jonathan Rosembaum, reviewing *Roger Rabbit* in the fall 1988 issue of *Film Quarterly,* plays with this idea of moral culpability by assuming a mock-prosecutorial tone, arguing that the film's director, Robert Zemeckis, may be "the main culprit" but that he should not be "convicted" on the basis of "circumstantial evidence."[17]

These hybrid works tend to provoke moral indignation or summary dismissal on grounds of absurdity—or both. In "The Long Pause," the chapter of *The Disney Version* dedicated to the late 1940s, Richard Schickel quotes Bosley Crowther, usually a staunch Disney fan, panning *The Three Caballeros* because it "dazzles and numbs the senses without making any sense." Schickel's own assessment mixes moral censure with terminal agnosticism:

> It is fair to say that the film reflected Disney's own mood. Nothing made sense to him. . . . Since he had never really known what he was doing culturally, he, particularly, could not find his own roots. Between him and his past he had erected a screen on which were projected only his own old movies, the moods and styles of which he mindlessly sought to recapture at cut rates in the bastard cinematic form of the half-animated, half-live-action film.[18]

What is left for the cultural critic who prefers meaning to meaninglessness and a sense of historical accountability to arbitrary accusations of immorality? Perverse texts invite perverse readings. What better term for the attempt to extract a measure of meaning from chaotic excess, to discern the coherence underpinning an ungainly amalgamation obviously assembled by committee, to identify the ideological stance behind the innocuous comic gesture?

TEN PERVERSE PROPOSITIONS ON DESIRE IN DISNEY

First Proposition: Latin America as a Wartime Toontown

In *Roger Rabbit,* Toontown is a zone of marginality inhabited by the vulnerable and the victimized, literally "an/other world" / "an/Other's world" to be entered only with wariness and dread and seldom escaped intact. For the writers and animators of *The Three Caballeros,* Latin America is the 1940s equivalent of "Toontown," the seductive-repulsive zone of spectacular excess and excessive spectacle. In the sections depicting Brazil and Mexico, reason gives way to passion, order to disorder and incoherence, the logic of experience to the chaos of nightmare. It is this impression/projection of Latin-ness which unleashes both Donald's and Disney's libido. The Latin is rendered synonymous with license and licentiousness. The projection onto the other of what we most fear/reject/suppress/desire within ourselves lies at the root of the film's indulgence in excess—an excess which is, in this case, specifically, relentlessly sexual.

Certainly, I would be treading shaky ground if I were to attempt to (psycho) analyze the animators, but the uncharacteristic excess which erupts most overpoweringly in the final segment begins to seem somewhat less unfathomable once one tries to reconstruct the atmosphere at Disney Studios in the last years of the Great War. As noted above (see footnote 8), financial losses occasioned layoffs and strikes which in 1941 reduced the workforce by half. By the end of that year, the Studios had turned into the most extensive "war plant" in Hollywood, housing mountains of munitions, quartering antiaircraft troops, providing overflow office space for Lockheed personnel. By 1943, fully 94% of the footage produced at the studios was war-related. Disney had become a government contractor on a massive scale. The restrictions on costs and equipment applied to the other studios did not apply to Disney because animation was exempted.[19] It is not difficult to imagine, in this context of dreary war work, how the license implicit in the "surprise package" of *The Three Caballeros* project might have unleased creative juices which had been stored too long under pressure.

Second Proposition: Spectacular Packaging

The Three Caballeros packages Latin America (or, more accurately, depicts Latin America as packaging itself) as pure spectacle. Each gift is an artifact of and for visualization: a movie projector and film, a pop-up book, a portfolio of scenes from various regions of Mexico. Parts II and III begin by emphasizing the spectacle of the Latin American landscape (ideally populated by singing, dancing natives) and ultimately progress to "bodyscape"—the spectacle of the playful, alluring, receptive Latin female.

Third Proposition: An Allegory of Colonialism

The Three Caballeros offers an allegory of (neo-) colonialism: every story packaged here is a narrative of conquest or of enslavement. In the first narrative from Part I, Pablo Penguin sets out from the south pole to find "the isle of his dreams." Having resourcefully overcome numerous comic setbacks, he finally reaches the Galapagos, where he is last seen tanning himself in a hammock while a tray-bearing tortoise brings him one iced drink after another. (It comes as no surprise that the narrative of this hapless indigene's enslavement has been conveniently omitted.) In the first segment's closing narrative, Gauchito captures and enslaves the donkey-bird because the instant he stumbles upon the creature, he immediately perceives that he "must be worth a fortune!"

Fourth Proposition: Hierarchies of the Willing-and-Waiting-to-Be-Conquered

The chronology of conquest in *The Three Caballeros* recapitulates a hierarchy that goes from claiming territory (Pablo's tropical isle) to capturing and taming the local fauna (Gauchito's flying donkey) to Donald's designs on the female homo sapiens. Each rung in this hierarchy is represented as simply waiting to be taken; Donald's conquests fail not because his targets aren't willing but because he is not able.

Fifth Proposition: Donald's Un-Don Juanly Ineptitude As Sop to the Excessive Machismo of His Avian Accomplices

If Donald's conquest is displaced (from geography onto the female body), it is also disguised or "de-fused" by his ineptitude, his failure to consummate his desires. The mechanisms of geopolitical and sexual conquest here enjoy a convenient congruence. Anxious to allay potential fears that this "neighborly" North American presence will be too potent, too overpowering, the filmmakers place the brunt of the film's humor on the sheer ludicrousness of Donald Duck as Don Juan—his impotence, his childish polymorphousness or, in baldest Lacanian terms, his lack of the phallus.

The *charra* sequence, part of the climactic second half of the Mexican segment, makes Donald's phallic inadequacy most glaringly apparent. Dressed in a feminized version of a traditionally male costume and carrying a riding crop, the phallic woman (Carmen Molina) stomps her high boots in a self-confident *zapateo*. She is surrounded by a phalanx of dancing cacti which, as they deploy and metamorphosize, alternately squash, obscure, fragment and otherwise overpower Donald. At the end of the sequence, Donald runs through a forest of elongated cacti, their prominent appendages dangling high above him, in futile pursuit of Carmen Molina who has herself "congealed" into a cactus before he can reach her. Green, the color of lust for the Latins and envy for the gringos, dominates the sequence. The imagery of inadequacy has seldom been more overdetermined.

In marked contrast to Donald, Joe Carioca and Panchito are more generously equipped. Each comes armed with a pair of phallic objects: a cigar and umbrella in the parrot's case (in the Mexican sequence, the umbrella more than once turns into a machine gun); and a pair of pistols liberally deployed in the case of the rooster, whose species itself is—needless to say—an emblem of male sexual prowess.

As recently as 1982, a film historian wrote appropros of this film that Donald Duck's "camaraderie with the caballeros from Brazil and Mexico symbolized the idea of hemispheric unity."[20] In fact, this male camaraderie provides a thin pretext for (and eventually a major impediment to) Donald's real interest, the (hetero)sexual pursuit of "priddy girls" of uniformly pale complexion. Donald's feathered companions are first potential rivals, later indomitable restrainers and disrupters. The Disney team apparently felt the need to reassure their Latin American counterparts that they need feel no threat to their sexual hegemony from this North American neighbor who, for all his quacking up and cracking up, is clearly incapable of shacking up.

Sixth Proposition: Doña Juanita?

The ultimate reassurance regarding Donald's nonthreatening nature is the recurrent feminization which he undergoes immediately after his attempts to "connect" with the objects of his desire—a desire no less fickle for all its obsessive intensity. Donald's surrogate femaleness at key moments is underlined by visual puns that verge on the subliminal but compel an embarrassing blatancy on the part of anyone wishing to describe them. (Oh well. Here goes.)

Seconds prior to the conclusion of both the Brazilian and the Mexican sequences, Donald is literally swept off his feet by a stream of ejaculate. His concluding appearance in the Brazilian sequence comes when he tries to imitate Aurora Miranda, whose compelling gestures "animate" her cartooned surroundings, making buildings and plazas pulse to a samba beat. In response to Donald's pathetic attempt at mimesis, a fountain shaped like an elephant's head extends its flaccid trunk into a rigid horizontal pipe and proceeds to overpower Donald with its spray.

In the frenetic "climax" of the Mexican sequence, which also ends the film, Joe Carioca and Panchito combat Donald in a mock bull-fight. The inept Donald has trouble maneuvering the bull armature which, with the instantaneousness of nightmare, he suddenly inhabits. His assailants are considerably more agile: Pancho goads him with red flags and wisecracks while Joe sets a cluster of firecrackers alight on his tail and then skewers him with a pair of pokers. After his ejection (ejaculation?) from the make-believe bull, which magically and terrifyingly continues to rampage unaided, Donald redirects his combative fury away from its original target (the "friends" who have so persistently thwarted his amorous efforts) and toward this emblem of masculinity, charging the bull head-on as Panchito sings in ironic voice-over, "like brother to brother / we're all for each other . . ." The trail of spewing fireworks in the Mexican finale rockets Donald skyward; embracing this stream, he then slides back "down to earth." The film's concluding frames show Donald in one of his many feminized poses, draped head to foot in a Mexican serape and protectively flanked by his two cohorts.

Seventh Proposition: One Man's Dominance Is An/Other (Wo)Man's Subordination

The Three Caballeros, though appearing to challenge it, in fact fully conforms to what students of machismo have recently theorized to be the "colonial compact." Proponents of this theory ask, what did the indigenous and creole males receive in return for their disenfranchisement by their Spanish and Portuguese conquerors? After they were stripped of their leaders, rituals, sacred artifacts and traditional forms of social organization, was the promise of a Roman Catholic heaven sufficient compensation for sustained submission, even in the face of the Europeans' obvious military and technological superiority? Some of those who identify the most virulent strain of machismo (the cult of male superiority) as Latin American in origin trace it to the colonial experience. They theorize that the reward for male acquiescence to the will of the conqueror was his socially enforced superiority to and dominance over the female.[21]

Eighth Proposition: Pity the Poor Conqueror

Predictably perhaps, the "gift" which El Groupo's Good Neighbor project offers to its Latin American audience turns out to be at their expense. The emissary turns out to be not only "a wolf in duck's clothings" (to quote Panchito) but also a conquistador in compañero's clothings. Donald is a disarmingly inept but no less effective front man for the imperial machine. A discerning viewer might object here that the various conquests depicted in *The Three Caballeros* are incomplete, that they "fall short," to borrow Barbara Deming's phrase. Yet the effect of this narrative strategy is not to call acts of conquest into question nor much less to condemn them, but rather to "humanize" the agents of conquest by exposing their pathetic ineptitude and/or their inner ambivalence regarding their prize.

The perspective of the conquered is banished from this account. Deprived of subjectivity, the male is constrained to serve as informant and guide for the would-be conqueror. (The role of the female, as we have seen, is to be the compliant object of invasive desire, the exotic Other's even more exotic Other.) For want of a victim, the conqueror himself is here posited as the "little guy," the "underdog," a fellow "strange bird" who inspires sympathetic concern and playful amicality rather than dread, resentment, or resistance.

Ninth Proposition: Illusory Reciprocities and Other Deceptive Ways of Seeing Eye to Eye

The notion of reciprocity is deceptively evoked in the opening frames of the film when Donald, who has opened the first of his birthday gifts from Latin America to find a movie projector and screen, subjects the strip of celluloid to the close scrutiny of his naked eye. Cut to a point-of-view closeup of one of the frames, which animates: Pablo Penguin turns his telescope toward Donald/the camera/the viewer; its huge concentric circularity, a remote eye at its center, dominates the frame. This brief sequence embodies what might be called the "myth of the reciprocal gaze." The Other who gazes back at the gazer in fact "sees" nothing, since a figure imprinted on a single frame of celluloid cannot be either animate or sensate—except of course in a cartoon, and in a cartoon-within-a-cartoon . . .

But *were* Pablo Penguin to *see* the one who is seeing him (Donald Duck), he would arguably be merely mirroring himself. The Antarctic penguin is a notably "de-culturated" choice, a paradoxical bird if there ever was one: so terrestrial that he seems to be the antithesis of the avian; so southerly that he conveys the quintessence of northerliness. The "rare bird" given pride of place in the film's order of presentation is thus not in fact "one of them" but quite transparently "one of us." The further we travel, the more we stay at home—or some such paradoxical platitude—seems to be the subtextual invocation here.

Furthermore, Pablo's successful colonization of tropical America is rendered innocent because he comes from an ephemeral "nowhere." Without any attachment to terra firma, he simply cuts his igloo free from the icepack when he wants to navigate north to the tropics, and the ice floe which anchored him to his Antarctic community becomes the vehicle for his solitary migration. Similarly, he lacks the avian "ethno/specificity" conveyed by the coloration, symbolic accoutrements, and richly genuine accents of both Panchito and Joe Carioca. (To his credit, Disney insisted on native voices for these roles.) Even the frenetic Carmen Miranda-esque "song" of the mischievous and disruptive aracuan bird, who appears at "random" moments in parts I and II, connotes a cultural embeddedness of which Pablo is utterly devoid. Pablo has no voice at all: Sterling "Doc" Holloway, the vibrato-voiced narrator of *Peter and the Wolf,* is called in to tell his story for him in voice-over.

Tenth Proposition: Prefigurations of Things to Come

Illusory reciprocity constitutes the very core of this film. As we've seen, the production of meanings in *The Three Caballeros* is both explicit and veiled, brazen and coy. Much of the film's fascinatingly devious elusiveness derives from the intricacy of its reversals, from deceptive reciprocities in which there is no real exchange, or in which what is exchanged is not what has been promised. Anthony Wilden, writing in *System and Structure* on logical typing and the triangulation of binary oppositions, notes how the apparent symmetry of the binary pair is often governed by an "invisible" third term which converts difference into hierarchy.[22] In this case, the "third term" between the North American and the South American may be the neocolonizing ambition of the former.

A film which reportedly set out to be an offering of friendship toward Latin America adopts the reverse as its core premise. Latin America fetes Donald Duck, showering him with birthday gifts and hosting his visits to Bahia and Mexico, much as, in relation to the film's production, Latin Americans hosted Disney and his team and much as, in relation to the film's reception, Latin America was offered up as ready host to Donald Duck's successors, the American tourists. The perverse dialectic of economic aid, which rewards the donor while impoverishing the recipient, is replicated (one is almost tempted to say prophesied) here.

Disney's "gift" of intercultural understanding turns out to be the act of packaging Latin America for enhanced North-American consumption.[23] The unspoken pact which makes that package possible rests upon the equation of cultural expression with femininity and cultural exchange with heterosexual conquest, and upon the positing of a shared assumption between conqueror and conqueree: that the female of the species is a willing target of appropriation.

To its enduring credit, *The Three Caballeros does* utilize Latin American music, accents, performers, locales, artifacts, and modes of cultural expression more extensively than any previous Hollywood film. Disney's quest for cultural authenticity was to that extent both sincere and successful. The results are often dazzling, even by today's elevated technical standards. But all these good intentions cannot mask the discomforting evidence which hides just below the comic frenzy: all cultural reciprocities are not created equal.

NOTES

Versions of this essay were presented as part of Michigan State University's Modern Literature Conference, the University of New Mexico's International Cinema Lecture Series, and the Inaugural Lecture Series at the University of California, Santa Cruz. The oral presentation includes nearly a half hour of film clips. It would be an understatement to say that the clips are half the fun; without them, the arguments lose immediacy and impact. Verbal description cannot replicate the intricate, hyperstimulated exuberance of the Disney images which provoked this essay. So, unless *The Three Caballeros* is very fresh in your mind, read no further: hasten instead to the nearest video store, where it should be readily available. The essay can wait; first see the movie!

N.B.: The Walt Disney Company, having reviewed this essay for "content," refused us permission to reproduce images from *The Three Caballeros* that it holds in copyright (the editors).

1. In this eponymous 1941 feature, a *comedia ranchera* directed by Joseíto Fernández, it fell to the lusty-voiced Jorge Negrete to belt out the title song. His performance established his fame—not only in Mexico but throughout Latin America—as "the quintessential singing *charro*." See Carl J. Mora, *Mexican Cinema: Reflections of a Society, 1896–1988* (Berkeley: University of California Press, 1982, rev. ed. 1989), p. 56.

2. See for example Victor Valle, "The Latino Wave: More Show-Biz Doors Are Opening Since 'La Bamba,'" *Los Angeles Times*, April 2, 1988, Section VI, pp. 1, 11; and Duane Byrge, "Hollywood Goes Hispanic," *San Francisco Magazine*, May 1988, pp. 99–100.

3. For an introductory discussion, see Allen L. Woll, *The Latin Image in American Film* (Los Angeles: UCLA Latin American Center, 1980 rev. ed.).

4. *Para leer al Pato Donald* (Valparaiso: Ediciones Universitarias, 1971); translated into English by David Kunzle as *How to Read Donald Duck: Imperialist Ideology in the Disney Comic* (New York: International General, 1975).

5. Dorfman and Mattelart, *How to Read Donald Duck*, Chapter 1, "Uncle, Buy Me a Contraceptive," esp. pp. 33–34. Other writers have recognized the gender imbalance. Richard Schickel, in *The Disney Version: The Life, Times, Art and Commerce of Walt Disney* (New York: Avon, 1968), notes "the absence of the mother," "a theme that is implicit in almost all the Disney features" (225).

6. Cited in Schickel, *The Disney Version*, p. 233.

7. Woll, *The Latin Image,* p. 55. The terms of the contract were generous. According to Schickel, "The [State] Department would underwrite each film he made up to fifty thousand dollars and . . . the traveling expenses of Disney and his party [19 in all] up to the amount of seventy thousand dollars" (223).

8. From Disney's point of view, the timing of these trips could hardly have been more propitious. Disney Studios showed a million dollar deficit in 1941, largely due to the wartime collapse of foreign markets. To make matters worse, the union combatted the consequent layoffs with a prolonged and bitter strike. Though the strike was eventually successful, by its conclusion the staff was 50% smaller. Conveniently, Disney happened to be "south of the border" when the strike was concluded and the studio reopened. See Richard Shale, *Donald Duck Joins Up: The Walt Disney Studios During World War II* (Ann Arbor, MI: UMI Research Press, 1987), p. 20.

9. Robert Spencer Carr, "Ideas for More Walt Disney Films For South American Release," January 1942. Larry Geller found this studio report, submitted to the Council on Inter-American Affairs and later "leaked" to *Politics* magazine (July 1945, p. 212), among papers in the Walt Disney Productions Archive, Burbank, California. I am grateful to him for a photocopies of selected pages from this 40-page document.

10. According to Shale, *Saludos Amigos* "became the first Hollywood film to premiere in all Latin American countries before opening in the U.S." (*Donald Duck Joins Up,* p. 47). It reportedly drew record crowds, and the only protests it elicited appear to have been from Uruguay, a country included in the tour but not represented in the film. The Gauchito sequence in *The Three Caballeros* compensates for this oversight.

11. In his forthcoming book *Animating Culture: Hollywood Cartoons from the Sound Era* (New Brunswick, NJ: Rutgers University Press), Eric Smoodin notes the chauvinism which underpins the entire enterprise, calling it "the flawless calculus of cultural imperialism" according to which "Walt Disney, a representative of the United States, could tour a foreign culture [actually, *several* different cultures and subcultures], come to understand it in just a short time, film it, and then bring it back home with him, all with the blessing and thanks of the culture he had visited."

12. The live action footage suggests that in the mid-forties, the beaches of Acapulco were inhabited by a remarkably homogenous species: all female, all shapely and fair-skinned, all apparently between the ages of eighteen and twenty-two.

13. See Shale, *Donald Duck Joins Up,* pp. 3, 98, 101–102.

14. Working primarily under the direction of Donna Haraway, Brett Kaplan wrote

a fascinating undergraduate thesis on the kind of cross-species coupling (female homo sapiens to male of another order) that she first noted in a course of mine which included *The Three Caballeros*. See "The Animals and Their Women: A Sexy Species Story" (Literature Senior Thesis, University of California at Santa Cruz, Spring 1990, 58 pp.), which concentrates on *Who Framed Roger Rabbit?* and *Gorillas in the Mist.*

15. Cited in Shale, *Donald Duck Joins Up*, p. 106.

16. Barbara Deming, "Film Chronicle: The Artlessness of Walt Disney," *The Partisan Review* (Spring 1945), p. 226. This six-page essay is the most thoughtful and perceptive reading of the film that I have encountered. Shale's chapter on *The Three Caballeros* (in *Donald Duck Joins Up*, pp. 96–108), the other major essay on this film, is interpretively indebted to Deming while supplementing her account with essential historical and technical information.

17. Jonathan Rosembaum, "*Who Framed Roger Rabbit?*" *Film Quarterly*, 42, 1 (Fall 1988), p. 33.

18. Schickel, *The Disney Version*, pp. 234–235.

19. For the information in this paragraph I am indebted to Shale, *Donald Duck Joins Up*, pp. 20–24.

20. Ibid., p. 107.

21. Among the scholars who have begun developing new lines of thinking on these issues, see Marvin Goldwert, *Psychic Conflict in Spanish America: Six Essays on the Psychohistory of the Region* (Washington, DC: University Press of America, 1982); Roger Bartra, *La jaula de la melancolía: Identidad y metamórfosis del mexicano* (Mexico City: Grijalbo, 1987), especially Chapter 22, "A la chingada," pp. 205–244; and Charles Ramirez Berg, *The Cinema of Solitude: A Critical History of Mexican Film, 1967–1983*, Ph.D. dissertation, University of Texas at Austin, 1987.

22. Anthony Wilden, *System and Structure: Essays in Communication and Exchange* (London: Tavistock, 1980), pp. xxxiii-xxxv.

23. Empirical data on how these films were received in Latin America is difficult to locate; see note 10 above for a start. Schickel writes that "about the only government-sponsored project that worked out profitably was *Saludos Amigos*. . . . It returned almost $1.3 million in grosses" (*The Disney Version*, pp. 230–231).

Chapter 2

Misgendering the Nation: African Nationalist Fictions and Nuruddin Farah's Maps

Rhonda Cobham

"Living begins when you start doubting everything that came before you."

With this sweeping gesture of irreverence (borrowed, ironically, from Socrates), Nuruddin Farah announces his break with past precedent in the epigraph to his novel, *Maps*. Farah focuses the cryptic iconoclasm of Socrates' "everything" on the ambiguity surrounding the gender assignation of his novel's protagonist, Askar, and the uncertainties about the integrity of the boundaries that define the nation state, Somalia. These unstable categories of gender and nationality are situated in a contrapuntal relationship so that each term, in the course of the novel's development, comes to subvert or complicate the meaning of the other.

Some critics have complained that Farah's quirky, needling irreverence about fundamental categories becomes at times the intellectual game of an idiosyncratic writer who has never quite "fit in" to the available pigeonholes for African writers and who enjoys playing tricks on his readers. *Maps* is Farah's sixth novel in English, which is probably his fourth language, after Somali, Arabic and, possibly, Italian. His first novel *From A Crooked Rib* (1970) recreated the experiences of a young Somali girl so successfully that the author occasionally receives mail addressed to Ms. Farah asking for firsthand accounts of female circumcision. *A Naked Needle* (1976) records the experience of a Western woman living in Somalia as the wife of a Somali man, while in *Sweet and Sour Milk* (1980) the competition for influence over the Somali nationalist cause between Eastern and Western world powers is played out in the confusion of mistaken identities that plagues a pair of identical twins. Farah is consciously eclectic, drawing on sub-Saharan, European, Arabic, and Latin American traditions to create his fictions, and often stopping to greet or play games with his literary mentors in the course of his work.

This essay argues that the transformation of the anti-imperialist struggle in Africa into a nationalist movement exacerbated a crisis of individual and collective identity that is staged in the African novel. To date most critics have seen these two levels of trauma in terms of an allegorical correspondence between the psychic crisis of the (usually educated) individual and the socio-political crisis of the modern nation state. However, we can also read the crisis of individual identity as a crisis of gender and sexual identities that parallels and intersects with the socio-political manifestations of disorder, and it is this process of destabilization that Farah's novels enact. *Maps* in particular subverts identities and assumptions that in retrospect were never as unproblematic as they may have seemed in earlier African works of fiction. It forces us to ask difficult questions about our own willingness as critics to accept uncritically many of the myths surrounding nationalism and gender that were actually being contested rather than affirmed in some of these earlier works.

No one can know for sure exactly how precolonial societies imagined sexual identity or constructed social categories of gender. Early anthropological accounts of gender and sexuality in African societies reveal more about the anthropologist's assumptions than they tell us about those of their subjects. Such practices as the Igbo conferral of masculine status on powerful women who were then allowed to take wives and establish lineages in their own names, or the ritual assumption of feminine identities by male Yoruba priests, were either puzzled over as eccentricities that did not fit with Western social expectations or held up as bizarre aberrations which proved the depravity of the primitive subject. More recent work by African scholars in this area is itself a product of the continuing contestation of discursive space in postcolonial Africa.[1] As critics of modern African literatures with relatively limited access to an understanding of "traditional" African societies, we can only assume that the social construction of gender roles in precolonial Africa must have been as problematic and provisional as would seem to be the case in all human societies. At most we can be certain that these roles and identities differed somewhat from the ones we take for granted in modern Western societies, and that part of the process of integration into an international socioeconomic order organized around the existence of nation states in contemporary Africa has involved an accommodation to and reaction against new ways of mapping gendered objects and spaces.

The idea of the nation itself also has had a shifting and unstable significance within African political discourse. In the short historical span of one century since the Berlin Conference of 1884, African societies, whose previous systems of collective organization ranged from vast, complex empires to scattered bands of hunters and gatherers, have reconstituted their identities in terms of the nation state. In so doing, much of the energy that had been spent formerly on maintaining and expanding ethnic hegemony or fighting against European and Arab invasions has been diverted into the development and maintenance of national systems of government that are rarely adapted to the political and social complexities of African societies. Benedict Anderson, in his study of *Imagined Communities*, argues that the advent of print literacy is one of the factors which facilitated the development of the idea of the nation in the modern world.[2] From this perspective, the relative ease with which interethnic and anticolonial struggles in Africa were redefined as nationalist movements after World War II can be seen as a consequence of the control that a small, literate group was able to exert over the spread of mass media and the development of African literatures in European languages.

In the rhetoric of its emergence, the concept of African nationalism has been defined variously and contradictorily as a wholesale return to the "organic" values and assumptions of precolonial Africa; the progress of Africa out of the dark ages of traditionalism into the era of modern technology; the hegemony of one ethnic group over others; or the transcendence of these very ethnic differences as a way of countering the imperialist depredations of Europe in Africa. At one time or another, each of the competing definitions of nationalism has served the interests of emergent national elites within Africa, even as these interests have changed in response to challenges from internal and external forces. Fanon had anticipated the co-optation of the rhetoric of the anticolonial struggle by a new nationalist elite as early as 1960 in his chapter on "The Pitfalls of Nationalism" in *The Wretched of the Earth*. More recently, the political theorist Jean-Francois Bayart has elaborated upon the contradiction between the pursuit of hegemony by national regimes on the one hand and the aspirations of civil society in Central and West Africa on the other.[3] Yet there is little acknowledgement of these competing nationalist agendas in the critical response to African literature. National identities are invoked and ranged against each other in African literary discourse as unproblematically as we take for granted that human beings must eat and breathe to live, or as we "naturally" assume the impermeability of masculine and feminine gender boundaries.

Farah's refusal to accept the categories of gender and nationality as sacrosanct or mutually exclusive is not without precedent in modern African literature. From the vantage point of Farah's work, novelists writing as early as Camara Laye and from ideological perspectives as divergent as Ngugi and Achebe, Soyinka and Armah, can be seen as contributors to a debate about the efficacy of an identity built around contested "natural" categories. Conversely, the ways in which these writers have approached the question of identity elucidates Farah's method and the context for his concerns in *Maps*.

In Camara Laye's classic preindependence "novel of childhood," *L'enfant noir* (1953), the passage from childhood to manhood or womanhood—and, by implication, the values of precolonial Africa which govern this transition—are presented as if they were unproblematic. Laye's portrayal of his protagonist's parents, especially, makes use of schematic forms of gender representation which function as metaphors for the unquestioned integrity of traditional society. Like the writers associated with the Negritude movement, Laye evokes a moment of perfect social harmony before the chaos of colonialism. His novel legitimizes their struggle for independence and validates their claims to maturity as the leaders of new nations.

For other early African writers, however, the whole question of how such categories as "maturity" and "manhood" came to be constituted is itself the issue at stake. One thinks here of Chinua Achebe's *Things Fall Apart* (1958), or the early novels of Ngugi wa Thiongo. The notion that categories of maleness or femaleness could exist as unchallenged absolutes in precolonial Africa is still present in these works. However, their narratives express some degree of uncertainty about how individual characters inhabit these categories, albeit in terms of personal failure or lack of resolution on the part of the (male) protagonists.[4] In *The River Between* (1965), for example, Ngugi sets the affirmation of gender and ethnic identity articulated in Muthoni's final message to her sister—"Tell Nyambura, I see Jesus. And I am a woman beautiful in the tribe"—against the tragedy of Muthoni's death as a result of the circumcision which constitutes her ritual initiation into womanhood. Moreover, her dying words are spoken to Waiyaki, who remains profoundly ambivalent about the efficacy of either his circumcision *or* his christian education to turn him into a "true" Kikuyu man. Here the certainties imputed to traditional gender roles and traditionally buttressed nationalist aspirations are disrupted in the very moment that the author attempts to mutually reinforce each by appealing to the other.

Such works coincide with the closing decades of the anticolonial struggle in East and West Africa when, despite moments of ambivalence and self-doubt, most intellectuals remained more or less sanguine about the potential of their societies to create, in the aftermath of colonialism, just and equitable nation states grounded in intangible but vividly imagined values that were automatically labelled "traditional." Independence and the onset of postcolonial angst introduced new tensions and uncertainties around questions of gender and national ideals. The Biafran war novel, for instance, invokes the disappearance of the traditional docile and economically dependent African woman (itself a fiction created by an earlier generation of novelists) as a symptom of anomie in postcolonial society. As the new nation states disintegrate under the pressure of bureaucratic corruption and interethnic rivalries, so too are good wives corrupted and fine men emasculated in their prime. The figure of the Western homosexual preying on the defenseless African emerges in many texts as a way of externalizing disorder or of registering alienation from a more "natural" definition of self.

Ayi Kwei Armah and Wole Soyinka use different strategies to express their concern over the inadequacy of the social fabric to protect national and sexual values. Armah seeks to recuperate some semblance of national dignity from the horrifying chaos and decay he describes in postcolonial Ghana by asserting the stability of gender identities and heterosexual orthodoxy as qualities inherent to an Africa before colonialism. In *Two Thousand Seasons* (1973), first the Arab, then the European colonizers are presented as the sources of all evil and corruption in sub-Saharan Africa, as evidenced by their decadent sodomite practices and their corruption of the "natural" order as purveyors of sex and slaves. Like the monstrous births and unnatural couplings which anticipate gross deviations from the moral order in Shakespeare's plays, the sociopolitical malaise Armah depicts produces sexual "anomalies," like homosexuality and sado-masochism, as well as freaks, like the old manchild who completes the cycle of human life in a mere seven years in *The Beautyful Ones Are Not Yet Born* (1968).[5] Ethical travesties also inhibit the birth of "the beautyful ones" whose potential perfection comes to symbolize a hope deferred in the modern nation state. Armah challenges the modern African nation to rally its spiritual resources to fend off this onslaught of moral turpitude, and in *The Healers* (1978) he celebrates those who, over the centuries, have attempted to rid the body politic of externally intruded dis-ease.

In *The Interpreters* (1965) Soyinka offers a more open-ended approach, but for the most part he, too, sees the angry, eternally young men of his title, like the state they inhabit, as symbolically fragmented—sexually, intellectually and spiritually—in comparison to some implicit earlier state of nature. Indeed Chris Dunton claims, in his essay "Wheyting be Dat? The Treatment of Homosexuality in African Literature," that in the presentation of the African-American homosexual, Joe Golder, who alternately reveals and dissembles around the issue of his racial and sexual identities, Soyinka seems to suggest that the naming of self in terms of sexual orientation is as artificially constructed a notion as the self-conscious assumption of a national identity like "Nigerian," or a racial identity like "Black."[6] According to Dunton, Golder's role "establishes the novel's problematic because throughout the book the characters comment on that which eludes them: a condition of wholeness unbroken by self-consciousness, by the need to state one's case." For Soyinka, the homosexual role assumed by Joe Golder is unnatural not because the homosexual act is perverted, but because homosexuality must be consciously claimed as a distinct(ive) sexual category—just as, in his famous "tigritude" putdown of the Negritude movement, the cultural authenticity of the Negritude movement becomes suspect because it must be asserted rather than assumed.[7]

For all its latent homophobia, Soyinka's stance raises an important issue for the articulation of national and sexual identities in African literary discourse. The problem that many postcolonial African writers face in defining both national and sexual categories may be described as a problem, ultimately, of form. The modern novel, with its roots in the era that produced European nationalism and bourgeois notions of individualism, offers the African writer only limited scope for naming states of being beyond the parameters of modern Western cultural experience. The signifier "homosexual," for instance, only has meaning within a cultural context in which, verbally at least, a clear distinction exists between so-called homo- and hetero-sexual forms of sexual intimacy. When Joe Golder announces his sexual and racial identities, he demands of his African respondents that they define themselves within these terms. To the African interpreters, Golder looks and sounds white. For them to recognize him as racially African would involve a suspension of the category "African" as they define it—in itself an act of imperialism. The same, Soyinka's text suggests, is the case when, in response to Golder's claiming of the identity homosexual, the interpreters must decide whether what they wish to do or not do sexually with him necessarily involves a redefinition of their sexual identity. Several of the sexual acts by which Golder's social identity as a homosexual is defined are acts performed in specific social contexts between men in various African societies who, if pressed, would probably identify themselves as heterosexual.[8]

The African novelists' use of homosexuality as a marker for a social relationship between colonizer and colonized rather than as an aspect of sexual identity may also be read as an internalization of the process within orientalist discourse by which the subaltern "other" was constructed as feminine or effeminate as a way of representing the power imbalance in the relationship between Europe and its colonies. The existence of the social category "homosexuality" within

Western discourse makes it virtually impossible for African writers who make use of the novel form to write about sexual intimacy in their societies without positioning their narratives in relation to the meanings associated with the "foreign" term. It is as if, in their novels, these postcolonial writers seek to engage with Western categories of identity and identification around issues of gender, power and sexuality but find them, like the parliamentary models imported by the new nation states, inadequate for addressing the unique complexities of African societies.

Placed within the context of such works, Nuruddin Farah's *Maps* can be read as an extension and elaboration of a familiar theme within modern African literature. *Maps* tells the story of Askar, a Somali child, raised in the Ogaden after World War II when that territory changed hands repeatedly as the superpowers supporting first Selassie then Mengistu changed sides. Somalia is unique among African nations in that practically all its citizens belong to a single ethnic group, but ethnic Somali live in an area which extends across the national boundaries of Somalia into Djibouti, Ethiopia, Kenya and even as far south as Tanzania. The Ogaden is the region enclosed in the angle of the elbow-shaped provisional border between Somalia and Ethiopia. It was subjugated by Anglo-Ethiopian forces in wars at the turn of the century, at a time when France, Britain and Italy were competing for jurisdiction over the rest of Somali territory.[9] For a brief period after the Italian occupation of Ethiopia several ethnic Somali territories were consolidated under a single administration, but after World War II the Allied Powers ceded the Ogaden to Ethiopia and the region has been claimed by Somali nationalists ever since. Under the feudal regime of Selassie, Somalia's claims on the Ogaden were supported by the Soviet Union, but when in 1974 Selassie was toppled by Mengistu's purportedly Marxist revolution, the East changed sides. Overnight the Ogaden, which had been successfully recovered by Somali forces, was repossessed by Ethiopia. The bloody battles which characterized this reversal are pivotal to the action in Farah's novel.

Like the territory of his birth, Askar is without natural parents. Instead, he is brought up by an Oromo servant woman named Misra who is tolerated by the ethnic Somali community, despite her outsider status and use of Amharic, the language of the Ethiopian oppressor, because of her strong maternal, even erotic ties to the orphaned child. The novel opens with the recounting of Askar's birth, or rather Misra's discovery of him in the blood of his dead mother. The position of the narrator during this act of recall anticipates Askar's position at the end of the novel—that of a solitary young man trying to make sense of his past and a brutal murder:

> You sit, in contemplative posture, your features agonized and your expressions pained; you sit for hours and hours and hours, sleepless, looking into

> darkness, hearing a small snore coming from the room next to yours. And you conjure a past: a past in which you see a horse drop its rider; a past in which you discern a bird breaking out of its shell so it will fly into the heavens of freedom. Out of the same past emerges a man wrapped in a mantle with unpatched holes, each hole large as a window—and each window large as the secret to which you cling as though it were the only soul you possessed. And you question, you challenge every thought which crosses your mind.[10]

The figure of the old man, whose rags frame windows into an abyss of historical uncertainty, suggests an unravelling of the traditional social fabric presented as seamless in earlier nationalist fictions. The reader is given due warning, not only that the traditional cultural certainties with which Askar is surrounded are up for grabs, but also that Askar's role as a reliable narrator of his own history—his actions and their motivation—cannot be taken for granted.

One of the ways in which the language of the text mirrors this shifting uncertainty is in its use of three personal pronouns to narrate Askar's story.[11] Askar identifies these at the end of the novel as the voices of judge, witness, and audience (246), although, typically, the lines between these three perspectives are not always reliably indicated by the pronoun used. The "you" voice of the opening paragraph quoted above is clearly associated with the judgmental or accusatory presence in the narrative, as it repeatedly challenges Askar to account for his actions and take responsibility for them. Paradoxically, its outer-directedness also has the effect of challenging the reader, who feels uncomfortably included in its reiterative "you."

The "I" narrator is altogether more sympathetic toward Askar. For example, the "you" voice describes the moment of bonding between Askar and Misra as the moment in which Askar by his stare binds Misra to his will, making her "responsible" for his existence:

> To Misra, you existed first and foremost in the weird stare: you were, to her, your eyes, which, once they found her, focused on her guilt—her self! . . . She was sure, for instance, that you saw her the way she was: a miserable woman, with no child and no friends; a woman who, that dusk— would you believe it?—menstruated right in front of you, under that most powerful stare of yours. She saw, in that look of yours, her father, whom she saw last when she was barely five. (6)

Here, the "you" voice harps on the newborn male child's access to privilege which even in his infant stare establishes the imbalance of power versus powerlessness that, from the perspective of this narrator, characterizes Askar's relationship to the servant woman. By contrast, the "I" voice argues later in the text that it was Misra's touch rather than Askar's stare which established the bond of love between them—a bond so strong that it ultimately breaks down the ego boundaries between the boy and the woman:

> Misra never said to me that I existed for her only in my look. What she said was that she could see in my stare an itch of intelligence—that's all. She said she had found it commendable that I could meet death face to face and that I could outstare the Archangel of Death. For in my stare, there was my survival and in my survival, perhaps "a world's"— mine and hers. I remember how often she held me close to herself, and how, lamenting or plaintive, she would whisper into my ears, endearments the like of which I am not likely to hear ever again. One of these endearments, I recall, was, "My dearest, my little world"! She would then lapse into Amharic, her mother-tongue, and, showering me with kisses, she would utter more of such endearments I wouldn't understand. Then she would end them with the one she most often employed when teasing me or giving me a wash, one which, if translated, would mean, "my little man." (23)

This time it is the woman's love that defines the child. It creates the private world that joins the two, and in which he is offered the privilege of masculinity as a term of endearment rather than the prerogative of an oppressor. The "I" voice is the vehicle through which Askar tries to establish his identity, mostly by describing and assessing his responses to evanescent objects and sensations in relation to which he plots his position as fixed or at least stable: the feel of water, the taste of blood, his feelings of being connected to Misra as he lies between her breasts. In many ways this voice seems to articulate Askar's female self—the self which remembers having menstruated, for example (151); the self that has difficulty recognizing the boundaries between Misra's body and feelings and his own (40, 205); or the alter ego whom he meets in dreams in the body of a young girl who claims that all she is sure she owns is her shadow (129–30). When Askar recalls the visits of the hated Aw-Adan, Misra's lover, he remembers watching as Aw-Adan's penis came to life, creating a third leg and cancelling out the wooden leg that the Koran teacher always removed before he had intercourse with Misra (31–2). Curiously, Askar's "I" voice also uses the image of a third leg to describe Askar himself, as he sleeps in the space between Misra's spread-eagled limbs (24). It is as if, in taking on a feminized identity through his merging with Misra, Askar becomes Misra's penis or third leg. And we can read this either as Askar's masculinization (or empowerment) of Misra, or his erasure of her as he incorporates her entire feminine identity into himself.

The story narrated through the voice of the third person singular "he" seems to correspond to the perspective of an elusive audience. This voice provides a record of the political events in Somalia and the Ogaden which unfold parallel to the story of Askar's life, but it is also the form of narration most often used in recounting Askar's dreams. The third person voice moves more freely across chronological time, making connections that often go well beyond the realm of the protagonist's immediate experience. Perhaps this voice represents the consciousness of a mature Askar, rendered sadder and wiser by the inevitability of suffering. When the pain that follows Askar's circumcision becomes too intense, he experiences a sensation of disembodiment which the "you" voice describes as creating a self "stand[ing] out from the others, with a view to studying the activities, thoughts of your primary self" (66). Alternatively, aspects of the perspective of the third person voice correspond at times to that of Askar's uncle Hilaal to whose home in Mogadiscio Askar moves on leaving the Ogaden before the reversals of the war. Hilaal is an "enlightened" intellectual who has divested himself of traditional gender roles. He has had a vasectomy in solidarity with his wife, Salaado, who cannot bear children, and he stays at home to do the cooking while Salaado drives their car and teaches at the university. Hilaal provides a socio-political gloss of events through which Askar may contextualize his experience. However, his words, rather than reinforcing Askar's sense of connectedness with reality, are experienced as profoundly disorienting. As the "you" voice comments early in the narrative:

> At times, when your uncle speaks about you, in your presence, referring to you in the third person and, on occasion, even taking the liberty of speaking on your behalf, you wonder if your existence is readily differentiable from creatures of fiction whom habit has taught one to talk of as if they were one's closest of friends—creatures of fiction with whose manner of speech; reactions to situations; conditions of being; and with whose likes and dislikes one's folk tradition has made one familiar. (3)

Apart from his three narrative personae, Askar possesses other resources by means of which he identifies himself and tries to measure his distance from or proximity to Misra or his "feminine" self. Calendars are important to him because he can use them in Mogadiscio to chronicle the success or failure of the nationalist struggle in the Ogaden. They also are associated with sexual vulnerability, as after the horror of an abortion which Askar witnesses, Misra keeps a calendar in the room she shared with Askar during his childhood on which she charts in green the "safe" days for sexual intercourse. And then there are Askar's mirrors and maps:

> . . . the one to reflect my visage, showing me whether or not I've grown a beard after so many disastrous beginnings—including, do you remember? my saying that if Karin's menopausal hair-on-the-chin was 'manlier' than mine it

> was high time I did something about it; the other, i.e. the maps which give me the distance in scales of kilometrage—the distance that is between you and me. Which is to say that we are a million minutes apart, your 'anatomy' and mine. (18)

This passage appears in quotation marks within the discourse of the "you" narrator. As a result it is virtually impossible to deduce to whom the "you" addressed within the text refers. It could be an extract from a letter to Misra, in which case, the "do you remember" appeals to the corpus of memories about their neighbor Karin and life in the Ogaden which the boy once shared with Misra, before they were separated by "millions of minutes." But we know that Misra cannot read and that Askar's letters to Misra remain "unfinished and unposted," so perhaps the "you" within the quotation marks addresses Askar's other self, the self which was merged with Misra's before his coming to Mogadiscio; before his discovery that "it appears as though it were a great virtue to be self-sufficient [as] Uncle Hilaal and Salaado are" (18).

Farah's presentation of Askar's shifting selves can be read as a form of intertextual play on Ngugi wa Thiongo's political thriller *Petals of Blood* (1977). Like *Maps*, *Petals of Blood* takes its point of departure from the occasion of a murder whose perpetrator is revealed in the course of a self narrative. In Ngugi's novel, the death of a hated neocolonial comprador is recounted as the possible result of the action of one of four people: a prostitute, whom the comprador has violated; a trade unionist and a former freedom fighter, both of whom seek revenge for the comprador's crimes against the people; or the narrator himself, a sometime fellow traveller and alter ego of the murdered man. But in *Petals of Blood* the murder victim is clearly defined as "the Other": a hated representative of the corrupted neocolonial nation state. In *Maps*, not only are the accuser and the accused different aspects of the same person, but the victim of the murder—who it ultimately emerges is Misra—is also represented as an aspect of the accused. Time and again within the course of the narrative, one or another of Askar's selves threatens to kill all rivals for Misra's affection (77); to kill Misra herself (37); to be incapable of conceiving of an existence without Misra (75–6, 88); or incapable of finding himself without exorcising her presence (57). Askar's crossing and recrossing of the boundaries of his self make it virtually impossible for the reader to be certain whether or not he is implicated in Misra's death.

The inability of the narrative voices that define Askar to differentiate between Askar and Misra, between maleness and femaleness, and between age and youth or accuser and accused works also as a metaphor for the shifting status of the signifier "nation" within the Ogaden and for Somalia as a whole.

As Hilaal explains, Somalia is one of the few nations in Africa that can define itself in "specific" rather than "generic" terms:

> Ethiopia is the generic name of an unclassified mass of different peoples, professing different religions, claiming to have descended from different ancestors. Therefore, "Ethiopia" becomes that generic notion, expansive, inclusive. Somali, if we come to it, is specific. That is, you are either a Somali or you aren't. (148)

What seems at this point the only certainty in the text, however, is immediately undermined by Askar's logic. For though this definition makes it possible for Hilaal to assume the essential unity of the Somali nation, currently split between Kenya, Somalia, Djibouti and the Ogaden, it leaves Askar confused and uncertain about the status of Misra or, more precisely, the status of that part of himself which is inseparable from Misra. When Askar discovers that there is no mention of Misra on his newly acquired Somali citizenship papers, he asks Hilaal what the essential marker of Somali-ness is. Hilaal answers:

> A Somali . . . is a man, woman or child whose mother tongue is Somali. Here, mother tongue is important, very important. Not what one looks like. That is, features have nothing to do with a Somali's Somaliness or no. True, Somalis are easily distinguishable from other people, but one might meet with foreseeable difficulty in telling an Eritrean, an Ethiopian or a Northern Sudanese apart from a Somali, unless one were to consider the cultural difference. (166)

Misra speaks fluent Somali and has lived all her adult life within Somali communities. From Askar's perspective her cultural traits are identical with his own. Thus he reasons that she, too, could qualify for Somali citizenship. Hilaal responds with a hypothetical "yes" but counters that Somalis living outside the nation state are *unpersons* because "they lack what makes the self strong and whole" (167). Hilaal's caveat throws both Askar and Misra back outside the circle of national certitude and Askar is left as confused about where to draw the national boundaries around himself as he was before, unless he can find a way to distinguish between himself and Misra.

Askar's anxieties around questions of gender and national identity interface serendipitously in Farah's introduction of the term "misgenderer," applied to non-native speakers of Somali who confound "the masculine third-person singular wrongly replaced or displaced by the female third-person singular" (161). This grammatical conflation of the Somali words for "he" and "she" is most common in the speech of non-Somalis. But it is also a feature of the speech of ethnic Somalis like Askar and his fervently nationalistic tutor (the author of a doctoral dissertation on the subject of misgendering) who have been brought up in far flung corners of Somali settlement. The term misgenderer seems to apply equally to Askar's unstable gender identity as well as his growing sense in the months following the outbreak of war in the Ogaden that his national identity is in some way violated by his intimacy with the non-Somali Misra.

Askar's sense of violation is shared by his friend and alter ego, a boy of ethnic Somali extraction who was once raped by an Adenese interloper, and whose manhood as a result is constantly called into question. One of the first secrets Askar keeps from Misra is his membership with this boy in a small group of youths who train secretly to become guerilla fighters in the war against Ethiopia. Askar is infected by the general mood among Somalis within the Ogaden who see the non-Somalis in their midst as potential traitors and he struggles to distance himself from Misra: "What mattered, he told himself, was that now he was at last a man, that he was totally detached from his mother-figure Misra, and weaned. In the process of looking for a substitute, he had found another—Somalia, his mother country" (96). But Askar's sense of a separate identity is constantly undermined by the long history of his intimacy with Misra, which makes it impossible for him to remain untouched by her uncertainties and anxieties about the desired outcome of the war. "'It was as if you were born with a deformity that you had to carry with you everywhere you went,' he said to the boy whom the Adenese had raped. Indeed, who better could he say this to, than another boy who carried on his head another shame of another kind?" (109). Significantly, for one whose masculinity was first defined by Misra's touching of his genitals (35), Askar will no longer allow Misra to touch him when he bathes—or, as he puts it, "to wash the dirt my body has accumulated when training to kill my people's enemy" (109).

The novel ends soon after the reversal of the war in the Ogaden, known in Somalia as "The Tragic Weekend" (155). In the frustration and bloodshed that follow the reversal, Askar receives word that Misra, whom he has not seen for over a decade since he left the Ogaden for Mogadiscio at the beginning of the war, has become an informer. Misra is accused by the Somali community in the Ogaden of having betrayed the Somali freedom fighters to her new Ethiopian lover, an act which leads to the slaughter of 603 men, women and children. Gang-raped, brutalized and ill, Misra makes her way to Askar in Mogadiscio where he now lives with his uncle and aunt. Askar must decide whether to accept her story that she had merely helped the Ethiopian soldiers to find fresh supplies of milk or to believe she is a traitor. He must also decide whether to take revenge on her if she is a traitor, or to avenge her violation at the hands of his fellow Somalis if she is not. Predictably, within this narrative, Misra's veracity and her bludgeoned death remain shrouded in mystery, and it is only the fact of Askar's arrest by the Mogadiscio police that suggests that he may have been implicated in the crime. The text provides no certainties beyond the conflicting assertions and absences in the stories told by Askar's several selves.

By the end of the story, however, it is clear that Askar has simultaneously appropriated those aspects of Misra's person that he can not afford to live without. Her mastectomy shortly before her death is one of the more graphic metaphors for this process (207), as is the fact that when her body is found, its heart is missing. Whereas Armah represents the postcolonial malaise through images of predatory exploiters preying on the African body politic, Farah sees the engorging of the other as an activity associated with the new nationalist subject. Indeed, dismemberment and/or the feeding off the body of another are recurring features of Askar's fantasies. In one dream which he has around the time of Misra's disappearance, he encounters Misra at the edge of the ocean which she had always longed to see:

> She stood in the shallows and fishes came to her, playful fishes, going between her legs, the curve of her elbow; small and big fishes, and on occasion even a shark, timid as a lamb. She didn't see me. She was busy feeding the fishes with her blood, the flow of her period. She was busy tending to the sickly among the fishes, feeding them with motherly care.
>
> I was utterly in love with her. (214)

Conversely, we are warned that as a result of Misra's death Askar has in some ways become a living corpse. His thoughts and conversations become obsessed with the taste of blood in his mouth, and the fear that he is an extension of the corpse of his mother who died while giving birth to him.

The no-win contradictions of Askar's relationship with Misra come to represent the endless conundrum of the Somali nationalist struggle, where each shift in national status comes at the price of 603 more corpses. The morning after Askar dreams of feeding off Misra's menstrual blood, his uncle tries to talk to him about Misra. Hilaal's attention is diverted by a map in Askar's room on which the word Ogaden has been erased and replaced by the term "Western Somalia." Hilaal asks Askar if he finds truth in the maps he draws and Askar ultimately responds:

> I identify *a* truth in the maps which I draw. When I identify *this* truth, I label it as such, pickle it as though I were to share it with you, and Salaado. I hope, as dreamers do, that the dreamt dream will match the dreamt reality—that is, the invented truth of one's imagination. My maps invent nothing. They

> copy a given reality, they map out the roads a dreamer has walked, they identify a notional truth. (216)

Askar hopes here for a blueprint with which his lived experience will ultimately coincide: a notional truth that will map out a way for him once and for all to be one with Misra as well as his separate self; that will allow the Ogaden to live out its generic identity as a place of mixed ethnic populations as well as its specific destiny as part of Somalia. But even this provisional longing for a notional truth is undermined in his uncle's response: "The question is, does *truth* change?" (217).

Farah is unremitting in his insistence that there can be no easy certainties or identities in the Somali situation or about the historical events that have produced them. At every turn in the narrative we are challenged to call our assumptions into question: about imperialism (the "imperial" powers in the Somali conflict today are other African countries); about our sense of the "natural" justice of the nationalist cause, even where a nation state like Somalia can boast a specific rather than generic identity. Ultimately Farah calls into question the most cherished myths of modern African identity—from the "natural" moral superiority of oral pretechnological cultures over literate cultures (Ethiopia has had a written tradition for centuries, the Somali language had no orthography until 1972); to the inevitability of certain gender and ethnic categories.

The question remains to be asked, therefore, how if at all does Farah's deconstruction of African nationalist discourse differ from the strategies used by Western postmodern theorists. In a recent article entitled "Postcolonialism, Postmodernism and the Rehabilitation of Postcolonial History," Helen Tiffin claims for Third World postcolonial writers a reconstructing rather than deconstructive intent in their undermining of received cultural categories.[12] She critiques Western deconstructionists for using the notion of "the other" like explorers did "turkeys, parrots and Indians," as "innocent signifiers," devoid of cultural meaning outside of their role as boundary markers "enthusiastically embraced by a depleted (western) system" (172). Tiffin posits instead a version of African literature in which the ontology and epistemology of traditional African cultures act "to subvert the political and textual authority of the imperial European perspective with a view to cultural reclamation, the breaking of a mould to reveal a new potential for wholeness *based on, if not entirely composed of the resuscitated materials of the original culture*" (175). Although I agree with Tiffin's critique of the uses Western theorists have made of the notion of the colonial Other, the final portion of her argument that I have italicized runs the risk of fixing the African/Third World reality in some form of original prelapsarian innocence which can only ultimately infantilize the African subject. It is as if, for this type of critic, the notional truth represented by Askar's narcissistic "I" voice, which perceives its own subjectivity as stable in the midst of a world of flux, could exist independently of the perspectives offered by the accusatory "you" and the subconscious, disembodied or analytical "he" narrations.

Farah's destabilization of national and sexual boundaries forces a remapping of the terrain that would take more fully into account the complexity of the modern nation-state in Africa. In the process, the evocation of "traditional" truths as the paradoxically static yet organic point of departure for the nation state is replaced by a sense of the dynamic interaction and internal contradictions of both the traditional and the modern in today's African nation. Such a strategy could in Bakhtin's terms truly challenge a Western paradigm of linearity and consolidation; not merely by endlessly pulling out the deconstructionist's rug from under the feet of the dominant/imperial culture, but by confronting and accepting the way in which any act or identity within human culture situates itself in relation to the fluctuating social forces that constitute its specific historical moment.[13]

Farah's text offers no answers, but it challenges us to resist the reflexive urge to pin down a single version of the African reality as "true" without first attempting to take seriously the conflicts, tensions and absences inherent in any narrative of the past or present. His stance makes it possible to reread many of the earlier narratives of the nationalist era in ways that escapc the paternalism inherent in western notions of "otherness," as well as the uncritical assertion of essence that underlies much of the discourse around nationalism and sexualities in modern African fiction.

NOTES

1. See Biodun Jeyifo, "On the Nature of Things: Arrested Decolonization and Critical Theory," *Research in African Literatures*, 21, 1 (1990), pp. 33–46, for a thoughtful analysis of the ways in which this contestation of discursive space overdetermines all aspects of the opposing critical positions held by (mostly Western) "Africanists" and (mostly African) "Nationalists" in the field of African Studies.

2. See Benedict Anderson, *Imagined Communities: Reflections on the Origin and Spread of Nationalism* (London: Verso, 1983), pp. 190ff.

3. For a useful summary of Bayart's argument and an explication of his debt to Gramsci, see Paul Geschiere, "Hegemonic Regimes and Political Protest: Bayart,

Gramsci and the State in Cameroon," in W. van Binsbergen, Filip Reyntjens and Gerti Hesseling, eds., *State and Local Community in Africa* (Brussels: Centre d'étude et de documentation Africaines), 2, 2–4 (1986), pp. 309–345.

4. For an analysis of the ways in which both Okonkwo and his creator negotiate definitions of manhood in situations of socio-political flux, see my "Making Men and History: Achebe and the Politics of Revisionism in *Things Fall Apart*," in Bernth Lindfors, ed., *Teaching Things Fall Apart* (New York: Modern Language Association, 1991).

5. Armah's linking of homosexuality with a parallel range of decadent social and sexual practices has suggestive precedent in Renaissance Europe's demarcation between natural and unnatural acts within a cosmology of the Great Chain of Being. In this regard, see Alan Bray's *Homosexuality in Renaissance England* (London: Gay Men's Press, 1982), for a discussion of the ways in which the distortion of gender roles and deviation from the norms of heterosexual intercourse were explained in sixteenth-century England as bodily reflections of a disruption in the social and spiritual order.

6. Chris Dunton, "Wheyting be Dat? The Treatment of Homosexuality in African Literature," *Research in African Literatures*, 20, 3 (1989), pp. 422–448.

7. In a famous, if probably apocryphal, response to the Negritude movement's claims to have identified and articulated the essence of Africanness, Soyinka is said to have commented: "The Tiger has no need to proclaim his Tigritude."

8. Cindy Patton's paper at the Nationalisms and Sexualities Conference discussed the implications of this ambiguity surrounding sexual practices and social identity for AIDS education in Africa. Of course, discrepancies between sexual practice and social identity are not exclusively an African "problem." I'm indebted to Patton for another anecdote about her experience as an AIDS educator with a group of self-identified gay youths in America who, having presented themselves for AIDS education were horrified to learn that anal intercourse was considered a standard form of sexual intimacy between gay men. Their own sexual practices had merely involved forms of mutual masturbation which many self-respecting macho youths might consider a normal part of their heterosexual initiation.

9. For a summary of the checkered colonial and precolonial history of Somalia, see "Colonialism and the Struggle for National Independence", in David D. Laitin and Said S. Samatar, *Somalia: Nation in Search of a State* (London: Gower Press, 1987), pp. 48–67. For a more detailed analysis, see I.M. Lewis, *A Modern History of Somalia: Nation and State in the Horn of Africa* (Boulder, CO: Westview Press, 1988).

10. Nuruddin Farah, *Maps* (New York: Pantheon Books, 1986), p. 3. All subsequent citations are taken from this edition and will appear parenthetically in the text above.

11. I'm indebted to Adrienne Taptitch who, in a term paper entitled "Three Narratives of One Childhood," first drew my attention to the significance of Farah's trinity of narrators.

12. Helen Tiffin, "Postcolonialism, Postmodernism and the Rehabilitation of Post-colonial History," *Journal of Commonwealth Literature*, 23, 1 (1988), pp. 169–181. Subsequent citations will appear parenthetically above.

13. I'm thinking here of Bakhtin's argument in "Discourse and the Novel" (from *The Dialogic Imagination*, trans. Caryl Emerson and Michael Holquist [Austin: University of Texas Press, 1981], pp. 259–422), that any system of meaning must constantly reinvent itself in response to the centrifugal and centripetal forces that simultaneously seek to subvert it at its margins or reduce it to an incommunicable exclusivity at its center. Hilaal's concept of the generic and specific natures of the hypothetical nation state can be read as one expression of this dynamic.

Chapter 3

Bradford's "Ancient Members" and "A Case of Buggery . . . Amongst Them"

Jonathan Goldberg

Granting, with Benedict Anderson, that the nation is an imaginary construct, the same must be true of a national literature. Both thrive on retrospection and the invention of tradition. William Bradford's *Of Plymouth Plantation, 1620–1647* has, by U.S. literary critics, been accorded an originary status in a national imaginary; Francis Murphy concludes his introduction to the Modern Library edition by hailing Bradford as "the first in a long line of American writers . . . who grasped the imaginative possibilities of the essential American myth: the story of a people who set themselves apart from the rest of the world and pledged themselves together in self-sacrifice and love."[1] Several generations of scholars have turned to Bradford as the repository of the American essence, finding in the separatism of the Puritans a vision of the ideal American community. That view comes under scrutiny in Wayne Franklin's *Discoverers, Explorers, Settlers: The Diligent Writers of Early America*, which argues that despite its professed goal to represent a community insulated in its beliefs, Bradford's text points the way to a more pluralistic America composed of "competing views . . . an abundance of centers . . . rather than any old scheme of cultural domination."[2]

The limits to such a reading of Bradford are suggested by another vision of America, one ignored equally by traditional and revisionist Bradford scholars. In Jonathan Ned Katz's groundbreaking *Gay American History* and in his *Gay/Lesbian Almanac*, Bradford's 1642 chapter devoted to sodomy appears as a founding text for the oppression of gays in the U.S.A.[3] While it is true that it is as anachronistic to speak of gay identity in relation to a colonial text as it is to read Bradford's *Plymouth Plantation* as a national text, the reading is justified by subsequent history. The 1986 Supreme Court decision in Bowers v. Hardwick (478 U.S. 186) declaring that there was no "fundamental right to engage in homosexual sodomy" points in the direction of Bradford. For it made its decision a matter of national interest; fundamental rights are defined as those "'deeply rooted in this Nation's history and tradition' or 'implicit in the concept of ordered liberty'"; and the history and tradition to which the justices refer includes biblical prohibitions and the sixteenth-century English law that lies behind the statutes of the colonies, as Chief Justice Burger stressed in his concurring note to the majority decision.

The dissenting opinion filed by four Justices registered the moral and intellectual poverty of the majority view, and in terms similar to Franklin's opposition to prevailing readings of Bradford: "From the standpoint of the individual," Justice Stevens wrote, "the homosexual and the heterosexual have the same interest in deciding how he will live his own life. . . . A policy of selective application must be supported by . . . something more substantial than a habitual dislike for, or ignorance about, the disfavored group." The "love" that Murphy celebrates in the vision of America bequeathed by Bradford is found by the Supreme Court to be equivalent to heterosexuality. Franklin might seem to dispute this, when, listing the members of a "rogues' gallery" of grasping newcomers and strangers in Bradford, "along with worse figures like Weston, Allerton, Lyford, and Thomas Granger" (172), he assembles among those who have a place in a future America unimaginable to Bradford, the "bugger," Thomas Granger, who is the subject of the 1642 chapter. Franklin names him as if blandly equivalent to the others on his list, and his list is guilty of a blindness equally apparent in Justice Stevens' liberal faith: women are tacitly ignored in his celebration of individuality. Franklin follows Bradford here, just as he fails to remark the absence of Indians in his more diverse American future. Moreover, however much Granger is "in" Bradford's text, he is there as the other men are not, in a merciless paragraph describing his death. That difference cannot be ignored. It is, I will be suggesting in the pages that follow, related to the tacit limits to the American version of liberalism that Franklin fetches from Bradford. Why the Supreme Court minority view failed to sway the majority may also come into focus as we explore the erotic dimensions of Bradford's vision of community.

It is from a passage in Bradford mourning the loss of this community that Franklin derives the title to his chapter devoted to Bradford, "Like An Ancient Mother":

> And thus was this poor church left, like an ancient mother grown old and forsaken of her children, though not in their affections yet in regard of their bodily presence and personal helpfulness; her ancient members being most of them worn away by death, and those of later time being like children translated into other families, and she like a widow left only to trust in God. Thus, she that had made many rich became herself poor. (370–71)

For Franklin, the passage offers a "benchmark from which Bradford's most important historical measurements are run in the book. The ancient mother-church is still a point of uncorrupted ideals . . ." (168). Reading this passage, Franklin never asks about its gendering, about the role that the mother is made to play in this vision of relations between men, and the dispersal of the "ancient members," the original settlers of Plymouth that are Bradford's signal point of attraction and identification.[4]

The "ancient members" of this passage are pitted against those that came after, not only the newcomers, but also their own children. A fierce antagonism between generations operates as one of the dividing lines *within* the community. "Translated" names obliquely the regular practice of putting out children to be raised by other families, a division within the patriarchy that virtually operates to redraw class lines (it was not only the children of poor families who became servants in others' houses), and that ensures the division of labor (children are a commodity in this system) and the increase of wealth finally lamented in the passage.[5] Having crossed class lines, the children of the founding fathers are also allied with the so-called strangers (many of whom remained apart from the community), or the newcomers, or those who arrived on their "particulars" and who did not become incorporated within the "general" body. Despite all these removals, of children and ancient members, the widowed mother-church is represented as yet married—to God. Thus, an ideal of the family and of the enclosed community is preserved—as an ideological construct at some distance from and yet as the sustaining rhetoric for what actually happened at Plymouth. As Bradford records, the early attempt to form extended households—so that unmarried men, or men who arrived without their families, were incorporated into families—eventually had to be abandoned. That initial arrangement "farmed out" all single men—in the name of the family. It was, of course, in the name of the family that the Supreme Court came to its decision in Bowers v. Hardwick.

In Bradford, an ideal of union *between men* is represented through the union of the mother-church with God. The "ancient mother" in this passage—the woman—is represented as abandoned, and to serve as an ideal from which men depart never to return. That movement is virtually enacted in the passage when the "ancient mother" is transmuted into the "ancient members"; from the division between older and younger men, pilgrims and other men, pathos is generated by the yearning for the ancient members.

The founding fathers may have arrived with their families and servants, yet Bradford's record of tensions between the oldcomers and the newcomers, between the general and the particulars, hardly concerns family life except for questions of property; women appear remarkably infrequently in his account. In the "ancient mother" passage, women are translated into a trope of ideal femininity, a fantasmatic female that secures male-male arrangements and an all male history. Written under the sign of an ancient mother, those male arrangements are secured beneath a spirituality that is nominally female and which serves a normative heterosexuality that barely obscures the fact that Bradford's attention is always on other men, whether the rogues or his divided fellow members—on other white men, that is, since Bradford's text excludes Indians as much as it can.

Unlike most other accounts of the settlement of North America, Bradford's has no space for even a minimal ethnography; Indians figure only in the spheres of trade and war, treaties and betrayals; in this his text represents a kind of limit case in new world writing.[6] A purple passage on the burning of the Pequot Indians at Mystic (not listed, as the "ancient mother" passage is, as memorable at the end of Samuel Eliot Morison's edition of his text) records a genocidal impulse in Bradford:

> all was quickly on a flame, and thereby more were burnt to death than was otherwise slain. It burnt their bowstrings and made them unserviceable; those that scaped the fire were slain with the sword, some hewed to pieces, others run through with their rapiers, so that they were quickly dispatched and very few escaped. It was conceived they thus destroyed about 400 at this time. It was a fearful sight to see them thus frying in the fire and the streams of blood quenching the same, and horrible was the stink and scent thereof; but the victory seemed a sweet sacrifice, and they gave the praise thereof to God, who had wrought so wonderfully for them, thus to enclose their enemies in their hands and give them so speedy a victory over so proud and insulting an enemy. (331)

Anglo women and Indians are not identical in Bradford's text, except insofar as they must be effaced in order for history to move forward as the exclusive preserve of white men. While white women are "saved" by the figuration of the mother church (and this, in turn, saves male-male relations from sexual stigmatization), Indians never are idealized. They appear more often than women, especially in the opening and closing chapters of the book—as helpers, providing food or beaver pelts, or hindrances to the Puritans, who are always represented as innocent peacemakers; at best, there is occasional sympathy for Indians, especially when they are dying. For Bradford, they are always "savages." It is thus worth pointing to the ways in which women and Indians are joined, as Ann Kibbey does in her discussion of the Pequot War,[7] to take a full measure of Bradford's genocidal text. In his description of the bloody massacre at Fort Mystic (one that featured the slaughter of women and children), an impulse buried in Bradford's initial description of the new world as "vast and unpeopled" (26) begins to be realized—the impulse to *make* it unpeopled.

These lethal energies also can be found in the "ancient mother" passage, even when the next generation of Puritans is being represented. These energies are not only directed against women and Indians, but are also deflected onto the bodies of other white men. How this is related to the divided constitution of Plymouth is suggested by a "providential" story Bradford tells about the crossing on the Mayflower, when a "lusty" young man refuses to help those who are sick and helpless:

> It pleased God before they came half seas over, to smite this young man with a grievous disease, of which he died in a desperate manner, and so was himself the first to be thrown overboard. Thus his curses light on his own head, and it was an astonishment to all his fellows for they noted it to be the just hand of God upon him. (66)

When, two pages later, Bradford records that only one passenger died in the crossing, "William Butten, a youth, a servant to Samuel Fuller, when they drew near the coast" (68), the death "before they came half seas over" of the "lusty" young man has been expunged. The nameless young man is not the named youth—the designation of his master further assures that. Similarly, the "Civil Body Politic" (84) compacted on the Mayflower in the face of mutiny was signed only by those who represented the "better part" (84), the "ancient members." They have their dutiful servants, others' children, single men, housed under their roofs; nameless dissolute young men have no place in this compact except insofar as they are willing servants of their masters. One consequence of these arrangements (fearful to be named, Bradford would write) is just that division of the society between hierarchically disposed male bodies that, Alan Bray has convincingly argued, facilitated male-male sexual behavior, and the bodies of "lusty" and rebellious young men on whom the sin of sodomy could be attached.[8] No wonder then that age and generational tension mark Bradford's text.

It is thus worth pausing over the nature of the all-male ideal that Bradford espouses. *Plymouth Plantation* opens by situating the notion of "removal" (to Amsterdam, to Leyden, to Plymouth) as a strategy for narrowing the perimeters around the community, for ensuring the separateness of "the better part" (4). Theirs is the history of a true church whose removals made it possible for "the truth" to "spring and spread" (3). What necessitates removal to America is the fear of the "dissolution" and "scattering" (24–25) of the chosen seed, the "sowing" of the seeds of error, a worry manifest in what is said to be happening to the dispirited and wayward youth in Leyden. Bradford's terms—seed, fruit, sowing, scattering and dissolution—are fetched from the Bible; they are also insistently sexual. So read, they can help us understand both the energies that animate Bradford as he regards the "ancient members," but also the lethal energies unleashed on Thomas Granger. One might well wonder why a sixteen or seventeen year old boy caught having sex with a mare should figure as the last on Franklin's list of who are the "worst" in Bradford (this does not misrepresent Bradford in the least) and what he might share with Weston (the backer that failed Bradford), the "atheist" Morton (whose crime seems to have been his attempt to form an egalitarian community), or Allerton, Bradford's partner who cut his own deals, or the backsliding minister Lyford. One answer lies in seeing that there are networks of connection between these allowable figures (the excluded who can be included) and those who do not even figure in this list, women and Indians. By pursuing these connections, we can come closer to understanding the function of sodomy in Bradford and its relation to the ideal of community that animates his text.

Consider the case of Lyford, the minister offended by Puritan exclusivity, the rule of the so-called "better part"; "the smallest number in the Colony . . . appropriate the ministry to themselves" (177), Lyford is discovered to have written in an intercepted letter, and his wife is called upon to give the clinching evidence against her husband. "She feared to fall into the Indian's hands and to be defiled by them as he had defiled other women" (185). The good wife here (a woman entirely complicitous or represented as being so) is admitted into the community in order to voice Lyford's identification as an Indian, to represent the Indian as a fornicator bent on the capture and rape of white women. Lyford's willingness to extend the community of believers beyond the limits of tolerability is signalled by the case mounted against him, of his use of his ministry as a way to the bed of other women, usually serving women, but, in the most fully detailed instance, the future wife of one of his parishioners: "Lyford had overcome her and defiled her body before marriage"; even worse it seems, "though he had satisfied his lust on her, yet he endeavoured to hinder conception" (187).

Lyford's religious "crimes" are translated into sexual ones, fornication and adultery, but in "hindering conception," his crime could also fall under the label of sodomy (in the broad sense of the term, as any form of sexual activity without procreation as its ostensible aim).[9] The last charge, which seals the case against him for Bradford—it is the worst that can be said about Lyford—is also palpably excessive.

Yet it is how Lyford can come to be in a list that ends in Thomas Granger. Such associations can be found throughout the text. Thus, Morton's threat to the Puritans' "lives and goods" is represented as even more fearsome than that of "the savages themselves" (230). If the proof of his profligacy is the allegation that his followers (lowerclass men whom Morton rescued from being sold into slavery) take "Indian women for their consorts" (227),[10] Morton's "School of Atheism" implies even worse deeds. Just as Lyford's "bad" religion translates into sodomitical sex, "atheism," as Bray points out, is a charge regularly made against sodomites. Beyond the explicitly named debauchery of Indian consorting (a "savage" debauchery that could fall under the broad label of sodomy), "worse practices" are hinted, "the beastly practices of the mad Bacchanalians," the "fairies, or furies" whirling about their "idle or idol maypole" (227), as Bradford puts it in prose whose doublings and allusions—in its refusals to name more directly—circles about the unnameable crime, and about the maypole erected in defiance of the ancient members. Such locutions only imitate what Richard Slotkin has read in the multiply-named pleasures of Merrymount—Marrymount, where whites and Indians joined; Marymount, where high church and "pagan" rituals mixed; and Maremount, evoking, as Slotkin concludes, "the image of sodomy, or buggery, a crime that troubled New England not a little (by Bradford's account),"[11] and which found its only detailed representation in Thomas Granger, "discovered by one that accidentally saw his lewd practice towards the mare" (355).

Granger is thus the worst of these unclean members, the site towards which these representations move. Tensions of age, race, class, and gender fasten on his body to unleash homophobic energies that serve the all-white male ideal in Bradford. Why the threat should be crystallized there—how it is that Granger is even admitted into Bradford's text—can be further understood if we look at another of the purple passages in Bradford, a very late (probably the last) addition to his manuscript. On one side of the page, a letter jointly penned by John Robinson, the leader of the church in Leyden who never joined his congregation in Plymouth, and by William Brewster, whose death is lamented by Bradford in the chapter immediately following the one devoted to sodomy. "We are knit together as a body" (34), the letter declares; on the facing page, Bradford replies:

> O sacred bond, whilst inviolably preserved! How sweet and precious were the fruits that flowed from the same! But when this fidelity decayed, then their ruin approached. O that these ancient members had not died or been dissipated (if it had been the will of God) or else that this holy care and constant faithfulness had still lived, and remained with those that survived, and were in times afterwards added unto them. But (alas) that subtle serpent hath slyly wound himself under fair pretences of necessity and the like, to untwist these sacred bonds and tied, and as it were insensibly by degrees to dissolve, or in a great measure to weaken, the same. I have been happy, in my first times, to see, and with much comfort to enjoy, the blessed fruits of this sweet communion, but it is now a part of my misery in old age, to find and feel the decay and want thereof (in a great measure) and with grief and sorrow of heart to lament and bewail the same. And for others' warning and admonition, and my own humiliation, do I here note the same. (34–35)

The intensity of male bonds in this passage is unmistakeable. Women have no place here, not even figuratively. The "blessed fruits of . . . sweet communion" may look like a procreative metaphor, but these are sweets and fruits that flow between men, ideally between the "ancient members," who, in this fantasy either never would die or would be replaced by newcomers identical to the old. This is that fantasy of the seed and of the truth that opens Bradford's book, a fantasy about the spirit that has not been expended in a waste of shame. If this sacred bond looks like marriage, it is worth recalling that Bradford's first act as governor of Plymouth was to reinstitute marriage as a secular relation, taking it out of the hands of the church; the bond that ties men together is propagated in fruits that are not the children of heterosexual procreation but an overflow from member to member, a preservation of the chosen seed, here sadly dissolved and disseminated. Rather than spending their seed upon each other, those who have betrayed Bradford's vision have sowed seeds into the void. The death of the "ancient members" marks the end of the fantasy of the preservation of the "better part."

The sexuality that flows at such moments in the representation of the ideal male community suggests how close sodomy is to this discourse and why, when sodomy "breaks forth," as Bradford puts it (351)—when it becomes visible—it is violently repudiated. The fundamental nonrecognition in Bradford's text, I would argue, is the proximity of the ties that bind these men together and the possibility of literally enacting them. Let me be clear here: I am not suggesting that Bradford is secretly homosexual, or latently so. Rather, Bradford's text is (to follow Eve Kosofsky Sedgwick's use of the term in *Between Men*) eminently homosocial, and it preserves its fantasy of all male relations precisely by drawing the line—lethally— between its own sexual energies and those it calls sodomitical. The burst of energy in Bradford's evocation of the "sacred bond," like that in so many other of his purple passages, comes against the other more usual impulse in his prose: the desire not to say, the desire to efface which is variously aimed at women, Indians, and sodomites. "I omit," "I have been too long," "etc.," are the frequent marks in his text. "To cut things short" (167), this, despite its prolixity, is the desire of Bradford's text.

Bradford would, if he could, not tell anything. The case of Thomas Granger, and his unmentionable sin, is, Bradford writes, "horrible to mention" but must be told since "the truth of the history requires it" (355). The truth of the history, as I am reading it, is the entanglement of the "ancient members" with and the desire to separate from the figure of the sodomite who represents at once the negation of the ideal and its literalization. Even the mention of Granger, Bradford claims, goes only so far: "I forebear particulars" (356). His acts are not described, just the satisfaction of their punishment. "I forebear particulars" could be Bradford's refrain: "particulars" are also how he names all those who are not part of the "general," all the dissolute members that Bradford would cut off. Granger's execution is recorded in the middle of Bradford's 1642 chapter, devoted to the "breaking out of sundry notorious sins," drunkeness, incontinence, uncleanness, and "that which is worse, even sodomy and buggery (things fearful to name)" (351). His "buggery," as I've been suggesting, is the dense site of a series of crossings and displacements in Bradford. It's to those now that I turn.

Legally, sodomy and bestiality were synonomous, both "fearful to name," both warranting death. However, in New England, a distinction was made between male-male sexual misconduct and having sex with an animal. As Robert Oaks remarks, "Puritans were less hesistant to punish buggery with death than they were sodomy" (70). (Bradford's list of sexual crimes thus arrives at buggery last, as the worst.) This inconsistency between law and practice has been variously explained—usually by asking whether sodomy or bestiality was more likely to have been practiced in the period and thus more in need of policing, and by pointing to the fears of monstrous offspring that such matings with animals were thought to produce.[12] In those fears, "buggery" was given the potential to realize—literally—the debasement of procreative sexual behavior against which sodomy in general was measured. By killing someone for an act that was believed capable of bearing fruit, the tacit relation between prohibited and metaphorically idealized male-male relations could remain undisturbed. Thus, the body of the "bugger" could serve as the site for the assaultive energies against "sodomy," and at the same time preserve ideal male-male relations untouched by the crime—could, by displacing male-male sodomy onto male-animal buggery, fail to bring sodomy into relation with the overflow of spirit and seed Bradford favored.

By punishing an inter-species crime rather than one between men, the "unnaturalness" of sodomy is insisted upon, and thus its lack of relation to bonds between men. Granger, undistinguished in his punishment from that meted out upon the animals, is, in effect, not granted membership in the human race. The punishment is the one specified in Leviticus, but in equating Granger with his animal partners, Bradford's racist energies fasten on his body too. Bradford, after all, believes that Indians are "wild beasts," "savage and brutish men" (26). In his bestiality, Granger momentarily—and finally—steps into that lethal space in Bradford's text reserved for the bodies of Indians.

But Granger's act is with a female of the species, a mare, and the crossing of species serves to mark a gender crossing as well as a racial one. To see that, we need to recall that Granger's story only surfaces midway in Bradford's chapter. Bradford begins by lamenting the appearence of sodomy, but it seems at first as if a "letter from the Governor in the bay . . . touching matters of the forementioned nature" (352), as if Governor Bellingham's case of "uncleanness" (353), is motivating him, not Granger's case at all. (Retrospectively, they will be connected.) The case in Massachusetts Bay involved what would, in modern terms, be thought of as rape—two underage female children were said to have been violated numerous times over the course of a couple of years, and by several different men. Appeals were sent to Plymouth and elsewhere (there was no statute that covered the case) and opinions were solicited; "sodomy" seemed a capacious enough category under which the case might fall, and Bradford polled various divines (the opinions of three find their way into his text). "Besides the occasion before mentioned in these writings concerning the abuse of those two children," Bradford finally admits, "they had about the same time a case of buggery fell out amongst them, which occasioned these questions, to which these answers have been made" (355). Granger's case and the Bay case are thought of together. Much as Bradford acts as if the outbreak of sodomy really hasn't happened at Plymouth, he finally admits otherwise. But displacement still takes place: Granger's buggery is being thought of in relation to a crime against women.

In their opinions, the learned divines measure the Massachusetts case against their own. They are divided by many issues, particularly, as Bradford summarizes the documents, whether death is warranted for crimes of bestiality and sodomy "if there be not penetration" (354). In that case, there should not have been any question of the punishment apt for the rape of the two girls; that's not how the Plymouth minister John Rayner understood the issue, however, "because there was not the like reason and degree of sinning against family and posterity in this sin as in some other capital sins of uncleanness" (Morison 405). Sodomy and buggery, when penetration can be proved, are capital sins; rape is "uncleanness," a lesser charge. The "logic" here is the same that led Bradford to regard Lyford's unprocreative adultery as more horrific than a "natural" adulterous act. Raping girls is less criminal than *any* sexual act between men or between a man and an animal. Thus the men charged in the Bay case were whipped severely, and one of them had his ears mutilated. They did not receive Granger's punishment. Crossing species—sleeping with a female horse—Granger's case is nominally sodomitical but also, and more significantly, a violation of the procreative act between sexes. However awful the Bay case was, at least it recognized that the female body was a site of procreation—such is Rayner's opinion: I need hardly point out how this hideous misogyny countenances rape and yet "saves" women for their proper role. The Bay case therefore was not a case of sodomy. Granger's was and deserved death. But it deserved that punishment precisely because it represented the worst male-female sexual behavior.

Thomas Granger thus is a transfer point for energies directed against Indians and women; his crossing of species is also a racial and gender crossing. His death along with his barnyard companions would seem to mark an absolute point of termination (the polluted animals, following the dictates of Leviticus, are not even allowed to serve for food). But, as Bradford puts it, Granger's case "fell out amongst them" and it remains to be said that his case *is* theirs. However much Granger displaces the anxieties about male-male sodomy, he also is a locus for them. This explains why the learned divines were so troubled about questions of penetration. To understand this, we need to notice yet another retrospective recontextualization in Bradford's text. For, after describing Granger's death, Bradford backtracks to a summary of his examination. When questioned, Granger's story is linked to one told by someone else "that had made sodomitical attempts upon another"; both said they learned such wickedness "in old England":

> this youth last spoken of said he was taught it by another that had heard of such things in England when he was there, and they kept cattle together. (356)

As usual, Bradford forebears particulars; here he seems to be conflating a March 1642 sodomy trial with Granger's September 1642 case. The earlier case had decided that the two men involved, Edward Michell and Edward Preston, had been engaged in "lewd & sodomitical practices tending to sodomy."[13] Public whippings were their punishment, to be witnessed by their townsmen, and by John Keene, a boy they had attempted, who was not found guilty, but not exactly innocent either ("in some thing he was faulty"). Michell had also attempted to "abuse" Lydia Hatch, and she in turn was said to have shared a bed with her brother. She too was whipped, and the brother banished from the community. These are all acts "tending to sodomy," acts in which penetration was not proved; none of these "sodomitical practices" (whether male-male or male-female—and incest seems to be included here) lead to the death penalty. "Normal" sodomy, practices tending to sodomy, were part of the usual fabric of sociosexual life.

The men, Bradford reports, confessed that they learned their crime when "they kept cattle togther" (Bradford thus conflates their sodomy with Granger's buggery, misrepresenting the differences in their fates). Once, as Bradford tells the story, that was what all the Puritans did. "They were not acquainted with trades nor traffic," Bradford writes of those English who originally removed to Amsterdam, "but had only been used to plain country life and the innocent trade of husbandry" (11). They all started as Thomas Grangers. For Granger was, after all, a quite ordinary English boy, indeed one of those farmed-out children upon which Bradford's ideal community rests, "servant to an honest man of Duxbury, being about 16 or 17 years of age. (His father and mother lived at the same time at Scituate)" (355). His case testifies to the unspeakable *continuity* between Bradford's ideal and the unmentionable horror of sodomy. No wonder, then, for all its deflections and despite the condensations upon Granger's body as the site of all that must be repudiated, the question that Bradford keeps asking in his 1642 chapter—both in its opening and closing pages—is, how could this happen here?

Alan Bray has remarked how Bradford displays the characteristic Elizabethan belief that sodomy is something which anyone is capable of doing, an eruption in "our corrupt natures, which are so hardly bridled, subdued and mortified" (351). Incipiently, Bradford (and Bray following him) read sodomy as the repressed, as a component inherent in human sexuality. Dammed up, it will out.[14] Yet, Bradford's view is insistently social and it seems worthwhile taking that seriously; not, obviously, to endorse his analysis, but because it suggests the social conditions through which sodomy came to be that which is discovered as *the* repressed, conditions in which repression is invented. "They are here more discovered and seen and made public by due search, inquisition and due punishment, for the churches look narrowly to their members" (352). The final locution connects of course to the object of Bradford's most rapturous desire, the old members to which he is always looking. Not surprisingly, then, it has its locus in a letter from John Robinson, the love letter that serves as the founding document of Plymouth. Robinson preaches the necessity of "watchfulness" (56): "Let every man repress in himself and the whole body in each person" (57). Repression here is a means of production; sexuality is not inherently within, it is produced as that which is within, the unseen that corresponds to what is seen. The gaze of members upon members produces what must be repressed—by inquisition and punishment when made visible, but "ideally" never made visible at all: this invisibility preserves the "ancient members" from sodomitical penetration; this invisibility ensures the life of sodomites as well.

Thomas Granger is killed as a sodomite but the chapter does not end with his death: it is only part of the mechanism for the production of sexuality. Hence, the end of the chapter swarms with a multitude of bodies, those of the strangers, the profiteers, the servants, represented as those who have diluted the community of first comers. They are said to be the *origin* of sodomy, the outsiders who have insidiously undermined the true members of the body politic. This is the import too of the letter from Massachusetts Bay which asks for advice about three things, not only their case of "uncleanness," but also what is to be done about "the Islanders at Aquidneck" (the "heretics," including Roger Williams and Anne Hutchinson),[15] and about the beaver trade. These are only apparently nonsequiturs. So-called "heretics" and Indians occupy the same discursive space in colonial writing, as more than one historian has noticed.[16] What has further to be remarked is the insistent sexualization of the connection. The heretics are represented as "sowing the seeds of Familism and Anabaptistry" (353) and as spreading "infection"; the Massachusetts Bay colony fears that "the Indians will abuse us" in trade (353). In other texts, this sexual language implicates the bodies of women; in Bradford, the language is that of the sodomitical body with its bad seed, infection and abuse.

Bradford's answer to the multiple query from Boston is epitomized in his decisively singular reply about the "heretics": "We have no conversing with them, nor desire to have, further than necessity or humanity may require" (354). "Necessity" makes clear, in its understated way, that the community cannot be sealed off; it explains why there is room for the "rogues" in Bradford. Morton may be sent off, but Allerton brings him back; the lapsing Lyford is given more than one chance. And Allerton, of course, the figure who dominates page after page of Bradford's text, is the only one who is never directly accused of sexual crimes. The reason is not far to seek. He was one of the "ancient members," a signer of the Mayflower Compact; moreover, he was married to William Brewster's daughter. With Allerton, Bradford repeated a relation he celebrates in the eulogy of Brewster that fills the chapter after the one devoted to sodomy. Allerton was Bradford's right hand man, as Brewster had been when he served Elizabeth I's chief secretary: "he [Secretary Davison] esteemed him rather as a son than a servant, and for his wisdom and godliness, in private he would converse with him more like a friend and familiar than a master" (360). Such are the proper connections between "ancient members," and the fallen Allerton never falls so far as to be connected with stigmatized forms of male-male familiarity. But humane treatment has its limits, and Thomas Granger is beyond the pale.

Who was Thomas Granger? The court records tell what Bradford omits:

"late servant to Love Brewster" (Shurtleff 2:440). Love Brewster was one of two sons—the other was named Wrestling—that came over on the Mayflower with their father, William Brewster. Love and Wrestling: the names are too allegorically perfect to describe the tensions between generations, or the sacrifice of Granger made in the name of the love between men. "Your loving friend, William Bradford" (355), so the Plymouth Governor signs his letter to his fellow leader of the rival colony, "Your loving friend, Richard Bellingham" (353), he signs himself.

Is there penetration here? Penetration is supposedly requisite for the death penalty in cases of sodomy, but not in Granger's case. Hence the "sad spectacle" that Granger's death offered this community of loving friends eyeing each other:

> For first the mare and then the cow and the rest of the lesser cattle were killed before his face, according to the law, Leviticus xx. 15; and then he himself was executed. The cattle were all cast into a great and large pit that was digged of purpose for them, and no use made of any part of them. (356)

The large pit: the holes in Bradford's prose. The spectacle: they watch those brought before Granger's face, those animals that he had been seen to penetrate. Because in "that carnal knowledge of man or lying with man as with woman," Rayner writes, "it was a sin to be punished with death (Leviticus xx. 13) in the man who was lyen withall, as well as in him that lieth with him. . . . His sin is not mitigated where there is not penetration." Because bestiality and sodomy are fully analogous, and "if a woman did stand before or approach to a beast for that end, to lie down thereto (whether penetration was or not) it was capital." Because in these cases—when men lie with men *as* with woman, when a woman *looks* to an animal as she might to a man—it is "equivalent to penetration" (Morison 404). Strange equivalence that must deny these equivalences, but no stranger than the gaze of the ancient members upon each other, or upon the bugger, Thomas Granger. No stranger, to return to (and rewrite) Murphy's characterization of Bradford, than the selves that must be sacrificed in the name of love or for the sake of fundamental (heterosexual) rights, for not to do so would entail a recognition even the most liberal Justices or literary critics might shirk: that there always is penetration.

NOTES

Michael Moon first taught me how to read Bradford; I'm grateful to him and to Eve Kosofsky Sedgwick for her generous and incisive comments on several drafts of this essay.

1. Francis Murphy, ed., *Of Plymouth Plantation* (New York: Random House, 1981), pp. xxiii–xxiv. All citations from Bradford will be taken from this edition, an abridgement of Samuel Eliot Morison's edition (New York: Alfred Knopf, 1952), which will be cited for materials omitted by Murphy.

2. Wayne Franklin, *Discoverers, Explorers, Settlers* (Chicago: University of Chicago Press, 1979), pp. 180–81.

3. See Jonathan Ned Katz, *Gay American History* (New York: Thomas Y. Crowell, 1976), pp. 20–22; *Gay/Lesbian Almanac* (New York: Harper & Row, 1983), pp. 86–87 for Bradford. The place of "sodomy" in colonial America is discussed at length in the introduction to the *Almanac*, and supporting documents are included in both volumes of these invaluable sources. For an incisive discussion of the Supreme Court decision, see the Harvard Law Review volume, *Sexual Orientation and the Law* (Cambridge, Mass.: Harvard University Press, 1990), pp. 1–30.

4. Bradford's abiding interest in the "First Comers" can be seen in the records he kept of their genealogical histories; see Morison edition, "Appendix XIII," pp. 441–48.

5. On the practice of putting out children, see Edmund Morgan, *The Puritan Family* (New York: Harper & Row, 1966 revision of 1944 edition), pp. 75–78. Morgan reads the practice as designed to ensure the creation of distance between parents and children, to guard against too much affection; this view is endorsed by John Demos in *A Little Commonwealth* (London: Oxford University Press, 1970), pp. 71–75, who tentatively suggests that the "ancient mother" passage in Bradford may relate to family tensions that were displaced into neighborly disputes about property (see p. 189).

6. Revisionist historians like Francis Jennings, *The Invasion of America: Indians, Colonialism, and the Cant of Conquest* (Chapel Hill, NC: University of North Carolina Press, 1975) and Neal Salisbury, *Manitou and Providence: Indians, Europeans, and the Making of New England 1500–1643* (New York: Oxford University Press, 1982), have begun to write the side of the story Bradford fails to tell. One limit to this undeniably valuable work is its blindness to questions of gender and sexuality; the remediation offered, the setting straight of the historical record, still operates within the confines of war and trade and towards a reversal of accounts like Bradford's.

7. See Ann Kibbey, *The Interpretation of Material Shapes in Puritanism: A Study of Rhetoric, Prejudice, and Violence* (Cambridge: Cambridge University Press, 1986), ch. 5 passim, esp. pp. 105–110.

8. See Alan Bray, *Homosexuality in Renaissance England* (London: Gay Men's Press, 1982), ch. 3 passim, esp. pp. 67–80.

9. For this broad definition and its significance for the American colonial situation, see Katz, *Gay/Lesbian Almanac*, pp. 31–65 passim.

10. For an account sympathetic to Morton, see Richard Drinnon, *Facing West: The Metaphysics of Indian-Hating and Empire-Building* (Minneapolis: University of Minnesota Press, 1980), p. 361; Drinnon pronounces sexual behavior with Indian women "good clean fun" (p. 57). More puritanically, but equally offensively, Neal Salisbury attempts to "save" Indian women from the charge of promiscuity (see *Manitou and Providence*, p. 160).

11. Richard Slotkin, *Regeneration Through Violence: The Mythology of the American Frontier, 1600–1860* (Middletown, CT: Wesleyan University Press, 1973), p. 61. In "'Things Fearful to Name': Sodomy and Buggery in Seventeenth-Century New England," *Journal of Social History*, 12 (1978), pp. 286–81; reprinted in Elizabeth H. & Joseph H. Pleck, eds., *The American Man* (Englewood Cliffs, NJ: Prentice-Hall, Inc., 1980), from which I cite, Robert Oaks also associates the "worse practices" with homosexuality, opining their likelihood in an all-male community (p. 58). This rather flattens the notion of sodomy, and fails to see its connections with the variety of practices associated with Morton in Bradford. Oaks thinks the "homosexuality" at Merrymount may have been either "situational" or a matter of "preference"— either compelled or freely chosen, alternatives that only appear, I believe, to cover all the possibilities in that dichotomy, and that depend moreover on the quite problematic notion that any man in the period would have self-identified as a homosexual.

12. See, e.g., Oaks, "Things Fearful," pp. 70–71, and Bradley Chapin, *Criminal Justice in Colonial America, 1606–1660* (Athens: University of Georgia Press, 1983), p. 128. Both authors think that the horror of bestiality was connected to the belief that monstrous offspring could come from such unions.

13. I cite the case as transcribed in Katz, *Gay/Lesbian Almanac*, pp. 84–85, derived from Nathaniel Shurtleff, ed., vol. 2, pp. 35–36 of *Records of the Colony of New Plymouth*, 11 vols. (Boston: William White, 1855–61).

14. See Bray, *Homosexuality in Renaissance England*, pp. 25–26. In *Facing West*, pp. 28–29, Drinnon finds the metaphor of damming in Freud, and treats Bradford's text as presciently modern in its articulation of repression.

15. As might be expected, Hutchinson's name never appears in Bradford; when Williams' does, Bradford expectedly writes: "I shall not need to name particulars" (286).

16. See Drinnon, *Facing West*, p. 55, indebted, as he notes, to Larzer Ziff, *Puritanism in America* (New York: Viking Press, 1973). See also Roy Harvey Pearce, *Savagism and Civiization* (Berkeley: University of California Press, 1988 revision of 1953 edition), p. 24. It is of course Kibbey's important recognition in the texts she studies of the ways in which this equation implicates the bodies of women.

Chapter 4

Nationalism, Gender, and the Narrative of Identity

R. Radhakrishnan

In a recent essay entitled "The Nationalist Resolution of the Women's Question," Partha Chatterjee elaborates the complex relationship between women's politics and the politics of Indian nationalism. His point is that while the women's question "was a central issue in some of the most controversial debates over social reform in early and mid-nineteenth century Bengal," this very issue disappeared from the public agenda by the end of the century. "From then onwards," Chatterjee observes, "questions regarding the position of women in society do not arouse the same degree of passion as they did only a few decades before. The overwhelming issues now are directly political ones—concerning the polities of nationalism." Chatterjee concludes that "nationalism could not have resolved those issues; rather, the relation between nationalism and the women's question must have been problematical."[1] Though these critical comments are made in the highly specific context of Indian nationalism in the nineteenth century, they express a general truth concerning the relationship among different forms and contents of political struggle and the problems that emerge when any one politics (such as "the women's question") is taken over and spoken for by an-other politics (such as nationalism).[2]

The conjuncture wherein the women's question meets up with nationalism raises a number of fundamental questions about the very meaning of the term "politics." Why is it that the advent of the politics of nationalism signals the subordination if not the demise of women's politics? Why does the politics of the "one" typically overwhelm the politics of the "other"? Why could the two not be coordinated within an equal and dialogic relationship of mutual accountability? What factors constitute the normative criteria by which a question or issue is deemed "political"? Why is it that nationalism achieves the ideological effect of an inclusive and putatively macropolitical discourse, whereas the women's question—unable to achieve its own autonomous macropolitical identity—remains ghettoized within its specific and regional space? In other words, by what natural or ideological imperative or historical exigency does the politics of nationalism become the binding and overarching umbrella that subsumes other and different political temporalities?[3] For according to Chatterjee, the ideology of nationalist politics in its very specificity acts as the normative mode of *the political as such,* and "the imagined community" of nationalism is authorized as the most authentic unit or form of collectivity. Consequently, the women's question (or the *harijan* question, or the subaltern question . . .) is constrained to take on a nationalist expression as a prerequisite for being considered "political." Faced with its own repression, the women's question seems forced either to seek its own separatist political autonomy or to envision other ways of constituting a relational-integrative politics without at the same time resorting to another kind of totalizing umbrella.

The questions that I've already raised lead to still others, which will be posed here in all their political and epistemological generality: What does it mean to speak of "one" politics in terms of an "other"? How is a genuinely representative national consciousness (and here I have in mind the distinction that Frantz Fanon draws between the official ideology of nationalism and nationalist consciousness) to be spoken for by feminism and vice versa? Is it inevitable that one of these politics must form the horizon for the other, or is it possible that the very notion of a containing horizon is quite beside the point?[4] Can any horizon be "pregiven" in such an absolute and transcendent way? Isn't the very notion of the horizon open to perennial political negotiation? Since no one politics is totally representative of or completely coextensive with the horizon, should we not be talking about the ability of any subject-positional politics to inflect itself both regionally and totally? In other words, isn't the so-called horizon itself the shifting expression of equilibrium among the many forces that constitute and operate the horizon: gender, class, sexuality, ethnicity, etc.? If one specific politics is to achieve a general significance, it would seem that it has to possess a multiple valence, i.e., enjoy political legitimacy as a specific constituency and simultaneously make a difference in the integrated political or cultural sphere. Without such access to an integrated cultural politics, any single subject-positional politics risks losing its interventionary power within that total field.

In their vigorously argued introduction to the volume *Recasting Women: Essays in Colonial History*, Kumkum Sangari and Sudesh Vaid advance the cause of feminist historiography towards "the integrated domain of cultural history." Claiming that "feminist historiography may be feminist without being, exclusively, women's history," they go on to say that "such a historiography acknowledges that each aspect of reality is gendered, and is thus involved in questioning all that we think we know, in a sustained examination of analytical and epistemological apparatus, and in a dismantling of the ideological presuppositions of so called gender-neutral methodologies." Carefully avoiding the pitfalls of both separatism and academicism that are only too ready to embody feminist historiography as a separate discipline based on a gender-coded division of labor, Sangari and Vaid contend that "feminist historiography rethinks historiography as a whole," and in this sense make feminist historiography "a choice open to all historians." Such a choice is understood, however, not "as one among competing perspectives" but rather "as a choice which cannot but undergird *any* attempt at a historical reconstruction which undertakes to demonstrate our sociality in the *full* sense, and is ready to engage with its own presuppositions of an objective gender-neutral method of enquiry."[5]

There is so much being said in these passages that I wish to unpack some of it in detail before describing nationalism as a subject amenable to deconstructive investigation. In speaking for a particular feminist historiography, it would seem that Sangari and Vaid empower it in a double-coded way,[6] i.e., feminist historiography is made to speak both representationally and post-representationally.[7] In other words, the articulation and the politicization of gender as an analytic category belongs initially with feminism narrowly conceived as exclusively women's questions, but does not and cannot merely stop with that. If indeed gender is a necessary category in the context of cultural and historical and political analysis, how can its operations be circumscribed within the narrow confines of its origins? Just as the elaboration of "class" is in some sense intrinsic to the history of Marxism but is by no means exclusively Marxist, "gender" has a particular placement that is local and specific to "women's questions" but is by no means merely a regional concern.[8] Feminist historiography is representational in the sense that it speaks, by way of gender, for those questions and concerns that stem from women's issues initially; but in doing so it understands "gender" as a category that is much more comprehensive in its scope. In this sense, feminist historiography speaks post-representationally, activating the category of "gender" beyond its initial or originary commitment to merely one special or specific constituency. This point needs emphasis, for as we have already seen in the context of nationalism, it is precisely because the women's question was kept from achieving its own form of politicization that it was so easily and coercively spoken for by the discourse of nationalism. Whereas with the arrival of gender as a fully blown historical/cultural/political/epistemic category, the women's question (which in and by itself was not yet a *politics*, but merely a constituency by description) is renamed and transformed as feminism. From this point on, feminist projects are interpellated by feminist ideology and not just covered under other and alien ideologies of patronage, amelioration and redemption. But as has been observed already, this move in itself does not go far enough: true, it succeeds in politicizing the women's question in terms of its own ideology, but this very politics runs the danger of limiting itself as a form of "micro-politics."

Sangari and Vaid's formulation of the project of feminist historiography is refreshingly different from (and more far-reaching than) a number of current poststructuralist, radically subject-positional versions.[9] Unlike many of these versions that seem happy to accept their positional separateness and difference, Sangari and Vaid's elaboration of the project boldly and relevantly raises questions concerning the "full" and "total" rethinking of historiography as such. In opening up feminist historiography in a way that concerns all historians, it would appear that they are surrendering the specificity of the feminist project to other grand theories and ideologies. But a close reading of their text tells us something entirely different: the very openness of the "choice" is conceptualized as a form of historical and political inevitability. For the choice is not just any choice, or even one among many possible choices, but a choice that cannot but be made. In repudiating the very notion of gender-neutrality, they integrate the category of gender into every aspect of reality; and in opening gender out to all historians, they make it impossible for other historians (who for example historicize along axes of nationality, class, race, etc.) not to integrate the feminist imperative within their respective projects. To put it differently, the field of historiography as such is made to acknowledge the reality of the feminist intervention as both micropolitical and macropolitical. In my reading, Sangari and Vaid forward the very strong claim that the feminist project cannot be considered complete or even sufficient unless it takes on the project of the "feminization" of the total/full field of historiography as such.[10] So much of poststructuralist feminism, rooted in epistemologies of relativism and difference, renounces global and macropolitical models on the basis of "epistemological purity," but Sangari and Vaid's analysis points out that such theories in themselves cannot be devoid of global projections and commitments. The category of "gender" in its particularity resonates with a general or universal potential for meaning (why else would it be a category?), and the task is not to eschew universality or globality in favor of pure difference or heterogeneity, but to read and interpret carefully the many tensions among the many forms of "particular-universal" categorical claims.

If we now put together the critical trajectories of Chatterjee's essay and Sangari and Vaid's historiographic agenda, we find ourselves confronting, with problematic urgency, the question we started out with: how is any one politics to be spoken in terms of an-other politics? If feminism or nationalism are expressions of "particular-universal" ideologies, and if furthermore, each of these ideologies (from its own specificity) makes general claims on the entire social formation, how are we to adjudicate among these relativist discourses, none of which is legitimate enough to speak for the total reality? As I have suggested, the strategy of locating any one politics within another is as inappropriate as it is coercive. If that is the case, then from what space or within what domain does any historiography speak? Neither strategies of radical separateness nor those of hierarchic and organic containment do justice to the relational nature of the "absent totality" whose very reality, according to Ernesto Laclau and Chantal Mouffe, is "unsutured."[11] The task facing the many subject positions and their particular-universal ideologies is that of envisioning a totality that is not already there. Nationalist totality, we have seen, is an example of a "bad totality" and feminist historiography secedes from that structure *not to set up a different and oppositional form of totality, but to establish a different relationship to totality*. My objective here, as I loosely conflate Sangari and Vaid with Laclau and Mouffe, is to suggest both that no one discourse or historiography has the ethicopolitical legitimacy to represent the totality, and that the concept of "totality" should be understood not as a pregiven horizon but as the necessary and inevitable "effect" or function of the many relational dialogues, contestations, and asymmetries among the many positions (and their particular-universal ideologies) that constitute the total field.

A model that sees hegemony articulated among multiple determinations obviously poses serious representational problems. If the categories of gender, sexuality, nationality, or class can neither speak for the totality nor for one another but are yet implicated in one another relationally, how is the historical subject to produce a narrative from such a radical relationality, a relationality without recourse? For once we accept the notion of relational articulation, two consequences follow: a) inside/outside distinctions become thoroughly problematized and displaced (for example, the idea of a feminist or an ethnic or a class-based historiography pursued entirely from within itself becomes highly questionable), and b) the conception of relationality as a field-in-process undermines possibilities of establishing boundaries and limits to the relational field; in other words, relationality turns into a pure concept, an end in itself.

So, when Sangari and Vaid make *their* transformative claims on behalf of feminist historiography, it is not immediately clear if by "feminist historiography" they mean Indian feminist historiography, or postcolonial feminist historiography, or subaltern feminist historiography, or Third World feminist historiography. There is a certain lack of situatedness, a certain rejection of the politics of location (in Adrienne Rich's sense of the term) in the manner in which "feminist historiography" resists being located in terms of Indianness, subalternity, postcoloniality, etc. But clearly, judging from the general thrust of their essay, they do mean to situate feminist historiography in the specific context of colonial and nationalist history. So in this sense, feminist historiography cannot become its own pure signifier, nor can it avoid the project of interpreting itself in relation to other given discourses and ideologies. Thus, in seeking to recast women against the backdrop of colonial history, Sangari and Vaid enact an oppositional relationship between their discourse and colonial history and, by extension, nationalist history. In a similar vein, the entire school of South Asian subaltern historians intentionally revises colonialist and nationalist historiographies, seeking all along to expose patterns of "dominance without hegemony" in these discourses.[12] This sense of historical specificity bounds and gives determinate shape to a project that would otherwise remain a rarefied and contentless exploration of relationality as such. What helps these historians in negotiating the boundaries among feminism, colonialism, nationalism, capitalism, Eurocentrism, metropolitanism, etc., is their commitment to the production of a critical history that has to acknowledge "realities" in the very act of challenging and discrediting them. In directing the revisionist deconstructive energies of gender and subalternity at colonialist and nationalist historiographies, these historians acknowledge the force of a prior placement, what we could term "the assigned nature" of their subject position. By thus taking a critical Gramscian inventory of their own historical positions, they deal with nationalism earnestly rather than dismiss it outright as a failed and flawed phenomenon: the history of nationalism is not easily bypassed just because it has been the history of a failure.[13]

But why study nationalism at all, especially at a time when avant garde, metropolitan theory has passed the verdict that like "the voice," like "identity," like "representation," nationalism is or should be dead? There are several reasons why nationalism must continue to be studied:

> A) Like all complex historical movements, nationalism is not a monolithic phenomenon to be deemed entirely good or entirely bad; nationalism is a contradictory discourse and its internal contradictions need to be unpacked in their historical specificity. The historical agency of nationalism has been sometimes hegemonic though often merely dominant, sometimes emancipatory though often repressive, sometimes progressive though often traditional and reactionary.

B) While banished by certain theories, nationalism is back today with a vengeance all over the world. Western theorists cannot in good faith talk any more about the ugly and hysterical resurgence of nationalisms "out there and among them," whereas "here and among us" nationalism is a thing of the past. The unification of the two Germanies in Europe and the separatist claims of a variety of ethnic nationalisms against the centralized authority of the USSR have brought nationalism and the national question back into the very center of the historical stage. Neither the deracinating multi- or inter-national spread of capitalism nor the Marxist theoretical assimilation of the national question within an internationalist Communism has been able to do away with the urgencies of the imagined communities of nationalism. Right here in the United States (which would seem to have surpassed the nationalist threshold of universal history), we witnessed televisual images of jingoistic self-celebration during the American bombing of Libya. And all along, political commentators and media reporters were condemning the madman Khaddafy and the violent behavior of the Libyan zealots "out there."

C) The international community of nations continues to bear the shame and guilt of not yet acknowledging the Palestinian right to nationhood and self-determination. The Palestinians continue being submitted to and brutalized by the duplicitous international consensus (spearheaded largely by the United States) that refuses to listen to the Palestinians because they are not yet a nation and at the same time frustrates their every attempt to become a nation.

And finally, D) stalemates such as the Salman Rushdie affair and the international impasse over Iraq's Saddam Hussein demonstrate yet again the poverty of a so-called international but in fact a Western metropolitan framework when applied to other and different forms of collective identity.

It is with these polemical pointers that I would like to resume my analysis of the problems of nationalism; the particular structure that concerns me here is the dichotomy of the inside/outside that nationalist discourse deploys with telling effect. My point here is not to condemn or endorse *in toto* the politics of "inside/outside," but rather to observe the strategic and differentiated use of this dichotomous structure within nationalism. For instance, are we evaluating the Rushdie affair from within the spaces of Western secularism or from some place else? Are we viewing the conduct of Arab politics from within the Arab nationalist umbrella, or from within an Arab but non-nationalist umbrella, or from yet another site? Our very mode of understanding is implicated in our mode of partisanship and our mode of partisanship is an expression or function of our location: what that location includes and excludes. Inside/outside perceptions are indeed very much alive and there is no transideological free space of arbitration to adjudicate among multiple nonsynchronous boundaries.

The particular instance of Indian nationalism makes use of the inner/outer distinction as a way of selectively coping with the West, and it is not coincidental that the women's question is very much part of this dichotomous adjustment. Here again, by mobilizing the inner/outer distinction against the "outerness" of the West, nationalist rhetoric makes "woman" the pure and ahistorical signifier of "interiority."[14] In the fight against the enemy from the outside, something within gets even more repressed and "woman" becomes the mute but necessary allegorical ground for the transactions of nationalist history. I turn again to Partha Chatterjee who describes this effect in scrupulous detail. Chatterjee observes that nationalism could neither ignore the West completely nor capitulate to it entirely: the West and its ideals of material progress had to be assimilated selectively, without any fundamental damage to the native and "inner" Indian self. In other words, questions of change and progress posed in Western attire were conceived as an outer and epiphenomenal aspect of Indian identity, whereas the inner and inviolable sanctum of Indian identity had to do with home, spirituality, and the figure of Woman as representative of the true self. As Chatterjee puts it:

> Now apply the inner/outer distinction to the matter of concrete day-to-day living and you get a separation of the social space into *ghar* and *bahir,* the home and the world. The world is the external, the domain of the material; the home represents our inner spiritual self, our true identity. The world is a treacherous terrain of the pursuit of material interests, where practical considerations reign supreme. It is also typically the domain of the male. The home in its essence must remain unaffected by the profane activities of the material world—and woman is its representation. *And so we get an identification of social roles by gender to correspond with the separation of the social space into ghar and bahir* (my emphasis).

Chatterjee goes on to say that once "we match the new meaning of the home/world dichotomy with the identification of social roles by gender, we get the ideological framework within which nationalism answered the women's question."[15] The rhetoric of nationalism makes use of gender from its own ideological perspective and frames women narrowly in the way that feminist historiography, as articulated by Sangari and Vaid, soundly rejects. Like any framework whose finitude is the representation of its own limited and ideologically-biased interests, the nationalist framework too thematizes its own priorities: the selective appropriation of the West and the safeguarding of one's essential identity. Unfortunately, in authorizing such a schizophrenic vision of itself, nationalism loses on both fronts: its external history remains hostage to the Enlightenment identity of the West while its inner self is effectively written out of history altogether in the name of a repressive and essentialist indigeny. And Woman takes on the name of a vast inner silence not to be broken into by the rough and external clamor of material history. Chatterjee's reading of the nationalist paradigm makes us acutely aware that the postcolonial project and its many narratives are still in search of a different political ethic or teleology (if that term is still permissible), one that is underwritten neither by the Western subject of Enlightenment nor by a reactionary and essentialist nativism. It is important to notice how nationalist ideology deploys the inner/outer split to achieve a false and repressive resolution of its identity. Forced by colonialism to negotiate with Western blueprints of reason, progress and enlightenment, the nationalist subject straddles two regions or spaces, internalizing Western epistemological modes at the outer or the purely pragmatic level, and at the inner level maintaining a traditional identity that will not be influenced by the merely pragmatic nature of the outward changes. In other words, the place where the *true* nationalist subject *really is* and the place from which it produces historical-materialist knowledge about itself are mutually heterogeneous. The locus of the true self, the inner/traditional/spiritual sense of place, is exiled from processes of history while the locus of historical knowledge fails to speak for the true identity of the nationalist subject. The result is a fundamental rupture, a form of basic cognitive dissidence, a radical collapse of representation. Unable to produce its own history in response to its inner sense of identity, nationalist ideology sets up Woman as victim and goddess simultaneously. Woman becomes the allegorical name for a specific historical failure: the failure to coordinate the political or the ontological with the epistemological within an undivided agency.

In his book *Nationalist Thought and the Colonial World,* Partha Chatterjee addresses in great depth the politico-epistemological predicament faced by nationalism. Nationalism, Chatterjee submits, should result in a double decolonization. Mere political decolonization and the resultant celebration of freedom, however momentous, does not by itself inaugurate a new history, a new subject and a new and free sense of agency.[16] It is of vital importance that nationalist thought coordinate a new and different space that it can call *its* own: a space that is not complicit with the universal Subject of Eurocentric Enlightenment, a space where nationalist politics could fashion its own epistemological, cognitive, and representational modalities. The break from colonialism has then to be both political and epistemological. The nationalist subject in its protagonistic phase of history (as against its antagonistic phase when the primary aim was to overthrow the enemy) has to break away from the colonial past, achieve full and inclusive representational legitimacy with its own people—the many subspaces and the many other forms and thresholds of collective identity (such as the ethnic, the religious, the communal)—and fashion its own indigenous modes of cultural, social and political production in response. Can nationalism as commonly understood fulfill these obligations?

The problem with nationalism in Chatterjee's view is that it sustains and continues the baleful legacies of Eurocentrism and Orientalism. The received history of nationalism argues for two kinds of nationalism: Eastern and Western.[17] By the logic of this Us-Them divide,[18] Western nationalisms are deemed capable of generating their own models of autonomy from within, whereas Eastern nationalisms have to assimilate something alien to their own cultures before they can become modern nations. Thus in the Western context, the ideals of Frenchness, Germanness, or Englishness—national essences rooted in a sense of autochthony—become the basis of a modernity that re-roots and reconfirms a native sense of identity. On the other hand, Eastern nationalisms, and in particular "Third World" nationalisms, are forced to choose between "being themselves" and "becoming modern nations" as though the universal standards of reason and progress were natural and intrinsic to the West. In this latter case, the universalizing mission is embued with violence, coercion, deracination and denaturalization. We can see how this divide perpetrates the ideology of a dominant common world where the West leads naturally and the East follows in an eternal game of catch-up where its identity is always in dissonance with itself.

The real tragedy, however, is when postcolonial nationalisms internalize rather than problematize the Western blueprint in the name of progress, modernization, industrialization, and internationalism. This process seems difficult to avoid since the immediate history of these nations happens to be Western, and there are no easy ways available to reclaim a pure and uncontaminated history prior to the ravages of colonialism. Even if such recovery were possible, it would serve only to render the postcolonial nation hopelessly out of sync with the "international" present of modernity. How inevitable is this scenario? Is nationalism then "always already" corrupt and defective in its agency? Whatever the answer may be in the long run, Chatterjee reminds us that it is crucial for the postcolonial subject to produce a critical and deconstructive knowledge about nationalism. Only such a critical knowledge will help us identify and elaborate the complicity of the nationalist project with that of the enlightened European subject. It is on the basis of such knowledge that postcolonial subjects can produce a genuinely subaltern history about themselves and not merely replicate, in one form or another, the liberal-elitist narrative of the West. And it is in this context that Chatterjee makes a sharp distinction between what he calls the "problematic" of nationalism and the "thematic" of nationalism.

Drawing on the work of Edward Said and Anouar Abdel-Malek and routing it through the phenomenology of Sartre and Merleau-Ponty and the structural Marxism of Althusser, Chatterjee makes his unique contribution to our understanding of the two terms: thematic and problematic. His purpose is to "make a suitable distinction by which we can separate, for analytical purposes, that part of a social ideology . . . which asserts the existence of certain historical possibilities from the part which seeks to *justify* those claims by an appeal to both epistemic and moral principles." The distinction takes the following form. The thematic "refers to an epistemological as well as ethical system which provides a framework of elements and rules for establishing relations between elements; the problematic, on the other hand, consists of concrete statements about possibilities justified by reference to the thematic." Applying this distinction to nationalist ideology, Chatterjee finds that "the problematic of nationalist thought is exactly the reverse of that of Orientalism." The only difference is that whereas in Orientalism the Oriental is a passive subject, in nationalism the object has become an active "subject" but one that remains captive to categories such as "progress," "reason," and "modernity," categories that are alien to him/her. Rather than being acted upon by these categories from the outside, this new subject internalizes them. Within such an ideological interpellation (that does not spring from the history of the postcolonial subject), the subject thinks that his/her subjectivity is "active, autonomous and sovereign." "At the level of the thematic, on the other hand," continues Chatterjee, "nationalist thought accepts the same essentialist conception based on the distinction between 'the East' and 'the West,' the same typology created by a transcendent studying subject, and hence the same 'objectifying' procedures of knowledge constructed in the post-Enlightenment age of Western science." The result is a constitutive contradictoriness in nationalist thought: its daring political agenda is always already depoliticized and recuperated by the very same representational structure that nationalist thought seeks to put in question. Hence, as Chatterjee concludes, the inappropriateness of posing the problem of "social transformation in a post-colonial country within a strictly nationalist framework."[19]

If we accept Chatterjee's analysis (I for one find it eminently persuasive), we have to conclude that the nationalist problematic preempts the nationalist thematic. The thematic of nationalism in a postcolonial country is constrained to remain a mere instantiation of a generalized nationalist problematic developed elsewhere. In other words, the processes and the procedures of the post-Enlightenment project are made to become the hallmark of the nation-building thematic in the postcolonial country. The post-Enlightenment telos begins to function as a freefloating signifier seeking universal confirmation. What remains concealed in such a false universalization is of course the fact that Western nationalism itself took shape under highly determinate and limited historical circumstances. In Chatterjee's terms, the thematic, justificatory rhetoric of

Western nationalism is naturalized as an integral part of the very algebra of *nationalism as such.* In instantiating without historical relevance the second-order history of nationalism developed elsewhere, postcolonial nationalism forfeits its own thematic agenda. If in Western nationalism the thematic and the problematic are reciprocally and organically grounded, in the case of postcolonial nationalism the thematic and the problematic remain disjunct from each other.

What it all comes down to is the betrayal by nationalism of its own "inner" realities. Obsessively concerned with the West and other forms of local elitism, nationalism fails to speak for its own people; on the contrary, it suppresses the politics of subalternity. Paralyzed by the ideological view of its inner reality as merely a bulwark against excessive Westernization, nationalism fails to historicize this inner reality in its own multifarious forms. The very mode in which nationalism identifies its inner identity privileges the externality of the West, and the so-called inner or true identity of the nation takes the form of a mere strategic reaction formation to or against interpellation by Western ideologies. This inner self is not allowed to take on a positive and hegemonic role as the protagonist or agent of its own history. Nationalism as a mode of narration thus fails both to represent its own reality and represent its own people.[20] The ideological disposition of nationalism towards its people or its masses is fraught with the same duplicity that characterizes its attitude to the women's question. To elaborate this thesis in the Indian context, I turn now to Chatterjee's critical analysis of the two great leaders of twentieth-century India, Mohandas Karamchand Gandhi and Jawaharlal Nehru and their very different orientations towards people's politics: Gandhi (the Father of the nation) who is Indian and of the people, and Nehru (Gandhi's beloved protégé), the modern intellectual trying to bridge a nationalism of the people and a progressive internationalism based on Western reason, science, technology, and industrial-economic progress.

One of the first moves Gandhi makes on his return to India from South Africa is to repudiate the urban politics practiced by the Indian National Congress. Gandhi locates his politics in the villages of India where the majority of India's population resides (and this is basically true even today). He seeks an active common denominator with the people of India, he changes his attire, his very mode of living so that he can become one with the people. And this is not merely a vote-catching political stunt but Gandhi's vision of India: it is in the villages that India is to be experienced and discovered. It is in this context that the discovery of India becomes a major theme in nationalist history. Where and what is the real India? Sure enough, it exists, but how is it to be known? From what perspective is the real India to be represented so that the representation may be unified, inclusive, even total? How is national consciousness to be generated when it does not yet exist as such? The problem here is that the narrative cannot pre-know its subject, which has itself to be the product of the narrative. The question that Gandhi raises is: Whose narrative is it going to be? The answer is certainly the "people's," but the term "people" covers a wide spectrum of positions, identities, and bases. How should nationalism forge from these many "sub-identities" a unified identity to work for the common national cause?[21]

It is in this spirit that the discovery of India is undertaken, albeit differently, by Gandhi and Nehru. To dwell just a little longer on the semantics of the term "discovery," this theme presupposes that a certain India exists already waiting to be touched, known, narrativized. In a narratological sense, the real India can only be the *a posteriori* effect of the narrative process, but ontologically, the reality of India is prior to the narrative. In other words, not any and every narrative can claim to be the signifier of the real India. Also, the criterion of reality serves two purposes: first, of demystifying the existing urban-elitist versions of India, and second, of securing an ethico-political alignment between the knowledge produced about the real India and the socio-political transformations that are to follow on the basis of such knowledge. The Gandhian thesis is that no worthwhile plan of action can be based on a knowledge that is spurious and nonrepresentative. The people of India become the subject of the independence movement and Gandhi's political ethic is to empower the people in a way that will enable them to lead themselves.

But a number of problems and contradictions arise here. Are the people the means or are they the end in the nationalist struggle? The contradiction lies in the fact that the unification of the people is going to be undertaken not in their own name, but in the name of the emerging nation and the nation state that is to follow. The subaltern valence of the people has to be reformed as a prerequisite for their nationalization. The people thus become a necessary means to the superior ends of nationalism. The masses can neither be bypassed (for they are the real India) nor can they be legitimated *qua* people. And here, Gandhi's and Nehru's visions vary. Gandhi's advocacy of the people carries with it their full moral force. His model of independent India makes the people the teachers, and leaders such as himself become the pupils. Hence Gandhi's stern refusal of progress as an end in itself, and his rejection of all indices of growth and prosperity developed in the West. Hence, too, his insistence on decentralization, simple modes of production, the ethic of self-sufficiency, and his moral indictment of capital, accumulation, greed, and the systemic proliferation of want and desire. We must also remember that Gandhi was a rare leader who, in the name of the people, prescribed that the glorious Congress party that had won India its independence should self-destruct once the aim of independence was achieved. But this of course was not to happen.

Jawaharlal Nehru's perspective on the masses of India is quite different. His discovery of India is much more ambivalent and doubt-ridden. He passionately admires the way in which Gandhi spontaneously establishes rapport with the people and becomes "one of them." But he often doubts whether he himself is capable of such organic identification with the masses.[22] Here then is Nehru in *The Discovery of India*:

> India was in my blood and there was much in her that instinctively thrilled me. And yet, I approached her almost as an *alien critic*, full of dislike for the present as well as for many of the relics of the past I saw. To some extent I came to her via the West and looked at her as a friendly *Westerner* might have done. I was eager and anxious to change her outlook and appearance and give her the garb of modernity. And yet doubts rose within me. Did I know India, I who presumed to scrap much of her past heritage? (my emphases)[23]

A number of interesting tensions are played out here between India and her loving patriot. First, there are visceral references to "instinct" and "blood" whose strength has nothing whatsoever to do with Nehru's rational and theoretical understanding of India. Second, India figures both as a transcendent and marvellous identity awaiting ecstatic comprehension and as malleable raw material awaiting transformation by an act of production. A kind of mystical essentialism confronts a certain secular constructionism. While the present, the past, and the future of India are imperfectly aligned, the present through which India is being perceived is both the pure moment of nativism/indigeny and the contaminated perspective underwritten by the West. And finally, there is an aporetic tension between Nehru's strong visions on behalf of India and his uncertainties about his knowledge of India. Is it conceivable that Nehru, the architect of modern India, may in fact *not know* his country?

It is from such a divided consciousness that Nehru attempts to account for the "spellbinding" agency of Gandhi. It is somewhat surprising that Nehru's viewpoint comes very close to Marx's devaluation of the "idiocy of rural life." Yet Nehru is divided in his response, at once touched and disheartened if not intimidated by the Indian peasant. On the one hand, intimate exposure to the peasants and "their misery and overflowing gratitude" fills him "with shame and sorrow, shame at (his) own easy-going and comfortable life and (our) petty politics of the city which ignored this vast multitude of semi-naked sons and daughters of India."[24] But on the other hand, there is Nehru's strong and almost ruthless evaluation that the peasants were "dull certainly, uninteresting individually," and that "they needed to be led properly, controlled, not by force or fear, but by 'gaining their trust,' by teaching them their true interests."[25]

The vexing question is how to mobilize the masses in this nationalist-modernist cause? And the answer seems to be: Gandhi.

In Partha Chatterjee's words: "On reading the many pages Nehru has written by way of explaining the phenomenon of Gandhi, what comes through most strongly is a feeling of total incomprehension." Gandhi becomes the voice of the people, a voice that is powerful, persuasive, legitimate, and yet inscrutable in its spellbinding effectivity. This voice intervenes successfully in the history of India precisely because it speaks for the masses and yet this very voice is considered misguided. Gandhian economics, Gandhian sociology, all of Gandhi's blueprints for independent India are all wrong, but Gandhi is the one who can inspire the masses; leaders like Nehru have the right facts, the right models for India's development, but are "powerless to intervene" in the history of the Indian masses. Gandhi thus becomes that mystical and incomprehensible genius exclusively responsible for India's independence, and yet Nehru has no hesitation in declaring that once *swaraj* is achieved, Gandhi's fads must not be encouraged. The affirmative project of building India finds itself thoroughly disconnected from the ethicopolitical modality of the independence movement. In a strange way, Nehru's understanding of Gandhi's historical agency lines it up with the "otherness" and the "unreason" of peasant consciousness, whereas the future of modern India becomes identified with the rationality of Western thought.

Nationalism is thus valorized as an inaugural moment precisely because it is also a project of deracination from an unreasonable prehistory. As Chatterjee sums it up:

> And so the split between two domains of politics—one, a politics of the elite, and the other, a politics of subaltern classes—was replicated in the sphere of mature nationalist thought by an explicit recognition of the split between a domain of rationality and a domain of unreason, a domain of science and a domain of faith, a domain of organization and a domain of spontaneity. But it was a rational understanding which, by the very act of its recognition of the Other, also effaced the Other.[26]

In a real sense, then, the subject of nationalism does not exist. Conceived within this chronic duality, the nationalist subject is doomed to demonstrate the impossibility of its own claim to subjecthood. The inner and the outer in mutual disarray, the nationalist subject marks the space of a constitutive representational debacle.[27]

The project that the subaltern historians are engaged in is the production of a subaltern critique of nationalism: a critique both to liberate those many spaces foreclosed within nationalism and to enable a nonreactive, nonparanoid mode of subjectivity and agency in touch with its own historically constituted interiority: a prey neither to the difference of the Western subject nor to the mystique of its own indigenous identity. In opening up new spaces, "the critique of nationalist discourse must find for itself the ideological means to connect the popular strength of the people's struggles with the consciousness of a new universality, to subvert the ideological sway of a state which falsely claims to speak on behalf of the nation and to challenge the presumed sovereignty of a science which puts itself at the service of capital."[28] Clearly, such a critique undertaken in the name of subalternity has to bear many different signatures within a universal and relational space: a space very much like the one invoked by Sangari and Vaid's feminist historiography.

NOTES

1. Partha Chatterjee, "The Nationalist Resolution of the Women's Question," in Kumkum Sangari and Sudesh Vaid, eds., *Recasting Women: Essays in Colonial History* (New Delhi: Kali for Women, 1989), p. 233. This collection has since been reprinted as *Recasting Women: Essays in Indian Colonial History* (New Brunswick, NJ: Rutgers University Press, 1990).

2. For a spirited articulation of the need to realize the women's question as its own autonomous form of politics, see Shulamith Firestone, *The Dialectic of Sex* (New York: Bantam Books, 1970).

3. I am using the term "temporalities" here as developed by Chandra Talpade Mohanty in her essay, "Feminist Encounters: Locating the Politics of Experience," *Copyright*, 1 (Fall 1987), p. 40.

4. Fredric Jameson argues in *The Political Unconscious* that Marxism does and should continue to operate as the ultimate semantic horizon within which other political struggles are to be located. But the very notion of any single ideology operating as a containing horizon is deeply problematic. For a poststructuralist critique of Jameson's position, see my essay "Poststructuralist Politics: Towards a Theory of Coalition," in Douglas Kellner, ed., *Postmodernism/Jameson/Critique* (Washington, DC: Maisonneuve Press, 1989), pp. 301–332.

5. Sangari and Vaid, "Recasting Women: An Introduction," in *Recasting Women*, pp. 2–3.

6. For an insightful account of the double-coded nature of postcolonial narratives, see Kumkum Sangari, "The Politics of the Possible," *Cultural Critique*, 7 (Fall 1987), pp. 157–186.

7. For an in-depth discussion, in the context of Michel Foucault and Antonio Gramsci, of the implications of representational and post-representational politics, see my essay, "Toward an Effective Intellectual: Foucault or Gramsci?" in Bruce Robbins, ed., *Intellectuals: Aesthetics, Politics, Academics* (Minneapolis: University of Minnesota Press, 1990), pp. 57–99.

8. I am referring here to a growing body of work by such feminist theorists as Gayatri Chakravorty Spivak, Teresa de Lauretis, Nancy Fraser, Linda Nicholson, Chandra Talpade Mohanty, Donna Haraway, and many others who elaborate gender both as a specific domain and as a general category of experience within the body politic.

9. My point here is that whereas postcolonial strategies of the politics of location are eager to take on macropolitical and global issues, Western conceptions of subject-positional politics (practiced in the manner of a Foucault or a Deleuze) tend to overlook global and macropolitical concerns. As Edward Said points out, there is a certain asymmetry that governs the relationship between discourses emanating from the world of excolonizers and those that rise from the world of the excolonized; see his essay "Intellectuals in the Post-Colonial World," *Salmagundi*, 70–71 (Spring-Summer 1986), pp. 44–81.

10. The tension between the local valence and the general or total valence of any constituency is illustrated powerfully in the American context where "ethnicity" plays a constitutive role in the shaping of American identity. The concern of each ethnic group is both to legitimate its own form of ethnicity and to influence the general platform where different ethnic groups renegotiate the nature of American identity.

11. See Ernesto Laclau and Chantal Mouffe, *Hegemony and Socialist Strategy*, trans. Winston Moore and Paul Cammack (London: Verso, 1985).

12. See Ranajit Guha, "Dominance without Hegemony and its Historiography," in Ranajit Guha, ed., *Subaltern Studies VI: Writings on South Asian History and Society* (Delhi, Oxford and New York: Oxford University Press, 1989), pp. 210–309.

13. For an important exchange about nationalism as a threshold in the development of a transnational and non-essentialist feminism, see the essays by Julie Stephens and Susie Tharu in *Subaltern Studies VI*.

14. In much the same way Freudian psychoanalysis makes feminine sexuality "unknowable" without raising the question of knowledge itself as a gender-inflected category. French feminists such as Luce Irigaray, Helene Cixous, Julia Kristeva, and Catherine Clement have raised the question of a feminine epistemics/*écriture* both within and without the economy of psychoanalysis.

15. Chatterjee, "The Nationalist Resolution," pp. 238–39.

16. See Gayatri Chakravorty Spivak, "Reading *The Satanic Verses*," *Public Culture*, 2, 1 (Fall 1989), pp. 79–99 for a suggestive distinction between "subject formation" and "agency formation."

17. See John Plamenatz, "Two Types of Nationalism," in Eugene Kamenka, ed., *Nationalism: The Nature and Evolution of an Idea* (London: Edward Arnold, 1976), pp. 23–36. The body of work on nationalism is too rich and complex to be fully represented, but here are a few significant (and of course, problematic) contributions: Benedict Anderson, *Imagined Communities: Reflections on the Origin and Spread of Nationalism* (London: Verso, 1983); John Breuilly, *Nationalism and the State* (Manchester: Manchester University Press, 1982); Horace B. Davis, *Toward a Marxist Theory of Nationalism* (New York: Monthly Review Press, 1978); Ernest Gellner, *Nations and Nationalism* (Oxford: Basil Blackwell, 1983); Elie Kedourie, *Nationalism* (London: Hutchinson, 1960); Anthony D. Smith, *The Ethnic Origin of Nations* (Oxford: Basil Blackwell, 1986); Kumari Jayawardena, *Feminism and Nationalism in the Third World* (London: Zed Press, 1986); E. J. Hobsbawm, *Nations and Nationalism since 1780* (New York: Cambridge University Press, 1990); Partha Chatterjee, *Nationalist Thought and the Colonial World* (Delhi: Oxford University Press, 1986).

18. See Satya Mohanty, "Us and Them: On the Philosophical Bases of Political Criticism," *Yale Journal of Criticism*, 2, 2 (Spring 1989), pp. 1–31.

19. Chatterjee, *Nationalist Thought and the Colonial World*, pp. 38–39.

20. For a brilliant and varied discussion of the complicated relationship between nationalism and narration, see Homi K. Bhabha, ed., *Nation and Narration* (London and New York: Routledge, 1990), in particular the essays by Homi K. Bhabha, Timothy Brennan, Doris Sommer, Sneja Gunew, and James Snead.

21. The fact that in 1990 India still has not resolved the separatist political problems of the Sikhs, the Gurkhas and the Hindu-Muslim communal tensions (the battle in Ayodhya between Hindus who wish to build a temple to Rama and the Muslims who legitimately do not want their existing mosque to be brought down) only goes to prove

that the historicization of an authentic national consciousness has nothing to do with the sovereignty of the nation-state.

22. Here I use the term "organic" as developed by Antonio Gramsci in his essay "The Formation of Intellectuals," in *The Modern Prince & Other Writings*, trans. Dr. Louis Marks (New York: International Publishers, 1957), pp. 118–25.

23. Jawaharlal Nehru, *The Discovery of India* (New York: John Day, 1946), p. 38.

24. Jawaharlal Nehru, *An Autobiography* (London: Bodley Head, 1936), p. 52.

25. Nehru as quoted in Chatterjee, *Nationalist Thought and the Colonial World*, p. 148.

26. Ibid., pp. 150, 153.

27. For a complex reading of the nature of representation in the postcolonial context, see Homi K. Bhabha, "Signs Taken for Wonders: Questions of Ambivalence and Authority under a Tree Outside Delhi, May 1817," *Critical Inquiry*, 12, 1 (Autumn 1985), pp. 144–65.

28. Chatterjee, *Nationalist Thought and the Colonial World*, p. 170.

Chapter 5

Woman in Difference: Mahasweta Devi's "Douloti the Bountiful"

Gayatri Chakravorty Spivak

[Douloti is the daughter of a tribal bonded worker. India has an aboriginal tribal population of nearly seventy million. A bonded worker offers free work as "repayment" of a small loan, at extortionate rates of interest, often over more than one generation. Douloti is abducted by an upper-caste (nontribal) Indian from her home with a false promise of marriage. She is sold into bonded prostitution, ostensibly to repay her father's loan. She descends down the hierarchy of "favor" in the house of prostitution. Devastated by venereal disease, she accomplishes a journey to a hospital, only to be directed to another hospital, much farther away. She decides to walk home instead and dies on the way. The rhetorical and narrative details are filled out in the following essay.][1]

The vast group that spans, *in the metropolis*, the migrant subproletariat at one end, and the post-colonial artist, intellectual, academic, political exile, successful professional or capitalist at the other, is articulate in many different ways. It is not surprising that it claims, in one way or another, a paradigmatic importance in the contemporary socius. By contrast, Mahasweta Devi lingers in post-coloniality in the space of difference, *in decolonized terrain*. Her material is not written with an international audience in mind. It often contains problematic representations of decolonization after a negotiated *political* independence. Sometimes this offends the pieties of the national bourgeoisie. A great deal can be said on this issue. Marie-Aimée Hélie-Lucas's words will suffice to make a closure here:

> In Algeria, many of us, including myself, kept silent for ten years after Independence, not to give fuel to the enemies of the glorious Algerian revolution. . . . I will certainly admit that Western right-wing forces may and will use our protests, especially if they remain isolated. But it is as true to say that our own rightist forces exploit our silence.[2]

The sheer quantity of Mahasweta's production, her preoccupation with the gendered subaltern subject, and the range of her experimental prose—moving from the tribal to the Sanskritic register by way of easy obscenity and political analysis, will not permit her to be an isolated voice.

Let me explain, somewhat schematically, what I mean by "post-coloniality in the space of difference, in *decolonized terrain*."

Especially in a critique of metropolitan culture, the event of political independence can be automatically assumed to stand in-between colony and decolonization as an unexamined good that operates a reversal. But the political goals of the new nation are supposedly determined by a regulative logic derived from the old colony, with its interest reversed: secularism, democracy, socialism, national identity, capitalist development. Whatever the fate of this supposition, it must be admitted that there is always a space that cannot share in the energy of this reversal. This space had no established agency of traffic with the culture of imperialism. Paradoxically, this space is also outside of organized labor, below the attempted reversals of capital logic. Conventionally, this space is described as the habitat of the *sub*proletariat or the *sub*altern. Mahasweta's fiction focuses on it as the space of the displacement of the colonization-decolonization reversal. This is the space that can become, for her, a representation of decolonization *as such*. "Decolonization" *in this context* is a convenient and misleading word, used because no other can be found.

This space is not indeterminate or uninscribed. In Virginia Woolf's *Mrs. Dalloway*, for example, the historically invested cartography of London, charged with the task of positioning and cathecting the proper names inhabiting that novel, entails an unproduced mass variously named India or Empire. Curiously enough, "Douloti"'s structuring can be compared to this. In "Douloti" too the historically produced proper name "India" is the name of a relatively unproduced and undifferentiated mass. However, in "Douloti" the alias of "India" is not "Empire," as in *Mrs. Dalloway*, but "Nation." Mahasweta invites us to realize that, in the context of this fiction, "Empire" and "Nation" are interchangeable names, however hard it might be for us to imagine it. If *Mrs. Dalloway*'s London is supported by the name and the implicit concept-metaphor "Empire" *from below*, in "Douloti" the socially invested cartography of bonded labor is animated and supported by the space of decolonization and implicit presupposition "Nation," *from above.*[3] In this fiction, the space of decolonization is displaced out of the received version of the relay race between "Empire" and "Nation," between Imperialism and Independence. If contemporary neocolonialism is seen only from the undoubtedly complex and important but restrictive perspective or explanatory context of metropolitan, internal colonization of the post-colonial migrant or neo-colonial immigrant, this particular scenario of displacement becomes invisible, drops out of sight. (The solution is not necessarily to privilege the self-defensive liberal elite in the "new" nation.)[4]

Keeping this methodological proviso in mind, I should like now to cut the context in a different way, and focus on three points:

1) How does Mahasweta inscribe this space of displacement, if not with the lineaments of the nation?

2) What does it mean to say "socially invested cartography of bonded labor"? and,

3) How does Mahasweta suggest that, even within this space, the woman's body is the last instance, it is elsewhere?

INSCRIPTION OF DISPLACED SPACE

As is her custom, Mahasweta uses a brilliantly simple strategy to inscribe the space of active displacement of the Empire-Nation or colonialism-decolonization reversal. She names.

On the very first page we read, "In Palamu, the communities of Nagesias and Parhuas are small. The bigger communities are Bhnuias, Dusads, Dhakis, Ganjus, Oraons, Mundas." We have not yet received the full treatment of naming or renaming. But the reader can already sense, if she will, that this is different from the admittedly most urgent theatre of the U.S. or Britain (and Australia and Canada) as unacknowledged multiracial cultures, which view India as one of the minorities that must be affirmatively acted upon or mobilized into collective resistance. Without minimizing the importance of that other, metropolitan struggle, attending to this one allows the reader to grasp that the word "India" is sometimes a lid on an immense and equally unacknowledged subaltern heterogeneity. Mahasweta releases that heterogeneity, here by restoring some of its historical and geographical nomenclature. We will have to go a little further into the text to grasp that this naming is not an invitation to monumentalize precapitalist tribal formations. Here the reader can prepare at least to think that, if in the metropolitan migrant context the invocation of heterogeneity can sometimes work against the formation of a resistant collectivity among all the disenfranchized, in the decolonized national context the strategic deployment of subaltern heterogeneity can make visible the fantasmatic nature of a merely hegemonic nationalism. Even a further step can be taken: to apply the requirements of the first case to the second is to be part of the problem, however innocently. The two cases are perhaps, even, *différends*.[5]

The *découpage* of "internal colonization"—colonization inside a metropolitan nation-state—can claim a normative globality only by leaving out this delicately outlined, displaced shadow space.

If the name "India" is undone here, the undoing is not coded in the terms regularly to be encountered in the international press—many languages, many religions. That scene of strife, again not to be ignored, is still within the hegemonic struggle over so-called national identity; still, that is to say, in the space of the Empire-Nation reversal. No Indian, expatriate or otherwise, could bypass the issue of violence in the subcontinent in the name of religious *identity*. But we must also keep our eye on the differences, where tribal animism does not even qualify as a religion.

In our childhood and adolescence, Indian history textbooks used to begin with the invocation of "unity in diversity." This by now somewhat tired slogan is, quite understandably, still on the agenda of the "builders of the nation," even as the consumer elite is being constituted as the definitive citizen. As she inscribes this other displaced space, Mahasweta appropriates and transforms this worthy generalization by positing a unity in exploitation and domination, by giving in her story the generic name "bond-slave" (not the miraculating name "citizen") in many of the modern Indian languages. This is the unity in diversity of the many named groups of tribals and outcastes. If we look at the official map of India, we can see how meticulously the territory is covered and reinscribed; I have italicized the official proper names of the spaces of the newish nation:

> In *Andhra* the people of Matangi, Jaggali, Malajangam, Mahar and other such castes become Gothi. In *Bihar* Chamar, Nagesia, Parhaiya, Dusad become kamiya or seokiya. In *Gujarat* the Chalwaris, Naliyas, Thoris and such others become halpati. In *Karnataka* the low of birth become jeetho, in *Madhya Pradesh* haroyaha. In *Orissa* Gothi and in *Rajasthan* sagri. The Chetty Rayats of *Tamilnadu* keep bhumidases. In *Uttar Pradesh* the bhumidasas of the *Laccadive Islands* are Nadapu (emphasis mine).

Not an exhaustive list, just an indication of multiplicity. Over against this is the Brahman and the Rajput, the contractor and the government, hereditary divinity indistinguishable from more recent forms of mastery: Boss—Gormen [government]—lord—Sir—Sarkar [government]—god.

These lists are scattered throughout the text and the effect of the reinscription is sustained. It is through them that we can approach the second proposed question:

SOCIAL INVESTMENT OF THE CARTOGRAPHY OF BONDED SPACE

Among these passages of lists, there are a few where Mahasweta rather unexpectedly uses the Bengali word customarily used for "society": *shomaj*. (Since the English words are not exact equivalents, *shomaj* is quite appropriate for describing caste- or tribe-*communities*. It undergoes a startling transcoding into a broad collectivity when used in the context of the far-flung *society* of bonded labor.) The two following passages are spoken by Bono Nagesia, an "unconventional personalit[y] . . . [a] fissure . . . for restructuring," to quote Kalpana Bardhan on the "strategies of indirect power within the authority hierarchy"[6]:

> Before I had left Seora [his village] I didn't know how many kamiyas there were in Chiroa, Chatakpur, Ramkanda, Daho, Palda, Chandoa, Banari. . . . Oh I didn't know before how large *my* society [*shomaj*] was" (emphasis mine). And again, "that's why I no longer feel alone. Oh the society [*shomaj*] of kamiyas is so large. Very large. If you call it a society, there is no accounting for the number of people in it.

This access to collectivity, and the repeated use of *shomaj* to mark the access, might remind the Bengali reader that *shomaj* is also the word that gives us "socialism" in *shomajbad* or *shomajtantro*. All Eurocentric predictive scenarios to the contrary, it is not unreasonable to see here the prefiguration from primitive communism to the ground of socialism in the most general sense.

The youthful Marx had suggested that, if the Hegelian system were wrenched into the sphere of political economy, its predictive morphology would prove itself wrong. Many readers still hold the implicit evolutionary assumption, sometimes in contradiction with their overt politics, that the true formation of collectivity travels from the family, through society, into the possibility of the ethico-rational abstraction embodied in the nation-state. If this evolutionary narrative is wrenched into the sphere of decolonization or displaced into the sphere of transnational capitalism, the precariously manipulative *function* called "the nation-state," coded and re-territorialized with the heavy paleonymic (historically stuffed) baggage of reason and affect, reveals how problematic this assumption might be, both from the global and the local perspectives. We hear a good deal these days about the *post*-national status of global capitalism and post-coloniality. This ignores the ferocious re-coding power of the concept-metaphor "nation-state," and remains locked within the reversal of capital logic and colonialism. If this entire way of thinking is displaced, the formation of a collectivity in bondage can accommodate an ethical rationality. Sharing this conviction, yet taking a distance from it, Mahasweta moves us further, further even from Bono Nagesia's access to *shomaj*, indeed to a space where the family is broken. Here the reader must recall that by the logic of the evolutionary narrative that is being displaced, the family is the first step toward collectivity.[7] Mahasweta moves us to a space where the family, the machine for the socialization of the female body through affective coding, has itself been broken and deflected to see that, even in the displaced imaginings.

THE WOMAN'S BODY IS THE LAST INSTANCE, IT IS ELSEWHERE

There is no avoiding this, even if the story is read by way of the broadest possible grid: in modern "India," there *is* a "society" of bonded labor, where the only means of repaying a loan at extortionate rates of interest is hereditary bond-slavery. Family life is still possible here, the affects taking the entire burden of survival. Below this is bonded prostitution, where the girls and women abducted from bonded labor or kamiya households are thrust together as bodies for absolute sexual and economic exploitation. These bodies are connected to bond-slavery but are yet apart. Detail by detail, in a spare narrative style that often resembles the schizo's "and then . . . ," "and then . . . ," Mahasweta relentlessly emphasizes this separation.

> The social system that makes Crook Nagesia [the father of the central character] a kamiya is made by men. Therefore do Douloti [the central character, a woman], Somni, Reoti have to quench the hunger of male flesh. Otherwise Paramananda [the boss of the house of prostitution] does not get money. . . . In the bond-slavery trade . . . the recourse to loans is the general regulator.[8]

Woman's body is thus the last instance in a system whose general regulator is still the loan: usurer's capital, imbricated, level by level, in national industrial, and transnational global capital. This, if you like, is the connection. But it is also the last instance on the chain of affective responsibility, and no Third-World-Gramscian rewriting of class as subaltern-in-culture has taken this into account in any but the most sentimental way:

> [Her father] stumbled on his face when he tried to pull the cart, with the ox yoke on his shoulders, at Munabar [his boss]'s command. His broken body gave him the name Crook. And Douloti has taken the yoke of Crook's bond-slavery on her shoulders. Now Latia is her client, her body is tight. Then going down and down Douloti will be as skeletal as Somni. She will repay the bond-slavery loan as a beggar.

The reader knows that Douloti will end her life not as a beggar, but "destitute in quite another way." And, to begin the last movement of the story, which leads to this particular end, Mahasweta marks the impersonal indifference of the space of the woman in difference elsewhere, in a simple sentence starting the shift to this last sequence: "Douloti didn't know this news."

The "news" that Douloti doesn't know is the outcastes' and tribals' plans to appropriate and transform state and national legal sanctions for legitimizing armed struggle. The regular revolutionary line here is to suggest that, if women are drawn into national liberation, feminism is advanced. I have already spoken of the precariousness of the adjective "national" in this context. Further, if one considers recent historical examples, one is obliged to suggest that, even if, in the crisis of the armed or peaceful struggle, women seem to emerge as comrades, with the return of the everyday, *and in the pores of the struggle*, the old codings of the gendered body, sometimes slightly altered, seem to fall into place. Mahasweta's "Draupadi" is a reminder of that.[9] Here she attends to the separate place of the woman's body.

In the previous paragraph, then, Mahasweta has been describing the politicization of male untouchables. Bono Nagesia has just joined Prasad Mahato's Freedom Party. Prasad, an untouchable who was associated with the now often impotent legacy of Gandhian nationalism—*Harijan* (god's people was Gandhi's new name for the Hindu outcastes)—has just broken away and founded this militant Party. Mahasweta treats these men with the sympathy they deserve. Yet, she assures us:

> The object of this account is not Prasad's quick transformation. Just as its object is not Bono Nagesia joining Prasad's party. Bono didn't value Prasad so much before. But the day Prasad, the son of a harijan, left the Gandhi Mission and the Harijan Association and gave witness in the Freedom Party, Bono sought him out and mingled with him. . . . Douloti didn't know this news.

The final movement of the story will be considered later in this essay. Here let us note its place apart and continue the discussion of woman's relatedness to bond-slavery and the separateness or difference in the woman's body, by way of a few more examples.

In my view, then, there is an accession to sociality and collectivity through the male militants' survey of the cartography of bondslavery. Yet the first invocation of collectivity is in the women's voice, through the first of the few strange "poems" in the text that resemble somewhat the ritual choruses sung at folk-festivals and ceremonies, but cannot be explained away as such. They are certainly not conventional to modern Bengali fictional narrative. They are beside the site of this narrative as well, where groups or an individual customarily speak or speaks with typicality.

Thus, early in the story, it is the old kamiya women by the fire who provide the answer to the question: by what force does the Boss turn human beings into slaves? "Then they say":

> By force of loans, by force of loans.
> Two rupees ten rupees hundred rupees
> Ten seers of wheat five of rice.

At the end of seventy-four lines they conclude

> He has become the government [or lord, *sarkar*]
> And we have become kamiyas
> We will never be free.

The women and men are collectively connected by this regulative logic of loans. But, I am arguing that in this fiction woman's body is apart, elsewhere. This is made visible by another couple of "poems."

The first "poem" gives us the sociologist, producing knowledge about kamiyas within his context of explanation. (*Shomajbigyani*—"social scientist"—is also built on *shomaj.*) The poem speaks the well-known fact that the so-called "green revolution" has operated the transformation of a rural economy into agri-capitalism and created a Kulak class.[10]

This poem comes from the position of the author analysing the analysts, who wish to make a science out of structures that may be random. It is especially interesting to me that, whereas the old kamiya women speak the regulative cause of their condition with conviction, the author, parodying social scientific assignment of cause, first invokes "nothing," and then simply breaks off.[11] First the sentence about the experts: "The sociologists travel around Palamu and write in their files, every sonofabitch is becoming a kamiya because of weddings-funerals-religious ceremonies." Then the corrective poem:

> These savants want government support.
> The government wants the Kulak's support
> Land-lender, this new agri-capitalist caste
> This caste is created by the independent government of India
> The government wants the support of the Kulak and the agri-capitalist
> Because of nothing, nothing, nothing
> Bhilai-Bokaro-Jamshedpur—[again, places on the map]
> And Kulak, agri-capitalist, the king-emperors
> Want free labor, free land—
> So they recruit kamiya-seokia-haroaha
> One mustn't know this, or write this, because—

When another authorial "poem," a bit later in the text, using a similar peculiar narrative, speaks woman's body, the narrative is not of the modes of production, land is *not-yet-and no-longer*-capital, the question is *not-yet-and-no-longer* "what is productive labor?," but "what is called work?":

> These are all Paramananda's kamiyas
> Douloti and Reoti and Somni
> Farm work, digging soil, cutting wells is work
> This one doesn't do it, that one doesn't do it—
> The boss has turned them into land
> The boss ploughs and ploughs their land and raises the crop
> They are all Paramananda's kamiya.

There is a break in the poem here. The next line is "They are all I don't quite know whose *maat*." *Maat* is one of the names for the bonded worker on Bono Nagesia's researched reinscription of the map of the nation-state. In the case of the woman's body defined and transformed into the field of labor, the author's diagnostic voice, inscribing "them" into a collective sociality they already inhabit, apart, is vague:

> They are all I don't quite know whose *maat*.
> Near the foot of the Himalayas in Jaunnar-Bauar
> They don't say kamiya, they are called *maat*—
> Tulsa and Bisla and Kamla
> Kolta women are I don't quite know whose *maat*
> Only farm work and shoveling soil is work
> This one doesn't do it, that one doesn't do it, the other one doesn't do it

> The boss has made them land
> He ploughs and ploughs their bodies' land and raises a crop
> They are all I don't quite know whose *maat.*

Mahasweta's fiction is impeccably researched. There is no "poetic license" here. But its rhetorical conduct shows me that it will not compete with "science." I have spent so long in discussing woman's logical connectedness and the separateness of woman's body in that connectedness because these problems are still sometimes "scientifically" dismissed as feudal, not feminist. Some feminists have described the broad spectrum of women's issues—from anorexia as resistance in the U.S. to the dowry system in India—as subsumable under the feudal mode of production.[12] Such gestures are, I think, mistaken. The woman is fully implicated in the mode of production narrative and, at the same time, also distanced from it. To quote Kalpana Bardhan again:

> In a stratified society, discrimination of wages and jobs/occupation by caste and sex is not a feudal remnant but perfectly consistent with the play of market forces. . . . If the wage-and-access differentials follow the lines of traditional privilege, then attention gets conveniently deflected from the adaptive dexterity of capitalist exploitation processes to the stubbornness of feudal values, when it is actually a symbiotic relationship between the two.[13]

I have suggested that Mahasweta displaces the woman's body even from the reversal logic of labor and capital. Kishanchand, a man who runs a house of prostitution on principles of Taylorism, says to one of the kamiya-whores: "Paramananda is boss, and this whorehouse is the factory. Rampiyari is Paramananda's overseer [in English] and you are all labor"; Jhalo, the most outspoken of the women's group, dismisses him with "Again that nonsense!"

This part of my paper, then, has been an extended discussion of three points: 1) Inscription of displaced space, 2) Social investment of bonded labor, and 3) The woman's body as last instance, and elsewhere. I would like now to go back to the phrase I began with: "post-coloniality in the space of difference, in decolonized terrain."

PARLIAMENTARY DEMOCRACY AND NATIONALISM

One of the gifts of the logic of decolonization is parliamentary democracy. Mahasweta treats with affectionate mockery the kamiyas' peculiar misunderstanding of the voting booths and the Census. Of the voting booths, she writes:

> What sort of thing is this that each person is put into an empty pigeonhole? However much the election officer explains, shall I put the mark on the paper or on my hand? . . . The officer scolds him loudly. So Mohan Dusad says, now run away. No doubt there will be fighting. Everyone runs for their life. The representatives of the candidates run to catch the voters. The police runs to help them. When the police runs, then Mohan Dusad says, the government doesn't mean well. In such glory do the General Elections come to an end.

And of the Census:

> You'll write my age? Write write, maybe ten, maybe twenty, eh? What, I have grandchildren, I can't have so few years? How old are people when they have grandchildren? Fifty, sixty? No, no, how can I be sixty? I have heard that our brave master is fifty? I am Ghasi by caste, and poor. How can I have more age than he? The master has more land, more money, everything more than me. How can he have less age? No sir, write ten or twenty. The 1961 Census took place in this way.

Where everything works by the ruthless and visible calculus of super-exploitation by caste-class domination, the logic of democracy is thoroughly counter-intuitive, its rituals absurd. Yet here too, the line between those who run and those who give chase is kept intact.

Here, for example, is Latiya, on the occasion of the Sino-Indian war. Latiya is, among other things, a government contractor. He is also the first and sole owner and user of Douloti's body for as long as his taste for her lasts—serial monogamy pared down to its bare bones. He is noted for his physical prowess, of which an unbounded sexual appetite is an important part:

> Such a Latiya contributes a truck and gives a speech himself.
> Calls out, give whatever you have into this shawl.
> Why sir?
> Isn't there a war on?
> Where, I don't know.
> You will never know, bastard motherfucker. China has come to contaminate India's truth.
> Yes, yes? But where is China? Where again is India?
> [Then the] Mye-lay or MLA [Member of the Legislative Assembly] says, this country is India.
> No, no, Madhpura.
> What! Contradicting the Mye-lay Sir?
> Latiya jumps into the sea of people with his club in hand and the people run away in every direction.

> Then Latiya comes again to Douloti's room.
> Here, too, the women keep their distance.
> Somni returned most troubled from the meeting.
> No, no this is not a good circus. What's the fight?
> Who knows? They're fighting some China.
> Whose fight?
> Someone called India, his. I didn't understand anything.
> Rampiyari [the manageress of the whorehouse] said, did you see Latiya?
> He is shouting the most.
> Then it's the contractor's fight. Come, make some tea.

Over against this, somewhat later in the story, is the tribal and outcaste political activists' debate: "what is to be done?" With them is the white missionary Father Bomfuller. These are seriously committed men. They speak of the advisability of nonviolent intervention, of armed struggle, and of agitating for legislation. The conversation is taking place in the whorehouse, after the group has taken statements from the women, and after we have heard that Douloti, simply one example among the women, taken for three hundred rupees ostensibly to repay her father's original loan, has brought in 40,000 rupees for the boss in eight years and is still taking five to twenty clients a day. In this context, the advocate of nonviolent intervention is found to be caste-specific. The women in his caste never enter bonded prostitution. Bomfuller's careful survey, entitled "The Incidence of Bonded Labor," is filed away in New Delhi and consigned to oblivion. It is agreed that since government officers in these areas themselves keep bond-laborers and since the police will not offend the bosses and moneylenders to enforce the law, mere legislation is no use. Only the untouchable Prasad Mahato understands that the law can be effectively claimed as justification for armed struggle. And only Bono Nagesia, with a strong affective tie to Douloti, understands the difference between the long haul and immediate action. "We will leave after hearing all this?" he asks twice, and then asks

> Who will light the fire Prasadji? There is no one to light the fire. If there was, would the kamiya society be so large in Palamu? There are people for passing laws, there are people to ride jeeps, but no one to light the fire. Can't you see the kamiya society is growing?

And, as we have heard, "Douloti didn't know this."

The alternative to this is not simply electoral education. And the most appropriate critique of that position does indeed come from migrant resistance in the metropolis.[14]

Let us move to the women's house, away from activist national debates, where Mahasweta meticulously charts a diversity of positions. First there is Rampiyari, who manages the house and is herself a former bonded prostitute. Bardhan's statement can be used to analyze this character's situation:

> Female conservatism . . . is often explained in terms of "false consciousness" (or cognitive dissonance, an euphemism for underdeveloped psyche). . . . However, female conservatism develops logically out of women's strategies of influence and survival within patrilocal, patriarchal structures. They are . . . the product of resourceful behavior under extremely disadvantageous circumstances.[15]

For example, when her power is taken away from her by the man, she leaves, "promising to open another business."

The other women are differentiated not only in terms of themselves, but also in terms of their attitudes to their children. As Mahasweta writes, "Even under such circumstances, children are born." Jhalo saves money. She says, "My husband is a kamiya, I am a kamiya, but I don't want my children to be kamiyas." Somni wants to put them in Father Bomfuller's Mission, since she is not allowed to keep them with her.

The affective coding of mothering extends from sociobiology all the way to reproductive rights. Before the mobilization of the reproductive rights debate in the West, demanding the full coding of the woman's body in constitutional abstractions had got off the ground, Simone de Beauvoir had suggested that, in the continuum of gestation, birthing, and childrearing, the woman passes through and crosses over her inscription as an example of her species-body to the task of producing an intending subject.[16] Of gestation, Beauvoir remarks that, however much the woman might want *a* child, however much she may bestow an intentionality upon it, she cannot desire *this* child. Beauvoir suggests that the rearing of the child, once it is born, is a chosen commitment, not the essential fulfillment of a woman's being.

I defer here the necessary critique of Beauvoir's existentialist notion of commitment, in order to use her figuration of mothering as a site of passage.[17]

Among the women of this fiction, pregnancy as the result of copulation with clients allows the working out of the inscription of the female body in gestation to be economically rather than affectively coded. The obligation to abortion is deflected into that code, of maximum social need, and not written into the rational abstraction of individual rights. Children are not written into mother right. Somni scrupulously distinguishes between my man's or husband's children and Latiya's children. Yet these women are absolutely committed, in the best sense of *engagement*, to the future of their children where they "can never do more than create a situation that only the child . . . can exceed."[18]

As is usual in Mahasweta's fictive texts, we are allowed an (impossible) step before the already coded value. (In "Breast-Giver," for example, we see cancer rather than the clitoral orgasm as the excess of the woman's body. There, too, the minute particulars of mothering are under scrutiny by way of foster-mothering as labor.[19])

How do such gestures show up the fault lines in critiques that must assume a civil society to posit struggle and in the efforts to recode? Let us consider Teresa de Lauretis's recent powerful essay "Sexual Indifference and Lesbian Representation."[20] One of the logical consequences of Beauvoir's figuration of the mother is the possibility of reading gay parenthood as philosophically normative.[21] De Lauretis, implicitly presupposing a multi-cultural Euro-American agent for the political struggles of this century, proposes:

> The discourses, demands, and counter-demands that inform lesbian identity and representation in the 1980s are more diverse and socially heterogeneous than those of the first half of the century. They include, most notably, the political concepts of oppression and agency developed in the struggles of social movements such as the women's movement, the gay liberation movement, and third world feminism, as well as an awareness of the importance of developing a theory of sexuality that takes into account the working of unconscious processes in the construction of female subjectivity. But, as I have tried to argue, the discourses, demands, and counter-demands that inform lesbian representation are still unwittingly caught in the paradox of socio-sexual (in)difference, often unable to think homosexuality and hommo-sexuality at once separately *and* together.[22]

"Douloti the Bountiful" shows us that it is possible to consider socio-sexual (in)difference philosophically prior to the reversal of the established codes, before the bestowal of *affective* value on homo- or hommo- or yet hetero-*sexuality*. To think therefore that the story is an evolutionary lament that *their* problems are not yet accessible to *our* solutions and they must simply come through into nationalism in order then to debate sexual preference is, I think, a mistake. On the other hand, this prior space, prior to the origin of coded sexual difference/preference, is *not* the neutrality of the Heideggerian *Geschlecht.*[23] This space is "unmotivated" according to the presuppositions of naturalized sexuality. (It reveals the lingering presence of such presuppositions even in our resolutely non-foundationalist discourses.) Although unmotivated, this space bears the instituted trace of the entire history and spacing of imperialism.[24]

It is not inappropriate to consider here the question not only of lingering presuppositions of naturalized sexuality but of naturalized subject-agency. I am referring, of course, to the use of psychoanalysis in the study of colonialism and post-coloniality.

Frantz Fanon and O. Mannoni set the model for the diagnostic use of psychoanalytic types produced by colonialism. Both were practicing psychoanalysts. We must put their written work in the perspective of the limits set by Freud's classic essay "Analysis Terminable and Interminable."[25] By the logic of that essay, all psychoanalytic practice is founded in an originary limiting "mistake" about the presuppositions of psychoanalysis as a "science." When we use psychoanalysis in the production of taxonomic descriptives in literary and cultural critique, the arena of practice, which persistently norms the presuppositions of psychoanalysis, becomes transparent. Put another way, the shifting dynamics of the ethical moment in psychoanalysis, which is lodged in the shuttling of transference and counter-transference, is emptied out.[26] What, apart from intelligibility, is the ethico-political agenda of psychoanalysis as a collective taxonomic descriptive in cultural critique? Lacan's simple and playful admonition to Anika Lemaire comes to mind: "Each of my *écrits* is apparently no more than a memorial to the refusal of my discourse by the audience it included: an audience restricted to psychoanalysis."[27] The current work being done in France on the implications of negative transference should also be kept in mind. And, finally, the powerful suggestions made by Deleuze and Guattari should generate an autocritique. Their suggestion, summarized, is that, since capital de-codes and de-territorializes the socius by releasing the abstract as such, capital-*ism* manages the crisis by way of the generalized psychoanalytic mode of production of affective value, which operates via a generalized system of affective equivalence, however spectacular in its complexity and discontinuity.[28]

By active contrast, the relationship between Marxist cultural critique and postimperialist practice is a thoroughly foregrounded theatre of contestation, not only in Western Marxism, but also in China, South and South-East Asia, Central and South America, Central and Eastern Europe. I have attempted to indicate how Mahasweta's representation of woman in difference is apart even from this negotiation. I will now quote an example of how she makes visible a certain critique of a marxian axiom against romanticizing "the rural commune." This will take me back to where I left off, mothering as commitment among the bonded-labor prostitutes.

Douloti is the only member of the group of bonded-labor prostitutes who does not share in this commitment. She has only ever been a child, not a mother. Her relationship to her mother, who is still in the village, is filled with affect. In terms of the critical implications of our argument, it has to be admitted that this affective production, fully sympathetic, is yet represented *within* rather than prior to an accepted code. Here are mother-and-daughter when Douloti is about to leave with her powerful abductor by way of a fake proposal of marriage:

> Douloti and her mother were two stones clasping each other. The mother was running her hand gently and constantly over her daughter's body. A split

> broken hand. Running her fingers she was weeping and humming, what is this, my mother, I never heard such a thing? The Boss-moneylender always takes away our daughters-in-law from field and barn. When does a Brahman marry a daughter of ours?

Douloti, like the unresisting majority of the male outcastes, comes to terms with her existence by accepting bond-slavery as a law of nature. Mahasweta does not represent Douloti as an intending subject of resistance. Her ego splits at her first rape and stays split until nearly the end. We will see at the end that Douloti is not represented as the intending subject of victimage either. The coding of intention into resistance and the resisting acceptance of victimage animates the male militants, and the fierce bonded prostitutes, for whom there is no opportunity for collective resistance.

Let us follow the build-up of Douloti as "character" through to the end. Like the affection between mother and daughter, Douloti's affect for her village, again gently and beautifully written, is *within* a recognizable coding of sentiment. And indeed, as we see in the following passage, this unresisting nostalgia, dismissing planned resistance as futile, seems to rely on a conservative coding of the sexual division of labor.

Bono has come with the white missionary and other militants to take depositions from the bonded-labor prostitutes. Here is Douloti's silent communion with him:

> Douloti sat by Bono and started rubbing his feet with great sympathy. . . . Douloti's fingers said, why grieve Uncle Bono? . . . Why don't you rather speak to me silently just as I am speaking to you in silence? Let the gentlemen twitter this way. Those words of yours will be much more precious. Remember that banyan tree. . . . Speak of it. When winter came . . . mother would put the little balls of flour into the fire. How sweet the smell of warm flour seemed to me. . . . Then I didn't know Bono Uncle that the world . . . held Baijnath, that it had so many clients. I lost those days long ago. I get all of it back when I see you.

Faithful to this characterlogical style, Douloti is here a catalyst to the passion of male militancy. It is at the end of *this* movement that Bono is made to burst out: "There are people for passing laws, there are people to ride jeeps, but no one to light the fire. Can't you see the kamiya society is growing?"

Douloti's affect for her home is thus staged carefully by Mahasweta as the regressive bonding that works against social change and ultimately, therefore, against the achievement of national social justice, a project in which the author is deeply involved as an activist. Mahasweta dismisses neither side but presents Douloti's affect, and ultimately Douloti herself, as the site of a real aporia. You cannot give assent to both on the same register. I am also arguing that, in terms of the general rhetorical conduct of the story, you cannot also give assent in the same register, to the evocation of a space prior to value-coding on the one hand, and the sympathetic re-presentation of Douloti as a character, recognizable within a rather banal value-coding, on the other.

(An aporia is *not* a statement of preference, certainly not a dismissal. One genuinely cannot decide between the two determinants of an aporia. It is the undecidable in the face of which decisions must be risked.)

Mahasweta sublates both the coded nostalgia and the separate space of Douloti at the end of her story. The movement of sublation or *Aufhebung*, destroying the nostalgia and the space of displacement as well as preserving it, transformed, starts working through a lyrical celebration of the nostalgic affect. With a body broken by absolute exploitation, Douloti is stumbling home at night. "The smell of catkins by the wayside, around the necks of cattle the homecoming bells are chiming. Gradually the fireflies flew in the dark, the stars came out in the sky! People had lit a fire, the smoke was rising."

Marx wrote of the Hegelian *Aufhebung* that it was a graph of the denegation of political economy.[29] Derrida has suggested the undoing of the *Aufhebung* by setting wild the seedbed of the *seminarium* through acknowledging the Saturnalia—progressive parricide—of Absolute Knowledge.[30] In "Douloti the Bountiful" the *Aufhebung* of colony into nation is undone by the figuration of the woman's body before the affective coding of sexuality. This can be seen as follows: the rural schoolmaster, again sympathetically portrayed, tries to teach his students nationalism by inscribing a large map of India in the clay courtyard of the schoolhut, in preparation for Independence Day. Douloti finds the clean clay comforting in the dark and lies down to die there. In the morning the schoolmaster and his students discover Douloti on the map.

As she reinscribes this official map of the nation by the zoograph of the unaccommodated female body restored to the economy of nature, Mahasweta's prose, in a signature gesture, rises to the sweeping elegance of high Sanskritic Bengali. This is in sharpest possible contrast to the dynamic hybrid medium of the rest of the narrative, country Hindi mixed in with paratactic reportorial prose. Echoes of the Indian national anthem can also be heard in this high prose. Contemporary Bengali, although descended from Sanskrit, has in its historical elaborations by and large lost the quantitative measure of the classical parent language. In this sentence, however, the manipulation of the length of the vowels is to be felt. Mahasweta's sentence is scandalous in the planned clash between content and form. Not the least of the scandal lies in the fact that most of these words are, of course, so-called Indo-European cognates: "Filling the entire Indian peninsula from the oceans to the Himalayas, here lies bonded labor spreadeagled, kamiya-whore Douloti Nagesia's tormented corpse, putrified with venereal disease, having vomited up all the blood in her desiccated lungs."

The space *displaced* from the empire-nation negotiation now comes to inhabit and appropriate the national map, and makes the agenda of nationalism impossible: "Today, on the fifteenth of August [Indian Independence Day], Douloti [not as intending subject but as figured body] has left no room at all in the India of people like Mohan [the schoolmaster] for planting the standard of the Independence Flag."

The story ends with two short sentences: a rhetorical question, and a statement that is not an answer: "What will Mohan do now? Douloti is all over India."

In his book *Through Our Own Eyes: Popular Art and Modern History*, Guy Brett has described a kind of art

> that cross[es] over between . . . [the] silence . . . [for which] Paulo Freire invented the term "the culture of silence" to describe the condition in which the impoverished majority of the world's people are living—powerless, and with little access to the means of communication. . . . There is also [Brett continues] the silence and ignorance in which the affluent minority of the world is kept.[31]

In these last appropriative moments, I believe we are witnessing such a cross-over. "Paradoxically," Brett says further, "the more intensely these images express a local reality and a local experience, the more global they seem to become." And indeed the last sentence of the story pushes us from the local through the national to the neo-colonial globe.

The word *doulot* means wealth. Thus *douloti* can be made to mean "traffic in wealth." Under the last sentence—"Douloti is all over India" [*Bharat jora hoye Douloti*]—one can hear that other sentence: *Jagat* [the globe] *jora hoye Douloti*. What will Mohan do now?—the traffic in wealth [douloti] is all over the globe.

I end, somewhat abruptly, with a text for discussion: such a globalization of douloti, dissolving even the proper name, is not an overcoming of the gendered body. The persistent agendas of nationalisms and sexuality are encrypted there in the indifference of super-exploitation.

NOTES

1. This story, "Douloti the Bountiful," is forthcoming in Mahasweta Devi, *Imaginary Maps*, trans. Gayatri Chakravorty Spivak (New York: Routledge).

2. Marie-Aimée Hélie-Lucas, "Bound and Gagged by the Family Code," in Miranda Davies, ed., *Third World, Second Sex*, Volume 2 (London: Zed Books, 1987), p. 14.

3. "Invested" is used here as an alternative for "cathected," or "occupied in desire." Mapping one's terrain is certainly a matter of "investment," in a whole spectrum of the senses that this meaning of the word can take on board. Preliminarily one can say that Mahasweta wants to occupy with a desire for sociality the area of "India," the general principle of whose cartography is quite different from bonded labor. In cartography "proper," by contrast, "physical geography" or "politics" do not need the effort of social investment as does "bonded labor."

4. The notion of cuts (*découpages*; not "circumscription" as in the English) is borrowed from Jacques Derrida, "My Chances/*Mes Chances*: A Rendezvous with Some Epicurean Stereophonies," in William Kerrigan and Joseph H. Smith, eds., *Taking Chances: Derrida, Psychoanalysis, and Literature* (Baltimore: Johns Hopkins University Press, 1984), p. 27.

5. Jean-François Lyotard, *The Differend: Phrases in Dispute*, trans. Georges van den Abbeele (Minneapolis: University of Minnesota Press, 1988).

6. Kalpana Bardhan, "Women, Work, Welfare and Status: Forces of Tradition and Change in India," *South Asia Bulletin*, 6, 1 (Spring 1986), pp. 3–16.

7. This is an enormous network of arguments. Let me just cite the Engels-Gayle Rubin circuit on the one hand (*Origin of the Family, Private Property, and the State* [New York: Pathfinder Press, 1979]; "The Traffic in Women: Notes on the 'Political Economy' of Sex," in Rayna R. Reiter, ed., *Toward an Anthropology of Women* [New York: Monthly Review Press, 1975]); and the Britain-India circuit on the other (Anna Davin, "Imperialism and Motherhood," *History Workshop*, 5 [1978]; Kumkum Sangari and Sudesh Vaid, eds., *ReCasting Women: Essays in Colonial History* [New Delhi: Kali for Women, 1989]); and let that mark the place of a footnote unwritten because of the limits of my knowledge.

8. Let us remember that the "schizo" marks the spot where the papa-mama-baby explanations, consolidating the romance in the nuclear family, find their limit. This is somewhat different from noticing a similar structure more aggressively foregrounded in *The Satanic Verses*, a novel of identity-formation in culture/ideology/religion/nation (Spivak, "Reading *The Satanic Verses*," *Public Culture*, 2, 1 [Fall 1989], p. 85).

9. In Spivak, *In Other Worlds: Essays in Cultural Politics* (New York: Routledge, 1987), pp. 187–196.

10. The continuity between Empire and Nation can be seen in this sphere. Imperialism is regulating land—creating private property in land. See Ranajit Guha, *A Rule of Property for Bengal*, 2nd ed. (New Delhi: Orient Longmans, 1981). For a mere sampling of the spectrum of debate around local rural self-government (Panchayati Raj), see Arun Ghosh, "The Panchayati Raj Bill" and Indira Hirway, "Panchayati Raj at Crossroads," *Economic and Political Weekly*, 24.26 (July 1, 1989) and 24.29 (July 22, 1989).

11. Judging from reactions to Spivak, "Can the Subaltern Speak?" in Cary Nelson and Lawrence Grossberg, eds., *Marxism and the Interpretation of Culture* (Urbana: University of Illinois Press, 1988); and to Spivak, "Three Women's Texts and A Critique of Imperialism," in Henry Louis Gates, Jr., ed., *"Race," Writing, and Difference* (Chicago: University of Chicago Press, 1986), it seems necessary to say that such a breaking-off does not mean a bad mark for me. One might describe these break-offs as the opposite kind of *découpage* to the ones that "arise in the place where, between the movement of science—notably when it is concerned with random structures—and that of philosophy or the arts—literary or not—the limits cannot be actual and static or *solid* but rather only the effects of contextual *découpage*" (Derrida, "My Chances," p. 27).

12. This is particularly true of the Rethinking Marxism group at the University of Massachusetts-Amherst, with whose general positions I am broadly in sympathy.

13. Bardhan, "Women, Work, Welfare and Status," p. 5.

14. Since this piece was first written, the use of the rational abstractions of "democracy" as "alibis" have become so abundant that this point is either not worth making or has been disproved if placed against the rational abstractions of communism.

15. Bardhan, "Women, Work, Welfare and Status," p. 12.

16. Simone de Beauvoir, *The Second Sex*, trans. H. M. Parshley (New York: Vintage, 1952), pp. 541–588.

17. For a study of international feminist theory that stands the test of decolonization, it is useful to see which bits of metropolitan theory can retain their plausibility "outside." This is not ahistorical theorizing about universals "from above," but contact with a space so intimate that it is both random and inaccessible, "below." (See Spivak, "French Feminism Revisited: Ethics and Politics," forthcoming in an anthology edited by Judith Butler and Joan Scott.)

18. Beauvoir, *The Second Sex,* p. 583.

19. See Spivak, "A Literary Representation of the Subaltern: A Woman's Text from the Third World," in *In Other Worlds,* pp. 241–268.

20. Teresa de Lauretis, "Sexual Indifference and Lesbian Representation," *Theater Journal,* 40, 2 (May 1988), pp. 155–177.

21. This argument is developed in Spivak, "French Feminism Revisited." I also argue that, unlike Sartrian existentialism, which must presuppose man with a European history as agent, Beauvoir's figuration of the mother as existentialist is not race-specific.

22. De Lauretis, "Sexual Indifference," pp. 175–177.

23. See Derrida, "Geschlecht: différence sexuelle, différence ontologique," in *Psyché: Inventions de l'autre* (Paris: Galilée, 1987), pp. 395–414.

24. This is an illegitimate thematization of Derrida, *Of Grammatology,* trans. Spivak (Baltimore: Johns Hopkins University Press, 1976), p. 47.

25. Sigmund Freud, *The Standard Edition of the Complete Psychological Works,* trans. James Strachey *et al.* (London: Hogarth Press, 1961), vol. 23, pp. 210–253.

26. On the other hand, if we see this move toward literature and culture precisely as marking a substitute-wish for "the dramatic character that one has so often wished to have lie down on the couch," we can say "literature [or culture] perhaps need not resist this clinic" (Derrida, "My Chances," p. 28). To this wish the nationalist backlash to expatriates writing about post-coloniality is an unacknowledged accomplice rather than an adversary.

27. Anika Lemaire, *Jacques Lacan,* trans. David Macey (London: Routledge, 1977), p. vii.

28. Gilles Deleuze and Félix Guattari, *Anti-Oedipus: Capitalism and Schizophrenia,* trans. Robert Hurley, Mark Seem and Helen R. Lane (Minneapolis: University of Minnesota Press, 1983).

29. Karl Marx, *Early Writings*, trans. Rodney Livingstone (New York: Viking Press, 1976), p. 324.

30. Derrida, *Glas*, trans. John P. Leavey, Jr. and Richard Rand (Lincoln: University of Nebraska Press, 1986).

31. Guy Brett, *Through Our Own Eyes: Popular Art and Modern History* (London: GMP Publishers, 1986), pp. 7–8.

Part II
Tailoring the Nation

Chapter 6

The Occidental Tourist: M. Butterfly *and the Scandal of Transvestism*

Marjorie Garber

> A former French diplomat and a Chinese opera singer have been sentenced to six years in jail for spying for China after a two-day trial that traced a story of clandestine love and mistaken sexual identity. . . . M. Boursicot was accused of passing information to China after he fell in love with Mr. Shi, whom he believed for twenty years to be a woman.
>
> —*New York Times*, May 11, 1986

This story, which scandalized and titillated Western journalists and readers, was—perhaps predictably—received slightly differently in different parts of the West. The British press treated it as another homosexual spy scandal, analogous to those involving gay men like John Vassall, Kim Philby, Donald Maclean, Guy Burgess and Anthony Blunt. Boursicot's explanation for his gender "mistake," that the couple had always had sexual relations in the dark, was dismissed as a thin cover for something else. According to one British chronicler of spy activities, "the likeliest explanation" for this unlikely story was "that Boursicot knew the truth and was hopelessly entangled in a web of lies begun to hide his homosexuality, which he continued to deny."[1] In other words, the "secret" here was homosexuality, the denial of which became so important for Boursicot that he was willing to be branded a fool and a traitor.

The French, not surprisingly, had a slightly different view as to where the shameful secret of this story really lay. A panel of French judges sentenced both Boursicot and his lover to six years in prison. Their treason in itself was not considered very serious—only minor documents were leaked. But at least one French judge seemed less appalled by the evidence of treachery than by the apparent fact that a Frenchman was unable to tell the difference between a man and a woman.[2]

As for the American press, its attitude may perhaps be examplified by the spectacular coverage afforded the incident by *People* magazine. *People* arranged for interviews with the two principals in the scandal—a coup it trumpeted with understandable self-congratulation ("Until now" neither man had been willing to discuss their relationship; "finally last week they agreed to talk"; "theirs is a story of East meeting West, and of political upheaval, sexual ambiguity and betrayal"; "It is a conundrum, finally, that will never be solved") and so on and on. But underneath this veneer of wide-eyed openness *People*, too, offered a social critique of sorts. And *People's* contempt, unlike that of the British or the French, was directed not at Boursicot, the now openly gay French man, but at Shi, the Asian "woman" in the story, now living, like Boursicot, in Paris. "A delicate man of 50 whose most striking features are his tiny hands," writes *People*,

> he leads his life like an exiled, impoverished princess, living in apartments provided by friends whom he calls "protectors," carrying himself like a faded diva.
>
> "My life has been *très triste, très triste,* don't you agree?" he asks, in the dramatic French he favors. "But one cannot fall into *une vie de désespoir.*" With a sigh, catching his middle-aged reflection in the mirror, he adds, "I used to fascinate both men and women. What I was and what they were didn't matter."[3]

What *does* matter to *People*'s readers, of course, is the question that underlies every account of this story: what did they *do*? And how could Boursicot possibly *not have known*? The British accounts imply that he did know, and was ashamed to admit it; the French judge exhibited consternation at an ignorance that seemed to reflect badly on a prized national trait, heterosexual connoisseurship. The American press, at least as represented by the voice of the *People*, applies a characteristic investigative technique: American know-how.

> Shi says he kept himself covered with a blanket in a darkened room and never allowed Boursicot to touch his crotch. He hid his genitalia by squeezing them tightly between his thighs. Even today [Boursicot] still cannot explain why sex with Shi seemed "just like being with a woman." He does not believe he had anal intercourse with Shi; he thinks his lover might have "put cream between his thighs," and that he penetrated Shi's closed legs. In any case, Boursicot stresses, they had sex only rarely. (96–97)

Thus to the British, the answer to the "conundrum" was that Boursicot was gay; to the French, the answer—shameful to admit—was that he was a nerd; to the Americans, he was merely a dupe, misled by the tactics of a "faded diva" with a tube of K-Y jelly.

What is particularly interesting to me in all of these readings is that none of these accounts is willing to recognize the role of the central figure in the story, the transvestite. Attention focuses on sexual object choice (gay or straight) and on erotic style (dominant, submissive) rather than on the cultural "fact" at the center of the fantasy: the fact of transvestism as both a personal and a political, as well as an aesthetic and theatrical, mode of self-construction. Once again, as so often, the transvestite is looked through or away from, appropriated to tell another kind of story, a story less disturbing and dangerous, because less problematic and undecidable.

That Boursicot could fall in love with a man, or be duped by a spy—these are tales for which we have cultural contexts and cultural stereotypes. But that Shi could be—professionally, as an actor and a spy—and personally, as Boursicot's lover—a transvestite, whose entire persona put in question the cultural representation of gender—this was a "truth" too disturbing not to be explained away. And the masterstroke of *M. Butterfly*, the play based upon this affair, is that it puts in doubt, in question, the identity *of* "the transvestite." For by the end of the play it is the Western diplomat, and not the Chinese spy, who wears the wig, kimono, and face paint of the (deliberately ambiguous) "*M.*" Butterfly.[4]

Both the original casting and the playbill of *M. Butterfly* drew attention, in different ways, to gender undecidability. The part of the diplomat, René Gallimard, was played by John Lithgow, who had appeared in a celebrated performance as the transsexual Roberta Muldoon (formerly a pro football player called Robert) in the film version of *The World According to Garp*. As for the Oriental actor/spy, that part was taken by a newcomer, B.D. Wong, whose gender was concealed by a playbill bio that carefully avoided all gendered pronouns. Until

B.D. removed his briefs onstage at the end of Act 2—the spy's final debriefing—it was not possible to know—unless one had read the play, or the news stories—what his gender "really" was. A. Mapa, the actor who succeeded Wong in the role, used the same device of onamastic occlusion, which had become by that time—if it was not originally—part of the mystification of gender and sexuality disclosed (and dis-clothed) on the stage.

When playwight David Henry Hwang heard about the Boursicot-Shi story, he was determined to write a play about it. He was equally determined not to find out any of the (disputed) details, since to him the events suggested a particular, and familiar, story about nationalism and sexuality—a story that he thought of as a "deconstructivist *Madame Butterfly.*" Over dinner one evening, he reports, a friend asked him if he had heard about "the French diplomat who'd fallen in love with a Chinese actress, who subsequently turned out to be not only a spy, but a man?" He then found a two-paragraph account in the *New York Times* that quoted the diplomat, Boursicot, as explaining that he had never seen his "girlfriend" naked because "I thought she was very modest. I thought it was a Chinese custom" (94).

Hwang, a Chinese American, was well aware that this was *not* a Chinese custom—that Asian women were no more shy with their lovers than are women of the West. He concluded that Boursicot had fallen in love with a stereotype, the image of the "Oriental woman as demure and submissive" (the word "Oriental" itself, he explains, is an imperialistic term imposed by Western discourse; "in general . . . we prefer the term 'Asian'" [94]). Hwang had never seen or heard Puccini's opera, but he was familiar with the derogatory remark frequently made about Asian women who deliberately presented themselves to men as obedient and submissive: "She's pulling a Butterfly." He was also familiar with the personal ads that run in magazines and on cable TV advertising "traditional Oriental women" as mail-order brides, and with the gay stereotype of the "Rice Queen," a gay Caucasian man primarily attracted to Asians, who always plays the "man" in cultural and sexual terms, while the Asian partner plays the "woman."

When Hwang consulted Puccini's libretto, therefore, he was gratified to find it a repository of sexist and racist cliches. From his point of view, he notes, the "'impossible' story of a Frenchman duped by a Chinese man masquerading as a woman always seemed perfectly explicable; given the degree of misunderstanding between men and women and also between East and West, it seemed inevitable that a mistake of this magnitude would one day take place" (98). Inevitable, that is, that racism and sexism should intersect with one another, and with imperialist and colonialist fantasies. The idea that good natives are feminized—submissive and grateful—and that the passive, exotic, and feminized East is eager to submit to the domination of the masculine West—this is a story so old that, in Hwang's play, it became new.

Now, what I want to argue here is that the figure of the cross-dressed "woman," the transvestite figure borrowed from *both* the Chinese and Japanese stage traditions, the Peking opera and the Kabuki and Noh theaters, functions simultaneously as a mark of gender undecidability and as an indication of category crisis—in literary and cultural formations in general, but to a particularly high degree in *M. Butterfly*. By "category crisis" I mean a failure of definitional distinction, a borderline that becomes permeable, that permits of border crossings from one (apparently distinct) category to another. The presence of the transvestite, in a text, in a culture, signals a category crisis elsewhere. The transvestite is a sign of overdetermination—a mechanism of displacement. There can be no culture without the transvestite, because the transvestite marks the existence of the Symbolic.

Man/woman, or male/female, is the most obvious and central of the border crossings in *M. Butterfly*, and the fact that the border is crossed *twice*, once when Song Liling becomes a "woman," and the second time when René Gallimard does so, indicates the play's preoccupation with the transvestite as a figure not only for the conundrum of gender and erotic style, but also for other kinds of border crossing, like *acting* and *spying*, both of which are appropriations of alternative and socially constructed subject positions for cultural and political ends. "Actor" and "spy" both become, like "transvestite," "third terms," or, more accurately, terms from within the third space of possibility, the cultural Symbolic, the place of signification. And that space of "thirdness" is marked, tagged, signalled, by the presence (or, as explicitly in this play, the construction) of the transvestite.

In order to make this argument, I will briefly summarize the action of *M. Butterfly*, and then take up a number of key and related issues: specific category crises within Hwang's play—crises of nationalism and sexuality troped on the transvestite figure; the Peking opera and the European infatuation with Oriental transvestite theater; the concept of "saving face" and the overestimation of the phallus; and the formal and theoretical interrelationships among acting, spying, diplomacy, and transvestism.

For reasons both political and theoretical, I will be using the pronouns "she" and "her" to describe the Chinese actor when dressed as a woman, and the pronouns "he" and "him" when the actor is dressed as a man. This may at first seem confusing, but that is, of course, part of the point.

Hwang's play begins with the diplomat, René Gallimard, in his French prison cell, and proceeds by flashback to tell the story of his love affair with

Song Liling, the Chinese opera star he calls "Butterfly." His first encounter with "her," at an ambassador's residence in Peking where "she" performed the death scene from Puccini's opera, had convinced him that "she" was a woman. She quickly perceives both his ignorance and his fascination, and invites him to attend performances of the Chinese opera. As their relationship develops, giving him a new sexual confidence in his own dominant manhood, he becomes more successful in his diplomatic career as well, and is promoted to Vice Consul. Always shy and inept in his relationships with Western women, and now fearing that his relationship with a Chinese will exposure him to ridicule, he finds himself instead—because he has a "native mistress"—the envy of the consular office. He discovers that he can treat Song Liling with cavalier neglect, and this further strengthens his sense of masculinity. Briefly he engages in another affair, this one with a young Danish woman student whose name is the feminine twin of his: Renée. (Denmark here is presumably chosen for its connotations of sexual freedom, and "Renée"—as with "Renée Richards"—in part because it means "reborn.")

But Renée, who is eager to parade naked before him, and whose language is as frank as her sexual behavior, strikes him as paradoxically "*too* uninhibited, *too* willing, . . . almost too . . . masculine." In other words, the play provides Gallimard with *two* narcissistic "female" doubles: the "masculine" Danish woman with the beautiful body, and the "feminine" Oriental who turns out to be a transvestic man.

When Song Liling writes him an imploring note, saying "I have already given you my shame," René knows he is in command. "Are you my Butterfly?" he demands, requiring her to acknowledge the scenario of cultural domination and submission. When she assents ("I am your Butterfly") he takes her to bed—in the dark, and clothed, for she protests that she is "a modest Chinese woman." In this first section of the play, then, Gallimard becomes—as he tells the audience—the Pinkerton of Puccini's opera, exploiting and abandoning his Oriental mistress.

In the second half of the play, the roles will be reversed. René is sent back to France; none of his predictions about the war in Indochina have come true. The Cultural Revolution comes to China, and after being put to work in the fields and renouncing his "decadent profession" the actor Song Liling is sent by the Mao government to Paris, to resume his work as a spy, by resuming his women's clothes, and his relationship to Gallimard. At "Butterfly's" urging, René becomes a courier, photographing secret documents, which Song passes on to the Chinese embassy. Then comes the trial. In front of the audience the Chinese actor removes his kimono, wig, and makeup, and appears before René and the audience as a man in an Armani suit. The French judge asks the question the audience has wanted to ask all along: "Did Monsieur Gallimard know you were a man?" And Song Liling answers with two rules. "Rule One": "Men always believe what they want to hear." And "Rule Two": "The West has sort of an international rape mentality towards the East." And he defines "rape mentality" this way: "Her mouth says no, but her eyes say yes."

> The West thinks of itself as masculine—big guns, big industry, big money—so the East is feminine—weak, delicate, poor . . . but good at art, and full of inscrutable wisdom—the feminine mystique.
>
> Her mouth says no, but her eyes say yes. The West believes the East, deep down, *wants* to be dominated—because a woman can't think for herself. . . . You expect Oriental countries to submit to your guns, and you expect Oriental women to be submissive to your men. That's why you say they make the best wives. (3.1)

But why, the judge asks, would that make it possible for Song Liling to fool Gallimard?

> One, because when he finally met his fantasy woman he wanted more than anything to believe that she was, in fact, a woman. And second, I am an Oriental. And being an Oriental, I could never be completely a man.

Yet there is another power reversal to come. Before Act 3 is over, and before René can stop him, he has completely removed his clothes, and stands naked, revealed as—in René's words—"just a man—as real as hamburger" (3.2). And René chooses "fantasy" over "reality." If his "Butterfly" is not the Perfect Woman he has thought her to be, he will become that perfect oriental woman himself. Song Liling—revealed at last to be a man—becomes the Pinkerton figure, and Gallimard literally transforms himself into "Madame Butterfly," dressing himself in the kimono and wig Song has discarded, making up his face in the traditional Japanese fashion, and ultimately committing ritual suicide—*seppuku*—plunging a knife into his body as the music from the "Love Duet" blares over the speakers. The final stage picture is a reversal of the first: Song, dressed as a man, stares at a "woman" dressed in Oriental robes, and calls out "Butterfly? Butterfly?"

BORDER CROSSINGS

M. Butterfly itself stands at the crossroads of nationalism and sexuality, since the axes along which it plots its dramatic movement are those of West/

East and male/female. These two principal binarisms are brought immediately into both question and crisis, for one cultural fact of which René and his wife Helga—a diplomatic couple stationed in China—are blissfully ignorant, is that the Peking Opera is a transvestite theater: that all women's roles are played by men. After his first encounter with Song Liling, Gallimard reports that he met "the Chinese equivalent of a diva. She's a singer at the Chinese opera." In other words, he is convinced that the performer he met was a woman. His wife is surprised to hear that the Chinese even *have* an opera. Informed by René that the Chinese hate Puccini's opera "because the white man gets the girl," Helga is dismissive ("Politics again? Why can't they just hear it as a piece of beautiful music?") and only mildly curious: "So, what's in their opera?" *Gallimard*: "I don't know. But whatever it is, I'm sure it must be old" (1.7).

Undoubtedly, much of the Broadway audience shares this cultural indifference, which will be René's downfall. ("I asked around," he says. "No one knew anything about the Chinese opera.") Only much later in the play does the play offer enlightenment, in a conversation between Song Liling and her female confidant-superior in the Chinese Communist Party:

Song: Miss Chin? Why, in the opera, are women's roles played by men?

Chin: I don't know. Maybe, a reactionary remnant of male—

Song: No. Because only a man knows how a woman is supposed to act. (2.7)

One category crisis leads to another, as Gallimard, voicing the indifference of the West to distinctions of national and cultural tradition in a region romanticized simply as "the Orient" or "the East," conflates China and Japan. Captivated by Song Liling's performance as Cio-Cio San, the heroine of *Madame Butterfly*, he assumes that what he is seeing is "authentic," and that an Oriental actress can bring Puccini's character to life in the way no Western diva could. After the performance, he seeks out Song Liling to tell her so:

Gallimard: I usually don't like *Butterfly*.

Song: I can't blame you in the least.

Gallimard: I mean, the story—

Song: Ridiculous.

Gallimard: I like the story, but . . . I've always seen it played by huge women in so much bad makeup.

Song: Bad make-up is not unique to the West.

Gallimard: But who can believe them?

Song: And you believe me?

Gallimard: Absolutely. You were utterly convincing. [. . .]

Song: Convincing? As a Japanese woman? The Japanese used hundreds of our people for medical experiments during the war, you know. But I gather such an irony is lost on you.

Gallimard: No! I was about to say, this is the first time I've seen the beauty of the story.

Song: Really?

Gallimard: Of her death. It's a . . . a pure sacrifice. He's unworthy, but what can she do? She loves him . . . so much. It's a very beautiful story.

Song: Well, yes, to a Westerner.

Gallimard: Excuse me?

Song: It's one of your favorite fantasies, isn't it? The submissive Oriental woman and the cruel white man.

Gallimard: Well, I didn't quite mean . . .

Song: Consider it this way: what would you say if a blonde homecoming queen fell in love with a short Japanese businessman? He treats her cruelly, then goes home for three years, during which time she prays to his picture and turns down marriage from a young Kennedy. Then, when she learns he has remarried, she kills herself. Now, I believe you would consider this girl to be a deranged idiot, correct? But because it's an Oriental who kills herself for a Westerner—ah!—you find it beautiful.

(Silence)

Gallimard: Yes . . . well . . . I see your point . . .

Song: I will never do Butterfly again, M. Gallimard. If you wish to see some real theatre, come to the Peking Opera sometime. Expand your mind. (1.6)

We might notice that even though Gallimard knows nothing at all about the Peking Opera—clearly he has no idea that its women's parts are all played by men—he assumes that "the Orient" can be represented in a single, and conventional, way. He conflates China and Japan.

But if *M. Butterfly* deliberately challenges the conflation of China and *Japan* as some mystical element called "the Orient," it also offers up another, less obvious conflation of national qualities between China and *France*. "What was waiting for me back in Paris?" Gallimard asks, rhetorically. "Well, better Chinese food than I'd eaten in China . . . And the indignity of students shouting the slogans of Chairman Mao at me—in French" (2.11). Like the exchange of roles between Song and Gallimard, between culturally constructed "woman" and culturally constructed "man," this apparent paradox is presented as not really a paradox at all. In a global cultural economy all constructions are exportable and importable: recipes for food, slogans, and gender roles are all reproduced as intrinsically theatrical significations.

The crossover from China to France, as from "female" to "male," is underscored theatrically by the presence onstage, during the scene of Song Liling's testimony and confession in the French court, of the actor who had played the French consul in China, and who now "enters as a judge, wearing the appropriate wig and robes" (3.1). Moments before in this same scene Song Liling had removed "her" wig and robes, the formal black headdress and embroidered kimono of Butterfly, and appeared for the first time onstage as a man, in a "well-cut Armani suit." In the courtroom scene "wig and robes" take on a new set of vestimentary significations, now the accoutrements of Western (specifically French) maleness as power and authority, the traditional costume of the judge. In the scene that follows, to the blaring music of the "Death Scene" from *Butterfly*, Gallimard will enter, "crawling toward Song's wig and kimono," while "Song remains a man, in the witness box, delivering a testimony we do not hear."

These border crossings, then, present binarisms in order to deconstruct them. As the figure of the transvestite deconstructs the binary of male and female, so all national binaries and power relations are put in question.

THE ORIENT-ATION OF TRANSVESTITE THEATER

In fact the traditions of the Peking Opera and of Japanese Kabuki theater, though both are transvestite theaters, are otherwise quite different, as we should expect, despite the efforts of some European and North American observers to conflate them (rather like René Gallimard), producing an idealized image of pure "theater" or "theatricality" that is analogous—and not coincidentally—to the idealization of "woman" derived from certain transvestic representations and certain cultural fantasies.

The European infatuation with "Oriental" theater as the antitype of (and antidote to) the psychologized theater of the West was memorably expressed by Artaud in *The Theater and Its Double*, first published in 1938. Artaud, responding in part to a visit by a Balinese theater troupe, wrote rapturously about the death of the author: "It is a theater which eliminates the author in favor of what we would call, in our Occidental theatrical jargon, the director; but a director who has become a kind of manager of magic, a master of sacred ceremonies . . . the actors with their costumes constitute veritable living, moving hieroglyphs. And these three-dimensional hieroglyphs are in turn brocaded with a certain number of gestures—mysterious signs which correspond to some unknown, fabulous, and obscure reality which we here in the Occident have completely repressed."[5]

Artaud's romanticized and mystified account of the difference of Oriental theater focused on clothes, on doubleness—and on the image of the *butterfly*.

> Those who succeed in giving a mystic sense to the simple form of a robe and who, not content with placing a man's Double next to him, confer upon each man in his robes a double made of clothes—those who pierce these illusory or secondary clothes with a saber, giving them the look of huge butterflies pinned in the air, such men have an innate sense of the absolute and magical symbolism of nature much superior to ours. (Artaud, 62)

The influence of Artaud could still be felt in France when, in 1955, the Peking opera came to the Théatre des Nations, to be greeted by the press with hyperbolic praise. (In fact, had he wished to, the model for *M. Butterfly*'s Gallimard, Bernard Boursicot, could have seen this cultural event during this visit, or on subsequent occasions when the troupe returned to Paris, in 1958 and 1964. As it happens, he did not.)

One of the Chinese opera's most important works is a traditional piece called *The Butterfly Dream*, or *The Story of the Butterfly*: a folktale about a beautiful girl who impersonates her lazy brother so that she can get an education. Like Shakespeare's Rosalind (or I. B. Singer's Yentl, whose story hers resembles), the girl in the opera falls in love with a young man who thinks she is a boy. It was this part, in fact, that made Shi Pei Pu a star in China. And at least according to one account it was looking at a scrapbook containing pictures of Shi in his cross-dressed *Butterfly* role that led the French diplomat Boursicot to believe he was really a woman, when the two men first met at a party at the French embassy. Although Shi was dressed in men's clothes at the time, the photographs of him in women's costume apparently persuaded Boursicot that he had detected his "real" gender.

(The two mens' stories differ slightly on this point. Boursicot says that Shi took him aside after they had become friends and confided that he was actually a woman, just like the character in *The Story of the Butterfly*—that his mother, having borne two daughters, was afraid to tell his father the third child was also a girl. Shi contends that he was showing Boursicot the scrapbook and that

Boursicot—rather like d'Albert in Gautier's *Mademoiselle de Maupin*—leapt to the conclusion that he was really a woman, with expressions of relief and delight.)

Many observers during the opera's European visit commented on similarities between the Chinese and the Elizabethan theaters, including the paucity of scenery, the absence of stage lighting to indicate night, and the commotion of eating, drinking and talking that took place in the audience during the performance. But there are obvious dangers about conflating Chinese opera, Elizabethan acting companies, and Japanese Kabuki as "transvestite theater," dangers that Hwang's play continually points up in the way it reverses even expectations of reversal. In Chinese opera, the *tan*, or female impersonator, wears a mask corresponding to the class of woman he is portraying: *chingyin*, the elegant lady, *huatan*, a woman of the lower classes, or *taomatan*, an Amazon or militant.[6] There is, then, no *one* fixed and inevitable role for woman; in fact, this tripartite division, with the inclusion of the woman as militant or Amazon, suggests the same kind of splitting and refusal of binarism explored by Hwang's *M. Butterfly*.

Furthermore, the Chinese theater also includes a tradition of *female* transvestism. All-female troupes were popular during the Ming and Qing dynasties,[7] and in the plays of that period the cross-dressed "man's" true gender is often detected by her tiny feet. This sign of "nature" was in fact a sign of culture, since the cultural aesthetic of foot-binding produced an ideal of beauty that was the effect of mutilation and deformity. The *small* size of the appendage is a mark of femininity, artificially and painfully wrought. Theatrically produced as a device of discovery, the female foot that trips up the masquerading "general" or "statesman" becomes a displacement *downward* that marks the site of anatomical gender. Thus, for example, in the play *Ideal Love-Matches* by dramatist Li Yu, a woman disguised as a man discloses her gender identity when she takes off her shoes. "With those black boots off, his feet are little 'three-inch lotuses.' It means he must be a girl!"[8]

Similarly, in a tale called "Miss Yan" or "Yanshi" by the seventeenth-century author Pu Songling, an intellectually gifted woman who has disguised herself as a man in order to substitute for her less studious husband at the candidate's examinations reveals her gender to an incredulous aunt by pulling off her boots and displaying her bound feet; the men's boots have been stuffed with cotton wool. Another tale by the same author, subsequently expanded by him into a long vernacular play, describes a young woman's quest for revenge on her father's murderers. Disguising herself as a young male entertainer, the heroine Shang Sanguan takes the fancy of the murderer, a village bully; they retire together for the night, and in the morning servants discover that the bully has been beheaded, and the young "boy" has hanged himself. When they attempt to move the "boy's" body the servants discover to their surprise that "his socks and shoes felt empty, as if there were no feet inside. They took them off and found a pair of white silk slippers as tiny as hooks, for this was in fact a girl."[9] As Judith Zeitlin notes, "bound feet, those manmade fetishes which had become the locus of the erotic imagination in late Imperial China, are transformed into a *natural* and *immutable* proof of true femininity."[10]

In Japan, as in China, female transvestite theater has at times coexisted with the male Kabuki tradition. The Takarazuka Young Girls Opera Company, for example, presents all-female productions in which the male roles are played by women. Recent films like Shusuke Kaneko's *Summer Vacation: 1999* (1990) starring four young actresses as schoolboys in a drama of uncanny homoerotic substitutions problematize gender roles and sexual fantasies.

But Kabuki remains the best-known, and the dominant, form of transvestite theater in Japan. The tradition of the *onnagata*, the male actor of female roles, is an honored position passed down, at least adoptively, in theatrical families. The present *onnagata*, Tomasaburo IV, has become a celebrity in the U.S. as well as in Europe and Japan. The *onnagata* is heir to an interpretative tradition centuries old, and so stylized that it demands a certain way of walking, of moving the head and hands, of managing the kimono. "Were a woman to attempt to play a Kabuki female role," writes one scholar, "she would have to imitate the men who have so subtly and beautifully incarnated woman before her." "But it is unlikely that a woman has the necessary strength to play a Kabuki female part; the Japanese claim that only a man possesses the steel-like power hidden by softness which is requisite to a successful *onnagata* creation. Besides, with many layers of heavy kimonos, and a wig weighing as much as thirty pounds, a woman would probably not have the physical stamina to hold up such a weight for ten or twelve hours a day."[11]

These comments by one of the most careful observers of modern "Theater East and West" exhibit the very essentialism that he describes Kabuki theater as putting in question. The idea that women would inevitably play cross-dressed women's parts less well than men, and would lack even the physical strength to wear the traditional woman's stage costume, suggests not a harmonious blending of male and female, as he later contends ("whether the spectator is aware of it or not, the *onnagata* stirs in his unconscious a dim memory of some perfection partaking of both feminine and masculine . . . the divine androgyn in whose bisexuality both dark and light are harmonized"[12]) but a reimposition of gender hierarchy. Only the *onnagata* is the real or true stage woman.[13]

The great eighteenth-century *onnagata* Yoshisawa Ayame declared that "if an actress were to appear on the stage she could not express ideal feminine beauty," for she could only rely on the exploitation of her physical characteristics, and therefore not express the synthetic ideal. "The ideal woman," wrote

Ayame, "can only be expressed by an actor."[14] In the same years, in England, where the reopening of the theaters presented women onstage after decades of transvestite performance, the Restoration actor Edward Kynaston, who specialized in women's roles, was praised by his contemporaries as superior to any actress: "It has been disputable among the judicious whether any woman that succeeded him so sensibly touched the audience as he."[15] The question seems to be, as Ayame expressed it, one of "ideal" and transcendent womanhood, an abstraction politically inflected so that it can only be conceptualized and embodied by men. Goethe, applying similar criteria, produced a celebrated praise of the castrati of Italian opera: "a double pleasure," he said, "is given in that these persons are not women but only represent women. The young men have studied the properties of the sex in its being and behaviour; they know them thoroughly and reproduce them like an artist; they represent, not themselves, but a nature entirely foreign to them."[16] Nor is this an attitude that can be safely consigned to the past. Not too long ago, for example, Kenneth Tynan remarked about Shakespearean theater that Lady Macbeth was "basically a man's role," and that "it is probably a mistake to cast a woman [in the part] at all."[17] Meantime in modern Japan, where Shakespeare is much admired, we are told that audiences "enjoy seeing Lady Macbeth played by a famous [male] Kabuki star, precisely because it is more artificial, thus more skilful, in a word, more beautiful."[18]

I should note that David Hwang himself is far from immune to this kind of sentiment. "What interested me most from the start," he reflected in an interview, "was the idea of the perfect woman. A real woman can only be herself, but a man, because he is presenting an idealization, can aspire to the idea of the perfect woman. I never had the least doubt that a man could play a woman convincingly on the stage." And he added, "I also knew it would not hurt in commercial or career terms to be able to create a great part for a white male." As for "real" women, Hwang is less interested in their "perfection," or, indeed, in their subjectivity: "Pleasure in giving pain to a woman is not that far removed, I think, from a lot of male experiences," he says. "As an Asian, I identify with Song," but "as a man, I identify with Gallimard."[19]

There is, then, a certain amount of double-speak that goes on in the discussion of "transvestite theater," even as an approach that verges on cultural anthropology valorizes these Eastern traditions, not only Peking opera and Kabuki but also the older and more stylized Noh drama, in which women never appear, and Balinese cross-gender ritual dances, to name only a few of the best known instances. The twentieth-century Western infatuation with Noh, and to a certain extent with Kabuki and the Chinese opera, reinstitutionalizes as "traditional" and "culturally authentic" a form of drama that writes out women and replaces them with men.

SAVING FACE

As we have noted, makeup, costume, gesture, symbols, and stylization are the key elements of the "Oriental theater" (whether Chinese, Japanese, or Balinese) that captivated Europe. Significantly, they are also the key elements of female impersonation as it is practiced in the West. What David Henry Hwang did, in writing his play about the seduction of a Western diplomat by a Peking opera star, was to demystify, and then remystify, the material basis of female impersonation. In so doing he recast the roles, allowing Gallimard to see that it was he, and not Song Liling, who was playing the woman in the piece, and thus revealing the mechanism of female impersonation as a political and cultural act.

One of the faults Gallimard found with Puccini's opera was that the part of Butterfly was always played by "huge women in bad makeup." At the end of *M. Butterfly,* Gallimard seats himself at the same dressing table where Song Liling had unmasked himself, and smears his face with white face-paint. The whiteness of the makeup is traditional in Japanese theater as a sign of the ideal white complexion of the noble who can afford to keep out of the sun, and the pallor of the protected young woman (or trained geisha) even today.[20] Since *Butterfly* is the story of a *Japanese* woman, the makeup is appropriate, but Song also wears white makeup whenever s/he is dressed as a woman, and we might note that in *Chinese* opera face-painting participates in an entirely different sign system, in which white on an actor's face symbolizes treachery, as red does loyalty, yellow piety, and gold the supernatural.[21] In this story of spies and treason the Chinese signification is over- or underlaid on the Japanese, and Song has already given Gallimard fair and explicit warning not to conflate the two.

For Gallimard himself, of course, the white makeup has yet another significance, since he is continually described as a "white man" throughout the play, even in France where "There're white men all around." When he covers his face with dead white paint Gallimard demonstrates the inexactness of this cultural shorthand. His already pale face takes on a dramatic sharpness, as he continues his painting. A red slash of mouth, dark black lines for eyebrows—this is not the careful and seductive adornment of acculturated woman or trained actor, but something that verges on tragic parody. He lifts the wig—which has remained onstage on a wig stand since Song's unmasking—onto his head, and slips his arms into the kimono. And as he makes up his face, he talks to himself, and to the audience:

> Love warped my judgement, blinded my eyes, rearranged the very lines in my face . . . until I could look in the mirror and see nothing but . . . a woman.

Dancers help him put on the Butterfly wig.

I have a vision. Of the Orient. That, deep within its almond eyes, there are still women. Women willing to sacrifice themselves for the love of a man. Even a man whose love is completely without worth.

Dancers assist Gallimard in donning the kimono. They hand him a knife.

Death with honor is better than life . . . life with dishonor.
(*He sets himself center stage, in a seppuku position.*)
The love of a Butterfly can withstand many things—unfaithfulness, loss, even abandonment. But how can it face the one sin that implies all others? The devastating knowledge that, underneath it all, the object of her love was nothing more, nothing less than . . . a man.
(*He sets the tip of the knife against his body.*)
It is 19—. And I have found her at last. In a prison on the outskirts of Paris. My name is René Gallimard—also known as Madame Butterfly. (3.3)

"Death with honor is better than life with dishonor." These lines from Puccini's opera have been quoted throughout the play. When juxtaposed to Gallimard's transformation, they underscore the fact that the dramatic use of face makeup in *M. Butterfly* is a remarkable literalized commentary on the concept of "saving face" in Chinese culture. It should come as no surprise to learn that this term, "saving face," is an invention of the English community in China, and not, strictly speaking, a Chinese phrase at all—although, equally significantly, it is common enough in Chinese to speak of "losing face" or doing something "for the sake of one's face." To "save face" in *M. Butterfly* it is necessary to "lose face." Song Liling in the character of Butterfly signals this in her letter to Gallimard: "I have already given you my shame." When Song Liling goes to a mirror at the end of Act 2 and starts to remove her makeup—and when Gallimard reverses this procedure in Act 3, sitting at the same mirror to make up his face—the figure of face is laid bare. And of course "figure" means "face."

Let me again emphasize that it is the omnipresent question of transvestism that makes this translation possible. Nationalisms and sexualities here are in flux, indeed in crisis, but what precipitates the crisis is the conflicting intertextual relationship between a transvestite theater that traditionally presents "woman" as a cultural artifact of male stagecraft (in the Chinese opera; in Kabuki theater) and a Western tradition of female impersonation that defiantly inverts the criteria for assertive individual "masculinity."

Transvestite theater in England and the United States, both Shakespeare's theater of "boy actors" and more recent manifestations like the Hasty Pudding

Show or the chorus of hula-skirted sailors in *South Pacific* (another East-West borderline marked by rampant cross-dressing), often turns on a stage rhetoric of phallic reassurance. And what I want to suggest here is that phallic reassurance, and its theatrically "comic" underside, the anxiety of phallic insufficiency, is the Western transvestite theater's equivalence of "saving—or losing—face." By a familiar mechanism of displacement (upward or downward) which is in fact the logic behind Freud's reading of the Medusa, "face" and "penis" become symbolic alternatives for one another. And this, in turn, suggests a reason for the presence, throughout *M. Butterfly*, of an insistent and anxious language of phallic jokes—jokes about phallic inadequacy.

For example: René, remembering himself as a boy of twelve having discovered his uncle's cache of girlie magazines, imagines a pinup girl in a sexy negligee stripping in front of him: "My skin is hot, but my penis is soft. Why?" *Girl*: You can do whatever you want. *Gallimard*: I can't do a thing. Why?" (1.5). He reflects that when a woman calls a man "friend" she's calling him "a eunuch or a homosexual" (1.11), and his friend Marc jokes about having had to set up René's first sexual encounter. The play establishes him clearly as a man unsure of his own sexual attractiveness and adequacy. The one relationship that make him feel like "a man" is that with Song Liling, and the more he neglects her, the more male and potent he feels. We may recall that his affair with the Danish girl Renée was predicated on her difference from "Butterfly": "It was exciting to be with someone who wasn't afraid to be seen completely naked. But is it possible for a woman to be *too* uninhibited, *too* willing, so as to seem almost too . . . masculine?"

The female Renée's "masculinity" extends itself not only to nakedness but also to unadorned language, as they discuss the difficult question of what to call his penis.

> *Renée*: You have a nice weenie.
>
> *Gallimard*: What?
>
> *Renée*: Penis. You have a nice penis.
>
> *Gallimard*: Oh. Well, thank you. That's very . . .
>
> *Renée*: What—can't take a compliment?
>
> *Gallimard*: No, it's very . . . reassuring. [. . .] what did you call it?
>
> *Renée*: Oh. Most girls don't call it a "weenie," huh?
>
> *Gallimard*: It sounds very—
>
> *Renée*: Small, I know.

Gallimard: I was going to say, "young" . . .

Renée: There's "cock," but that sounds like a chicken. And "prick" is painful, and "dick" is like you're talking about someone who's not in the room.

Gallimard: Yes. It's a . . . bigger problem than I imagined. (2.6)

Furthermore, Renée has a sartorial theory about war that hinges on the unknowability of phallic supremacy:

> I think the reason we fight wars is because we wear clothes. Because no one knows—between the men, I mean—who has the bigger . . . weenie. So, if I'm a guy with a small one, I'm going to build a really big building or take over a really big piece of land or write a really long book so the other men don't know, right? But, see, it never really works, that's the problem. I mean, you conquer the country, or whatever, but you're still wearing clothes, so there's no way to prove absolutely whose is bigger or smaller. And that's what we call a civilized society. The whole world run by a bunch of men with pricks the size of pins. (*She exits*)
>
> *Gallimard* (*to us*): This was simply not acceptable. (2.6)

Renée's exhibitionism is thus directly contrasted with Butterfly's modesty. When Gallimard, stung by humiliation at work (his political prophecies have not come true) decides to return to Butterfly and displace his humiliation onto *her*, he demands that she do the one thing she has consistly refused him: to strip. But before she can comply, he withdraws his request: "Did I not undress her because I knew, somewhere deep down, what I would find? Perhaps" (2.6). The phallus can play its role only when veiled.

Transvestism, in fact, theatrically literalizes Lacan's famous statement that the relations between the sexes "turn around a 'to be' and a 'to have,' which, by referring to a signifier, the phallus," both "giv[e] reality to the subject in this signifier" and "dereliz[e] the relations to be signified."[22] In effect, transvestism becomes the middle term, the "to seem," that Lacan suggests will intervene to protect both the fantasy of having and the fear of losing (or having lost) the phallus. Since in Lacanian terms "having" is always a fantasy, "seeming," which speaks at once to the situation of theater (what Lacan calls "the comedy") and of psychoanalysis, does represent an effective "intervention." When the theater involved is *transvestite theater*, or when the intervention is that of *the transvestite* within the context of a (hypothetically) nontransvestite dramatic or cultural moment, the effect can be stunning.

Consider this example from Hwang's play, which may help to make the theoretical point more clearly. Song Liling, determined to keep Gallimard's affections from straying, tells him she is pregnant, and then produces a child she says is his son (following, as it happens, the scenario of the Boursicot-Shi relationship).[23] She announces that she will name the child "Peepee." And to Gallimard's appalled remonstrance she offers the reproach of cultural difference:

> *Gallimard*: You can't be serious. Can you imagine the time this child will have in school?
>
> *Song*: In the West, yes.
>
> *Gallimard*: It's worse than naming him Ping Pong or Long Dong or—
>
> *Song*: But he's never going to live in the West, is he? (2.9)

We may recall that the Chinese actor-spy on whom Song Liling's part was based was named Shi Pei Pu. The name Pei Pu may have suggested to the playwright the joke on "Peepee." But in any case little "Peepee," the detachable phallus (who may someday grow up to be Long Dong) is the "proof" of Gallimard's "masculinity." In an earlier scene, his wife had urged him to see a doctor to find out why they were unable to have children. "You men of the West," said Song Liling to him on that occasion, "you're obsessed by your odd desire for equality. Your wife can't give you a child, and *you're* going to the doctor?" "Promise me . . . you won't go to this doctor. Who is this Western quack to set himself as judge over the man I love? I know who is a man, and who is not" (2.6). There could be no better example of the translation of "saving face" into phallic terms. "Of course I didn't go," Gallimard comments to the audience. "What man would?" (2.6).

TURNCOATS, OR WHAT PASSES FOR A WOMAN IN MODERN CHINA

Most transvestites are not spies. Indeed, recent statistics in Massachusetts suggest that most transvestites in that state, for example, are married heterosexual truck drivers or computer engineers.[24] But some of the most famous transvestites in history have been "actresses," diplomats and spies. Why should this be?

In the seventeenth century, for example, the Abbé de Choisy, who cross-dressed in women's clothes from his earliest childhood, had a highly successful career on the stage (and off) as an actress in a Bordeaux theater. Indefatigably heterosexual, he dressed himself in a gown and his mistress as a boy and attended the opera with her, attracting more attention from the audience than the lesser spectacle on the stage. Sent to Rome to attend the election of the Pope, he dressed as a woman at the coronation ball—and for the next several years while he lived in Italy. When he visited Siam in the entourage of Louis XIV's ambassador, we are told, he "went gorgeously arrayed in a feminine evening gown, make-up and jewelery. The Siamese thought it was a European custom of some sort."[25] This is the inverse of the East/West stereotype: instead of the West feminizing the East, the East feminizes the West, or, rather, naturalizes the "feminine" it sees.

The most famous transvestite in Western history, the personage after whom Havelock Ellis wished to name the transvestic syndrome *eonism,* was the Chevalier d'Eon de Beaumont, a French diplomat who early in his career went to Russia as a cross-dressed spy, then was sent to England, where bets were laid about which sex he was. Based on anatomical observation, an English court ruled that d'Eon was a woman. Recalled to France by an increasingly restive King, d'Eon was required as part of his repatriation to dress and live like a lady of the court, which he did for years. Tiring of this restrictive life, the Chevalière, as she was then styled, began a theatrical career as a female fencer, which enabled her to use the military skills she had acquired in her earlier years. Tended by a faithful female companion for years, she died a woman—and was then revealed, to the astonishment of her companion, to have been a man.[26]

Perhaps the most celebrated brief description of treason is the terse little epigram ascribed to Elizabeth I's godson, Sir John Harington:

> Treason doth never prosper, what's the reason?
> For if it prosper, none dare call it treason.
> —Harington, *Epigrams*

What is being described here is a hermeneutic of *passing* or *crossover.* If treason *works,* it gets mainstreamed or translated into another, nonoppositional category, a new political orthodoxy. This will come as no surprise to any reader of George Orwell—or of history. But the mechanism that is here being described is also the mechanism of gender impersonation, transvestic passing. If we were to take Harington's epigram about treason and replace "treason" with some metrically equivalent word—like "passing"—we would be characterizing a social and sartorial inscription that encodes (as treason does) its own erasure. Successful treason is not treason, but governance, or diplomacy. Is successful cross-dressing, when undertaken as a constant rather than an episodic activity, and when undetected, still cross-dressing? In other words, was Bernard Boursicot wrong, to believe that Shi Pei Pu was a woman? If we are serious about describing gender as constructed rather than essential or innate, the lifelong transvestite puts this binarism (constructed/essential)—like so many others—to the test.

The most direct revelation of Song Liling's activities as a spy in *M. Butterfly* comes, significantly, in a conversation that also addresses the question of cross-dressing and the essence—or construction—of womanhood. The scene is the flat shared by the lovers in Beijing, 1961. Gallimard has left for the evening, and Comrade Chin, Song Liling's female government contact, is interviewing Song about American plans for increased troop strength in Vietnam—all information passed through the French embassy. Chin, writing as fast as she can, can hardly keep up with the numbers of soldiers, militia, and advisors. "How do you remember so much?" she asks. "I'm an actor." "Is that how come you dress like that?" "Like what . . . ?" "You're wearing a dress. And every time I come here, you're wearing a dress. Is that because you're an actor? Or what?" "It helps me in my assignment," says Song.

"Remember," cautions Comrade Chin, "when working for the Great Proletarian State, you represent our Chairman Mao in every position you take." "I'll try to imagine the Chairman taking my positions," replies Song, with an irony entirely lost on her interlocutor. "Don't forget," says Chin as she is leaving, "there is no homosexuality in China." And Song answers, "Yes, I've heard." And then to the audience, after the departing Miss Chin in her Mao suit, he comments, "What passes for a woman in modern China." What *passes* for a woman—this is the real question. And, in René's horrified recognition that "the man I loved was a cad, a bounder," what passes for a man.

Song's ironic and disparaging aside, "What passes for a woman in modern China," marks a crucial dissymmetry in the playtext. Focusing on male pathos and male self-pity, *M. Butterfly* is intermittently antifeminist and homophobic, ridiculing the *female* cross-dresser, Miss Chin, while it elevates Gallimard's plight to the plane of high drama. The other women in the play, like Renée and Helga, are likewise presented in caricature rather than in sympathetic depth. This is a critique frequently made of contemporary male transvestite theater, that it occludes or erases women, implying that a man may be (or rather, make) a more successful "woman" than a woman can. In Hwang's play cross-dressed men are emblematic of cultural crisis (or even of the "human condition"), but the cross-dressed woman is a risible sign of failed "femininity."

Here too, though, it is worth recalling that the "women," like the "men" in Hwang's play, are gendered *in representation* rather than in "reality." Making Miss Chin the butt of broad jokes about uniforms, bureaucratic dress-for-success and the totalitarian erasure of difference offers a sharp contrast between the impossibility of androgyny by sartorial fiat and the subversive power of transvestism both to undermine and to exemplify cultural constructions. Nonetheless, the easy laugh elicited by Song's put-down on "passing for a woman" is too anti-butch not to let the fear of women, and women's difference, come through. What is really at stake here, it seems to me, is a subconscious recognition that "woman" in patriarchal society is conceived of as an artifact—and that the logical next step is the recognition that "man" is likewise not fact but artifact, himself constructed, made of detachable parts. This is the anxiety that lies beneath the laughter; and it is on this anxiety of artifactuality that the aesthetic claims of transvestite theater are, paradoxically, based.

That acting, espionage, and, indeed, diplomacy should be formally or structurally cognate with transvestism is not really surprising. Using the language of vestimentary codes, actors, spies, and transvestites could be characterized as potential or actual *turncoats.* Another suggestive sartorial term popularly in use to describe espionage activities is *cloak and dagger*—again, pointing to the element of disguise, but also of theatricality virtually for its own sake, and of displacement onto clothing—away from the body. Remember that Artaud's praise of Oriental theater was literally a praise of cloak and dagger—of "those who succeed in giving a mystic sense to the simple form of a robe and . . . pierce these illusory or secondary clothes with a saber, giving them the look of huge butterflies pinned in the air." What these activities have in common, however, is more than metaphorical or literal change of costume. It is an ideology of construction.

"The woman of Fashion," says Roland Barthes in *The Fashion System,*

> is a collection of tiny, separate essences rather analogous to the character parts played by actors in classical theater; the analogy is not arbitrary, since Fashion presents the woman as a representation, in such a way that a simple attribute of the person, spoken in the form of an adjective, actually absorbs this person's entire being. . . . The paradox consists then of maintaining the generality of the characteristics (which alone is compatible with the institution of Fashion) in a strictly analytical state: it is a generality of accumulation, not of synthesis: in Fashion, the *person* is thus simultaneously impossible and yet entirely known.[27]

We might compare this to what Diderot says about the paradox of acting: that the actor, the great actor, must not feel.

> At the very moment when he touches your heart he is listening to his own voice; his talent depends not, as you think, upon feeling, but upon rendering so exactly the outward signs of feeling, that you fall into the trap. He has rehearsed to himself every note of his passion. . . . The broken voice, the half-uttered words, the stifled or prolonged notes of agony, the trembling limbs, the faintings, the bursts of fury—all this is pure mimickry, lessons

> carefully learned, the grimacing of sorrow, the magnificent aping which the actor remembers long after his first study of it, of which he was perfectly conscious when he first put it before the public, and which leaves him, luckily for the poet, the spectator, and himself, a full freedom of mind. . . . He puts off the sock or the buskin; his voice is gone; he is tired; he changes his dress, or he goes to bed; and he feels neither trouble, nor sorrow, nor depression, nor weariness of soul. All these emotions he has given to you.[28]

This (de)construction or (de)composition of the fantasy of "character" is precisely what is at work and on display in *M. Butterfly*. Barthes' description of the fashion system suggests that "personality" in the discourse of clothing is an illusion, made up of an accumulation of signifying "essences": "in Fashion, the *person* is thus simultaneously impossible and yet entirely known." In David Henry Hwang's play the vestimentary codes of stage, gender, nation and race conspire together to make the person of the play's title, the *dramatis persona*, likewise, in Barthes' terms, both "impossible" and "entirely known." As Song Liling changes costume, from the "traditional Chinese garb" of the opening tableau to the "Anna May Wong" black gown from the twenties and the chong sam in which "she" appears at home to Gallimard (1.10) to the Armani slacks and gold neck chain in which "he" reveals "his" true gender in the courtroom in France, s/he also changes "character," becomes, as s/he has always been, unknowable, unknown.

"What passes for a woman." And what passes for a man. *Passing* is what *acting* is, and what *treason* is. Recall that the French diplomat Boursicot was accused of *passing* information to his Chinese contacts. In espionage, in theater, in "modern China," in contemporary culture, embedded in the very phrase "gender roles," there is, this play suggests, *only* passing. Trespassing. Border crossing and border raids. Gender, here, exists only in representation—or performance.

This is the scandal of transvestism—that transvestism tells the truth about gender. Which is why—which is one reason why—like René Gallimard, we cannot look it in the face.

NOTES

1. Chapman Pincher, *Traitors* (New York: Penguin Books, 1987), pp. 104–105.

2. The (London) *Times*, May 6, 1986; *The Daily Mail*, May 6 and 7, 1986; Pincher, *Traitors*, p. 105.

3. Joyce Wadler, "For the First Time, The Real-Life Models for Broadway's *M. Butterfly* Tell of Their Very Strange Romance," *People*, 30, 6 (August 8, 1988), p. 91.

4. David Henry Hwang, *M. Butterfly, with an Afterword by the Playwright* (New York: New American Library, 1989). Citations from the play (by act and scene) and references to the afterword (by page number) will be incorporated directly in the text above. I am grateful to David Henry Hwang, to Andreas Teuber and to John Lithgow, who graciously allowed me to see the playscript before *M. Butterfly* appeared in published form.

5. Antonin Artaud, "On the Balinese Theater," *The Theater and Its Double*, trans. Mary Caroline Richards (New York: Grove Press, 1958), pp. 60–61.

6. Peter Ackroyd, *Dressing Up* (New York: Simon and Schuster, 1979), p. 94.

7. See Colin P. Mackerras, *The Rise of Peking Opera, 1770–1870* (London: Oxford University Press, 1972), pp. 45–47.

8. Patrick Hanan, *The Invention of Li Yu* (Cambridge, MA: Harvard University Press, 1988), p. 175.

9. *Liaozhai's Records of the Strange*, 3.374. I am indebted to Judith Zeitlin and her forthcoming book *The Painted Wall: Pu Songling's Records of the Strange* for this reference, and for much other fascinating information on cross-dressing and sexual transformation in Chinese literature and culture of this period. My thanks as well to Ellen Widmer, who first drew my attention to the bound foot in Chinese drama in a discussion after the Nationalisms and Sexualities Conference at the Harvard University Center for Literary and Cultural Studies in June 1989.

10. Zeitlin, *The Painted Wall* (unpub. MS), p. 167. As will be evident, Zeitlin's reading and mine agree on many points. As she notes, "It is almost irresistible to explore the allure of bound feet in Freudian terms as representations of the female genitals—as mutilated appendages with *something missing*" (p. 167).

11. Leonard Cabell Pronko, *Theater West and East* (Berkeley: University of California Press, 1967), p. 195.

12. Ibid., p. 196.

13. Yet even here things are not quite what they seem—or rather, what they seem

always to have been. For the earliest form of Kabuki was in fact the so-called Women's Kabuki (*onna-kabuki*) of the late sixteenth century. But women were prohibited from the stage in 1629 because of allegations of immorality, political as well as sexual; many were prostitutes, and actors were by edict officially to be segregated from the general populace. After a brief interlude in which Kabuki actresses attempted to evade this regulation by reversing the theater's previous practice, and having men play men's roles, and women, women's roles, women disappeared from the stage altogether, and did not reappear as performers in Japan until after 1868.

The women were succeeded on the stage by long-haired, handsome boys, in what was known as Young Men's Kabuki (*wakashu-kabuki*), but these boys proved, apparently, too attractive to some of the samurai in the audience, and in 1652 Young Men's Kabuki was also forbidden. The present form of all-male theater therefore derives from the "Male" Kabuki (*yaro-kabuki*) of the seventeenth century, in which boys and young men were required to cut off their forelocks and shave their foreheads in order to appear less seductive. See Earle Ernst, *The Kabuki Theater* (Honolulu: University of Hawaii Press, 1974), pp. 10–11.

14. Ibid., p. 195.

15. Ashley H. Thorndike, *Shakespeare's Theater* (New York: Macmillan, 1960), p. 420.

16. Quoted in Ackroyd, *Dressing Up*, p. 98.

17. Kenneth Tynan, *Tynan on Theater* (Harmondsworth, UK: Penguin, 1964), p. 108.

18. Ian Buruma, *Behind the Mask* (New York: New American Library, 1984), pp. 117–118.

19. Jeremy Gerard, "David Hwang: Riding on the Hyphen," *New York Times Magazine*, March 13, 1988, p. 87.

20. Pronko, *Theater West and East*, p. 151.

21. Ibid., p. 44.

22. Jacques Lacan, "The Signification of the Phallus," in *Écrits: A Selection*, trans. Alan Sheridan (New York: W. W. Norton, 1977), p. 289.

23. Wadler, "For the First Time . . . ," p. 96.

24. Sally Jacobs, "'You Do What You Need to Do,'" *The Boston Globe*, August 2, 1988, p. 2.

25. Ackroyd, *Dressing Up*, p. 9. For more on Choisy, see *The Transvestite Memoirs of the Abbé de Choisy and the Story of the Marquise-Marquis de Banneville*, trans. R. H. F. Scott (London: Peter Owen, 1973), and also the extended treatment in my *Vested Interests: Cross-Dressing and Cultural Anxiety* (New York: Routledge, 1991).

26. I discuss D'Eon, like Choisy, at much greater length in my *Vested Interests*. See also, among the many books and articles on this enigmatic figure, J. Buchan Telfer, *The Strange Career of the Chevalier D'Eon de Beaumont* (London: Longmans Green, 1885); Ernest Alfred Vizetelly, *The True Story of the Chevalier D'Eon* (London, 1895); Marjorie Coryn, *The Chevalier d'Eon, 1728–1810* (London: T. Butterworth, 1932); Edna Nixon, *Royal Spy: The Strange Case of the Chevalier D'Eon* (New York: Reynal and Co., 1965); Cynthia Cox, *The Enigma of the Age: The Strange Story of the Chevalier d'Eon* (London: Longmans, 1966); Michel de Decker, *Madame le Chevalier d'Eon* (Paris: Perrin, 1987); and Gary Kates, "D'Eon Returns to France: Gender and Power in 1777," in Julia Epstein and Kristina Straub, eds., *Body Guards: The Cultural Contexts of Gender Ambiguity* (New York: Routledge, 1991).

27. Roland Barthes, *The Fashion System*, trans. Matthew Ward and Richard Howard (New York: Hill and Wang, 1983), pp. 254–255.

28. Denis Diderot, *The Paradox of Acting*, trans. William Archer (New York: Hill and Wang, 1957), p. 19.

Chapter 7

Fashioning Cuba

Norman S. Holland

Over a decade before Mallarmé discovered that a national style encompasses both the literary and the fashion worlds, the first version of *Cecilia Valdés* appeared in two installments in the Cuban magazine *La Siempreviva.*[1] This twenty-six page story by Cirilio Villaverde already displayed the remarkable fascination with fashion that would permeate the definitive edition, *Cecilia Valdés o La Loma del Angel: novela de costumbres cubanas*, published by the exiled author in New York City in 1882. More than half of the four hundred pages of this novel of failed romantic love are devoted to descriptions of dressing and dancing. In arguing below that these descriptions helped to promote an independent Cuba by advancing a pleasure-seeking consumerism,[2] I follow a mode of analysis which seeks both to evoke and dismantle the workings of the novel's fashion world. As we move from the political conventions of romance to the equally binding rules of fashion, the elements of a singular national style—*lo cubano*—will emerge.

Nineteenth-century Latin American novels like *Cecilia Valdés* have been frequently treated as historical documents that realistically transcribe "local color." Even the most acute critics of these novels seldom question their writers' documentary intentions. In the case of *Cecilia Valdés*, critics tend to accept at face value Villaverde's subtitle: "una novela de costumbres cubanas" (a novel of Cuban customs). Typically, these critics celebrate the novel's realistic depiction of slavery, focusing on such passages as: ". . . allí reinaba un estado permanente de guerra, guerra sangrienta, cruel, implacable, del negro contra el blanco, del amo contra el esclavo" ["there reigned a permanent state of war, a bloody war, cruel and implacable, of black man against white man, of master against slave"] (292/406).[3] But since Villaverde fails in the end to propose concrete strategies for the liberation of the slave Dionisio and his other oppressed characters, the novel has been often dismissed as a politically-compromised if sociologically-accurate portrait of the period. Underlying this dismissal is the notion that a novel must be more than a realistic recording of social injustices—it must be nothing short of utopian in its ambitions.

Other readers focus on the romance that shapes the plot.[4] Subtitled "A Romance in Old Havana" in the American translation, the novel traces the incestuous affair of an unsuspecting half-brother and sister, Leonardo and Cecilia. This love story between Leonardo, the only son of one of the leading sugarcratic families, and his half-sister Cecilia, the almost white mulatta, might have formed the model for a nation building project, a model implicit in many other nineteenth-century Latin American novels. Yet when Villaverde has José Dolores, Cecilia's other suitor, kill off Leonardo, he short-circuits this possibility. And although the sign of incest always hovers over Cecilia and Leonardo's affair, the text seems scarcely invested in exploring its narrative consequences.[5] It would seem, indeed, that in all respects the novel fails to fulfill the generic expectations it arouses in its readers. Hence its odd place in the formation of a national literature: an acknowledged masterpiece often praised for its wealth of historical detail, it has otherwise been ignored or condemned since its narrative conflicts and contradictions remain unresolved at any level. I will argue below, however, that *Cecilia Valdés* successfully narrates its historical moment but not simply in any mimetic or derivative way. The novel constructs a national subject in the all-but-neglected character of the tailor while simultaneously producing a mechanism—a concern for style—that at once liberates and polices the desired political body: an integrated, independent Cuba.

Through *Cecilia Valdés*, Villaverde participates in the contemporary Cuban debate on the formation of a national subject. Following his mentor, the progressive Cuban thinker Domingo del Monte, he advocates the integration of the various racial minorities that constitute the island's population. While Villaverde is aware of the need to establish a national hegemony as a precondition for independence, he also recognizes as did his male continental counterparts (or perhaps because of them) the political dangers of independence run riot.[6] Not surprisingly, then, *Cecilia Valdés* opens with its heroine running loose in the streets of Old Havana: "¿Qué hacía, pues una niña tan linda azotando las calles día y noche, como perro hambriento y sin dueño? ¿No había quien por ella hiciera ni rigiera su índole vagabunda?" ["What was such a pretty little girl doing, wandering about the streets day and night, without food or rest like a homeless dog? Was there no one to care for her nor to guide her footsteps?"] (17/29). This paternalist preoccupation suggests the parallel quandary of who will guide Cuba after independence.

Cecilia's need to be brought under masculine guidance can be traced to the moment when her father denied her his name at birth, an act which makes him incapable of functioning as her legitimate shield. But neither can the other familial figures of the romance assume this protective role. Leonardo is discredited when he turns out to be his father's clone. And when José Dolores kills Leonardo, he destroys at the same time any future connection with Cecilia, for she had wanted him to kill her rival Isabel instead:

> Cecilia, a poco, con el pelo desmedejado y el traje suelto, corrió a la puerta y gritó de nuevo:
>
> ¡José! ¡José Dolores! ¡A *ella*, a *él* no!
>
> Inútil advertencia. El músico ya había doblado la esquina de la calle de las Damas.
>
> [Cecilia ran to the door and cried at the top of her voice: José, José Dolores! Her, not him!" A useless entreaty. The musician had already turned the corner.] (402/544)

In the end, the novel refuses any match with either the colonial lover (Leonardo) or the noble black lover (José Dolores), the latter recalling a narrative solution which earlier in the century had conquered a (white) reading public.[7] In rejecting both of these possibilities, the romance cannot bring closure to the novel because Cuba's liminal political status demands a similarly transitional figure who can mediate between private and public realms. José Dolores's enterprising employer, the tailor Señor Uribe, will turn out to fit this bill.

In the tailor, Villaverde creates a figure who is, strictly speaking, positioned outside the familial and hierarchical settings that dominate the novel. And yet because of his profession he can intervene in various social practices to which, by virtue of his race and class, he is marginal. In other readings of the novel, this figure has been ignored or neutralized as part of the background or setting, as if "Cuban customs" were not a construct but rather a given. I propose, however, that the novel celebrates the creations of this black tailor not merely to engage in *costumbrismo* but to produce a model of national unity and civic pride, a model which will have the added "benefit" of safeguarding class and racial differences in the new nation. Such attention to style will serve, moreover, to distinguish Cuba from Europe. Though Cuba's stratified, colonial society hardly seems to resemble the Enlightenment democracy of the European bourgeoisie, the novel's preoccupation with fashion constructs an inclusive social contract in which all the participants are invited to dress and dance. This invitation does not mean, however, that all dresses and dances are the same. If we listen to the inconsistencies within and between the voices that consume the novel's fashions, we will learn to appreciate how compelling and pernicious the tailor's work becomes. He himself is amply aware of fashion's possibilities, limits and duplicities.[8]

When the reader first meets Señor Uribe, he is advising the unhappy José Dolores, distraught upon learning that Cecilia has fallen for Leonardo: "Deja correr, chinito que alguna vez nos ha de tocar a nosotros. Esto no puede durar siempre así" ["Let 'em alone, my boy, and someday it'll be our turn. It can't last forever like that"] (106/147). Linking romance with food, he sketches his understanding of the politics of consumption: "Los blancos vinieron primero y se comen las mejores tajadas, nosotros los de color vinimos después y gracias que roemos los huesos" ["The white people came first, and they're eating the choice cuts; we, the coloured people, came later, and we gnaw the bones"] (106/147). But what appears passive in his strategy is redefined by the kind of mimicry the tailor proposes: "Haz lo que yo. ¿Tú no me ves besar muchas manos que deseo ver cortadas?" ["Copy me. Don't you see me kiss many a hand that I'd like to see chopped off?"] (106). The tailor, however, never *simply* copies. He has earned his reputation for being able to reproduce the latest European fashions but always with a difference—*ese yo no sé que* which Benítez Rojo convincingly argues is the essence of *lo cubano.*[9] *Ese yo no sé que* made him "favorito en aquella época de la juventud elegante de La Habana" ["the favourite of the fashionable young men of Havana"] (102/140). We could almost say then that Señor Uribe is a kind of Caliban, the Caliban who dialogizes with (if we think of Bakhtin) or cannibalizes (if we think of Haroldo de Campos) other—especially British and French—fashions.

Still, Villaverde's narrative strategy always runs the risk of turning out to be a daydream—just an inferior imitation of the European—when the novel shifts from the conventions of romance to the rules of fashion. The tailor thus takes pains to reassure José Dolores of the overriding importance of (sartorial and hence social) distinction: "Pues qué, . . . , ¿te figurabas que porque le hago el *rande vú* a todos cuantos entran en esta casa, es que no sé distinguir y que no tengo orgullo?" ["Because I seem delighted to welcome everybody who enters this shop, (don't think) I draw no distinction between people and that I have no pride"] (106/147). Although Señor Uribe may not resolve in his character the profound racial and ethical crisis of the colonial order, he insists that to be Cuban is among other things to have pride [*orgullo*]. Paraphrasing the tailor, we could say that to be Cuban is among other things to be proud of dress, to know *how* to dress. So it should not surprise us that the novel celebrates the tailor and the sites where his creations circulate: dances. Fashion and music will mutually reinforce one another in Villaverde's construction of the Cuban national subject.

While the novel does not endorse their union, Leonardo and Cecilia's preoccupation with dressing and attending balls creates the space in which these morally bankrupt protagonists are constituted as "modern" nationals. Of the two, Leonardo is the most obsessed with fashion. He spends his days getting himself ready to see and be seen by Cecilia. While the romance fixes him as his father's degraded copy, his concern with fashion turns him into one of Villaverde's figures for *lo cubano*.

Leonardo's interest in fashion initially emerges with his elaborate ruse to obtain a new Swiss repeating watch from his mother after being scolded by his father for arriving late the night before. He begins his deception by remarking the reliability of Swiss watches and thus indirectly blaming his tardiness on his unreliable English watch: ". . . los legítimos ginebrinos son otra cosa, casi todos salen buenos, exactos" ["Swiss watches are always accurate and reliable"] (93/131). Though the true cause of his late hours is of course his amorous pursuit of Cecilia, the novel's point is that time itself is of no concern to this representative of the ruling slavocracy. He is instead all about style: "Todavía sirve el inglés que tú me regalaste el año pasado, sólo que no es de moda" ["The English watch you gave me last year is perfectly all right, except it's no longer in style"] (92/130). The consumption of fashion in and by this text not only registers the protagonist's, and by extension the colony's, wealth but also the importation of the foreign ideas and aspirations embodied in the objects thus consumed.[10]

Yet Leonardo's obsession with European watches is not simply another sign of a colonial mentality at work. Strikingly, at the level of dress, Leonardo favors the "native" over the "foreign." Rather than patronize one of the foreign tailors whom Leonardo's oldest sister constantly praises, Leonardo engages a black freeman. His advocacy of national "difference" surfaces as well when he discovers that his sister is being courted by a Spanish officer, with whom he nearly comes to blows. Though in these instances the text inscribes Leonardo as the potential national subject, he is never fully constituted as such. It is as if his speech acts never succeed in escaping the narrative conventions of romance. In fact, they serve only to impress our heroine Cecilia who, in turn, is oblivious to anything beyond the licenced pleasure seeking and day-dreaming of the romance in which she is emplotted. Unlike her rival Isabel, who is painfully aware that a union with Leonardo would symbolically affirm his slavocratic identity, Cecilia cannot even acknowledge her own skin coloration. Until the very end she cares solely about herself; she never sees herself as a prefiguration of national unity. The only characters who attempt to destabilize the rhetorical system that constrains our privileged pair are the married slaves Dionisio and María de Regla. And yet their interventions fall short: by rushing to reveal the true identities of the parties involved, they fail to understand how fashion binds those caught in its thrall.

When Dionisio tries to inform Cecilia of her true lineage, she—like the reader—refuses to listen to him not so much because he is a slave (albeit the love plot dictates this ignorance) but because he is not properly attired. Even before the reader knows who and what Dionisio is up to, the reader has already been instructed not to trust him as well. "Aunque se vestía como se había dispuesto el frac le venía algo estrecho, el chaleco se le quedaba bastante corto, las medias estaban descoloridas por viejas, carecían de hebillas sus zapatos, no tenía vuelos la camisa y el cuello le subía demasiadamente hasta cubrirle casi las orejas . . . ["Though he wore the required dress, his coat was too small for him, his waistcoat too short, his stockings were yellow with age, his shoes lacked buckles, his shirt had no ruffles, and the collar came up so high that it nearly covered his ears"] (225/314). His clothing signals clearly that he does not belong.

Dionisio does not belong for both literal and figurative reasons. First, his clothes do not belong to him; they are his master's. Secondly, Dionisio is not aware (as are our protagonists) that costume in modern Cuba has evolved into fashion. No longer does it suffice to wear the required dress to a ball; one must be aware of the details—"buckles," "ruffles"—which turn dress into fashion. By fashion here I mean a recognizably codified but dynamically changing style; costume, on the other hand, speaks of a static, timeless code. At this stage of the development of Cuban society, fashion is not strictly associated with women; men have not yet renounced fashion like their European counterparts. While Dionisio thinks that he is appropriately dressed, that he is wearing the required costume, throughout this episode his unfashionable clothing discloses his identity as a slave. Though his dress identifies him as other, it also blocks all identification with the Other.

Just as Dioniso's clothes trap the reader into his/her own racial and familial biases, the outward signs of skin coloration blind Cecilia to the truth of her lineage. This difference between outer appearance and inner identity constitutes the essential erotic appeal of Cecilia for the reader. Yet the novel demonstrates that outsides and insides might well be impossible to distinguish, for modern Cubans are shown in effect *to wear their identities*. Inasmuch as the fashion system depends upon the interweaving of codes concerning gender, race, and class—external signs that put into question the concept of inner identity as a coherent category—tailoring Cuba into a nation does not require the revelation of "true identities" as much as a newly stylish incorporation, the amalgamation of various minorities into an encompassing plural voice. Although compelling in its apparent inclusiveness, this national voice also serves to police the emerging national body.

This policing function can be discerned, for example, in María de Regla's telling of Cecilia's story. Unlike her husband Dionisio's version, we are more prone to listen to hers since her motivation is safely kept in place by her desires. Although she too hopes to exchange the tale about Cecilia for her liberty, her freedom reaffirms rather than threatens Villaverde's political project. She waxes to her niñas: "¡La libertad! ¿Qué esclavo no la desea?" ["Freedom! What slave does not long for it"] (315/436). And what is this a desire for? To go dancing, all dressed up: ". . . voy a los bailes vestida de ringo rango, con manillas de oro, aretes de coral, zapatos de raso y medias de seda . . ." ["I go to balls, all dressed up with gold mantillas, coral earrings, silk stockings and satin slippers"] (316/436). Dressed in this way María de Regla will of course be an object of scorn, no different than the other women who arrive at the balls "vestidas estrafalariamente" ["for the most part overdressed in gaudy clothing of the worst taste"] (32/50). To paraphrase Stephen Greenblatt, it is by dressing in bad taste that cultural boundaries are distinguished and enforced most powerfully. The novel thus does not fear this slave's desire for freedom since a fashion system is already in place to mark her social difference. Not unlike the prescribed movements of dances, fashion promises mobility while masking a highly rigid social order.

I have been suggesting that such concern for the codes of fashion cannot simply be understood as "realism" but as the novel's attempt to construct a space and a body that the desired political order—an independent Cuba—will consolidate: the modern consumer as national subject. The fashion system further reassures the reader that, after independence, class and racial differences will continue to be respected. Recall that the novel is set during the period 1812–1831, the years when Cuba replaced Haiti as the foremost sugar-producing island and became extremely wealthy. The novel's actual composition, on the other hand, virtually spanned the entire century, the period when Cuba, while still politically a Spanish colony, was being transformed into a modern bourgeois state. This antagonism between colonial and market economies mark a tension in Villaverde's writing that issues ultimately in *lo cubano*. The novel assembles a unique system of fashion and music that differentiates Cuba not only from Spain, but also from the other Caribbean islands that share its colonial history.

In presenting a highly elaborate system of fashion and representing it as the new order of things in Cuba, Villaverde effectively intervened in national culture. Within the powerful constraints of colonialism, he was able to devise a narrative that sought to integrate the island's voices into the fabric of an independent nation. Crucial to this integration is the tailor whose very marginality turns him into a central figure in the fashioning of a postcolonial subjectivity. Yet Señor Uribe also alerts us to the holes in the national cloth: ". . . porque lo cierto y verídico es que en verbo de blanco no quiero ni el papel" ["the honest truth is that for a white man's word I wouldn't give a centavo, not even for the paper it's written on"] (106/147). If my aim was to register the power of Villaverde's fashion system, I have also attempted to follow some of the other threads that weave Cuba into nationhood.[11]

NOTES

1. Stephane Mallarmé began to publish his magazine *La Mode* in 1854. Eight years earlier in Buenos Aires, the foremost Argentine political theorist Juan Bautista Alberti edited a magazine devoted to fashion and society news, *La Moda.* After Villaverde published his first draft of *Cecilia Valdés* in 1839, he contributed articles on Cuban fashion and custom to various magazines. What interests me here is how this overlap reveals some of the political concerns that inform Villaverde's writing.

For information on Villaverde, see Cirilio Villaverde, *Cecilia Valdés,* ed. Ivan Schulman (Caracas: Biblioteca Ayacucho, 1981). I have also employed the translation by Sidney G. Gest, *Cecilia Valdés or Angel's Hill: A Novel of Cuban Customs* (New York: Vintage Press, 1962). Citations, first to the Spanish and then to the English editions, will be incorporated in the body of the text.

2. See Colin Campbell, *The Romantic Ethic and the Spirit of Modern Consumerism* (Oxford and New York: Basil Blackwell, 1988). Although his subject is Romanticism (and its links with leisure, desire, and speculation), Campbell's argument can be translated more forcefully to romance. Other primary sources on fashion that I consulted are Roland Barthes, *Système de la mode* (Paris: Seuil, 1967), and Valerie Steele, *Fashion and Eroticism: Ideals of Feminine Beauty from the Victorian Era to the Jazz Age* (New York: Oxford University Press, 1985).

3. For an exemplary reading in this mode, see Selwyn R. Cudjoe, "The Liberation Movement," in his *Resistance and Caribbean Literature* (Athens, OH: Ohio University Press, 1980).

4. Jean Franco labels these novels' plots "conventionally Romantic." What distinguishes them from their European predecessors is their inevitable articulation of the

question of race. Just as their lovers are doomed to failure, so too do these novels fail in becoming "national epics." See Jean Franco, *A Literary History of Spain: Spanish American Literature Since Independence* (London: Ernest Benn Limited, 1973), ch. 3, "The Inheritance of Romanticism," from which these ideas are drawn.

In her forthcoming book on foundational fictions in Latin America, Doris Sommer has challenged this traditional reading by focusing on how the romances create what Benedict Anderson calls "imagined communities." For a preliminary discussion see her "Foundational Fictions: When History was Romance in Latin America," *Salmagundi*, 82–83 (Spring-Summer 1989), pp. 111–141.

5. In contrast, no apocalyptic baby with a pig's tail dooms Villaverde's novelistic world as in García Márquez's masterpiece *Cien años de soledad* (*One Hundred Years of Solitude*). But even in García Márquez's novel, the pig's tail functions as a "diversion." For a convincing exposition of this argument, see Michael Wood, *Gabriel García Márquez: One Hundred Years of Solitude* (Cambridge: Cambridge University Press, 1990), p. 24.

6. From the Argentine Bartolomé Mitre's *Soledad* (1847) to the Venezuelan Rómulo Gallego's *Doña Bárbara* (1929), we find in many Latin American novels feminist protagonists who are simultaneously loved and feared. While these female characters prefigure national unity, they a pose a threat to the desired (male) symbolic order if they are not reinscribed within a readable, that is, a recognizable generic convention. This reinscription is usually accomplished through a character marginal to the plot. In the case of Mitre, his protagonist Soledad operates at first within a sixteenth-century comedy of cuckoldry but then is replotted within the contours of traditional romance. The figure of the doctor who displaces the priest at the end of the novel presides over this change in emplotment. The tailor assumes a similar function in *Cecilia Valdés*. My work in progress argues that these marginal male figures mark out a subjectivity distinct from the totalizing concept of *machismo*.

7. For this idea, I am indebted to Doris Sommer's reading of the Cuban national epic *Sab*, which is part of her forthcoming book *Foundational Fictions: The National Romances of Latin America* (Berkeley: University of California Press, 1991).

8. The fashion system offers in miniature the model of culture that Greenblatt describes: "if culture functions as a structure of limits, it also functions as the regulator and guarantor of movement." See Stephen Greenblatt, "Culture," in Frank Lentricchia and Thomas McLaughlin, eds., *Critical Terms for Literary Study* (Chicago: University of Chicago Press, 1990), pp. 225–232; the concept is defined on p. 228.

9. See Antonio Benítez Rojo, *La isla que se repite* (Hanover, NH: Ediciones del Norte, 1989), from which this idea is drawn.

10. Spain well understood that the importation of foreign goods into its colonies, what economists call "an open market," presupposed the consumption not only of luxury items but also of the ideology that fostered these consumer goods, that is, a nascent liberalism. Hence, its trade policy. The English had to use force to open the Cuban market.

For a brief history of Cuba, see Hugh Thomas, "Cuba from the Middle of the Eighteenth Century to c.1870," in Leslie Bethell, ed., *Cambridge History of Latin America* (Cambridge: Cambridge University Press, 1985), vol. 3, pp. 277–296. And for an overview of the Cuban sugar industry, see Manuel Moreno Fraginals, "Plantation Economies and Societies in the Spanish Caribbean 1860–1930," in Bethell, vol. 4, pp. 187–231. Both essays can be read as abridged versions of their authors' respective authoritative histories, *Cuba, or the Pursuit of Freedom* and *The Sugarmill: The Socioeconomic Complex of Sugar in Cuba, 1760–1860.*

11. A version of this paper was first read at the conference on Nationalisms and Sexualities at Harvard University (June 1989). I wish to thank my colleague Mary Russo for her valuable suggestions and editorial help as I was revising the paper for publication. I also would like to thank Doris Sommer for the stimulus of her pioneering work and for my many conversations with her.

Chapter 8

Dismantling Irena: The Sexualizing of Ireland in Early Modern England

Ann Rosalind Jones and Peter Stallybrass

In 1537, "An Act for the English Order, Habit and Language" was published in Ireland which, even as it acknowledged cultural differences between English and Irish, attempted to erase them. The Act claimed that there was

> nothing which doth more contain and keep many of [the English king's] subjects of this his said land in a certain savage and wild kind and manner of living, then the diversity that is betwixt them in tongue, language, order and habit, which by the eye deceiveth the multitude, and persuadeth unto them, that they should be as it were of sundry sorts, or rather of sundry countries, where indeed they be wholly together one body, whereof his Highness is the only head under God. . . . Wherefore be it enacted . . . that no person or persons, the King's subjects within this land being . . . shall be shorn or shaven above the ears, or use the wearing of hair upon their heads, like unto long locks called "glibes" . . . and that no person or persons . . . shall use or wear any mantles, coat or hood made after the Irish fashion. . . . And be it enacted that every person or persons, the King's true subjects, inhabiting

> this land of Ireland, . . . to the uttermost of their power, cunning and language, shall use and speak commonly the English tongue and language.[1]

As we shall show, the problems of hair, clothes and language were returned to again and again by English colonizers and commentators in Ireland in the sixteenth and seventeenth centuries. But by the 1590s, the New English, as they came to be called, adopted a radically different perspective on cultural diversity. Their whole enterprise depended upon the *denial* that Ireland was "wholly together one body," governed by English common law. While the New English, and particularly writers like Edmund Spenser, Barnabe Rich and Fynes Moryson, repeated the concerns of the 1537 Act, they did so to insist that there was no hope of a gradual assimilation of the Irish to English customs and manners. On the contrary, for them conquest, through military repression, starvation, dispossession and plantation, was the desired goal. And to justify the expense of such repression, as well as to justify its moral necessity, they insisted upon the absolute difference between English and Irish.

If England and Ireland were together members of the same body, then Ireland was, according to Fynes Moryson, "the heele of the body" and had become "the sincke of England."[2] But the weight of such writing went into establishing the absolute otherness of the Irish. This may not seem very novel. In 1188 Giraldus Cambrensis had completed his influential *Topographia Hibernica,* in which he wrote that the Irish were a "*gens inhospita, gens ex bestiis solum et bestialiter vivens . . . et omnes eorum mores barbarissimi sunt* (an unhospitable people, entirely descended from beasts and living in a beastly manner . . . and all their customs are extremely barbarous)."[3] The novelty of the claim that the Irish were barbarous in the late sixteenth century lay in the attempt to use antiquarian research to provide a historical ethnography of this barbarism, and in particular to locate the origins of the Irish in the Scythians. One reason for developing this theory of national origins was to argue that the Irish, like the Scythians, were nomads and therefore had no claim to have settled the land. Johann Boemus, in *The Manners, Laws and Customs of All Nations,* had written that the Scythians were barbarous precisely because they "neither possessed any grounds, nor had any seats or houses to dwell in, but wandered through wilderness and desert places driving their flockes and heardes of beasts before them."[4] In 1610, Sir John Davies, the Attorney General for Ireland, used the "Scythianism" of the Irish as an argument for dispossession and plantation. The Irish, he claimed, were more "hurtfull and wilde" than "wilde beastes," and he argued that if they were

> suffered to possess the whole country as their septs [tribes] have done for many hundreds of years past, they would never (to the end of the world)

> build houses, make townships or villages, or manure or improve the land as it ought to be; therefore it stands neither with Christian policy nor conscience to suffer so good and fruitful a country to lie waste like a wilderness.[5]

One of the most extensive parts of Spenser's *A View of the Present State of Ireland* (1596) is dedicated to the proof that the Irish are Scythians. Although Spenser admits that the Irish are "not of one nation" but "of many different conditions and manners," he is intent to show that "the cheifest which have first possessed and inhabited" Ireland were the Scythians.[6] Yet this claim leads him into a series of difficulties located in the existing ethnography of the Scythians. On the one hand, the term "Scythian" was used loosely to suggest any kind of barbarism. In his *Description of Britain*, William Harrison writes that "these Scots were reputed for the most Scithian-like and barbarous nation;"[7] and Shakespeare's Lear, disowning Cordelia, says

> . . . the barbarous Scythian
> Or he that makes his generation messes
> To gorge his appetite, shall to my bosom
> Be as well neighbour'd, pitied and reliev'd
> As thou my sometime daughter. (I.i.115–9)

The Scythian, in this sense, is a monster whose cannibalism extends to the eating of parents by children or children by parents. On the other hand, as Spenser was well aware, the early history of the Scythians records their triumph over foreign invaders: Book 4 of Herodotus' *Histories* describes the successful guerrilla tactics which the Scythians used against Darius' invading Persian army.[8] Moreover, as Spenser himself argues, the later history of the Scythians is of their successful sweep through Europe, their conquest of Spain, their migration to Ireland and their spread "into all countreys in Christendom, of all of which there is none but hath some mixture and sprinckling" (628).

But seen from this perspective, the Scythians begin to emerge less as nomadic vagrants than as models of military valor. This is made explicit in Spenser's argument that the Irish should *want* to be descended from the Scythians, and secondarily the Gauls, because they are worthier ancestors than the Spaniards whom the Irish chronicles claimed were the settlers of Ireland. There's a particular point to this, of course. One of the main aims of the English in the late sixteenth century was to disarticulate the Irish from the Spanish. But in the process, Spenser is forced to devaluate supposedly civilized peoples and to ennoble barbarian tribes. The Spanish, who are at first imagined as a "very honorable people" in contrast to the Irish, "nowe accounted the most barbarous nation in Christendome," have to be reconceptualized by Irenaeus, one of the two speakers in Spenser's dialogue on Ireland: "Of all nations under heaven (I suppose) the Spanyard is the most mingled, most uncertayne, and most bastardly" (628). The Scythians and Gauls, in contrast, are "two as mightye nations as ever the world brought foorth." It is particularly around the image of the Scythian-Irish warrior that Spenser is most ambivalent. The kerns, or common Irish soldiers, had long been viewed as the very exemplars of barbarism, and Spenser claims:

> they doe use all the beastly behaviour that may be to oppress all men; they spoyle as well the subject as the enemy; they steale, they are cruell and bloudye, full of revenge and delighting in deadly execution, licentious, swearers, and blasphemers, common ravishers of women, and murtherers of children. (640)

But this catalogue of evils is immediately followed by the claim that "they are very valiaunte and hardye, very great scorners of death." And Eudoxus sums up: "It seemes the Irishman is a very brave soldier" (640). In other words, if the Irish are models of Scythian barbarity, they are also models of a military virility that Spenser admires in Irish and Scythian alike.

The Irish, indeed, suggest to Spenser the "antique ways" of the English: "for the English were, at the first, as stout and warrelike a people as ever were the Irish" (613). But the English have been "brought unto that civility" from the perspective of which the stout and warlike is reinscribed as "licentious barbarism" (613). Civility, though, does not emerge through cultural evolution but through military conquest. The English had to be "*brought unto*" civility. By arguing that it is necessary to put Ireland to the sword, Spenser is forced to reimagine the formation of English civility in ways which directly contradict the genealogy he constructs in *The Faerie Queene*. In *The Faerie Queene*, Englishness is traced on the one hand to the mists of Arthurian legend, as a survival from time immemorial, and on the other to the supposed immigration of the Trojan Brute (Brutus). In Book II, Arthur and Guyon enter a library, where they see "old records from auncient time deriv'd, / Some made in books, some in large parchment scrolles" (II.ix.57). While Guyon reads *Antiquities of Faerie land*, Arthur picks up a book called *Briton moniments* and is "quite ravisht with delight" at the genealogy that traces Britain's imperial rule back to the Trojan Brute, who "spred his empire to the utmost shore," to Constantine and his successors. This "remembraunce" is the "perpetuall band" that attaches Arthur to his "deare country." But in the iron world of *A View of the Present State of Ireland*, that perpetual band is smashed. In the Ware ms. of the *View*, the Irish claim to be descended from the Spanish is compared to the English claim to be descended from the Trojans, and both claims are denounced as "vain" (704). Civility now emerges not out of the mists of time but out of a specific moment of conquest. William the Conqueror, writes Spenser, "*layed upon the neck* of England" the common law.

Civility is thus reinscribed as the necessity of military subjugation. And it is only if Spenser can imagine the Irish as barbarically/heroically resistant to all change that he can justify his own insistence that the English must be more Scythian than the Irish, pursuing a policy of terror. What Spenser imagines as the barbarism of the Irish reemerges as the necessary strategy of the English conqueror. Thomas Churchyard praising Sir Humphrey Gilbert, Spenser praising Lord Grey, Sir John Davies praising Lord Mountjoy—all praised the supposed courage of an oppressor who came increasingly to resemble the Scythian Tamburlaine, the tyrant king who had won such fame upon the English stage through Marlowe's depiction of his rise and rise and rise. If the New English apologists *imagined* the barbarism of the Irish, they advocated—and witnessed—the barbarism of the English. Churchyard, for example, praised Gilbert's policy of total war in Munster in 1569, where the English killed "manne, woman and childe," it being necessary to slaughter civilians, in Churchyard's view, as "the waie to kill the menne of warre by famine." Churchyard justified the efficiency of Gilbert's policy when the latter ordered that

> the heddes of all those (of what sort soever thei were) which were killed in the daie, should be cutte of[f] from their bodies and brought to the place where he incamped at night, and should there be laied on the ground by eche side of the waie ledyng into his own tente, so that none could come into his tente for any cause but commonly he muste passe through a lane of heddes which he used *ad terrorem*, the dedde feelyng nothyng the more paines thereby: and yet did it bring greate terrour to the people when thei saw the heddes of their dedde fathers, brothers, children, kinsfolke and freindes, lye on the grounde before their faces, as they came to speake with the said collonell.[9]

The imagined terror of the Scythians was met with the terror of English colonialism.

But it is worth noting just how fully Spenser *failed* to imagine the Scythians. Or, to be more precise, in a tract that parades his ethnographic sources (Aristotle, Herodianus, Pliny, Olaus Magnus, etc.), it is striking what he chooses to ignore. Certainly, the Scythians of Herodotus are nomadic, trained for war and despising the plough and trade, averse to foreign customs. All of this Spenser repeats. What he effaces is that for Herodotus, and even more for Hippocrates, the consideration of the Scythians is also part of a meditation on gender and sexuality. In the nineteenth century one aspect of that meditation was to be formalized under the names of "the Scythian disease," defined as "the atrophy of the male organs of generation, accompanied by the loss of masculine attributes," and "Scythian insanity," defined as "the mental perversion occurring in the Scythian disease, manifested in the assumption of female dress and habits." What a later age named the Scythian "disease" first emerges in Herodotus' *History*, where he describes how, after the Scythians marched upon Egypt, some of them plundered the temple of Aphrodite Urania. Herodotus wrote, "Now, on these Scythians who plundered the temple at Ascalon and on their descendants forever, the goddess has sent the 'female sickness' . . . the Scythians say that this is why these people have fallen sick; and they also say that those who come to their country of Scythia can see the condition of those whom the Scythians call 'Enareis.'"[10] In Herodotus, the nature of the "female sickness" is certainly not clear; some nineteenth-century scholars translated it as pederasty.

But Herodotus, in his tract on *Airs, Waters, Places*, gives an extended discussion of the sickness. "The great majority among the Scythians," he writes, "become impotent, do women's work, live like women, and converse accordingly. Such men they call Anaries."[11] Hippocrates dismisses the Scythians' explanation of the disease as the result of "a divine visitation" because he is intent upon giving a physiological or environmental explanation. He first argues that "The men have no great desire for intercourse because of the moistness of their constitution and the softness and chill of the abdomen, which are the greatest checks on venery. Moreover, the constant jolting on their horses unfits them for intercourse" (125). But he later suggests that through riding the Scythians get swollen joints, to alleviate which they cut veins behind their ears. He continues,

> by the side of the ear are veins, to cut which causes impotence, and I believe these are the veins which they cut. After this treatment, when the Scythians approach a woman but cannot have intercourse, at first they take no notice and think no more about it. But when two, three or even more attempts are attended with no more success, thinking they have sinned against heaven, they attribute thereto the cause, and put on women's clothes, holding that they have lost their manhood. So they play the woman, and with the women, do the same work that women do. (127–8)

It's perhaps worth noting in passing that Hippocrates suggests that the elite are more afflicted with the malady than the poor, since the former ride more. No doubt, it is this last account that is reworked into a theory of heredity in Aristotle's *Nichomachean Ethics*. He argues there that "we are surprised when a man is overcome by pleasures and pains which most people are able to withstand, except when his failure is due to some innate tendency, or to disease: instances of the former being the hereditary effeminacy of the royal family of Scythia, and the inferior endurance of the female sex as compared with the male."[12] Aristotle thus takes an account which problematizes gender and turns it into the exception that proves the rule of female inferiority.

Why does Spenser have no interest in the supposed effeminacy of Scythian men, despite the fact that it is so central a concern of his Greek sources? We suggest that Spenser wished to construct a notion of the Irish as innately warlike so as to support his argument for their brutal suppression. To do that, he constructed them (as Shakespeare did Caliban) as marauding males, prone to theft, torture and rape. In this account, unlike the accounts in his sources, the instability of categories, as of purpose, was attributable to the English, not the Scythians. If the so-called wild Irish were imagined in terms of a supposedly resolute virility, the fantasy of a degenerate masculinity was displaced from the barbarian onto the Catholic Anglo-Irish, or the Old English, as Spenser called them. These early settlers had, in Sir John Davies' view, "become degenerate and metamorphosed like Nebuchadnezzar, who although he had the face of a man, had the heart of a Beast; or like those who had drunke of Circes Cuppe, and were turned into very Beasts; and yet tooke such pleasure in their beastly manner of life, as they would not returne to their shape of men againe."[13] While the Gaelic Irish presented to the New English a picture of unreformable barbarism, the Old English suggested the possibility of rapid cultural transformation. But it was the colonizer, not the colonized, who was being transformed.

At the root of this transformation, for Spenser and Davies alike, was the question of language. The Old English, Davies wrote, "did not only forget the English language, and scorne the use thereof, but grew to bee ashamed of their very English Names" (181). But why should the English give up their language? Spenser gives two answers, both depending upon "effeminacy" in its dominant Renaissance sense: that is, the "contamination" of men by women. First, the Old English are said to have adopted the Irish habit of fostering out their children, who were thus brought up by Irish-speaking nurses. Second, the Old English (here imagined as all male) have intermarried with Irish women. In the first case, "the child that sucketh the milke of the nurse, must of necessity learne his first speache of her"; and, "the speche being Irish, the harte must needs be Irish." In the second case, "the child taketh most of his nature of the mother, besides speache, manners and inclination. . . . For by them they are first framed and fashioned, soe as what they receave once from them, they will hardly ever after foregoe" (638). The denial that the Irish are transformable is set in odd juxtaposition to the total permeability of English civility by the "wild Irish." And that permeability is itself inscribed in the power of Irish women to speak, to control language through love ("children . . . will affect and imitate what they see done afore them, specially of their nurses whom they love soe well") and to control love through language ("the mynde must needs be affected with the woordes").

What Spenser conjures up, then, is a parody (for him, grotesque) of the colonial enterprise, a parody in which the domestic triumphs over the state, female over male, Irish over English. Pandora's box, Circe's cup—these insistent figures of female misrule are embodied in the very homes of the English elite in the Irish wet-nurse and the Irish mother. And outside the house, in the streets and fields, the language of state is mocked and undone by the "wandering women," called "*Beantoohle*" or "*Monatshutt*," "great blasphemers of God" who "run from country to country, sowing sedition amongst the people" (631). It is perhaps as compensation for such a fantasized domestic subversion of the colonizer that Spenser imagines a subversion of the Irish warrior. If the English are transformed from within through language, perhaps the Irish can be transformed from without through their costume, "for mens apparrell is commonly made according to theyr conditions, and theyre conditions are oftentimes governed by their garments" (639).

If Spenser and other Englishmen writing to argue for all-out recolonization manipulated gendered histories to justify plans for containing the Irish, they seem also to have recognized, at least at an unconscious level, the difficulty of that project. From the early sixteenth century, in common with colonialist discourse in the New World as well as the old, English writers figured Ireland as a virgin inviting penetration by virile explorers.[14] But by the end of the century, this metaphor was taking on problematic coloring in relation to Ireland. Luke Gernon, for example, in his 1620 *Discourse of Ireland*, writes: "Ireland is at all poynts like a young wench that hath a green sickness"[15] (that is, the pallor symptomatic of a wandering womb, supposedly needing to be fixed in place by intercourse). But as Gernon elaborates the conventional link between woman and landscape, his analogy becomes more specific and more anxious: "She is very fayre of visage, and hath a smooth skinn of tender grass. Indeed she is somewhat freckled (as the Irish are) [with] some partes darker than others." The transparent purity conventionally attributed to Elizabeth I as royal English virgin here becomes—literally—spotted. What are the "darker partes" of Ireland, which interfere with the hymeneal fantasy of a territory awaiting its master?

Gernon probably means the bogs and forests that darken the predominantly meadow-green of the country. But those bogs and forests are signs of human activity: English colonizers constantly associate them with armed men in hiding. Moryson, for example, deplores the nomadic habits of the Irish lords, who, rather than raising their cattle in fixed fields, "commonly retyre them within thick woods not to be entred without a guide, delighting in this Rogish life, as more free from the hand of Justice, and more fitt to committ rapines" (198). He condemns Irish horsemen for their hit-and-run attacks and sneers at the foot soldiers, who "dare not stand in a playne feild but always fight upon boggs . . . and skirts of woods" (236). Yet this technique is clearly effective. In his next sentence Moryson acknowledges, "the Irish Foote without any help of horse are exceeding swift and terrible Executioners." He also makes an unintentionally revealing point about language. Unlike the colonizers, the Irish use a positive term to describe their compatriots' resistance to the English: "these outlawes are not by them termed Rebles, but men in Action, living in the woods and Boggy places" (194). What is fearful in the Irish is their slipperiness, their ability to disappear, their capacity to disturb even the certainties of the invaders' tongue.

Polyvalence and deception are seen, as well, in Irishmen's style of letting their hair grow. The "glibe" (also "gleb," "glebe"), the long hank of hair worn over the forehead, was read as a provocation because it permitted two kinds of disguise: the Irishman could pull it down to conceal his features or cut it off to change his appearance entirely. Either way, English order is baffled: not to be able to identify the enemy is to be at his mercy. Hence the otherwise puzzling obsession with controlling Irish haircuts, registered in the edict of 1537. If the "rebels" cannot be pursued into the woods and bogs, the colonizer can attempt to pursue them into their very bodies, to strip bare the faces that otherwise resist through disguise.

A related suspicion that the Irish conceal valuable as well as dangerous possessions from the English runs throughout the tracts of colonial advisors. Barnabe Rich, in a revealingly contradictory passage of *A New Description of Ireland* (1610), argues that the Irish hide their iron mines from the English: "To speake truly, the Irish are so malicious that they will not suffer men of art and skill to make search for them."[16] But he then concludes that there are probably neither mines nor minerals in the country, in any case: "for those are . . . to be sought after, in those Countries that are warme, or at the least very dry, but not in those places that are so overcharged with raine, and so much given to moisture as *Ireland*" (7). Spenser writes of rich lands concealed from the English crown; he argues that the "bolys," or summer pastures to which nomadic groups climb in the mountains, provide hiding places for criminals and sites for licentiousness (630). And, perhaps by a train of association from that fantasy of sexual disorder, he compares the Irishman's "glibe" to the mantle worn by both sexes as a means of disguise.

In fact, most colonizing tracts fixate on the Irish mantle as a garment that masks and veils men and women alike. Rich mentions it in a list meant to establish the general physical grotesqueness of the wild Irish: "in the remote places the uncivill sort . . . disfigure themselves with their *Glybs*, their *Trowes* [trousers] and their misshapen attire" (15). Spenser condemns the garment as an accessory in crime for the outlaw, the rebel, and the thief: the outlaw uses it to hide his face, the rebel to hide his weapons, the thief to hide his stolen goods. Spenser goes on to associate the mantle with the prostitute—by which he means any vagrant Irishwoman. Wearing only a "smocke and mantle," he asserts, makes her quickly ready "for her light services" (631–2).

Irishwomen wearing the mantle are widely invoked as figures of disorder who confuse family and class categories as well as political ones. Spenser typifies the view that the Irishwoman hides her illegitimate pregnancies under her woolen cloak: after her "lewd exercise, when she hath filled her vessel, under it she can hide both her burden and her blame." He adds that once her "bastard" is born, she can cradle and clothe it in the mantle, which he further condemns as a means of avoiding proper "howse-wiverye" (631–2). Moryson represents Irishwomen as transgressors of class as well as sexual decorum, both forms of disorder arising from their enmity to Englishmen. There is not one of them, he says, who will not "sooner yeald . . . those ill fruites of love to an Irish horsboy, then to any English of better condition" (235). He goes on to associate the mantle with the lowest category of Irish woman he can imagine, even as he describes it as a garment that crosses boundaries of class and sex: "In the remote parts where the English Lawes and manners are unknowne, the very cheefe of the Irish, as well men as women, goe naked in very Winter time, onely having their privy parts covered with a ragge of linnen, and their bodies with a loose mantell, so as it would turne a mans stomacke to see an old woman in the morning before breakefast."[17] Sartorial difference is read here through a lens of ageist misogyny that reinforces hostility to cultural difference. Cartographic efforts to identify and control the Irish also suggest that their dress frustrated English concepts of social hierarchy. Six etchings of Irish costume printed with a map of the country for English readers in 1616 show men and women of three ranks—nobles, city-dwellers and rural wanderers—all dressed in the mantle.[18] Despite several details signaling class status, the similarity of this major garment as worn by all six figures tends to minimize the perception of both class and gender differences.

We suggested that edicts forbidding the "glibe" to Irish men served the practical purpose of preventing them from changing their appearance and thereby escaping capture. Attacks on the mantle, however, are part of a symbolic as well as material politics. The mantle represents Irishness as the refusal to adopt English order, English social categories, English style. The mantle, that is, not only constructs a veil that requires penetration (like the "green-sick virgin"); it is also read as a sign of defiance. So whether it is actually dangerous or not, it must be suppressed.

This form of oppression fell particularly on Irish men called to English-dominated public hearings. One example: a long narrative of the Parliament held in Dublin in 1585 begins by reporting the decree that no Irishman was allowed to attend in the native attire previously worn on such occasions. The English governor, Sir John Perrot, "bestowed upon Tirlough Luineach [O'Neill], the prinicipal lord of Ulster, and on some others, chief of the Irish, gowns and other robes fit for that place, and their degrees; which they embraced like fetters."[19] The English chronicler then shifts into a anti-Irish anecdote, but one that reveals the Irishman's reciprocal attempt to mock his Protestant rulers. One Irish chieftain, "weary" of the English garb imposed on him, "came to the Deputy and besought him, that one of [the Deputy's] chaplains, which he called priests, might go with him along through the streets, clad in his Irish 'trouses': for then, quoth he, the boys will laugh as fast at him, as they now do at me." There is a good deal of sly wit in this request, perhaps a further reason that the Deputy refuses it; he tells the Irishman that if he is laughed at, it is only because he has not learned to wear English clothes as "civil custome" requires. He should ignore his compatriot's objections to this coercive measure: "If any idle or ill-affected person shall put the contrary into your head, believe it to be done out of ill-meaning to the State and worse unto your person, for contempt of order and decency will in the end be your downfall." The tale ends with the narrator's statement that it is not simply Irish character but deliberate strategy that accounts for resistance to such an order: "It is to be observed in the proud condition of the Irish, that they disdain to sort themselves in fashion unto us, which in their opinion would more plainly manifest our conquest over them." He concludes with satisfaction, "Willing or unwilling, they were constrained to come to the Parliament in that civil habit, which did best fit the place and present service." If clothes make the man, as Spenser claimed of the Irish mantle, then English clothes must unmake him. We are back to a form of symbolic castration—or, literally, rehabilitation. For the colonizer, the mantle, a confuser of appearance and reality, is nonetheless a reality that must be repressed. The Dublin Parliamentarians were made to dress not only in "civil" robes but in deference to their English governors.

Back home in England, in a more obvious fiction, Ben Jonson asserted the same principle: the costume makes the actor. In the fantasy setting of his *Irish Masque at Court*, performed twice for King James in the winter of 1613–4, four parody Irishmen are finally silenced after a dance to "rude music" by a gentleman who sings the praises of King James.[20] The gentleman invites the character of the Irish bard to "sing some charm" that will enchant James's Irish subjects into obedience; the bard obliges, inviting masquers dressed in Irish mantles to drop their outer covering to demonstrate their new loyalty: "'Tis done by this; your slough let fall,/ And come forth newborn creatures all" (212). The masquers "dance forth," magically transformed into English nobles, while the bard proclaims their metamorphosis as a triumph of spring over winter. This pastoral discourse asserts a "natural" process through which Irish resistance melts away under the beneficent gaze of James I as Sun King: "And all get vigor, youth and sprite,/ That are but looked on by his light." What was at issue in the Dublin Parliament is at issue again here, but this time, Irish stubbornness is resolved with elaborate ease: the mantles fall to the ground, the "civil" gentlemen underneath celebrate the power of the English king. Costume here, too, embodies social identity. But its meanings have been wrested away from the Irish in the Jacobean dramatist's appropriation of the mantle and of the Irish bard, a poet now made to sing not the resistance of Irish warlords but the triumph of English order.

If Jonson imagines a magical vestimentary undoing of a barbaric nation, Spenser imagines a more literal undoing of supposed Irish virility. He repeats the story, told by Herodotus and retold by Aristotle, of the Persians' conquest of the Lydians: "When Cyrus had overcome the Lydians, that were a war-like nation, and devised to bring them to a more peaceable life, he chaunged theyr apparrell and musick . . . clothed them in long garments like women . . . appoynted to them certayne lascivious layes, and loose gigges, by which in shorte space theyr myndes were so mollyfyed and abated, that they forgate theyr former fierceness, and became most tender and effeminate" (639). If Irish women had effeminated the old English, perhaps the Irish could in turn be effeminated. At the same time, effeminating the conquered would be a way of reasserting the masculinity of the conqueror. Cyrus *enforces* civility: that is, while civility is itself imagined as an effeminating process, the conqueror stands *outside* that process while enforcing it. Finally, in the tale of Cyrus and the Lydians, Spenser attempts to exorcise the fantasy that shadows his colonial project: miscegenation, a creole Anglo-Irish,[21] paradoxically interpreted as wilder than the wild Irish yet subordinated to Irish women. In the story of Cyrus and the Lydians, we are returned to an all-male world, in which femininity has been transformed into the enforced masquerade of the colonized male and women have been magically erased.

This story of gender fantasy and sartorial law ends on a strange note, a historical irony that suggests that the English could not banish the Irish mantle and the powers it stood for as easily as Jonson's masque imagines. A miscegenation of clothes returns to haunt the colonizer. In 1599 the English occupiers of Ireland drew up a list of supplies needed by their soldiers, who had arrived in the north shoeless and badly apparelled. The supplier recommends that the queen give each soldier an "allowance for an Irish mantle, which costeth but 5s."[22] This will

> be his bed in the night, and a great comfort to him in sickness and in health; for the mantle, being never so wet, will presently, with a little shaking and

> wringing, be presently dry; for want of which the soldiers, lying abroad . . . in cold and wet in the winter time, die in the Irish ague and flux most pitifully.

English fears of internal colonization, of "corruption" by the Irish, could never be put to rest: Irish diseases, the "ague and the flux," were constant dangers. And if clothes make the man, what did it mean that the Englishman was now dressed like the wild Irish? What instability, mixture of categories and undoing of clear boundaries is occurring in this exchange? The new English were imposing a violent hierarchy through military subjugation. But their own identity was put culturally at risk as their soldiers deserted in unprecedented numbers, as the imagined boundaries between English and Irish were mantled over.

NOTES

1. "An Act for the English Order, Habit and Language," in Constantia Maxwell, ed., *Irish History from Contemporary Sources (1509–1610)* (London: Allen and Unwin, 1923), p. 113.

2. Fynes Moryson, "On the Commonwealth of Europe," in Charles Hughes, ed., *Shakespeare's Europe, being unpublished chapters of Fyne Moryson's "Itinerary"* (New York: Benjamin Bloom, 1967), p. 211; further citations will be incorporated into our text.

3. Giraldus Cambrensis, *Topographia Hibernica*, in J. F. Dimock, ed., *Rerum Brittanicarum Medii Aevi Scriptores* (London: Rolls, 1867), vol. 5, pp. 150, 153. For a study of early modern uses of classical history, see Hugh MacDougall, *Racial Myth in English History: Trojans, Teutons and Anglo-Saxons* (Hanover, NH: University Press of New England, 1982).

4. Johann Boemus, *The Manners, Laws and Customs of All Nations*, cited in Nicholas Canny, *The Elizabethan Conquest of Ireland: A Pattern Established, 1565–76* (New York: Barnes and Noble, 1976), p. 126.

5. Sir John Davies, Letter to the Earl of Salisbury, November 8, 1610, cited in Canny, *Conquest*, p. 119. See Hans Pawlisch, *Sir John Davies and the Conquest of Ireland: A Study in Legal Imperialism* (Cambridge: Cambridge University Press, 1985).

6. Edmund Spenser, *A View of the Present State of Ireland* (1596), in R. Morris, ed., *The Works of Edmund Spenser* (London: Macmillan, 1899), p. 625; further citations

will be incorporated into our text. Two important studies of Spenser's Irish politics are Nicholas Canny, "Edmund Spenser and The Development of an Anglo-Irish Identity," *Yearbook of English Studies*, 13 (1983), and Ciaran Brady, "Spenser's Irish Crisis: Humanism and Experience in the 1590's," *Past and Present*, no. 111 (May 1986). See also the Canny/Brady debate in *Past and Present*, no. 120 (1988).

7. William Harrison, *An Historicall Description of the Iland of Britaine*, in *Holinshed's Chronicles: England, Scotland and Ireland*, London, 1587; facsimile of the 1809 reprint (New York: AMS Press, 1976), p. 10.

8. Herodotus, *The Histories*, ed. A. R. Burn, trans. Aubrey de Selincourt (Harmonsdworth, UK: Penguin, 1954; rev. ed. New York: Viking Penguin, 1986), p. 310ff.

9. Thomas Churchyard, "The Unquietness of Ireland," cited in Canny, *Conquest*, p. 122.

10. Herodotus, *The Histories*, trans. David Grene (Chicago: University of Chicago Press, 1987), p. 204.

11. Hippocrates, *Airs, Waters, Places*, in *Hippocrates*, trans. W. H. S. Jones, Loeb Classical Library (London: Heinemann, 1923), vol. 1, p. 127; further citations incorporated in our text.

12. Aristotle, *Nichomachean Ethics*, trans. H. Rackham, Loeb Classical Library (London, Heinemann, 1926), pp. 415–17.

13. Sir John Davies, *A Discovery of the Reasons Why Ireland Was Never Entirely Subdued* (London, 1612), p. 182; further citations incorporated in our text.

14. For a study of lands figured as women from the sixteenth to the early eighteenth centuries, see Patricia Parker, "Rhetorics of Property: Exploration, Inventory, Blazon," in *Literary Fat Ladies: Rhetoric, Gender, Property* (New York: Methuen, 1987).

15. Luke Gernon, *Discourse of Ireland*, in James Carty, ed., *Ireland from the Flight of the Earls to Grattan's Parliament (1607–1782): A Documentary Record* (Dublin: C. J. Fallon, 1949), p. 3.

16. Barnabe Rich, *A New Description of Ireland* (London, 1610), p. 6.

17. Fynes Moryson, *An Itinerary* (London, 1617; rpt. Glasgow: James MacLehose, 1902), vol. 2, p. 237.

18. For a reproduction of the 1616 map, see Liz Curtis (for Information on Ireland), *Nothing But the Same Old Story: The Roots of Anti-Irish Racism* (London: Information on Ireland/Russell Press, 1984), pp. 15–16.

19. Maxwell, *Irish History*, p. 350.

20. Ben Jonson, *The Irish Masque at Court*, in Stephen Orgel, ed., *Ben Jonson: The Complete Masques* (New Haven: Yale University Press, 1969). For an incisive study of this masque, see David Lindley, "Embarrassing Ben: The Masques for Frances Howard," *English Literary Renaissance*, 16, 2 (Spring 1986), pp. 350–59.

21. Benedict Anderson, *Imagined Communities: Reflections on the Origin and Spread of Nationalism* (London: Verso, 1983).

22. "Irish Clothes Recommended for the Soldiers" (1599), in Maxwell, *Irish History*, p. 215.

Part III

The Other Country

Chapter 9

Plague in Germany, 1939/1989: Cultural Images of Race, Space, and Disease

Sander L. Gilman

The question of the national qualities ascribed to an illness has not been widely addressed in the debates about the social construction of the idea of AIDS.[1] Indeed, there has been an assumption that there is a "Western" (read: Christian or read: medical) tradition which has determined the basic structure of the ideas of disease.[2] My intent with this study is to illustrate some of the discontinuities in such overreaching models and to show the national variations on such themes. I will be looking at the cultural and social implications of "plague" in German culture under National Socialism and in Germany (both East and West) in the 1980s.

My point of departure will be the cultural representation of disease.[3] I shall use two novels as my artifacts in order to examine the fantasies of contagion and disease within German culture of 1939 and 1989. The first is the best-selling novel by Rudolf Heinrich Daumann, *Patrouille gegen den Tod* (Patrol against Death) of 1939,[4] and the second, the first "AIDS-novel" in German, Peter Zingler's 1989 *Die Seuche* (The Plague), published half a century later.[5]

These two novels reflect a basic set of attitudes present in German culture concerning the relationship between ideas of national space and ideas of race, between representations of the body and concepts of difference. These concepts are, of course, "Western" and make use of the basic paradigms of "race," of "difference," of the "normal" and the "pathological" which are to be found in other "Western" (read: Christian and/or scientific) cultures (not all of them in Europe and North America). But what I would like to stress here is the singular construction of ideas of race and ideas of sexuality within the German context.[6]

The texts I have selected bear striking similarities. Both Daumann and Zingler's novels are "science fiction" dystopias/utopias,[7] each set in a designated (but not too distant) future moment which extrapolates certain qualities of a constructed "present" into an image of the future. They are "science fiction" in that they both deal with the "science" of medicine. Both deal with the idea of "plague," indeed both use the term "plague" ("Seuche") as their central metaphor. It is therefore important to contextualize the idea of plague as represented in these two books in order to examine the image of the "disease" which is constructed in this context. Let me begin with a cursory reading of the Daumann text, just to sketch the plot and to stress the construction of the representation of ideas of race, space, sexuality and disease in utopian novels as distanced in time as 1939 and 1989.

Rudolf Heinrich Daumann's novel begins in a research institute for tropical medicine in Hamburg in 1969—thirty years into the future from the actual publication of the novel. We are introduced to one of the new employees, an out-of-work "Russian" ballerina, Maxie Perussenko, called "Maxie" in the novel. Through one of her female friends she has been appointed as a factotum at the institute and we are shown its daily routine—the counting of lice, the feeding of white mice and lab rats—through her horrified eyes. The head of the institute is the microbiologist Dr. Robert Dobbertin, but the true "hero" of the novel is his assistant Dr. Alfried Kalsten. The laboratory is given the task of identifying the nature of and, of course, finding the cure for an unidentified tropical epidemic which has broken out in a mining camp at Kanda-Kanda in the Belgian Congo. Kalsten and Perussenko are sent to Africa to gather tissue samples from the victims of this disease. In Africa the reader learns the true background of the "Russian" assistant. She is really a German ballerina, the daughter of an out-of-work army officer and a German countess, who has adopted a "Russian" identity because of the cachet associated in Germany with Russian dancers such as Pavlova. We also learn that Kalsten had refused a senior academic position because of his desire to work in the field. His banker-father had offered to buy such an appointment for him by funding his own research institute.

In the Belgian Congo our protagonists experience the Africa of the European settlers who understand contagious disease as part of their experience of

Africa (108). They meet Alver Reemerzijl, the Flemish physician who is in charge of the health care facilities at the mine. With him they see and marginally interact with a group of cannibalistic and/or marijuana-smoking "natives" whose "hysterical" fear of the disease has made them "revert" to the beliefs and practices of their precolonial past. Finally, flying on their way out of the Congo with a box full of infected white mice, they crash in the tropical jungle and are guided through it by a "faithful native" guide. During their escape each of them (unknown to the other) inoculates him and herself with one of the strains of the disease so that their research will not be jeopardized by the death of their specimens in the jungle.[8] This altruism causes them to admit their love for each other. They return to Hamburg at the conclusion of the novel, bearing the disease within them. Kalsten, through pure intelligence, uncovers the "cure" for the disease and thus saves them both. At the end of the novel a cure for the disease is linked with the "happy end" of their relationship. The lovers find themselves at a hotel in Aswan (Egypt) and are there informed of the successful end of the epidemic but also the death, through overwork, of their Flemish counterpart, Alver Reemerzijl.

The plot for this novel is a standard one for the mass and/or "trivial" literature of the 1930s. These novels are heavily indebted to British models, such as the Tarzan novels of Edgar Rice Burroughs, as well as to the image of Africa in the extraordinarily popular novels of Karl May.[9] (The popularity of both novelists remains high in Germany even today.) Present within this tradition is the image of the diseased nature of the black and the need for the colonial master to serve the cause of "healing" the black. This "meaning" of this topos shifted radically during the 1930s. Imperial Germany had been stripped of its African (and South Pacific) colonies as a result of the treaty of Versailles. After 1919 the British became the main villains for the Germans in their struggle for colonial "living space." It was the British who had destroyed the careful work of the Germans in their colonies, specifically in the area of public health. The health of the natives, part of the rationale for colonial rule (a healthy native is a healthy worker), became a touchstone for the image of the failure of colonial policy.[10]

After 1933, under the leadership of General Franz Ritter von Epp, the head of the Office for Colonial Politics of the NSDAP, a conscious attempt was made to associate the British (and by extension the South African) mandates over the former German colonies with the abdication of this role in maintaining the "hygiene" of the "natives."[11] But after 1933 the ideological context of the term "hygiene" had taken on a different implication.[12] In the German Colonial Yearbook for 1940, entitled "Africa needs Greater Germany," there is a long essay by Ernst Janisch, a state secretary in the National Biological Institute on the abdication of "racial hygiene," on the need to maintain the pure race of the black inhabitants.[13] The direct accusation was that the other colonial powers, including the British and the French, permitted racial mixing with the inevitable weakening of the pure racial qualities of the black.[14]

All of these commonplaces about "race" and "difference," about "racial mixing" and the "degeneration of pure races," are reflected in the novel. Thus it is the German pilot, Konrad Steen, who is disgusted (after the fact) by the suggestion of his Belgian acquaintance to visit a black house of prostitution (174). Indeed, the very love story between Alfried Kalsten and Maxie Perus-senko which stands at the center of the book reflects the "pure racial model," for the object of desire reveals herself in the course of the novel to be a "pure" German rather than a mere Slav and thus the relationship can be consummated.

The discourse about race and difference, especially in a German reading of 1939, can be more highly contextualized. The "Africa" of German fantasy with its racial struggle played out within the strict confines of the model of colonialism also reflects the daily preoccupation of the Germans of the period from 1933 to 1939 with another model of race in which the image of difference was not as visibly written upon the skin, but had rather to be even more carefully constructed in order to identify the Other.

It is evident that Daumann sees 1969 as an extension of a pre-1932 world. Real Germans, such as Maxie's ex-soldier-father, are employed in menial jobs or, like Maxie herself, have to disguise themselves as foreigners, such as Russians, to have any role in the cultural life of Germany. A strong Germany dominates Europe only because of its role in science. "Science" fiction becomes thus a manner of speaking about the centrality of a German identity rather than a means of escape. But this is a novel published in 1939, not in 1932. It is novel of fulfillment not of longing (two genres which can easily be found within the official NSDAP party literature before and after the Nazi seizure of power).[15] In this rear-view mirror image of the future there is an axiom for the construction of ideas of difference and of disease. It is in the immediate events of the past that such images are to be sought, not in an image of the present. For specific images of the past are internalized as part of the discourse of the thought collective about the "origin" of the present. These images are usually represen-tations of trauma— such as the post-World War I image of the collapse of the body politic in Germany—and within the German tradition of 1939 are closely linked to the search for the origin of the collapse of that "healthy" body politic in the defeat at Versailles, in ideas of race and infection.[16]

The quality ascribed to the world of 1969 (22) which is quite missing from the world of 1939 is that the outsiders, the pollutants, are present only "outside"—in Africa, not in Europe. Thus we are confronted with an image of German science which deals with tropical medicine but in a model of disease which has a series of very specific racial connotations. The construction of the image of the disease represented in the novel starts at the very opening when Alfried Kalsten attempts to assuage Maxie's fears of working in the Institute by pointing out to her the ubiquitousness of infection in the "real" world outside the clinic. "Imagine" he says, "that your legs have failed and that you have to work as a bar-girl from eight in the evening to four in the morning. How do you know who is sitting near you in this shady bar? Old travelers with flattened noses, in whom the Spirochaete palladia, the white spirochaete, wends its quiet and secret path, transforming human tissue into rubber, destroying the brain and creating the most horrible paralysis" (19). It is syphilis which is the model for the idea of disease in this novel. Thus the "unknown disease" is a "brand-new type of infectious disease" (43), a "plague" (58) which has made "thousands of brown and black people" in the mines unable to work (35). And it is no surprise that when Alfried looks into his electron microscope the source of this mystery disease in Africa is revealed to be a "tiny, cork-screw shaped virus-like spirochaete" (72). Syphilis and the "unknown disease" found in Africa are linked through the very word "spirochete" with its "scientific" province. Indeed, the discussion of infected specimens of liver, brought to Hamburg as tissue samples, are immediately described as "full of unknown spirochete" (90). The disease is thus associated throughout the novel with syphilis and, in the German context, with a very different idea of "race" and "disease."[17]

But syphilis, as with all stigmatizing diseases, had to be "seen," it had to be as evident in its signs and symptoms as the signs of "race," it had to be written on the skin. In the realm of German science, as in American medicine during the very same period,[18] syphilis was associated with a racial (as well as a pathognomonic) image of difference. And if we remember the very first mention of syphilis in Daumann's novel, the sign with which it was to be identified was the very shape of the nose (19).[19] In Germany it was the Jewish nose rather than the nose of the black that was the salient sign of difference. Within the German proverbial tradition the shape and nature of the nose and that of the phallus are inexorably linked. Sexually transmitted disease, especially syphilis, was mythically associated with the Jewish (read: circumcised) penis, the physical aspect ascribed to the Jew (read: Jewish male) which in the German eye defined the Jew as readily as skin color defined the inhabitants of Africa. This in an age in which more and more German Jews (as defined racially by the Nazis) actually remained uncircumcised! Thus the need to construct another "mark" of difference in the concentration camps of the 1930s—the tattoo—an "indelible" mark upon the body which uniformly signified difference.

In Daumann's novel the Jew seems to be strangely missing. It is Jewishness, this central category of "racial" difference for the German reader and writer of 1939, which has vanished from the world of "1969." Of course, the sole exception is the name of the Jewish bacteriologist August von Wassermann, whose 1906 discovery of the sero-diagnosis of syphilis led to the test which bore his name.[20] While ennobled in 1913, he remained in the anti-Semitic handbooks of the day as well as in public mind the "Jew" associated with syphilis.[21]

For the Jew in European science and popular thought was closely related to the spread and incidence of syphilis.[22] Such views had two readings. The first model saw the Jews as the carriers of sexually transmitted diseases who transmitted them to the rest of the world, as in Adolf Hitler's treatment of syphilis in *Mein Kampf* (1925), the central discussion of race and disease for German culture in 1939. Hitler's views linked Jews with prostitutes and the spread of syphilitic infection. Jews were the arch-pimps; Jews ran the brothels; but Jews also infected their prostitutes and caused the weakening of the German national fiber.[23] But Jews are also associated with the false promise of a "medical" cure separate from the social "cures" which Hitler wishes to see imposed—isolation and separation of the syphilitic and his/her Jewish source from the body politic. Hitler refers to the belief that the specialty of dermatology and syphilology was dominated by Jews, who used their medical status to sell quack cures.[24]

The second model which associated Jews and syphilis postulates exactly the opposite—that Jews had a statistically lower rate of syphilitic infection—because they had become immune to it through centuries of exposure. In the medical literature of the period, reaching across all of European medicine, it was assumed that Jews had a notably lower rate of infection. In a study of the incidence of tertiary lues in the Crimea undertaken between 1904 and 1929, the Jews had the lowest consistent rate of infection.[25] In an eighteen-year longitudinal study H. Budel demonstrated the extraordinarily low rate of tertiary lues among Jews in Estonia during the pre-war period.[26] All of these studies assumed that biological difference as well as the social difference of the Jews were at the root of their seeming "immunity."[27]

The marker for such a view of the heightened susceptibility or resistance to syphilis is the basic sign of difference of the Jews, the circumcised phallus. The debates within and without the Jewish communities concerning the nature and implication of circumcision surfaced again in Germany during the 1840s. German Jews had become acculturated into German middle-class values and came to question the absolute requirement of circumcision as a sign of their Jewish identity. Led by the radical reform rabbi Samuel Holdheim and responding to a Christian tradition which denigrated circumcision, the debate was carried out as much in the scientific press as in the religious one. There had been four "traditional" views of the "meaning" of circumcision after the rise of Christianity.[28] However, in the medical literature during the course of the early twentieth century only two of these views dominated, those which bracketed the images of "health" and "disease." These views saw circumcision either as the source of disease or as a prophylaxis against disease—and in both cases syphilis plays a major role. In the first case there is a detailed literature which discusses the transmission of syphilis to newly circumcised infants through the ritual of metsitsah, the sucking on the penis by the mohel, the ritual circumciser, in order to staunch the bleeding.[29] The opposing view, also seen as an aspect of "hygiene," the favorite word to critique or support the practice, sees circumcision as a mode of prevention which precludes the transmission of sexually transmitted diseases because of the increased capacity for "cleanliness."[30]

The need to "see" and "label" the Jew at a time when Jews were becoming more and more "invisible" in Germany made the association with socially stigmatizing diseases which bore specific visible "signs and symptoms" especially appropriate. In the German Empire of the late nineteenth century all of the arguments placed the Jew in a "special" relationship to syphilis and, therefore, in a very special relationship to the "healthy" body politic needed to make the Jew visible. Jews had been completely acculturated by the end of the nineteenth century and thus bore no external signs of difference (unique clothing, group language, group-specific hair and/or beard style). They had to bear the stigma of this special relationship to their diseased nature literally on the skin, where it could be seen. Indeed, Jews bear the salient stigma of the black skin of the syphilitic, the syphilitic rupia.

The Jews are black, according to nineteenth-century racial science, because they are "a mongrel race which always retains this mongrel character." That is Houston Stewart Chamberlain arguing against the "pure" nature of the Jewish race.[31] Jews had "hybridized" with blacks in Alexandrian exile. They are, in an ironic review of Chamberlain's work by the father of modern Yiddish scholarship, Nathan Birnbaum, a "bastard" race the origin of which was caused by their incestuousness. But the Jews were also seen as black.[32] Adam Gurowski, a Polish noble, "took every light-colored mulatto for a Jew" when he first arrived in the United States in the 1850s.[33] Jews are black because they are different, because their sexuality is different, because their sexual pathology is written upon their skin. Gurowski's "German-Jewish" contemporary, Karl Marx, associates leprosy, Jews, and syphilis in his description of his archrival Ferdinand Lassalle (in 1861): "Lazarus the leper, is the prototype of the Jews and of Lazarus-Lassalle. But in our Lazarus, the leprosy lies in the brain. His illness was originally a badly cured case of syphilis."[34] Jews = lepers = syphilitics = blacks.

By the 1930s the pathological image of the Jew was part of the general cultural vocabulary of Germany. Hitler used this image over and over in *Mein Kampf* in describing the Jew's role in German culture: "If you cut even cautiously into such an abscess, you found, like a maggot in a rotting body, often dazzled by the sudden light—a kike! . . . This was pestilence, spiritual pestilence, worse than the Black Death of olden times, and the people were being infected by it." "Plague" [*Seuche*] and "pestilence" [*Pestilenz*]—a disease from without which, like syphilis, rots the body—was the model used to see the role of the Jew. The syphilitic weakening of the pure race of the Germans by the Jews was likened by Hitler to the corruption of the blood of the race through another form of "mammonization," interracial marriage.[35]

If the Germans (Aryans) are a "pure" race—and that is for turn of the century science a positive quality—then the Jews cannot be a "pure" race. Their status as a mixed race became exemplified in the icon of the "Mischling" during the 1930s. The Jewishness of the "Mischling," to use the term from racial science parallel to "Bastard" (the offspring of a "Black" and a "White" "race"), "looks" and sounds degenerate. They can have "Jewish-Negroid" features.[36] And this is often associated with their facile use of language, "the use of innumerable foreign words and newly created words to enrich the German language in sharp contrast to the necessary simplicity of the language of Germanic students."[37] This is in no way to be understood as a sign of strength.[38] The Jew's language reflects only the corruption of the Jew and his/her discourse. It is the sign of the "pathological early development" of the "Mischling," who, as an adult, is unable to fulfill the promise of the member of a pure race. The weakness, but also the degenerate facility of the "Mischling," is analogous to the image of the offspring of the syphilitic. Thus Hitler's image of the "Mischling" is of the offspring of a "Jewish" mother and an "Aryan" father—hidden within the name and Germanic lineage of the child is the true corruption of the race, the maternal lineage of the Jew. And as Jews claimed their lineage through the mother (rather than through the father as in Salic law), the "Mischling" becomes the exemplary hidden Jew just waiting to corrupt the body politic.

The weakness of the offspring of Jews as well as syphilitics is especially evident in the nervousness of the offspring. One of its most salient signs and symptoms is the decay and collapse of language. But this sign is also part of the image of the black in Daumann's assumption of the general discourse of colonialism. And the "boy"—to use Daumann's term—like the pseudo-Russian dancer is marked by a discourse of difference. The Other speaks differently, reveals him or herself in his/her discourse. The blacks in Daumann's novel speak a mix of German, Flemish and French, all represented in a broken grammar, a language similar in its structure to that affected by Maxie early in the novel. But unlike them she continually lapses back into "real" German. The blacks' hidden fault manifests itself in the symptom of the degeneration of language; Maxie's "pure" race manifests itself in her inability to maintain this sign.

Like the syphilitic, marked by the collapse of language and discourse and the "hidden language of the Jew," the image of discourse is also a marker of pathological difference in this world, a signifier which links race and difference. Daumann's image of the infected and hysteric blacks has them revert to the primitive religion of their forefathers, to cannibalism and drugs, to a reversion to the older, "pre-Christian" world. For German-language scholars (like the psychiatrist Richard Krafft-Ebing or the anthropologist Wilhelm Schmidt), this primitive stage of Christian Europe was to be found frozen in the world of the Jews. For the discourse about "Jewish hysteria," as Jan Goldstein has so well shown, is already part of the medical discourse of high science in the nineteenth century.[39] By the 1930s the myth of the Jewish sacrifice of Christians (as part of a therapy to rid them of specific sexually-related pathologies) had reappeared.[40] The real plague among the "blacks" was the response to the epidemic for "as bad as or even worse than the illness is the spiritual crisis, the fear, horror, anxiety, and doubt . . . the best example is inner Africa today. An area almost as big a Germany can be seen as plague-ridden (*verseucht*). . . . The quarantine (*Pestkordon*) is a paper fiction" (280).

Maxie's observation, having learned from her time in the jungle the "truth" about the world in which she now lives, reflects two salient images of the syphilitic and of the Jew. First, the Jew's madness, especially apparent in the "Mischling," and second, the impossibility of creating impermeable barriers to eliminate the presence of the "disease" from society.[41] By 1939 the anti-Jewish laws in Germany had excluded Jews from virtually every sphere of public life, and yet the very isolation of the Jews called forth greater and greater anxiety about their presence in Germany, an anxiety which had its first major release on "Kristallnacht" in 1939. The Jews could not be kept cordoned off, they could slip through the jungle of the cities (to extend Daumann's metaphor in a viable image of the time) and continue to spread infection.

The image of the body politic and the politics of race are inexorably linked in the novel. The presence of "strange blood" in the body causes death, as we learn very early in the novel (45–46) from Professor Klading's "scientific" excursus about the impossibility of putting "eel's blood" in a test rabbit. This is associated by him with the need for every race to be in its proper place. His "scientific" metaphor is that each race must consume its appropriate protein, seeing the primeval German diet of swine and fish as growing out of the Germans' appropriate place. This view is articulated in the concept of *Lebensraum*—living space, the basic philosophy which underpins the German rhetoric about their need for African colonies during the late 1930s but which is also closely related to specific ideas of the absolute location of race. In the work of the nineteenth-century anthropologist Friedrich Ratzel, the founder of the ecological theory of race, the Jews are seen as the one race "out of place." In the Near East they were productive (for example, creating monotheism) but in

Europe they can have no real cultural meaning.[42] The association of place and race is linked in the rationale of the German in Africa or the Jew in Europe. They are presented as mirror images, for while the German in Africa "heals," the Jew in Europe "infects." No quarantine is truly successful in controlling the Jew. The image of the "plague" presented in this novel is paralleled to the Black Plague (52–54) which is described as coming from the Middle East and which proceeded to decimate European civilization, an image which also appears in *Mein Kampf.* Again the subliminal message is that disease comes from outside, from "Byzantium" or from "Kanda-Kanda," and can destroy Europe (55). The traditional association—in Hitler's presentation as well as in the "historical" studies cited in Daumann's novel[43]—is the association with the Jews as the "cause" of the Black Plague. These parallels between the medieval plague and a potential future outbreak would not have been lost on the reader of 1939.

In early 1989 the icon of "plague" in the German context should have been very different. At that time we had two clearly differentiated "Germanies"—the Federal Republic of Germany (FRG) and the German Democratic Republic (GDR)—each of which, in its own manner, repudiated everything about the Nazi period (at least in their official rhetoric). Westberlin was a space belonging ideologically to the BRD (even though it maintained its status as a four-power city) but it was also a place which was always understood as on the margin between cultures. It was a "dangerous" place as it was neither truly "west" nor "east." The public perception of this status was radically altered after November 9, 1989. The special function which Westberlin played in fanatasies about disease and its control was a reflex of that special status.

Perhaps the best place to begin with an examination of the fantasies about "plague" which haunt the contemporary German idea of AIDS is with a very different text from a very different world: the first gay book of belles-lettres officially to appear in the GDR, Ulrich Berkes' 1987 "diary" *Eine schlimme Liebe* (An Evil Love), published by the premiere publishing house of the GDR. In this text, part literary manifesto on the nature of modernism and part autobiographical catalogue of the daily life of a gay poet in the GDR during 1984, there are two passing mentions of AIDS. Dated 7 April 1984 and 30 October 1984, they describe the disease first, in an American context and second, in an African one.[44] These fragmentary mentions of the disease are represented as but one of the building blocks in the self-image of the gay in the GDR of 1984. But they also localize the disease as coming from "out there." The disease which by 1987 had taken a substantial hold on the imagination of German gay as well as straight readers is seen on the historical periphery without any seeming context.[45] While the first mention of AIDS is used to justify the practice of mutual masturbation, the second mention in the text is reported as part of the daily "static" heard through the airwaves which the gay individual assimilates because it relates directly to his sexuality. The USA and Africa are the "source" of AIDS for German culture.[46] It is this web of associations—and the absence within Berkes' text of a set of overt associations which reappear in Peter Zingler's AIDS novel (as well as elsewhere in the discourse about AIDS in German in the past few years), a novel written for a "straight" audience and published by a self-consciously "liberal" press (the Eichborn Verlag).

If Rudolf Heinrich Daumann's novel of 1939 deals with a "heroic" image of medicine, with its emphasis on high-tech research (including fantasies of laser-surgery [41]) and cure, Peter Zingler's *Die Seuche*, a 1989 science fiction account of AIDS in Germany in 1999, presents the reader with the model of medicine as public health, with all of its negative associations after the Nazi period. It is this seeming rejection, but also the maintenance of parallel ideological structures, which have shaped the idea of AIDS in Germany. For the image of Nazi medicine in Germany—especially during the 1980s—was inexorably linked with social control and placed into a special category remote from "good" clinical treatment. For the German public "medicine" under National Socialism was tied to the icon of the "concentration camps," to the annihilation of groups labeled by the society of the time as different and, therefore, diseased (Jews, gays, the mentally ill).[47] The immediate association between the death camps and concentration camps, the association between images of social control and mindless, cruel experimentation was made. Medicine as an agent of control was seen as a negative, destructive force and the image of the clinician and that of the police were one. The sense of collective responsibility of the society was here resolved as the acts of brutality in the camps became (in part) linked to the sterile and inhumane image of a "science" treating all human beings as if they were laboratory animals. Science fiction or at least the fiction of futuristic medicine became a nightmare and the day residue in that nightmare came from the representation of the Nazi past.

Let us turn to Peter Zingler's AIDS novel and see how his image of plague is realized. The plot is set on New Year's Eve of 1999, the beginning of a "new age," and we are confronted with the scene at a border crossing from Westberlin to the FRG. The "Hiffies" (HIV-infected) are marching in a column hundreds strong out of the "AIDS-Ghetto Berlin" (5). For Berlin as of 1992 with the passage of the "Rules for the Health of the German People" [*Anordnungen zum gesundheitlichen Wohl des Deutschen Volkes* (21)] had become the largest German AIDS internment camp [*Intenierungscamp*]. The allies had pulled out and only those labeled as AIDS-carriers or AIDS-infected were left in Berlin. ("I'm proud to be in Berlin West, in Hiff-Town" [103] sings a street singer in English.) Only these, the criminals who live off of the "Hiffies," and the "Turks" who have nowhere else to go except back to "Istanbul" (50) remain in Westberlin. The "Hiffies" are shipped to Westberlin once they are found to be "positive." Even the GDR began quietly to expel its "positive" cases into Westberlin (101). By 1999 4 million in the FRG are in "camps" with over 400,000 "SSD" police in place to guard them. Of these, 3 million "Hiffies" are in Westberlin. The "SSD" is the "Seuchen-Sicherheitsdienst," the Plague-Security Force, the "wasps," who are dressed in clearly identifiable black uniforms with a yellow stripe, and are armed with "heavy Israeli 44 magnum automatics" (19). The border guards observe the movement of this column of the "plague-ridden" and "undertake nothing. The Hiffies can carry their viruses 'back into the Reich'" (8).

Into this world comes Judith Bahl, daughter of the Minister of Health, Hans Kaufmann (the most important member of the cabinet) and the estranged wife of Harald Bahl, an "AIDS careerist" (20), the head of Frankfurt's city "plague-control-institute" (18). By 1999 everyone in the FRG must carry a recent HIV test result as his/her identity card and all public facilities were open only with the presentation of such an identity card. Judith is tested and is revealed to be "positive." She is immediately swept off into the machinery which takes her to Westberlin.

Westberlin is a German fantasy of Alfred Döblin's Berlin of the 1920s—it is the locus of the most extraordinary excesses, drugs of all types are openly sold on the streets (103) and sex (of all types) is the rule (173). For the inhabitants of Westberlin are beyond caring about anything except their physical pleasure (173). Westberlin has become a huge concentration camp. Indeed the very idea of Westberlin as a camp is created in 1992 when the Bavarians reopen Dachau as an AIDS internment camp. "The other states were more discrete" (55). In Westberlin Judith arranges to meet with an escape specialist, Max Isslacker, who for 50,000 Marks has offered to help her escape from Westberlin. Max, whose tattooed body is revealed to us when he and Judith have sex (138), eventually does help her escape. She returns to Frankfurt to retrieve her daughter and flees with her to a asylum, a "Campo de Sida" in Spain. There we learn that she was indeed always "negative." Her husband had rigged the test so as to claim their daughter, discredit his father-in-law, and remove his unfaithful wife.

The parallel story to the adventures of Judith is the attempt of an international pharmaceutical concern KREM to steal the secret of a Japanese "cure for AIDS." The debate about the nature of the disease reveals the mercenary nature of the drug companies' interest in medication, any type of medication, which could be sold to this huge and ever growing population. But acquiring AIDS in this novel is not random; it has meaning. It is a disease which is closely linked, in the "scientific" discourse of the physicians and researchers in the novel, to those individuals who have already "ruined" their immune system through their "unnatural habits" and their resultant extreme use of medication.

The examples cited are "homosexuals, who have to have their syphilis cured every fourteen days" through the use of penicillin and who "eat antibiotics as others eat peppermints," and "whores" who constantly use penicillin to cure their "professional gonorrhea" (26). These social deviants are as "different" from the scientists as are the inhabitants of Africa, who, according to another theory outlined in the novel, "have an immune system quite different than ours and based on their way of life. Then the whites came and introduced diseases that were unknown to them: grippe, colds, syphilis" (26). Here Africa becomes the land—not of the origin of disease—but of the victim. This reversal was quite different from the popular German view in 1988 that the disease was caused, not only by Africans, but by African black women who had had sex with monkeys.[48] This is quite in line with the post-war German image of the "sexual deviancy" of the black, especially the black out of her own space, the black in Germany.[49] But where does AIDS come from in this novel? As in other images of the origins of the disease in contemporary German culture, it is American. It is Rock Hudson "who fifteen years earlier admitted to being gay" (77) who brought the disease into German consciousness. Since then it has been an "American" disease.

One of the scientists, Alfred Droege, has kept the fact that his daughter Manuela has developed AIDS a secret, and is using every means to acquire the drug and treat her. She has developed AIDS through being exposed to her father's research. The research centers are themselves huge concentration camps, with the "Hiffies" serving both as the researchers as well as the subjects for their own research. This is seen as an economically sound manner of using this huge interned labor pool. They are supervised by scientists such as Droege, who lives in a large house with his own laboratory. At the very end of the novel (217) the existence of the daughter is revealed to the "wasps," the house is stormed, but the daughter has died of the effects of the drug which has turned her into a hemophiliac. The effect of the drug is to turn everyone into a "bleeder," and the image in German is even stronger: "Alle Menschen werden Bluter" (215), a grotesque pun on the line from Schiller's (and Beethoven's) "Ode to Joy": *Alle Menschen werden Brüder!*—everyone will be brothers. This reversal of the image of infection—"corrupt" AIDS carriers give "innocent" hemophiliacs *the* disease—becomes the leitmotif for the novel. But such simple reversals of stereotypes leads to the continuity of images of the locus of corruption with a very specific cultural significance.

The discourse about difference in this novel is on the surface antithetical to that in Daumann's world. It is an image of the world as a concentration camp with all of the self-conscious evocation of the Nazi period in its response to the actual debate during the mid-1980s about the "Bundesseuchengesetze" (actually the "Law for the Prevention and Control of Infectious Disease in

Human Beings"), the German law concerning contagious diseases in the FRG.[50] Already in 1984 the weekly news magazine *Der Spiegel* could write of "the plague breaking out of the gay-ghetto."[51] In an entry dated 28 August 1987 in his autobiographical account of his struggle with the social stigma of being a person with AIDS, Helmut Zander recounts the publication of an essay which revealed that a number of West German municipal officials had approved the idea for a new "AIDS-camp" the plans for which turned out to be plans for the infamous concentration camp at Sachsenhausen.[52] In Fred Breinersdorf's 1989 novel *Quarantäne* (Quarantine), also set in "a German metropolis in the near future," this image haunts the idea of AIDS.[53] There AIDS hospitals are the solution to the "problem of hygiene" (*Hygieneprobleme*) and are compared to the concentration camps (267). These metaphoric equations were given a "real political" dimension in the suggestion in 1987 by Peter Gauweiler, the Minister of Health of the Bavarian "Republic," for the wide-scale compulsory testing of groups such as foreigners, prostitutes, drug users, prisoners, and the intimation of potential quarantine for those who tested positive.[54] In the retelling of the plot of Peter Zingler's novel it is evident that this construction of the idea of plague contains a series of analogues to an understanding of "plague" shaped by the revulsion to but also the format of the vocabulary of disease in the Nazi period. This immediate association is reflected in the use of a vocabulary of images which has its origin in a West German understanding of the past. Indeed, the very phrase "home into the Reich" (8) with which the border guards describe the marching column of "Hiffies" reflects the Nazi rhetoric accompanying the Austrian Anschlu. Evoking the Nazi associations present in the late 1980s with Kurt Waldheim's Austria, in this novel the rhetoric of political space refers to an Austria of the spirit; the "disease" habored in Westberlin reflects the "sick" society of the BDR.

The central "fact" of both the novels by Daumann from 1939 and Zingler from 1989 is that the protagonists do not belong in the "place" of the novel. Daumann's scientists "visit" Africa and are infected. But they arrive at a cure from the African disease only when they are back in Hamburg. The disease becomes proof that they really do not belong in "Africa." Judith Bahl is never "positive"—she belongs to none of the categories at risk—but she has had sex with a man outside of her marriage. Thus we expect her to be "punished" by contracting AIDS, much like the audience expectation in the eighteenth-century German tragedy that a single act of coitus must lead to pregnancy, infanticide, and suicide. She is shown as intensely "heterosexual." And that category seems to be problematized by her status as a "Hiffie" since she does not belong to any of the high-risk categories known to the reader in 1989. But she does not act in the light of her own knowledge of her status as a "social pollutant," indeed she has sex with a man she knows to be "negative" when she believes herself to be positive without informing him of that fact (66). She is beyond the category of disease and, therefore, the revelation that she is truly "safe" comes to reify our sense that her actions are intuitively correct and she really does not belong in this world of disease. She no more belongs in this world of disease than Maxie does in Africa.

The question of why she does not belong is important. It is the association of the "normal"—of her roles and identity as created in the novel which "saves" her. Judith becomes the baseline for the healthy in contrast with the society in which she dwells. Her desire to escape from Westberlin is tied to her image as a mother. She is obsessive about returning to rescue her daughter—she is a good mother. And that, within the discourse of difference in the novel, means that she is heterosexual. The sexual contacts described in the novel, both the "good" ones (mutual seductions) and the "bad" ones (unwanted sexual approaches or rapes), are all heterosexual. Indeed, the one overtly lesbian figure described in the novel commits suicide after an attempted rape by exposing herself to freezing weather while she compulsively tries to cleanse herself in a public fountain.

It is through the background given this "deviant" figure that we can begin to tie the structure of representation in Zingler even tighter to Daumann's world. For what is central about Judith is that she is in no way directly tied to the world of the Nazi past. All of the ironization of the vocabulary of difference in the novel, all of the self-conscious evocation of the Nazi past provides a model for difference which is tied to the idea of race. We can begin with that one image of the sexually "deviant" presented in the novel, the "positive" image of the lesbian who befriends Judith when she arrives in Westberlin, but who ends in suicide. Birgit Sattler is in Westberlin because she had acquired AIDS from her gay roommate (130). Her "deviancy" is explained by the factoid that her father had had his health destroyed in a concentration camp and that she had spent her youth on the streets as a result of his early death (132). Her "disease," i.e., her sexual identity, is tied to the world of gay men and is explained by her tie to the Nazi past. She is a lesbian because the Nazis destroyed her father, made him into less a man so that he could not serve her as a true parent—and therefore as a model for the ideal male. She becomes the image of the person with AIDS represented in the novel. Gay men are virtually invisible.

Nowhere in this novel do we "see" any ill gay men; any more than we "see" the hoards of the ill Blacks in Africa. They form the frame of the novel, but we are "exposed" only to those "deviants" from the diseased norm, who turn out, like Birgit Sattler, to exhibit their "deviance" because of an association with the realties which lay behind the metaphors of the AIDS-Ghetto and the internment camps. The gay males, like the blacks, are the excuse for the novel, not its focus. The "liberal" intent of the novel is to draw the absolute boundary of difference between the "sick" dystopian German society which condemns people with AIDS and a "healthy" utopian German society which would accept them. But in creating these boundaries Zingler reverts to a historically determined model of "health" and "illness." The association of the "normal," i.e., heterosexual, with the "healthy" and the "abnormal," i.e., the gay, with the diseased is presented here within an environmental model. This is, of course, the liberal fantasy which represses the "realities" of disease, realties which in German culture are associated with the oppression of Jews and gays in the Third Reich through the imposition of a medical model, and which stresses the "diseased" nature of those exposed to the forces of evil, such as the camps. The pseudoscientific arguments about the theoretical basis of "plague" parallel the discussions in Daumann's book. The central difference is that they are presented in an ironic mode. But simple reversals of images lead to their structural perpetuation.

The association of the "persecution" of "Hiffies" through a future German response to AIDS is elided with the image of the persecution of the Nazi victims. And for the West German reader the representative victim of the Nazis are the Jews. This is stated quite directly in the novel in both an ironic mode and an unself-conscious one. "All human beings are brothers," but some are more human, less diseased than others. Thus we are given a long monologue by a muckraking newspaperman on the search for a new AIDS scandal. He notes that in the last issue of the newspaper there was a full column about the fact that "circumcised males are especially at risk from the plague" (141). This is ironic—and repeats quite literally the special status of the Jews as especially at risk for sexually transmitted disease which, as we have seen, is part and parcel of the literature of the biological determinism of Jewish pathology. But it is clear that this "rumor" is presented in a self-undercutting mode. Zingler is presenting in this entire monologue the sort of scandal sheet stories that one finds in the FRG in the *Bild-Zeitung*. It is nevertheless startling to find this "repressed" image from the past reappearing in the phantasized future represented in this novel. This image never vanished from German discourse. After the war Jews were accused of having imported the most horrific sexually transmitted diseases into the German-speaking world.[55] In the novel it becomes part of the stereotypical representation of difference which is supposed to characterize the horror and inflexibility of German society toward those suffering from AIDS.

But Zingler also presents an unself-conscious association of the Jew with disease, feeling that he is giving a "positive" image of the Jew. In the "Campo de Sida" in Spain we meet the owner of the local bar who speaks in "an accent which lead us to believe that he was a German" (79). But he speaks only Spanish, as he explains in "clumsy Spanish" (80), because we are "guests, whether welcome or tolerated matters not. But we live here and live free. One should speak the language of the country if just for this reason" (80). But he looks "like a vulture . . . his nose looks like a bent saber" (80). It turns out that Alfons is a German Jew, of over seventy, who had been forced to leave Germany first with his parents under the Nazis and then fifty years later again because his lover, with whom he had lived for thirty years, had contracted AIDS. They fled Hamburg and opened the bar in Spain. The lover had died two years before. Since then Alfons had "refused to speak a word of German." Most importantly: "He is not sick" (80). At the very end of the novel we return to the "Campo de Sida" and attend Alfons' funeral: "It is pleasing to be able to accompany some one like Alfons on his last journey, someone who died quite naturally of old age" (215). At the cemetery "only the voice of the Rabbi could be heard" (216). After the burial service, the crowd breaks out in lamentations while one of the participants observes: "It is perverse . . . but I really enjoy crying at the cemetery. Afterwards I feel relaxed and full of life" (216).

Here we have the other side of the argument—circumcised Jews (and male Jews in this myth of the body are by definition circumcised) are immune. They do not get AIDS when they live monogamously together with someone who has an active case. Such Jews are not "perverse," they are "healthy" since they do not bear the stigma of "Jewish hypersexuality." The special discourse of the Jews, the rejection of "German" here for "Spanish" as a sign of the necessary adaptability of the Jew is contrasted in the novel with the fragments of clumsy German spoken by the Turks in Westberlin. The Turks have to speak German; the Jew adapts out of instinct. The images are precisely those displaced from the past. Indeed, there are even some slight hints of the left anti-Semitism which constantly surfaces in the FRG under the guise of anti-Zionism. The "SSD," an acronym which immediately recalls the Nazi SS, are armed with Israeli weapons (19). But in general the reader in this novel which parallels the treatment of the person with AIDS with the Jews is given a "positive" reversal of the negative stereotype of the Jew. This reflects the image of the Jews as the agent of infection which dominated Hitler's association of Jews and disease. The "realities" of the person with AIDS or even the person who is HIV positive are confused with the attributes associated with the Jews. The Jew, who is labeled as "sick," is exactly equated with the person with AIDS who is ill.[56] In Zingler's text this association, with all of its power for the German reader of the 1980s, whose sense of the Nazi past is limited to media clichés, overwhelms any sense of the difference between the Jew and the person with AIDS. The Jew thus acquires a special status in the subtextual structure of this world of images. He is immune as the desired sign of the ultimate reversal of the Nazi stereotype of the Jew as disease carrier or organism, a status which is now attributed to the "Hiffie," a term which comes to replace "kike" in the vocabulary of difference in this text.

One additional argument should be brought up at this point—the fact that AIDS is not a "Jewish" disease in the FRG and the GDR but an "American" one. Here too the association of the intensely negative image of the American and the vicious anti-Americanism present in both Germanies after the Vietnam War is evident. But there is an older association with the image of the pathological representation of the American and its equation with the image of the Jew which should be cited. For the nineteenth century, cities are places of disease and the Jews are the quintessential city dwellers, the Americans of Europe. Richard von Krafft-Ebing's remarked that civilization regularly brings forth degenerate forms of sexuality because of the "more stringent demands which circumstances make upon the nervous system" and which manifest themselves in the "psychopathological or neuropathological conditions of the nation involved."[57] For him the Jew is the ultimate "city person" whose sensibilities are dulled, whose sexuality is pathological, whose goals are "American."[58] It is also the city which triggers the weakness hidden within the corrupted individual. It is its turbulence, its excitement, what August Forel in his *The Sexual Question* (1905) calls its "Americanism," which leads to "illnesses" such as degenerate neurasthenia:

> Americanism.—By this term I designate an unhealthy feature of sexual life, common among the educated classes of the United States, and apparently originating in the greed for dollars, which is more prevalent in North America than anywhere else. I refer to the unnatural life which Americans lead, and more especially to its sexual aspect.[59]

This is an image seen by physicians of the period as "Jewish" in its dimensions. Jews manifest an "abnormally intensified sensuality and sexual excitement that lead to sexual errors that are of etiological significance."[60] Just like gays in the 1980s. Thus hidden within the image of the American origins of AIDS is a further association with the Jew, an association made through the image of the city (and for late nineteenth-century Germany, Berlin is the exemplary city). Berlin is the biblical Sodom and Gomorrah and, after World War II, the image of Westberlin—as can be seen in Zingler's novel—is closely associated in German fantasy with the image of the American.

But as we have seen, both sides of this issue are present within the medical discourse of the twentieth century concerning the special nature of the Jews' relationship to sexually transmitted diseases. In the dystopia of the world of plague represented in the novel the simple reversal of images, the ironization and projection of the past, recreates the stereotypical perception of difference. In placing Judith's misdiagnosis, a "mistake"—purposeful and cruel—but a "mistake" at the center of this novel, Zingler undertakes the rescue of the

German heterosexual as surely as Daumann rescues his protagonists. It is "science"—in the case of AIDS the now "accurate" AIDS test—which frees the heterosexual woman from the stigma of the disease and permits her to return to her role as mother; in the case of the African plague, it is the heroic activities of the scientist who develops a cure which enables Maxie to undertake the ultimate role in German society, that of the "German" mother "with a little house with a red roof and a green garden, a good husband, and little children who cry 'mama' and suck on their thumbs" (168). Judith's cleanliness is now paralleled to that of her lover Max. While she had sex with him when she believed she was positive—and he knew he was negative—this is revealed to have been a nonpathological act. Even though in terms of the law on contagion in force in 1989 this would be understood as inflicting "grievous bodily harm." And we "knew" that she was not dangerous even during the sex scene. For Max's "tattoo" is not a camp tattoo—it is a tattoo of Mickey Mouse (138). Here the "American"/"Jewish" danger of disease is defused and represented as an icon of childlike innocence. The representation of the "private" sphere in this novel is "safe"; it is only in the "public" sphere that danger in the form of the mentality of the Nazi past lurks. We are made to contrast Max's tattoo with the image of a bellicose, pre-WW II Germany in the pub in Frankfurt where Judith waits to meet Max. It is called the "Iron Cross" and "naive paintings of tanks, war ships, and fighter planes of the Third Reich" hang on the walls (199).

The cultural image of "plague" in Germany in 1989 is very different from that of 1939. It tries to be an antithetical presentation of the past in its evocation of a distopic future. And yet the romanticism of the past, of the Jew as the essential victim, moves the image into the same structure of discourse as is found under the Nazis, a discourse which creates images of the "normal" and the "diseased" with absolute boundaries. Such boundaries are to be expected in any case. But in these German texts they are constructed with an eye toward the German past which is quite unique. In Germany the evocation of a socially stigmatizing disease seems to be difficult without the evocation of past metaphors of disease and political persecution. The vocabulary of difference employed in 1989 cannot abandon the imagery of 1939, an imagery empowered by a fantasy of the past and reflecting a basic understanding of the nature of difference expressed within a vocabulary of images taken from that of the past.

NOTES

A slightly different version of this essay appeared in *MLN*, 104, 5 (December 1989), pp. 1142–71.

1. See Lynn Payer, *Medicine and Culture: Varieties of Treatment in the United States, England, West Germany, and France* (New York: Henry Holt, 1988).

2. Roy Porter, "Ever since Eve: The Fear of Contagion," *Times Literary Supplement*, 27 May–2 June 1988, p. 582; Susan Sontag, *AIDS and its Metaphors* (New York: Farrar, Straus & Giroux, 1989); Sander L. Gilman, *Disease and Representation: Images of Illness from Madness to AIDS* (Ithaca, NY: Cornell University Press, 1988). On the general background of the image of the person with AIDS see Casper G. Schmidt, "The Group-Fantasy Origins of AIDS," *Journal of Psychohistory*, 12 (1984), pp. 37–78; Casper G. Schmidt, "AIDS Jokes, or Schadenfreude around an Epidemic," *Maledicta*, 8 (1984–85), pp. 69–75; Dennis Altman, *AIDS in the Mind of America: The Social, Political, and Psychological Impact of a New Epidemic* (New York: Anchor/Doubleday, 1986); David Black, *The Plague Years: A Chronicle of AIDS, the Epidemic of Our Times* (New York: Simon & Schuster/London: Picador, 1986); Graham Hancock and Enver Carim, *AIDS: The Deadly Epidemic* (London: Gollanz, 1986); Richard Liebmann-Smith, *The Question of AIDS* (New York: New York Academy of Sciences, 1985); Eve K. Nicols, *Mobilizing against AIDS: The Unfinished Story of a Virus* (Cambridge, MA: Harvard University Press, 1986); Lon G. Nungasser, *Epidemic of Courage: Facing AIDS in America* (New York: St. Martin's, 1986); Simon Watney, *Policing Desire: Pornography, AIDS and the Media* (Minneapolis: University of Minnesota Press, 1987); Randy Shilts, *And the Band Played On: Politics, People, and the AIDS Epidemic* (New York: St. Martin's, 1987); Gary Alan Fine, "Welcome to the World of AIDS: Fantasies of Female Revenge," *Western Folklore*, 46 (1987), pp. 192–97; Elizabeth Fee and Daniel M. Fox, eds., *AIDS: The Burdens of History* (Berkeley: University of California Press, 1988); Mirko D. Grmek, *Histoire du sida* (Paris: Payot, 1989). See George L. Mosse's brilliant study *Nationalism and Sexuality* (New York: Howard Fertig, 1985) for the national context of much of this literature.

3. See Douglas Crimp, ed., *AIDS: Cultural Analysis/Cultural Activism* (Cambridge, MA: MIT Press, 1989), and Cindy Patton, *Inventing AIDS* (New York: Routledge, 1990).

4. Rudolf Heinrich Daumann, *Patrouille gegen den Tod: Ein utopischer Roman* (Berlin: Schützen-Verlag, 1939). Within the first year of publication, 70,000 copies of the book had been sold.

5. Peter Zingler, *Die Seuche: Roman* (Frankfurt a. M.: Eichborn, 1989). The German literature on AIDS is not as extensive as the Anglo-American. Of importance is the 94th issue of the *Kursbuch* (November 1988) entitled "Die Seuche."

6. See Sander L. Gilman, *On Blackness without Blacks: Essays on the Image of the*

Black in Germany (Boston: G. K. Hall, 1982), pp. 119ff. See also Rosemarie K. Lester, *Trivialneger: Das Bild der Schwarzen im west-deutschen Illustrietenroman* (Stuttgart: Heinz, 1982).

7. Bernard Blanc, "Lexique à l'usage des voyageurs en S. F.," *Le Français dans le Monde*, 193 (1985), pp. 32–33, and Charles R. Saunders, "Why Blacks Don't Read Science Fiction," in Tom Henighan, ed., *Brave New Universe: Testing the Values of Science in Society* (Ottawa: Tecumseh, 1980), pp. 160–68.

8. On the history of self-experimentation and the legends associated with it, see Lawrence K. Altman, *Who Goes First?: The Story of Self-Experimentation in Medicine* (New York: Random House, 1987).

9. Everett Franklin Bleiler, "Edgar Rice Burroughs, 1875–1950," in his, ed., *Science Fiction Writers: Critical Studies of the Major Authors from the Early Nineteenth Century to the Present Day* (New York: Scribner's, 1982), pp. 59–64; Dieter Ohlmeier, "Das psychoanalytische Interesse an literarischen Texten," in Jochen Horisch and Georg Christoph Tholen, eds., *Eingebildete Texte: Affairen zwischen Psychoanalysse und Literaturwissenschaft* (München: Fink, 1985), pp. 15–25; Gert Ueding, "Die langandauernde Krankheit des Lebens," *Jahrbuch der Karl-May-Gesellschaft* (1986), pp. 50–68.

10. See Oliver Ransford, *"Bid the Sickness Cease": Disease in the History of Black Africa* (London: John Murray, 1983). For a description of a yellow fever epidemic as evidence of English colonial misrule, see also Hans Poeschel, *The Voice of German East Africa: The English in the Judgment of the Natives* (Berlin: August Scherl, 1919), esp. p. 65.

11. See Prosser Guifford and William Roger Louis, eds., *Britain and Germany in Africa: Imperial Rivalry and Colonial Rule* (New Haven: Yale University Press, 1967), and L. Smythe Barron, ed., *The Nazis in Africa* (Salisbury, NC: Documentary Publications, 1979).

12. See the general discussion and background in Hans-Walter Schmuhl, *Rassenhygiene, Nationalsozialismus, Euthanasie: Von der Verhütung zur Vernichtung lebensunwerten Lebens, 1890–1945* (Göttingen: Vandenhoeck & Ruprecht, 1987); Robert Proctor, *Racial Hygiene: Medicine under the Nazis* (Cambridge, MA: Harvard University Press, 1988); Peter Weingart, Jürgen Kroll, Kurt Bayertz, *Rasse, Blut und Gene: Geschichte der Eugenik und Rassenhygiene in Deutschland* (Frankfurt a. M.: Suhrkamp, 1988).

13. Ernst Janisch, "Selbstbehauptung und Verpflichtung der weßien Rasse in

Afrika," *Afrika braucht Grossdeutschland: Das deutsche koloniale Jahrbuch 1940* (Berlin: Wilhelm Süßrott, 1939), pp. 60–64.

14. This charge was a mainstay of German discussions about the need for the return of the German colonies. H. W. Bauer made the point in his broadside of 1938 that the "Germans had been on the way to creating the most valuable type of black on the black continent" through the "cultural and hygienic care of the native population" at the point their colonies were taken away from them. See his *Deutschlands Kolonialforderung und die Welt: Forerungen der deutschen Raum- und Rohstoffnot* (Leipzig: Richard Bauer, 1938).

15. Helmut Vallery, *Führer, Volk, und Charisma: Der nationalsozialistische historische Roman* (Rugenstein: Pahl, 1980).

16. See in this context Klaus Theweileit, *Male Fantasies*, trans. Stephan Conway, 2 vols. (Minneapolis: University of Minnesota Press, 1987).

17. There was a real fear in the 1920s and 1930s of a substantial increase in the number of cases of syphilis and of the development of a new form of "metalues." Such a fear was also coupled with a sense that this increase would drastically effect the offspring of the present generation. See Max Nonne, *Syphilis und Nervensystem* (Berlin: Karger, 1921), p. 6; on the impact on various foreign countries, especially in Africa, see p. 679.

18. James H. Jones, *Bad Blood: The Tuskegee Syphilis Experiment—A Tragedy of Race and Medicine* (New York: The Free Press, 1981).

19. On the pathological meaning of the nose in German science of this period see Hans Leichner, *Die Vererbung anatomischer Variationen der Nase, ihrre Nebenhöhlen und des Gehörorgans* (München: J. F. Bergmann, 1928), p. 81. As important was the general discussion of "types" in medicine spinning off of Ernst Kretschmer's theory of constitution (itself in opposition to ideas of race yet incorporated in these ideas) which saw specific types—among them the types normally associated in racial science with the image of the Jew—as particularly at risk for syphilis. See Richard Stern, *Über körperliche Kennzeichen der Disposition zur Tabes* (Leipzig: Franz Deuticke, 1912).

20. Ludwik Fleck, *Entstehung und Entwicklung einer wissenschaftlichen Tatsache* (1935; Frankfurt a. M.: Suhrkamp, 1980). I am indebted to Fleck's work for the basic conceptual structure presented in this essay.

21. Theodor Fritsch, *Handbuch der Judenfrage* (Leipzig: Hammer, 1935), p. 408.

22. See M. J. Guttmann, *Über den heutigen Stand der Rasse- und Krankheitsfrage der Juden* (München: Rudolph Müller & Steinicke, 1920) and Heinrich Singer, *Allgemeine und spezielle Krankheitslehre der Juden* (Leipzig: Benno Konegen, 1904). For a more modern analysis of the "myths" and "realities" of the diseases attributed to the Jews, see Richard M. Goodman, *Genetic Disorders among the Jewish People* (Baltimore: Johns Hopkins University Press, 1979).

23. Compare Edward J. Bristow, *Prostitution and Prejudice: The Jewish Fight against White Slavery, 1870–1939* (Oxford: Clarendon, 1982). Such a view of the Jew as the syphilitic was not limited to the anti-Semitic fringe of the turn of the century. It was a view which possessed power even over "Jewish" writers such as Marcel Proust (whose uncomfortable relationship to his mother's Jewish identity haunted his life almost as much as did his gay identity).

24. Fritsch, *Handbuch der Judenfrage*, pp. 406–7.

25. N. Balaban and A. Molotschek, "Progressive Paralyse bei den Bevölkerungen der Krim," *Allgemeine Zeitschrift für Psychiatrie*, 94 (1931), pp. 373–83.

26. H. Budul, "Beitrag zur vergleichenden Rassenpsychiatrie," *Monatsschrift für Psychiatrie und Neurologie*, 37 (1915), pp. 199–204.

27. Jewish scientists also had to explain the "statistical" fact of their immunity to syphilis. In a study of the rate of tertiary lues, the final stage of the syphilitic infection, undertaken during World War I, the Jewish physician Max Sichel responded to the general view of the relative lower incidence of infection among Jews as resulting from their sexual difference. He responds—out of necessity—with a social argument. The Jews, according to Sichel, evidence lower incidence because of their early marriage and the patriarchal structure of the Jewish family, but also because of their much lower rate of alcoholism. They were, according to the implicit argument, more rarely exposed to the infection of prostitutes whose attractiveness was always associated with the greater loss of sexual control in the male attributed to inebriety. The relationship between these two "social" diseases is made into a cause for the higher incidence among other Europeans. See Max Sichel, "Die Paralyse der Juden in sexuologischer Beleuchtung," *Zeitschrift für Sexualwissenschaft*, 7 (1919–20), pp. 98–104.

28. Following the writings of Paul, the first of these views saw circumcision as inherently symbolic and, therefore, no longer valid after the rise of Christianity (this notion was espoused by Eusebius and Origen); the second saw circumcision as a form of medical prophylaxis (as in the writing of Philo but also in the work of the central German commentator of the eighteenth century, Johann David Michaelis); the third saw

it as a sign of a political identity (as in the work of the early eighteenth-century theologian Johann Spencer); and the fourth as a remnant of the early Jewish idol or phallus worship (as in the work of the antiquarian Georg Friedrich Daumer—this view reappears quite often in the literature on Jewish ritual murder). There is no comprehensive study of the German debates on circumcision. See J. Alkvist, "Geschichte der Circumcision," *Janus*, 30 (1926), pp. 86–104; 152–71.

29. See for example the discussion by Em. Kohn in the *Mittheilung des Ärtzlichen Vereines in Wien*, 3 (1874), pp. 169–72 (on the Jewish side) and Dr. Klein, "Die rituelle Circumcision, eine sanitätspolizeiliche Frage," *Allgemeine Medizinische Central-Zeitung*, 22 (1853), pp. 368–69 (on the non-Jewish side).

30. See the discussion by Dr. Bamberger, "Die Hygiene der Beschneidung," in Max Grunwald, *Die Hygiene der Juden. Im Anschluß an die internationale Hygiene-Ausstellung* (Dresden: Verlag der historischen Abtteilung der internationale Hygiene-Ausstellung, 1911), pp. 103–12 (on the Jewish side) and W. Hammer, "Zur Beschneidungsfrage," *Zeitschrift für Bahnärzte*, 1 (1916), p. 254 (on the non-Jewish side). This question of hygiene is closely associated with the therapeutic use of circumcision throughout the nineteenth century as a means of "curing" the diseases caused by masturbation, with, of course a similar split in the idea of efficacy: circumcision was either a cure for masturbation as it eliminated the stimulation of the prepuce and deadened the sensitivity of the penis, *or* it was the source of Jewish male hypersexuality.

31. Houston Stewart Chamberlain, *Foundations of the Nineteenth Century*, trans. John Lees, 2 vols. (London: John Lane, 1910), 1, pp. 388–89.

32. Nathan Birnbaum, "Über Houston Stewart Chamberlain," in his *Ausgewählte Schriften zur jüdischen Frage*, vol. 2 (Czernowitz: Verlag der Buchhandlung Dr. Birnbaum & Dr. Kohut, 1910), p. 201.

33. Adam G. de Gurowski, *America and Europe* (New York: D. Appleton, 1857), p. 177.

34. Saul K. Padover, ed. and trans., *The Letters of Karl Marx* (Englewood Cliffs, NJ: Prentice-Hall, 1979), p. 459.

35. Adolph Hitler, *Mein Kampf*, trans. Ralph Manheim (Boston: Houghton Mifflin, 1943), pp. 57–58.

36. W. W. Kopp, "Beobachtung an Halbjuden in Berliner Schulen," *Volk und Rasse*, 10 (1935), p. 392.

37. M. Lerche, "Beobachtung deutsch-jüdischer Rassenkreuzeung an Berliner Schulen," *Die medizinische Welt,* 17 September 1927, p. 1222.

38. See my *Jewish Self-Hatred: Anti-Semitism and the Hidden Language of the Jews* (Baltimore: Johns Hopkins University Press, 1986).

39. Jan Goldstein, "The Wandering Jew and the Problem of Psychiatric Anti-semitism in Fin-de-Siècle France," *Journal of Contemporary History,* 20 (1985), pp. 521–52.

40. See my *Disease and Representation* (note 2 above), pp. 190–91.

41. See the discussion in Sander L. Gilman, *Difference and Pathology: Stereotypes of Sexuality, Race, and Madness* (Ithaca, NY: Cornell University Press, 1986).

42. Friedrich Ratzel, *The History of Mankind,* trans. A. J. Butler, 3 vols. (London: Macmillian, 1898), 3, p. 183 (on the Near East) and 3, p. 548 (on Europe).

43. Daumann, pp. 53–54 cites Justus Hecker, *Der schwarze Tod im 14. Jahrhundert* (Berlin: Herbig, 1832).

44. Ulrich Berkes, *Eine schlimme Liebe: Tagebuch* (Berlin: Aufbau, 1987), pp. 40–41 and 214. On the background to the question of AIDS in the GDR see Günter Grau, ed., *Und diese Liebe auch: Theologische und sexualwissenschaftliche Einsichten zur Homosexualität* (Berlin: Evangelische Verlagsanstalt, 1989), as well as John Parsons, "East Germany Faces its Past: A New Start for Socialist Sexual Poltics," *Out/Look,* 5 (1989), pp. 43–52.

45. See the extensive coverage in the news magazine *Der Spiegel* during 1987, for example, the cover story of the February 9, 1987 issue, pp. 30–53.

46. For a detailed overview see John Borneman, "AIDS in the Two Berlins," in Crimp, ed., *AIDS: Cultural Analysis/Cultural Activism,* pp. 223–37.

47. On the treatment of gays in the Third Reich see Richard Plant, *The Pink Triangle: The Nazi War Against Homosexuals* (New York: Henry Holt, 1986), and Hans-Georg Stümke, *Homosexualle in Deutschland: Eine politische Geschichte* (München: Beck, 1989).

48. See the Berlin *Tageszeitung (TAZ)* rebuttal of this on June 6, 1989, p. 13.

49. Karin Obermeier, "Afro-German Women: Recording their Own History," *New German Critique*, 46 (1989), pp. 172–80.

50. See Wiebke Reuter-Krauß and Cristoph Schmidt, *AIDS und Recht von A-Z* (Munich: dtv/Beck, 1988).

51. *Der Spiegel*, 5 November 1984, p. 100.

52. Helmut Zander, *Der Regenbogen: Tagebuch eines AIDSkranken* (München: Knaur, 1988), pp. 235–36.

53. Fred Breinersdorfer, *Quarantäne* (Stuttgart: Weitbrecht, 1989).

54. *Der Spiegel*, 25 May 1987, pp. 25–32.

55. Ruth Beckermann, *Unzugehoerig: Oesterreicher und Juden nach 1945* (Vienna: Lockner, 1989), p. 83.

56. This is not to confuse the fact that both Jews and gays can internalize the same sense of social difference in their confrontation with exactly such stereotypical structures. See Paul Parin, "'The Mark of Oppression': Enthnopsychoanalytische Studie über Juden und Homosexuelle in einer relative permissiven Kultur," *Psyche*, 39 (1985), pp. 193–219.

57. Richard von Krafft-Ebing, *Psychopathia Sexualis: A Medico-Forensic Study*, rev. trans. Harry E. Wedeck (New York: Putnam, 1965), p. 24.

58. Compare Otto Binswanger, *Hysterie* (Wien: Deuticke, 1904), p. 82.

59. August Forel, *The Sexual Question: A Scientific, Psychological, Hygienic and Sociological Study*, trans. D. F. Marshall (New York: Physicians and Surgeons Book Co., 1925), pp. 331–32.

60. Richard von Krafft-Ebing, *Text-Book of Insanity*, trans. Charles Gilbert Chaddock (Philadelphia: F. A. Davis, 1905), p. 143.

Chapter 10

"White Slavery," Citizenship and Nationality in Argentina

Donna J. Guy

The history of citizenship has often lost sight of women, understandably, since women have been so often excluded from the fraternal imaginings that constitute a citizenry. This essay hopes to fill in some of that spotty history by reviewing how female nationality came to be (re)defined at the turn of the century as a result of international conflict. In what was sensationalized as the Argentine "White Slave Trade," European and Latin American women became more than simply vehicles for sexual traffic; they were the pretexts for defining one nation's sovereignty against another's.

Before the twentieth century only a few republics granted citizens' rights to women. Women generally were denied such rights even though the nation depended on their participation in various ways. Floya Anthias and Nira Yuval-Davis have identified some of these basic roles women have played in the formation of the nation. Women, they argue, not only give birth to future members of national groups but also reproduce the ideological constructs of the nation by transmitting its culture to new generations. Women serve, moreover, as a "focus and symbol in ideological discourse used in the construction, reproduction, and transformation of ethnic/national categories." And finally, women help defend the nation by participating in its political, economic, and social struggles.[1]

Despite this variety of reproductive and civic roles typically assigned to women, their participation in national life has often been severely limited. Women can be most useful to the nation as passive wards who require the state's protection. Under certain circumstances they may even be called upon to protect, or rather to demand the protection of, their sexuality as a patriotic gesture. As Christine Obbo commented:

> Women's security is often the last frontier men have to defend when all the other battles against colonialism and imperialism are lost. Human societies always portray their women as more virtuous than women of other groups and therefore in need of protection. Never mind that each society also coerces women to be "good women" through imposing a number of sanctions against "bad women."[2]

Women who emigrated and sometimes married beyond the geographic boundaries of the modern nation state were expected—regardless of their social or economic status—to maintain the honor of their nation by safeguarding their sexual virtue. If these women were placed in a situation where their honor was threatened, the nation's honor would be compromised as well: patriots felt compelled to defend their female citizens, even if their citizenship and virtue had first to be constructed in order to be defended.

The issue of "bad women" triggered the discourse on female nationality and citizenship as thousands of women left their European homelands from the 1870s onward in search of a better life in the Americas, South Africa, and other parts of Europe. From the last quarter of the nineteenth century until the outbreak of World War II, modern European nations carved out empires, fought to preserve national interests, and sought innovative ways to construct national identity. As male legislators and military leaders devised strategies to manifest national strength, the condition of their women living abroad, whether as respectable wives or as socially marginal prostitutes, affected the rights and inherent restrictions of citizenship beyond national frontiers, as if nationality were an inviolable identity. These "loose" emigrant women would play a major role in defining European citizenship and national responsibility.

Soviet Russia was the only European nation before World War Two which granted married women the same access to citizenship as men. The potential disabilities that affected other European women did not become an issue until they began to migrate to new countries in search of work and a better life. Almost as soon as women began to arrive in great numbers at foreign ports, troubling stories appeared about European females in legally-sanctioned bordellos in colonial or postcolonial cities. For many Europeans it was inconceivable that their female compatriots would willingly submit to sexual commerce with foreign, racially varied men. In one way or another these women must have been trapped and victimized. So European women in foreign bordellos were construed as "white slaves" rather than common prostitutes, and the campaign to rescue them became a glorious battle pitting civilization at home against barbarism beyond. In this way "bad women" were rehabilitated to become "good women" as their homelands rushed to defend their imputed, nationally inalienable virtue.

To these European nations—influenced by racism and Victorian sexual values—it was deeply disturbing, probably humiliating, to watch prostitutes freely migrate to foreign barbarous lands where they were ignominiously required by local laws to register in local bordellos. And stories of European women working in foreign houses of prostitution triggered the debate about female citizens' rights. At home in Europe—where prostitution was not always considered a criminal offence—even the lowliest prostitute had a national identity and enjoyed certain civil rights unless convicted of breaking the law. To complicate the offense felt by European patriots and moral reformers, there were, certainly, desperate fellow countrywomen who were forced into prostitution through coercion by family members or by strangers, particularly those lured by offers of better employment in a new land. In response to such compromising situations, outraged reformers and diplomats pressured their governments to rescue their countrywomen, whether or not those women wanted to be rescued.

One way or another, the modern nation state was drawn into the plight of female nationals who apparently needed succor from home. But the rescue efforts were hampered by the modern—yet seemingly premodern—definition of female citizenship in Europe that owed more to paternal rights in the family than to the paternalism of the state. Children inherited their national identity not only because of where they were born, but also through their father's citizenship. And a married woman's citizenship was determined by that of her husband, not by her parents or place of birth. Female nationals who married foreigners encountered another type of problem: they lost their citizenship and could not be protected by their homelands. Instead they were subjected to the laws and customs of their husband's nation. The situation became even more critical if women were divorced, abandoned, or abused by their husbands, because being husbandless meant being stateless. Even women who married foreigners and remained at home lost their citizenship in most European countries where foreigners were allowed to follow the civil codes of their own homelands.[3]

Thus when nations were partitioned or conquered, or parents were divorced, both women and children found themselves just as stateless as if they had actually emigrated. Protecting children as well as married women was an opportunity to construct new definitions of citizenship as corollaries to the paternalist state. But of course it was not the plight of married women living abroad that first prompted European diplomats and politicians to contemplate the protection of female citizens as a function of national honor, a need that invested the home country with international authority. The rights of married women were paradoxically defined in an *a fortiori* manner only after the rights of whores had been posited.

Throughout this process of definition the sexuality of both the prostitute and the married woman generated anxious debate. This was especially so in the case of Argentina, where female citizenship was being defined in terms of sexuality, and where a centralized and intrusive state needed to assume civic and moral authority to bolster its political legitimacy.

European nations had many reasons to both fear and admire Argentine laws that focused upon prostitutes and wives. As women whose sexual practices and relationships represented each other's antithesis, these two groups jointly defined the parameters of female citizenship in modern Argentina. Prostitutes determined the limits of socially-acceptable female sexual behavior so that self-identified female prostitutes lost the right to move freely within cities, work without medical inspection, and live wherever they pleased. In contrast wives, by law and religion sworn to remain sexually faithful, enjoyed all those privileges taken from prostitutes though they still suffered other civil restrictions. Until 1926 married female Argentines could not keep the money they earned nor work without permission of their spouse. Nor could they assume parental authority over their children. Yet despite these differences, after 1926 the combined civil rights of females born in Argentina enabled their nation to boast having the most inclusive nonpolitical female citizenship laws found among pre-World War II modern nation states.

Benedict Anderson observed that nineteenth-century Latin American politicians were unique in their quest to include minority groups within the newly formed nation. In order to do so they had to create, as Anderson put it, "an imagined political community—and imagined as both inherently limited and sovereign." Argentina, one of these newly sovereign nations, imagined its community not only by identifying as citizens all males born in Argentine territory, but also by granting the same rights and privileges, according to its 1853 Constitution, to women born in Argentina. Even foreign-born residents were granted most citizenship privileges except military service. This meant that female Argentine and foreign born women might be restricted in some of their activities, but most Argentine women could obtain passports or other identity documents that reaffirmed their Argentine citizenship.[4]

Traditionally, citizenship has been conceived as a political right which often reflects unequal access to power in societies that differentiate male and female roles. The mere possession of the right to vote, hold office, and serve in the military—all male prerogatives until recently—may tend to obscure, however, other important rights women have possessed as citizens within the nation state, which include the ability to marry, work, own property, and make a will. The Argentine 1853 Constitution, indeed, guaranteed these civil rights to all inhabitants, although subsequent local, civil and commercial codes placed limitations on prostitutes, minors and married women. Discussions concerning the negation of constitutional rights for females, however, became important only after European women began to migrate in significant numbers to Argentina, which by the 1880s had become an extremely attractive destination for both women and men.

Inexpensive ocean passages, high wages for agricultural labor (mostly male), as well as a rapidly growing capital city, prompted Europeans to seek their fortunes there. Thousands of poor European women emigrated between 1870 and 1914 in search of work and marriage partners, and they were treated in the same way that the nation dealt with its own countrywomen. Their ability to work, particularly in medically-supervised municipal bordellos opened in 1875 to control venereal disease, and their freedom to marry foreign men led to stories of "white slavery"—the international traffic in women and children for purposes of sexual exploitation—and prompted international concern about the plight of European women reputedly forced into a life of vice in Argentina.

In order to work in legal bawdy houses, these women forfeited rights both inside and outside the bordello. They had to undergo biweekly medical examinations, keep away from bordello windows and doors during working hours, and carry identity cards when outside. No other urban inhabitants were monitored so strictly. Yet the only legal issue that separated whores from married women or mistresses—one might put it provocatively—was the fact that prostitutes accepted cash in exchange for sexual favors with a variety of men.[5]

Many civil libertarians in Argentina questioned the legality of depriving women, even sexually dangerous ones, of basic civil rights such as the freedom of movement and work. In response, a French physician resident in Argentina, Dr. Benjamin Dupont, wrote *Pornografía de Buenos Aires* in 1879 to defend the existing system. He argued that it was in fact legal to restrict the civil liberties of prostitutes because they "violate fundamental social laws, therefore they cannot expect the freedom that society assures all its members." Dupont, whose native land created the system of medically-supervised prostitution in the early nineteenth century, provided little comfort to those back home who organized to keep French women out of foreign bordellos.[6]

The passage of laws to legalize prostitution in Buenos Aires coincided with the formation of a European moral reform association whose aim was diametrically opposed: to close down state-licensed bordellos within and outside Europe. The group called itself "The British, Continental and General Federation for the Abolition of the Government Regulation of Prostitution." Led by the British feminist Josephine Butler, the federation set out to combat the injustice of state-supported prostitution where women, but not their customers, were subjected to medical exams and special restrictions. Relatively unsuccessful at prohibiting bordellos in Europe, this group, as well as subsequent organizations, soon identified South American countries, especially Argentina, as morally and politically offensive because European women became "sexual slaves" there.[7]

The campaign to extirpate "white slavery" is usually viewed as one component of the social purity campaigns that swept Europe and North America by the turn of the century. Other factors such as "the changing role of women, domestic and international migrations and rapid urban and industrial growth,"[8] have also been identified as issues that fed the often hysterical cries to save white slaves entrapped abroad. This concern of European nations to protect their citizens, even the most marginal, must also be kept in focus. After all, at a time of great international jockeying or strength, what nation could afford to allow foreigners to exploit its countrywomen? Where did national duty or citizenship end?

The international anti-white slavery movement was organized to promote treaties to protect foreign women from sexual exploitation. The emphasis on international agreements was an acknowledgement that by itself, no nation was powerful enough to protect its own, let alone a foreign, damsel in distress. In 1890 the Subcommittee for the Suppression of Foreign Traffic of the National Vigilance Association, the principal British anti-white slavery society, recounted a story of futile diplomatic efforts:

> We received most reliable and accurate information that a foreigner had left London with three Polish girls, professedly to find them good situations in Buenos Aires, but really to sell them into profligacy there. The vessel . . . had already left Southampton, but we were informed it would be detained for one day at a Continental port taking in cargo. We immediately telegraphed to the British Consul at that port, and asked him to take steps. . . . The Consul's reply was that as neither the man nor his victims were British subjects, he

> could not interfere. . . . If we had an international Act . . . the whole business might be stopped within a month.[9]

Stories such as these led the National Vigilance Society and other anti-white slavery groups to lobby for an international treaty that would restrict the emigration rights of female citizens in order to protect them. The first phase of that goal was realized in 1904. Delegates of thirteen nations, Belgium, Denmark, France, Germany, Great Britain, Italy, the Netherlands, Norway, Sweden, Portugal, Russia, Spain and Switzerland, all European nations and many of which had state-licensed bordellos, ratified an agreement to create agencies to monitor the movements of people suspected of importing or exporting "women and girls destined for an immoral life." These women, within "legal limits," were to be repatriated if they so desired. Countries were also asked to monitor employment agencies specializing in the recruitment of women for jobs abroad.

A second international document was signed in Paris in May 1910. This time the countries agreed to prosecute those who procured women and girls for immoral purposes. Representatives came from thirteen countries: Austria-Hungary, Belgium, Brazil, Denmark, France, Germany, Great Britain, Italy, the Netherlands, Portugal, Russia, Spain and Sweden. For the first time a Latin American nation was among the signatory nations.[10]

But international cooperation proved insufficient to keep European women out of foreign houses of prostitution. Reported incidents of involuntary sexual slavery in third-world port cities led foreign communities to emulate measures already taken in railway stations and docks across Europe. They hired social workers to meet incoming ships and offer assistance to women travelling alone or under suspicious circumstances. By 1913 two were working the ports of Buenos Aires, one hired by the Jewish community who reported to the Jewish Association for the Protection of Girls and Women, and another hired by the resident British community, linked to the National Vigilance Society. In addition to the efforts of these stalwart reformers, an Argentine anti-white slavery committee, the *Asociación Nacional Argentina contra la Trata de Blancas*, was founded in 1902. It distributed flyers to disembarking passengers proclaiming in Spanish, Italian, French, English, German and Yiddish, "This is a free country. No one is forced to be a prostitute. The woman who wishes to give up this profession should advise 'The National Association against the white slave traffic,'" and then listed the group's address. The municipality of Buenos Aires after 1904 allowed social workers to interview women who wished to sign up at the Prostitute's Registry.[11]

Despite the efforts of such groups, both foreign and national, to protect European women in Argentina, this country became the principal target in Latin

America for anti-white slavery campaigns because so many Europeans enrolled in the Buenos Aires Prostitutes' Registry. Furthermore, the Argentine state whose internal campaign for moral hygiene depended on isolated outlets for occasional sexual excess by otherwise decent male citizens,[12] conspicuously failed to sign international anti-white slavery agreements. At the tenth International Abolitionist Federation meeting in September 1908, Argentina was accused of encouraging the world traffic in women. According to Sir Percy Bunting, nationality statistics published by the Prostitutes' Registry proved that "prostitution is controlled by the international traffic and [in Buenos Aires] it is fed by the houses that receive these women and live off their sexual commerce."[13]

These accusations were lodged against Argentina again and again. In 1913 when Samuel Cohen, Secretary of the Jewish Association for the Protection of Girls and Women, went to Buenos Aires to ascertain the veracity of white slavery incidents there, he noted in his report that South America was considered a haven for white slavers, and that "There is no doubt whatever, that immorality exists to a very large extent in South American States." As for Argentina, he believed that "Immorality is still bad, but it is not so flagrant . . . as it was formerly," yet licensed houses of prostitution remained a "black spot," a hindrance to the rehabilitation of the nation's reputation.[14]

The outbreak of World War I quickly ended the exodus of Europeans to Latin America and temporarily quelled the clamor to protect foreign women through the international regulation of houses of prostitution. Following the war, however, the creation of new European nation states, each with its own claims to national honor and set of codes regarding nationality, made the problem of the female citizen even more complicated than before. Not only were women beginning to emigrate to South America again, those still in Europe had to confront new political realities that often left them at risk. Ironically Argentina—the country that had been the international pariah due to its licensed bordellos filled with Europeans—would come to serve as a model for protecting the nationality of married female citizens.

In the postwar period new international organizations took up the banners and slogans of earlier anti-white slavery movements and worked to enforce existing treaties and create new ones. The League of Nations was the most significant international organization prior to the formation of the United Nations. By 1921 it had a special committee authorized to explore the international traffic in women and children. In an effort to separate itself from the racist implications of earlier anti-white slavery campaigns, it called the problem the "international traffic in women and children."[15]

At the Sixth International Congress for the Suppression of Traffic in Women and Children, delegates returned to the prewar agenda of trying to pass an international agreement to restrict foreign women's employment and pursued a new proposal from the League of Nations Committee on the Suppression of Traffic in Women and Children to ban foreign women from legal houses of prostitution. Dr. Paulina Luisi, representative from Uruguay, opposed the idea because it embodied all the problematic aspects of female citizenship. If women sought work, they or their pimps could lie about the women's nationality. Furthermore, children born in many South American countries of European heritage would not be considered citizens of their parents' homeland (even though European laws did not necessarily concur). Equally important, if work in such businesses was unacceptable to foreigners, why then should nationals be allowed to engage in them?

> I would like to know how my Government could expel a woman merely on the grounds that she is a foreign prostitute? Is prostitution a crime? In my country only people guilty of offenses against the law can be deported. The foreign women are to be expelled because they commit a crime in leading a life of prostitution? In that case prostitution is a crime; then why should we allow our nationals to commit crimes?[16]

In 1927 the next International Congress expanded the number of occupations deemed immoral or unacceptable for foreign women. "Posts offered abroad to domestic servants, maids, governesses, teachers, milliners, dressmakers, and more especially posts as entertainers or 'artistes'" were listed among the most dangerous, and incidents reported by the League of Nation's Committee on the Traffic in Women and Children provided the evidence. Clearly moral reformers were intent upon keeping foreign women from engaging in any gainful occupation abroad lest they be forced into sexual slavery, and they relied on the League of Nations to prove that foreign countries threatened their female compatriots.[17]

By the time the League of Nation's Committee on the Traffic in Women and Children published its mammoth two volume report in 1927, a wealth of documentation had evidently been compiled. Originally the Committee intended to study only the traffic from Western Europe to Central and South America. Eventually investigators went to twenty-eight countries and one hundred twelve cities in North America, the Mediterranean, North Sea and Baltic countries as well as in South America.[18]

South America, however, was the first area examined. More time was spent in cities in Argentina and Brazil than anywhere else, and nationality statistics from the Buenos Aires Prostitutes' Registry provided convincing proof that many foreign-born women registered in Argentina almost as soon as they arrived. After apprising the reader that Argentina had signed no international agreements regarding the international traffic in women and children, the Committee carefully studied Argentine municipal and national laws relating to prostitution; at the same time it ignored the laws of countries or cities where few foreign women were engaged in sexual commerce. By the end of the second volume, which treated the outward bound traffic as well as importation of women to foreign brothels, it was clear that despite efforts to reduce exploitation and limit the number of women in each bordello, Argentina deserved nothing but criticism.[19]

In fairness to the League of Nations, it should be made clear that the organization did not criticize Argentina without considering the nation's merits in other committee investigations. In addition to studying the status of "bad women," the League of Nations endeavored to defend the rights of "good women," namely married women. When it came to the issue of married women's citizenship rights, the League was quick to commend Argentina for its progressive laws and this helped rehabilitate Argentina's international image.

The concern for the citizenship status of married women did not arise specifically from governmental responses to emigration, but rather from the formation of new national entities during and after World War I. To deal with citizens residing in new countries, European reformers looked for innovative citizenship models. This quest began in 1917 when the International Alliance of Women for Suffrage and Equal Citizenship was founded. Comprised of representatives of thirty-nine countries and representing diverse "races, creeds, and political parties," it worked to "secure for the married women under the laws of every state her own independent nationality and the same right as a man to retain or change her nationality." The Alliance was particularly concerned that a woman's nationality not be changed without her consent when she married.[20] It proposed two ways to guarantee the citizenship of a married woman. One was through the principle that geographic locality of birth determined citizenship (*jus soli*); the other held that the citizenship of both parents could be conferred upon the child. As of 1917, however, only a few Latin American nations proved to be exceptions to the general rule that the nationality of a married woman was determined by that of her husband.

Argentina, from this perspective, was an admirable model. In addition to its 1853 Constitution, a subsequent Law of Citizenship explicitly identified as citizens all children born in Argentina, regardless of their parents' nationality. Others had to apply for citizenship, and certain circumstances such as marriage to an Argentine woman or the petition of a child born outside the country of Argentine parents would be given preference. By 1935 Argentina was commended along with nine other Latin American nations (Brazil, Chile, Paraguay, Uruguay, Colombia, Guatemala, Panama, Ecuador and Cuba) listed by the International Alliance of Women for Suffrage and Equal Citizenship. These Latin

American nations comprised nine of the fourteen nations in the world that not only offered equal terms of citizenship for married citizens, male and female, but also did not force citizenship upon women who married their male citizens.[21]

European nations made an effort to agree on the issue of married women's citizenship, and the result was the Hague Nationality Convention of 1930. Designed to protect women from becoming stateless, it still did not achieve the goals set by the Alliance despite the efforts of Latin American women that were strongly supported by male diplomats from the region. According to the Alliance:

> A woman to whom the Convention applies who has kept her own nationality and also by marriage automatically acquired her husband's may find herself when abroad in her husband's country, or even in a third country, deprived of the privileges belonging to her own nationality and without redress, because her own State, by ratifying the Convention, has waived its right to protect her in some particular difficulty in which she may find herself. Ratification of this Convention is therefore against the interests of women.[22]

Evidently many European nations could not even agree to these terms and few in any case had ratified the convention before World War II.

The Pan American Union, predecessor to the Organization of American States, proved more successful at proposing international nationality conventions because the aims of the treaty did not conflict with the concepts of nationality and citizenship espoused by its members. This made it feasible for Latin American diplomats to support the work of Latin American feminists who, in 1928, had formed the Inter-American Commission of Women and presented an Equal Rights Treaty to the plenary session of the Sixth International Conference of American States held in Havana.[23]

By the time the Seventh International Conference of American States met at Montevideo, Uruguay in December, 1933, members of the Inter-American Commission of Women were allowed to address the plenary sessions and two major conventions were approved that affected the status of women in their respective countries. The first related to general nationality issues. Article VI, however, specifically referred to the issue of marriage and it forbade any change in nationality status of any member of the family as a result of contracting marriage. The second convention eliminated sex as a factor that determined nationality: "There shall be no distinction based on sex as regards nationality, in their legislation or in their practice." Together these two proposed conventions stood as a challenge to existing European law.[24]

Latin American diplomats did not merely sign these conventions; many worked to have national civil codes reformed to accord women equal nationality rights if they did not already possess them. According to the *Report* issued by the Inter-American Commission of Women to the 1938 Eighth International Conference of American States held in Lima, Peru, great strides had been made to promote the rights of women in Latin America. In five years ten countries had ratified the Convention on the Nationality of Women, and six adhered to the Convention on Nationality. In contrast, the weaker Hague Convention on Nationality, signed in 1930 by delegates of thirty-one of the forty-eight countries represented, had been ratified only by eleven countries, one of them Latin American (Brazil). The Inter-American Commission of Women proudly commented: "It will be seen that the greatest advance in this hemisphere has been made in the mother's right to transmit her nationality to her legitimate child. . . . The Commission rejoices to be able to report to you that now 15 American Republics of the 21 members of the Pan American Union guarantee to the mother as well as to the father this right over the legitimate child."[25]

In Argentina great improvements in the status of women had been made before the 1933 Conventions were signed. In 1926 a major revision of the nation's Civil Code had eliminated almost all the restrictions of married women found in earlier codes that had been in direct contravention to the 1853 Constitution. Thus, even though Argentina had not ratified the Conventions, its laws were the models praised by the Inter-American Commission of Women.[26]

The League of Nations also took up the issue of female citizenship. In 1935 the Secretary-General proposed that the views of women's international organizations on the status of women be circulated to members of the Assembly since "the questions of nationality and of the status of women had been placed on the agenda of the Assembly." The reports included those of the Alliance of Women for Suffrage and Equal Citizenship, the World's Young Women's Christian Association, the Women's Consultative Committee on Nationality, and Open Door International.[27]

The thirty-seven page report expressed opinions held by international women's organizations on a wide range of topics. From the outset it was obvious that just as it had been difficult to build consensus among men, women were also in disagreement about the merits of absolute equality between men and women. The World's Young Women's Christian Association, for example, opposed an international convention on equal rights because "Such a method cannot take into account the claims of motherhood and of the family nor can it allow for the great variety of social and economic conditions in different countries." The Association was particularly concerned about the prospects of losing existing benefits afforded women if protective labor legislation were enacted.[28]

In contrast the League of Nation's Women's Consultative Committee on Nationality heartily endorsed the Latin American Conventions and argued that the 1930 Hague Nationality Convention be amended to conform to the provisions of the two Montevideo Conventions "to ensure that all future codification of international law undertaken under the auspices of the League shall be free from inequalities based on sex." The Committee concluded its statement by arguing that the legal status of female nationals be considered "only one phase of the whole issue of equality between men and women."[29]

Among the diverse topics covered by the Alliance of Women for Suffrage and Equal Citizenship was the issue of prostitution. It seemed that no international discussion of women's rights could avoid the issue. As the Alliance put it, "In the domain of morals, inequality is universal. There exists to some extent in every country a class of women, the prostitute, who is subject to special laws which make her more or less of an outcast." If they had removed the word "prostitute," it could have been replaced by "married women." The fact that prostitution was mentioned in this context firmly linked the status of married women, political restrictions against female suffrage, and the battle to close down bordellos that registered only women. Together wives and prostitutes formed the objects of a series of prescriptive measures designed to limit the civil rights of women not only outside, but also within the nation.[30]

The linkage between the prostitute and the married woman was again made evident in yet another League of Nations report. In 1939, just as World War II was breaking out, the League's Advisory Committee on Social Questions published its findings on the prospects for rehabilitating prostitutes. The study had been prompted by the success of the League of Nation's campaign to end state-licensed prostitution. Even Argentina had passed a law in 1936 to close down all municipal houses. Once the bordellos closed, however, what happened to their employees? Information regarding rehabilitation practices came in from all over the world. Most reports were discouraging because prostitutes refused to be rehabilitated if the alternative to commercial sex was a life of poorly paid jobs such as domestic labor and laundry work. For that reason, some officials believed, the only way to rehabilitate prostitutes was to marry them off: "There is complete agreement that a happy marriage is the ideal solution and many reports concur in stating that a surprisingly high proportion of the marriages of former prostitutes prove successful."[31]

In the long run, the reluctance of European nations to adhere to the Hague Convention, along with the advent of World War II, did little to assure prostitutes that marriage would bring them greater security and more civil rights. Even after the United Nations took up the cause of female equality in issues of citizenship and civil rights, many countries still refused to adhere to earlier or to subsequent conventions. The strength of patriarchal rights, as well as the unwillingness of countries to grant women equality within marriage, resulted in the inability of any international group to guarantee equal citizenship rights for women in many countries.[32]

For countries like Argentina, however, the debate over married women's citizenship served an important purpose. It enabled a postcolonial nation to rehabilitate its international reputation as a haven for white slavery and transform it into a pioneer in progressive citizenship legislation. Allied with its Latin American neighbors, Argentina and other adherents of the Pan American Union showed more powerful imperialist nations that national identity could be constructed in ways that enabled newly independent nation states to protect their women at home and abroad more effectively than could the empires that originally had conquered and colonized them. In this way Argentina managed to redefine itself from recalcitrant pariah to a vanguard model of married women's rights and modern nationality.

NOTES

1. Floya Anthias and Nira Yuval-Davis, "Introduction," in Yuval-Davis and Anthias, eds., *Women, Nation, State* (London: Macmillan Press, Ltd., 1989), p. 7.

2. Christine Obbo, "Sexuality and Economic Domination in Uganda," in Ibid., p. 85.

3. A comparative analysis of citizenship laws in Europe and Latin America, particularly in regard to female citizenship, can be found in *Encyclopedia Jurídica Omeba* (Buenos Aires: Bibliográfica Omeba, 1964), xx, pp. 36–37.

4. Benedict Anderson, *Imagined Communities: Reflections on the Origin and Spread of Nationalism* (London: Verso, 1983), pp. 15, 52.

5. The history of municipal and national legislation regarding legalized prostitution in Argentina can be found in Donna J. Guy, "White Slavery, Public Health, and the Socialist Position on Legalized Prostitution in Argentina, 1913–1936," *Latin American Research Review*, 23, 3 (1988), pp. 60–80. See also Donna J. Guy, "Public Health, Gender, and Private Morality: Paid Labor and the Formation of the Body Politic in Buenos Aires," *Gender and History*, 2, 3 (1990), pp. 297–317.

6. Dr. Benjamin Dupont, *Pornografía de Buenos Aires. De la necesidad imprescindible de un dispensario de salubridad y de una oficina de costumbres para reglamentar y reprimir la prostitución* (Buenos Aires: Imprenta de Pablo E. Coni, 1879), pp. 12–13. It was fortunate for Dupont that the French anti-white slavery movement was relatively

weak. See Steven C. Hause and Anne R. Kenney, *Women's Suffrage and Social Politics in the French Third Republic* (Princeton: Princeton University Press, 1984), p. 257.

7. Edward J. Bristow, *Vice and Vigilance; Purity Movements in Britain since 1700* (Dublin: Gill and MacMillan; Rowman and Littlefield, 1977), p. 78.

8. Ibid., p. 175.

9. National Vigilance Association, *Fifth Annual Report* (London, 1890), p. 35.

10. League of Nations, *Report of the Special Body of Experts on Traffic in Women and Children,* Two Parts (Geneva, 1927), Part II, Annex IV, pp. 197–98.

11. The story of the Jewish social worker in Buenos Aires can be found in the Jewish Association for the Protection of Girls and Women's report to the National Vigilance Association, December 3, 1934 (NVA Archives, Box 111, File No. 3, Fawcett Library, London Polytechnic University), while the British social worker's story was published in the *Vigilance Record,* 11 (November 1914), p. 82 and 12 (December 1914), p. 86. The organization of the Asociación Nacional Argentina contra la Trata de Blancas can be found in its first report: *Memoria de la "Asociación Nacional contra la Trata de Blancas" correspondiente al ejercicio 1902 a 1903* (Buenos Aires: Tipografía Pablo Gadola, 1904), pp. 3–4. The flyer was found in Great Britain, Public Record Office, FO 371/4477. A more general analysis of these groups can be found in Donna J. Guy, *Sex and Danger in Buenos Aires: Prostitution, Family, and Nation in Argentina* (University of Nebraska Press, forthcoming), chapters 1 and 2.

12. Argentine physicians tended to view women's desire for money as a more important justification for regulated prostitution than an unhealthy desire for men. For an early but cogent opinion see Dr. Carlos Gallarani, "Reglamentación de la prostitución. Fundamentos de esta importante medida de higiene pública. Proyecto adaptable a la ciudad del Rosario (República Arjentina)," *Revista médico-quirúrgica,* 6 (1869–70), p. 271.

13. Fédération Abolitionniste Internationale, *Dixième Congrès tenu a Genève, le 7–11 Septembre 1908* (Geneva: Secretariat Générale de la Fédération, 1909), pp. 264–65.

14. Jewish Association for the Protection of Girls and Women, *Report of the Secretary on his Visit to South America, 1919* (Oxford: Privately Printed, 1913), pp. 1–2, 14–15.

15. *Vigilance Record*, May 1921, p. 38.

16. Speech of Dr. Paulina Luisi, *Report of the Sixth International Congress for the Suppression of Traffic in Women and Children held in Graz (Austria)* (Graz, 1924), pp. 108–11.

17. *Report of the Seventh International Congress for the Suppression of Traffic in Women and Children* (London, 1927), pp. 36–37.

18. "Extent of the Enquiry," League of Nations, *Report of the Special Body of Experts on Traffic in Women and Children*, 2 Parts (1927), I: 6.

19. Ibid., Annex I. List of Countries and Towns in Which Enquiry was Conducted and Time Spent by Investigators in Observing Traffic Conditions, II: 195; I: 11. The Argentine report can be found in II: 11–18.

20. Statement from the International Alliance of Women for Suffrage and Equal Citizenship, League of Nations, *Nationality and Status of Women; Statements Presented by Women's Organizations* (Geneva, 1935), p. 2.

21. Ibid., p. 3; Part I, Article 14, Argentine Constitution of 1853, including reforms of September 23, 1860. Arturo Enrique Sampay, compiler, *Las constituciones de la Argentina (1810–1972)* (Buenos Aires: EUDEBA, 1975); Law No. 346, Ley de Ciudadanía, October 1, 1866, found in Argentine Republic, Cámara de Diputados, *Diario de Sesiones*, 1869, pp. 478–79.

22. League of Nations, *Nationality and Status of Women; Statements Presented by International Women's Organizations*, p. 4.

23. Francesca Miller has examined the role of Pan American Scientific Conferences in organizing Latin American feminists for the 1928 International Conference of American States; see her "The International Relations of Women of the Americas 1890–1928," *The Americas*, 43, 2 (October 1986), pp. 171–81.

24. Seventh International Conference of American States, *Final Act Including the Conventions and Additional Protocol Adopted by the Conference* (Uruguay: J. Florensa, Impresor, 1933).

25. *Report of the Inter-American Commission of Women to the Eighth International Conference of American States on the Political and Civil Rights of Women* (Lima, 1938), pp. 85–87.

26. Ibid., p. 98.

27. League of Nations, *Nationality and Status of Women; Statements Presented by International Women's Organizations*, p. 2.

28. Ibid., p. 10.

29. Ibid., p. 15.

30. Ibid., p. 8.

31. League of Nations, *Advisory Committee on Social Questions; Enquiry into Measures of Rehabilitation of Prostitutes*, 2 Vols. (Geneva, 1939), II: 112.

32. "National Ratification of Selected International Conventions on the Rights of Women," in Ruth Leger Sivard, *Women—A World Survey* (Washington, DC: World Priorities, 1985), pp. 30–31.

Chapter 11

From Nation to Family: Containing "African AIDS"

Cindy Patton

Current AIDS-control efforts have invented a heterosexual "African AIDS" that promotes a new kind of colonial domination by reconstructing Africa as an uncharted, supranational mass. Whatever the overt concerns of international health workers for containing AIDS in (within?) the continent, their construal of "Africa" as the margin of economic/cultural "development" and as the "heart" of the AIDS epidemic helps to stabilize a Euro-America adrift in a postmodern condition of lost metanarratives and occluded origins. As a totalizing grand history of nations has given way to a transcendent account of chance intersections of germs and bodies, the map of the postcolonial world has now been redrawn as a graph of epidemiologic strike rates. Because international AIDS policy has discouraged or overlooked serious attempts to prevent HIV transmission through health education, community organizing, and improved bloodbanking, this new Africa-with-no-borders functions as a giant agar plate, etched by the "natural history" of the AIDS epidemic.[1]

The very labelling of "African AIDS" as a heterosexual disease quiets the

Western fear that heterosexual men will need to alter their own sexual practices and identity. If the proximate (homosexual) AIDS allows such men to ignore their local complicity in "dangerous" practices that lead to the infection of ("their") women, then a distant "African AIDS," by correlating heterosexual danger with Otherness/thereness, performs the final expiative act for a Western heterosexual masculinity that refuses all containment. Erased in this process are the colonially inscribed borders of sub-Saharan countries while new borders are drawn between the "African family" and a "modernizing society" populated by "single people" who have been dying at an appalling rate throughout the epidemic. The nation, once the colonial administrative unit *par excellence*, has been replaced in the minds of healthworkers with (an image of) the bourgeois family, thereby constituting what had never truly existed before in Africa as the only defense against modernization and its "diseases." In what follows I explore some of the implications of this movement from nation to family as the preferred prophylaxis in the catastrophe of "African AIDS."

MAPPING "AFRICAN AIDS"

Accompanying a recent *New York Times* article "AIDS in Africa: A Killer Rages On" (whose headline continues "AIDS Is Spreading Rapidly and Ominously Throughout Africa") is a nearly full page chart, "AIDS in Africa: An Atlas of Spreading Tragedy."[2] These headlines displace responsibility for the epidemic—who exactly is this killer? what is the tragedy?—and elide the disease's biological mechanics in exploiting its symbolic resonances. The article's spatialization of AIDS in its accompanying map of the continent simultaneously locates countries and underscores the irrelevance of their borders: in *this* Africa, disease transcends nation. Replacing what had been colonialism's heart of darkness is the calculated horror of a new interior density, represented on the map by dark-to-light shadings corresponding to HIV attack rates. The "AIDS belt" supposed to exist in central Africa is depicted here not only as the "heart" of the regional epidemic but as the imagined origin of the entire global pandemic. Yet the "evidence" employed by the map reveals the duplicities of Western discourse about AIDS in Africa: seroprevalence rates for the continent are concocted from sensationalist media accounts of specific locations and from the records of epidemiologists working from strictly limited samples (often as few as 100 people) of pregnant women, prostitutes, and clients with sexually-transmitted diseases. When not enough AIDS is found, it needs to be imagined, as the key to the *Times*' map suggests:

> The shadings on this map indicate the percentage of sexually active adults believed to be infected with the AIDS virus in major urban areas. Rural rates tend to be much lower. The numbers are based on the latest available data, which may understate current rates. Blank spots do not necessarily mean an absence of AIDS.

Despite its disclaimers about "missing data," there are in fact no "blank spots" on the map; the *Times* fills in the *entire* surface, lumping together countries with "infection rates less than 5 percent" with those for which "data [is] not available." Although we are told that high attack rates (of HIV, which is consistently conflated here with AIDS) are characteristic only of urban areas, whole countries are shaded to indicate "At least 5 percent to 10 percent," "At least 10 percent to 20 percent," and "At least 20 percent." The curious use of the non-exclusive "at least" for the increasingly darker/denser shadings suggests that errors in data will always underestimate "AIDS" for a country. But the note on "sources" at the bottom of the map gives us a clearer indication of the accuracy of the epidemiologic data from which the map is derived:

> Surveys of subgroups are useful but must be interpreted with caution. Urban infection rates cannot be extrapolated to rural areas. Rates among prostitutes, soldiers, hospital patients and patients at clinics for sexually transmitted diseases tend to be far higher than in the population at large. Blood donor figures may overstate prevalence if donors are recruited among high risk groups or understate it if efforts are made to avoid high-risk donors. Often, surveys of pregnant women visiting prenatal clinics are considered the best indicator of infection among the adult population.

In this brief summary of data offered for the twenty-four countries which appear to have data (this leaves as "blank spots" another twenty-nine, which include some of the continent's largest[3]), the *Times* acknowledges that seroprevalence studies vary from nation to nation, but all of these studies have been used indiscriminately to present the worst case scenario within any given country.

While HIV is certainly an important African health concern, seroprevalence rates are rising *everywhere* and not just in African locales. The *Times*, however, suggests no reason for singling out Africa as exceptional and offers no comparative data on rates in Euro-American or other global regions (Asia, the Pacific Rim, Eastern Europe, Central and South America, and the Caribbean are the real "blank spots" on the *Times*' map). The article's one comparison to the U.S. serves to inscribe "their AIDS" as heterosexual in comparison with "our AIDS":

> In contrast with the pattern in the United States, AIDS in Africa is spreading mainly through heterosexual intercourse, propelled by long-neglected epi-

> demics of venereal disease that facilitates viral transmission. . . . In the United States, gay men and residents of a few inner-city pockets face comparable devastation, but over all, fewer than 1 percent of adults are believed to be infected with the AIDS virus.

"Inner-city pockets" is of course a reference to poor people of color, the internal blank spot of the U.S. If the horror of the American crisis is the confrontation (of white heterosexuals) with both homosexuality and the feared black underclass, the tragedy in Africa seems rather more unthinkable: "Strange new issues are in the air. Where the disease spread earliest and large numbers have already died, as in Uganda, frightened young men and women are starting to realize that even marriage may be risky."

If AIDS has been thought to sail or jet[4] between the Euro-American countries, it is represented by the *Times* as travelling by truck throughout Africa. An insert showing trucks on a dusty road and entitled "Dangerous Traffic" tells us that:

> The highways of East and Central Africa, such as this one west of Kampala, Uganda, have been major conduits for AIDS. A study in Kenya of 317 truck drivers of varied nationalities found that three-fourths frequently visited prostitutes but that only 30% ever used condoms. One in four was infected with HIV. In 1986, 35% of drivers studied in Kampala were infected. Most prostitutes and barmaids along trucking routes are infected.

While the direction of infection is obscured here (truck drivers to prostitutes or prostitutes to truck drivers?), the conflation of truckers with their penises and of roads with vaginas is abundantly clear. If truck drivers "unloading" their "dangerous cargo" is a more compelling trope than the usual evocation of urban prostitutes spewing germs to hapless clients, this is because the spread of AIDS in Africa is itself hardly unrelated to the spread of "modernization."

INVENTING AFRICAN AIDS

By 1986, Western media and scientists worldwide had created the linguistic distinction between "AIDS" and "African AIDS" that makes the *Time*'s map readable. These designations are informal names for the more technical World Health Organization terms, Pattern One and Pattern Two. Pattern One describes epidemiologic scenarios where "homosexual behavior" and "drug injection" are considered the primary means of HIV transmission. Because Pattern One (or, as the unmarked category, simply "AIDS") is coded racially as "white," African-American communities—where homosexuality is presumed to be absent—are now said to exhibit features of Pattern Two ("African AIDS"). Pattern Two indicates places where transmission is held to be "almost exclusively heterosexual."[5] Synonymous with "African AIDS," Pattern Two is a linguistic construction confusing an epidemiologic description (however unuseful) with an emerging "history" of the epidemic. The Caribbean has "African AIDS" but Latin America has "AIDS," an unprecedented if barely conscious recognition of indigenous homosexualities. A third category, Pattern Three, recognizes the emergence of "heterosexual" AIDS outside Euro-America and Africa in places where HIV arrived "late" and largely through postcolonial sex tourism and international bloodbanking.

The "history" of the epidemic reflected in these categories inverts the crucial epidemiologic issues. Rather than asking how HIV moved from the Pattern One countries (where AIDS was diagnosed first by epidemiologists' accounts) to the Pattern Two countries, the scientifically endorsed history of AIDS shows HIV originating in Africa and then moving to North America.[6] The scientific distinction between AIDS/gay/white/Euro-American and African AIDS/heterosexual/black/African/U.S.-inner-city neatly fails to inquire how HIV travelled from the bodies of U.S. homosexual men into the bodies of "Africans" a continent and ocean away, or how "African AIDS" then returned to diasporal African communities in the U.S. The blank spot within the Euro-American mind makes it far easier to imagine an alternative causal chain running from monkeys to Africans to queers than to recall the simple fact that the West exports huge quantities of unscreened blood to its Third World client states (much less acknowledge that black and white Americans have sex—gay as well as straight—and share needles with each other).

This difference between Patterns One and Two thus helps white, Euro-American heterosexuals evade the idea that they might themselves be vulnerable since African (and African-American) heterosexuality is so evidently different than Euro-American. Euro-American heterosexuality is "not at risk" as long as local AIDS is identified as homosexual and heterosexual AIDS remains distant. This projected difference of African heterosexuality and the asserted absence of African homosexuality[7] continue to drive not only the forms of epidemiologic research (for example, researchers have been more interested in finding bizarre and distinctive "African" sexual practices[8] than in documenting transfusion-related cases) but also the forms of educational intervention whose focus in Africa is almost exclusively on promoting monogamy or, in more "sensitive" campaigns, "stable polygamy."

My earlier work on "African AIDS" investigated how Western scientific representations of the national and sexual cultures of postcolonial Africa direct the international AIDS research agenda. Reading conference documents and media reports on "AIDS in Africa," I marked the links between apparently innocuous or obviously fantastic assumptions made about Africa(ns) within Western discourse and the conduct and direction of Western science. In particular, I showed how the persistent Western description of Africa as a "catastrophe" and as "heterosexual" justified as altruistic genocidal Western practices and policies toward their client-state "Others."

Because "African AIDS" is simultaneously "different" and "similar," conflicts in Western AIDS discourse, ethics, and medical research can be rationalized by drawing upon research undertaken throughout the continent. For example, while data from African clinics convinces Westerners that heterosexual transmission is possible (because all intercourse is the same), this same data is also read as suggesting that widespread transmission among heterosexuals is not likely enough to require the universal adoption of the condom (because Africans engage in other exotic sexual practices and polygamy).[9] Diagnosis of AIDS in Africa is said to be unreliable because medical facilities are alleged to be poor; this licenses demographers to multiply known cases by exorbitant factors in order to obtain a "true" (i.e., catastrophic) picture of AIDS in "Africa." But "African" diagnosis becomes a problem (and for epidemiologists rather than clinicians) only because the definition of AIDS is derived from the U.S. experience of largely well-cared-for middle-class men who become inexplicably weak and unable to fight common illness. The fall from "previous health" is not a feasible diagnostic distinction in countries (or among U.S. women or those living in the inner city, for that matter) where people have received little health care or where infectious diseases and nutritional deficiencies make it difficult to distinguish between clinical AIDS and malaria, anaemia, tuberculosis, etc.

An important note on the terms I've employed here: in Western discourse, Africa, a continent of roughly eleven and a half million square miles and fifty-three countries, is treated as a homogeneous sociopolitical block. Yet this supposedly "unknown" continent—unknown, that is, to its pale neighbors to the north—is in fact far more culturally, linguistically, religiously, and socially diverse than North America and Europe. Collapsing the many cultures residing on the continent into "Africa" is an act of political and cultural violence. In order to complicate "Africa" as a Western construction, I employ the equivalent constructions "North American" and "Euro-America" to indicate the collection of relatively homogeneous northern administrative states as we appear to our southern neighbors. The resultant vagueness Euro-Americans will experience in this strategy should be read back from the "Other" point of view: "North Americans" in particular should consider their own discomfort at having their cultural space discursively reduced in this way.

But this is not the only critical reduction occurring in Western discourse about Africa: as a term, "Africa" can mean both the land mass and its people precisely because the people of Africa have been considered to be coextensive with the continent, a conflation I evoke through the shorthand "Africa(ns)." This conflation has been eloquently described by Frantz Fanon: what is done to the "African body," especially woman's body, is a metaphor for what is to be done to the continent, and visa versa.[10]

IMPLODING BORDERS

The flattening out of the racial, ethnic, and cultural diversity of non-European-descended Africans into a singular autochthonous people performed an important function during the era of colonialism. Carving up the land was not sufficient; a narrative reconstruction of Africa's "uncivilized" prehistory was necessary to justify the colonial presence. The colonial taxonomist's "racial" distributions—"semites," "hamites," "negroes," "nilotes," "half-hamites," "bantus," "khoisans," not to mention "Italians" and peoples of the Asian subcontinent ("Indian," another site of colonialist reduction through arbitrary racial taxonomic schemes)—mapped an Africa prior to colonial border construction in order to deny the social orders and political/cultural groups of *people* ("Zulus," "Sabaeans," "Berbers," "Ibos," etc.) who lived, intermarried, fought battles, and traded culture and religion with one another before the incursion of Europeans. These are peoples whose racial and sexual histories seemed always to defy the new administrative borders, but the Europeans still insisted that "natives" must be placed somewhere—spatialized—and organized properly through sexual and genealogical successions—temporalized.

Such a displacement of the political and social onto the sexual and racial has returned today, with similarly self-justificatory motives, as the narrative logic underwriting Western accounts of AIDS among the peoples of Africa. Again, spatial demarcation and temporal sequence organize historical narrative. In obvious ways ("AIDS began in Africa"), insidious ways ("AIDS 'jumped species' from green monkeys to 'African' humans"), and subtle ways (persistent descriptions of truck drivers, miners, "prostitutes," and soldiers traversing the continent), the Euro-American story of "African AIDS" concerns not only racial difference but also territory transected and borders gone out of control. But rather than continuing to adduce African "backwardness" as an excuse for colonial plunder, AIDS epidemiology offers "African sexuality" as a rationale for unethical experimentation and unwillingness to pursue education and community organizing projects that could decrease transmission of HIV. No longer content to carve up a massified Africa into "proper" nations, AIDS media reportage offers a view of African sexuality—alternately described as traditional (polygamy) or condemned as modern (rural-urban social breakdown resulting in "prostitution")—which now requires rapid reorganization into bourgeois families.

This is the side of "African AIDS" I wish to take up here: "containment" through the promotion of racist and heterophobic conceptions of "safe sex." Reading the *Times*' map alongside the new pamphlet series "Strategies for Hope," collaboratively produced by British international relief organizations and two African national AIDS committees,[11] I want to show how "self-help" manuals for use in Anglophone communities in Africa recall previous border constructions in seeking to promote as "safe sex" a bourgeois "African family" that has never in fact existed.

STRATEGIES FOR HOPE

With an international recession underway, the only capital-intensive educational projects possible in poor countries are collaborative ones with (largely) European international relief organizations. The set of concepts underlying "African AIDS" have become so naturalized today that such projects must rewrite local experience to conform to the internationally adopted narrative. The Euro-American fascination with a "different" African sexuality can routinely be glimpsed in epidemiologic studies and newspaper accounts (witness this sidebar to the *Times* article discussed previously):

> Studies in the United States show that transmission of the AIDS virus during vaginal intercourse is usually quite difficult, especially from female to male. But research in Africa has revealed conditions that multiply the danger. . . . One is the rampant extent of sexually transmitted diseases . . . above all, chancroid, which causes festering ulcers. . . . A second major factor . . . is the lack of male circumcision in much of Africa. . . . Researchers are just now turning attention to little-known sexual practices that might also raise transmission odds. . . . In parts of Central Africa . . . women engage in a practice know as "dry sex." In variations of the practice, designed to increase friction during intercourse, women use herbs, chemical powders, stones or cloth in the vagina to reduce lubrication and cause swelling. . . . Promiscuity helps drive the epidemic. While data do not exist for comparing sexual behavior on different continents, surveys do show that extramarital sex is commonplace in Africa.

The Western imaginary runs wild in these few lines: the easy slide between the gaping vagina and the gaping hole that, on the map, is the "heart" of African AIDS; the undisguised preoccupation with the shape and size of African penises; the assertion of a relative promiscuity which even the author admits has no data to support it; the conflation of "extramarital" and "promiscuous"—all of these together form a shorthand litany of the "difference" of African sexuality. Such accounts, however, are not limited to the Western media but can be discovered in educational materials designed specifically for "African" use. The following is taken from the "Strategies for Hope" pamphlet series:

> HIV infection in Africa is spread primarily by *heterosexual intercourse.* It affects sexually active men and women in equal numbers, rather than subgroups of the population such as male homosexuals or intravenous drug users. (Homosexuality and intravenous drug use are rare in Africa.) High-risk sexual behavior therefore consists of sexual intercourse with more than one partner. (Pamphlet 1, 3)

The claim in the colonial voice-over to this ostensibly "local" pamphlet that "African" homosexuality is rare is extraordinarily duplicitous. Indeed, same-sex affective and domestic relations were not at all unusual in many precolonial cultures. When colonial and especially British administrators arrived, they were distressed by these relationships which often played key roles in the distribution of goods and the maintenance of lineages. Colonial law grouped these disparate practices together under one name, "homosexuality," which it pronounced uncivilized and banned by law. Thus contemporary denials by African leaders of the category "homosexuality" are as often a refusal of the European notion of static homosexual identity as they are a denial of same-sex affective and domestic relations. Neo-colonialists now can denigrate homosexuality as a Western import and thereby gain increased control over indigenous economic and social relations by tightening control over the remaining cross-sex relations.[12]

In the context of the reigning transnational distinctions between "AIDS" and "African AIDS," (bad) individuals are routinely figured against (good) families, a strategy that both denies the existence of Euro-American gay people's social networks and excommunicates them from their blood relatives. The language employed in the pamphlets—"HIV infection in Africa is primarily a *family disease,* rather than a disease affecting mainly single people" (Pamphlet 1, 3; emphasis in original)—begins to reveal what is at stake. The homophobic Section 28 in Britain (similar to the Helms Amendments in the U.S.) was not content to refuse government funding to projects that "promote homosexuality" but also derided "pretend families." The unit to be sanctioned and protected is thus the statistical minority, the bourgeois family—white, heterosexual, mother and father, small number of children. The logo for the 1987 International AIDS Conference in Stockholm proposed a similarly compacted description of the AIDS epidemic: here was a stylized (and nude) mother and father, each holding a hand of the small child who stood between them. To the Western mind, AIDS is most importantly a threat to the family, and a double one—not simply the threat of an entire family being infected, but also the threat of growing numbers of single people challenging the supremacy of the family unit.

Besides "African AIDS," the only other media image of a "family with AIDS" that has received wide attention focuses on the hemophiliac, the less celebrated Other whose "feminine" bleeding shores up heterosexual masculinity. The October 1988 *Scientific American,* a special issue entitled "What Science Knows About AIDS," presents a full-page picture of a white, North American family (the Burkes, who were outspoken advocates for the rights of people with HIV). We are told that the father is a hemophiliac who "infected" his wife before he knew he was himself infected, and she in turn gave birth to an infected son. Even as the Burkes' membership in a community of blood-product users is completely elided in the magazine's account, this apparently isolated family encodes the story of the tragic innocence of those who lack knowledge, pitted against those who do or should have had it (gay men and drug users are said to infect "knowingly" or recklessly). Though the article's passive constructions describing how wife and son "became infected" minimize the heterosexual component of the "Burke's AIDS," the fact of the matter is that, throughout this account, Mr. Burke's hemophilia has itself been sufficient to undercut his masculine identity. We have a glimpse here of the power of heterosexual culture's own heterophobia: the horror of this North American "family with AIDS" is that the unit was actually engaging in the identity-bestowing activities of a small, well-disciplined family.

The African family's purported problem is its similar inability to construct itself properly as a small, well-disciplined unit. Oddly enough, the families (that is, everyone defined as "not an individual") in the "Strategies for Hope" pamphlets are comprised of multiple adults, not just "polygamous" units but "sisters" who "often visited the nearby rural bar, where they sold chicken . . . and sexual favours" (Pamphlet 1, 19). Like homosexuality, the Euro-American category of "the prostitute"—an individual with a professional identity as a sex worker—is seen as distinct from those who engage in the traditional practice of "selling favors." Located outside the confines of the family proper, "prostitutes" are singled out by the media to bolster support for "family values" and by epidemiologists to mark the historical progress of HIV through a country or city. Such "prostitutes" are said to have "Western" AIDS since they are constructed as "single people"; they are not as recuperable into families as are the women who seem to mimic traditional female roles by selling chicken and sexual favors. In the "Strategies for Hope" series, the various extramarital and nonmarital sexual relations that have resulted in "family AIDS" (as represented in the thirteen "true story" inserts in the pamphlets) are considered, in contrast, to form part of "family life." The issue, it becomes clear, is not sex per se but the failure to organize it within the disciplined borders of the bourgeois family.

The pamphlets invoke a nostalgia for a less urban Africa in which "traditional family values" once prevailed—and this despite the reality that polygamy and age-specific sexual experimentation were the dominant organizational strategies in the many different cultural strands of this "tradition." In a gesture remarkably like Thatcher's privatization and Reagan's New Altruism, the pamphlets posit the family as the idealized site for support, care, and education: "Even in urban communities the family retains much of its cohesive power, although weakened to some extent by the spread of 'modern' attitudes and values" (Pamphlet 3, 3). Instead of noticing how this conception of the family-as-primary-political-unit disempowers both women and the community, this odd *recto-verso* history of the rise of the bourgeois family in Africa secures as "traditional" the mother-father-child unit by conflating the image of the single urban person ("prostitute" and perhaps migrant workers and truck drivers) with the image of "the modern." But what, after all, could be more modern than the bourgeois family?

Legible throughout the pamphlets is the heterophobic dread of the condom. The litany that "Africans won't use condoms," which formed a crucial part of Western rationalizations for pursuing vaccine trials,[13] is repeated under the guise of "cultural sensitivity" in this Christian missionary/British neo-colonial collaboration:

> *Sexual attitudes and habits* are different from those of industrialized countries. Resistance to the idea of using condoms is widespread, especially among men. Many years of intensive health education and attitude-forming would be required to achieve sustained attitudinal and behavioral change in this area.
>
> Condoms do have a significant—but limited—role in AIDS control in Africa, but promoting the use of condoms is a diversion from the central issue of *sexual behavior*. The practice of having multiple sexual partners is the main causal factor in the transmission of HIV in Africa. Promoting the use of condoms does not address this issue. It advocates a technical solution to a problem which can be addressed only through fundamental changes in social attitudes, values and behavior. (Pamphlet 3, 21)[14]

Such distinctions are of course completely ludicrous—Euro-American heterosexual men seem no less resistent to condom use than African men; condom use and sexual behavior are scarcely two separable matters; the spatial dispersions invoked in the image of HIV infected truck drivers and wandering prostitutes are only slightly more imaginative than the idea of mobile yuppies with bicoastal lifestyles transporting HIV around the U.S. or, as Pattern Three implicitly suggests, around the world. The crucial point here is that bourgeois family units in Africa—understood, from the outset, to be free of infection—must not rely upon condom use to prevent infection, for how otherwise could they succeed in reproducing themselves? Conversely, since those outside the family must be prevented from reproducing, it is they alone who must be urged to use condoms. The already-infected persons, especially women, in their haphazard, defamilialized units are thus to be "eliminated" in a kind of final prophylactic solution. Advocated only for "people already infected with HIV or those who engage in recognizably high-risk sexual behaviour" (such as sex with "prostitutes"), condoms "reduce but *do not eliminate the risk of transmission*" (Pamphlet 3, 21). "Elimination" of transmission slides easily into elimination of persons: what is implicit here is a brave new world of monogamous or faithful polygamous relationships[15] that will rise from the ashes of the "modernization" which, in its destruction of "traditional values," becomes the "cause" of AIDS.

If any doubts remain about the nature of the pamphlet series, its descriptions of AIDS counselling make it clear that the "cure" for AIDS in Africa lies in the proliferation of bourgeois families. "Communication" is repeatedly proscribed for counsellors and families. Although noting that other social support networks continue to exist (though always fractured by "modernization"), the pamphlets urge one-on-one, paraprofessional counselling to replace functioning social relations involving grandmothers, cousins, or jokesters who teach about sexuality. In the abstract, such programs seem desirable in a crisis setting, but their longer-term effect is to destroy existing social relations while promoting disciplining interventions from the local clinic.

The TASO project of Uganda (Pamphlet 2) follows precisely from this model of the reconstructed bourgeois family and describes how the transition "back" to the family and the "elimination" of the already-infected will be managed. I do not want to undercut the important work of TASO, modelled on the grassroots "self-help" (though largely gay male) people-living-with-AIDS movement in the West.[16] Instead, I want to underline what is presented here as "appropriate" AIDS work. While this organization has been enormously helpful, it is crucial to realize that the conception of "self-help" as employed in its project is as culture-bound as the idea of the bourgeois family. *Self*-help arises only in the context of already existing (or already denied) *state*-mediated services, hence the emphasis on "self-" rather than on community mobilization. Not surprisingly, most of the TASO clients whose stories appear in this pamphlet are men who are themselves both counsellors and clients of the five-year-old organization. These stories suggest in effect that the organization has become a kind of surrogate family; indeed, a client named Gilbert has moved to a house near the TASO office where he now works part time, so that he "can see a lot more of his children. . . . As a father I feel much closer to my children" (Pamphlet 2, 24). These transitional family units, "victims" of the modernization which permitted the disease of Western single people to invade the African family, are presented as evidence for the "safeness" of bourgeois families to come. Though never specifically addressed in the pamphlet, the paradigmatic act that defines the bourgeois family—regulated heterosexual intercourse—is itself to be protected from the condom. In one sweep, the pamphlet's refusal to promote universal condom use paves the way for the virtual genocide of anyone outside the chastity-before-marriage-monogamous-couple and enables Euro-American epidemiologists to name the "difference" constitutive of "African AIDS." *If only they'd had proper families.*[17]

African social patterns once were deemed unnatural or hypernatural (uncivilized) by the West, but African sex is still considered profoundly natural, too close to the body and its supposedly prediscursive desires to be able to accommodate the inhibiting condom. Having failed to demonstrate anatomical, behavioral, or even sociomedical differences between Euro-American and African sex acts, international AIDS workers now conclude that intercourse itself must ultimately be declared safe, and the "risk" situated in its practice outside the legitimate borders of the bourgeois family. Those who cannot be contained within this family will be simply left to die, but such an outcome will be rapid because "African AIDS" seems inexplicably to move faster than "AIDS" (largely because the Western drug companies cannot make any money there). "Africa" is thus once more experiencing border constructions that mask state-sponsored genocide as indigenous social and cultural formations are elided in the interests of a brave new world of disease-free—and controllable—bourgeois family units.

NOTES

This essay differs in its focus from the version given at the Nationalisms and Sexualities Conference, a version which has already appeared at several stages and in different forms: "Inventing African AIDS," *City Limits* [London], 363 (September 1988); "Inventing African AIDS," *New Formations*, 10 (Spring 1990); and "Inventing African AIDS," in my *Inventing AIDS* (New York: Routledge, 1990). I am indebted to Erica Carter who spent a good deal of time preparing the latter two manuscripts, and to Andrew Parker who helped with this new version. I am grateful as well to Eve Kosofsky Sedgwick for hosting a symposium on this topic at Duke University in September 1989.

For related analyses see especially Paula A. Treichler, "AIDS and HIV Infection in the Third World: A First World Chronicle," in Barbara Kruger and Phil Mariani, eds., *Remaking History* (Seattle: Bay Press, 1989); Treichler, "AIDS, Africa, and Cultural Theory," *Transition*, 51 (1991); and Simon Watney, "Missionary Positions," *Critical Quarterly*, 30, 1 (Autumn 1989).

1. "Natural history" is the term employed within epidemiology to describe the development of a disease, epidemic, or pandemic if left to run its course. The desire to learn the natural history of HIV/AIDS has resulted in debates, for example, about whether the few remaining long-time infected but asymptomatic men in a San Francisco "natural history" cohort should now "be allowed" to take prophylactic AZT or pentamidine, two of the most widely accepted life-prolonging drugs. Researchers in Africa have expressed a similar wish to allow existing conditions to continue to "see what happens." In one study of the effectiveness of contraceptive sponges for interrupting HIV transmission, researchers gave half of the targeted women (who were sex workers) placebos—in essence a wad of cotton. Despite early data suggesting that both groups in the study were becoming infected at a rapid rate, the experiment continued for three years until "statistically-sound samplings" were obtained. Tragically, the same research data showed that sex workers in an adjoining district had been able to get many of their male clients to use condoms, thereby decreasing not only HIV transmission in these women but other sexually-transmitted diseases overall. For more on such experiments see my *Inventing AIDS*.

2. *New York Times*, September 16, 1990, pp. 1, 14. The map and accompanying article, "What Makes the 2 Sexes So Vulnerable To Epidemic," appear on p. 15.

3. Specific information is given for: "Most Severely Affected" —Malawi, Rwanda, Uganda, Zambia; "Urban Rate 10% to 20%"—Burundi, Ivory Coast, Tanzania, Zimbabwe, Central African Republic, Congo, Guinea Bissau, Kenya, and Zaire (Rwanda has the same percentages but is placed in the "Most Severely Affected" category apparently because of a single study showing a 30% rate of seroprevalence in a cohort of pregnant women in the capital city); and "Ominous Signs"—Angola, Burkina Faso, Mali, Ethiopia, Ghana, Namibia, Nigeria, Senegal, Sierra Leone, South Africa, and Sudan.

4. I am alluding here to the highly publicized accounts which suggest (based on fantasy) that either Tall Ships sailors who toured the world in 1976 or "Patient Zero," a steward on Air Canada in the early 1980s, brought AIDS to the U.S. See Randy Shilts, *And the Band Played On* (New York: St. Martin's Press, 1987).

5. This assumption of heterosexuality seems to be based only on the simple statistical fact that the male to female ratio in Africa as a whole is about 1:1. Scientists

have been slow to recognize, however, that the number of women who receive transfusions (and thus the transfusion-related HIV infection) has been grossly underestimated. Since it is standard medical practice throughout much of Africa to give whole blood transfusion for malarial, nutritional, or maternal anaemia, scientists have consistently conflated pregnancy with transfusions as "risk" factors. See Alan Fleming, "Prevention of Transmission of HIV by Blood Transfusion in Developing Countries," Global Impact of AIDS Conference (London, March 8–10, 1988).

6. A scientist of the stature of Luc Montaigne has persistently maintained, despite contrary epidemiologic data, that "AIDS" started in "Africa." His claim is based on the genetic similarity of a simian immunodeficiency virus found in monkeys. This insistence is an updating of racist evolutionary theory, only in place of the old missing link between apes and homo sapiens, the new missing link connects monkeys with North Americans. By a clever sleight of hand, the AIDS-came-from-Africa theory first situates the virus as more or less dormant in Africa and then transports it to Europe and/or America, where it rapidly disseminates. At the same time, so this theory runs, a variant of the virus suddenly proliferates in Africa (urbanization is cited as an explanation—but this process was already well underway before the onset of the epidemic).

7. I remain perplexed by Westerners' insistence that there is no homosexuality in Africa—after all, it would have been much simpler to lay AIDS at the door of a single "perversion." Yet Western homosexual panic works overtime in AIDS discourse: homosexuality is more controllable if it can be retained as a category of Western bourgeois culture. To acknowledge other homosexualities would implicitly challenge Western notions that homosexuality is a symptom of cultural decadence, even if "primitive" homosexualities can be written off on that basis. But such panic also enables the denial of miscegenation through the denial of cross-race homosexual congress. This is nowhere clearer than in South African AIDS discourse, where both "white (homosexual)" AIDS and "black (heterosexual)" AIDS are said to exist. Well into the 1980s, South African commentators would wryly note that apartheid may have "saved" South African blacks from AIDS. Studies of male relations in the mines, conducted as gay history, were appropriated as "proof" of the effectiveness of sexual apartheid (perhaps the least violent but most fundamental aspect of racial separation): black miners, it was argued, did not acquire AIDS while in the male-only dormitories since they had "intercourse" only with their female partners.

8. The persistent effort to establish an African heterosexual "difference" began with allegations that Africans favored anal intercourse because it is, as many media reports called it, "a primitive form of birth control." This assumed that HIV transmission was paradigmatically sodomitic; the handful of Army cases in which men alleged that they had been infected by prostitutes also rested on this idea since, as one researcher

told me, "their wives wouldn't do it (permit anal intercourse)." Sadly, for the Western sexual imagination, epidemiologists failed to find higher rates of anal intercourse, or any other exotic practice, to explain differences between "African" and "Euro-American" heterosexual practice. But researchers and journalists are still searching, as can be seen in a passage from the *Times* on "dry sex" that I discuss below. Who knows what lurks in the Euro-American male imaginary here—"African" penises smaller than fantasized? "African" vaginas even larger than feared?

9. See, for example, Robert E. Gould, "Reassuring News About AIDS: A Doctor Tells Why *You* May Not Be at Risk," *Cosmopolitan* (January 1988), p. 147: "The data I gathered concerning heterosexual intercourse in Africa show marked differences from the way it is usually practiced in the United States."

10. See especially Frantz Fanon, "Unveiling Algeria," in *A Dying Colonialism* (New York: Monthly Review Press, 1965). I am also indebted here to Kirstin McDougall, whose unpublished manuscript on maternal metaphors in AIDS discourse confirms that such slippage occurs not only in Western and but also in Anglophone African media.

11. The three "Strategies for Hope" pamphlets, published jointly by ACTIONAID in London, the African Medical and Research Foundation in Nairobi, and World in Need in Colchester (U.K.), are now distributed widely by the World Health Organization Global Program on AIDS. The series includes two pamphlets about Zambia and one about Uganda; these have been reviewed, respectively, by the National AIDS Surveillance Committee of Zambia and the National AIDS Control Programme of Uganda. Pamphlet One is entitled *From Fear to Hope: AIDS Care and Prevention at Chikankata Hospital, Zambia*, authored by U.K.-based Glen Williams, who is also the series editor. Pamphlet Two, by U.K.-based Janie Hampton, is called *Living Positively with AIDS: The AIDS Support Organisation (TASO), Uganda*. The third pamphlet is *AIDS Management: An Integrated Approach*, by Williams and Capt. (Dr.) Ian D. Campbell, Chief Medical Officer of the Salvation Army Hospital in Chikankata, Zambia.

12. For more general information on the inscription of sexual cultures as subaltern, see especially T. Dunbar Moody, "Migrancy and Male Sexuality in South African Gold Mines," *Journal of South African Studies*, 14, 2 (January 1988), pp. 228–56; Lourdes Arguelles and B. Ruby Rich, "Homosexuality, Homophobia, and Revolution: Notes Toward an Understanding of the Cuban Lesbian and Gay Male Experience," in Martin Duberman, Martha Vicinus and George Chauncey, Jr., eds., *Hidden From History* (New York: New American Library, 1989); Pat Caplan, ed., *The Cultural Construction of Sexuality* (New York: Tavistock, 1987); "Homecoming," *Black/Out*, 2, 1 (Fall 1986); and Alfred Machela, "The Work of the Rand Gay Organization," Conference on Homosexual Identity Before, During, and After HIV (Stockholm, June 1988).

13. For the longer argument on Western medical ethics and proposed vaccine trials, see my *Inventing AIDS*.

14. To their credit, in Pamphlet 3, the authors emphasize that condoms are not currently being supplied to African countries in sufficient supply to meet potential demand (21). However, this can hardly be used as an excuse not to promote condom usage at all, since it is probably easier and quicker to increase condom supplies than it is to promote "monogamy." Indeed, the ease with which the lack-of-supply argument becomes an excuse for not promoting condoms is rooted in the widespread notion that "In Africa, AIDS is a disease of poverty."

15. See Pamphlet 1, which invokes "traditional values and norms of sexual behavior, which have been lost in the recent wave of 'modernization,'" and which defines "stable polygamy" as a form of "safe sex" (20).

16. It is critical to recognize how limiting are the terms of the international health regime; many local strategies remain "unreadable" because they defy the standardizations favored by the World Health Organization.

17. I am indebted here to the brief sections on the construction of the "Algerian" family in Malek Alloula, *The Colonial Harem*, trans. Myrna Godzich and Wlad Godzich (Minneapolis: University of Minnesota Press, 1986). A similar pattern occurs in the media reportage about AIDS in Africa, where the existing "African" family is often implicitly denigrated for having, besides a surfeit of children, either too many parents or too few (usually the father has died or has run off).

Chapter 12

Nationalisms and Sexualities in the Age of Wilde

Eve Kosofsky Sedgwick

for Doris Sommer

In September 1988, I was involved with a conference at my home institution on Liberal Arts Education in the Late Twentieth Century. The speakers at the three-day conference mostly represented an emerging mainstream-left consensus on issues such as pluralization of canons and curricula. I participated in the conference in two ways. On the second day, Skip Gates and I were on a panel about emerging canons, where I gave a talk about antihomophobic pedagogy and the difficult question of defining a gay canon. And on the last day, in the round-up discussion period that concluded the conference, I tried to articulate a serious unease that I had had with the whole proceeding. What was disturbing me then was the way the term "America" had come, unbidden and unremarked, to occupy a definitional center for almost every single one of the papers, and for the conference as a whole, in a way that no one could even seem to make visible enough to question. That the conference, whose title did not specify "America" and whose topic was by no means *necessarily* circumscribed by any boundaries of the national, had lined up so neatly in the current train of contestations about what exclusive or inclusive, white or non-white, gay or straight, homogeneous or heterogeneous visions are to constitute a *national* culture, a *national* identity, about where we are to look for the special *American* values—be they good or bad—of America and American education, seemed a striking datum to the very degree that it was taken for granted. It seemed to me that to the social archaeologist of the future, a conference like this one might figure not most saliently as an agonistic moment in the history of the liberal arts, nor as the nexus of a conflict between a political left and a political right, but as a moment of the heavy, uncontestable re-engraving of nationalism—or more accurately, of what Benedict Anderson refers to as "nation-ness"[1]—as the invisible outline whose unquestioned boundaries could only be strengthened by the apparent fierceness of the battles fought in its name and on its ground. Why, I asked at that final session, when we talk about all the very disparate things we have been talking about, do we always seem to find—do we always seem to fail to notice or query—that we are also talking about, and ratifying—by appealing back to different versions of it to ratify *us*—the primary realness of, of all imaginary things in the world, "America"?

A few days later, the conference was written up in the *New York Times.* Given the framework of recent controversy over the liberal arts, our write-up was miraculously positive; it seemed clear that everything that could be done, had been done, to bathe the goings-on in North Carolina in a benign and edifying light. The headline, for instance, was, blandly, "Liberal Arts Scholars Seek to Broaden Their Field." The picture run with the article, for another instance, was a nicely emblematic one of me lecturing forcefully, with Skip Gates as an appreciative listener, our proximity buffered by the brow-furrowed head of a white man. The list of topics discussed, for a third instance, though voluminous, was kind enough to omit any mention whatever of so alarming a subject as homophobia or gay and lesbian culture, on which I was in fact lecturing when the picture was taken. Instead, a quotation, quite possibly accurate, from the last session of the conference was attached to my name, as a sort of clincher to prove the sincerity and unimpeachable good faith of all the participants in this conference. "Eve K. Sedgewick, an English professor at Duke, said: 'What we're really talking about is America, our vision of what the country is, what the country should be.'"[2]

I expect that the kind of process that went into disappearing the gay/lesbian content of that conference from the *New York Times* felt completely different from the kind of process that led to the 180-degrees miscontextualization of the remark on America. Someone, I am sure—be it the author of the article or some person or persons elsewhere in the editorial line-up—someone must have given conscious thought to whether it would be possible to name gay issues in the article without disrupting the bland homogeneity of the legitimating aegis it aimed to throw over the work of the conference. Such person or persons decided, obviously, *no*—but at least I feel confident that they did have to decide, in a discursive context where, in the elegant formulation of Congressman Barney Frank, homosexuality has gone from seeming to public arbiters a "no way" issue, where there is only one articulated side and that side is negative, to being what he calls an "oh shit" issue, with two highly articulated opposing sides each one of which is now eager and able to make a federal case. Concerning "America," however, I am just as confident that nothing that felt in the least like a decision had to be made, by writer or editor, in order to misrepresent as a legitimating, populist appeal to national identity what was in fact an attempt to put into question the grounds of any such appeal. To the contrary: it can only have seemed (quite literally) the most natural thing in the world to anyone at the *Times* to assume, not only that any labor of intellectual legitimation must necessarily, sooner or later, be channeled through an appeal to the national, but conversely that any mention whatsoever of the national must necessarily, sooner or later, reveal itself as an appeal for legitimation.

Finally—to come to the end of this particular journalistic saga—the difference between the precisely contestable current status of gay definition and the completely uncontestable current status of national definition was brought, as they say, home to me with the next Sunday's *Times*, where the News of the Week section carried a second, this time virulently negative article about the same conference. Where our friends may politely, protectively—and of course, obliteratingly—omit the mention of gay studies and antihomophobic constituencies, our enemies have no such hesitation about naming us; the "homosexual" component of the conference was salient in the attack on it, by a different calculation in the same arithmetic that had elided us from its defense. What the second article shared unquestioningly with the first, on the other hand, was the assumption that to discuss the future of the humanities is coextensive with discussing the Americanness of America: that the national question is both the grounding origin and the necessary terminus of any understanding whatsoever of consciousness or production, perhaps *especially* insofar as those are also carried out in the name of the universal. The second article ends with a telephone interview with Lynn V. Cheney, chair of the National Endowment for the Humanities:

> I have the conviction that great literature, no matter whom it is written by, speaks to transcendent values that we all share, no matter what our time and circumstance," Mrs. Cheney said. . . . There is everything to be gained, she said, from studies by and about women, blacks, and other elements in American culture. Still, she maintained that American history and values derive

> primarily from the great thinkers of Europe, and not from Asia or Africa. "In the West," she argued, "the first responsibility is to ground students in the culture that gave rise to the institutions of our democracy.[3]

What we're really talking about is America, our vision of what the country is, what the country should be. Is there any way to stop? In his impressively suggestive book on this subject, *Imagined Communities: Reflections on the Origin and Spread of Nationalism,* Benedict Anderson points out that while "nationalism" is usually discussed as *an* ideology, like liberalism or fascism, against which an alternative ideology might be posed, to the contrary "it would, I think, make things easier if one treated it as if it belonged with 'kinship' and 'religion'" (15)—by implication, as the name of an entire underlying dimension of modern social functioning that could then be organized in a near-infinite number of different and even contradictory ways. The work, I should more accurately say the struggle, of defamiliarizing and thereby rendering visible the nationalism that forms the overarching ideology of our age is difficult to the extent that one or another nationalism tends to become the form of last resort for *every* legitimizing political appeal—whether right or left, imperialist or anti-imperialist, religious or secular, elitist or populist, capitalist or anti-capitalist, cynical or utopian, and whether or not on behalf of an ideology that has any account whatsoever to offer of the status of the "nation" as such. (No analysis through Marxism, capitalism, religion, or race, for instance, offers any intelligible justification of national form, yet each of these kinds of power today takes national or nationalist shapes.)

My sense is that an underlying liberal understanding of nationalism as *an* ideology, as something *against which* there exist conceptual tools to fight, is currently shaping our sense of the relations between nationalism and sexuality in circumscriptive ways. It's characteristic of mainstream-left thought (when it is not in the grip of utopian misunderstandings of foreign nationalisms, whose *un*masking as "ordinary" nationalisms always performs another extension of the same cynical narrative) to associate nationalism in the first place and definitionally with a nineteenth-century reactionary European project of bourgeois boundary-consolidation: with rightist projects of racial, gender, sexual and other scapegoating around borders shaped by a quasi-familial ideal of purity, that would at the same time distance and justify the inflictions of overseas empire. The topos of the creation, reification, and expulsion of the Other, and signally the Orientalized other, in the emergence of the modern European state, has become a central tool of liberal analysis; and it is the explanatory aegis of the Other or Othered that has, for the most part, allowed people of variant sexualities, along with non-Christian, non-white, and medically-disadvantaged people, to become visible in liberal narratives about the origins of nationalism. Roughly, one could say that the trope of the Other is to current understandings of nationalism what the repression hypothesis was to pre-Foucauldian understandings of sexuality. Like the repression hypothesis, it is in fact true to a certain irreducible core of suffering, denial, and crude reification whose historical and contemporary traces are everywhere to be seen and felt. Also like the repression hypothesis, however, the trope of the Other in relation to nationalism must almost *a priori* fail to do justice to the complex activity, creativity, and engagement of those whom *it* figures simply as relegated objects—their activity, creativity, and engagement with and on behalf of, among other things, that protean fabric of public discourse that does also figure their own relegation. Beyond the always accurate but spectacularly unanalytic diagnosis of, say, "internalized homophobia"—diagnosis to which, like the diagnosis of "Jewish" or "colonial" "self-hatred," the trope of Otherness necessarily has ultimate recourse—beyond the search for "internalized homophobia," what questions may we learn to ask about the extremely varied kinds of importance of national questions in the sexual politics—in those, for instance, to take some complicated examples into which I have been inquiring, of a Wilde, a Forster, a Nietzsche, or a Proust?

"In the modern world," Benedict Anderson writes, "everyone can, should, will 'have' a nationality, as he or she 'has' a gender" (14). The implication, I think, is that just as every culture has *some* mechanism—different mechanisms—to constitute what Gayle Rubin refers to as a "sex/gender system,"[4] a way of negotiating back and forth between chromosomal sex and social gender, so every *modern* culture and person must be seen as partaking of what we might (albeit clumsily) call a "habitation/nation system." The "habitation/nation system" would be the set of discursive and institutional arrangements that mediate between the physical fact that each person inhabits, at a given time, a particular geographical space, and the far more abstract, sometimes even apparently unrelated organization of what has emerged since the late seventeenth century as her/his national identity, as signalized by, for instance, citizenship.

Practically, the existence of habitation/nation systems, and their great variety worldwide, tend to become visible most easily as "exceptional" stresses on a system (thereby) taken as normal: through personal and political crises concerning exile and expatriation, sanctuary, guest-workers whose status is for some reason deroutinized, changes in the laws of Aliyah, emerging or resurgent nationalisms within previously established states, etc. But let us, for a minute, consider some consequences of Anderson's analogy between modern nationality and gender. To suggest that everyone might "have" a nationality as everyone "has" a gender presupposes, what may well be true, and may well always have been true, that everyone does "have" a gender. But it needn't presuppose that everyone "has" a gender *as* everyone else "has" a gender—

that everyone "has" a gender in the same way, or that "having" a gender is the same kind of act, process, or possession for every person or for every gender. It wouldn't be contradicted, even, by something like Nancy Chodorow's finding that female and male gender were by definition different kinds of things attainable by different kinds of process—normative female gender by a primary *identification with* a mother, say, and normative male gender by a secondary *differentiation from* female gender. Under such a finding (and while I don't assume it's either true or exhaustive, I don't think it particularly implausible), while everyone could be said to *have* a gender, while gender would certainly constitute a first category of the "normal," and while there would be an availability of so-called normal female gender and so-called normal male gender, there nevertheless could not be any such thing as *the* normal way to "have" a gender. Under the Chodorovian supposition, the definitional Other of gender—the answer to "gender as opposed to what?"—would be different in each case: "normal" female gender would be *as opposed to* no gender; "normal" male gender *as opposed to* female gender.

Something similar may be true of "nation-ness" and nationality. Even a simple exercise like attempting to compare the "nationality" of a Gypsy in Germany (formerly East or West Germany), that of a Turkish guest-worker in France, and that of a person who works in Johannesburg, lives in Soweto, and has an official assignment to a "homeland" s/he may never have seen, suggests how ragged and unrationalizable may be not only the rights and entailments, but the definitional relations of the habitation/nation systems of the modern world.

Benedict Anderson suggests that if any one thing defines the modern "nation" as opposed to "the older imagining, where states were defined by centres, borders were porous and indistinct, and sovereignties faded imperceptibly into one another," it is that "in the modern conception, state sovereignty is fully, flatly, and evenly operative over each square centimetre of a legally demarcated community" (26)—and so is "that remarkable confidence of community in anonymity which is the hallmark of modern nations" (40). Thus it should not surprise you when at the Buffalo airport, waiting for your little commuter flight to Toronto, and starting to wonder what the weather there is likely to be like, you notice that the *New York Times* and *USA Today*, whose weather maps are bounded by the precise, familiar outlines of the 48 contiguous United States, both assume that, as an American, you participate in the sunshine, clouds, and flurries of Salt Lake City, Miami, Fargo, Billings, and L.A. in a sense that you simply couldn't in those of a city fifty miles away across a national border. (In fact, *USA Today* goes even further in naturalizing the exclusion of Canada: since its snappy graphics give the weather map the illusion of projecting into three dimensions, a viewer of it receives the "information" that the North

American continent dramatically drops off into the sea across the top of the United States.) What might surprise you is the powerful familiarizing effect of nation-ness: that you could have failed to notice this before. In a sense, according to Anderson, these weather maps with all their apparent naturalness would be *the* defining icon of modern nationality. But the "same" experience at the Toronto airport turns out to be completely different. The *Globe and Mail*, and indeed every other Canadian newspaper I have seen, runs a weather map that extends southward at least as far as the Mason-Dixon Line in the United States. There is no presumption that the Toronto reader would (as it were) identify more with the fog over Vancouver than with the blizzard approaching Detroit. Does this mean that Canada does not have "nation-ness"? Or instead that its nation-ness, having a different history from that of the United States, may well therefore have a structure different enough to put into question any single definition of the quality "nation-ness"?

The very blandness of the "American" compacting of borders—the, as it were, bad pun between the name of a continent and the name of a nation—how much must it not owe to the accidents of a history of geographic, economic, imperialist entitlement, a path into "nation-ness" no more "normal," no more *as opposed to* the same set or even the same *kinds* of definitional others, than that of the nation-ness of Canada, the different nation-ness of Mexico, of the Philippines, of the Navajo Nation (within the U.S.), of the Six Nations (across the U.S.-Canadian border), the nationalism of the non-nation Quebec, the non-nationalism of the non-nation Hawaii, the histories of African-American nationalisms, and so forth and so forth and so forth. The "other" of *the* nation in a given political or historical setting may be the pre-national monarchy, the local ethnicity, the diaspora, the trans-national corporate, ideological, religious, or ethnic unit, the sub-national locale or the ex-colonial, often contiguous unit; the colony may become national vis à vis the homeland, or the homeland become national vis à vis the nationalism of its colonies; the nationalism of the homeland may be coextensive with or oppositional to its imperialism; and so forth. Far beyond the pressure of crisis or exception, it may be that there exists for nations, as for genders, simply no normal way to partake of the categorical definitiveness of the national, no single kind of "other" of what a nation is to which all can by the same structuration be definitionally opposed.

When it occurs to us, then, to run this question of national definition athwart some already articulated questions of turn-of-the-century sexual definition, we must be prepared to look in more directions at once than one. For instance, as I have discussed at more length in *Epistemology of the Closet*,[5] it is more than possible—it is almost unavoidable—to read *The Picture of Dorian Gray* as an intensely and rather conventionally orientalizing text. This is played out in both the lavishly exhibitionistic openness, and the techniques of coverture, of the novel's homosexual subject. It can be seen, for instance, in the intertwining mutual camouflage and mutual expression of the novel's gay plot with its drug-addiction plot. The heavily exoticized and glamorized opium commodity condenses many of the problematics of the natural vs. the unnatural/artificial, voluntarity vs. addiction, and the domestic scene vs. the foreign substance, that seem in the first place to have to do with the novel's modes of framing gay male identity. Yet the very patency of Wilde's gay-affirming and gay-occluding orientalism renders it difficult to turn back and see the outlines of the sexual body and the national body sketched by his *occidentalism.* With Orientalism so ready-to-hand a rubric for the relation to the Other, it is difficult to resist seeing the desired English body, on the other hand, as simply the domestic Same. Yet the sameness of this Same—or put another way, the *homo-* nature of this sexuality—is no less open to question than the self-identicalness of the national borders of the domestic. After all, the question of the National in Wilde's own life only secondarily—though profoundly—involved the question of overseas empire in relation to European *patria.* To the contrary: Wilde, as an ambitious Irish man, and the son, intimate, and protégé of a celebrated Irish-nationalist poet, can only have had as a fundamental element of his own sense of self, an exquisitely exacerbated sensitivity to how by turns porous, brittle, elastic, chafing, embracing, exclusive, murderous, in every way contestable and contested were the membranes of "domestic" national definition signified by the ductile and elusive terms England, Britain, Ireland. Indeed, the consciousness of foundational and/or incipient national *difference* already internal to national *definition* must have been part of what Wilde literally embodied, in the expressive, specularized, and symptomatic relation in which he avowedly stood to his age. As a magus in the worship of the "slim rose-gilt soul"—the individual or generic figure of the "slim thing, gold-haired like an angel" that stood at the same time for a sexuality, a sensibility, a class, and a narrowly English national type—Wilde, whose own physical make was of an opposite sort and (in that context) an infinitely less appetizing, desirable, and placeable one, showed his usual uncanny courage ("his usual uncanny courage," *anglice* chutzpah) in foregrounding his own body so insistently as an index to such erotic and political meanings. The decades around the turn of the century marked the precipitous popularization, not only of the new word "homosexual," but of the very conception of male-male desire as a desire based on sameness. I have argued, also in *Epistemology of the Closet,* that a central trajectory in, for instance, *Dorian Gray,* is toward the establishment of men's love for men, no longer as a classicizing pedagogic/pederastic relation structured, like Basil's and Lord Henry's relations to Dorian, by diacritical differences between lover and beloved, but instead in the relatively modern terms, as slim rose-gilt Dorian's inescapably narcissistic mirror-relation to his own figured body in the portrait. Wilde's alienizing physical heritage of unboundable bulk from his Irish-nationalist mother, of a louche swarthiness from his Celticizing father, underlined with every self-foregrounding gesture of his person and *persona* the fragility, unlikelihood, and strangeness—at the same time, the transformative reperceptualizing power—of the new "*homo*-" homosexual imagining of male-male desire. By the same pressure, it dramatized the uncouth nonequivalence of an English national body with a British or with an Irish, as domestic grounds from which to launch a stable understanding of national/imperial relations.

Of course, Wilde's very hyper-indicativeness as a figure of his age means that there's no one else like him, but I do want to suggest that the mutual interrepresentations of emerging national and sexual definitions must be looked for at no less a level of complexity for other important figures, as well. Roger Casement's would be an obvious career in which to look for a heightening and contrastive braiding-together of exoticizing British imperialist/anti-imperialist, with Irish-nationalist, with homosexual identifications and identities. For him, as for Wilde, the question of the Other of a national, as of a sexual, identity was an irreducibly—and *sometimes* an enablingly—complex one. But even for someone like Forster whose national identity can in no sense have been a colonized one, the erotically expressive anti-imperialism of *A Passage to India* has as its other face the also anti-imperialistic, highly problematized English nationalism of *The Longest Journey*, whose shepherd nature-hero refuses an imperialist future in the colonies in favor of the homoerotically anthropomorphic, body-scaled and nationally-figured landscape of his native valley. "I can't run up the [Druidic] Rings without getting tired, nor gallop a horse out of this view without tiring it, so what," he asks, "is the point of a boundless continent?"

For Proust, on the other hand, whose plots of Dreyfusism and of gay recognition are the organizing principles for one another as they are for the volumes through which they ramify, the numinous identification of male homosexuality (which he figures in terms of a diaspora from the original homeland in Sodom) with a *pre*-national, premodern dynastic cosmopolitanism, through the figure of Charlus as much as through the Jews, is haunted by the spectre of a sort of gay Zionism or pan-Germanism, a normalizing politics on the nominally ethnic model that would bring homosexual identity itself under the sway of what Nietzsche called "that *nervose nationale* with which Europe is sick." At the climax of his disquisition on "the men-women of Sodom," Proust explains,

> I have thought it as well to utter here a provisional warning against the lamentable error of proposing (just as people have encouraged a Zionist movement) to create a Sodomist movement and to rebuild Sodom. For, no sooner had they arrived there than the Sodomites would leave the town so as not to have the appearance of belonging to it, would take wives, keep

> mistresses in other cities where they would find, incidentally, every diversion that appealed to them. They would repair to Sodom only on days of supreme necessity, when their own town was empty, at those seasons when hunger drives the wolf from the woods. In other words, everything would go on very much as it does to-day in London, Berlin, Rome, Petrograd or Paris.[6]

And what finally to say of the virulently anti-German Nietzsche himself, with his homoerotic luxuriances of Europeanized sickness, the homosexual-panic-charged epistemologies of his political diagnostic techniques, his more than Proustian resistance to every nationalism as to every form of gay minority identity, and the more than Wildean passions of vicariousness with which he invested so rich a variety of male national bodies? I don't think any of these accounts will be simple ones to render—even to render visible. But we need to do so lest we continue to deal numbly around and along the eroticized borders of this apparently universal, factitiously timeless modern mapping of the national body.

NOTES

1. Benedict Anderson, *Imagined Communities: Reflections on the Origin and Spread of Nationalism* (London: Verso, 1983), p. 13; further citations incorporated in the text.

2. [Spelling unmodified.] Lee A. Daniels, "Liberal Arts Scholars Seek to Broaden Their Field," *New York Times*, September 21, 1988, p. 23 (national edition).

3. Richard Bernstein, "Academia's Liberals Defend their Carnival of Canons Against Bloom's 'Killer B's,'" *New York Times*, September 25, 1988, p. 26E.

4. Gayle Rubin, "The Traffic in Women: Notes on the 'Political Economy' of Sex," in Rayna R. Reiter, ed., *Toward an Anthropology of Women* (New York: Monthly Review Press, 1975), pp. 157–210; the term is defined on p. 159.

5. Eve Kosofsky Sedgwick, *Epistemology of the Closet* (Berkeley: University of California Press, 1990), ch. 3, from which this paragraph is drawn.

6. Marcel Proust, *Remembrance of Things Past*, trans. C. K. Scott Moncrieff and Terence Kilmartin (New York: Vintage, 1983), vol. 2, pp. 655–56. It is too early to gauge the meaning of the national referent in a newly emerging New York political group,

Queer Nation, a more concertedly antihomophobic offshoot of the AIDS activist group ACT UP-N.Y., that seems ardently and ingeniously to be taking up the challenge flung down by Proust in this passage—a rhetorical move anticipated, of course, by, among others, Jill Johnston in *Lesbian Nation.* Part of what will be most interesting to see in the emergence of Queer Nation is how the moment of denominating a political movement as a *nation* intersects with whatever will turn out, under this new definitional pressure, to be the meaning of *queer.* For it is not self-evident that "queer" is identical even in denotation to "lesbian and gay." An early controversy stimulated by Queer Nation has had to do with their distribution (at the 1990 Gay Pride march in New York) of an anonymously-written broadside one of whose essays is headlined, "I HATE STRAIGHTS." A lesbian writer who found this a potently liberatory gesture writes in an article about it,

> In a voice ringing with the vision of a new queer courage, "I Hate Straights" urges lesbians and gay men to retire self-abnegating tolerance of straight indifference in favor of honesty, because, the piece argues, the therapeutic value of unleashing peculiarly queer emotions will ultimately free us to act in our own splendid interests.

(Nina Reyes, "Queerly Speaking," *OutWeek*, 59 [August 15, 1990], pp. 40–54, quoted from p. 44.) Another view might be that the yoking together, as inaugural gestures for a new political grouping, of two words seldom found in gay/lesbian politics but common elsewhere, *nation* and *hate*, is the opposite of "peculiarly queer." But perhaps the most productive aspect of the controversy will be its potential for unfolding, as opposed (I hope) to foreclosing, the "as opposed to what?" explorations of queer self-definition in the context of antihomophobic activist concentration.

Chapter 13

Revolution Must Come First: Reading V. Aksenov's Island of Crimea

Greta N. Slobin

That this was the only essay presented on a Russian topic at the Nationalisms and Sexualities Conference should hardly be surprising. Problems of nationalism and sexuality in the Soviet Union and Eastern Europe are radically different, for example, from the issues explored in current postcolonial theory mainly focused on the first and third world, with little to say about the second. In James Clifford's succinct formula, it is always "The West and the rest," but how does Russia fit in here? Which one is she, positioned between the East and the West? From the eighteenth century on, enlightened Russians were often torn between their European allegiance and their Scythian or Eastern heritage. Historically, Russia has been the "other" for Western Europe, yet however distant, exotic, and mysterious, Russia was a neighboring colonial power to be reckoned with. Its relationship to Europe has always been that of a conflicted symbiosis, defined by both geopolitical enormity and presumed cultural inferiority, all of which has been further compounded by ideological difference since the Revolution.

The idea of the Revolution came to Russia from the West and the earliest Russian revolutionaries were aware of the problems this translation entailed, since Russia was not an industrial but largely a peasant society. In a famous letter of April 23, 1885 to Vera Zasulich who asked his opinion on Plekhanov's book *Our Differences*, Engels acknowledged Russia's particular situation but admitted having limited knowledge about it. He was nevertheless quite certain that "the Russians are approaching their 1789. The revolution must break out there within a given time; it may break out any day."[1] Yet when the Revolution took place in 1917, many Russian poets and writers perceived it as a uniquely Russian conflagration, a cleansing storm emanating from the Scythian East rather than from the West. Until Gorbachev's critical reforms and the bloodless revolutions in Eastern Europe, this relationship of "difference" vis à vis Europe would remain largely unchanged as the Soviet Union became the hardly-ever mentioned "second" world existing in a vast, mythic expanse of land East of Vienna, aligned with the equally ignored "fourth" world of Central Europe.

To understand the reasons why Slavists do not recognize themselves in much contemporary theoretical discourse would require a separate and lengthy study.[2] Here instead I hope to shed light on the peculiarities of the Soviet situation through a reading of Vasily Aksenov's novel *The Island of Crimea*, one of the most probing and subversive works of contemporary Russian fiction. Written in the late seventies during the Brezhnev era of political stagnation, artistic repression and general malaise, the novel explores the potentially lethal tensions inherent in Russian formations of nationalism, state ideology, and sexuality. Too irreverent to be published in the USSR in the eighties, *The Island of Crimea* appeared first in the West in 1981.[3]

Aksenov was a leading member of the first generation of writers who broke with the constraints of Socialist Realism in the post-Stalinist thaw. The young characters of Aksenov's early stories embody Soviet counter-culture, while in the novels of the seventies he is concerned with the repressions of the Stalinist period and the gradual recovery of his generation from that inheritance. This recovery takes place through language, a blatantly subversive counter-discourse which frankly relishes the forbidden fruits of slang, unofficial popular culture, and the artistic-intellectual bohemia of Aksenov's generation, displacing and parodying the official, ideologically correct idiom.[4] Language becomes the harbinger of change at the moment when the dominant discourse is threatened by "subversion" from within (Soviet youth culture of the sixties) and without (new contacts with the West).

The Island of Crimea is a masterpiece of rhetorical and political daring: official Soviet ideology is clearly dead and nationalism, demystified, emerges as a cynical vehicle for domination capable of destroying anything in its path. The novel's action shifts between the USSR and an imaginary independent and capitalist island off the the Black Sea coast, whose relationship to the USSR resembles that of Taiwan and Hong Kong to China. Aksenov takes stock of the cumulative effects of more than a half century of Party control by placing the Soviet Union in provocative proximity to a thriving, multi-ethnic, libertine democracy across a rather permeable border. The construction of this potentially "explosive" situation allows him to juxtapose popular Western mythologies of the "monolithic" socialist East with the official and popular socialist mythologies of the "decadent" West.

Reunification with the motherland is the overarching ambition of the novel's hero, Andrei Luchnikov. The editor of the island's main newspaper, the *Courier,* he is a glamorous forty-six-year-old jet-setting playboy, a cross between JFK and James Bond, able to travel freely in and out of the USSR. As the son of one of the White Army officers who took over Crimea during the Civil War and installed themselves as its ruling elite, he represents the traditions of Russian aristocracy still alive on the island. As a link not only between the USSR and the West, but also between Imperial and Soviet Russia, Luchnikov is a perfect instrument for the novel's stab at nationalism.

Andrei's nationalist nostalgia for "reunification" is figured sexually in the novel through his romantic involvements with two female embodiments of Mother Russia, Tanya and Krystyna. In Aksenov's scenario, nationalist and libidinal urges erupt in conflicts played out in a thoroughly modern, intense and frenzied plot, unusual in Soviet fiction. Emphasizing the sexual politics that underlies Soviet state power, the novel offers a brilliant deconstruction of nationalism by superimposing two of Russia's traditional "others": Crimea, a colonized region of Imperial Russia, and women, whose low status reflects the patriarchal and colonialist ideology that continues today in the Soviet Union. Below I will recount briefly some pertinent history of these two "others" and then consider their continuities as they affect the course of the novel.

WOMEN, THE STATE, AND MOTHER RUSSIA

The "woman's question" and particularly a woman's right to be sexually active outside marriage were declared "bourgeois" and "obsolete" in Lenin's famous letter of 1915 to his fellow revolutionary, Inessa Armand. Lenin was unequivocal on the issue of adultery. In an extensive early statement on this question, entitled *What Can Women Expect from Socialism* and published in Stuttgart in 1903, A. A. Isaev conceded that the future woman was to enjoy male companionship but made it clear that "sex, in any case, would not play an excessively large role in the life of the socialist couple . . . since much of [women's] energy would be deflected into public activity"—a point of view described by a recent historian as "an early adumbration of the theory of 'revolutionary sublimation.'"[5]

Male theorizing about socialist sexuality has been clearly on the side of revolutionary sublimation ever since, despite the brief period of sexual freedom in the early twenties and the writings of Bolshevik feminists, especially Alexandra Kollontai, calling for radical changes in the status of women. In the subsequent struggle of the young Soviet Union to constitute its national identity, the women's question was no longer deemed an important issue. As early as 1923 Stalin suggested that women could either impede or promote the progress of the nation. This paternalistic attitude is reflected in later official policies regarding women's place and role in society, and in laws that made abortion illegal and divorce all but impossible: "This double view of woman—as an active economic and political agent of society and as a mother and nurturer of new communists—remained unchanged and was the basis for Stalin's support of a policy bent upon curbing the sexual energies of a revolutionary generation."[6]

This suppression of women's rights remained in force through Stalin's rule as post-Revolutionary freedom was succeeded by a Soviet-style puritanism that conformed more to the nineteenth-century European model of "respectability" than to any new socialist understanding of sexual relations. The irony of this situation seems to have been missed by the Bolsheviks, for whom control over sexuality and reproduction was tied to political power, labor productivity, and order.[7]

While the concerns of Russian women have thus been marginalized since the Revolution, the myth of Mother Russia—the kind of archaic structure, analogous to religion and kinship, that Benedict Anderson finds pervasive in nationalism[8]—has remained very much alive throughout the modern period with the nation commemorated, for example, in the ambivalent, gendered images of pre-Revolutionary poetry as suffering or religious, as a holy fool or whore. Traces of this mythical Holy Russia were sought in the late fifties by Solzhenitsyn's freed prisoner-hero of "Matryona's Home." And Aksenov's Andrei finds them on his trip to the provinces of the USSR, bringing back to Crimea a tape of conversations and sounds from that "lost" religious Old Russia. The words of Andrei's filmmaker friend, Gangut, emphasize the gendered quality of the myth: "Love, love for the glorious, the pitiful, the powerful, the vulnerable, the one-and-only motherland and what a—you'll excuse the expression—what a mother she is, our Mother Russia" (95). The epithets Gangut uses attribute oxymoronic, incompatible, paradoxical qualities to this female entity to which power and weakness, poverty and plenitude are ascribed. Even in the socialist present, Mother Russia continues to combine the threatening and abject affects we associate with misogyny.

Andrei's "nostalgia" for the motherland shapes his relationship with the two women in his life. Tatyana and Krystyna walk the tightrope between the extreme aspects of the "Mother Russia" myth, the virgin and the whore. Their characterization recalls Dostoevsky's formula of female beauty, Sodom and Madonna. Indeed, this opposition dominates Andrei's attitude to both women: he is suspicious of the sexually-liberated American Krystyna, but seduces the virtuous Soviet Tatyana into becoming a Western-style sex symbol.

For Luchnikov, the encounter with Tatyana marks the beginning of "expectation and hope. The island and the continent. Russia. The center of life where all roads converged" (49). Tatyana becomes a celebrity in Moscow: a wife and mother, she is also a star athlete, a television personality (tanned, chic in her French suit bought by Andrei). She appears to be an anomaly, a liberated Westernized Soviet woman. When Andrei's highly placed friend Marlen Kuzenkov sees her on TV, he notes with pleasure that hers is a "new face," not burdened by "social problems." Despite this, she cannot escape becoming the traditional object of "barter" in a primitive fistfight between Andrei and her oaf-like husband, the Hub, who asserts his marital rights over her island lover. The husband's rights are, in turn, subsumed by those of the KGB, represented by colonel Sergeev, who knows the intimate details of Tanya's affair with Andrei and forces her to spy on him. These events render Tatyana passive and push her toward what she perceives as her "fall": she is forced to betray Andrei as she sleeps with an old millionaire for money.

Krystyna is a young Polish-American who has a casual one-night affair with Andrei at the beginning of the novel. Their lovemaking scene takes place to the sounds of the tape from Andrei's recent Russian journey, with folksy voices of religious believers and holy fools. Did the tape affect her subliminally during this scene when Andrei achieved dominance over her? She responds to the call of her Slavic blood and reappears on the eve of the invasion to join Andrei and serve the Idea: "I decided to exorcise you by deromanticizing you, studying you. I did some serious research on your Idea and what happened? You won me over. The articles I read called it a typical manifestation of Russian Sadomasochism, but I saw it as something much deeper, more important than that. It may even have a religious tinge to it. . . . In any case I started feeling disgusted with myself for leading the silly, dissolute life I led." Andrei responds to the new Krystyna in a similar vein: "Amazing . . . but why such asceticism? He looked over at her pleasant oval face and her long graceful neck. She did have a kind of monastic freshness about her. The discovery stirred his imagination; she reminded him more and more of Old Russia . . ." (299).

With both female characters, Andrei's sexual conquests foreshadow the island's imminent takeover. Just before the invasion, the local opposition group headed by Andrei's enemy kidnaps and rapes Tatyana to take revenge on Luchnikov. And during the invasion, the same group will dose Krystyna with gasoline and set her on fire. The women die shockingly as nationalist martyrs, victims of the violence that will soon engulf Crimea as well.

RUSSIAN ORIENTALISM

Crimea is an exotic Southern coastal region with a strategically desirable access to the Black Sea, long considered indispensable for the Russian Empire. Populated by fiercely independent, semi-nomadic, horseback-riding natives of various small ethnic groups, Crimea became a prime target for imperial expansion in the nineteenth century. For Russian Romanticism, Crimea was a site of bloody violence and romantic seduction, a counterpart of the Orient in the European literary imagination. Crimea's ancient lore and dramatic landscape with snow-covered mountain peaks, gorges, and dangerously narrow passes colonized the Russians' imagination as it was being colonized. Pushkin's narrative poem, "The Fountain of Bakhchisarai," is a classic example of Russian Orientalism, with its depiction of ancient ruins and a vision of an absent heroine. In Lermontov's poem "The Captive," a young Russian officer is taken prisoner and then freed from his chains by a beautiful but silent Circassian maiden. By the latter part of the century, Tolstoy's programmatic stories in *The Cossacks* parody this tradition and deromanticize the site: written in measured lucid prose and pacifist in temperment, these stories attempt to see "natives" as an indigenous culture rather than as blank slates waiting to be inscribed by the civilized conqueror.

In the twentieth century, from Chekhov on to the Silver Age, Crimea became a writers' gathering place, first in Yalta and then in Koktebel, in the home of the poet Maksimilian Voloshin who is mentioned in the novel (47). The Southern seashore offered respite and escape during the ravages of Revolution and Civil War. Literary reminiscences are scattered throughout Aksenov's novel in which Crimea remains the traditionally desired, exotic, sensuous "other." Aksenov does not dwell upon its strategic significance, but ascribes its present independence to a mere accident of history due to an English lieutenant, Bailey-Land, who fought for Crimea during the Civil War, for no particular reason, "just so."[9]

Aksenov's imaginary island is everything the mainland is not, all that it wishes to be but would never dare, nor be allowed, to admit: it is Western, capitalist, decadent, a cosmopolitan multiethnic "Mecca of world anarchism" (168) and "carnival of freedom" (153). Though clearly modeled on Los Angeles (where Aksenov had recently visited), the island is not a particular place in the West but a part of the East, a composite projection of *its* own long-repressed desires. As in Said's analysis of European orientalism, "it has less to do with Orient that it does with 'our world.'"[10]

Marlen Kuzenkov, Andrei's friend and the general consultant to the Institute for the Study of the Eastern Mediterranian Region reporting directly to the Central Committee, confesses a "secret, desperate love—Crimea . . . I love this island; I love its memory of the old Russia and the dream of a new one; I love its rich and dissolute democracy, the ports of its rocky south open to the entire world, the energy of historically doomed but eternally resilient Russian capitalism; I love the girls of Yalta and its bohemian atmosphere . . ." His love for Crimea is no less passionate than Andrei's for Russia. But Kuzenkov maintains that "its fall can help no one, not even our country, and the rest of our leadership has formed no set opinion on the subject. O God, I won't survive it" (310). Indeed, he does not.

The American millionaire Baxter, who is Kosygin's golf partner and a pragmatist (a takeoff on Armand Hammer), discloses the Soviet stake in Crimea: "At present the rigid Soviet system has more or less made peace with the idea of a miniature, tinselly Russia on its underbelly, made peace with it ideologically, strategically, and most of all, economically. Confidential sources report that a full third of Russia's hard currency enters the country via Crimea" (210). Baxter refers to Andrei's Idea as "aristocratic romanticism . . . psychology of noble impulses . . ." (211). Marlen Kuzenkov's disgust with "that sadomasochistic Idea, that snobbish guilt gone berserk!" (317) contrasts with Krystyna's infatuation when she returns to Andrei. For her, the Idea stems from the nineteenth-century Russian "spiritual messianism" to which Andrei reverts after he realizes how culturally and politically bankrupt the Soviet Union has become. In his last speech, Andrei celebrates the "bond with our Historical Homeland . . . toward the greater spiritual development of mankind . . . unique moral and mystic mission of Mother Russia and the nations that have chosen to follow her path." He has a grand vision of Russia's leadership role in the world: "Perhaps Crimea will provide the spark to ignite the Russian engine in the world rally of History . . . a vote of sacrifice . . . active participation in Russia's messianic future—that is, in the spiritual development of our time" (291). Through Andrei's nationalist rhetoric Aksenov implicitly underscores the danger of reviving nineteenth-century Slavophile ideas: "I thought of Russia, of her sacred path, of Your path, of redemption" (345).

The relationship between the mainland and the island illuminates the novel's construction of Crimea and women as Russia's "others." The one thing the island "lacks" and the mainland "possesses" is national identity. The nationalist longing of the Russian "islanders" is a great irrational drive, stronger even than ideological rifts or the mortal danger of being pitted against brute forces bent on domination. Crimea is the source of everything the mainland both fears and desires: passion and excess, freedom and erotic play, miscegenation and cosmopolitanism. It is the "feminine" counterpart of the Fatherland. In the context of the novel, gender difference offers a pretext for both nationalism and colonialism, as women figure only as pawns in the always-lethal male power game.

BATHOS IN THE BATHHOUSE

Aksenov provides an unambiguous glimpse into an impregnable site of male power where members of the Central Committee gather. Located in the heart of Moscow, this is a "masonic lodge" of the Russian Party, a stronghold of the kind of Russian nationalism represented by the group Pamyat today. The exclusive Russian Club, informally referred to as "the womb," is "a State-owned dacha with a Finnish bath run by fat-assed sluts." It is the scene of "the twilight of the Third Rome," recalling Moscow's medieval formula of imperial and religious messianism as the Third Rome after the fall of Constantinople. Here in the Finnish bath Aksenov stages carnival Soviet style: "Disrobed, they were even more friendly, more cordial . . ." (172). Luchnikov gains access to this secret retreat through Kuzenkov and observes his hosts as carefully as they observe him:

> They represented real power, he could see that. . . . The main topic of their conversation was levels (hierarchy) . . . Climbing out of a pool, he had a chance to see them at a remove. From that perspective, they reminded him of something, but he could not quite put his finger on it. Eight men with towels carelessly draped over them sitting at a long, artificially roughed table of expensive wood, one leisurely pouring his friends some Gordon's gin, another pouring himself a Tuborg, a third winding a slice of smoked salmon onto his fork, a fourth giving Liuda's terried behind a hug as she sat down a tray of tropical fruit. (173)

This homosocial scene reminds Luchnikov of another familiar image of power: "No, not Roman senators. Why, of course! The Mafia! That's it. Chicago, the roaring twenties, a Hollywood B-movie, the nouveau riche combination of ferocity and flab, the sense of power usurped." Aksenov's reference to this cinematic icon of corruption and power in American capitalism is hardly accidental since post-Brezhnev critics indeed alluded to the Mafia in condemning the excesses of the previous regime.

A neophyte nationalist, Oleg Stepanov, is thrilled to have finally been admitted to the secret bathhouse and makes a speech in which he updates the traditional Russian imperial triad "Orthodoxy, Autocracy, and Nationality":

> So in its infinite wisdom our people combined ideology and power, faith and a strong hand, and astounded the whole world with a new form of power: the soviet! And here we have it, the Russian triad of our times: communism, Soviet power, and nationality! Only nationality remains untouched, for nationality is our blood, our spirit, our strength, our mystery! (175)

Aksenov is truly inspired in this scene. Mystery, the last word in the passage, is the basis of the imposed power of the church that seeks to dominate its people in Dostoevsky's "Legend of the Grand Inquisitor." But Aksenov's final touch of bathos is revealing: "In the first flush of inspiration Stepanov himself had not noticed his penis rising, and now with a gasp he tried to cover it with his hands. But his erection was so powerful that the little red head on the end kept peeping out triumphantly through his fingers" (175). This scene leaves no doubt but that Soviet state power and male sexuality are inextricably bound.

THE RHETORIC OF GENDER AND NATIONALISM

Andrei's erotic longing for the motherland functions as a counterpoint to the Soviet desire for the decadent island. Stock images of Russia are at the heart of Andrei's quest: "cold, foreign, distant as it was, it was the land of his forefathers, Russia, and there was nothing dearer to him" (31). The heterosexual component of Luchnikov's desire for Mother Russia leads him to dismiss as "mere politics of glands" a plot to assassinate him by island nationalists opposed to reuinification, a plot led by an old enemy who is tellingly figured as homosexual. Andrei returns from his last trip to the Historical Homeland, elated: "I have returned from Russia full of hope. For it is like a field, which shall never be barren" (216). The metaphor becomes literalized in Andrei's conversation with the film director, Gangut (Tarkovsky): "Why do you refuse to see further than your nose? Is it because they won't let you make those shitty potboilers of yours? Yes, that's it, pure spite. You're a fucking reject of history, you know? Russia *needs new sperm!*" (61).

As in the bathouse scene described above, nationalism is identified once more with virility. When Andrei's son Anton, an island nationalist, argues with his father he also resorts to sexual metaphor: "We shall never merge with you, you law-abiding, monumental, hulking, northern, Russian swine, you! We're not Russian by ideology, we're not communist by nationality; we're Yaki Islanders, we have a fate of our own. Our fate is the carnival of freedom" (153). Baxter comes to the island to warn Luchnikov senior of the impending annexation: "It will consist of a simple, unconscious physiological act, the big swallowing the small" (210). And at the grand reception held to celebrate the reunification, the paparazzi question Tanya in similar terms: "Have you ever thought of the male element in the idea of a Common Fate? I mean the yearning of something hot and hard to plunge into boundless female flesh?" (294).

The invasion, following in the wake of the islanders' vote for reunification, is a concretization of this metaphoric series. An ultimate betrayal, it is staged like a rape, an affair "between men" that proceeds from seduction to violence, as Baxter had forseen: "The thing is it will be forced into it; it will do it against its will" (211). Indeed, explicitly linking colonial ambition and male sexual aggression, the colonial takeover is staged as a cinematically projected vision of a violent pornographic act televised for viewers everywhere. The romantic vision of reunification is thus succeeded by the deadly reality of the invasion as Andrei watches the humiliating scene of his father and his old friends, the gentlemen soldiers of the White Army, capitulating to the invaders. The two women are brutally killed and Andrei fears he is going mad, hoping it is all a film in the genre of *Apocalypse Now*.

Aksenov's Luchnikov emerges as a hero with fatal flaws and bankrupt ideas, a striking contrast with the obligatory "positive heroes" of Socialist Realism who fight for their "ideals" and always win. Heir to the nationalism and sexism underlying both the Westernized aristocratic culture of the Russian Enlightenment as well as that of the USSR, Andrei responds to the atavistic call of blood, sexuality and race in a world where political bankruptcy is the expression of male lust and where femaleness can only be its victim. Aksenov stresses the impossibility of change in a motherland enthralled by a morally-depleted Stalinism that can be salvaged neither through peaceful coexistence with the West nor through the kind of nationalist Russian messianism espoused by the most famous exiled writer, Solzhenitsyn.

In Aksenov's novel both Russia and the West appear mired in their (suspiciously symmetrical) ideologies of capitalist "liberalism" and communist "control." Aksenov is sceptical about the longterm consequences of Khrushchev's politics of coexistence and of Western "convergence" theory which, as Olga

Matich pointed out, were reactions to Stalin's long-standing isolationist policies rather than signs of real change.[11] The only hope the novel envisions lies with the "flower children" of the sixties and with the jazz musicians who are the cultural heroes of Aksenov's generation, the harbingers of liberalization in the post-Stalinist thaw. Their appearance is marked as "the dawn of the new youth subculture," dated after the Hungarian Revolution of 1956. The underground jazz-rock commune in the Old Arbat section of Moscow forms the "only one escape where they can't get you—music!" (162). Indeed, the commune becomes a haven where Luchnikov can hide and it eventually helps him leave the Soviet Union when he is in danger from the authorities. The novel ends with Andrei's son Anton playing his favorite tunes on the horn, the song of Aksenov's generation, "My Melancholy Baby," and also the title song of his recent autobiography:

> Gonna take a sentimental journey,
> Gonna set my mind at ease,
> Gonna make a sentimental journey,
> To renew old memories . . . (332)

The tune expresses Aksenov's own nostalgia for the bygone sixties, with its sexual revolution and new hope for "coexistence," when change was in the air and freedom seemed genuinely possible. Anton sums up the apolitical mood of that time: "I am not going to swap my freedom for a political idea . . . Jazz is a free and independent country. It doesn't need any of that politics crap" (334). Anton, his wife and newborn baby escape to Turkey in a boat steered by a jazz musician, Ben Ivan, an expert at getting across difficult borders, while Andrei remains behind to bury his dead.

Crimea represented Anton's ideal of a nation, a libertine democracy for all people and races: "It is a nation currently taking place here on the Island of Crimea and includes descendants of Tatars, Italians, Bulgarians, Greeks, and Turks, of the Russian army and the British navy. The Yaki nation is a nation of youth" (22). He argues against the traditional nationalism of his father's generation: "You have no right to call the Island Russian. That's imperialism. Less than half the population is Russian by blood" (275). Andrei offers a lame but by now ominous justification in response: "The same holds for the Soviet Union."

TOWARDS PERESTROIKA

Aksenov's scathing satire on post-Stalinism appears in some respects remarkably prophetic in its incisive critique of nationalism, state ideology, and gender politics. Gorbachev's reforms have opened the possibilities for radical change as the Russian Empire, both within the borders of the USSR and in Eastern Europe, begins its gradual disintegration. The hope of Aksenov's generation has come back to life with the political and cultural change of the "velvet revolutions" of 1989, in which music, jazz or rock, preserves the counter-culture spirit of the sixties, especially for the Czechs.[12] At the same time, the rise of nationalism in the country where "less than half the population is Russian" brings to surface ethnic violence that threatens the reforms. But most significantly, the secondary status of women in the USSR, long suppressed by socialist ideology, has also reemerged as an urgent problem.

The low status of women is reflected in the continuing Soviet prejudice against prostitution, expressed in distinctly Victorian formulations that seem as outdated as the Soviet economy. In her essay "Restructuring the 'Woman Question': Perestroika and Prostitution," Elizabeth Waters quotes from a great number of newspaper articles from all over the Soviet Union that uniformly blame the women themselves for engaging in prostitution. The existence of this social phenomenon, considered an "aberration," was not even admitted legally until 1987 when it was declared an administrative offense. Waters writes that "'the woman's question' does not figure in the government's list of political priorities" and that "the prostitute has become one of the scapegoats for the failure of reality to measure up to ideals."[13]

As perestroika proceeds amidst growing turbulence and uncertainty, with the boundaries of new freedoms constantly expanding and being tested, the mistakes of the past are revealed but without a clear program for the future. Aksenov ends his account of a recent trip to Russia with a rhetorical question: "I merely wish to know this: is there, behind all the tragicomic turns of our Russian tale—all the revolutions, counterrevolutions, Stalinisms, neo-Stalinisms, revisionisms, thaws, freezes, perestroikas, glasnosts—is there, behind all this, some enchanted playwright, some divine author who knows how the story ends?"[14] While no one knows of course the answer to this question, the process of change is considered "irreversible" by its active participants.

NOTES

1. *Marx-Engels: Selected Correspondence,* trans. I. Laskar, ed. S. W. Ryazanskaya (Moscow, 1975), p. 361. I am grateful to Gayatri Spivak for this suggestion.

2. For some insight into the theoretical incommensurability between Slavic and Western scholarship, see Peter Steiner, "Slavic Literary Studies Yesterday and Tomorrow," *Profession 87* (1987), pp. 2–9.

3. Michael Henry Heim's excellent translation of the novel was published in 1983 by the Vintage Library of Contemporary Literature. All further citations from this edition will appear parenthetically in the text above.

4. See Greta N. Slobin, "Vasily Aksenov Beyond 'Youth Prose': Subversion through Popular Culture," *Slavic and Eastern European Journal*, 31, 1 (Summer 1987), pp. 50–64.

5. Richard Stites, *The Women's Liberation Movement in Russia: Feminism, Nihilism, and Bolshevism, 1860–1930* (Princeton: Princeton University Press, 1978), p. 262.

6. Ibid., p. 385.

7. See Vera Dunham, *In Stalin's Time: Middleclass Values in Soviet Fiction* (Cambridge: Cambridge University Press, 1976). Dunham aptly refers to Stalin's "Big Deal": "It was the middle class which offered itself as the best possible partner in the rebuilding of the country. . . . It was with the middle class that the regime entered a concordat" (13).

8. Benedict Anderson, *Imagined Communities: Reflections on the Origin and Spread of Nationalism* (London: Verso, 1983), p. 15.

9. On Crimea's colonial history and the British role in the Crimean Wars, see Cecil Woodham-Smith, *The Reason Why* (New York: McGraw Hill, 1954). After the Revolution, Crimea was considered a possible place of settlement for Russian Jews; see Zvi Gitelman, *Jewish Nationality and Soviet Politics: The Jewish Sections of the CPSU, 1917–1930* (Princeton: Princeton University Press, 1972), p. 430. In Stalin's time, Crimea suffered the forced resettlement of the Tatar population.

10. Edward Said, *Orientalism* (New York: Pantheon Books, 1978), p. 12.

11. Olga Matich, "Vasilii Aksenov and the Literature of Convergence: *Ostrov Krym* as Self-Criticism," *Slavic Review*, 47, 4 (1988), pp. 642–51.

12. See John Tagliabue's recent article on the John Lennon commemorative wall

in Prague: "Prague's Velvet Revolutionaries Recall John Lennon," *New York Times*, December 9, 1989, p. 9.

13. Elizabeth Waters, "Restructuring the 'Woman's Question': *Perestroika* and Prostitution," *Feminist Review*, 3 (Autumn 1989), p. 4.

14. Vasily Aksenov, "Not Quite a Sentimental Journey," *The New Republic*, April 16, 1990, p. 25.

Part IV

Spectacular Bodies

Chapter 14

Tearooms and Sympathy, or, The Epistemology of the Water Closet

Lee Edelman

On October 16, 1964, a correspondent for *The Times* of London made the following observation about the intertwining of sexuality and nationalistic ideology in the United States: "In the post war political primer for beginners, perversion is synonymous with treason. A surviving McCarthyism is that homosexuality and other sexual aberrations are both dangerous to the national security and rife in Washington."[1] These remarks were prompted by the disclosure, less than three weeks before America's Presidential election, that Walter Jenkins, Lyndon Johnson's chief of staff, had been arrested with another man (identified, significantly, as "Hungarian-born") and charged with performing "indecent gestures" in a basement restroom of the Y.M.C.A. two blocks from Jenkins' office in the White House. This arrest, which Laud Humphreys would later characterize as "perhaps the most famous tearoom arrest in America,"[2] precipitated the furor of a political scandal, one that some thought capable of swaying the election, when it was learned that Jenkins had not only been arrested in the very same men's room five years earlier—leaving him with a police record on which had been marked "disorderly conduct (pervert)"—but also that this prior arrest had escaped detection by both the White House and the F.B.I. Jenkins, therefore, had had access to a variety of classified materials, including documents that were submitted to the National Security Council, and he had been granted the top-secret "Q" clearance from the Atomic Energy Commission.

The paranoid logic that echoed throughout the clamor provoked by these revelations found canonical expression in a column written by Arthur Krock for the *New York Times*. After sympathizing with Jenkins and his family, and asserting with self-congratulatory satisfaction that "sympathy in such circumstances is a foremost trait of the American people," Krock went on to admonish his readers: "But it would be irresponsible if the American people felt no anxiety over the fact . . . that a Government official to whom the most secret operations of national security were accessible . . . is among those unfortunates who are most readily subject to the blackmail by which security secrets are often obtained by enemy agents."[3] For this reason—and because, as the editor of the *New York Times* observed, "sexual perversion," like alcoholism and drug addiction, "is increasingly understood as an emotional illness"—America's paper of record, the public voice of "liberal" sentiment, editorialized in support of the anti-gay policies that had informed the federal government's hiring practices for over a decade: "there can be no place on the White House staff or in the upper echelons of government," the *Times* declared, "for a person of markedly deviant behavior."[4]

For several days the Jenkins affair earned front-page attention in newspapers throughout the country before being dislodged by events that seemed more immediately to threaten the nation's well-being: events such as the overthrow of Khrushchev in Russia, and China's first explosion of a nuclear device. Aspects of the Jenkins case resurfaced in news reports during the weeks leading up to the election, but the political ramifications of the scandal were largely contained within ten days of the initial revelations. As soon as the story broke (and it did so despite efforts by Clark Clifford and Abe Fortas to persuade Washington editors to suppress it) Jenkins resigned as special assistant to the President; said to be suffering from "high blood pressure and nervous exhaustion,"[5] he was admitted to George Washington University Hospital where his room was kept, with appropriate irony, under twenty-four hour surveillance. On October 14, the day Jenkins resigned, President Johnson, under pressure to protect his campaign from the scandal, ordered the F.B.I. to "make an immediate and comprehensive inquiry"[6] into the affair. The document generated by that investigation, released on October 22 and consisting of some 100 pages of text under the chillingly broad and encompassing title "Report on Walter

Wilson Jenkins,"[7] reassuringly offered its official conclusion that Jenkins at no time had "compromised the security or interests of the United States."[8]

In the process, however, the report inadvertently offered tantalizing insights into the discursive contexts within which it was possible in 1964 to conceptualize both homosexual activity and the susceptibility to participation in such activity of men not overtly homosexually-identified: Jenkins himself, after all, had been married for some nineteen years at the time of the scandal and was the father of six children. According to Victor Lasky, President Johnson personally insisted that the final report "state that Jenkins was overly tired, that he was a good family man and a hard worker, and that he was not 'biologically' a homosexual."[9] Consequently, even though the incident in 1964 involved Jenkins' arrest for a second time in a men's room that *Time* magazine would describe as "a notorious hangout for deviates";[10] and even though Jenkins acknowledged to the F.B.I. that he had had "limited association with some individuals who are alleged to be, or who admittedly are, sex deviates";[11] and even though he admitted his participation in "the indecent acts for which he was arrested in 1959 and 1964"; and even though he severely qualified his denial of participation in other homosexual encounters by saying that "he did not recall any further indecent acts" and that "if he had been involved in any such acts he would have been under the influence of alcohol and in a state of fatigue and would not remember them";[12] despite all of this it was possible for the F.B.I. to reinforce the rationale for Jenkins' sexual behavior as publically set forth by the White House: Jenkins had been suffering from high blood pressure, nervous tension, and physical exhaustion as a result of being severely overworked.[13] As Lady Bird Johnson expressed this notion in one of the earliest official responses to the scandal: "My heart is aching for someone who has reached the endpoint of exhaustion in dedicated service to his country."[14]

Though I will return to this framing, in every way *political*, of the interpretive context within which, according to the White House and the F.B.I., Walter Jenkins' homosexual encounters were properly to be construed, my interest here extends beyond the specific events that followed from the public disclosure of his arrests. I want in this essay to consider three apparently heterogenous pieces of information, each related in some way to the Jenkins affair, and then see what sort of analysis they permit of the interpenetration of nationalism and sexuality, or rather, of nationalism and the figurations of sexuality—and, in particular, the figurations of homosexuality—in dominant cultural expression at that historical moment in America. For insofar as it marked a turning point in the formulation of nationalistic ideology in the United States—insofar, that is, as it signalled the end of what Michael Rogin has called the "cold war consensus"[15] and initiated the period of national redefinition provoked by the emergence of a sizeable middle-class culture of opposition that would crystallize around the incipient anti-war movement—1964 constitutes a signal moment in which to examine the shifting ideological frameworks within which homosexuality could be read in relation to American national identity.

I would begin, then, by calling attention to the fact that Jenkins was apprehended in 1964 by two members of the District of Columbia vice squad who had placed the restroom of Washington's G-Street "Y" under surveillance on the evening of October 7 by concealing themselves behind the padlocked door of a shower room no longer in use. *Time* magazine explained the mechanics of the policemen's stake-out in the following terms: "They . . . stationed themselves at two peepholes in the door that gave them a view of the washroom and enabled them to peep over the toilet partitions. (There are two peepholes in this and several other washrooms in the area because two corroborating officers are required in such cases)."[16] Let me place a second item beside this description of the State's operations in the public men's rooms of our nation's capitol: this one a statement made six months earlier, in May of 1964, by Senator Barry Goldwater as he set his sights on the White House. Responding to national anxiety about America's technological prowess—an anxiety that had dominated our forays into space since the Soviet triumph with the Sputnik satellite in 1957—Goldwater, implicitly acknowledging the connection between space exploration and the military development of missle and weapons technology, declared with characteristic immoderation: "I don't want to hit the moon. I want to lob one into the men's room of the Kremlin and make sure I hit it."[17] Finally, I would adduce one further item for consideration as a cultural text: the words with which Lyndon Johnson, in a televised comment, expressed his reaction to the discovery that his oldest and closest advisor and friend had been arrested for engaging in homosexual activities in the restroom of the Y.M.C.A.: "I was as shocked," he said, "as if someone had told me my wife had murdered her daughter."[18]

In order to sketch some relationship among these fragments of the historical record, I want to consider another event that took place in 1964; for *Life* magazine, in June of that year, entered thousands of middle-class homes across the country with a photo-essay offering a spectacular view of what it called the "secret world" of "Homosexuality in America."[19] In thus breaking new ground for a family oriented, mass circulation American periodical—and in the process establishing the journalistic conditions that would enable *Time* magazine to present so explicit and sensational an account of the Jenkins affair—the editors of *Life* felt compelled to provide some contextualizing remarks that would justify their devotion of so much attention to what that they identified as a "sad and often sordid world" (66). The terms in which they framed that justification, presenting it in a sort of exculpatory preface to the two essays on homosexuality that followed, are worth considering here:

> Today, especially in big cities, homosexuals are discarding their furtive ways and openly admitting, even flaunting, their deviation. Homosexuals have their own drinking places, their special assignation streets, even their own organizations. And for every obvious homosexual, there are probably nine nearly impossible to detect. This social disorder, which society tries to suppress, has forced itself into the public eye because it does present a problem—and parents especially are concerned. The myth and misconception with which homosexuality has so long been clothed must be cleared away, not to condone it but to cope with it. (66)

The prurience with which *Life*'s writers and photographers produced the spectacle of the gay male body for consumption by an audience they presumed to be heterosexual finds its warrant here in the editors' claim that nine out of ten homosexuals are "nearly impossible to detect." *Life*, therefore, undertakes to expose the gay male body as social "problem" by exposing the problem of seeing or recognizing the gay male body itself: a purpose tellingly figured in the editors' insistence upon "clear[ing] away" the obfuscating garb with which homosexuality has, in their words, "so long been clothed." Whatever else this fantasy of an unclothed homosexuality may bespeak, it establishes a sociological justification for the journalistic depiction of gay men, and in the process it draws attention to the physicality of their bodies, in terms of which the notion of a "homosexual difference" continues to be construed; for even that ninety percent of homosexuals whose sexuality is not immediately "obvious" are only, the preface informs us, "nearly" impossible to detect. As the magazine later tells its readers, with the goal of making them *better* readers of homosexuality and homosexual signs: "Often the only signs are a very subtle tendency to over-meticulous grooming, plus the failure to cast the ordinary man's admiring glance at every pretty girl who walks by" (77). Thus a certain falseness in relation to the body, a disparity between the "truth" of gender as articulated by anatomy and the ways in which that gender is represented by the individual, can serve to assist the heterosexual in the recognition of the gay male body and to effect the cultural reification of "the homosexual" itself. That is, as a "secret" or unarticulated condition that demands journalistic scrutiny and exposure, homosexuality falls from the outset of the article under the aegis of inauthenticity and of a difference all the more subversive because simultaneously threatening ("parents especially are concerned") and potentially unidentifiable.

Through all of this *Life* engages in the ideological labor of constructing homosexuality as a problem or social concern that cannot be disentangled from the processes by which "homosexuals become more visible to the public" (74). Insofar as the magazine participates in those processes by making the "secret world" of homosexuality visible to its (presumptively heterosexual) readers, it does so in order to encourage their internalization of the repressive supervisory mechanisms of the State—an internalization that it seeks to effect by reproducing in its readers the magazine's interest in learning to recognize those denizens of the gay world who are "nearly impossible to detect." Moreover, by conjuring homosexuality as an often invisible yet omnipresent concern, the magazine evokes the cold war equation of homosexuality with Communist infiltration and subversion—an equation that becomes explicit when Ernest Havemann begins one of the magazine's articles by inquiring, provocatively: "Do the homosexuals, like the Communists, intend to bury us?" (76).

Now it is significant that when Guy George Gabrielson, the Republican National Chair, helped to popularize that equation by warning that homosexuals in the government's employ were "perhaps as dangerous as the actual Communists"—and the word "actual" in this phrase is worth noting—he also explained the public's relative ignorance about the extent of this "problem" by pointing to the moral constraints that prevented the mass media from exploring the issue: "The country would be more aroused over this tragic angle of the situation," he wrote, "if it were not for the difficulties of the newspapers and radio commentators in adequately presenting the facts, while respecting the decency of their American audiences."[20] With this the question of textual representation, especially in the journalistic media that shape popular opinon, finds itself enmeshed in the cold war rhetoric that conflated homosexuality with communism. The very possibility of a public, nonmedical discourse of homosexuality comes to depend upon the political interests that such a discourse can be made to serve. Far from disallowing, therefore, the discussion of homosexuality, remarks such as Gabrielson's *encouraged* public consideration of the issue to the extent that such consideration furthered the promotion of a homophobic—and therefore, at least metonymically, anti-communist—agenda sufficient to "arouse," to use his word, the unwary American public. The result, of course, was that Senator McCarthy's campaign against subversives in the American government had the effect of focusing public attention on the unrecognized pervasiveness of homosexuality.[21]

Less constrained in 1964 by the representational "difficulties" to which Gabrielson alluded, the media were able to flesh out or give body to the abstract cold war rhetoric of homosexuality as public and political threat by resituating it within the framework of concern about the definitional barriers between the social and the privately domestic—a concern that had served implicitly to support the ideological construction of American nationalism at the end of the forties and throughout the fifties. For the backward looking ideology of domesticity that governed the American national consciousness in the wake of World War II sought not only to achieve such regressive social policies as the return of white middle-class women to the unpaid labor of heterosexual homemaking, it also attempted to establish for America the fictive cohesiveness of a suburban national-cultural identity. Even as American cities expanded, the white middle-class imaginary was enthralled by the consumerist fantasy of the "American Dream": the bourgeois family safely ensconced in a home that was detached and privately owned. This national self-image can be viewed as a reaction against the political realities of a postwar world in which American power could no longer detach itself from military involvement in international affairs, a world in which atomic bombs and the pirated missile technologies of the Nazis, technologies simultaneously undergoing development by East and West alike, made American isolationism strategically impossible and therefore all the more powerful as a spur to ideological formation.

As the development of weapons technology deprived America of the geopolitical privilege of its distance from powerful enemies, the idealization of domestic security, for both the nuclear family and the nuclear state, became an overriding national concern. Yet that ideal of a private domestic preserve could only be articulated through an insistence upon the need for new technologies of social control. Refinements in techniques of interrogation, surveillance, and security examination marked the dependence of the white bourgeois family's expectation of a privileged domestic space upon the state's girding up of that notion even—or especially—by ceaselessly violating the domain of domestic privacy itself. Such violations, however, gained considerable acceptance as necessary weapons in the effort to expose the activities of subversives who were widely depicted as using (and hence abusing) their constitutional liberties in order to bring the United States under foreign domination. Thus the postwar machinery of American nationalism operated by enshrining and mass-producing the archaic, bourgeois fantasy of a self-regulating familial sanctuary at a time when the idea of the domestic was embroiled in an anxious and unstable relation to the manifold social imperatives of the State.

If the reactionary aftermath of World War II, then, saw a massive intensification of the State's efforts to control homosexual behavior, those efforts responded to the widespread perception of gay sexuality as an alien infestation, an unnatural because un-American practice, resulting from the entanglement with foreign countries—and foreign nationals—during the war.[22] And as the importance of international and domestic surveillance became a central preoccupation of postwar America, so the campaigns against gays by local police departments, spurred by the national political identification of homosexuality with domestic subversion, made use of new modes of subterfuge and dissimulation, including the surveillance of public rest rooms that would lead to the arrest of Walter Jenkins in 1964.

Now in the twentieth-century American social landscape, the institutional men's room constitutes a site at which the zones of the public and the private cross with a distinctive psychic charge. That charge, of course, carries, at a stronger voltage, the tension of ambivalence that the bathroom as such is sufficient to evoke. In May of 1964, for example—the same month that Senator Goldwater declared his interest in making a preemptive strike against the men's room of the Kremlin—*Life* published an article in which it noted with satisfaction that "Americans already have nearly 50 million bathrooms, more than the rest of the world put together. Now they are demanding even more—and are demanding that they be bigger and fancier."[23] Yet if this metonymic index of American cleanliness—itself, proverbially, a metonym of godliness—suggests an element of national pride that centers on the ongoing proliferation of its bathrooms, the opening sentence of the article sounds a note potentially more ominous: "Bedecked, bejeweled and splashed with color, the bathroom is blossoming with a flair unapproached since the fall of the Roman Empire." Caught between its honorific associations with industrial progress and hygienic purity, and its more pejorative associations with weakness, luxury, and aesthetic indulgence of the perverse, the American bathroom in 1964 constituted an unacknowledged ideological battleground in the endless—because endlessly anxious—campaign to shore up "masculinity" by policing the borders at which sexual difference is definitionally produced.

Nowhere are the psychic stakes in that conflict more intense than when the bathroom in question is a public or institutional facility. Already set aside as a liminal zone in which internal poisons are cast out and disavowed, the institutional men's room typically emblematizes the uncertainty of its positioning between the public and the private through its spatial juxtaposition of public urinals and private stalls. Indeed, the effort to provide a space of privacy interior to the men's room itself, a space that would still be subject to some degree of regulation and control, had encouraged by 1964 the increasing popularity of that monument to capitalist ingenuity, the coin-operated toilet stall in the public washroom. And it was in the anticipated privacy of just such a stall that Walter Jenkins would be spied upon by representatives of the D.C. police department as he engaged in illegal sexual behavior with a Hungarian-born veteran of the U.S. armed services.

The transformation of Walter Jenkins from retiring and camera-shy chief of staff to a man whose sexual behavior was subject to sensationalized depiction, however, was accomplished not so much by the police as by the social policing carried out by the press. For when Jenkins chose, on the night of his arrest, to forfeit his $50 bond, he waived his right to trial (without confessing guilt) and, as far as the law was concerned, thus brought the matter to a close. Only when the news of his arrest was leaked to the Republican National Committee, and then leaked again by the RNC to members of the press, did Jenkins become the central figure in what many called Johnson's Profumo scandal[24]—and only then because the media coverage of the case re-enacted on an enormously magnified scale the regulatory surveillance that the vice squad detectives carried out from behind the shower room door.

Yet the scandal that led editors to pontificate about its ominous implications for American security produced a radically different response among the public at large. *Time* magazine acknowledged "a nationwide wave of ribald jokes" while *Newsweek* referred to the widespread outpouring of "sick jokes and leering sloganeering." Johnson's reelection motto—"All the way with LBJ"—was parodistically rewritten as "Either way with LBJ";[25] and wags insisted that Johnson was determined to stand "behind" Jenkins to the bitter end. Like the media's sensationalistic fascination with the case—*Time,* for instance, even gave its readers the measurements of the "notorious" restroom, describing it as a "9-ft. by 11-ft. spot reeking of disinfectant and stale cigars"—these jokes symptomatize a cultural fascination that can help to illuminate Senator Goldwater's remark ("I want to lob one into the men's room of the Kremlin and make sure I hit it") in which he implied a symbolic connection that defined the "men's room" no less than "the Kremlin" as the source of his anxiety.

The public staging of the men's room in Goldwater's flamboyantly militaristic comment, as in the surveillance operations of the vice squad and the journalistic narratives of the Jenkins affair, takes much of its significance from the concern about the indeterminacy of "homosexual difference" in postwar America. Consider, for example, the language with which *Time* contextualized, in 1959, the social invisibility enjoyed by the majority of the gay men examined in a contemporary book by Dr. Edmund Bergler: "Despite all the washroom jokes, most of Dr. Bergler's homosexuals look and act perfectly masculine."[26] It is not insignificant that it is the washroom here that serves as the scene of a universally recognizable heterosexual mythologizing (no specification of these "jokes" is necessary since the audience can be assumed already to know them) that defensively seeks to establish those signs by which homosexual difference can be determined—signs that would establish such a difference as unambiguously as the sign on the washroom door seems to point to the certainty of distinctions between the sexes.

But that latter sign, of course, figures crucially in a celebrated diagram employed by Lacan: a diagram in which what he designates as "the laws of urinary segregation" produce the signifiers "Ladies" and "Gentlemen" in order to differentiate identical doors. It is not insignificant that Lacan should elaborate a fable from this diagram in which "Ladies" and "Gentlemen" become, through the misrecognitions of a boy and girl sitting opposite each other on a train, "two countries" that are subject to "the unbridled power of ideological warfare," even though, as Lacan assures us, "they are actually one country."[27] Nor is it insignificant that in this fable "anatomical difference," as Jacqueline Rose observes, "comes to *figure* sexual difference," so that, as she goes on to note, "the phallus thus indicates the reduction of difference to an instance of visible perception."[28] For I want to suggest that the men's room, whose very signifier in this fable enshrines the phallus as the token not only of difference, but of difference as determinate, difference as knowable, is the site of a particular heterosexual anxiety about the inscriptions of homosexual desire and about the possibility of knowing or recognizing whatever would constitute the "homosexual difference."

This can be intuited more readily when the restroom is considered, not, as it is by Lacan, in terms of "urinary segregation"—a context that establishes the phallus from the outset as the token of anatomical difference—but as the site of a loosening of sphincter control, with the subsequent evocation of an anal eroticism undifferentiated by gender, in Freudian etiology, because anterior to the genital tyranny that raises the phallus to its privileged position. Precisely because the phallus marks the putative stability of the divide between "Ladies" and "Gentlemen," because it articulates the concept of sexual difference in terms of "visible perception," the "urinary" function in the institutional men's room customarily takes place within view of others—as if to indicate its status as an act of definitional display; but the private enclosure of the toilet stall signals the potential anxiety at issue in the West when the men's room becomes the locus not of urinary but of intestinal relief. For the satisfaction that such relief affords abuts dangerously on homophobically abjectified desires, and because that satisfaction suggests an opening onto difference within the signifier on the men's room door, it must both be isolated and kept in view lest its erotic potential come out, as it were.[29] The Freudian pleasure or comfort stationed in that movement of the bowel overlaps too extensively with the Kristevan abjection that recoils from such evidence of the body's inescapable implication in its death; and the disquieting conjunction of these contexts informs, with predictably volatile and destructive results, the ways in which dominant American culture could interpret the "meaning" of male-male sexual relations in 1964.

Consequently, in the representations of the Jenkins case and in Senator Goldwater's remark, the historical framing of the men's room as theater for heterosexual anxiety condenses a variety of phobic responses to the interimplication of sphinctral relaxation and the popular notion of gay male sexuality as a yielding to weakness or a loss of control—a notion invoked in the Jenkins scandal when James Reston, in the pages of the *New York Times*, defined Jenkins' behavior as "personal weakness."[30] In fact, in a novel that first appeared on the *New York Times*' best-seller list the week of Walter Jenkins' arrest, the title character of Saul Bellow's *Herzog* watches as a young man is brought before a magistrate to answer charges stemming from his pursuit of erotic gratification in the men's room beneath Grand Central Station. Reasserting the heterosexual identification of the men's room with epistemological crisis and the anxiety of lost control, Herzog observes, "You don't destroy a man's career because he yielded to an impulse in that ponderous stinking cavern below Grand Central, in the cloaca of the city, where no mind can be sure of stability."[31] The threat to stability—that is, to the security of (heterosexual) identity and (heterosexual) mastery of the signifiers of difference—portended here by the men's room itself, gains figural reinforcement from its contiguity to the image of the "cloaca," a term that designates not only a sewer or a water-closet, but also, as the *Random House Dictionary* phrases it, "the common cavity into which the intestinal, urinary, and generative canals open in birds, reptiles, amphibians, many fishes, and certain mammals." The "stinking cavern" of Grand Central Station recapitualtes the anatomical "cavity" to which the "cloaca" refers, and together these displaced but insistent spatial tropes suggest the anxiety of an internal space of difference, an overdetermined opening within the male, of which the activity of defecation may serve as a disquieting reminder. Indeed, it is worth recalling in this context the words of Kristeva: "It is . . . not lack of cleanliness or health that cause abjection but what disturbs identity, system, order. What does not respect borders, positions, rules."[32]

It should come as no surprise, therefore, that in the sex-segregated environment of the institutional men's room the act of defecation remains, in most circumstances, discreetly closeted. For a host of reasons—including childhood fantasies of phallic detachability that are linked with the release of the faeces; the substitutability in the unconscious, according to Freud, of "the concepts *faeces*, . . . *baby*, and *penis*";[33] and a psychic ambivalence "memorialize[d]" in the anus, as Eve Sedgwick puts it, as the site of a struggle "over private excitations, adopted controls, the uses of shame, and the rhythms of productivity"[34]—the heightened awareness in the men's room of this internal space of difference threatens to vitiate the assurance of those identities that the signifiers "Ladies" and "Gentlemen" would affirm. And by threatening the stable relations between those two heavily defended "countries," the disturbing psychic configurations for which the public men's room serves as the arena make possible the figurative interchangeability of a (perceived) threat to the integrity of the nation's (male) bodies and a (perceived) threat to the integrity of the body of the nation, especially when that nation, like America in the fifties and early sixties, confronts the fact that its defenses and its borders are now subject to penetration by the missle technology of its foes.

In a sense, then, the arrest of Walter Jenkins can be viewed as one spectacular instance of the "false arrest" of what Herman Rapaport describes, in another context, as "the sliding that occurs between signified and signified, door one and two" in the Lacanian representation of the restroom doors.[35] For Jenkins, like thousands of other men—not all of them gay or gay-identified—booked on similar charges before and after, could be understood by his contemporaries in one of three ways: a) as a homosexual whose identity *as* a homosexual reinforced the binarism of "Ladies" and "Gentlemen" precisely by standing outside that binarism as the recognizable "mistake" within the system itself; or b) as the victim of some illness, physical or emotional, whose transgressive behavior, therefore, did not symptomatize his (homosexual) identity but rather bespoke an exceptional *falling away* from his true (i.e. heterosexual) identity;[36] or c) as a threat to the interpretive certainty invested in the phallus as the privileged signifier of that "identity" upon which patriarchal epistemology definitionally depends. That is to say, insofar as male homosexuality continued to signify as a condition indissociable from the category of gender, the only alternative to defining Jenkins as, essentially, "a homosexual" or to explaining his behavior in terms of some sort of illness or mental breakdown, was to posit a category-subverting alterity within the conceptual framework of "the masculine" itself. But it was, after all, to secure the integrity of that always embattled framework that the surveillance of public restrooms was undertaken in the first place, and that same defensive imperative determined the strategic response to the Jenkins affair as orchestrated by President Johnson and the members of his staff.

In seeking, however, to circumscribe the scandal by defining it outside the context of homosexuality as such—by insisting, for instance, as Victor Lasky reports President Johnson to have done, that Jenkins was not "biologically" a homosexual—the White House entered into the unavoidable contradictions that permeate the discourse on homosexuality in America. Thus the image of Jenkins that it disseminated was that of a family man victimized by the extraordinary demands that were placed, by his profession and by his own sense of responsibility, on his energy, time, and attention. As one former insider subsequently wrote: "Whatever the nature of Jenkins' difficulty, he was obviously no simple or habitual homosexual. He was a man who for years had been destroying himself in the service of Lyndon Johnson, ten to sixteen hours a day, six or seven days a week, and finally something had snapped."[37] *Newsweek*, in its presentation of this reading of the affair, quoted from the F.B.I. report in which a colleague asserted that Jenkins "would walk 'on his hands and knees on broken glass to avoid giving President Johnson any problem,'"[38] while *Time* cited a "friend of Jenkins'" who declared, "There were two great devotions in his life: L.B.J. and his own family."[39] These testimonials, of course, endeavor rhetorically to "protect" Jenkins from any assumption that his acknowledged participation in male-male sexual acts should be read as an indication of "homosexuality." By presenting him as man whose difficulties sprang from an excess of those celebrated American attributes of industriousness and loyalty, they dissociate him from a homosexuality conceived in terms of indolence, luxury, and the lack—or worse, the repudiation—of generative productivity. Those same testimonials, however, produce retroactively an inescapable question about the "meaning" of such excess and such "devotion." They produce, that is, an epistemological doubt about the legibility of homosexuality that generates what I have elsewhere described as a homographic imperative—an imperative to read experience (often retroactively, and always with an emphasis on the signifying potential of the male body) for the inscriptions (understood to have been present all along) that convey a "meaning"—homosexuality—that one could and should have read from the outset.

In the context of the Jenkins affair, the burden of this epistemological doubt found its most loaded expression in President Johnson's assertion that the news of Jenkins' arrest was as shocking to him "as if someone had told me my wife had murdered her daughter." This phrasing suggests that while the scandal itself led some members of the public to question their ability to know or trust the President, the President here could figure the shock of his response to Jenkins' homosexual involvement only in terms that put into play his own ability to know or trust his wife. The news, that is, of an unrecognized "crime" committed by one of his intimates finds displaced expression through his rhetorical conjuring of a different crime committed by someone we presume to have been a different sort of intimate. The unspeakable scene of desire between two men must be represented through a scenario of violence between two women, and the "shock" that responds to the "foreignness" of the homosexual encounter in the men's room is translated into a betrayal interior to the structure of heterosexual marital domesticity. Johnson thus images his advisor's arrest as a violation of trust, and hence as a blow to the possibility of cognitive security, by dwelling on its exposure of an unrecognized quality that calls into question the knowledge and familiarity on which his relationship with Jenkins was based. By emphasizing the defamiliarization effected by such a sudden revelation, the comment implicitly diverges from the official explanation that Jenkins had strayed from the straight, if not the narrow, as a result of too much work; instead, it positions the shock of the affair in the disclosure of what should have been known in advance. The shock, therefore, derives as much from the President's having to receive from someone else ("as if someone had told me") such information about his friend (a friend close enough to be represented in the figure by Johnson's wife), as it does from the specific nature of the information he receives. Significantly, moreover, the logic at work in the mobilization of this figure places homosexuality in a conceptual space contiguous with, and impinged upon by, an anxiety-producing image of the power that women wield as mothers.

This bespeaks not merely the popular assumption of the interchangeability of same-sex desire and the disturbance of gender distinctions and roles, but also the psychological truism of the period that male homosexuality both resulted from, and constituted an inappropriate identification between, the mother and her son. The President's comment invokes the contradictory reasoning whereby gay men were assumed, derisively, to be overly fond of and close to their mothers, even as they were assumed, projectively, to hate women—"especially," as the editors of the Catholic journal, *America*, wrote in 1962, "the woman who is a mother."[40] Tellingly, those who charged gay men with denigrating women and "especially" mothers, did not scruple to read homosexuality as a "problem" for which mother herself should be blamed. It was, after all, the too loving mother that heterosexual culture loved to hate, the smothering mother who destroyed her son through overprotection or overindulgence. Just four months before the Jenkins affair, Ernest Havemann, borrowing heavily from the work of Irving Bieber, summarized these notions in his article for *Life*: "On the one hand, the homosexual's mother kept him utterly dependent on her, unable to make his own decisions. On the other, she pampered him, catered to his every whim and smothered him with affection" (78). As the language of this passage makes clear, the mother stands accused here of effeminizing her son, of preventing his "natural" development into heterosexual manhood and thus, effectively, of consigning him to a life of nongenerative sexuality. The abjection of male homosexuality, therefore, carries the burden of an archaic patriarchal anxiety about the mother's relation to power; as Kristeva puts it: "The abject confronts us . . . with our earliest attempts to release the hold of *maternal* entity even before ex-isting outside of her, thanks to the autonomy of language. It is a violent, clumsy breaking away, with the constant risk of falling back under the sway of a power as securing as it is stifling."[41] If the security of that power allows homosexual relations to be figured in terms of indulgence and weakness—in stark contrast to the masculinizing rigor and renunciation involved in the break from maternal control—the "stifling" that the mother allegedly effects provokes a "violent" disavowal that gets displaced and reenacted in the phobic response to male homosexuality. Hence the logic by which Johnson's comment can substitutively represent homosexual eros and desire in terms of violence; hence too its anxious evocation of the slippage from "wife," a position of subordination within the dynamics of heterosexual marriage, to mother, a position of power within the mother-child dyad.[42]

It should come as no surprise that the same social pressures that conspired to "blame" the mother for male homosexuality produced the cold war discourse of "momism" that implicated mothers in narratives of subversion through the weakening of masculine resolve against communism. In his compelling and well-documented analysis of cold war cinema in America, Michael Rogin demonstrates how films of the fifties and early sixties "identif[y] Communism with secret, maternal influence. . . . The films suggest that the menace of alien invasion lay not so much in the power of a foreign state as in the obliteration of paternal inheritance."[43] Brilliantly exposing the contradictory implications of domestic ideology, Rogin shows how the security state of cold war America adopted the very mechanisms of illicit power that it anxiously identified with its enemies: "Men comprise the state, to be sure; but they use the techniques of motherhood and Communism—intrusion, surveillance, and secret domination" (21). These technqiues, as Rogin makes clear, were then turned against motherhood and Communism both so as to prevent the disappropriation of American masculinity. It is within this context that I want to suggest that by representing male homosexuality through the figure of a mother who murders her child, and who therefore participates in the destruction of (patriarchal) familial continuity, Johnson's comment not only restages the cultural abjection of the mother, it also recapitulates the anxiety invoked when *Life* magazine inquired if "the homosexuals, like the Communists, intend to bury us." It figurally positions homosexual behavior in the context of "the obliteration of paternal inheritance" and signals an interpretation of male-male desire not only through the filter of sentimental self-pity writ large in the melodrama of (domestic) betrayal that President Johnson so vividly imagines, but also in a specific relation to history that equally informs Senator Goldwater's remark and the staging of the men's room in the Jenkins affair.

For when homosexuality enters the field of vision in each of these fragments of the social text it occasions a powerful disruption of that field by virtue of its uncontrollably figuralizing effects; and that disruption of the field of vision is precisely what homosexuality comes to represent: so radical a fracturing of the linguistic and epistemic order that it figures futurity imperilled, it figures history as apocalypse, by gesturing toward the precariousness of familial and national survival. If momism is the theory, then homosexuality is the practice, for it is seen as enacting the destabilization of borders, the subversion of masculine identity from within, that momism promotes. Such a reading of male homosexuality, of course, is not unique to America in the early sixties; my point, however, is that the historical pressures upon the nationalistic self-image of postwar America found articulation through the portrayal of homosexual activity as the proximate cause of perceived danger to the nation at a time of unprecedented concern about the possibility of national—and global—destruction. Employing late nineteenth-century arguments about racial degeneration in the context of contemporary sociopolitical conflicts, historically deployed readings envisioning male homosexuality in terms of the abjection associated with the men's room could bemoan the threat that homosexuality posed to the continuity of civilization itself. Norman Mailer, in an essay from 1961, offers one blatant formulation of this idea: "As a civilization dies, it loses its biology. The homosexual, alienated from the biological chain, becomes its center."[44] Mailer clarifies the phobic logic that underlies this statement in an essay titled "Truth and Being: Nothing and Time," published in 1962 and reprinted (ironically?) in *The Presidential Papers* as part of a section labeled "On Waste": ". . . if excrement is the enforced marriage of Tragic Beauty and Filth, why then did God desert it, and leave our hole to the Devil, unless it is because God has hegemony over us only as we create each other. God owns the creation, but the Devil has power over all we waste—how natural for him to lay seige where the body ends and weak tragic air begins."[45] Heterosexuality alone possesses the divine attribute of creativity here; homosexual activity, by contrast, leads only to waste, as Mailer insisted in an interview in 1962: "I think one of the reasons that homosexuals go through such agony when they're around 40 or 50 is that their lives have nothing to do with procreation. . . . They've used up their being."[46]

The erotic behavior proscriptively associated with the men's room as the scene of the voiding of waste thus gets entangled in the national imaginary with a fantasy of cultural and historical vastation. But the surveillance by which the law expresses the state's "need" to see homosexuality, like the sensationalism involved as that "need" is reenacted by the popular media, reveals a scarcely suppressed *desire* to see, to recognize, and to expose the alterity of homosexuality and homosexual tendencies. That desire bespeaks a narcissistic anxiety about the definition of (sexual) identity that can only be stabilized and protected by a process of elimination or casting out. It betokens, that is, a cultural imperative to anal sadistic behavior that generates the homophobic definition of masculinity itself—that generates, for our culture, masculinity as such through the anal sadistic projection or casting away that inheres in homophobia. Little wonder, then, that Senator Goldwater should aim his missles at the Kremlin and the men's room both, for in the process he makes visible the aggressive anality of a culture compelled to repudiate the homosexuality it projectively identifies with the very anality it thus itself enacts. That abjectifying—and therefore effeminizing—anality is a condition that homophobic masculinity repudiates by construing it as the distinguishing hallmark of a recognizable category of homosexual person. As the various texts drawn together here suggest, though, that reification of homosexuality is inherently unstable, its markings always subject to doubt and the anxiety of retroactive interpretation. Homosexuality, therefore, remains subject to figuration as that which threatens the catastrophic undoing of history, national and familial both, by opening an epistemological gap, a space, a void, in maleness itself—a gap in which, in the end, as it were, there is nothing to be seen, and no assurance, therefore, that the visual display of masculinity's phallic ensign can suffice as evidence of the heterosexuality for which "masculinity" has become a trope. For the public insistence on the visible organ in the open space of the urinal can never dispel the magnetizing pull of the dangers seated in that unseen space, that cavity concealed by the toilet stall door that leads, as Lacan's fabulation would have it, toward another "country" whose agents are always already operating within—always already operating even, or even *especially*, within the men's room itself, in which, for heterosexual men, it is never sufficient for one to be in order to be, with any certainty or security, a "man."

NOTES

The version of "Tearooms and Sympathy" printed here is significantly shortened from the essay that grew out of my presentation at the Nationalisms and Sexualities Conference. The full text of that essay will be forthcoming in Henry Abelove, Michèle Barale, and David Halperin, eds., *Lesbian/Gay Studies: A Reader* (Routledge, Fall 1992); it will also appear in my own book, *Homographesis: Essays in Gay Literary and Cultural Theory*, forthcoming from Routledge.

1. *The Times*, October 16, 1964, "President Johnson's Cause Threatened by New Scandal," p. 11.

2. Laud Humphreys, *Tearoom Trade: Impersonal Sex in Public Places* (Chicago: Aldine Publishing Company, 1975), p. 19, n. 10.

3. Arthur Krock, "The Jenkins Case," *New York Times*, October 18, 1964, Section E, p. 11.

4. Editorial, "The Jenkins Case," *New York Times*, October 18, 1964, Section E, p. 10.

5. This quotation from Dr. Charles Thompson, Jenkins' physician, is cited by *Time* magazine, October 23, 1964, p. 22. The *New York Times*, in its first story on the Jenkins case, October 15, 1964, observed that Dr. Thompson had been quoted "by The

Associated Press as saying that Mr. Jenkins was suffering from 'insomnia, tensions and agitation' and that he was 'just worn out'" (31).

6. Cited in the *New York Times*, October 16, 1964, p. 1.

7. *Newsweek*, November 2, 1964, p. 26.

8. Cited in the *New York Times*, October 23, 1964, p. 1.

9. Victor Lasky, *It Didn't Start with Watergate* (New York: The Dial Press, 1977), p. 192.

10. *Time*, October 23, 1964, p. 21.

11. *New York Times*, October 23, 1964, p. 1.

12. *New York Times*, October 23, 1964, p. 1 and p. 31.

13. A similar sort of reasoning was used to explain the suicide of Lord Castlereagh. As Louis Crompton observes, Castlereagh's suicide responded to his concern that he would be charged with sodomitical offenses, but "the official account given out was that overwork from his arduous duties had led to a mental breakdown in the throes of which Castlereagh had opened his carotid artery while unattended" (Louis Crompton, *Byron and Greek Love* [Berkeley: University of California Press, 1985], p. 302).

14. *Time*, October 23, 1964, p. 22.

15. Michael Rogin describes the period "between 1943 and 1964" as "the years of the cold war consensus." During these years, as he notes, subversives, who "signified control by a sophisticated, alien order," could no longer be recognized by their racial or ethnic differences; they "melted into their surroundings." And the reactionary response to the threat this was thought to pose to dominant cultural values was twofold: "One was the rise of the national security state. The other was the production and surveillance of public opinion in the media of mass society" ("Kiss Me Deadly: Communism, Motherhood, and Cold War Movies," *Representations*, 6 [1984], p. 2).

16. *Time*, October 23, 1964, p. 21.

17. Cited in the *New York Times*, October 22, 1964, p. 45.

18. Cited in *Newsweek*, November 2, 1964, p. 27.

19. *Life,* June 26, 1964, pp. 66–80. Subsequent page references to this article will be given in the text.

20. *New York Times,* April 19, 1950, p. 25.

21. The publication of the Kinsey Report in 1948, of course, provided a context in which the concern about widespread and unrecognized homosexual behavior could be mobilized.

22. This sort of argument about the "sources" of homosexual behavior in a given society is, of course, quite common historically. Louis Crompton cites a passage from the British antiwar newspaper, the *Morning Chronicle,* from 1810, which offers a strikingly similar analysis by ascribing the "prevalence" of homosexuality in England to "the unnecesssary war in which we have been so long involved. It is not merely the favour which has been shewn to foreigners, to foreign servants, to foreign troops, but the sending of our own troops to associate with foreigners, that may truly be regarded as the source of evil" (*Byron and Greek Love,* p. 167).

American fiction of the fifties suggests in a number of different ways the connection between war-time experiences and homosexual behavior. In Dennis Murphy's novel, *The Sergeant,* for instance, published in 1958, the title character's coercive expressions of his erotic interest in the private, Tom Swanson, signify in terms of the text's initial recollection of the sergeant's decoration-earning bravery during an ambush in World War II; the narrative, evoking that primal moment, lingers provocatively over the sergeant's violent and intimate struggle with a German soldier and thus underscores the element of desire that first finds expression in this lethal encounter. Allen Drury's *Advise and Consent,* published the following year, similarly implies a link between homosexuality and the war by situating Senator Brigham Anderson's fateful exploration of his homosexual tendencies during a rest period in Honolulu in the midst of World War II. When this episode, which Anderson has concealed throughout his subsequent marriage, finally surfaces as his political opponents attempt to control the Senator's vote, Anderson finally must try to explain his homosexual encounter to his wife: "People go off the track sometimes, under pressures like the war" (*Advise and Consent* [Garden City, New York: Doubleday & Company, 1959], p. 432). More interestingly, the novel establishes a structural analogy between homosexuality and communism by pairing them as the guilty secrets that "come out" in the course of the political maneuvers prompted by the effort to confirm Robert Leffingwell as Secretary of State.

23. "Elegant Décor in Bathrooms," *Life,* May 15, 1964, p. 68.

24. In a front-page article in the *Wall Street Journal* of October 16, 1964, for instance, Henry Gemmill quotes "one prominent Republican Senator," as follows: "It

seems to me there's now a direct parallel to Britain's Profumo case—except here it's boys instead of girls." The coverage of the scandal in *Newsweek*'s article on October 26, 1964 also features a photograph in which demonstrators at a Johnson rally in Pittsburgh raise an enormous banner that queries, "Jenkins, LBJ's Profumo?" (32).

25. Shelley Ross, *Fall from Grace: Sex, Scandal, and Corruption in American Politics from 1702 to the Present* (New York: Ballantine Books, 1988), p. 213.

26. "The Strange World," *Time*, November 9, 1959, p. 66.

27. Jacques Lacan, "The Agency of the Letter in the Unconscious," *Écrits: A Selection*, trans. Alan Sheridan (New York: Norton, 1977), p. 152.

28. Jacqueline Rose, "Introduction-II," in Juliet Mitchell and Jacqueline Rose, eds., *Feminine Sexuality: Jacques Lacan and the école freudienne* (London: MacMillan Press, 1983), p. 42.

29. Significantly, one common response, especially in the fifties and early sixties, to the fear of homosexual activity in men's rooms, particularly in those on college campuses, was the removal of the doors from toilet stalls so as to produce a space enclosed on three sides which thereby continued to gesture toward privacy, while simultaneously functioning, as the absent fourth wall hints, as a stage upon which the actor could always be subject to surveillance.

30. October 15, 1964, p. 31. Note how close the expression of this sentiment comes to the words with which Lyndon Johnson's brother described the arguments made by Fortas and Clifford as they tried to persuade the Washington press not to publish the reports of Jenkins' arrest: "You can't condemn a man for one single moment of weakness" (Sam Houston Johnson, *My Brother Lyndon*, ed. Enrique Lopez [New York: Cowles Books, 1969], p. 175).

31. Saul Bellow, *Herzog* (New York: Viking Penguin, 1964), p. 227.

32. Julia Kristeva, *Powers of Horror: An Essay on Abjection*, trans. Leon Roudiez (New York: Columbia University Press, 1982), p. 4.

33. Sigmund Freud, "On Transformations of Instinct as Exemplified in Anal Erotism," in *On Sexuality*, trans. James Strachey, The Pelican Freud Library, Volume 7 (Harmondsworth, UK: Penguin, 1983), p. 296.

34. Eve Kosofsky Sedgwick, "A Poem is Being Written," *Representations*, 17 (1987), p. 126.

35. Herman Rapaport, "Lacan Disbarred: Translation as Ellipsis," *Diacritics*, 6, 4 (Winter 1976), p. 58.

36. Three days after Walter Jenkins resigned, the *New York Times* carried a story under the headline: "Ex-Homosexual Got U.S. Job Back." The article reports that the administrator of the Federal Aviation Agency, Najeeb H. Halaby, had ordered reinstatement of a 32 year old employee who had been fired in 1960 when he admitted having engaged in four homosexual acts when he was 18. Mr. Halaby explained that the employee was "fully rehabilitated and competent" and "should not be scarred for life for a youthful mistake." The article substantiated this notion by then observing: "The employe [sic], now 32 years old, is married and the father of three children. The Government, in effect, conceded that he now had a normal sex life and that the homosexual incidents had been youthful indiscretions." In addition, however, the article offers two other interesting pieces of information: first, although the employee was ordered to be reinstated, the report concludes by asssuring the public, "He will not actually control air traffic"; second, the article notes that despite the reinstatement, a memorandum from the White House had recently been circulated calling for more stringent security screening prior to hiring workers in order to avoid other cases in which such questions could arise. The memorandum, in an ironic twist that the author of the article clearly relished, turns out to have been, of course, none other than Walter Jenkins.

37. Eric F. Goldman, *The Tragedy of Lyndon Johnson* (New York: Knopf, 1969), pp. 250–51. It is worth noting that the concept of bisexuality does not enter into the discursive framing of Jenkins' psycho-sexual identity.

38. "The Jenkins Report," *Newsweek*, November 2, 1964, p. 26.

39. "The Senior Staff Man," *Time*, October 23, 1964, p. 21.

40. Editorial: "The 'Mother' Image," *America*, May 12, 1962, p. 227. In this virulently homophobic article the editors endorse an assertion by Eric Sevareid that homosexuals exercise pernicious international control over the worlds of fashion, theater, film, and design. The implications of a conspiracy are reinforced by Sevareid's description of homosexual power imposed through "loose but effective combines." Sevareid's vehement denunciation of gay men, as quoted in the editorial, touches so many of the familiar bases in this sort of rhetorical outburst that it seems worthwhile to quote from it here: "The homosexual is usually capable of neither loving nor understanding a woman; so, in his fashions, the woman's body is merely a skeletal frame for his

artistic experiments in design; in his films the woman is generally a prostitute or an overbearing clod. In the theatre, they [homosexuals] portray neither high triumph nor high tragedy, for these involve acts of will and decision. In their world there is no decision and no will; there is only a degraded helplessness against 'forces,' because being sick themselves, they must see society as the sickness" (227). The occasion for this outburst in the pages of *America* was the celebration of a "antidote," one described as "providential," to the "malevolent . . . influence of the homosexual" in "defiling the image of mother." That "antidote" was the decision of Pope John XXIII to allow the 1964 World's Fair in New York to exhibit the "Piéta" of Michelangelo. The irony of *such* an "antidote," as the language of the article would have it, can hardly fail to recall Derrida's reading of the *pharmakon* in "Plato's Pharmacy."

41. Kristeva, *Powers of Horror*, p. 13.

42. It may be worth noting that the name by which Johnson's wife was known, "Lady Bird," foregrounds the distinction of sex that bears so decisively on the question of power. The fact that the mother's destructive force is unleashed upon the female child responds, of course, to the historical circumstance that Johnson had two daughters and no sons. His naming of those daughters, however, suggests his eagerness to perpetuate the paternal inheritance insofar as both daughters were given names that made their initials identical to his own (and to his wife's after her marriage to him): LBJ. The murderousness of the mother in this figure might position "Lady Bird" in the role of another lady, "Lady MacBeth," in which case she, as a tropological substitution for Walter Jenkins, articulates male homosexuality as a condition of being "unsexed."

43. Rogin, "Kiss Me Deadly," p. 9.

44. Norman Mailer, "Theatre: *The Blacks*," *The Presidential Papers* (New York: G. P. Putnam's Sons, 1963), p. 210.

45. Mailer, *Presidential Papers*, p. 275.

46. Mailer, *Presidential Papers*, p. 144.

Chapter 15

Lovers and Workers: Screening the Body in Post-Communist Hungarian Cinema

Catherine Portuges

Eastern Europe's emergence from its Stalinist past is dramatically inscribed in the politics of its recent cinema. Relegated to a secondary status in favor of more pressing economic priorities, filmmakers accustomed to the security of a state-supported industry now find themselves competing for scarce resources in the midst of accusations of complicity with and defenses of opposition to former regimes. In Hungary as elsewhere, cinema continues nonetheless to play a vital role as public forum for the ongoing reassessment of the nation's political past.[1] Yet despite—or perhaps on account of—the transformations that have overtaken East-Central Europe, there persists in Hungarian cinema a lingering double vision, a depressive symptom of the profound alienation that is a legacy of the post-totalitarian psyche.[2]

In the vanguard of the "other Europe's" increasingly oppositional stance throughout the 1980s, Hungarian filmmakers boldly represented contested political terrain, especially the central event of Hungary's postwar history: the uprising of 1956. The status, nomenclature and ultimate reclaiming of that event by the opposition movement became a cornerstone of Hungary's "quiet revolution" of 1989, finding its way into nearly every film produced that year. The urgency displayed by artists and intellectuals to examine, with obsessional repetition, that period of their country's history with its stories of deceit and accommodation, collaboration and resistance, seems in fact to have displaced other, more contemporary projects that had been on the agenda, creating a transitional space between collective discourse and individual subjectivity, between official narrative and private memory.[3]

Suppressed under the aegis of Stalinist internationalism, culturally-specific questions of gender, sexuality and politics invite today renewed articulation, cloaked though these questions may be in the mantle of a Western "look" that bears little resemblance to the Stalinist aesthetic of previous decades.[4] Although economic constraints are likely to foreclose temporarily the exploration of these issues, whether in the cinema or in other cultural media, an enduring (albeit seldom examined) dialectic of sexuality and nationalism may well become the site of future representational enactments. Joining the ever-increasing list of joint capitalist ventures and "limited corporations" that characterize Hungary's post-communist transitional moment, the culture of cinema has been forced to reinvent itself if indeed it is to survive under a new order. To that end, such 1989–90 films as *The Dokumentator, Sexploitation* and *Fast and Loose* suggest that some Hungarian filmmakers have responded to the demands of liberalization by embracing the more commercially viable trajectory of the eroticized spectacle.[5]

Long banned by the Communist Party as a symptom of the more decadent aspects of Western capitalism, pornography now can be found at local kiosks graphically displayed on the covers of such publications as *Sexexpress, Apollo,* and *Lesbi Girls.* X-rated videos constitute a new growth industry, as suggested in *The Dokumentator* in which a successful video-store owner, having profitted by trafficking in black-market trade, spends his time suturing video footage of international catastrophes before turning the camcorder on his own suicidal impulses. A pornography kingpin celebrates this tendency, hoping customers will "spend their sorrow" and thereby enrich his successful enterprise consisting of sex magazines, massage parlors, and sexual tourism. A female teacher, aware that the repressive sexuality of Stalinism is in part accountable for the escalation of such images, nevertheless voices a concern, familiar to Western feminists but far less so in Eastern Europe, for the exploitation of women: "But what is missing from the debate is the articulation of the view that this is offensive to women. People are mixing liberty with bad taste."[6]

One of the most popular of the newly "liberated" films, Gyorgy Szomjas's *Fast and Loose* (*Konnyu Ver*) features the adventures of two platinum-blonde "models" in search of foreign clients with hard currency. Compensating in audience appeal for its good-natured lack of high production values, the film is an index of current spectatorial cravings for uninhibited exploration of heterosexual titillation in the wake of puritanical censorship. For representation of the body is inseparable from political discourse, implicated as it is in the circulation of desire between production and spectatorship.[7]

In these and other works in which youthful bodies are exhibitionistically fetishized, the ardently sought free-market economy is both symptom and cause, and the Western observer acustomed to the more subdued look of films of the 1970s and early 1980s is understandably confused by this appearance of eroticized excess. Among the few filmmakers who have consistently addressed the intersections of state ideology, sexuality, and everyday life—rural and urban, workplace and domestic—Márta Mészáros has courageously and consistently explored the highly charged intersections of gender and nationality. After a distinguished career as a documentary filmmaker trained in Moscow at the Institute of Cinematographic Art, she made her first feature films in the late 1960s and early 1970s. These works, which catapulted her to a degree of international celebrity hitherto unequalled by any other East European woman director, established the concerns for which she is now recognized: the representation of the struggle of working women and men attempting to create a new society against the background of modern political and socioeconomic life in postwar Hungary.[8]

In contrast to most of her male colleagues, Mészáros's films raise issues of class relations and gender, love and sexuality, deception and honesty in an unsentimental and at times even ruthless fashion. They have been particularly troubling for Hungarian audiences and critics discomfited by her uncompromising meditations on the double imperatives of national identity and gender inscription in post-Stalinist and post-communist Eastern Europe. One of over a dozen features released between 1968 and 1988, her 1980 film *The Heiresses*, with Isabelle Huppert as the leading actress, received favorable notices in France for its audacious treatment of such subversive issues as infertility, class difference, and the solidarity of female friendship. Unable to produce an heir, a wealthy Jewish couple contracts a young working-class woman to act as surrogate mother while fascism overtakes the country. It is worth noting that this highly controversial topic emerged in Hungarian cinema more than half a decade before the "Baby M." case, anticipating contemporary debates on surrogacy and maternity within the politically and historically charged atmosphere of wartime Nazism and the historical specificity of East European anti-semitism. Cinematic references to this topic are rare in Hungary, and Mészáros did not endear herself to critics of the time by focusing on highly controversial—and officially denied—problems of class, religion, ethnicity, and gender. The unorthodox arrangement backfires in the film, transgressing its purported object—the perpetuation of the married couple's upper-class family—as the husband and his wife's friend fall in love.

The film's reception was far from welcoming; critics and audiences in Hungary were resistant, if not outraged. Communist Party leaders displeased by its portrayal of a "decadent" bourgeois relationship and its exploitation of a working-class woman saw in it a distinction officially discouraged and, for that matter, denied by the socialist state. Critics and spectators alike read the film as a confirmation of their deepest fears of the consequences of the weakening of family bonds and the amorality of contemporary Hungarian domestic life.[9]

At once encoding and disclosing a critical stance with regard to the interpenetration of sexuality and the state, Mészáros's films may, to be sure, be seen as consistent with other East European cinematic discourses previously compelled to perform their textual operations through nuance, subversion, and covert systems of reference. But her cinema diverges inescapably from those representations, I think, by virtue of the specificity of its inscription of masculinity and femininity compared, for example, to the work of an Agnieska Holland in Poland or of a Vera Chytilova in Czechoslovakia.[10] For Mészáros's texts embody an unrelenting conflict and persistent sense of unease between men and women, be they factory workers (as in *The Girl*, 1968, and *Nine Months*, 1976), communist party officials (as in *Diary for My Children*, 1983), or bourgeois intellectuals (as in *Mother and Daughter*, 1981, and *The Heiresses*, 1980). Intimacy and sensuality, Mészáros seems to suggest, are possible primarily between female coworkers or in solitary moments of respite from the unceasing turmoil of the rigors of contemporary socialist life:

> I am an East European director, and my whole life, unfortunately, has been filled with politics. It is a tradition that, good or bad, you must deal with politics, especially for my generation educated under Stalinism. . . . An independent woman—one who finds herself in a situation where she must make a decision on her own—is the central character in each of the pictures I have made so far.[11]

In *Adoption* (1975), two women are framed together, at first contentedly drinking and smoking in a bar, later harrassed by the mocking laughter and gestures of male patrons. The men appear envious of the women's obvious pleasure in their own conversation and are discomfited by the obvious display of intimacy between them. Visually and semiotically, these sequences foreground the women's friendship while acknowledging their vulnerability in a society whose socialist party rhetoric of sexual equality is often dramatically at odds with traditional cultural practice.[12]

Like *The Heiresses*, *Adoption* trangresses codes of national and sexual chauvinism, opening with a long sequence that portrays a woman in her forties named Kata awakening alone, preparing breakfast, showering and leaving for work in the practiced gestures of solitary habit. Later she is examined by a male physician: we suspect from her rather haggard appearance that she might be suffering from tuberculosis; yet as the doctor pronounces her fit, it becomes clear that she wishes to conceive a child, a fact she subsequently announces to her married lover when they arrange to meet in a cafe. The scene is played without pathos or self-pity, and Mészáros's characteristic restraint evinces not blame but painfully realistic acceptance of the lover's limitations, unwilling (and, we are meant to understand, unable) as he is to commit himself fully to his mistress. Encouraged later by her friendship with a young woman from a nearby orphanage, Kata finds herself able to adopt a baby on her own. The camera tracks back in the final sequence of *Adoption* as Kata boards a bus with her newly acquired infant; they appear all the more vulnerable in an urban landscape indifferent to the middle-aged woman's subjective drama.

But there is in Mészáros's cinematic construction an affecting visual ambiguity, for, however great the cost, Kata has triumphed over entrenched priorities of nation and gender to achieve the "object of her desire"—the opportunity to raise a child as a single, older woman, without the family or male companion normally considered as prerequisites for adoption by the values of the socialist state of the time. Seen today in a Western context, this gesture of defiance should be inserted within its proper historical frame in a national agenda that, while encouraging natalism and gender equality under socialism, was only beginning to emerge from a legacy of communism that privileged collectivity above individual psychology and hence offered little opportunity for emotional support for such social experiments. The woman's body becomes, for Mészáros, a sign of opposition to prevailing post-Stalinist gender policies in which sexual difference was to be elided in favor of the project of building "socialist man" and "socialist woman." Mészáros's treatment of gender thus contrasts markedly with the work of Miklós Jancsó, Mészáros's husband at the time and an internationally renowned film director, celebrated for historical dramas portraying Hungary's nineteenth-century revolutionary period in films such as *Red Psalm* (1971), in which long-haired young peasant women are made to undress before the gaze of uniformed soldiers who then encircle and run toward them across the vast *puszta*. Jancsó's camera appropriates the female body both as provocation and erotic object, and never grants it the measure of authorial subjectivity which it is accorded in Mészáros's diegetic universe.[13]

Like many Hungarian films of the past twenty years produced in the wake of a socialist-realist aesthetics, Mészáros's works bear the traces of an implicit critique of the problematics of desire, of male domination and female suffering. Almost seductively engaged with the political issues of their time, these films also strike many Western audiences as inordinately depressing, hopeless, or resigned. Erotic encounters are often represented as pleasurable only when illicit—whether because of class differences or oedipal triangulation, as in *The Heiresses* (1980)—or as mythical, idealized by the temporal distance of childhood memory, such as in her later *Diary* trilogy. Mészáros's lovers are often young workers seeking relief from foreclosed possibilities in the early period of Stalinism, as in *Riddance* (1973); middle-aged couples growing apart under the weight of unrealized hopes, as in *The Two of Them* (1977), and older people attempting to reconcile harsh objective conditions with thwarted individual desires, as in the *Diary* films.

Mészáros's first feature film, *The Girl* (1968), initiates the interrogation of parentage and family history that has persisted throughout the director's work to date. Symbolically, parentage converges with the Stalinist state in the 1950s when Matyas Rákosi, the country's leader from 1948–56, followed Stalin's example by proclaiming himself the metaphorical progenitor of all Hungarian children.[14] A number of her feature films employ the narrative strategy of a child or young girl who accuses her parents—and, through them, the state—of lying about the past, and, in so doing, insists on discovering the truth at great personal cost. In sexual, familial, and political matters, then, the evasions and half-truths typical of Stalinist culture are investigated with unflinching vision, whether they concern the trauma of a little girl witnessing her father's degrading alcoholic cure in a detoxification clinic (as in *The Two of Them*), or the more abstract ideological consequences of repression (as in the *Diary* trilogy). Such relentless probing testifies eloquently to the prescience of Mészáros's agenda; further, it demonstrates the leading role of filmmakers in opening the discursive boundaries that gave voice to that which had so long been silenced far in advance of the transformations in East-Central Europe and the Soviet Union.

The Two of Them (1977), Mészáros's seventh feature, shifts its focus to concentrate on a friendship between two women, and is, according to the director, the first of her narrative films to have a "sympathetic male character—albeit an alcoholic . . . a sensitive person who sees life in its complexity and profundity."[15] As the self-possessed director of a working women's hostel, Marina Vlady as Mari maintains her composed serenity in principled stands against the hostel administration's inhumane regulations on behalf of a troubled younger woman still deeply attracted to her alcoholic husband. But it is Juli's daughter Zuzsi whose point of view indicts the adult world of deception and compromise, and the child actress who plays her, Zsuzsa Czinkoczy, in fact becomes the central protagonist in Mészáros's subsequent films, an alter ego for the director's fascination with the experience of a child abandoned by her parents.[16] Despite Mari's efforts to shelter and assist her friend, Juli finds it difficult to resist her irresponsible, childlike husband. In a darkly lit yet revealing sequence, they make love on a kitchen chair, two bodies hopelessly lost, acting out a primally brutal physical attraction. In contrast, Mari's own deteriorating middle-class marriage has become psychologically abusive through her husband's absences and is devoid of the erotic passion that controls Juli and her husband. This difference is demonstrated in a sequence of visually shocking sexual humiliations when Mari is left lying on the floor, legs spread, by her usually passive husband after a brief and, we are meant to suspect, typical moment of intercourse. Afterward, we see Mari, water streaming from her blonde hair, enjoying herself in a steamy shower, joined by her fully-clothed friend Juli, as the two women embrace and share a moment of sensuous release through the complicit laughter that momentarily transcends even the barriers of class and gender.

Such sensual moments portraying a woman nude in the shower recur frequently in Mészáros's work, often counterbalancing anguished episodes of distress resulting from the material as well as the sexual conditions of existence. The female body is imaged—but not, I think, fetishized—through the purificatory ritual of bathing, either alone or in the company of other women. While the unclothed female figure was hardly unknown in post-Stalinist East European cinema, other Hungarian renderings, among which the most celebrated are those of Miklós Jancsó, are clearly presented primarily for the visual, erotic pleasure of the male spectator. A telling sequence of shots from *Riddance* (1973) dramatically integrates issues of class, domestic abuse, and gender within a state-socialist context. A young factory worker ashamed of her working class origins pretends to be a university student in order to please a young man she meets at a dance and to rid herself of her working-class boyfriend. When she confronts the latter by admitting she does not love him, he slaps her face several times in the presence of patrons at an outdoor cafe. Only after repeated blows does a nearby waitress come to her aid, while onlookers (both male and female) appear either to ignore or to take pleasure in her humiliation. Mészáros cuts again to a shower sequence where the young woman is framed in close-up, the camera panning unhurriedly down small, graceful breasts toward her trim belly as the water's spray mingles with her tears. It is obviously a pleasurable moment for the protagonist, and we share her complicated yet enjoyable sense of catharsis and renewal. Such unflinching cinematic representation of domestic violence mirrored social conditions perhaps rather too accurately, and as a result was met with particularly hostile reception in the popular and critical press. That the director was a woman willing to express such truths in uncompromising visual terms may have left audiences with a sense of unbearable exposure.

The critical realism of Márta Mészáros's method works to situate her bourgeois women and factory workers in the homes, offices, and factories in which they spend much of their time; we learn in deliberate, documented detail about the machines they operate, the domestic tasks they accomplish, the financial, political, and sexual anxieties that preoccupy them. We are allowed, for instance, to see women of all ages and physical types showering together in the factory washroom at the end of a shift, arguing heatedly about working conditions and teasing each other about their love lives.

Even the rural and urban antagonisms characteristic of Hungarian society are examined with cinematographic rigor and the impeccable editing attributable in part to Mészáros's documentary training. When a young urban woman worker returns to her village to seek her father in *Binding Sentiments* (1969), Mészáros gives the story a twist that highlights urban-rural tensions with regard to gender: a peasant mother, now remarried, denies her own daughter, now a city dweller, thereby illustrating as well the deeper suspicion with which each group has traditionally regarded the other in Hungarian society. The young woman is subjected first to the unwelcome advances of her mother's husband and then to those of her half-brother at a village dance, suggesting the family's acceptance of this form of incestuous behavior and its rejection of her as both class traitor and now unattainably sophisticated, desired object. Mészáros thus combines several layers of social critique by foregrounding the alienation between mother and daughter as inescapably embedded within the complexities of class tension, national antagonisms between city and countryside, and the gender politics that encompass both.

Within those contexts, disparities and affinities between generations emerge as young village women come to live and work with older women in workers' hostels in Budapest, a common theme of Mészáros's early features. At first glance, these women appear to gain autonomy because of their excursion into the labor force. But at a deeper level, Mészáros's treatment is grounded in the reality of the sexual antagonism of Hungarian working class relations: these women are depicted as increasingly alienated from familial ties because of their displacement into urban workers' hostels, thereby making them more vulnerable to the advances of similarly solitary males.[17]

Subverting the official party program of an East European state claiming to have created a homogeneous society in which gender as well as class contradictions have been eliminated, Márta Mészáros places the cinematic apparatus in the service of a deconstruction of that ideology. In so doing, she reveals how deeply embedded within the culture such contradictions remain, how resistant to transformation by purely external dictates. But her most searching critique thus far emanates from the two completed segments of her *Diary* trilogy, the director's autobiographical *magnum opus*.

Having been denied permission for fifteen years to embark upon that project, Mészáros was able to complete the first installment in 1984. *Diary for*

My Children, its 1986 sequel *Diary for My Loves,* and the last of the trilogy *Diary for My Father and Mother* (1990) represent the director's return to Hungary following several years of international coproductions. As such, they exemplify the conflict facing many East European artists—and, for that matter, any exiled artist—trapped between the desire to return to the site of national origin or leave it behind, perhaps forever. Confronting her own past by returning to Budapest, she once more chronicles through these films the tumultuous period of Hungarian and East European history between 1949 and 1989. More important still, they narrate the director's own life story from the perspective of her adolescent alter ego, Juli, using what was a highly innovative and, since, much-imitated combination of semi-fictionalized and documentary material.

By validating the importance of reconciliation with what had been repressed or denied—be it family, political affiliation, or inequalities inadmissible under Stalinism and in its aftermath, these films affirm the right and responsibility of both individual and nation to claim their experience, no matter how fraught with guilt, betrayal, or fear. And as in her first feature, Mészáros again focuses upon the protagonist's quest for her lost father, according him a more overtly political role. For this time, not only the small Hungarian but also the mighty Soviet state is interrogated and indicted: Juli's father disappears in the Stalinist purges, as did Mészáros's own father, the sculptor László Mészáros, who vanished in 1938. Juli subsequently returns to Hungary as an orphan, unwilling to accept the powerful influence, potential support, and concomitant control of Magda, a devoted communist party cadre in search of a surrogate daughter. In the final installment of the *Diary* trilogy, Mészáros restages the destruction of a monumental statue of Stalin as her heroine completes the odyssey of reassessment begun a decade earlier in *Diary for My Children.* The completion of the *Trilogy* corresponds with the end of an era of Hungarian filmmaking, opening new directions for filmmakers and spectators at the site of the border crossings between sexuality and nationality.

NOTES

1. For an overview of the effects of *glasnost* on film culture in the USSR, East Germany, Hungary, Poland, Czechoslovakia, Yugoslavia and Rumania, see Daniel J. Goulding, ed., *Post New Wave Cinema in the Soviet Union and Eastern Europe* (Bloomington: Indiana University Press, 1989). My comments on current developments in Hungarian film are based in part on screenings of 43 feature and documentary films

produced in 1989 and presented February 2–8, 1990 in Budapest at the 22nd Hungarian National Film Festival, at which I was an invited observer.

2. See Timothy Garton Ash, *The Uses of Adversity: Essays on the Fate of Central Europe* (New York: Random House, 1989); also Milan Kundera, "The Tragedy of Central Europe," *New York Review of Books*, April 26, 1984, for further elaboration of this syndrome.

3. This spatial metaphor originates with the British psychoanalyst and pediatrician D.W. Winnicott in *Playing and Reality* (London: Routledge & Kegan Paul, 1986) and refers to his theory of the psychological distance between mother and infant presumably indispensable to the development of the child's sense of creativity and cultural experience.

4. According to *Variety* (May 23, 1990), Universal Pictures plans to schedule release of some 200 American films on Hungarian screens in 1990 alone, more than eight times the total number of films produced in an average year by Hungarian studios.

5. Screened at the 22nd Hungarian National Film Festival in Budapest, February 2–8, 1990.

6. Quoted in the *New York Times*, May 12, 1990, p. 6.

7. Szomjas' *Fast and Loose* was Hungary's only feature entry in the 27th International Film Festival at Karlovy Vary, Czechoslovakia, in July 1990, a decision suggestive of how the country wishes to see itself represented in the international market.

8. Best known among Mészáros's films of this period are *Riddance* (1973), *Adoption* (1975), and *The Two of Them* (1977). See my *Screen Memories: The Hungarian Films of Márta Mészáros* (Bloomington: Indiana University Press, 1991).

9. French critical reception was considerably more positive (the film was a Franco-Hungarian coproduction), and Mészáros's reputation continued to rise in that country as elsewhere in Western Europe, in contrast to the negative view a number of her Hungarian colleagues evinced in response to her work. This may have been due in part to the dissolution of her marriage to Miklós Jancsó, the best-known Hungarian filmmaker of that period, whose avant-garde works such as *The Red and the White* (1967) and *Red Psalm* (1971) were highly esteemed by such influential journals as *Cahiers du Cinéma*.

10. See Peter Hames, *The Czechoslovak New Wave* (Berkeley: University of California Press, 1985); and Boleslaw Michalek and Frank Turaj, *The Modern Cinema*

of Poland (Bloomington: Indiana University Press, 1988), for discussions of these and other Polish and Czechoslovak filmmakers.

11. From a series of interviews conducted by the author in Budapest between 1986 and 1990.

12. I am grateful to Prof. F. T. Zsuppan of St. Andrews University, Scotland, for his illuminating presentation on the seeming anachronism of the history of feminist activism in Hungary (cf. "Rozsika Schwimmer and Hungarian Feminism, 1904–1918," Conference of the American Association for the Advancement of Slavic Studies, October, 1990, Washington, DC).

13. It should be noted that Jancsó's experimental avant-garde work was nevertheless an instrumental intervention in the rupture of contemporary Hungarian cinema from the stronghold of post-Stalinist puritanism.

14. A fascinating example of this tendency may be found in *Somewhere in Europe,* the classic Hungarian film by Radvanyi in which homeless children—mostly boys—are cared for by the state, a powerful reference to the ideology of the then-new socialist state's function *in loco parentis.*

15. See Barbara Koenig Quart, *Women Directors: The Emergence of a New Cinema* (New York: Praeger, 1988), pp. 191–208.

16. Like François Truffaut's use of the twelve-year-old Jean-Pierre Léaud in *The 400 Blows*—the actor who became the primary figure of the director's autobiographical Antoine Doinel cycle of films—Mészáros has sustained with Czinkoczy (at first a nonprofessional actress and a village girl) an evolving on-screen relationship of extraordinary depth and delicacy.

17. See for example Miklós Haraszti, *A Worker in a Worker's State* (New York: Universe Books, 1978), for an insightful overview of the 1960s in Hungary; and László Kürti, "Hierarchy and Workers' Power in a Csepel Factory," *Journal of Communist Studies,* 6, 2, special issue on Market Economy and Civil Society in Hungary, ed. C. M. Hann (London: Frank Cass, June 1990), pp. 61–84, for an excellent analysis of working-class youth in a socialist firm during this period.

Chapter 16

From Foreground to Margin: Female Configurations and Masculine Self-Representation in Black Nationalist Fiction

Joyce Hope Scott

Nationalism among the African people of the United States had its genesis in the various acts of rebellion carried out by slaves in attempts to free themselves from tyrannical violence and oppression at the hands of white masters and their collaborators. In essence, it expressed itself in the late eighteenth and early nineteenth centuries in two distinct ways: first as the individual acts of runaway slaves whose rebelliousness was commemorated in later "acts of language" through personal narratives, and secondly as discursive attacks aimed at provoking mass action on the part of slaves and liberal-thinking whites. In the former we recognize primary figures like Frederick Douglass, William Still, Williams Wells Brown and Harriet Jacobs, to name a few.

From the mid-nineteenth century to the Civil War, we see the emergence of the latter group. The landmark appearances of David Walker's "Appeal to the Coloured Citizens of the World" in 1829 and Henry Highland Garnet's "Address to the Slaves of the United States" in 1843 epitomize the charismatic nationalist writers and theorists of this time. A black nationalist theme which ran concurrently with the idea of slave revolt was that of the emigration of former slaves to more favorable countries of Africa, the Caribbean, and South America, particularly after the 1850 Dred Scott Decision when more and more blacks became disillusioned with the promise of American democracy.

Wilson Jeremiah Moses refers to the black radicalism of the mid- to late nineteenth century as "The Golden Age of Black Nationalism" and suggests that nationalist tendencies at this time were invariably linked to religious ideology: "Black nationalism was absolutist, civilizationist, elitist, and based on Christian humanism . . ." Proponents espoused also a messianic self-conception or "Ethiopian mysticism accompanied by an authoritarian collectivism." Moses argues further that, "After World War I, new tendencies arose that were relativist, culturalist, proletarian, and secular." This latter characteristic, Moses claims, defined the structure of "Elijah Muhammad's movement of the 1930's which departed from the Christian humanist tradition of his predecessors."[1]

Imaginative literature of Afro-Americans, taking its cue from the broader sociopolitical exigencies at various periods of the nationalist movement, has tended to situate the black woman in fictive locations relative to and reflective of popular notions of the time. Gayle Tate suggests in her study on black nationalism in the nineteenth century that blacks' focus on freedom and liberation contained the same sentiments of liberty and equality that inspired the American revolutionaries. Black theologians merged nationalism with theology and political protest, and challenges to slavery were synonymous with the struggle for justice, virtue and divine grace. In short, there remained a clear connection between religious and political struggle. The overall theme of collective elevation and moral uplift embodied all of the nationalist strivings of blacks of this period; in essence, "Religion and spirituality were the sources for its perpetual dynamism," according to Tate.[2]

Rosalyn Terborg-Penn points out in her study of "Black Male Perspectives on the Nineteenth-Century Woman" that many of the most prominent black male nationalists "were inclined to be sensitive to the demands of other groups similarly disfavored. [Thus] in reacting to the 'woman question' on the basis of their own images of women in general and black women in particular, [some] perceived women as being in need of male protection, while most perceived them as equal to men. Some sought to uplift the women of the race, while others included women and men in the uplift process . . . [Indeed] black organizations with both men and women in attendance were prevalent long before the 'woman question' became prominent in white reform circles."[3]

A clear indication of the views of black men toward women was their attitude concerning education, often seen as a means of bettering civilization in general, the race in particular. Both Frederick Douglass and Martin R. Delany emphasized the importance of educating black women. Delany expressed his attitude about education and the black woman in his book *The Condition, Elevation, Emigration and Destiny of the Colored People* and in articles in the *North Star* where he noted that black men must abandon their ideas about the traditional role of women as they were the backbone of the race and needed to prepare themselves for facing the inconsistencies of life as well as for passing on appropriate values of racial uplift to their children.[4] Other prominent black nationalists like Robert Purvis, James Forten, Charles Lenox Remond, and William C. Nell all advocated through their oratories and their writings the centrality of women in the struggle for freedom and justice in America. T. Thomas Fortune, addressing The Afro-American League's National Convention in Chicago in 1890, entitled his speech "Salvation Through Negro Women":

> We complain of the hardships of our women when we never do one thing to relieve them. Our female element, under mother influence attends school and church, eschews the brothels, stays at home, works and to our shame is the backbone of the Negro race today. Were it not for the Negro woman the outlook would be dark. I am aware of the breadth of my speech when I say that the world has never furnished a higher woman-hood under like conditions than the Negro woman of the South today. With strong appetites and passions, penniless, houseless, working on "starvation wages," practically left to shift alone, amid stumbling, falling, rising, fleeing—she goes on washing, cooking, plowing, sowing, reaping—educating her daughter, building the cottage, erecting churches and schools, often supporting husband and son—this black woman deserves the admiration of the gods . . .[5]

Black women had indeed positioned themselves firmly at the forefront of the nationalist movement as early as the late eighteenth century with their benevolent and mutual relief societies followed by antislavery societies in the 1830s. Maria Stewart of Massachusetts was one of the first women of any color in the country to speak in a public assembly. In a speech delivered at Franklin Hall, Boston in 1832, she called on black women to rise up and take charge of their own destiny: "O, ye daughters of Africa, awake! Awake! Arise! No longer sleep nor slumber, but distinguish yourselves. Show forth to the world that ye are endowed with noble and exalted faculties."[6] The outspoken Anna Julia Cooper, it might be argued, was one of the first black women to introduce a black feminist philosophy. In her book *A Voice From the South,* published in 1892, she championed the cause of black women and proclaimed that the race as a whole could not rise out of its despair and degradation until the black woman is given her due as the categorical imperative of all black liberation efforts. Black male leaders who were attempting to improve the condition of the race exclusive of the black female, she warned, would soon realize that "all such attempts would prove abortive unless so directed as to utilize the indispensable agency of elevated and trained womanhood." Cooper further notes:

> The fundamental agency under God in the regeneration, the retraining of the race, as well as the ground work and starting point of its progress upward, must be the *black woman*. . . . The cycles wait for her. No other hand can move the lever. She must be loosed from her bands and set to work. Our meager and superficial results from past efforts prove their futility . . . A stream cannot rise higher than its source. The atmosphere of homes is no rarer and purer and sweeter than are the mothers in those homes. A race is but a total of families, the nation is the aggregate of its homes . . . Only the BLACK WOMAN can say, "When and where I enter, in the . . . undisputed dignity of my womanhood . . . then and there the whole *Negro race enters with me*."[7]

Collectivism, where nationalist efforts were carried out by an elite class of highly literate and liberally educated men and women in the nineteenth century, gives way in later periods to an attempt to resecure the black female in a patriarchal, gendered economy. Such revisioning and repositioning of the feminine role in the nationalist struggle is clearly evident in the discourse of Black Arts and Black Power advocates of the Civil Rights movement and poignantly depicted in fictive texts of Afro-American male writers of the period.

I examine here three literary works: *Black Thunder* by Arna Bontemps (first published in 1936 and later reprinted in 1968); *The Spook Who Sat by the Door* by Sam Greenlee (1969); and *The Last Days of Louisiana Red* by Ishmael Reed (1974). These texts, I argue, show a paradoxical movement of the black female from her earlier vocality and centrality to the movement to a position of silence as the phallocentric and patriarchal vision of Black Power advocates relocate the black woman in the margins of the struggle for freedom and equality in the United States.

First, a look at the Harlem Renaissance era. Assessing the black artistic movement in Harlem during the 1920s and 30s, Alain Locke noted that the creativity of the period reflected a spirit of cultural nationalism based on pride in the Afro-American's own traditions, folk arts and folk heros, i.e. a desire for self-determination which paralleled America's struggle to throw off European cultural hegemony and develop its own artistic forms. Thus a transformed and transforming psychology permeated the masses. The major political activism of the NAACP, Urban League, churches and even of Marcus Garvey tended to privilege what Wilson Jeremiah Moses has referred to as Christian humanist values coupled with a nostalgic romanticism of Africa and the mystical Ethiopia.

The intellectual struggle of the Harlem Renaissance between the "New Negro" and the old vanguard testified to the conflict between the factions of the black nationalist movement to define the character of the next phase of the struggle.

Though their contributions have until recently been overlooked by scholars and critics of the period, black women were situated firmly in the forefront of the literary and political activism which characterized this creative period. Black male writers like Jean Toomer, Langston Hughes and Arna Bontemps in particular depicted the black woman with sensitivity, underscoring her brown beauty and ancient sensuality so long degraded by the general Euro-American populace. Arna Bontemps infuses an especially powerful and unique portrait of the black woman into his fictive account of the historical revolt of Gabriel Prosser in Virginia in 1800. In his text, Bontemps reconstructs the events of the Prosser slave insurrection, which shattered the security of the slave plantocracy throughout the South and gave rise to a plethora of repressive laws and acts of brutality by whites trying to regain control of their "peculiar institution." Gabriel is depicted as the romantic hero, a freedom-loving slave who is inspired to fight to the death for his and his people's liberation. The plot develops in fragments through short chapters which open with the name of the character under consideration. These constant shifts in point of view mean that the reader must piece together the full panorama of events.

What is most striking about Bontemps' revisioning is his portrayal of the female as a metaphor for the revolution and as prophetess and keeper of ancestral wisdom. Gabriel systematically recruits men from all over the county through a clever and brilliant strategy of deception and subterfuge. He is a man larger than most, young and strikingly handsome. The night for the planned revolt arrives and Gabriel tells the men that the sign which will foretell of the time for the attack will be a rider wearing Marse Prosser's boots and riding his favorite horse, Araby. On this night, the county experiences its worst storm in history. Rain falls in torrents and thunder and lightning fight a frightening duel in the heavens. Yet it is not Gabriel who signals the attack by riding up on Araby wearing the master's boots, but rather Juba, his girl described by the narrator as a "thin-waisted brown girl with a savage mop of hair"[8]:

> The streaks moved faster and faster across the sky. Then suddenly there were flashes playing on the rushing clouds. Araby whimpered, his lovely head at the open window of his stall. He was bridled and ready. The stables were peopled with shadows slipping from place to place . . . There was a girl's hand on the colt's bridle. She wore a shiny pair of men's riding boots and a cut off skirt that failed to reach her knees. "Not yet," she said, seeking the colt's forelock. "Not yet, boy." Presently it was full night, full night with heavy clouds, scudding up the sky. Rain or no rain, wet or dry, it was all the

> same to Juba. . . . She sat astride Araby's bare back, her fragmentary skirt curled about her waist, her naked thighs flashing above the riding boots, leaned forward till her face was almost touching the wild mane and felt the warm body of the colt straining between her clinched knees. Juba heard the footfalls now, heard the sweet muffled clatter on the hardened earth and her breathing became quick and excited . . . She was giving the sign. Those were shadows running down to the roadside, pausing briefly and then darting back into the thickets. Those were not shadows, merely. Juba knew better. She understood. (79–80)

Juba's figure becomes the apocalyptic revelator. She is indeed the fifth horseman/woman of the apocalypse, signalling the time to rise up and destroy the evils of oppression. Juba or Diuba in Bantu signifies the marking of the time, the sun or the hour. And mark the time she does as she tells the shadowy crowd:

> Y'all see me, every lasting one of you. And you knows what this here means . . . Dust around now, you old big foot boys. Get a move on . . . You got to get around like the wind. Quick. On'erstand? Always big talking about what booming bed-men you is. Always trying to turn the gal's heads like that. Well, let's see what you is good for sure 'nough. Let's see if you knows how to go free; let's see if you knows how to die, you big-footses, you. (81)

The unnatural storm does indeed rout the insurrectionists. People from the outlying farms cannot get across the swollen river and streams, and talk circulates throughout the ranks about the bad omen that all the rain and thunder represents. Gabriel is determined to continue and so is Juba. The crowd fizzles out, however, and the insurrectionists are betrayed by Ben and Pharaoh.

The symbolic implications of Juba in this revolt must be noted here. She wears the master's boots. J. E. Cirlot explains that shoes (to wit, boots) are symbols of the female sex organ. For the ancients, they were also a sign denoting liberty. Earlier, we were led to believe that it will be Gabriel who will give the sign as he rides up on Araby wearing John Prosser's boots. Yet Bontemps foregrounds the mystic feminine as primary in this adventure. While Cirlot points out that the sudden appearance of a horse is a symbolic foreshadowing of war, Jung wondered at the possibility that the horse might be a symbol for the Mother in that it expressed the magic side of man, "the mother within us," innate understanding.[9] Near the beginning of the insurrection, Gabriel tells Juba, "It's a man's doings, Juba. You ain't obliged to [follow] along" (68), to which she replies, "I hears what you say . . . but I'm in it. Long's you's in it, I'm in it too," and he understands as he tells her, "Well it ain't for me to tell you no, gal" (68).

When the revolt fails, Juba goes back to the Prosser plantation. There she finds a circle of slave women discussing the event. One older woman "wrinkled and witchlike" (165) and reminiscent of the African "Earth Goddess" speaks with the mystical wisdom of the West African Mazoes of the secret female societies. In searing and prophetic tones, she explains why Gabriel's insurrection failed: "A man, do he 'spect to win, is obliged to fight the way he know. That's what's ailing Gabriel and all them. He is obliged to go at it with something he can manage" (166). When Juba scornfully asks her what she means, the old woman explains the failure in terms of the Afro-American's abandonment of the ancient gods, spirits, and ancestors of the African past. Gabriel has made the fatal error of subscribing to the whiteman's god through the religious rhetoric of the Bible: "Too much listening to Mingo read a white man's book. . . . They ain't paid attention to the signs. They talks about Toussaint over yonder in San Domingo . . . Toussaint and them kilt a hog in the woods. Drank the blood; they [Gabriel and the others] done forgot something . . . Gabriel done forget to take something to protect hisself. The stars wasn't right. See? All the rain. They ain't paid attention to the signs" (166).

This reference to the signs is made again and again by the circle of women. Although it is historically true that bad weather routed Prosser and his insurrectionists, Bontemps privileges this "folk reading" as the cause for the failure of the revolt. The "stars" which "wasn't right" symbolize according to Cirlot the spirit (light) struggling against forces of darkness. Going back to Egyptian hieroglyphics, the five-pointed star signifies "a raising upward to the point of origin. As they appear in clusters, they are associated with destiny."[10] Gabriel seeks to return the people to their point of origin, freedom and existence as respected human beings.

Indeed, the North Star has traditionally symbolized freedom for the southern slave. It was this brilliant beacon in the sky that was often the only signal to the runaway that he was headed north and thus toward liberty. Frederick Douglass, in fact, chose to name his abolitionist newspaper *The North Star*. As the stars (or signs) were primarily the only affirmation of truth for the bondsman, it would truly have been perceived as dangerous to disregard or misread them. That Gabriel has not been wise is emphasized by the old woman, who could have given him the "power" to ensure his success. Juba understands this and asks the old woman to make her "a hand" for Gabriel to keep him safe while he continues to run. And although the old Mazoe makes one for her, she knows it will not matter, "He ought to come hisself," she says, "that's the most surest way. He should of come long time ago, did he have any sense" (167–168). Here with the old wise woman of the ancient African village, Bontemps suggests the need for the black male revolutionary to defer to this traditional feminine wisdom as it ensures appropriate mystical knowledge and protection in the dangerous business of confrontation with the Euro-American power structure.

Gabriel remains the proud, god-like hero until his death, and Pharaoh, one of the main traitors of the revolt, is "fixed" by the voodoo of the women in the circle, climbing up a tree and barking like a dog, while Ben the old traitor and faithful slave retainer, waits for the knives that he knows will soon come to cut him to pieces. Juba is savagely stripped and beaten by Marse Prosser, refusing to cry even as her thighs turn to cut beef. But she is observed on the auction block: "Her feet were bare. Her clothes were scant. And there was something about her figure, something about the bold rise of her exposed breasts that put gooseflesh on a man. But her look was . . . bitter, almost threatening" (224).

John Henrik Clarke and Wilson Moses both argue that the black nationalist movement experienced a hiatus after the fall of Marcus Garvey. This pause in the struggle for liberation gives way to a resurgence of creative energy with the Civil Rights and Black Power movements of the 1960s and 70s. The militancy and violence of the period not only shaped new leaders of the black cause, but a new breed of activist writer who, far from belonging to an established black intellectual elite, wrote of the passions and experiences that emerge from people in direct conflict with society.

Freedom and liberation during this latter phase of the black nationalist movement in America become equated with power roles—political office, economic control, and, yes, even military might. Kate Millet points out in *Sexual Politics* that

> In a money economy where autonomy and prestige depend upon currency, [woman's work or economic rights] is a fact of great importance. In general the position of women in the patriarchy is a continuous function of their economic dependence. Just as their social position is vicarious and achieved (often on a temporary or marginal basis) through males, their relation to the economy is also typically vicarious or tangential.

Millett further explains why, given this context of dependency, black men could often hold public forums "to mimic that staggering contempt white patriarchy habitually reserves for the black female."[11]

Like their white male counterparts, black male novelists often tended to portray black women in their fictive worlds with ambivalence at best and at worst, within the Euro-American, male-dominated, exploitative framework where the male is superior, owner, controller, and defender of the female who is owned, inferior. In this latter category, black women have appeared as the bitch or ancient "terrible mother" who, as Moynihan put it, emasculates and tyrannizes the black male, depriving him of his opportunity to flourish and grow into a healthy American man.

In her book of black feminist criticism *Ain't I a Woman*, bell hooks argues that black men indeed have absorbed the same sexist socialization white men succumb to:

> At very young ages, black male children learn that they have a privileged status in the world based on their having been born male; they learn that this status is superior to that of women. As a consequence of their early sexist socialization, they mature accepting the same sexist sentiments their white counterparts accept. When women do not affirm their masculine status by assuming a subordinate role, they express the contempt and hostility they have been taught to feel toward nonsubmissive women. [Thus] that black men should begin to see the black woman as their enemy was perfectly logical given the structure of patriarchy.[12]

Indeed, much leading black literature of the late 1960s came from men bred in the conflict of the streets and prisons. This literary discovery of the black urban masses focused on the lower-class blacks of the city streets who (in the views of writers like Hughes, Fisher, and McKay of the 1920s) "represented virility and vitality of which white American culture was almost devoid."[13]

The Black Arts movement, fostered by artists like Larry Neal and Imiri Baraka, sought to locate a new black aesthetic grounded in the secularism of a proletarian rather than elitist culture. Charles Johnson writes in *Race and Being* that the Black Arts movement is a "child of cultural nationalism." Proponents of the movement saw the need for black cultural reconstruction, a reenvisioning of the lived black world. Here, "The artist . . . is the guardian of image: the writer is the myth-maker of his people." "Image control," according to Johnson, "has been the aim of black fiction—and perhaps its problem from the very beginning of black literary production."[14] In this endeavor, black male writers often took their cue from their political counterparts. This is especially worth noting where depictions of the black woman in the black nationalist struggle is concerned.

The Black Muslim movement, Stokely Carmichael, Imiri Baraka, and Maulana Ron Karenga—all key opinion shapers of the turbulent 1960s and 70s—uniformly espoused a rhetoric of female subordination and role assignment based on traditional biological function. In the 1967 tract *The Quotable Karenga*, Ron Karenga speaks of his black ideology of change called "Kawaida." In the section called "House System," he gives his view of the role of women in the black nationalist struggle:

> What makes a woman appealing is femininity and she can't be feminine without being submissive.

> There is no virtue in independence. The only virtue is in interdependence. Black women . . . should remember this.

> Insecurity is a constant preoccupation with every woman. Only the hardest woman, and she's jivin', doesn't want to be secure.[15]

Carmichael's position relative to the black woman's role in the nationalist movement has become ingrained in the hearts of all through his immortal words: "The only position for the woman in the revolution is prone."

Sam Greenlee's novel, *The Spook Who Sat By The Door,* is a fable about the first black man to enter the CIA, who learns all he can there and uses the knowledge to train an urban guerilla force. Dan Freeman, the hero, is a protagonist well-grounded in "historical literacy" in that he is aware of his "inside and his outside" and the duplicity needed to succeed in the white man's arena. At the CIA Dan's "job was to be black and conspicuous as the integrated Negro of the Central Intelligence Agency of the United States of America."[16] The general attitude of the whites in the novel toward the presence of blacks in the CIA is that they are essentially "misplaced cotton pickers" (23).

Freeman manages to complete the training program and get hired through careful masking of his real ability and his real motive for joining the CIA. He "Yes, Sir's" his way into the good graces of the "Senator" who first uses criticism of the CIA's poor affirmative action record as part of his campaign strategy. Freeman's Tomming and accommodation serve to give meaning and purpose to his posturing for the audience and to highlight his effectiveness as the age-old trickster who inverts the universe of the master because the master fails to understand that words on the tongues of the oppressed can become tools that initiate a reversal of roles and subversion of the system which he (the master) has so carefully crafted.

While Dan Freeman as portrayed here can be seen as the classic nationalist hero, it is the configuration of women in the novel on which my discussion will center, for it is with their depiction that the departure from the Christian humanism of which Moses spoke as characterizing the black nationalist movement of the nineteenth century and the later tendencies toward secularism and cultural relativism can be seen. The two women in Freeman's life are Joy, his middle-class lover, and the Dahomeyan Queen, a prostitute with whom Freeman strikes a lasting relationship. Joy is a former ghetto dweller like Freeman, but she has gone to school and managed to elevate herself above her former existence. She is portrayed as selfish, materialistic and unresponsive to the needs of her people back in the teeming ghettos of Chicago. The nameless prostitute is the woman who is seen as most fitting and acceptable for the black male revolutionary. She, like Freeman, is a detachable individual having no discernible family or friends. She is equally ambivalent where her sexual preference is concerned. While she professes abhorrence for men, she is undoubtedly taken with Freeman. She is also sufficiently subservient and obedient to Freeman, allowing him essentially to "rename" her. That she accepts this revisioning of self is evident in that she goes to the library to read about the Dahomeyan queens and slowly transforms her appearance to match that of the women pictured in the book.

Freeman's relationship with both women is purely sexual, although we sense that he probably loved Joy, but found it necessary to negate this potential source of male/female unity through shared power. In her unpublished paper "The Argument with Oedipus: Romantic Sons in Joyce Carol Oates' Fiction," Marilyn C. Wesley looks at the question of gender structure which strictly separates the attributes of sympathy and power. She argues that the adult gender structure demands that "in order to become a man the boy must 'smash' the only nurturance he has encountered [the mother, significant other woman] however imperfectly, in order to enter a position of power supported by violence." As the focus of the Black Power movement shifted away from preoccupation with liberty and redress of grievances to the seizure of power (power over the definitions, the community institutions, the social and economic exigencies which affected black people's lives), such a repositioning of the female seems inevitable. A number of black male fictional texts from the period of the 1960s and 70s privilege the black-female-as-sex-object image alongside configurations of the black male as revolutionary/sex master. A specific example of this is Imiri Baraka's (LeRoi Jones's) play *Madheart: A Morality Play*, where the black woman is beaten to the floor in submission as the ultimate act of black-male affirmation.

After leaving the CIA, Freeman returns to Chicago and Joy reappears smugly secure in her materialistic, comfortable—though loveless—marriage to a black doctor. Her conversation is shallow and callous and centers on her hired help, her new car, wardrobe, and her husband's drinking and womanizing—which she, of course, does not mind. Such estrangement and alienation between black man and woman places Freeman squarely in the tradition of the modern male hero in that he is a prototype of the contemporary sense of existential dislocation, carrying out his quest in a lonely, alien landscape. In this respect, the black nationalist hero, in his journey toward power, is not so unlike his prototype in Euro-American literature since both males' quests must be achieved by banishing to the margins all that is of the mother and the feminine.

Freeman's choice of street gangs for training in urban guerilla warfare is the Cobras. His decision to select them over all the other gangs rests on the fact that he had himself been one in his youth and that they possessed the "right characteristics" for successful underground revolt. The Tigers are discredited because they "even got chicks in the gang"; as Dean says, "The tigerettes, man them chicks as bad as they are!" Freeman notes, however, that they could "use women; they can often go places and do things men can't do" (96). The type of "things" that they can do are demonstrated by the Dahomey queen who comes to Chicago later to warn him that the CIA is launching a powerful attack on the guerrillas and their leader. She is now the mistress of the CIA general, Freeman's old boss, and she, unlike Joy, feels a genuine commitment to Dan. For all her self-sacrificing, she expects nothing in return and is apparently content just to be able to spend the night with Freeman in his flat.

As the urban unrest intensifies, Joy becomes even more of the stereotyped, middle-class black bitch, expressing bitterness over the fact that the rioters have put respectable blacks in jeopardy. Her husband has been fired from the hospital and she fears for her job: "It's those damn Freedom Fighters," she moans. "You can't go to a cocktail party nowadays without running into someone who has lost his integrated job" (237). "People are losing jobs they worked and sacrificed to get, all because of ignorant niggers who know nothing but hate" (238). In fact, it is she who ultimately turns Freeman in to the police at the end of the novel. Greenlee, indeed, makes her a metaphor for the failure of the black revolution, a direct inversion of Arna Bontemp's Juba, whom he turns into the very harbinger of black insurrection.

Reed's 1974 novel *The Last Days of Louisiana Red* attempts to promote a Hoodoo aesthetic for liberation of Afro-American minds and psyches. Louisiana Red is an attitude, according to Reed, which makes it impossible for blacks to unite and work for common goals in the best interest of the whole community. It results in racial betrayal and intraracial strife. He further charges through the text that Black Power politics of the 1960s and 70s was reduced to a commodity and coopted by the media. Interestingly enough, it is in black women that Louisiana Red seems to have taken root. In a fable form which parallels the tragedy of Oedipus Rex of Thebes and his daughter Antigone, Reed delineates the destruction of the Yellings family primarily as a result of the Hoodoo hierarchy's manipulation of Minnie Yellings, known in the story as "Minnie the Moocher." Her brand of liberation ethics is referred to as Moocherism. Although it is never really clear just what Moocherism is, the reader surmises that it refers primarily to Minnie and her followers' apparent disregard for the efforts undertaken by Solid Gumbo Works, which was begun by Minnie's father, Ed Yellings. Minnie the Moocher comes from Cab Calloway's song of the same name. In the song, she is portrayed as "a strong, glamorous female with hustling powers whose old man is her inferior, or a cokey." Papa LaBas (a name referencing the Hoodoo deity Legba) is sent by the "Board" to deal with Minnie after her father Ed is assassinated. Ed's Solid Gumbo Works has found a cure for cancer and he is on the way to finding a cure for drug addiction when he is eliminated by the agents of Louisiana Red.

A character called Chorus infuses the story of Antigone and Creon into the text through a rereading of the play and the events surrounding the tragedy of the family. Chorus gives us the subtext that inheres in Reed's Hoodoo ethics of Solid Gumbo Works. Antigone is, in fact, a beautiful and clever "man killer": "Antigone was after bigger game. She wanted to be a sphinx: head and breasts of a woman; bird's wings; lion's feet and a snake's ass. A hissing, barking, distorted, eye-balling bitch is what she was out for."[17] Supposedly, a cult sprang up as a result of Antigone's act. She herself, according to Chorus, was saved in time and became a ball-busting tyrant using her lies and good looks to get her way. She went around with her Nanny who made a reputation for herself through her "readings" where she portrayed Theban males as weak simpering nothings. This is unmistakably an assessment of Minnie and black women like her, educated, vocal and beautiful. She is characterized by Chorus and Labas as a spouter of theories, "an emotional vamp" (34) who has been influenced by a Louisiana Red agent posing as her Nanny. This agent tells her stories of Marie or the great Hoodoo Mambo Marie LeVeau and Doc John, her male counterpart. It is Nanny's privileging of Marie over Doc John which is said to have corrupted Minnie's mind as a child. Because of this mis-training, Minnie's Moocherism is held responsible for the warped minds of those black men who steal from each other or commit other "incestuous crimes."

Minnie is constantly surrounded by her Dahomeyan Softball team, a group of "fierce rough-looking women led by . . . a big . . . 6-foot bruiser . . . called Big Sally." Chorus (or the voice of black manhood) charges Antigone/Minnie with crowding out his lines, i.e., emasculating the black man through her aggressive vocality in the black nationalist struggle. Papa LaBas (Legba) observes that "Typically the black woman is infected by the promise of white liberalism. And if I [LaBas] can interpret her through African witchcraft, then a lot of people's eyes will be opened" (35). He continues, "She is an agent of the sphinx's jinx, an acolyte of an ugly cause. . . . She was sent to destroy the patriarchy—notice how her victims are connected with Royalty and the Theocracy" (35). Chorus continues, "She's the worst of tyrants. Like the black widow spider that draws its prey, loves it, then drains it. Only she doesn't drain it physically, she drains it emotionally. She deprives her victim of the ability to express itself . . ." (36), which is a profoundly powerful comment by Reed on his perception of the black woman.

Like Antigone, Minnie is "extremely good with words" and, as Chorus says, "She could argue a man to a stand still" (87). This prevailing opinion that women who are allowed prominence in the black nationalist movement will ultimately use their verbal and sexual power to challenge the position of the black male is expressed in the text by Street Yellings, Minnie's estranged brother and leader of a radical group called "the Seven" (obviously for the *Seven Against Thebes* play delineating the conflict between Oedipus' two sons Eteocles and Polynices). "Knowing you [he says to Minnie] you'd probably want to sit down but only stand because I asked you to sit down—a man asked you to sit down. You want to defy me like you did Dad . . . You could never come to a man in peace" (89). Minnie, on the other hand, tells him that she is prepared to hand over leadership of the Moochers to him, but Street scolds:

> Then why don't you get rid of those scurry skuzzy skanks who follow you around [the Dahomeyan Softball Team]? Our Argivians are enough muscle for the Moochers. Let them make themselves useful. Mimeographing my speeches, licking stamps, fixing drinks, giving massages, cooking our dinner, giving up some drawers . . . giving up some PUSSY. Lying down like a woman . . . You're my sister, all right, scared to get fucked. Scared to do anything. Trembling. Whatever gave you the right to think you could lead a man! You better try and get some dick and take your mind off this bullshit. (89)

As though echoing the sentiments of his "brother" in the patriarchal struggle for power, Chorus vents his spleen over being upstaged by Antigone: "In former time when the Theban elders had manhood, a man would have leaped across the stage and whipped the shit out of this bitch, but this is considered bad form these days. . . . In Brazil they would have left Antigone in a temple until all of her psychic poisons were flushed out. . . . What did Creon say? 'O Zeus, what a tribe you have given us in woman'" (105). And further, referring to the popular belief about the collaboration between white men and black women to keep the black man down, Chorus comments, "The conqueror always sends Antigone. She gets the biggest honorariums. She is on her way to becoming: 'The Sphinx who ate men raw'" (105).

Perhaps the most poignant example of this misogynistic blaming of women for all that is wrong with the black man is illustrated by Papa LaBas himself, the mystic head of Solid Gumbo Works, when he finally brings Minnie in for a confrontation:

> A woman uses her cunt power to threaten and intimidate, even to blackmail—to cause brother to kill brother . . . women use our children as hostages against us. We walk the streets in need of women and make fools of ourselves over women; fight each other, put Louisiana Red on each other. . . . The original blood-sucking vampire on this earth, and you know it, and you know

> how to use it. I can't understand why you want to be liberated. Hell. You already free—you already liberated. Liberated and powerful. We're the ones who are slaves; two thirds of the men on skid row were driven there by their mothers, wives, daughters, their mistresses and their sisters. (125–126)

Papa LaBas goes on to pose the argument heard since slavery that there are "lucrative benefits" to being a black woman in America, and that black female prostitution is just a continuation of the age-old clandestine (and I might add, "cooperative") meetings between "ancient lovers," black women and white men (128). As to why black men run off and leave their families, LaBas comments that they are "harassed and pursued by court warrants . . . that help [black women's] vengeance" (128). Black women's vocality in the revolutionary movement, in short, is portrayed as a conspiracy between the black woman and the white man to put the black man "in the kitchen and to death" (129).

True to the Oedipus/Antigone parallel, the two Yellings brothers, Wolf and Street, kill each other in a duel at the San Francisco Marina, a tragedy which, by the way, is attributed to Minnie's doings. Minnie is shot by Chorus as she boards a plane, and LaBas returns to the mystical domain of the Hoodoo divines to plead for Minnie's release from death, since, as LaBas often notes, Minnie is not totally responsible as she is a pawn in a spiritual power-play between the forces of Louisiana Red and Solid Gumbo Works. He succeeds as Minnie is kicked out of the afterworld by Blue Coal, the Chairman of the Board, and seeks the reassuring arms of her new protector, Papa LaBas, finally resecuring the female in a more appropriate role in the gender-based patriarchal economy and insuring the prosperity of Solid Gumbo Works. The black woman has, indeed, been resituated from the foreground of the black nationalist struggle to the margins.

Perhaps Albert Memmi's observations about oppressed peoples in his book *The Colonizer and the Colonized* merits our consideration here for its prophetic vision of the colonized in relation to the black nationalist manifestation in America:

> The [oppressed will ultimately come to fight] in the name of the very values of the [oppressor]; [they] use his techniques of thought and his methods of combat. It must be added that this is the only action that the oppressor understands.

Furthermore, the painful irony is that,

> To expect the [oppressed] to open his mind to the world and be a humanist and internationalist would seem to be ludicrous thoughtlessness. He is still

> regaining possession of himself, still examining himself with astonishment, passionately. . . . Moreover, it is remarkable that he is even more ardent in asserting himself as he tries to assume the [very] identity of the [oppressor].[18]

NOTES

1. Wilson Jeremiah Moses, *The Golden Age of Black Nationalism, 1850–1925* (New York: Oxford University Press, 1978), pp. 6, 7, 11.

2. Gayle T. Tate, "Black Nationalism: An Angle of Vision," *Western Journal of Black Studies*, 12, 1 (1988), pp. 41, 44, 47.

3. Rosalyn Terborg-Penn, "Black Male Perspectives on the Nineteenth-Century Woman," in Sharon Harley and Rosalyn Terborg-Penn, eds., *The Afro-American Woman: Struggles and Images* (Port Washington, NY: National University Publications, Kennikat Press, 1978), pp. 28–29.

4. Ibid., pp. 30, 31.

5. John H. Bracey, Jr., August Meier, and Elliott Rudwick, eds., *Black Nationalism in America* (Indianapolis, IN: Bobbs-Merrill, 1970), p. 226.

6. Tate, "Black Nationalism," p. 42.

7. Anna Julia Cooper, *A Voice from the South*, intro. Mary Helen Washington, The Schomburg Library of Nineteenth-Century Black Women Writers (New York: Oxford University Press, 1988), pp. 28–31.

8. Arna Bontemps, *Black Thunder* (Boston: Beacon Press, 1936; rpt. 1986), p. 68. All further references will be incorporated in the text above.

9. J. E. Cirlot, *A Dictionary of Symbols* (New York: Philosophical Library, 1962), pp. 152, 295.

10. Ibid., p. 309.

11. Kate Millet, *Sexual Politics* (New York: Ballantine, 1969), pp. 55, 455.

12. bell hooks, *Ain't I a Woman: Black Women and Feminism* (Boston: South End Press, 1981), p. 102.

13. Moses, *The Golden Age of Black Nationalism,* p. 260.

14. Charles Johnson, *Race and Being: Black Writers Since 1970* (Bloomington, IN: Indiana University Press, 1988), p. 17.

15. Maulana Karenga, *The Quotable Karenga* (Los Angeles: Temple of Kawaida, U.S., Inc., 1967), p. 27.

16. Sam Greenlee, *The Spook Who Sat by the Door* (New York: Bantam, 1969), p. 47. All further references will be incorporated in the text above.

17. Ishmael Reed, *The Last Days of Louisiana Red* (New York: Random House, 1976), p. 62. All further references will be incorporated in the text above.

18. Albert Memmi, *The Colonizer and the Colonized* (Boston: Beacon Press, 1965), pp. 129, 135.

Chapter 17

The Parricidal Phantasm: Irish Nationalism and the Playboy *Riots*

Stephen Tifft

When the curtain first rose on J. M. Synge's *The Playboy of the Western World* at the Abbey Theatre in Dublin on Saturday, January 26, 1907, the directors of the Theatre—W. B. Yeats, Lady Gregory, and Synge—had been sufficiently schooled by previous spasms of nationalist discontent with the Abbey's overly aestheticized political outlook to anticipate an uneasy reception. Yet few could have foreseen the tumult that greeted the play, and only grew more furious during its week-long run. Even in the first, relatively quiet performance, the groaning and hissing of the audience gathered force and finally erupted in a riot that obliterated most of the last act. The play was ferociously denounced in the press, and word of the outrage spread so quickly that the disturbances of opening night proved to be a mere dumbshow to the hectic events that followed. Monday's performance was interrupted within minutes by choirs of chanting, thumping demonstrators, many of whom had come equipped with tin trumpets. "Now," reports the *Freeman's Journal*, "the uproar assumed gigantic dimensions, stamping, boohing, vociferations in Gaelic, and the striking of seats with sticks were universal in the gallery and pit."[1] Some spectators, apparently unwilling to sink to new depths of depravity, shouted, "What would not be tolerated in America will not be allowed here!" From time to time the curtain was lowered, and W. G. Fay, the Abbey's Manager and leading actor, advanced to the footlights to appeal for a fair hearing and offer refunds to the dissatisfied, but he was shouted down. The audience drowned out the play with Gaelic songs and patriotic anthems. The second act got underway at 10 o'clock; it proved to be as inaudible as the first, and the company resigned themselves to performing the rest of the play in pantomime.

This got to be a regular thing. The following performances were if anything still more turbulent; not until the fifth evening, when the rioting began to abate slightly, were audiences able to hear more than a few sentences in succession. Even this respite, according to Willie Fay, was achieved only by padding the floor of the theater with felt, in order to muffle the protestors' rhythmic stamping.[2] Such sustained outbursts could only be the result of a combination of spontaneity and design. By the second performance it seemed clear to many observers that the demonstrations were being organized, apparently by Irish nationalists, some of them brought in from the Gaelic West. Counter-gangs of supporters started to appear (including some Trinity College students, invited by Lady Gregory,[3] who did not make matters any calmer by standing up at the end of the performance to sing "God Save the King"), and shouting matches and fistfights broke out between them and the protestors.

It was Yeats and Lady Gregory themselves, however, who most dramatically exacerbated the tumult, as early as Monday: they called in the police to quell the riots, in what was read as an imperious appeal to British power by the erstwhile vanguard of Irish cultural nationalism. This gesture, perhaps even more than the play itself, proved impossible for Yeats's and the Abbey's nationalist opponents to forgive, particularly after they heard "our dreamy poet swearing in the Northern Police Court that he distinctly heard a boo."[4] Yeats remained resolute in championing the rights of sympathetic spectators and of playwrights to hear and be heard, and he claims that later in the week, when rival gangs were marching through Abbey and O'Connell streets shouting their slogans, some five hundred police were called out to keep order.[5] But disillusioned nationalist leaders such as Arthur Griffith and Pádraic Pearse, convinced that the Abbey's Ascendancy leaders had at last shown their true British colors, publicly called upon the Abbey to give up its pretensions to the title "The Irish National Theatre," and one antagonist declaimed bitterly after the trials that this "was not the first time in our history that a wrongly administered English law had violated Irish freedom."[6]

Yeats saw the riots as the decisive outbreak of a long-simmering conflict over the political status of art, between the writers of the Abbey and those nationalists who expected the Theatre to serve as an instrument of propaganda.[7] It is surely true that the riots served nationalists as the explosive release of several years of accumulated discontent with the Abbey's stubborn artsiness, and conversely provided the Abbey with a chance to insist upon its independence from programmatic politics. But the most intimate sources of outrage should be sought in the play itself. The rioters felt quite strongly about this; for them, *The Playboy* amounted to defamation: "It is not too much to say that no traducer of the Irish people ever presented a more sordid, squalid, and repulsive picture of Irish life and character. It is calumny gone raving mad."[8] Synge's raving calumny was embedded in the essential elements of his plot. The protagonist, Christy Mahon, thinks that he has killed his father in an argument and flees to a peasant community in County Mayo. When the local people learn his secret, far from turning him in, they lionize him for his heroic deed. The publican's daughter in particular, Pegeen, virtually generates Christy's heroism—and with it, an object for her own romantic aspirations—retroactively; and Christy, schooled by her seductive lyricism, comes actually to embody in the present the ideal power and grandeur that are fictively ascribed to him in the past. (As it turns out, the father has only been wounded, and he shows up to spoil Christy's fun, turning the disillusioned peasants against the newfound playboy for failing his image. Christy finally retains his claim to heroism in a ritual repetition of the parricidal gesture, but the villagers, once so enamored of a phantasmatic image of father-slaying, are now shocked by the violent immediacy of its reenactment, and stubbornly persist in repudiating Christy.) For most of the play's opponents, the very idea that Irishmen and Irishwomen—especially peasants from the honored Gaelic West—would dote on a parricide constituted an "unmitigated, protracted libel upon Irish peasant men and, worse still, upon Irish peasant girlhood."[9]

It is striking that rioting of so distinctly nationalist a cast should focus on intimations of sexual license, as the last phrase suggests. The principal metaphors of *The Playboy*—the slain father, libido run amok—almost ostentatiously invite the Oedipal idiom of a Freudian reading, and the ideology of nationalism is equally bound up with psychoanalytic inflections of parricide. But it is not at all clear why the notion of rising up in violent retribution against a tyrannical father (albeit in comic phantasy) should seem outrageous to nationalists who themselves paid lip-service, at least, to the Fenian revolutionaries of former days who had sacrificed their lives in rebellion against their British rulers—why these nationalists should rally behind the banner of the law-abiding—nor why the seductiveness of Christy's exuberant phantasy should prove so alarming for Irish nationalism at a crucial moment of its history. In what follows I will examine parricidal phantasy as a provocation to Irish nationalism, especially in libidinal terms; for in the riotous economy of representation and reception initiated by

The Playboy, erotic energy is in effect the currency of choice: let us say, the yen.[10]

The rioters' most vocal grievance verged on sexual hysteria: for all the moral turpitude of harboring a parricide, it was the amorous attention that the young girls of the village lavish on their hero which especially shocked the audience. Above all, according to the popular wisdom, a week of riots was touched off by what one observer called Synge's "wanton indecency" in having a female character utter the word "shift." "Shift," as one indignant letter to the editor from "A Western Girl" reminds us, is "a word indicating an essential item of female attire, which the lady would probably never utter in ordinary circumstances, even to herself."[11] It is often assumed that hints of sexual license inflame sensitive patriots simply by offending ideals of purity and respectability on which nationalism depends (Hugh Kenner observes that "Irish womanhood [is] in its pure state a revolutionists' utility like gunpowder"[12]), but even contemporary observers sensed a strain of hysterical overreaction that warns us of something more volatile at stake than respectability. Attitudes such as those of the Western Girl or of the Belfast reviewer who called Synge's female characters "vulgar, shameless, unnatural viragoes with the soul and tongues of strumpets," were immediately challenged in the press.[13] Moreover, the response to the scandalous "shift" was itself curiously inconsistent: the word is actually used three times in *The Playboy,* by both Pegeen and the Widow Quin in Act II and by Christy in Act III, and despite the indignation of the Western Girl, on the opening night it was apparently not until the third instance that the audience took violent notice.[14] If they were offended at Synge's realist candor in producing what Griffith, grudgingly conceding its colloquial currency, denounced as "the foulest language we have ever listened to from a public platform,"[15] they nodded strangely in their vigilance—until, interestingly, "shift" was reiterated in a context of parricidal violence.

The allergic reaction to "shift"—a word that is at once highly charged for the rioters and oddly bland considering the effect it produces—resembles an effect of the psychoanalytic process of deferred action: a total evacuation of the affect of an early, properly traumatic moment (not yet experienced as such), by means of the displacement of that affect onto the banal triggering elements of a later scene, in which the trauma belatedly emerges in all its original force.[16] But if "shift" might thus be understood as the displaced irritant of a more obscure trauma or anxiety to which it gives voice, what is the trauma? Evidently it concerns an intuitive association of libidinal excess with parricide; but although it may be tempting to suppose that nationalists were given scandal by the simple assertion of this Oedipal scenario, their vexed relations to its various positions, as well as anomalies in their response to the play, oblige us to search for more convoluted causes.

Such vexations may be measured by the conflicted attitudes toward female figures that the rioters adopt in their squeamishness about Pegeen's doubly licentious seduction of a murderer. Christy's rebellion against his father was instigated by the latter's insistence that for mercenary reasons Christy marry the Widow Casey, whom Christy describes as "a walking terror from beyond the hills," who "did suckle me for six weeks when I came into the world, and she a hag this day with a tongue on her has the crows and seabirds scattered, the way they wouldn't cast a shadow on her garden with the dread of her curse."[17] This maternal hag—strangely foisted upon the Oedipal son by an overbearing father—resembles the mythical figure called *Shan Van Vocht*, "The Poor Old Woman," an exorbitantly nostalgic trope for a victimized Ireland as the maternal object of nationalist devotion. If Yeats, in the wildly popular *Kathleen ni Houlihan*, had stirred Fenian hearts by portraying the Poor Old Woman as an aged seductress who for those devoted to her is transformed into a beautiful young queen, Synge more sardonically presents such a figure as an antique horror to be shunned at all costs, and Christy's dalliance with young Pegeen as a defiant alternative. In this respect the rioters' reaction against Christy's shunning makes sense, but it is puzzling that they should not fall in with his efforts to desexualize this maternal figure. Christy is burdened with an Oedipal ambivalence that emerges in the undertone of jealous resentment in his reproof of the Widow Casey as "a woman of noted misbehaviour with the old and young," and that Synge reinforces by introducing young Widow Quin as a plausible match. Christy's steadfast rejection of both widows, in favor of a romance with Pegeen that is both more amorous and less highly charged sexually, may be read as part of an entirely orthodox (if unusually literal) move to foreclose this play of Oedipal desire. But in denouncing Pegeen as a virago, the rioters not only reject this attempt at resolving Oedipal tensions, but also risk exacerbating their own parallel tensions toward the Poor Old Woman, by mimicking Christy's panicky reaction and directing it toward Pegeen instead of the mother figure.[18]

In reacting against the play's implicitly Oedipal logic, then, the rioters only enter into that logic while further destabilizing its terms. This impulse to exacerbate the volatility of illicit desire even in protesting it repeatedly marks the nationalists' outrage. Occasional frank acknowledgements of a threat to manliness, for instance (Synge was charged with betraying the duty of the Abbey to support "the forces of virile nationalism" against an insidious decadence),[19] echo with an interesting edginess when the "shift" furor touches on sexual license and hypocrisy, a knot of investments that Yeats instinctively associated with a strident new voice of nationalism: "As I stood there watching, knowing well that I saw the dissolution of a school of patriotism that held sway over my youth, Synge came and stood beside me, and said, 'A young doctor has just told me that he can hardly keep himself from jumping on to a seat, and pointing out in that howling mob those whom he is treating for venereal disease.'"[20] Yeats is shrewd to notice the link between a moment of crisis for Irish nationalism and a form of male sexual hysteria which Neil Hertz has illuminated in other contexts,[21] and the poet's observation is none the less salient for his own obvious participation—as Hertz's argument would predict—in much the same hysteria (where the rioters' anxiety about sexual and political loss lashes back at the play's scandalous protagonists, Yeats's anxiety issues doubly in the elegiac pathos of his introductory lament and the subsequent disgust with the "howling mob" of licentious hypocrites[22]). A panicky reversibility, endemic to the riots, emerges in the central figure of Yeats's anecdote, the prude with VD: one who fears and loves the evil he denounces with an oppositional intimacy.

It is a dangerous instability of desire, then—in some way their own desire, come alarmingly home to roost—that underlies the rioters' puzzling and significant recoiling from a usual mainstay of nationalist ideology: the phantasy of revolutionary heroism. One might expect a nationalist ideologue to welcome the example of Christy's mythic parricide as a transfiguring endowment from the past. Initially the slaying of his father was for Christy a mere pettish reflex, and he enters the Flaherty public-house a doleful, shrinking, guilt-ridden fellow; it is the poetic speculation of Pegeen and the others that swells the act into something Promethean, engendering in him a delightful new sense of triumph and even a number of strikingly physical prepotencies. The ability to draw present power from myths of an epic past is surely central to the nationalist investment in the Gaelic Revival at this period. Irish revolutionaries were remarkable for being "myth-possessed men who willingly perish into images," and in fact it was Arthur Griffith himself who saluted the Abbey in its early years as "a Theatre where the heroic past of Ireland can be made to live again for us and give us inspiration and aspiration."[23] Militant nationalists who had long relied on popular admiration for, precisely, their terrorist violence—which many Irish people felt was their sole recourse in the face of injustice—might thus be expected to welcome the call to bloody revolt that Christy seems allegorically to offer, or else to reject it only because of its burlesque qualities.[24] Yet Dubliners were strangely obstinate in failing to recognize the allegory, and loudly denounced the play's evocation of much the sort of whole-hearted violence that in contemporary nationalist circles was not only openly espoused by militant activists as an essential political weapon, but also tacitly relied upon by moderate parliamentary nationalists for the pressure it could apply to an intransigent government.[25]

There were specific political reasons for this Gertrudian bad conscience. In 1907 militant nationalism was in some disarray; Fenian terrorists had found it increasingly necessary to stay their hand, partly because of the adverse publicity attending such glamorously ill-starred conspiracies as the Phoenix Park murders, and partly because of the surprising success of more moderate strategies, above all the Parliamentary maneuvering of Charles Stewart Parnell before his calamitous fall. In the comparative power vacuum which followed that fall, various forms of cultural nationalism had begun to flourish, which called for the staging of revolution in the minds of the Irish people: for reimagining the civilization, often on the model of ancient legends.[26] Christy carries out on a small scale a quite similar project, but one problem for cultural nationalists is that he does so precisely by reinstating the First Cause of parricidal violence. The recoiling from a rhetoric of violence which marked the riots, even at *their* most violent, might thus be seen as a sign of the ascendancy of cultural over militant nationalism: nationalists whose field was discourse felt keenly that imputations of violence could only imply either that their cultural policies were ultimately impotent, and would have to give way to the militancy of their Fenian counterparts, or that cultural nationalism was to begin with only a front for schemes of revolutionary violence. What is worse, the peasants in the play are implicitly ridiculed for just the same sort of self-contradiction, when they recoil from the actual bloody deed that they had praised in phantasy; and one wonders whether the rioters, contrary to all their rhetoric, also felt affronted at the idea that the nationalist not only fabricates myths of violence with extraordinary zeal and desperation, but then turns out after all to be unable to stand the sight of blood.

Not just anyone's blood, however: it is the father's blood in particular that so gets under the nationalist's skin. Psychoanalytic theory offers a partial explanation: since the son's hostile wish to oust the father is inseparable from the desire to be the father, to occupy his position, a nationalist's revolutionary impulse to be, as Pegeen puts it, "a fine lad with the great savagery to destroy [his] da" is likely to encounter a backlash of identification with the paternal opponent. Freudian theory also suggests, however, that the son's triumph in the Oedipal conflict ultimately allays this ambivalence by consolidating both positions. But for the rioters, the apparent specularity of the Oedipal contest is distorted, before it can achieve this resolution, by a vexing quirk of the psychodynamics of Irish nationalism. Most simply put, the nationalist has an embarrassment of fathers: in order to assert his rebellion against the tyrannical British father, he needs to invoke the heritage of a beneficent (if defunct) Irish one. Hence the very formation of a national identity—a seemingly rebellious act—amounts to cooptation by the father, or a father, and impels the nationalist instinctively to combat signs of filial revolt and (what seems to amount to the same thing) libidinal disorder, even in himself and his representations. Because the nationalist externalizes two mutually hostile fathers, with each of whom he has the usual ambivalent relations, insurrection can never deliver him to the purity of aggrieved filiation without simultaneously letting him in for renewed internal conflict with the alternative father, into whose position the rebellion has propelled him without having given him the chance to sublate it.

There are plenty of practical examples of this impasse. Pearse, the most ardently revolutionary of all Ireland's sons, could only work himself and his listeners up to the proper rebellious pitch by claiming a "virility" drawn from its dead fathers, whose example, however, in some ways oppresses him.[27] Griffith's misleadingly named *Sinn Fein* ("Ourselves") policy, which was strongly to influence the emergent form of an independent Irish government (under his presidency) within fifteen years, replicates the same ambivalent structure still more clearly. It calls for the Irish to set up a shadow-government of their own (complete with a sort of Parliament, whose decrees would be executed by County Councils) within the British jurisdiction. A figure of phantasmatic uprising within actual submission, this Irish shadow-structure acts like a rebellious son whose behavior and institutions replicate those of the oppressive father, with whom he thus identifies, ambivalence intact, as completely as could be imagined. But the nationalist's troubled Oedipal status is illustrated most dramatically in the fate of Parnell. His fellow nationalists accepted him as an Irish father as long as he directed any rebellious filial energies solely toward the British, and sublimated libido into an abstract devotion to the Poor Old Woman; but when they witnessed his betrayal of this devotion, and this role, for that of the adulterer trespassing against the parental unity of Captain and Mrs. Kitty O'Shea, they turned against him with a fury appropriate to their solidarity with the married man in the story. Surely there is no mere coincidence in the fact that the crowds who turned on Parnell when the scandal broke taunted him for his libidinal excesses by waving in the air the tokens of his affair with the young mother: shifts.[28]

We can therefore see in the denunciations of Christy's parricide and of all who sympathize with it the fury of the nationalist who has become a father in the very name of a nationalism which otherwise looks like the epitome of the desiring son. An untoward third party that hovers disturbingly between the opposed positions of Irish son and British father, the phantasmatic nationalist ideal no sooner holds out to the embattled son—or, in another mood, father—the promise of supportive identification than it seems to go over to the other side. This shiftiness parallels the uncontrolled reversibility revealed in Yeats's venereal anecdote, and more subtly conforms to the riots' highly charged figure of betrayal from within the ranks. In the treachery of the seeming nationalist like Synge or Yeats, or of the false Christy, a version of the self, "one of us," splits off as "one of them"; but given the heightened Oedipal double bind of nationalist ideology, this calamitous traduction inevitably replays an intrapsychic self-betrayal implicit in nationalist rebellion. The function of trauma is to convert a betrayal (exposure) *of* one's conflicted desires to a betrayal *by* the Other;[29] but for the rioters this reaction fails in its primary motive of foreclosing ambivalence.

This suggests that the nationalist's desire can at best drive him on to Pyrrhic victory. Pyrrhic victory is an insistent feature of *The Playboy*, appearing not only in Christy's second thrashing of Old Mahon, which only results in a more vehement rejection by Pegeen and in his final relegation to the company of the defeated father, but also in the logic by which Pegeen's extravagant phantasy of a heroic suitor bears fruit so desirable that it is impossible for her to eat. *The Playboy* might seem most exasperatingly perverse just in its suggestion that such losses and prohibitions are immanent in the phantasy of parricide. In post-Lacanian psychoanalytic accounts of the nature of phantasy in general, desire is not impelled toward a natural object that might satiate it; rather, it originates as a function of sexuality in the splitting off of a felicitous surplus pleasure initially "propped" on the satisfaction of an instinctual need: "sexuality detaches itself from any natural object, finds itself delivered over to the phantasm, and even by that means creates itself as sexuality."[30] From its inception, then, sexual desire absorbs itself in the phantasmatic experience of prohibition and loss. One might regard the phantasm itself as the desired object; this would preserve the illusion of possible even if immaterial fulfillment. But as Laplanche and Pontalis point out, the phantasm of desire in fact preserves the splitting and loss of its origin by taking the more complex form of a *scenario*, encompassing not only an externalized object, but an entire narrative in which complicating elements and troubling permutations—or, we may say, "shifts"—appear: notably, the phantasm includes both an insistent gesture of prohibition against its own attainment and, above all, the forlorn desiring subject himself, caught in the act of yearning for the phantasm of which he is fated to remain a part.

The allegory of a heroic power generated in Christy by the sheer energy of desire may seem promising for the nationalist, but ultimately the parricidal phantasy-scenario can only strike him as alarming: not only because phantasmatic gestures of projection and prohibition frustrate desire, but also because of the more unsettling sense Christy conveys that it is just this baffled phantasy, this trap of its own short-circuiting, toward which his desire perversely gravitates. In accepting this he in effect identifies with, or commits his desire to, all the positions of the phantasy (Pegeen's, Old Mahon's, Shawn's, for example); his subjectivity shuttles erratically, always a third party, always on the move, and thus further evokes—as if the allegory were not sufficiently pointed already—the nationalist's perpetually mobile Oedipal crisis. In balking at the desire displayed or triggered by *The Playboy*, then, the repressive nationalist both denounces the indignity of such phantasy, and takes his proper place in it.

If Christy, by contrast, appealingly succeeds in deriving a certain practical power from his cathexis of such a phantasm, he himself recognizes that this power is grounded not in stubbornly cheerful wish-fulfillment, but in his steadfast desire for the phantasmatic dilemma itself, as not an object but rather a staging, of loss as well as gain. This is not, after all, a comfortable basis for political action—how it can issue in action at all will demand our attention in the remainder of this essay—but what Christy may expose most alarmingly for nationalists is the danger that their desire will find no other itinerary.

To desire a phantasm fretted with figures of loss and prohibition, and to identify with all the positions of such a phantasm, is to neutralize the figure of the female as object of desire, still more as agent. Thus Christy's dogged Oedipal victory finally reveals the libidinous son to be after all in league with the defeated and admiring father who accompanies him offstage at the end of the play, as sexuality is sublimated into rhetorical empowerment: the two have no other prospect than to thrive on the phantasmatic satisfactions of telling their story. Father and son share an embittered victory that inevitably comes trailing clouds of defeat, in the form of the defection of both the prize of the victory and the admiring audience. To the extent that this fretful logic of phantasy perfectly suits the double jeopardy of nationalism's Oedipus complex, we might say that the riots complete the phantasmatic movement of Synge's play, even that he has in effect solicited this repudiation: both by coopting the ideals of his audience, thus provoking their reactionary rage, and by schooling their response in the nearly identical reactions of their surrogates in the play.

But might not the play, conversely, be made to order for the nationalists? If so, they would have not merely to recoil from but to profit by their sense of the ambiguous phantasm it discloses. Still, such profit might conceivably lie in the galvanizing effect of their resistance to the phantasm, announced in rioting—in some conjuncture of loss and violence with the power to foreclose the paralyzing ambivalence that besets Irish nationalism. Perhaps Pegeen provides the necessary tutelage for the rioters, through her plausibly outraged reply to loss: at the moment of Old Mahon's appearance, Pegeen answers the failure of her love-idyll with Christy by an active (for Christy nearly lethal) rage that mirrors, or more accurately anticipates, that of the riots. This fury—repudiating a story that she had done more than he to fashion—tries its best to reject the phantasm that she has all too much reason to regard as one with her in her desire. Outrage thus takes the form of violent reversal, of a traumatic disavowal of that which has apparently been, as now seems, so intimately a portion of one's being as not to have been noticeable as such.

Hertz finds such reversals symptomatic of political crisis generally, and especially of that reflex of "male hysteria" by which "a complex of historical factors can be ignored in favor of a thrilling encounter in which intimations of sheer weakness and sheer power are exchanged."[31] In Hertz's account women both trigger and represent the thrilling exchanges of weakness and power to which the panicked male responds so violently, but *The Playboy* short-circuits these gender dynamics: it is Christy who purveys such exchanges, as the basis of his acceptance of phantasmatic loss and of wilful sublimation at the end of the play, while Pegeen recoils from them; she is flattened and used as a means of objectifying and thus discharging both the malevolent affect of Christy's rejection and the flat-footed resistance to ambivalence that he has superseded. Thus Pegeen rivals the rioters in the shameless denials by which she responds to the thrilling exchanges of weakness and strength that pervade *The Playboy* as well as its reception. Much as she accuses Christy of treachery even while working herself up to turning him over to the authorities, the audience evinces horror at Christy's parricide, then at the peasants' violent treatment of him, yet moments later proceeds to egg the peasants on by shouting "Brain him!"—and finally denounces the Mayo women as unnatural viragoes. Such moments of bad faith are triggered by abrupt topplings from and returns to power: Christy's rebounding, in overmastering his father a second time, provokes Pegeen to have him tied up and to burn his leg with a flaming peat-sod; and strikingly, the precise flashpoint of irremediable rioting on opening night was this spectacle of Christy bound, abased, and (therefore) dangerous. Interchanges of sheer weakness and sheer power such as these fill the annals of Irish heroism, with its myths of betrayed heroes, of powerful and ruthless but ultimately doomed English tyrants, of a transfigured and omnipuissant Poor Old Woman. The play's reversals vividly enact the alarmingly mixed nature of the phantasm; Pegeen's sudden and flabbergasting violence is meant to put an end to them.

Specular violence, with its illusory consolidation of self versus other, might readily yield to a nostalgia for its losses—the loss of the other that was the self—that is its after-effect for Pegeen. The final lines of the play announce yet another reversal (her third in fifteen minutes) generated by Christy's Pyrrhic victory, and by its restoring to her phantasy the patina of nostalgic loss. When he walks out, blessing the people with hostile irony for their part in his minimalist triumph, she wails, "Oh my grief, I've lost him surely. I've lost the only playboy of the western world." While her rage had enacted a trauma of internal splitting, her nostalgia, smug in its histrionic lamentation, regards the expelled heroic figure of her phantasm from a distance, its separateness a fait accompli. A similar nostalgia, elevated to sublimity by the glamor of fated loss, holds a place of honor in the Irish imagination, according to several of the more cynical literary commentators on Ireland during this period. Matthew Arnold's patronizing yet admiring essay "On the Study of Celtic Literature" had started with an epigraph from Ossian that announced the lure of a mesmeric fatalism: "They went forth to the war, but they always fell"; and in *Ulysses*, Joyce's Professor MacHugh confirms the obsession, with an astute account of its appeal: "We were always loyal to lost causes, the professor said. Success for us is the death of the intellect and of the imagination."[32] If Pegeen's nostalgia marks the success of her rage, a few moments before, as an apotropaic gesture, perhaps the riots serve a like function for the nationalist audience, preparing the way for a nostalgic retrenchment.

Yet it is precisely the nationalists' rioting that signals the frustration of such a gesture, and thus foretokens a different reaction to loss. The violence with which they inconsequently condemned Synge's defamation of the Irish as lovers of violence culminated in an astonishing moment at the height of the riots, when they were moved to cry out, "Kill the Author!"—thus fully yielding, in reference to Synge, to the very parricidal impulse they denounced. This gesture is, on one level, a reactionary move like Pegeen's, a way of recuperating the threat to the rioters' autonomy and stability posed by their being drawn into the self-contradictory positions to which the play solicits them. It resembles the "end of the line" moment described by Hertz, involving a subject drawn to an object that comes to seem disturbingly split: "the poised relationship of attenuated subject and divided object reveals its inherent instability by breaking down and giving way to scenarios more or less violent, in which the aggressive reassertion of the subject's stability is bought at some other subject's expense."[33] But in the case of the rioters, this purchase is doubled over, giving Hertz's scenario a curious self-mirroring effect: the split object, as well as the other subject who pays for the reassertion of stability, converge in a figure (Christy) whose nature coincides in crucial ways with that of the endangered, violent subject, and whose story mimics proleptically the dilemma of the latter. Though the rioters' unthinking enactment of the Oedipal gesture might seem reassuring,[34] then, their affinity with Christy, who occupies *all* the positions of an end-of-the-line moment, prevents a violent gesture of foreclosure from having its usual monolithic efficacy. Both affinity and prevention are witnessed in their voicing the parricide's cry, even in denouncing him so as to foreclose their double bind. But if Pegeen's more effective gesture of foreclosure merely results in her being transfixed by a nostalgic sense of loss, how can the nationalist discover any greater promise of power in finding such a gesture balked?

Christy plays out one possible answer, when his father returns in the flesh and explodes the easy version of his parricidal phantasy (even in fulfilling, as we by now suspect, one of its subtler fallen permutations): he applies the logic of reversal to loss itself, converting the energy of desperation to renewed action, turning Pyrrhic victory inside out—Roman loss, one might call it, except that he is the underdog. Christy oddly enacts his second parricidal gesture as almost a rider to his concession that Old Mahon has succeeded in foiling his son's phantasmatic liberation. Yielding—but with a difference—to his father, who wants to collar Christy in the old patriarchal way and remove him from the community that Mahon has now spoiled for him, Christy says, "I'm going but I'll stretch you first"; and so he does. Loss, then, is absorbed into—or even inspires—a more somber but equally empowering phantasy-scenario. Such a strategy, if that is what it is, accedes to endemic exchanges of weakness and power, without succumbing to Pegeen's specular obstinacy—but also, within Synge's psychical economy, thanks to her reduction to that obstinacy. The contrast to Hertz's scenario illuminates the implacable logic of this transaction: in committing himself to the exchanges of weakness and power, rather than resisting them through specular reaction, Christy appropriates the threat of powerful victimization usually ascribed to the female, and consequently shoulders Pegeen out of the way; in her fierce rejection, she becomes inseparable from, or more accurately, exchangeable with the oppressive paternal authority he had grossly resisted in the past.

Christy, by contrast, rides what looks like capitulation to a kind of victory—suggesting that they amount to much the same thing—with a productive perversity such as the rioters unconsciously adopt in their "Kill the Author!" To engage with, to gain momentum from, the dialectical exchanges on which phantasy thrives is to avoid the narcotic desire of Pegeen or of Professor MacHugh's Irishman, whose rage and bitterness project their phantasm and distance them from it in a continuous and costly suppression. In these terms we might surmise that the rioters, as involuntary partners in a common venture, stand to learn from Christy's fate the glimmer of a way out of their own Oedipal impasse, which echoes his despite being voiced in terms of outrage. Such a conjecture would have to interrogate the power of loss as a revolutionary instigation: for in its most material form (the kind that gives fathers renewed headaches) Christy's final power of abandoned action springs not from parricidal wish-fulfillment, but from his acceptance of phantasmatic prohibition and loss.

Yet there is something self-effacing—something which does not so much frustrate action as obviate it—about Christy's final victory, visible in his having to pair up with his father and depart from the community that he had briefly dominated. This complicity of filial transgression and paternal limit parallels Michel Foucault's account,[35] but only so far as to reveal the limitations of Christy's transgression. Tethered to a preexisting Oedipal paradigm which it has never annulled, Christy's success is established through both the "violence in a divided world (in an ethical world)" and the "victory over limits (in a dialectical or revolutionary world)" that for Foucault palliate most putative forms of transgression, and that finally attest to Christy's attenuated complicity with that paradigm. Both violence and victory are ultimately bracketed (not transcended or abolished) in *The Playboy*, perhaps to assist the attenuation, but at the cost of projecting transgressiveness to a decidedly figurative level, on which he neither smashes the Oedipal structure nor gives in to it, but identifies with it as a "scene."[36] Any practical nationalist would wish to carry Christy's logic of triumphant loss, of gaining power *through* having failed to kill one's father, one step forward—or backward—to an, if not more radical, at least more material conclusion. Nationalists of such a kidney were among Synge's audience, but it took them a couple of years to digest his thinking.

The *Playboy* riots themselves might be seen as a preliminary enactment of the difficult strategy by which the nationalist will learn to accommodate Christy's parricide, a strategy of unbracketing violence and victory while avoiding the paralyzed nostalgia that is their usual result, and of accepting Christy's logic of reversal yet preserving the simplicity of instrumental imperatives necessary for effective political action. But this enactment is first felt as a trauma; the play's more productive effects are deferred. The power of *The Playboy* in instigating them, its significance to the nationalist movement as a phantasy of initiation, can be felt nowhere more vividly than in the imposing figure of Pádraic Pearse, and in his changing relation to the career of Christy's phantasmatic action. In 1907, in a review in the Gaelic League's newspaper, Pearse denounced the play for reasons suggested above; by 1913, in "From a Hermitage," he publicly repented of this attack, and even portrayed Synge as the latest victim of that chronic ingratitude which Pearse, like Joyce, acknowledged for Irish nationalism.[37] In that essay, Pearse implied that he, with most of Synge's public, had simply not understood Synge's "strange symbols," but Pearse's own rapidly developing interest in a mythic phantasy deceptively combined with political shrewdness suggests that he was absorbing something of Synge's way of thinking. Pearse's friend Stephen MacKenna wrote that Pearse "hoped no less than to see Ireland teeming with Cuchulains," and in the Easter Rising of 1916 he deliberately invoked that mythic hero in proclaiming, from the steps of the General Post Office, the achievement of an Irish Republic.[38]

There is good reason to seek in the Rising part of the legacy of an evolving nationalist reading of *The Playboy*. There are obvious parallels. The aesthetic, symbolic impetus of the venture is suggested by the striking prominence of poets and thespians among the revolutionaries.[39] More specifically, the carefully invoked religious resonances of the Easter Rising recapitulate many of the figurative patterns of the play: the rising up from the dead—an uncanny return of the repressed, like the bloody resurgence of Old Mahon—of a son who is consubstantial with the father, a rising up, too, against a tyrannical power, hence a parricidal gesture. What is less obvious is that Pearse in particular follows Synge's logic that the success of this gesture must be found in its failure, in loss. For Pearse did not suppose that the Rising would work militarily—he saw with clairvoyant vividness that its success would depend upon a Pyrrhic triumph of the British.[40] On a psychic level, his strategy entailed two perhaps unconscious ruses, meant to avoid a stalemate like that of Christy absconding with his father at the end of the play: entangled in a logic by which son is also father, and victory also loss, Pearse tries to cast the father or limit outside his doubled self—to give it decisively the form of the British tyrant—and then to tempt that externalized father to the Pyrrhic victory which the son now knows well enough to avoid, in favor of a defeat which will amount to victory. If this is "transgression," it takes a curious form: in fact, Pearse aims at a *failed* transgression, one which will avoid the trap of crossing—and thus merely reconfirming and even in a sense embodying—the paternal limit. This failure rather serves to lure the externalized father into, as it were, crossing the limit himself, in the other direction, by annihilating the (passively) rebellious son and thus exceeding the limit *for* him. In this gambit, the nationalist claims the clarified single position of revolting son by the simple expedient of falling to the father; and the same stroke dispels any ambiguity in his identification with his Irish fathers, who, equally fallen, are equally nothing but sons (Christy's loss, by contrast, is too equivocal; it lacks the kamikaze zing that makes failed parricide work in practice).

Thus the Rising, as expected, contrived that the father achieve the transgression: it enticed the British into making martyrs of the failed rebellious sons by executing them—amid all the holy pathos they intended—and thus into founding for them their revolutionary success.[41] This was, to say the least, a public relations coup. Like Christy, the men of the Rising were jeered in the moment of their failure, as they were taken into custody; and yet their vanishing, like Christy's departure, produced in their mockers an intense pathos of identification, which gathered a revolutionary force that Britain proved unable to withstand. With perfect assurance, Pearse took the jeering in stride and the pathos of identification for granted; both were part of the plan. Just before his execution he wrote his mother, "People will say hard things of us now, but we shall be remembered by posterity and blessed by unborn generations. You too will be blessed because you are my mother."[42] Restaging the Oedipal dynamic wholly in his own terms, with no object remaining save the martyrdom that will dupe the British father, Pearse collapses the Oedipal triangle, even monopolizing the victim's role by which the Poor Old Woman had formerly exerted her power over her sons. Like the rioters, he suppresses the sexual stakes of the struggle (the potential of the Poor Old Woman to become a seductive Maud Gonne): much as Christy's sullen victory required a sublimation that left Pegeen keening, Pearse coaxingly reduces Kathleen ni Houlihan to the role of grieving mother, more knowing but just as passive. But this foreshortening—the price of his foxy Oedipal maneuver—carries a certain elemental rhetorical power; for while Pegeen's nostalgia was her own numbing end-of-the-line, the pathos that

Pearse knows will galvanize his followers is a bequest that the doomed son tricks the father into conferring, with all the force of a fresh exchange of power and weakness. The astonishing success of the fatal Easter Rising vindicated Pearse's strategy, and Synge's vision: this revolutionary gesture could never succeed by actually killing the father, nor actually becoming Cuchulain. Practical success would only be attained through the brilliant failure of a hopelessly, deliberately phantasmatic parricidal gesture.

NOTES

This essay is drawn from a study written in part under a fellowship from the National Endowment for the Humanities, whose support I gratefully acknowledge. I would also like to thank the editors for their helpful advice, and I am particularly grateful to Don Gifford, Anita Sokolsky, and Karen Swann for their valuable comments on earlier versions of the essay.

1. Quoted in James Kilroy, *The 'Playboy' Riots* (Dublin: Dolmen, 1971), p. 15. Kilroy's book reprints with commentary most of the Irish press coverage of the riots and of the debates carried on for the next fortnight. Except for accounts that he omits, further contemporary periodical sources will be cited simply by reference to his volume, where they are fully documented.

2. W. G. Fay and Catherine Carswell, *The Fays of the Abbey Theatre: An Autobiographical Record* (New York: Harcourt, 1935), p. 216.

3. Lady Gregory, *Our Irish Theatre* (New York: Capricorn, 1965), p. 114.

4. Kilroy, pp. 45–46. Not to be outdone by a dreamer, Irish-American nationalists bided their time, and five years later, when the Abbey first presented *The Playboy* on tour in the United States, they had the entire cast arrested in Philadelphia on charges of immorality.

5. William Butler Yeats, *Explorations* (New York: Collier, 1973), p. 226.

6. Kilroy, p. 83. On Griffith and Pearse, see David H. Greene and Edward M. Stephens, *J. M. Synge, 1871–1909* (New York: Macmillan, 1959), p. 253, and Kilroy, p. 61. Sean O'Casey sees the riots in terms of class in his satire "Song of a Shift," in his *Drums Under the Windows* (London: Macmillan, 1945).

7. See Yeats, "J. M. Synge and the Ireland of His Time" [1910], in his *Essays and Introductions* (New York: Collier, 1968), p. 311; and Hugh Hunt, *The Abbey: Ireland's National Theatre, 1904–1978* (New York: Columbia University Press, 1979), pp. 39–71.

8. Kilroy, p. 19. Dr. J. T. Gallagher struck much the same note during the American tour in 1911: "Nothing but hell-inspired ingenuity and a satanic hatred of the Irish people and their religion could suggest, construct, and influence the production of such plays" (Hunt, pp. 94–95).

9. Kilroy, p. 7. On the background of nationalist sensitivity to unflattering theatrical portrayals of Irish people, see Declan Kiberd, "The Fall of the Stage Irishman," *Genre*, 12 (1979), pp. 451–472. On the Abbey's own encouragement of such sensitivity, see Hunt, pp. 18–19, and F. S. L. Lyons, *Ireland Since the Famine* (London: Fontana, 1973), p. 235.

10. The tightness of this economy encourages readings of the play that emphasize its reflexive histrionics; see especially Thomas R. Whitaker, "On Playing with *The Playboy*," in Whitaker, ed., *Twentieth Century Interpretations of "The Playboy of the Western World"* (Englewood Cliffs, NJ: Prentice-Hall, 1969), pp. 1–20, and C. L. Innes, "Naked Truth, Fine Clothes and Fine Phrases in Synge's *Playboy of the Western World*," in Joseph Ronsley, ed., *Myth and Reality in Irish Literature* (Waterloo, ON: Wilfrid Laurier University Press, 1977), pp. 63–75. I extend this line of argument, in part through the terms of a theory of comedy, in a chapter of the work-in-progress from which the present essay is drawn, *Playing History False: Comedy in Political Crisis*.

11. Kilroy, p. 10. The "essential item" is a chemise or underslip.

12. *A Colder Eye: The Modern Irish Writers* (New York: Knopf, 1983), p. 24. See also George L. Mosse, *Nationalism and Sexuality: Respectability and Abnormal Sexuality in Modern Europe* (New York: H. Fertig, 1985).

13. Kilroy, p. 58. Synge noted in an interview that the word appears in the Irish verses of Douglas Hyde's "Love Songs of Connaught," beloved of Gaelic Leaguers. Dublin's premier satirist, Susan Mitchell, published an admirable lampoon of the furor in a pamphlet called *The Abbey Row* (see Greene, pp. 246–47).

14. Pádraic Colum's account (in *The Road Round Ireland* [New York: Macmillan, 1926], p. 368) supports this, as does Yeats's in "Synge," p. 311.

15. Kilroy, p. 66; or as Holloway forthrightly puts it, "the outpouring of a morbid,

unhealthy mind ever seeking on the dunghill of life for the nastiness that lies concealed there" (Robert Hogan and Michael O'Neill, eds., *Joseph Holloway's Abbey Theatre: A Selection from His Unpublished Journal, Impressions of a Dublin Playgoer* [Carbondale: Southern Illinois University Press, 1967], p. 81).

16. Freud remarks that deferred action is often experienced as an outward seduction—a parallel which illuminates the protestors' consternation at Pegeen's "shameless" behavior; see Sigmund Freud, "From the History of an Infantile Neurosis," *The Standard Edition of the Complete Psychological Works of Sigmund Freud*, vol. 17, trans. and ed. James Strachey (London: Hogarth, 1955), p. 109.

17. J. M. Synge, *The Playboy of the Western World*, in *J. M. Synge: Collected Works*, vol. 4, ed. Ann Saddlemyer (London: Oxford University Press, 1968), pp. 101–103.

18. An obverse process to that of Yeats's play, in which the antique Kathleen metamorphoses off-stage into the beautiful and fiery nationalist who first performed the role, Maud Gonne.

19. Greene, p. 148.

20. Yeats, "Synge," p. 312.

21. *The End of the Line: Essays on Psychoanalysis and the Sublime* (New York: Columbia University Press, 1985), pp. 160–215.

22. In a similar vein, Yeats concluded a speech chiding the rioters for their intolerance with the pronouncement, "Manhood is all." See Kilroy, p. 83.

23. William Irwin Thompson, *The Imagination of an Insurrection: Dublin, Easter 1916* (1967; rpt. West Stockbridge, MA: Lindisfarne, 1982), p. x; and *The United Irishman* [Dublin], April 12, 1902, p. 4. See also Robert Kee, *The Green Flag: The Turbulent History of the Irish National Movement* (New York: Delacorte, 1972), pp. 434–436. On the inevitable projection of fictive pasts for nationalisms, see Benedict Anderson, *Imagined Communities: Reflections on the Origin and Spread of Nationalism* (London: Verso, 1983), especially pp. 14–15.

24. For Synge's explicit recognition of the social and political origins of the propensity for violence attributed to peasants from the West, see Greene, pp. 167–168. For a deprecating view of the play's indirect and figurative bearing on political issues, see Seamus Deane, *Celtic Revivals: Essays in Modern Irish Literature, 1880–1980* (London: Faber and Faber, 1985), pp. 59–60.

25. One reviewer does suggest that "the parricide represents some kind of nation-killer," but immediately represses this line of thinking: "If it is an allegory it is too obscure for me" (Kilroy, p. 13).

26. Lyons gives a detailed account of this development (pp. 247–259).

27. Pearse, *Political Speeches and Writings* (Dublin: Talbot, 1966), p. 72; on this oppressiveness, see Thompson, p. 77. For *Sinn Fein*, see Lyons, pp. 255–256.

28. See Herbert Howarth, *The Irish Writers, 1880–1940: Literature Under Parnell's Star* (London: Rockliff, 1958), p. 231. The intriguing coincidence reminds us also that Kitty O'Shea's relation to the Poor Old Woman closely parallels that of Pegeen, and inverts that of Maud Gonne.

29. Even the title of Griffith's first newspaper reflects with extraordinary precision the nationalist's intrapsychic dilemma: in calling for the solidarity of Irish patriots, the "United Irish*man*" covertly speaks a prior anxious wish that the putatively individual Irish nationalist pull himself together.

30. Jean Laplanche and J.-B. Pontalis, *Fantasme originaire, fantasmes des origines, origines du fantasme* (Paris: Hachette, 1985), p. 72; my translation.

31. Hertz, p. 206.

32. *Ulysses*, ed. Hans Walter Gabler et al. (New York: Random House, 1986), p. 110.

33. Hertz, p. 223.

34. On the reassuring aspects of the Oedipal scenario, see Hertz, p. 230, and Julia Kristeva, "Freud and Love: Treatment and Its Discontents," in her *Tales of Love*, trans. Leon S. Roudiez (New York: Columbia University Press, 1987).

35. In the second section of "A Preface to Transgression," Foucault shows how the transgression of a limit does not merely reveal both transgression and limit as what they are, but even brings them mutually into being; see his *Language, Counter-Memory, Practice*, trans. Donald F. Bouchard and Sherry Simon (Ithaca: Cornell University Press, 1977), pp. 33–38.

36. "The phantasm is not the object of desire, it is the scene. Indeed, in the

phantasm the subject does not take the object or its sign as his aim; it is he himself who appears taken up in the sequence of images" (Laplanche, p. 74).

37. See Pearse, p. 145. On the earlier denunciation, see Thompson, p. 71.

38. MacKenna is quoted in Thompson, p. 76. Kee observes that "It was to be Patrick Pearse's own special contribution to Irish nationalism that by acknowledging unashamedly the mythical and even mystical nature of the Republic he paradoxically brought it closer to reality" (504).

39. Joseph Plunkett was a poet, Sean Connolly (the first man shot in the Rising) a leading actor at the Abbey, Pearse himself and Thomas MacDonagh poets and playwrights—indeed the latter's *When the Dawn Is Come*, produced at the Abbey in 1908, prophetically portrayed a war against England.

40. See Kee, pp. 551–552, and Thompson, pp. 89–99.

41. See Kee, p. 573.

42. Kee, pp. 578–579; see also Thompson, p. 75.

Part V

"To Govern Is to Populate"

Chapter 18

Some Speculations on the History of "Sexual Intercourse" During the "Long Eighteenth Century" in England

Henry Abelove

My purpose in this paper is simple. I intend to try to deduce, from the mathematically impressive recent scholarship on English demography, some conclusions about the development of English sexual behavior. Once I have explained these conclusions about sexual behavior, I shall also speculate just a little on their significance.

It has been known for many years that the population of England increased mightily during the period which is now called the "long eighteenth century"—the period stretching from the 1680s to the 1830s. In 1681 the population stood at about 4.93 million; in 1831, it was 13.28 million. But what hasn't been known with any certainty, at least until recently, was whether this extraordinary increase of people was due to a decline in mortality, to an increase in fertility, or to a combination of both. Historians, of course, have argued about the matter, some favoring one answer, some favoring another; but since their arguments have been based on scanty or broken data, nothing of what they have said could be really established and command general assent.

This arguing was stilled in 1981, when the demographers Wrigley and Schofield, both associated with the Cambridge Group for the History of Population and Social Structure, published their seven-hundred-some-page *magnum opus* on English population history. Their book virtually settled the question.[1] At last sufficient data had been gathered (the data came from more than four hundred parish registers), and a statistical technique sufficiently sophisticated for the job of interpreting them (the technique is called "back-projection") had been utilized. Two years later, in 1983, Wrigley repeated the findings of the book in short form in an article for the journal *Past and Present.* He called the article "The Growth of Population in Eighteenth-Century England: A Conundrum Resolved," and to that decisive-sounding title he may actually have been entitled.[2]

What the work of Wrigley and Schofield shows is that the mighty increase in English population during the long eighteenth century was due to a combination of a decline in mortality and a rise in fertility, but that of these two factors, a rise in fertility was much the more important. It isn't that the decline in mortality was a negligible matter. In the 1680s the average life expectancy, as Wrigley and Schofield establish it, was 32.4 years. By the 1820s it was 38.7 years.[3] So life had lengthened and mortality declined by a bit more than six years on average from the start of the period until the end. But Wrigley and Schofield can demonstrate mathematically that a rise in fertility, which occurred during the same period, contributed two and a half times as much to the outcome of population increase as did the decline in mortality, substantial as that was.[4]

The chief cause, then, of the increase in population in England during the long eighteenth century was a rise in fertility; and this rise was realized, as Wrigley and Schofield show, in several different ways. First of all, more women got married. At the start of the period, about 15 percent of all women who survived through the years of their fertility never married. By the end of the period, no more than half that percentage of all women who survived through the years of their fertility never married. This drop in the percentage of single women seems to have occurred mostly in the latter part of the eighteenth century.[5] Second, the average age of the first marriage for men as well as women fell by about three years, from twenty-six to twenty-three. This drop in the age of first marriage seems also to have occurred mostly during the latter part of the eighteenth century.[6] Finally, there was a marked increase in the rate of illegitimate births. At the start of the period only about 2 percent of all births were illegitimate. At the end of the period it was about 8 percent. This rise in the illegitimacy rate is more important than the figures may suggest. Another way of expressing the same rise, a way which may make its importance plainer, is to say that at the start of the period fewer than one-tenth of all first births were illegitimate but that at the end of the period about a quarter were.[7] I should add that an additional quarter were legitimate but prenuptially conceived, and that this figure, too, represented a marked increase.[8] Like the drop in average age of first marriage, like the increase in the percentage of women marrying, the rise in illegitimacy and in prenuptial pregnancy seems to have occurred mostly during the latter part of the century.

To sum up, a rise in fertility was realized in these ways: more women got married than had done before, women and men married earlier in their lives than they had done before, and women had more illegitimate children and prenuptial pregnancies than they had done before. Chiefly because of the rise in fertility so realized,[9] and only very secondarily because of a concurrent decline in mortality, England's population grew from 4.93 million to 13.28 million in the course of about 150 years, but with special acceleration during the latter part of the eighteenth century.

What all this means is that there was a remarkable increase in the *incidence* of cross-sex genital intercourse (penis in vagina, vagina around penis, with seminal emission uninterrupted) during the late eighteenth century in England. I mean that the particular kind of sexual expression which we moderns often name tendentiously "sexual intercourse" became importantly more popular at that time in England, and so much more popular that by means of that enhanced popularity alone, without any assistance from a decline in mortality, England's population could have doubled in a relatively short span. With the assistance of a decline in mortality, the population did actually more than double.

That is my deduction from the demographic data—that sexual intercourse so-called became importantly more popular in late eighteenth-century England—and I believe that the deduction is irresistible. It is, however, a deduction that the demographers do not make. They do not say it; they do not seem to see it. I should guess that for all of us, whether or not we are demographers, seeing, saying, deducing such propositions on the history of sexual behavior may be peculiarly difficult. It isn't primarily a matter of embarrassment, of a fear of indecorum, though embarrassment and fear may of course play a part in restraining some of us. It's more a matter of a very strong feeling we're likely to have that such deductions and observations are, first, too bizarre to be cogent, yet, second, too obvious to be worth seeing and saying. We can easily feel both ways simultaneously. On some other occasion I should like to talk further about that discomfiting dual feeling. For now, I want to remark that in my opinion the feeling is ideologically determined and that in the measure we give way to it and allow it to govern us we reinforce that essentialism which so disempowers us both as historians and as political beings.

If we take seriously the deduction I've put to you, then many lines of inquiry open before us. We may, for instance, want to ask *why* sexual intercourse so-called should have become so much more popular in late eighteenth-century England. Nor need we be deterred from asking that question by our realization that we don't in the least know how to go about answering it, that we don't even know what would constitute an adequate answer to it. By permitting ourselves to ask it, we may eventually learn how to answer it. We may also want to ask whether or not this change in sexual practice is related to any change in late eighteenth-century English conceptions of what sex is, what it is for.

Returning for the moment to the demographers, we may note that although they don't make the deduction I've put to you nor ask the questions I've just asked, they do try to account for their data by asking another question. Their question is: Why did people marry earlier in life, and why did more women marry?[10] One worrisome disadvantage to this question is that it doesn't save the appearances, that it doesn't fully respond to the data on fertility that they themselves present. Their data show not only a fall in the average age of marriage partners at first marriage, with consequences for population, not only a higher percentage of women marrying, with consequences for population, but also a rise in the rate of illegitimacy and prenuptial conception, with consequences for population—that is to say, their data show more sexual intercourse so-called both inside and outside of marriage. On the other hand, their question has also a certain advantage. Even if the answering of the question couldn't explain what needs explaining, the question is at least comfortable. The demographers imagine that they know, and maybe most of us would imagine that we knew, how to go about trying to provide an answer for a question such as theirs. When the point at issue is understood simply as earlier marrying and more marrying, then surely we would look almost automatically for a rise in the wage-rate as the likely cause. The demographers do look for a rise in the wage-rate, but to their obvious disappointment they cannot find the causal connection they expect. Wages go up, but they go up a good thirty years in advance of the fertility rate; and thirty years is, as the demographers concede, probably too long an interval to fit into a causal argument of the sort they want to make.[11] Still, their failure to answer the question they ask is less remarkable than their evading their own data with that question. What they do is defensively transform something that ought to be a problem in the history of sexual behavior into a problem in the history of nuptiality so that they can proceed comfortably, if unsuccessfully.

I'd like to suggest that the conclusion I've deduced from the demographers' data, that sexual intercourse so-called came to be importantly more popular in late eighteenth-century England, can perhaps be related to another contemporary experience. The new popularity of intercourse so-called doesn't follow from, or depend on, a rise in wages; and it is only when we misconceive the data to be understood as simply about marrying that we are tempted even to look to wage-rates for an explanation. But the new popularity of intercourse so-called does correlate rather well with a dramatic rise in virtually all indices of production, a rise which the textbooks call the onset of the Industrial Revolution and which as we know distinguished late eighteenth-century England. I don't mean to imply that this rise in production, which was probably the biggest since the invention of agriculture in prehistoric times, caused the rise in intercourse so-called, nor do I mean to imply that the rise in intercourse so-called caused the rise in production. Neither of these causal arguments would seem to me to be sound, and both would of course depend on a too-easy and conventional distinction between the sexual and material realms. What does seem to me at least conceivable, though I am just speculating in saying so, is that the rise in production (the privileging of production) and the rise in the popularity of the sexual act which uniquely makes for reproduction (the privileging of intercourse so-called) may be aspects of the same phenomenon. Viewed from different perspectives, this phenomenon could be called either capitalism or the discourse of capitalism or modern heterosexuality or the discourse of modern heterosexuality.

It is of course true that sexual intercourse so-called had been valued in some measure or another, on some grounds or another, before the late eighteenth century and in every previous European society about which we know anything. But it is also true that production had been valued before the late eighteenth century and in every previous European society about which we know anything. What happens to production in the late eighteenth century in England is nevertheless new. While production increases importantly, it also becomes discursively and phenomenologically central in ways that it had never been before. Behaviors, customs, usages which are judged to be nonproductive, like the traditional plebeian conception of time, according to which Mondays and maybe Tuesdays and Wednesdays as well are free days, play days, rest days ("St. Monday" was the plebeian phrase), come under extraordinary and ever-intensifying negative pressure.[12] If I should be right in speculating that the rise in popularity of sexual intercourse so-called in late eighteenth-century England is an aspect of the same phenomenon that includes the rise in production, then we should expect to find that sexual intercourse so-called becomes at this time and in this place discursively and phenomenologically central in ways that it had never been before; that nonreproductive sexual behaviors come under extraordinary negative pressure; and finally that both developments happen in ways that testify to their relatedness, even to their unity.

I cannot say that I have such findings to present to you. As I mentioned before, I am just at a point of speculative beginning. But I can say something about where my attention is currently directed. The earlier part of the long eighteenth century, before the big rise in production and in the incidence of sexual intercourse so-called, was an era of relatively late marriage, low illegitimacy and prenuptial pregnancy rates, and a relatively high rate of nonmarrying for women. According to some students of plebeian sexuality, like Flandrin, Quaife, and Bray, this was also an era of very diverse sexual practice. If outside of marriage plebeians typically avoided sexual intercourse so-called (penis in vagina, vagina around penis, with seminal emission uninterrupted), they were nevertheless typically sexually active. They practiced mutual masturbation, oral sex, anal sex, display and watching (or to use the more common and pejorative terms, "exhibitionism" and "voyeurism"), and much else besides, on a cross-sex basis and in some now uncertain measure on a same-sex basis as well.[13]

What happens to the tradition of same-sex sexual behaviors in the late eighteenth century is something that I shall put aside for now. It is an intricate problem and demands extended and separate treatment. As for what happens to the tradition of very diverse cross-sex sexual behaviors, my hypothesis is: They are reorganized and reconstructed in the late eighteenth century as foreplay. They don't disappear, they aren't ruled out, as the incidence of intercourse so-called increases, but they are relegated and largely confined to the position of the preliminary. From the late eighteenth century on, they are construed as what precedes that sexual behavior which alone is privileged, intercourse so-called. On this hypothesis, the invention of foreplay—an important passage in the making of modern heterosexuality—is to be understood as homologous with the crowding of St. Monday, Tuesday, and Wednesday into Sunday, the first day of the work week—an important passage in the making of capitalism. Rest doesn't disappear, isn't ruled out, as production rises; but rest is relegated and largely confined to the position of the preliminary. To put it differently, I hypothesize that the invention of foreplay is an aspect of the history of capitalism, that the invention of industrial work-discipline is an aspect of the history of heterosexuality, and that both developments are in an important sense the same.

NOTES

This is a slightly revised version of an article published originally in *Genders*, 6 (November 1989), pp. 125–30. I am grateful to *Genders* for permitting me to reprint the article here. I also want to thank Nancy Armstrong and Leonard Tennenhouse for their encouragement and Richard T. Vann for his helpfulness in pointing me to several pertinent publications.

1. E. A. Wrigley and R. S. Schofield, *The Population History of England, 1541–1871: A Reconstruction* (Cambridge, Mass.: Harvard University Press, 1981). Of course there has been *some* criticism. See, for instance, Peter Lindert, "English Living Standards, Population Growth, and Wrigley-Schofield," *Explorations in Economic History*, 20 (April 1983), pp. 131–55, and Louis Henry, "La Population de L'Angleterre de 1541 à 1871," *Population*, 38 (July–October 1983), pp. 781–826.

2. E. A. Wrigley, "The Growth of Population in Eighteenth-Century England: A Conundrum Resolved," *Past and Present*, 98 (February 1983), pp. 121–50. Wrigley has recently reprinted this essay with little revision in E. A. Wrigley, *People, Cities, and Wealth: The Transformation of Traditional Society* (Oxford and New York: Basil Blackwell, 1987), pp. 215–41.

3. Ibid., p. 129.

4. Ibid., p. 131.

5. Ibid., p. 132; Wrigley and Schofield, *Population History*, p. 263.

6. Wrigley, "Conundrum," p. 131; Wrigley and Schofield, *Population History*, p. 255.

7. Wrigley, "Conundrum," pp. 132, 133.

8. Ibid., p. 133; Wrigley and Schofield, *Population History*, pp. 266, 254.

9. This may be the right place to remark that family limitation was practiced very seldom in preindustrial England and so registers virtually no impact macrostatistically. See C. Wilson, "Natural Fertility in Pre-Industrial England, 1600–1799," *Population Studies*, 38 (1984), pp. 225–40.

10. Wrigley, "Conundrum," p. 134.

11. Ibid., p. 142. Wrigley suggests that the currently available data on eighteenth-century English wage-rates may be defective, and he may be right. But there is no reason to suppose that improved data would yield the conclusion that he wants.

12. See, for instance, E. P. Thompson, "Time, Work-Discipline, and Industrial Capitalism," *Past and Present,* 38 (December 1967), pp. 56–97.

13. Jean Louis Flandrin, *Families in Former Times: Kinship, Household, and Sexuality,* trans. R. Southern (Cambridge: Cambridge University Press, 1979); G. R. Quaife, *Wanton Wenches and Wayward Wives: Peasants and Illicit Sex in Early Seventeenth Century England* (New Brunswick, N. J.: Rutgers University Press, 1979); Alan Bray, *Homosexuality in Renaissance England* (London: Gay Men's Press, 1982).

Chapter 19

State Fatherhood: The Politics of Nationalism, Sexuality, and Race in Singapore

Geraldine Heng and Janadas Devan

Postcolonial governments are inclined, with some predictability, to generate narratives of national crisis, driven perhaps—the generous explanation—to reenact periodically the state's traumatic if also liberating separation from colonial authority, a moment catachrestically founding the nation itself *qua* nation. Typically, however, such narratives of crisis serve more than one category of reassurance: by repeatedly focusing anxiety on the fragility of the new nation, its ostensible vulnerability to every kind of exigency, the state's originating agency is periodically reinvoked and ratified, its access to wide-ranging instruments of power in the service of national protection continually consolidated. It is a post-Foucauldian truism that they who successfully define and superintend a crisis, furnishing its lexicon and discursive parameters, successfully confirm themselves the owners of power, the administration of crisis operating to revitalize ownership of the instruments of power even as it vindicates the necessity of their use.

If a postcolonial government remains continuously in office for decades beyond its early responsibility for the nation's emergence, as is the case in the Republic of Singapore, the habit of generating narratives of crisis at intervals becomes an entrenched, dependable practice. While the metaphors deployed, causes identified, and culpabilities named in the detection of crisis necessarily undergo migration, accusation by the government of Singapore—whose composite representation is overwhelmingly male, Chinese, and socioeconomically and educationally privileged—has been increasingly directed in recent years to such segments of society as do not give back an image of the state's founding fathers to themselves. Precise adequacy on the part of the citizenry to an ideal standard of nationalism then becomes referenced, metonymically, to the successful if fantasmatic reproduction of an ideal image of its fathers. Crisis is unerringly discovered—threats to the survival and continuity of the nation, failures in nationalism—when a distortion in the replication or scale of a composition deemed ideal is fearfully imagined.

NATIONALISM AND SEXUALITY: IDEOLOGIES OF REPRODUCTION

That an obsession with ideal replication in the register of the imaginary can lend itself to somatic literalization—transformed through acts of state power into a large-scale social project of *biological* reproduction—is the disturbing subtext of one of the most tenacious and formidable of state narratives constructed in Singapore's recent history, with consequences yet proliferating at the time of this article. Hinging precisely on a wishful fantasy of exact self-replication, this narrative of crisis posits, as the essential condition of national survival, the regeneration of the country's population (its heterogenous national body) in such ratios of race and class as would faithfully mirror the population's original composition at the nation's founding moment, retrospectively apotheosized. In an aggressive exposition of paternal distress in August 1983 that ranges authoritatively over such subjects as genetic inheritance and culture, definitions of intelligence, social and economic justice and responsibility, and gender theory, the nation's father of founding fathers, Prime Minister Lee Kuan Yew, levelled an extraordinary charge against the nation's *mothers*, incipient and actual—accusing them of imperiling the country's future by wilfully distorting patterns of biological reproduction. The disclosure of a reproductive crisis took place, suitably, on the anniversary of the state's birth, during the Prime Minister's annual National Day Rally speech, as part of the celebrations commemorating the country's emergence as a national entity.[1]

The crisis, as formulated by him, received this inflection: highly-educated women in Singapore, defined as those with a university degree, were not producing babies in sufficient numbers to secure their self-replacement in the population, either because of a failure to marry, or, having married, a failure to bear more than 1.65 children per married couple, he declared. On the other hand, poorly-educated women, defined as those who do not complete the equivalent of an elementary school education (women of "no education" or "no qualifications," as they came to be called), were reproducing too freely, generating 3.5 children each; women with only an elementary education, producing 2.7 children, were also outstripping the "graduate mothers," as the Prime Minister called them.

This was a problem, Lee reasoned, because graduate mothers produced genetically-superior offspring, the ability to complete a university education attesting to superior mental faculties, which would be naturally transmitted to offspring through genetic inheritance. Eighty percent of a child's intelligence, Lee explained, citing certain studies in genetics and sociobiology, was predetermined by nature, while nurture accounted for the remaining twenty percent. Within a few generations, the quality of Singapore's population would measurably decline, with a tiny minority of intelligent persons being increasingly swamped by a seething, proliferating mass of the unintelligent, untalented, and genetically inferior: industry would suffer, technology deteriorate, leadership disappear, and Singapore lose its competitive edge in the world. Since his was a tiny country of no natural resources and few advantages other than the talents of its people, if measures were not immediately taken to counteract the downhill slide caused by "lopsided" female reproductive sexuality, a catastrophe of major proportions was imminent a scant few generations down the line.[2]

It would seem that men did not figure prominently in the Prime Minister's dystopian vision because his statistics revealed to him that Singapore women as a rule selected mates of equal or superior academic standing; graduate mothers alone, therefore, could be relied on to guarantee the genetic purity of the tribe. Closer examination of his tables consequently revealed that class and race, however, were the major, suppressed categories of his anxiety, since the women of recalcitrant fertility were by and large Chinese, upper- and middle-class professionals, while those of inordinate reproductive urges and no university degrees comprised, by a stunning coincidence, working-class women of Malay and Indian ethnic origin—members, that is, of Singapore's minority racial groups. The Chinese majority, then 76%, was shrinking at the terrifying rate of 7% in each generation, even as Malays, a mere 15%, were wildly proliferating by 4% per generation, and Indians, then 6% of the population, by 1%. The threat of impending collapse in the social and economic order, for which an unruly, destabilizing, and irresponsible feminine sexuality was held to account, was covertly located at the intersecting registers of race and class. Chaos, in this prophecy of national disaster, was visualized as the random interplay of excess and deficiency among female bodies, which, left unregulated, would produce disabling, ungovernable, and unsafe equations of class and race.[3]

If Lee's articulation of genetic inheritance, culture, education, intelligence, and reproductive sexuality seems inordinately mechanical, his faith in the assumed infallibility (and univocity) of statistics oddly uncritical, and his commitment to the logic of racial and class regulation relentless, it is because he subscribes, without apology, to a projective model of society as an economic and social machine. His stated preference, on the controversial issue of intelligence, for genetic catalogues and theories of determination over such arguments as would consider the interplay of social, psychic, historical, cultural, environmental, *and* genetic forces operating on the human subject (the reductive impatience leading him to extract, from a small-scale study on identical twins by Thomas Bouchard of the University of Minnesota, easy, simplistic axioms and catch-phrases on universal essences of human nature, expressed in tidy percentages) merely evinces a concomitant desire for the human organism to function, also, like a machine. The language of eugenics is precisely for Lee a language of efficient automation—a syntax and grammar congenially identical to his own, and to that routinely employed by his ministers and cohorts in public discourse—the appeal of eugenics residing, for him, in its very promise, however fugitive it might seem to others, of state-of-the-art biological replication: a superior technology to guarantee the efficient manufacture of superior-quality babies (the machine of eugenics confirming the body machine).[4]

The investment in mechanical models of human reproduction, social formations, and the body, exposes, of course, the desire for an absolute mastery, the desire that mastery be absolutely possible. Functional machines in everyday life—machines as they are recognized by Lee, and used in Singapore society—are predictable and orderly, blessedly convenient: malfunctioning ones can be adjusted, faulty components replaced, and the whole made to work again with a minimum of fuss. Most pointedly, a machine presupposes—indeed, requires—an operator, since a machine commonly exists in the first place in order to be operated: relieving all suspicion that full supervisory control may be impossible (exorcising, that is, the specter of desire, instability, and an unconscious from human formations), the trope of the machine comfortingly suggests that what eludes, limits, or obstructs absolute knowability, management, and control, can be routinely evacuated.

The indictment of women, then—working-class and professional, Malay, Indian, and Chinese—inscribes a tacit recognition that feminine reproductive sexuality refuses, and in refusing, undermines the fantasy of the body-machine, a conveniently operable somatic device: thus also undoing, by extension, that other fantasied economy, society as an equally operable contraption. Indeed, the disapproval, simultaneously, of an overly-productive, and a non(re)productive feminine sexuality registers a suspicion of that sexuality as noneconomic, driven by pleasure: sexuality for its own sake, unproductive of babies, or babies for their own sake, unproductive of social and economic efficiency.[5] That women of minority races should stand accused of a runaway irresponsibility, moreover, neatly conjoins two constituencies of society believed to be most guilty of pursuing the noneconomy of pleasure (pleasure as, indeed, noneconomic): the female, and the "soft" Indian/Malay citizen, whose earthy sexuality, putative garrulousness, laziness, emotional indulgence, or other distressing irrationality conform to reprobate stereotypes of ethnicity and gender that have, in recent years, prominently found their way into public discourse.

In the months that followed his sketch of a future, feminine-instigated apocalypse, controversy of a sort arose around the issue, whose political volatility was at once and slyly undercut, however, by its characterization in the national press and electronic media (which are in Singapore either directly state-owned, state-dominated, or subject to severely restrictive licensing laws) as a "Great Marriage Debate." Its reduction to merely a "debate," and over merely an old, respectable, and comfortably familiar institution, marriage, strategically moved the issue away from any explicit recognition of or engagement with its deeply political, and politically extreme, content. The English-language newspapers would have it, moreover, that the vast majority of their readers were concerned merely to help the Prime Minister accomplish his goal of increased numbers of graduate babies; and since access to popular opinion through media uninflected by state control was, and still remains, unavailable, the character of public response could only be gauged from what was selected for publication in newspaper letters' columns, or broadcast on state-run radio and television programming.[6]

Even as public discussion began, however (a discussion mercilessly regulated by speeches and pronouncements from government cohorts of every description, all tirelessly repeating and expatiating at length on the Prime Minister's arguments in a concerted drive to overwhelm public opinion), the government moved with characteristic preemptive speed to launch a comprehensive system of incentives and threats, together with major changes of social policy, to bend the population in the direction of the Prime Minister's will. Cash awards of S$10,000 were offered to working-class women, under careful conditions of educational and low-income eligibility, to restrict their childbearing to two children, after which they would "volunteer" themselves for tubal ligation. The scheme was piously tricked out in the language of philanthropic concern and state munificence—one fawning newspaper headline even proclaiming it the "Govt's $10,000 Helping Hand for the Low Income Families" [sic]. At the same time as the formal statement from the Prime Minister's

Office grandly and unctuously trumpeted its benevolence, maternity charges in public (that is, government-run) hospital wards most frequently used by working-class mothers were increased for those who had already given birth to their state-preferred quota of two children.[7]

To entice graduate women to have more children, on the other hand, generous tax breaks, medical insurance privileges, and admission for their children to the best schools in the country were promised, *inter alia*—prompting legal scholars and others to object that such discriminatory, class-inflected practices were manifestly and blatantly unconstitutional.[8] Changes in school admissions policy to further privilege the privileged were nonetheless implemented, the government countering criticism with a massive disinformation effort which shamelessly sought to persuade the disadvantaged that their children, too, would profit from the new hierarchies ("Non-graduates Will Also Benefit," one newspaper headline soothingly cajoled the public; another announced, with unremitting cruelty, "More Good News for Non-graduate Mums: All Primary Schools are of Fairly Equal Standard").[9] Other transformations in social policy followed—altered entrance criteria to the country's only existing university to favor men over women applicants, since the Prime Minister's statistics had suggested to him that male more than female university graduates tended to marry and have children;[10] a revised family planning program that now urged *all who could afford it* to have at least three children (where its former policy encouraged the two-child family as the ideal norm for all, equally); and, more recently, the suggestion that certain restrictions may be placed on legalized abortion, freely available in Singapore since 1974[11]—but with their relationship to the priorities advertised in the so-called Great Marriage Debate officially denied, minimized, or simply passing unreported and undiscussed. Among its own employees, the government decided to require members of the Civil Service in the higher echelons—Division One officers, who no doubt qualify as intelligent—to submit detailed personal information on themselves and their families, including their "marital status, the educational qualifications of their spouses, and the number of children" they had; and at least one civil servant was summarily selected ("assigned") to undergo an experiment in the use of commercial matchmaking services abroad.[12]

Cabinet ministers began to exhort graduate women to marry and bear children *as a patriotic duty*. Obediently taking their cue from the government, two (nonfeminist) women's organizations accordingly proposed, in a disturbing collusion with state patriarchy, that women be *required* to bear children as a form of National Service—the equivalent, in feminine, biological terms, of the two-and-a-half year military service compulsorily performed by men for the maintenance of national defense.[13] A sexualized, separate species of nationalism, in other words, was being advocated for women: as patriotic duty for men grew out of the barrel of a gun (phallic nationalism, the wielding of a surrogate technology of the body in national defense), so would it grow, for women, out of the recesses of the womb (uterine nationalism, the body *as* a technology of defense wielded by the nation). Men bearing arms, and women bearing children; maternal and/as military duty: the still-recent history of Nazi Germany grimly but not uniquely reminds us that certain narratives of nationalism and dispositions of state power specifically require the exercise of control over the body, the track of power on bodies being visited differently according to gender. The demand that women serve the nation biologically, with their bodies—that they take on themselves, and submit themselves to, the public reproduction of nationalism in the most private medium possible, forcefully reveals the anxious relationship, in the fantasies obsessing state patriarchy, between reproducing power and the power to reproduce: the efficacy of the one being expressly contingent on the containment and subsumption of the other.[14]

As the Prime Minister himself spoke with ominous nostalgia of the traditional means by which women had been variously coerced into bearing children in most Asian cultures of the past, the dependence of paternal power—its assurance of regenerative survival—on the successful conscription and discipline of female reproductive sexuality within hierarchical structures dominated by patriarchs, explicitly surfaced. Lee spoke feelingly of the past, when families could enforce the marriage of their daughters by arranging marriages of convenience without their daughters' consent.[15] He expressed regret at his government's socialist policies in the heady days of early postcolonial independence, when women's suffrage and universal education relinquished to women some control over their biological destinies.[16] He speculated thoughtfully on the possibility of reintroducing polygamy (by which he meant *polygyny* rather than polyandry), outlawed in Singapore since the Women's Charter of 1961, and voiced frank, generous admiration of virile Chinese patriarchs of the past, whose retinues of wives, mistresses, and illegitimate children unquestionably testified, under principles of social Darwinism, to their own, and thus their children's genetic superiority.[17]

Men, it would seem, figured prominently in Lee's dystopian vision after all. Behind the ostensible crisis of maternity and reproduction—too much or too little, never exactly enough—was a crisis of *paternity* and reproduction. A few women suggested, with irony, that if increased numbers of superior children were exclusively the issue, then women ought to be encouraged, nay, urged to have children outside the institution of marriage, with all stigmatization of single mothers and illegitimate offspring removed. Many women, they challenged, did not wish to marry, but wished nonetheless to have children; should not the government in their urgent desire recommend moves toward women-headed families?[18] Recognizing the threat to patriarchal authority vested in the traditional Asian family—after which its own hierarchies and values were after all patterned—the government conspicuously failed to generate enthusiasm for this alternative. A future in which women might conceive and raise children with the support of society, but without the check of a paternal signifier, could not be thought, even in the name of putative national survival. Addressing as it did the hidden stake in Lee's narrative of crisis, whose undisclosed object of concern was precisely the stable replication of the paternal signifier and its powers, this vision of women-led families struck at the core of state fatherhood itself, the institutional basis on which governmental patriarchy was posited.[19]

The narrative behind Lee's narrative could then be read: a fantasy of self-regenerating fatherhood and patriarchal power, unmitigated, resurgent, and in endless (self-) propagation, inexhaustibly reproducing its own image through the pliant, tractable conduit of female anatomy—incidental, obedient, and sexually suborned female bodily matter. His sentimental indulgence in the saving visions of a reactionary past, selectively idealized, stages that past as the exclusive theatre of omnipotent fathers: state fathers, whose creative powers incorporate and subsume the maternal function, as attested by their autonomous birthing of a nation. The subsequent show of protective solicitude over the national offspring then aggressively, if fantasmatically, replays the cherished moment of paternal delivery: by arresting change and difference in the national body, and wishfully transfixing the population in its original composition at birth, a living testimony to the founding moment is made perpetually available, a constantly present reminder; and the fearful threat of material transmogrification—growth, alteration, difference, the transformations wrought by an undisclosed, never-certain future (imagined, conveniently, as issuing from mothers, that displaced, but ever-looming, ever-returning source of threat and competition)—is simultaneously warded off and disengaged.

Out of that obsession with a pastness ideologically configured had come, then, the script of a dangerous agenda of racial and class manipulation: the very agenda explicitly renounced by the publicly subscribed goals—democracy, equality, and social justice, regardless of race, gender, creed, or class—on which Lee's government had so prided itself, for which it had won the country freedom from Britain, and by which its public mandate to govern today is still declaratively based. It is as a defense against his fear of the future—a future which finds its representation and threat, for him, in a race-marked, class-inflected, ungovernable female body (so commonly figured as the receptacle of the future that it is the perennial locus of social accusation and experiment)—that Lee's Great Marriage Debate was invented. The past—that ground in which the powers of reproduction and the reproduction of power had seemed miraculously to converge in a self-legitimating moment of plenitude echoing through time—served, in this case, as in the case of so many other nations and nationalisms, as the imaginary treasure-house of a superannuated political fantasy.

NATIONALISM AND RACE: REPRODUCTIONS OF IDEOLOGY

Concurrent with the rhetoric of crisis identifying what might be called the threat from within the nation that inaugurates the "Great Marriage Debate," there has also been over recent years the discovery of a threat from without, a *cultural* crisis of an equally disturbing magnitude. Represented as the intensified danger of contamination by the West, this particular crisis has required the formulation of related themes in defense of the social body—the retrieval of a superior, "core" Chinese culture in the name of a fantasmatic "Confucianism"; the promotion of Mandarin, the preferred dialect of the ruling class of imperial China, as the master language of Chineseness; and the concoction of a "national ideology," grounded in a selective refiguration of Confucianism, to promote the interests of the state.

All three themes take shape as urgent national priorities to combat this other, external threat to the survival, prosperity, and identity of the nation: "Western" values, variously depicted as individualism, relativism and hedonism at worst, or as an unstable pluralism and a needlessly liberal democracy at best.[20] The decadent individualism of the West, cabinet ministers declare, has caused the economic decline of the United States relative to Japan, South Korea, Taiwan, and Singapore, the so-called "four Asian tigers"; concomitantly, these East Asian economies are said to owe their prosperity to their Confucian-based cultures, their "communitarian value system," industry, thrift, and social cohesiveness being attributed to a changeless Confucian *essence* that has been preserved intact through the ages, an essence which not only survives transmission without alteration, but which has made possible rapid industrial development. Taught in Singapore schools since 1982, Confucianism has been offered as an option to Chinese secondary students, who are encouraged to study it in place of a religion in "moral education" classes. Preceding this initiative by a few years is the "Speak Mandarin" campaign for the preservation of Chineseness: if all Chinese Singaporeans spoke Mandarin, this argument goes, they could communicate without the use of English across dialect boundaries; Chinese values would be disseminated without the dilution and distraction that multiple dialects threaten, and the auditory unity of a common tongue would assuage the dangers of the West.[21]

Like the script of the "Great Marriage Debate," racial and sexual categories are conjoined in the attribution of value and accusation in the detection of crisis. Prime Minister Lee has often reiterated his conviction that the industrial prominence of East Asian societies over the relatively less developed economies of the Indian subcontinent and Malay archipelago is rooted in the "hard" values of the former over the "soft" cultures of the latter, unapologetically proffering, in simultaneous praise and contempt, figures of phallocentric toughness and gynocentric laxity that are scarcely disguised. Indians, moreover, Lee confidently proclaims, are "naturally contentious"; like women, they are loquacious and theatrical, too indulgent and irresponsible ("soft") to be capable of the social discipline of "hard" Confucian cultures which renders East Asian societies increasingly potent as political powers to challenge the West. Lest one miss the point, Lee has mused aloud if Singapore could have achieved its economic and social strides if the population had been composed of an Indian racial majority and a Chinese minority, instead of the other way around. State policies instituted to manipulate female reproductive sexuality in preferred ratios of race and class leave no doubt as to what his government believes the answer to be.[22]

Because almost all Singaporeans under the age of forty speak English today with varying degrees of fluency—93% of primary-school age children are in schools where it is the language of instruction—they are deemed uniquely vulnerable to infection by the West, unlike Japanese, Koreans, and Taiwanese. Encouraged by British colonial policy for over a century, the dominance of English was institutionalized after decolonization by Lee's own government which established it as the preferred language of education and business, and as the *de facto* language of government: a privileged medium of access to Western science and technology which augmented the nation's attractions to multinational capital. In the 1950s and 60s, when the Malayan Communist Party was influential among the Chinese-educated in Singapore and Malaya, the policy of both the British colonial administration and the postcolonial governments that succeeded it involved the diminution in social and political status of Chinese education: "left-wing activist," "Communist," and "Chinese-educated" were virtually synonymous, interchangeable terms ("the English-educated," as Lee put it then, "do not riot"). The association of English with progress and economic enfranchisement resulted, by the mid-1970s, in a considerable reduction in the number of Chinese schools, and the closure of the only Chinese-language university in Singapore.

Ironically, thirty years after independence, the very political authority that had institutionalized the language now expresses "doubt about the wisdom of teaching Singaporeans English." "If one went back to Korea, Taiwan, or Hong Kong 100 years from now," Lee speculated in a wistful fantasy of paternal control, "their descendants would be recognizable because what they took in from the West was what their leaders decided to translate into their books, newspapers and t.v. programmes." In Singapore, on the other hand, "we have given everybody a translator in his pocket and all doors are open." In this nightmare vision—the unresisted seduction of a vulnerable, "soft," social body feminized by language ("all doors are open")—Lee saw "a wholesale revision of values, attitudes of good and bad, or role-models and so on."[23] English, once the conduit of rapid economic development that consolidated the power and legitimacy of the new state and its founding fathers, is now a dangerous passage facilitating an invasion of difference that would rupture the continuity of cultural identity, and alter the course of ideal generational propagation.

These changing fantasmatic definitions of threats to the state, requiring sporadic redeployment of valid and invalid identities, languages, and cultures in narratives of history and national survival, reveal, then, the essentialist counters of race and culture as amenable to arbitrary representations, inflected by interests of state power. Differences *within* cultures and races—and the conflation of these two terms is a necessary gesture in the essentialist discourse of nationalism—are converted into differences *between* cultures and races, into differences that strategically serve to distinguish valid, enabling, or potent cultural identities from those other identities represented as seductive and disabling, subverting the firmness of national purpose. Narratives of history and survival thus deployed in the production of differences support specific formations of power; the past itself becomes a category produced by present causes to legitimate the exigent directives of the state, and is punctually offered as a reusable counter to vindicate genealogies of state dispensation. Each construction of an essential identity requires a reconfiguring of the past: the equation of "Confucian Chineseness" with the interests of the state demands not only the discounting of Singapore history in the 1950s and 1960s, but also a radical retroping of the enabling conditions of economic development and modern nationhood. No longer is an absorption of Western values, liberal democracy, technological organization, and habits of objectivity deemed *sine qua non* the legitimizing prerequisites of a modern state. That Singapore, like Japan, Korea, and Taiwan, has "arrived" as a developed economy is to be traced instead to the presence in these societies of "core" Confucian virtues—to the efflorescence, as it were, of what has always been there, fully present, denying the perceived absence or lack that instigated the movement toward the West in the immediate postcolonial period. Locating the ideological source of the modern East Asian state in an unchanging Confucian essence allows, moreover, the idealized recuperation of the entire history of Chinese culture as a seamless narrative of continuity and cohesion, suffering neither a fall (as into communism) nor a lack—allows, that is, an ideological fantasy of transgenerational replication, where a signifying essence gendered in a particular modality of authority reproduces itself across history and national boundaries in unobstructed transcendent resurgence. The history of Singapore is then a single moment in the history of Chinese racial culture, written into an integrated script of transnational ideological revitalization.

The mystifications exercised in this figuration of (trans)national ideology should not, however, be read as implying irrationality. The very discovery of Confucianism is articulated by the need to manage, not to resist, an increasingly successful industrial nation. Confucianism accordingly is promoted in Singapore as constitutive of the rational organization of society, and has itself been submitted to stringent inquiry, that it might be systematically delivered as an object of knowledge, a rational and authoritative epistemology. Confucian scholars are hired from abroad (from metropolitan centers such as Harvard and Princeton, among others) to staff an Institute of East Asian Philosophy at the National University of Singapore: they help to formulate the syllabi and design the texts for school courses, sift Confucian tenets consciously for useful emphases and prescriptions, and systematize the propagation of the subject. Bizarre as this programmatic exercise might seem to Western eyes, it merely repeats, in effect, the modalities of producing and using knowledge long assumed in the West by the social sciences, including the discourse Edward Said calls Orientalism. Based on expertise and scholarly systematization, the knowledge produced is then delivered as a rational, objective, disinterested and coherent (philosophical) system, confering legitimacy on the state which establishes the promise of a truly rational organization of society, even as it enables the state to police the boundaries of permissible discourse through the continued regulation of knowledge. Thus mantled in objectivity and knowledge, the state assumes what Foucault calls its "pastoral" function, subjecting its citizens to a "set of very specific patterns" that totalizes the operation of an apparently benign, implicitly paternal power.[24] In Singapore, the paradigms of economic or corporate management and their protocols of rationality serve at once as the model and chief beneficiary of the state's pastoral power, submitting citizens to a structure of values which best subtends, with minimal fuss and resistance, the efficient working of state corporatism and multinational capital.[25] The location of this structure of values in Confucianism, moreover, and the figuration of Confucianism itself as racial and (trans)national identity, continuous with other East Asian societies and with an organically fecund past, stages the modern state and nationalism as merely the theater where a primordial paternal signifier can gather to itself new instruments of potency, without the irritation of difference to trouble its timeless sway. The description of history as the movement and repetition of the same discovers an aggressive and ruthless absorption of contemporary forms of power: few nations can boast the degree of thoroughness to which the founders of Singapore have carried the paternal logic of the modern state.

The policies of the Singapore government cannot therefore be dismissed as an instance of a peculiarly irrational but unique oriental despotism, for their exercise of power is enabled, in large measure, by the reinscription of *Western* modes of discourse in an Asian context. Represented as an invasive threat to Singapore society from without, Western modalities are in fact already operating as instruments of power for the local production of subjects *within* the nation. The strategic deployment of selective material from contemporary metropolitan disciplines such as genetics and sociobiology (in the fabricated exigency dubbed the "Great Marriage Debate") is one explicit instance of state collusion with Western institutions of power/knowledge. Indeed, the domestication of an economy of power operative and operable as rationality—knowledge as a technique, a circuit, of power—is crucially necessary to the constitution of a "native" center of authority. Though the ultimate horizon of complicity between authoritative knowledges in the metropolitan West and formations of power in the postcolonial state is beyond the scope of this article, a few of the productive effects of this complicity can be briefly described.

The institution of what can be called, for suggestive convenience, an "internalized Orientalism" makes available to *postcolonial* authority the knowledge-power that *colonial* authority wielded over the local population, and permits, in Singapore, an overwhelmingly Western-educated political elite to dictate the qualities that would constitute Chineseness. Internalized orientalism allows the definition of an idealized Chineseness fully consonant with the requirements of a modern market economy, and supplies the mechanism of justification by which qualities deemed undesirable (and projected as forms of racial and sexual accusation) may be contained or excised. Thus simultaneously concerned with replication and containment, internalized orientalism supervises the erasure of the rich cultural resources of dialects spoken over countless generations, and arbitrarily names Mandarin the single repository of core Chinese virtues so as to facilitate cultural dissemination and bring within the possibility of governance a Chineseness that might otherwise have remained, like female reproductive habits, too resistantly diverse and prolific.

Ignoring the materiality of Chinese history, internalized orientalism writes its own narratives of history and nationalism, in service to the state. In the effort to establish congruence between the individual's place in a "natural institution like the family" and the individual's loyalty to an "omnipresent government" (see note 20 above), the Singapore brand of Confucianism suppresses the fact that loyalty to family and clan functioned frequently in Chinese history to subtract from loyalty to the state.[26] State fatherhood specifically requires, of course, the intimate articulation of the traditional family with the modern state, and the ostensible homology of the one to the other, claimed by Singapore Confucianism, facilitates and guarantees the transfer of the paternal signifier *from* the family *to* the state, the metaphor of state as family then rendering "natural" an "omnipotent government."[27]

For all the anti-Western rhetoric that characterizes this detection of crisis, then, internalized orientalism in fact supplies state fatherhood with an efficient mechanism for the processing of Western culture—an apparatus of definition, selection, and control that manipulates the rationalizing power of Western modes of knowledge and organization for the efficient management of local capitalism, even as it sets aside as waste what is deemed seductively decadent and dangerous: in short, it presents the ideal regulative machine to the modern Asian state. Whether it provisions the state with a schematic Confucianist system of knowledge or selected statistics from genetics and sociobiology, internalized orientalism serves a paternal master: a gendered formation of power absorbed in fantasmatic repetition, and seeking a reliable machinery of efficient self-regeneration. Recent discoveries of national crisis—in female reproductive sexuality, and the social insufficiency that must be rectified by Confucianism, Mandarin and a national ideology—mark significant breaches, or failures of repetition. The narratives of identity, sexuality, history, culture, and nationalism officially issued with their discovery merely reinstate the proper mechanisms of correction.

In the reproductions of ideology contained in these narratives, then, a dream of a timeless paternal essence emerges, splendid, transcendant, immortal.[28] Masking its power in myriad forms, but somehow always managing to reveal itself, this paternal signifier moves across history, and national boundaries, harboring within itself a Chinese soul wielding a Western calculus of choice (so the fantasy goes). Triumphantly resurfacing through many ages, countries, and cultures, always appropriating to itself new, and ever-puissant forms of contemporary power, it finds that it is checked nonetheless in its primordial play, in one location on the globe, by a troublesome figure of difference. Invariably, that figure is feminine. Whether represented by actual women (as in the "Great Marriage Debate") or "other" races and cultures whose identifying characteristics are implicitly feminized—whether, that is, it is a sexual, or a social, body that haunts and threatens—the figure of threat, auguring economic and social disintegration, dismantling the foundations of culture, undermining, indeed, the very possibility of a recognizable future, is always, and unerringly, feminine. The Great Marriage Debate, and the great cultural crises in Singapore—the threats from within and without—merely reposition an age-old reminder, repeated in the scripts of many nations, many nationalisms:

Women, and all signs of the feminine, are by definition always and already anti-national.

NOTES

1. The trope of father and daughter is so commonly invoked in Singapore to express the relationship between the governing political party which won Singapore independence from Britain (the People's Action Party, or PAP), and the nation itself, as to be fully naturalized, passing unremarked. Singapore is never imagined, by its government or citizens, as a "motherland" or "mother country" (identifications reserved exclusively for the ancestral countries of origin of Singapore's various racial groups—India, China, etc.), but rather as a female child, or at best, an adolescent girl or "young lady." A letter to a national newspaper, entitled "Dear PAPa . . .", and signed by "Singapore, A Young Lady," in the persona of a respectful growing daughter petitioning for greater freedom from her stern father captures the tenor of the relationship perfectly (*The Straits Times* [Singapore], January 5, 1985). (An answering letter, fictitiously from "PAPa," subsequently appeared in the same newspaper.) The psychic economy of the nation prominently circulates between these two gendered positions, tropes of the mother appearing only as counters of facilitation in and reinforcement of the father-daughter dyad.

2. "If we continue to reproduce ourselves in this lopsided way, we will be unable to maintain our present standards. Levels of competence will decline. Our economy will falter, the administration will suffer, and the society will decline. For how can we avoid lowering performance when for every two graduates (with some exaggeration to make the point), in 25 years' time there will be one graduate, and for every two uneducated workers, there will be three?" ("Talent for the Future: Prepared Text of the Prime Minister, Mr. Lee Kuan Yew's Speech at the National Day Rally Last Night," *The Straits Times* [Singapore], August 15, 1983).

3. Lest anyone assume that Lee's articulation of race, class, and gender in the detection of reproductive crisis is unique to Singapore, attention might be drawn to the increasing number of articles in popular U.S. magazines which describe similar discoveries in alarmist, prophetic tones like his—see, e.g., "A Confederacy of Dunces: Are the Best and the Brightest Making Too Few Babies?" in *Newsweek* (May 22, 1989), and R. J. Herrnstein, "IQ and Falling Birthrates" in the *Atlantic Monthly* (May 1989), the latter glossed by the cover headline: "In this Issue: Why are Smart Women Having Fewer Children?" Lee, in the latter article, is admiringly played up as a stalwart example of farsighted and courageous leadership that dares to take measures to rectify envisaged future disaster. Significantly, he is cast in this favorable light with Arthur Balfour, the prime minister of Britain who moaned in 1905 that "Everything done towards opening careers to the lower classes did something towards the degeneration of the race." The

eugenic nightmare of a representative of British high imperialism is echoed thus across the century—the cadences of alarm, fear, and threat remaining unchanged—by the postcolonial prime minister of (a formerly British) Singapore. Nor is Lee's reductive faith in the genetic transmission of intelligence a subscription exclusive now to retrograde third world autocrats. Even as a redoubtable Jay Gould stirred himself to counter Lee's misuse of scientific arguments ("Singapore's Patrimony [and Matrimony]: The Illogic of Eugenics Knows Neither the Boundaries of Time nor Geography," *Natural History*, May 1984), U.S. genetic determinists Thomas Bouchard, Jon Karlsson, and the seemingly indefatigable William Shockley, lent themselves to eager support of Lee's vision: "The Singapore program, says Schockley, 'is discriminate in a very constructive way. Discrimination is a valuable attribute. Discrimination means the ability to select a better wine from a poorer wine. The word has become degraded. And social engineering? As soon as you've got welfare programs, where you prevent improvident people from having their children starved to death, you are engaged in a form of social engineering. Of genetic engineering even. We have these things going on now, but we're not looking at what effects they have, and that's where the humanitarianism is irresponsible'" (see "The Great Debate Over Genes," *Asiaweek*, March 2, 1984).

4. Lee has, on occasion, referred to the people of Singapore as "digits," their inherited attributes as "hardware" to be "programmed" with "software" (ideology, education, culture, etc.). A cohort of his recently suggested, in public, that people "interface" more with one another to increase human communication and understanding. Typically, Lee's National Day Rally speeches (the August 1983 one is no exception) begin with a report of the nation's economic progress for the year in a detailed statistical format, the machinery of statistics representing, for him, and for his government, the power of a penultimate, absolute, and unarguable force. That his statistics in this particular instance are not immovable, however, is suggested by curious vagrancies in the figures subsequently cited, with confident authority, by various government individuals in his support (the "1.6" children born to graduate parents sometimes mutating, for instance, into "1.3" or "1.7" children).

5. Thomas Laqueur's contention that feminine pleasure (and in particular the female orgasm) was historically read as essential to the economy of female reproductive sexuality suggests that its functional removal from that economy has specifically marked it as superfluous, irrelevant ("Orgasm, Generation, and the Politics of Reproductive Biology," in Catherine Gallagher and Thomas Laqueur, eds., *The Making of the Modern Body: Sexuality and Society in the Nineteenth Century* [Berkeley: University of California Press, 1987], pp. 1–41). The pleasurable and the economic are not only read as separate in Singapore today, but inimical (the trope of the machine allowing no role for pleasure, which by its very concession of unusefulness, nonnecessity and excess disables the fantasies of order and regularity on which a local notion of the economic must depend):

indeed, pleasure is tacitly suspected of subverting what would otherwise have been an economic reproductive sexuality, distorting this instead into its opposite, a self-indulgent noneconomy.

6. The *Straits Times*, publishing 31 of the 101 letters it received immediately following the Prime Minister's speech, defended its decision not to publish the remaining 71 letters thus: "Sifting through the pile, one can detect some misunderstanding of Prime Minister Lee Kuan Yew's message. Most of the correspondents did not address their thoughts to the main issue: The better-educated segment of the population should be encouraged to have more children (than what they are having now) to bring about a more balanced reproduction rate. Instead, they interpreted the speech as one more setback for the less intelligent in our society" (A. S. Yeong, "What the Others Said: An Analysis of Unpublished Letters on the PM's National Day Rally Speech," *The Straits Times* [Singapore], August 29, 1983). Among the letters published—no doubt because it was thought acute and useful—was an argument to do away with the right of every adult citizen to an equal vote in national elections: "If, at any stage, there is a threat to progress due to increasing numbers of incompetent people, government may even think of introducing a weightage factor for every vote that comes from a 'qualified' person so that power and administration are kept in the hands of truly competent persons. In a democratic set-up, the principle of 'one person one vote' is fast becoming a menace to society" (G. Rangarajan, "Maintain a Competent Majority," letter to *The Straits Times* [Singapore], August 19, 1983).

7. The statement from the Prime Minister's Office declares, in officialese borrowed from sociology: "Unless we break this low education large family cycle, we will have a small but significant minority of our people permanently trapped in a poverty subculture, whilst the rest of the population will move even further up the economic and social ladder" (Margaret Thomas, "Govt's $10,000 Helping Hand for Low Income Families," *The Sunday Monitor* [Singapore], June 3, 1984). The aim of this money incentive, according to the report, "is to encourage poorly-educated and low-income Singaporeans . . . to stop at two so that their children will have a better chance in life." The writer of this article, driven to notice the coincidence of class and race in the encouragement of this particular group of citizens, nonetheless finds in it an opportunity to play up the dewy-eyed innocence and ingenuous charity of the proposal: "Though it is not spelt out in the statement, a significant proportion of the people caught in the poverty trap are Malays . . . The relatively disadvantaged position of the Malay community is a matter of concern to both leaders of the community and the Government."

8. The relevant clause in the Constitution, article 16(1)(a), reads: "there shall be no discrimination against any citizens of Singapore on the grounds only of religion, race, descent or place of birth . . . in the administration of any educational institution

maintained by a public authority and, in particular, the admission of pupils or students or the payment of fees." Of six unnamed "legal experts" consulted by one newspaper, four agreed that the privileging of certain children over others in the proposed new admissions policy was in direct contravention of this clause (see Siva Arasu, "Unconstitutional? What Legal Experts Say," *The Sunday Times* [Singapore], March 4, 1984). Protests against the scheme were lodged by one government Member of Parliament (Tan Ban Huat, "A Violation of Constitution, Says Dr. Toh," *The Straits Times* [Singapore], February 13, 1984); the lone opposition-party Member then in Parliament (see "House Throws Out Motion by Jeya on Entry Scheme," *The Straits Times* [Singapore], March 14, 1984); the National University of Singapore Students' Union in a petition carrying 3,000 signatures (Hedwig Alfred, "NUS Students' Union Wants to Meet Dr. Tay," *The Straits Times* [Singapore], March 14, 1984); and "500 undergraduates, or nearly 40 per cent" of the student population of the Nanyang Technological Institute ("NTI Students Pen Protest Against Priority Plan: A Class System Would Arise, They Say," *The Sunday Times* [Singapore], February 19, 1984).

9. The Minister of State for Education at the time, Dr. Tay Eng Soon, repeatedly characterized the country's top schools (a description earned on the basis of examination results and the traditional reputation of the institutions) as schools that were merely "popular" as a consequence of public misconception (see "Equal Standard, Equal Chances" and Hedwig Alfred, "More Good News for Non-Grad Mums: All Primary Schools Are of Fairly Equal Standard—Dr. Tay," *The Sunday Times* [Singapore], March 4, 1984). In the midst of public anxiety, resentment, and anger over the proposed changes, the Minister admitted, in an interview with *The Straits Times*, that for all the fuss and trouble, only 200 children were eligible for the new privileges that year (June Tan, "Non-Graduates Will Also Benefit," *The Straits Times* [Singapore], January 24, 1984). Despite Tay's firm assurance in January 1984 that the new policy would be a permanent one, public opinion nevertheless triumphed, and the demise of the scheme was announced in March 1985: "Education Minister Dr. Tony Tan has decided that Singapore can do without the controversial priority scheme which favored the children of graduate mothers but made a whole lot of people angry" (see "Graduate Mum Scheme to Go," *The Straits Times* [Singapore], March 26, 1985).

10. In August 1983, Lee pronounced the larger number of male to female university graduates a source of satisfaction (Bob Ng, "PM: Watch This Trend: Talent Problem Will Worsen When Women Graduates Are No Longer in the Minority," *The Straits Times* [Singapore], August 22, 1983). By October, a change in university admissions policy was announced: "This more-girls-fewer-boys trend was worrying, [the Vice-Chancellor] said, on general principles. Asked if the new policy had anything to do with the Great Marriage Debate—that many women graduates are staying unmarried because a lot of male graduates are marrying less educated women—he said it was unfair to say

so. But if [the National University of Singapore] continued to take in more girls than boys, 'the problem of unmarried women graduates will be aggravated'" (June Tan and Abdullah Tarmugi, "NUS Relaxes Rule on Second Language: To Redress Imbalance between Male and Female Undergrads," *The Sunday Times* [Singapore], October 30, 1983).

11. "Whatever the changes, the two-child family will remain the norm, except that now well-educated parents who have the means to bring up children in a good home are encouraged to have more than two" (June Tan, "New Family Planning Slogan: Message Will Tell Different Things to Different People," *The Straits Times* [Singapore], January 31, 1984). A year later, in 1985, restrictions on abortion began to be publicly discussed (Irene Hoe, "When MPs Shake Their Heads Over Unwed Mums," *The Straits Times* [Singapore], March 17, 1985).

12. The information to be furnished compulsorily was formidably exhaustive: "They must state whether the spouse has a pass degree or is an honors graduate, and if so, which class, the year it was obtained and the name of the college or university. Those with spouses having a pass degree or lower qualifications have to furnish details of the examinations they sat for, the subjects taken, the grades achieved, the name of the school and the year they got their certificates" (see "Officials Asked to Disclose Spouses' Education," *The Straits Times* [Singapore], September 9, 1983, and Teresa Ooi, "Singapore Diplomat Is Asked to Try Out Match-Making Service," *The Straits Times* [Singapore], September 18, 1983).

13. Tsang So-Yin, "The National Service for Women," *The Straits Times* (Singapore), August 17, 1983. Sunday columnist Irene Hoe tartly responded: "if childbirth is indeed national service, the women in the S[ingapore] C[ouncil of] W[omen's] O[rganizations] should be the first to volunteer—before they seek to draft other women" ("The National Service for Women: If Childbirth Is That, These Women Leaders Should Set an Example," *The Sunday Times* [Singapore], August 21, 1983). For the homology between military service and maternal service in cultural representation, see Nancy Huston, "The Matrix of War: Mothers and Heroes," in Susan Rubin Suleiman, ed., *The Female Body in Western Culture* (Cambridge, MA: Harvard University Press, 1986), pp. 119–36.

14. Alice Jardine finds "a climate of sustained . . . paranoia" to exist whenever "the *regulation* of the mother's body . . . [serves] as ground for a monolithic, nationalistic ideology" ("Opaque Texts and Transparent Contexts: The Political Difference of Julia Kristeva," in Nancy K. Miller, ed., *Poetics of Gender* [New York: Columbia University Press, 1986], p. 108). Laurie Langbauer suggests that "the mother's confinement during delivery" in the nineteenth century represents an attempted immobilization of a certain

fear of feminine regenerative uncontrollability—the physical transfixing of the woman being itself an admission of her "controlling power" of reproduction ("Women in White, Men in Feminism," *Yale Journal of Criticism*, 2, 2 [1989], p. 223).

15. "In the old days, matchmakers settled these affairs . . . I remember, as a young boy, hearing my grandmother talk, and she got my aunt married off. She was already 20 plus . . . and there was a widow with no children. Well educated, highly suitable. The result is a family of five, all of whom made it to university. My cousins. . . . We are caught betwixt and between, from an old world in which these matters are thoroughly considered and carefully investigated and properly arranged, to this new world of hit and miss" ("Talent for the Future").

16. "When we adopted these policies they were manifestly right, enlightened and the way forward to the future. With the advantage of blinding hindsight, educating everybody, yes, absolutely right. Equal employment opportunities, yes, but we shouldn't get our women into jobs where they cannot, at the same time, be mothers. . . . You just can't be doing a full-time, heavy job like that of a doctor or engineer and run a home and bring up children . . . we must think deep and long on the profound changes we have unwittingly set off" ("Talent for the Future").

17. "Mr. Lee told an audience of university students that polygamy allowed the mentally and physically vibrant to reproduce. He said that in the old society, successful men had more than one wife. Citing the example of former Japanese Prime Minister Kakuei Tanaka as a man who had a wife and a mistress and children by both, he said the more Tanakas there were in Japan, the more dynamic its society would be" (Kong Sook Chin, "Woman MP Questions Notion of Polygamy," *The Sunday Times* [Singapore], December 28, 1986).

18. In a forum conducted by the *Sunday Times*, two women, who went by the pseudonymous names of "Veronica" and "Mrs. Chan," produced the following dialogue: "Mrs. Chan: 'No woman would support polygamy.' Veronica: 'But there are women like me who would love to have children even though we're unmarried.' Mrs. Chan: 'Yes, a lot of women would like that. Our laws should not penalize such women. Those who are professional and financially self-supporting are quite capable of bringing up their children alone. We should encourage single motherhood, allow such interested women to have artificial insemination.' Veronica: 'It needn't be by artificial means.' (Laughter)" (Tan Lian Choo, "Marriage and the Single Girl: The Sunday Times Roundtable," *The Sunday Times* [Singapore], July 20, 1986).

19. Single motherhood appears to make patriarchy of the first-world as much as the third-world variety equally queasy. In a *Newsweek* article (October 31, 1988) on

what seems to be a highly successful program of state-supported single motherhood in Sweden (the title of which—"What Price Motherhood? An Out-of-Wedlock Baby Boom in Sweden"—strategically projects an affect of doubt and skeptical disapproval), Neil Gilbert, "who heads the Family Welfare Research Group at the University of California at Berkeley," is quoted as saying piously: "If people aren't willing to make commitments . . . you wonder what kind of society you will have down the line."

20. Professor Tu Wei Ming of Harvard University, the government's most prominent Confucian "expert," has offered the view that "democratic institutions . . . are institutions that, if not diametrically opposed to, are at least in basic conflict with *natural* organizations such as family. . . . Some very deep-rooted Confucian-humanistic values are values that need to be fundamentally transformed to be totally compatible with democratic institutions." The newspapers that published the text of Professor Tu's talk glossed it thus: "Democratic institutions are opposed to basic Confucianist ideas like the primacy of the family, an *omnipresent* government, and a preference for a community of trust rather than an adversarial relationship" (emphasis ours). See "When Confucianism Grapples with Democracy," *The Sunday Times* [Singapore], November 27, 1988.

21. Singaporeans are commanded by the most prominent slogan in the campaign to "Speak More Mandarin, Less Dialects" [sic], as if Mandarin itself were not a dialect. Mandarin is now referred to as the "mother tongue" of all Chinese, though virtually all Chinese in Singapore, left to themselves, would likely identify their "mother tongues" as Teochew, Hokkien, Cantonese, Hainanese, Shanghainese, Hakka, or some other regional dialect spontaneously used in their family. Their official "mother tongue," by contrast, has to be acquired through formal education, a large percentage of Chinese schoolchildren proving so inept at it as to require extensive extracurricular private tuition. The government has gone to great lengths, nonetheless, to promote Mandarin, including dubbing Cantonese feature films and soap operas from Hong Kong into Mandarin for Singapore television, and instituting a campaign to discourage taxi drivers—notoriously resistant to government regulation—from speaking in dialect. By the government's own estimate, the measures have been successful; 87% of Chinese Singaporeans, they claim, can now speak Mandarin.

22. Recently, in defending a government policy to import up to 100,000 Chinese from Hong Kong to redress declining birth rates among Chinese Singaporeans, Lee repeated the scenario of crisis he sketched in inaugurating the "Great Marriage Debate" in marginally more delicate terms: "Let us just maintain the status quo. And we have to maintain it or there will be a shift in the economy, both the economic performance and the political backdrop which makes that economic performance possible" (see "Hongkongers' Entry Won't Upset Racial Mix," *The Straits Times Weekly Overseas Edition*, August 26, 1989).

23. See N. Balakrishnan, "Pledge of Allegiance: Core Values Touted as an Antidote to Westernisation," *Far Eastern Economic Review* [Hong Kong], February 9, 1989.

24. Michel Foucault, "Afterword: The Subject and Power," in Hubert L. Dreyfus and Paul Rabinow, *Michel Foucault: Beyond Structuralism and Hermeneutics* (Chicago: University of Chicago Press, 1983), pp. 213–14.

25. Significantly, the notion that East Asian industrial powers owe their prosperity to a Confucian essence circulates prominently also in the West, repeated so often in U.S. print and electronic media as to be naturalized as fact. The image of a ruthlessly efficient Confucianist Orient, with a highly commendable "communitarian value system," celebrated in the West chiefly, one suspects, for the purpose of promoting a particular reorganization within Western industrial societies, is shared by the Orient itself to promote a similar agenda: the efficient management of capitalism.

26. For instance, in *The Gates of Heavenly Peace: The Chinese and Their Revolution, 1895–1980* (New York: Viking, 1981), Jonathan Spence quotes a writer who blamed "Chinese faith in the family for having destroyed all possibilities of true patriotism" (340), and cites Lu Xun's contempt for Confucian scholars, the fictionist asserting in a story that these Confucianists had survived through the centuries because they "had never laid down their lives to preserve a government" (122).

27. Recently, speaking on the problem of escalating emigration from Singapore, First Deputy Prime Minister Goh Chok Tong introduced a plaintive inflection of the trope of state as family: "No country is perfect just as no family is perfect. But we do not leave our family because we find it imperfect or our parents difficult" ("The Emigration Problem," *The Straits Times* [Singapore], October 6, 1989).

28. Personal immortality is sometimes claimed by the representatives of paternal essentialism as well. An issue of *Newsweek* (November 19, 1990) quoted Prime Minister Lee as saying, in concern over the future of Singapore: "Even from my sickbed, even if you are going to lower me in my grave and I feel that something is going wrong, I'll get up."

Chapter 20

From Rough Lads to Hooligans: Boy Life, National Culture and Social Reform

Seth Koven

In the autumn of 1893, Hugh Legge, a member of one of England's ancient aristocratic houses and a recent graduate of Trinity College, Oxford arrived in Bethnal Green, the heart of the slums of East London. He came to live among the poor as a resident in Oxford House, the high Anglican university settlement established less than a decade before. In an age of fashionable slumming, settlement houses enabled young Oxford and Cambridge graduates to "peep into" the nether world of darkest London,[1] literally to settle among the poor, while recreating the relationships, comforts and rituals of the all-male world of the university. The men's settlement movement was a self-conscious attempt to create nation and community through vertical bonds of comradeship across class lines. Legge quickly established the Repton Club for boys in a notoriously unrespectable street and reserved an entire floor of the club for boxing, one of East Londoners' favorite pastimes. Legge found the respectability of collar-wearing boys "uninteresting," "not at all the sort my club was meant for." He referred to the "rough lads" who came to the club as "my lads" and "my boys."

The sort of boys Legge wanted "have been known to assault inoffending persons, and even to fall foul of the police." After noting the boys' smells, their physical prowess and amiable rituals of male violence, he concluded that "they are a class of lads from whom the army is largely recruited—tough wiry fellows, with tons of pluck, and with first rate fighting qualities." In short, the Repton boys made Legge "more optimistic about the rising generation of democracy."[2]

Only six years later, in 1901, the settlement shrilly defended itself against the charge that its Repton Club was a den of hooliganism.[3] Several former members had attacked club boys and property. The illusion of forging the nation on the bonds of love between elite men and working-class boys had been shattered. Legge had breezily used the pronoun "we" in discussing his rough lads. Now the settlement made clear that "hooligans" were menacingly apart from and opposed to the settlement, and by extension the nation. Writing as Head of the Trinity College Settlement in Stratford in July 1901, Legge confessed that "in view of possible military requirement, we have to remember that children bred in over-crowded cities tend to become a degenerate race; and, in spite of patriotic dreams, it is idle to suppose that the men of Whitechapel, Southwark, Hoxton, and the like, could lend much effective aid in repelling a foreign invasion—they have neither the physique nor the morale for such a purpose."[4] Alluding to the violent celebrations marking the relief of Mafeking in South Africa, C. F. G. Masterman, a young Cambridge man and settler in South London, asserted that "a new force, hitherto unreckoned"—the degenerate hooligan—had suddenly emerged from the bowels of the Abyss. This hooligan, he continued, "only rises to menacing gaity upon occasions of national rejoicing." Almost overnight, the "rough lad" had become the "hooligan."[5]

What precipitated this sudden transformation? Levels of juvenile crime may well have increased at the turn of the century. However, most scholars agree that the rise of hooliganism must be explained in terms of shifting attitudes toward and representations of working-class male youth behavior, and not youth practices *per se*.[6] How then should we interpret the sudden renaming of a "new" degenerate race of hooligans and its appearance at times of national rejoicing and national crisis? What are the links between shifting perceptions about working-class adolescent boys and concepts of national culture and nationalism—and how, in turn, do these relate to evolving conceptions of masculinity? I attempt in this essay to explore some of the ways in which heightened concern about masculine identity during and after the Boer War, coupled with the loss of confidence in Arnoldian conceptions of national culture, encouraged British social reformers to reimagine fundamental relationships between men, women and children, families, the state and the nation.[7] By charting interconnections between and (mis)appropriations of the homoerotic, national and imperial fantasies of male social welfare reformers in late-Victorian and Edwardian Britain, I hope to demonstrate that "private" sexual desires and "public" welfarist schemes did not have separate histories.

UPPER-CLASS MEN AND WORKING-CLASS BOYS: CLASS, CULTURE AND CITIZENSHIP

With the expansion of the electorate in 1867, theorists, reformers and politicians alike struggled to establish the terms by which working men would be allowed to share political power. Some, like the poet and school inspector Matthew Arnold, argued that it was the task of the "great men of culture" to combat the divisive forces of anarchy by using culture to reunite the two nations under their supposedly disinterested leadership.[8] T. H. Green, the leading Oxford Idealist philosopher, offered perhaps the most subtle and influential formulation of the problem of male citizenship, class and culture in the 1870s and 80s. The citizen was the man who stood above the prejudices of class, who performed his sacred duties for the benefit of the entire community and nation. Green asked that in exchange for the full privileges of membership in the political nation, working men should abandon class conflict in favor of harmonious and consensual social politics.[9]

The teachings of Arnold and Green found receptive audiences in Oxford and Cambridge in the 1880s. Culture, ostensibly outside of politics, offered an attractive solution to the problems an anomic working class posed for social integration. Green's Balliol protegé Arnold Toynbee proclaimed that only the student-citizen could mediate impartially between labor and capital to determine the best interests of the nation.[10] Colonizing the slums of London, young graduates established outposts of Arnoldian "sweetness and light": libraries and museums, social and literary clubs, cricket and rowing societies, university extension classes, working men's cooperatives, and clubs for working lads. They sought to stimulate working-class desire for a national culture which they, the reformers, had created in their own image. This national culture would bind men, women and children together to forge a community out of the impersonal anonymity of the metropolis.[11] The tasks of constructing a national culture and making citizens out of laboring people were linked by reformers who saw both as essential for the maintenance of a productive social and political order. While they enjoined working-class men, women and children to empower themselves as educated citizens, reformers insisted on maintaining tight control over the definition of what culture was—and more vitally, what it was not—and the setting in which working-class people had access to culture.

For several reasons, working-class boys played an unusually important role in male reformers' daily activities and in their vision of social regeneration. First, as environmentalist arguments about the impact of urban degeneration gained popularity, reformers saw working-class boys as the material out of which they could forge ideal citizens. The British Working Man was, many feared, already irrevocably degraded by slum life. Boys were made of more malleable material, and could be guided to realize a higher self. Reformers thus strove to make and shape men. For some, this task was complicated by personal struggles to make and shape their own masculine identities. A boys' club worker explained that "it is not the case of man and his work; for a boys' club the work must be the man, it must be the expression of himself."[12] The interdependence of reformers' self-identities and their vision of the children whom they hoped to save was further accentuated by their acceptance of a post-Wordsworthian understanding of children as agents capable of rescuing adults from their own corrupting experiences.[13]

Second, generational differences between reformers and boys masked class differences as the source of power that legitimated the reformers' claims to authority. In their programs for working-class men, reformers often cloaked their paternalism in the rhetoric of democratic citizenship. With boys, they felt no need to disguise their tutelary role. Guy Pearse, a Mansfield House Settlement resident and manager of the Fairbairn Club in West Ham, insisted that self-government for working lads meant "training in obedience to authority which they themselves have chosen."[14] A club manager in Whitechapel explained that the elaborate apparatus of boys' clubs elections and committees, like all meetings of "popular representatives," was "an old and reputable device for the concealment of an autocracy, but in a boys' club the committee should not be allowed, in imitation of the popular assembly, to usurp the functions of government."[15]

Third, the interests of parents and reformers often coincided in providing safe and inexpensive entertainment and instruction for working-class children. In a world where older siblings ("little mothers" and "little fathers") and women's informal neighborhood networks were the most prevalent forms of child minding available, clubs and activities for children provided by missions, churches, settlements and other community-based social welfare agencies offered inexpensive and reliable child-care alternatives.

Finally, children were readily accessible to reformers, in a way that working-class adults were not. Reformers met children in casual encounters in the crowded streets, courts, and alleyways, as well as through official positions such as managers of local schools.

These reformers were drawn largely from the all-male networks of the public schools, Oxford and Cambridge colleges, and the celibate communities of Anglo-Catholic slum priests. At a time when norms of male intimacy and friendship increasingly were constrained by anxiety about and medicalization of what Victorians called "sexual inversion,"[16] these networks provided socially acceptable settings for men to nurture and sustain relationships with one another—and with working-class boys. (Ironically, sexual proprieties dictated that female reformers should promote the welfare of working-class girls.)

The links between Anglo-Catholicism and departures from traditional heterosexual relationships date from the first generation of Tractarians who were criticized as effeminate by their ecclesiastical antagonists, most notably that exemplary "muscular Christian," Charles Kingsley.[17] By the late nineteenth century, the dogmas of high churchmanship and the ideal of engaged and masculine Christian social obligation combined in sexually ambiguous, reform-minded clergymen such as James Adderley, Scott Holland, Stewart Headlam, Osborne Jay, and Arthur Foley Winnington-Ingram. Of this group, only Headlam married. But his wife entered and quickly left their conjugal home with a woman friend rumored to have been her lover. Headlam and Adderley (who preceded Winnington-Ingram as Head of Oxford House Settlement) both came to Oscar Wilde's aid during and after his trials and espoused radical political and social causes that embarrassed the Church hierarchy.[18] Adderley, before taking orders, had dreamed of creating a celibate community of laymen devoted to the poor.[19] Jay, immortalized as Father Sturt in Arthur Morrison's stunning novel *A Child of the Jago,* combined love of priestly pomp with close familiarity with the lowest class of boys in London's infamous Old Nichol.[20]

Holland and Winnington-Ingram were closely associated with Oxford House Settlement and the reformist Christian Social Union. A visitor to Oxford House in the early 1890s observed that Ingram "like all that sect . . . was . . . as polite as a model, and laughed copiously if not heartily at everyone and everything." Ingram and his type were "the true hermaphrodites realised at last."[21] In descriptions and photographs, Ingram and his fellow slum priests were typically surrounded by boys, often costumed in ceremonial garb celebrating religious rites. As a young man, Ingram was as likely to be seen playing on the fives court as in leading prayer.[22] In some respects he embodied that peculiarly English fusion of what Theodor Adorno, visiting Oxford fifty years later, snidely identified as the two prevalent types of men he encountered there: the "tough guy" and the "effeminate intellectual" whose concealed homosexuality could only find expression in fraternal life and club sociability.[23]

Men's settlement houses were also committed to maintaining the forms of male sociability of Oxford and Cambridge. Samuel Barnett, the founder of Toynbee Hall and one of the most respected reformers of his generation, made "pal chats"—intimate *tête à têtes* with each settler—an integral part of life at Toynbee.[24] While he found in Henrietta Rowland Barnett a formidable and accomplished spouse, many of his contemporaries described Samuel as the more "feminine" of the two.[25] C. R. Ashbee, an early settler at Toynbee Hall, entered in his journal that Barnett was in fact "primarily a eunuch—in spirit and heart. . . . He plays fast and loose with the moral enthusiasm of young men, and has not the strength either to lead or to be led by them."[26]

Ashbee's views on Barnett are largely self-revelatory. Ashbee came to the settlement wrestling with incipient same-sex desires awakened at Kings College Cambridge where he, Roger Fry and Goldsworthy Lowes Dickenson had spent long evenings together in philosophical and personal reflection. Ashbee saw life in the slums of Whitechapel as an escape from the political, social as well as sexual conventions of bourgeois respectability. Hoping to avoid "devilish gentility" and the "quagmires of society," he revelled in meeting "men who are really men and not men plus top-hats, and to come whenever one will, in actual living contact with great ideas."[27] Toynbee Hall offered Ashbee a "chain of comrades" and ready access to the "rough boys" whose company he craved. Ashbee's circle included Hubert Llewellyn-Smith, later knighted for his pioneering work as an architect of the welfare state. Ashbee and Llewellyn-Smith took East End boys on idyllic weekend gambols into the countryside: Ashbee felt that "eternal love" had been "sealed between themselves [the boys] and men from the day we went to the Isle of Whight [sic] together."[28]

For Ashbee, comradeship with working-class boys *was* the vehicle for social reform, not merely an accident of settlement life in Whitechapel. Ashbee was not alone in basing social reform on cross-class male comradeship. In *Homogenic Love and Its Place in a Free Society*, Ashbee's idol, the Sheffield socialist Edward Carpenter, asserted that homogenic love between elite and laboring men would create an enduring and passionate bond that would transcend and thereby heal class conflict.[29] Neither Carpenter nor Ashbee defined this passionate bond as necessarily physical; their vision of comradeship was in many respects profoundly platonic and more than a little tinged with wishful idealism.[30]

Ashbee's fantasies about his relationships with his "lads" from Whitechapel chastely echo in a different key the violently pornographic account of a philanthropic gentleman's efforts on behalf of a beautiful, thirteen-year-old shoeblack recounted in the 1881 *Sins of the Cities of the Plain or Confessions of a Maryanne*. (Ashbee's father, perhaps the foremost collector of pornography of his time, may have owned a copy of this work, but there is no reason to suppose that his son ever read it.) The genteel protagonist in this story seduces the friendless boy by exciting his desire for fine food, clothes and comfortable lodgings; he then threatens to return the boy to a Ragged School if he does not "consent" to being raped. The story ends as the charitable gentleman takes the boy to Paris and sells him into a life of prostitution for £100.[31]

What makes this story so significant is its imaginative links between several ostensibly unrelated gentlemanly descents into the nether worlds of London. These descents are fueled by overlapping and yet seemingly contradictory impulses: lust and social rescue; a class-transgressive violation of bourgeois values which exposes philanthropy as a veiled system of coercion and control; and, ironically, a desire to reinscribe, even in the darkest depths of London, existing relations of domination and submission between social classes and between adults and children. Late Victorians worked and reworked a fairly limited stock of images of shocked revelation and shadowy uncertainty in describing the sexual and class underworlds of the metropolis. That Ashbee and *Sins of the Cities* both drew from this common stock adds a different dimension to relationships between elite male social reformers and the rough lad recipients of their charity. And just as the pornographer titillated his male readers by simultaneously defying and buttressing power structures, so too male social reformers at once criticized the status quo even as they struggled to prevent its overthrow by the forces of class warfare.

It would be misleading to imply that Ashbee's experiences, or rather, his candor in articulating them, were typical of most male social reformers in the late-nineteenth century. Ashbee's voluminous diaries and correspondence are exceptionally detailed and intimate; and Ashbee was willing to state openly thoughts and feelings that many of his contemporaries felt obliged to repress entirely or to express in other ways. The case of Robert Morant, Ashbee's near contemporary, is perhaps more illustrative precisely because the language he used to express his desires was so much more enshrouded in conventional ideas and diction.

The trajectory of Morant's career and the intense but restrained language he used to describe his feelings for boys suggest further links between sexuality and social welfare. An old boy of Winchester, Morant arrived at New College Oxford in the early 1880s just as the movement to form personal bridges of friendship between university men and slum dwellers came into fashion. He quickly befriended Cyril Jackson, just up from Charterhouse. Like Morant, Jackson later lived at Toynbee Hall, worked closely with working-class boys and played a leading role within social welfare bureaucracies. At the urging of Canon King and under the spell of Scott Holland and Father Dolling, Morant formed a "brotherhood" committed to studying theology. He taught Sunday School classes in Hinksey, a neighboring village famous as the scene of Ruskin's quixotic road-building adventure that had included Algernon Swinburne and Oscar Wilde. Morant felt that "I am getting to like my boys very much . . . we are quite friendly and happy." Later he noted that "it was so jolly to be all among boys again . . . I am fond of boys."[32] In a working-class parish of Oxford he taught working lads boxing and fencing. Instead of immediately joining a university settlement in London, however, Morant first went to Siam where he eventually became tutor to the royal family. Feeling isolated, Morant took two little boys with him on a holiday: one he described as "a dear little chap, about ten, very small, pearly white teeth and brown skin, but a perfect little gentleman."[33] This passage suggests Morant's need to efface the boy's difference—in this case a difference marked by his brownness, not by his class—into an anglicized paradigm of a "perfect little gentleman." He rationalized taking the boys with him on the grounds that "I was longing for something to be fond of . . . I do like someone to be happy with me, when I want to be happy, someone to care for, in fact." Morant's desire to appear sexually pure in the eyes of his Siamese employers was so extreme that he did not even allow his sister to visit him: "I know I have scored hitherto by having not even the shadow of a female even near my garden gate." Morant consoled himself by reading the "Noble Diary" of Colonel Gordon (better known later as General Gordon of Khartoum fame), one of a long line of English imperial heros free from heterosexual entanglements and obsessed with native boys.[34] In 1896 Morant married Helen Cracknell, with whom he remained happily and devotedly married until his death at the height of his fame and power.

At the turn of the century, when Charles Masterman and a group of his friends decided to live in South London and work nearby at Cambridge House Settlement, the path before them was clearly marked. In words strikingly reminiscent of Ashbee's, Masterman confided in his diary that he, along with Reginald Bray and Frederick Head, had gone up to Camberwell "to commence a new life." He came determined for "hard work, do *something* . . . to get to know people of all kinds, to help those that can be helped, to write, to comfort those that mourn."[35] A seeker after truth battling with manic-depression, Masterman recognized that his social work activities among the "bad but nice" children of Camberwell were, like all philanthropy, "only subtler selfishness, escape from boredom and desire for something novel."[36] At a meeting of the Church Lad's Brigade he was struck by the enthusiasm of the boys for Scott Holland, but doubted if any "had the slightest conception what it was all about."[37] In long letters to a few of his closest male friends, he addressed them as "Dear Childe," drawing a circle of Byronic attachment around one another.[38] He later used this form of address in his most tender letters to his well-connected future wife Lucy, suggesting an interchangeable intimacy between the "beloved" men and women in his life.[39]

In a notebook of inspirational excerpts Masterman collected in 1899, he copied some words from Ruskin's *Crown of Wild Olive*: "It is among children only, and as children only, that you will find your healing and true wisdom for your teaching."[40] In the late nineteenth century, a whole generation of elite male social reformers, clerical and lay alike, sought "healing" and "wisdom" among the rough lads of London's slums. While ostensibly these men came to heal the wounds of a class-divided nation, it seems probable that many were also driven by the need to come to terms with their own sexualities.[41]

THE CONTRADICTIONS OF THE ROUGH LAD

Social reformers in the 1880s and 90s frequently used the term rough lad to describe a particular type of working-class boy drawn from the poorest casual laborers of Charles Booth's classes B and C. At the same time, the phrase had other less precise meanings and usages. The Oxford English Dictionary devotes several pages just to the word "rough." Several definitions and examples associate "rough" with a young male. The OED documents that by the early Victorian period, "rough" could mean "a man or lad belonging to the lower classes and inclined to commit acts of violence or disorder; a rowdy." It also meant "lacking in refinement or culture." Certainly, late-Victorian social reformers' use of "rough lad" was freighted with these class and cultural connotations.

The word "rough" was frequently contrasted with "respectable" during the Second Reform Bill crisis in the 1860s. To whom or to what both terms referred depended largely upon context.[42] Thus, while settlement house workers in Whitehcapel used "rough" and "respectable" to elucidate fine distinctions between subgroups within the working class, "rough" could also used by a member of the well-to-do classes to describe any working-class person. In general usage, the social boundaries and composition of "rough" and "rough lads" were often loosely defined, allowing different groups to be clustered together without specificity depending on the needs of the speaker or writer.

The late-Victorian and Edwardian gay subcultures appropriated and reinvented the words "rough" and "lad" and added explicitly sexual meaning to them. Oscar Wilde, in a letter to Robert Ross in the spring of 1900, described one of his conquests on the street of Paris as "half rough, all Hylas."[43] The phrase "rough trade" referred to working-class, usually youthful, male prostitution. As Paul Fussell has argued, "lad" often signalled homoerotic attraction, especially in the works of writers such as Hopkins and Housman.[44] Joined together, "rough lad" could and did have homoerotic connotations. This does not give us license to impute a homosexual meaning or motive to every usage of the term; it does suggest that "rough lad" sometimes carried many more, and different, meanings than has generally been recognized. As part of an elaborate language of words, gestures, and places in gay London, it was a phrase whose sexual meanings would be fully understood only by those who had gained access to the code.

While male social reformers worked with and among working-class boys day to day, the "rough lad" was their peculiar discursive invention. The rough lad refused to conform to the blunted and stultifying conformity of Victorian respectability. He embodied the optimistic and romantic assumptions of reformers for whom he represented aboriginal boyhood uncorrupted by an emasculating civilizing process. C. R. Ashbee sought out rough lads to participate in his Guild and School of Handicraft, initially established as an off-shoot of Toynbee Hall. He strove to teach the boys practical skills in metalworking and design by infusing them with Ruskin's ideas about production and Edward Carpenter's vision of male comradeship across class lines. Carpenter sent Ashbee reassuring words: "I think you might do something some-day with your Guild ideas; and I believe you have a real love for the rougher types of youths among the 'people,' which of course will help you much—without which indeed one could do but little."[45] Ashbee and many other settlers were clear about the kind of boys they sought for their programs: "boys who are going to wear high collars and serve behind counters, or add up figures with white fingertips, or do penny-a-lining, or buying and selling or think themselves too grand to work with their hands or who expect to be waited on by others, or are in any other way haunted by the Demon Respectability, the great green middle class bogey in the top hat, such boys are not really very interesting."[46] The story of the founding of the Sydney Club for boys in Whitechapel in 1884 amplifies this theme. According to its manager, the club only prospered after its original members, five choir boys, were replaced by a lower, more "spirited and manly" group of boys.[47]

Reformers were remarkably candid in articulating class, age and gender specific values. Behavior encouraged in boys was threatening and undesirable in all females and working-class men. For example, William Smart approvingly described a typical boys' club scene run by settlers: "What first on entering strikes one accustomed to ordinary ways of regulating the amusements of the poor is the eager circle around the billiards table, the smoking everywhere, the good humored noisy discussion—for within the limits of decorum the boys are allowed to amuse themselves as they please, noise not being objected to."[48] C. E. B. Russell, a well-known expert on boy life in Manchester, insisted that while club boys frequented music halls and gambled every day of their lives, they were "in the main good natured, simple, generous, plucky, manly . . . the most human and pleasing types."[49] However, the independence, ingenuity and loyalty reformers treasured in rough lads were unbecoming in future wives and domestic servants. And such attributes were dangerous in future trade unionists and potential members of the emerging Independent Labour Party.

Through a wide range of morally uplifting and physically wholesome cultural and sporting activities, reformers sought to reconstitute "manly" communities with one another and with rough lads in the slums of London. However, their relationships with rough lads were neither as unproblematic nor as innocent as this account suggests. Their own writings, published and private, suggest deep if sometimes contradictory connections between their objects of social reform and their objects of sexual desire. Just as the reformers' democratic rhetoric about the creation of a common culture conflicted with their elitist political and economic agendas, so too their desires for rough lads led some to doubt their own "moral purity."

The very process of transforming rough lads into model adult citizens necessarily meant instilling qualities of deference, conformity, and respectability—"priggishness" in short—that the reformers so despised. W. J. Braithwaite, who later worked with Morant and Masterman in developing and implementing the 1911 National Health Insurance Act, summarized this process: "the object of a rough lads' club surely as that of every club should be, is to become respectable and cease to be a rough lads' club."[50] Success, defined in this way, promised to neutralize reformers' desires and admiration for the rough lad.

Reformers' idealizations of their relationships with rough lads in the 1880s and 90s were undermined not only by their own internal contradictions, but by events outside the narrow confines of East End boxing societies and South London working lads' clubs. In the mid-1890s, the spectacle of rough lad "renters" and blackmailers called to testify against Oscar Wilde became the touchstone for a virulent backlash against all forms of homoeroticism. The Wilde case reinforced anxieties about the existence of a "degenerate" homosexual subculture reaching across the social spectrum. More ominously, as Richard Ellmann has pointed out, the prosecution highlighted that cultural elitism and a varsity background were altogether too compatible with a democratic fondness for rough lads.[51] While there is no reason to assume that Wilde's rough lads and those who populated the clubs and fantasies of male social reformers shared much in common beyond their youth and their approximate class background, contemporaries easily confused the two.

If the Wilde case thus registered to the wider culture an explicitly sexual dimension to relationships between elite men and rough lads, the onset of the Boer War a few years later marked a kind of collective loss of innocence for many social reformers. For some, like Samuel Barnett, the mindless jingoism of the war seemed a complete negation of his vision of social reform and the nation. The atavistic emotions unleashed by the war dealt a powerful blow to his liberal optimism about the inevitability of social progress, and his stance as a pro-Boer isolated him even within his own circle of reformers.[52] While Barnett decried the moral depravity of the war, the British public was panicked by revelations about the physical degeneration of its soldier class. As army recruiting offices reported a widespread incapacity of working-class men to take up their duties as citizen-soldiers, news of defeats at the hands of the lilliputian forces of the Boers dominated the headlines. The relief of the siege of Mafeking in May 1900 galvanized spontaneous national celebrations accompanied by a terrifying display of mob violence and disorderly youth behavior. As many contemporaries and historians have since noted, the Mafeking riots allowed social commentators to link the degeneracy of the British working class with uncertainty about British imperial strength.[53] Mary (Mrs. Humphry) Ward explained in March of 1901 that "the 'spirited element' of boy nature must have its outlet. Train it, and it will serve your State. Let it run to waste and riot, and you will get your 'Hooliganism,' as you deserve." The upper classes must choose, she continued, "whether to create ' 'eroes' " to serve in battle in South Africa or "boys gangs of Southwark and Euston Road."[54] Control over boy nature was the key to the future of nation and empire. "Boy life" became a convenient shorthand for the assumption that working-class, adolescent, urban male behavior was necessarily a social problem.

THE HOOLIGAN IN THE ABYSS

Lord Meath, President of the Lads' Drill Association, declared that "the suppression of Hooliganism amongst the rough lads of our towns is one of the most pressing social questions of the day."[55] The need to protect the rough lad from the contagion of hooliganism was a recurrent and urgent theme among social reformers in the decade after the Boer War. Social reformers never doubted for a moment that a new kind of urban youth actually had come into existence who was distinct from and yet somehow also bound to his predecessor, the rough lad. Nonetheless, Meath's words seem to slide between the two categories, "rough lads" and "hooliganism" underscoring his confusion about the relationship between the two. A correspondent for the London *Times* assured readers that two conferences had been held by "experts" to determine how to deal with hooliganism. The experts were drawn overwhelmingly from men's settlements and Anglican suffragen bishops from the East and South London slums.[56] Those groups of men who had heralded the rough lad as the rising hope of democracy in the 1880s and 90s now shaped public perception and interpretation of his alter ego, the hooligan. In the aftermath of the Boer War, these same men would also play vital roles in laying the foundations of British welfare programs and policies. These professed experts served as witnesses before parliamentary commissions and wrote hundreds of scholarly and popular articles and books about boy life. The list of contributors to this literature is vast and distinguished, ranging from Rider Haggard to R. H. Tawney.

One of the works that influenced Edwardian debate about social reform, urban conditions and child life was *The Heart of the Empire*, edited by C. F. G. Masterman. It appeared in the summer of 1901, at the height of the public interest in hooliganism and the war effort.[57] It was the collective work of nine public school and university men who put themselves forward as at once visionary prophets and practical politicians of the new age. They claimed authority based on their "first hand knowledge of the new city race" acquired by living in settlements and block dwellings.[58] The book was intended to serve many purposes. It was a tirade against Victorianism and its survivals—foremost among them, Gladstonian liberalism—as mere "relics" of an outmoded way of seeing the world. It was a journalistic exposé, one of a long line of sensational pieces written by social reformers about "descending" into and "penetrating" the unknown world of the London slums. Its intensely apocalyptic tone and lurid invocation of Darwinian imagery were meant to startle readers about the emergence of a new degenerate race festering at the very heart of the empire. But the work was also written to draw attention to the authors. Masterman frankly admitted that he hoped to "sell the book, create interest and rescue ourselves from dismal obscurity."[59] His hopes for the volume were quickly realized. The book sold out and was then reprinted; Masterman began a meteoric rise in politics as a quintessential New Liberal protegé of Lloyd George and Winston Churchill.

The Heart of the Empire and a companion volume Masterman wrote in 1901, *From the Abyss*, powerfully illustrate interconnections between national culture and nationalism, social reform and hooliganism, race degeneration and imperialism, masculine identity and the state. Masterman's goal was to "combat the estranging forces, weld together into a compact and homogeneous people a *nation* [my emphasis] that seems breaking up into isolated atoms" (47). In the "incredibly distant" past of the 1880s, Masterman averred, settlement workers and slum priests had "essayed their hands" at building a nation on the bedrock of personal friendships, cultural philanthropy and Christian socialism (2, 5). All these efforts had failed and nowhere was this failure more apparent than in the conditions of child life. Life in the Abyss was a "long progress from the transitory vision of childhood to the dead futility of premature old age" (17). In language that recalled the optimistic assessment of the rough lad, Masterman celebrated the promise of the children of the slums: "Human nature, however stunted or dwarfed by cramped dwellings, poor food, or hereditary disease, seems perennially about to blossom into something holy and divine." But this promise, like childhood itself, was inevitably blighted by the unnatural conditions of city life—the aggregation of numbers, the segregation of classes, and the deadening conformity of mass culture (48–49). Contrasted with the manly pluck and attractiveness of the urban rough lad of the 1890s, the town dweller was "stunted, narrow-chested, easily wearied; yet voluble, excitable, with little ballast, stamina, or endurance." Cut off from the "virility and health of the country life," the new city race was effeminate, "bloodless" and incapable of performing the manly tasks of ruling Britain and her empire (8, 24).

The hooligan was the most notorious creation of this town life. Embodying a dangerous form of masculinity, the hooligan rejected not only the norms of bourgeois culture but the sublimated erotics of cross-class male comradeship and sociability. One still can find in Masterman's account of the hooligan traces of the rough lad's admirable audacity. For example, he recasts hooligan violence as a kind of "protest, however vague and uncontrolled, against a purely material satisfaction: a movement resistant to that stagnation which is the precursor of inevitable death."[60] But the overwhelming sense Masterman conveys is that hooligan behavior was a kind of cruel parody of reformers' hopes for the rough lad, the nation and the empire. Mirroring the corrupt policies of the British state in South Africa, hooligans were preoccupied with staking out territories in the interior wildernesses of the metropolis, a kind of counter-nationalism. "Those who have fought together," Masterman explained, "like the component parts of the Empire, become bound together with a new tie of comradeship."[61] Had this "new tie of comradeship" replaced the previous ties that reformers had sought to establish with "rough lads"? Masterman does not address this explicitly. But his rhetoric is saturated with images of sexual excess and revulsion. Gang warfare promoted "the lust of battle." The cycles of activity and quiescence of the Abyss resembled an episodic, even violent, pursuit of sexual gratification: "occasional outbursts of brutalising and unlovely pleasure." The generative power of the Abyss, their "continual impetuous multiplication," clearly frightened and repelled Masterman (28, 13).

Masterman did not attempt systematically to consider hooliganism in terms of sexuality. This task was left to a pioneering American psychologist, G. Stanley Hall. With the appearance of Hall's monumental study *Adolescence* in 1904, hooligan behavior ceased to be viewed exclusively as a function of class relations.[62] Instead, Hall proposed that adolescence was a peculiar phase in psychological and sexual development between childhood and adulthood, a revolutionary "new birth" characterized by change and contradiction. In connecting this adolescent phase to "distinctly school and city bred" diseases,[63] Hall placed the emergence of the physical and psychological attributes of manhood at the heart of debates about boy life and hooliganism. The hooligan was a victim not only of his environment and his poverty, but of the painful process by which all men and women achieved sexual identities. In this way, the sexual and psychological positions of hooligans and social reformers resembled one another as transitional stages between childhood and adult responsibilities. After all, the social reformers were still young men themselves, unmarried and living in all-male communities.

Many of the themes developed by Masterman and Hall were brought together in the works of Masterman's close friend and flatmate, Reginald Bray. Bray believed that the problems besetting slum children stemmed from an imbalance between the forces of "humanity" (the city) and "nature" (the country). The nature element promoted stability, the human element wildness and unrest. The hooligan resulted from an excess of the human element.[64] City life, Bray explained in 1907, gives "rise to action on the most trifling occasion, exploding like a pistol at the mere touch of the half trigger. In the face of the vast population, penned within the walls of the city, such possibilities of unpremeditated violence constitute a standing menace to the general welfare."[65] With school attendance mandatory only until the age of 14, the state relinquished its educational and social stewardship over children at precisely the age when it was most essential. From ages 15 to 18, "the greater part of adolescence," when "there is most risk of ugly and dangerous outbreaks," both parents and the state typically withdrew their supervision.[66]

Bray and many other reformers imagined that the key to transforming the sordid conditions that produced hooligans out of rough lads was the working-class family. Bray moralized that working-class people had been cut off from the home, "that fabric of memories and associations, simple and unpretentious in design."[67] But how could the conditions of home life be transformed? And what roles should working-class parents and social reformers play within this home? In short, was there a way out of the Abyss?

THE FATHERLY STATE AND SOCIAL WELFARE IN EDWARDIAN BRITAIN

In the years immediately preceding the Boer War, some reformers already had begun to question their vision of one-to-one cultural and moral philanthropy. As early as 1898, for example, Robert Morant believed the continued existence of the democratic British state depended on the recognition "*by* the democracy, of the increasing need of voluntarily submitting the impulses of the many ignorant to the guidance and control of the few wise." The few wise were "special expert governors or guides or leaders, deliberately appointed by itself for the purpose." These experts in "the science of national life and growth"—

civil servants—were essential if the democratic state were to survive "in the international struggle for existence." Only the civil servant, according to Morant, possessed an "outlook over the whole field of national growth."[68] Morant sought to balance love for democracy with elitist insistence that the democracy had to submit its ignorant impulses to the control of men like himself. He turned to the technology and resources of the state to implement his vision of the family and the nation.

This shift toward interventionist social politics was propelled by the experiences of the Boer War and the Report of the Inter-Departmental Committee on Physical Deterioration published in its aftermath. The Liberal Party after 1906, armed with a popular mandate for change and led by radicals Lloyd George and Winston Churchill, enacted an unprecedented range and quantity of social welfare legislation. A great deal of this legislation targeted children. From cradle to grave, the state now presumed to play an essential role in the working-class household. New legislation ensured that births were registered, "necessitous" school children fed and medically inspected. One rather cynical working-class view of all this legislation insisted that it was "essentially undemocratic . . . a gross and stupid insult, the outcome of sentimentality and ignorance, engineered by well-meaning busybodies."[69]

To an astonishing degree, these "busybodies"—key architects of social welfare legislation within the civil service—served apprenticeships in the slums of London working with rough lads. Hubert Llewellyn-Smith and Robert Morant were probably the two most influential permanent civil servants in Edwardian Britain. Smith transformed the Board of Trade into the administrative locus of state policy on labor and labor relations.[70] Smith worked closely with another former Toynbee man, William Beveridge, in laying out the structural characteristics of unemployment and in establishing Labour Exchanges as an integral part of British Unemployment Insurance.[71] Seeking to use his position to make policy both in the Education Department and then later as Head of the Insurance Commission, Morant worked closely with C. F. G. Masterman as they both schemed to create a new, more comprehensive social welfare agency, a Ministry of Public Health.[72] Masterman wielded his power as an elected member of parliament, not as a civil servant. A trusted lieutenant of Lloyd George, he was a key link between Liberal leadership and the civil service in developing and implementing the National Insurance Act of 1911. At the Insurance Commission, Masterman also worked with many other former male settlers, including William J. Braithwaite. Braithwaite had managed the Old Northeyites' Boys' Club in Whitechapel, and maintained a lifelong involvement with the club. He had inherited his club position from Cyril Jackson, a champion of child welfare measures on the London County Council as well as the author of the Boy Labour

Inquiry for the Poor Law Commission Report of 1909. Bray, like Jackson, also served on the London County Council for a short time.

Though this list is by no means exhaustive, it demonstrates that work with rough lads formed a vital part of the collective experiences of that generation of elite young men who wielded considerable influence in reimagining the nature and purpose of the state from 1901 to 1914. But how should we interpret these experiences and their impact on how male social reformers envisioned the state? We can only offer possible interpretations. No evidence directly and explicitly linked reformers' experiences with rough lads to their roles as state policy makers. Perhaps these men turned to the state, at least in part, in response to their perception that their rough lads had rejected their gift of friendship, citizenship and elevation, and had instead devolved into hooligans. It is also possible that reformers replaced one discursive invention, the rough lad, with another, the hooligan, to justify a shift from personal philanthropy to statism. This change may well have been galvanized by the immediate circumstances of the Boer War and motivated by broader political and social pressures. These two explanations are not of course mutually exclusive. The shift in the representation of working-class male youths from rough lads to hooligans may well have grown out of and responded both to the personal needs of reformers and to changing political exigencies. While these indeed are speculations, there is evidence suggesting that reformers remained deeply committed to the project of building the nation and state through the bonds of manly camaraderie.

The case of Benjamin Kirkman Gray is particularly illustrative. Disillusioned by his work in a London slum mission, Gray rejected the individualist basis of Victorian philanthropy. Only the state could respond to and understand the "national" (and not individual) basis of the ills confronting modern Britain.[73] The standards and conditions of adolescent boy life served as an important touchstone of the well-being of the nation. "The essential human business," he insisted, "from 13 to 18 is to make men" (185). Echoing G. Stanley Hall, he contended that "the boy is passing through rapid and critical changes, physiological and psychological, the result of which will determine his whole future. . . . In these years the boy enters into the tragic mystery of self and sex and social consciousness" (187). "When a man is a worker," he admitted, "as a worker he is an instrument. That seems to be in the nature of things. With the boy this ought not to be the case. When the nation is convinced of that, the evil of unregulated boy labour will cease." Citing the findings of the Report on Physical Deterioration, Gray believed that the failure of the state to regulate adequately the conditions of boy life against the "devitalising and dehumanising environment" forced boys to enter manhood "with perverted sex instincts and atrophied social consciousness . . ." (182, 187). The promise and power of boyhood threatened to degenerate into a "manhood twisted and awry" (189). For Gray, making men was a vital task of the collectivist state.

Reginald Bray shared many of Gray's hopes and assumptions. He envisioned a manly state that actively intervened in the lives of its citizens. "Where an environment requires transformation," he explained, "the broad and far reaching arm of the State is singularly effective."[74] In language that conjures up the image of the hero rescuing a damsel in distress, he argued that the "environment is too powerful for the individual to combat single-handed; he needs the strong arm of the State to lift him up from the Abyss where he is held in unresistant helplessness" (70). Bray elaborated on the state's role in regulating not only the public but the private roles of and relationships between men, women and children. He called for the creation of a minimum wage which would enable men to support their dependent wives and children. Bray believed the state was obliged to help beleaguered mothers not on the basis of their social and political rights as women, but as the best means to protect and promote the rights of infants. He demanded a vast expansion of state welfare to include meals for nursing mothers; municipal milk depots; registration of births; municipal creches; and the feeding of school children (92–116). Bray further stressed that the state should train boys and girls to develop class and gender specific identities as citizens and workers. "Boys must learn to use their hands, and girls be initiated into the mysteries of domestic duties" (178).

In the first decades of the twentieth century, male and female reformers alike turned increasingly to collectivist social politics to solve the intractable conditions of urban poverty. Most of their social welfare programs aimed to transform the conditions of family life—some indirectly through policies that targeted conditions at work and others directly through inspection of households and distribution of services and resources to families. Sex roles were so central to their project that they used explicitly gendered language to describe their vision of the state. An influential child-welfare organization asserted in its Annual Report for 1909 that "the twentieth century pleads that, besides his own parents, every child has in the State a social father who more and more controls and trains him, and in Society a social mother who daily seeks to love and tend him more truly."[75]

Most male social reformers in Edwardian Britain, even those who fancied themselves sympathetic to women's emancipation, were committed to perpetuating this division of labor between a fatherly state and a motherly society.[76] Their attitudes and actions as leading civil servants in developing the National Insurance Act of 1911 highlights their preoccupation with improving the status of men as heads of households, and their indifference to the claims of women.[77] In November 1911, a prominent newspaper editorialized that "we have admitted from the beginning that the (Insurance) scheme is grossly unjust to women. Its refusal to regard the family as a unit and marriage as a partnership entitling the widow to all the benefits the husband would have received had he lived, is a strange and cruel error on the part of a democratic ministry."[78] The bill virtually ignored the special needs of women as workers, mothers and widows. Lloyd George included a maternity benefit almost as an afterthought; even this benefit was paid to the husband, not directly to the mother, until women's organizations protested against its injustice.

Despite women's inroads in such selected areas as maternal and child health and factory inspection, the Edwardian civil service retained some of the characteristics of a men's club.[79] Women—and their interests—remained outside the inner circles of policy formulation. W. J. Braithwaite, as a junior civil servant at the Insurance Commission, drew explicitly on "my own experience in boys' club work" in lobbying for welfare legislation on a contributory basis.[80] According to Braithwaite, "whenever the women were talked of, they were thought of as unsatisfactory." His account of the women's deputations that met Lloyd George to discuss health benefits makes no attempt to hide his condescension: "Poor Mary MacArthur! We had told L. G. [Lloyd George] that Miss Tuckwell, the first speaker, was hysterical and must be left alone . . ."[81] In the heat of negotiations over the implementation of the Insurance Act, Lloyd George sent for Masterman to come to Wales. "You might bring Christabel [Pankhurst] with you," he disparagingly commented: "The clansmen at Llanystudmdwy are making her bath ready for her, and if she brings the whole of her WSPU [Women's Social and Political Union] with her there is plenty of room and to spare."[82]

The state, in its pose as neutral arbiter between the competing interests of citizens, has proven an enduring and powerful "imagined community" on which to build a nation.[83] Many factors contributed to the shift toward collectivism at the turn of the century including the rise of class-conscious labor movements, the increasing complexity of an urban and industrial society, the need to stabilize the work force and the Liberal electoral triumph in 1906. But historians of social welfare have overlooked the significant impact of the deep fissures in masculine and national identity revealed by the Boer War on both the ways in which reformers envisioned the state and the nature of the policies they encouraged. Fears about the conditions of life of the urban poor, the strength of the empire and the degeneration of male soldiers/citizens antedated the onset of the Boer War. However, the heightened tensions of war brought into stark relief the extent of these problems and suggested underlying connections between nationalism, sexuality and social welfare. The very existence of the hooligan—or, perhaps more accurately, his cultural representation—forced male reformers to confront the failure of their liberal-cultural vision of social change and affirmed the necessity of state intervention. Male reformers described this interventionist state as a newly potent member of the family and nation. In the 1880s and 90s, the future of the nation appeared to rest on the precarious comradeship of gentlemen and rough lads. In the aftermath of the Boer War, reformers imagined a new kind of male community—of fathers, sons and the state—clearly masculine and perhaps patriarchal.

NOTES

I would like to thank Adele Lindenmeyr and Chris Waters for their incisive and illuminating suggestions.

1. See Richard Whiteing's slum novel *No. 5, John Street* (New York, 1899), in which he describes settlements as mere "peep holes" (8) and hence accentuates the voyeurism implicit in upper-class scrutiny of working-class life.

2. Hugh Legge, "The Repton Club," in John Matthew Knapp, *The Universities and the Social Problem* (London, 1895), pp. 133–47.

3. See Annual Report, Oxford House, 1900, p. 15 and Annual Report, Oxford House, 1901, p. 32.

4. Rev. Hugh Legge, "The Education of Democracy," *Economic Review* (July, 1901), p. 299.

5. C. F. G. Masterman, *From the Abyss* (London, 1902), pp. 4–5.

6. See John Gillis, *Youth and History* (London, 1974), especially Chapters 3 and 4; Stephen Humphries, *Hooligans or Rebels? An Oral History of Working-Class Childhood and Youth, 1889–1939* (Oxford, 1981), Chapter 7; Geoffrey Pearson, *Hooligan, A History of Respectable Fears* (London, 1983), Chapter 5; and *The Deviant Imagination: Psychiatry, Social Work and Social Change* (London, 1977). On connections between youth movements (in particular the boy scout movement) and imperialism, see John Springhall, *Youth, Empire and Society* (London, 1977). On the social and economic debates over youth and labor, see Harry Hendrick, *Images of Youth, Age and Class and the Youth Male Problem, 1880–1920* (Oxford, 1990). Because the present essay was completed before the publication of Hendrick's book, I have not been able to incorporate its findings into my argument.

7. George Mosse investigated similar questions, focusing heavily on German materials, in his provocative *Nationalism and Sexuality: Middle-Class Morality and Sexual Norms in Modern Europe* (Madison, WI, 1985). Anna Davin examined the impact of the Boer War on conceptions of motherhood and female identity in "Imperialism and Motherhood," *History Workshop Journal*, 5 (1977). There is a burgeoning literature on the history of masculinity. J. A. Mangan and James Walvin, eds., *Manliness and Morality: Middle-Class Masculinity in Britain and America* (Manchester, 1987) is a particularly useful collection; see especially John Springhall's contribution, "Building Character in the British Boy: The Attempt to Extend Christian Manliness to Working-Class Adolescents, 1880 to 1914," which examines the Boy's Brigade. See also Peter N. Stearns's important general study on the construction of masculine identity, *Be A Man! Males in Modern Society* (New York, 1979).

8. Matthew Arnold, *Culture and Anarchy*, ed. R. H. Super (Ann Arbor, 1965), p. 113.

9. See Melvin Richter, *The Politics of Conscience* (Cambridge, MA, 1964) and Andrew Vincent and Raymond Plant, *Philosophy, Politics and Citizenship: The Life and Thought of the British Idealists* (Oxford, 1984).

10. Alon Kadish, *Apostle Arnold: The Life and Death of Arnold Toynbee, 1852–1883* (Durham, NC, 1986), p. 83.

11. The role of communitarian ideals in the settlement movement is explored in Standish Meacham, *Toynbee Hall and Social Reform 1880–1914: The Search for Community* (New Haven, 1987).

12. W. J. Braithwaite, "Boys' Clubs," in E. J. Urwick, ed., *Studies of Boy Life in our Cities* (London, 1904), p. 219.

13. See Peter Coveney, *The Image of Childhood, the Individual and Society: A Study of the Theme in English Literature* (London, 1967); see also Carolyn Steedman, *Childhood, Culture and Class in Britain: Margaret McMillan, 1860–1931* (New Brunswick, NJ, 1990), especially Chapter 3.

14. Guy Pearse, "Fairbairn House Boys' Club," Seventh Annual Report, 1897, Mansfield House, p. 23.

15. Braithwaite, "Boys' Clubs," p. 223.

16. Jeffrey Weeks's many works on this subject are indispensable. In particular,

see his "'Sins and Diseases': Some Notes on Homosexuality in the Nineteenth Century," *History Workshop Journal*, 1 (1976), and *Coming Out: Homosexual Politics in Britain, from the Nineteenth Century to the Present* (London, 1977), especially Chapters 1–3.

17. See David Hilliard, "Unenglish and Unmanly: Anglo-Catholicism and Homosexuality," *Victorian Studies*, 25, 2 (1982).

18. Where Headlam was extraordinarily attuned to sexual politics and openly supported feminist causes, his biographer F. G. Bettany was entirely reticent about Headlam's sexual relations. At the end of his life, Headlam lived with two women, one of whom was a school teacher named as a beneficiary in his will. Headlam's papers have never been located, despite the fact that he had them typed and organized before his death. As a consequence, it is difficult to reconstruct a full picture of his private affairs. In addition to Bettany's *Stewart Headlam, A Biography* (London, 1926), see also John Orens, "The Mass, the Masses and the Music Halls: The Radical Anglicanism of Stewart Headlam," unpublished Ph.D. dissertation, Columbia University, 1976.

19. See Adderley's revealing, loosely autobiographical novel *Stephen Remarx, The Story of a Venture in Ethics* (New York, 1894), as well as H. H. Henson's biting account of his involvement with Adderley during these years in his autobiography *Retrospect of an Unimportant Life* (London, 1942), p. 14. Henson later became Bishop of Durham and disavowed his youthful flirtation with High Anglicanism.

20. See Arthur Osborne Jay, *The Social Problem: Its Possible Solution* (London, 1893) and *A Story of Shoreditch* (London, 1896).

21. Henry Wood Nevinson Diaries, February 11, 1893, in the Nevinson Papers, Ms. Eng. misc.e 610/12, pp. 16–17, Bodleian, Oxford.

22. See S. C. Carpenter, *Winnington-Ingram* (London, 1949), especially Chapters 2, 3, 4 and 11.

23. Theodor Adorno, *Minima Moralia, Reflections from a Damaged Life*, trans. E. F. N. Jephcott (London, 1974), p. 46.

24. Henrietta Barnett, *Canon Barnett, His Life, Work and Friends* (London, 1919), Volume I, pp. 315–318.

25. G. P. Gooch, *Under Six Reigns* (London, 1958), p. 63.

26. C. R. Ashbee Papers, *Journals*, "Summing up of two years," end of 1888,

Kings College Cambridge. There are several good full-length biographies of Ashbee, including Alan Crawford's *C. R. Ashbee: Architect, Designer and Romantic Socialist* (New Haven, 1985), which is particularly outstanding on Ashbee's design contributions; see also Fiona MacCarthy, *The Simple Life: C. R. Ashbee in the Cotswold* (London, 1981).

27. Ashbee Papers, Ashbee to Roger Fry, February 28, 1887 in *Journals*, Kings College Cambridge.

28. Ashbee Papers, *Journals*, March 21, 1889, Kings College Cambridge.

29. See Edward Carpenter, *Homogenic Love and its Place in a Free Society* (Manchester, 1894).

30. Carpenter was much more open about his sexual relationships with men than Ashbee was, especially after Ashbee's marriage. On Carpenter's personal and sexual relations with men, see Sheila Rowbotham and Jeffrey Weeks, *Socialism and the New Life: The Personal and Sexual Politics of Edward Carpenter and Havelock Ellis* (London, 1977), pp. 75–91.

31. This scene is recounted in Neil Bartlett, *Who Was That Man? A Present for Oscar Wilde* (London, 1988), pp. 231–232. Only a few years later, W. T. Stead's exposé of the white slave trade graphically described similar scenes involving working-class girls and wealthy men. See Deborah Gorham, "The 'Maiden Tribute of Modern Babylon' Re-Examined: Child Prostitution and the Idea of Childhood in Late-Victorian England," *Victorian Studies*, 21, 3 (Spring, 1978).

32. These direct quotations from letters written by Morant are cited by Bernard M. Allen, *Sir Robert Morant, A Great Public Servant* (London, 1934), pp. 19, 20.

33. Ibid., p. 52.

34. Ibid., pp. 52, 60, 63.

35. C. F. G. Masterman Papers, Typescript of Camberwell Diary, April 23, 1900, A2/2/3. See also Lucy Masterman, *Life of C. F. G. Masterman* (London, 1968), p. 28. All quotations from the Masterman Papers are by permission of the University of Birmingham.

36. Ibid., entries for April 25 and 28, 1900.

37. Ibid., entry for April 29, 1900.

38. For an intriguing gay reading of *Childe Harold*, see Louis Crompton, "Byron and Male Love: The Classical Tradition," in Harry Brod, ed., *The Making of Masculinities: The New Men's Studies* (Boston, 1987), p. 327.

39. See letters of Masterman to Arthur Ponsonby, especially during 1905, A2/3/3; and Masterman to Lucy Talbot (Masterman), especially during 1908, A2/3/8.

40. C. F. G. Masterman, manuscript notebook of quotations, Masterman Papers, A2/1/6.

41. E. M. Forster's novel *Maurice* (written in 1913–14 but not published until after his death) offers another perspective on the writings and activities of men like Winnington-Ingram, Ashbee, Morant and Masterman. Forster's narrator was free to acknowledge explicitly connections between homosexual desire, social welfare work with slum youths, and empire that these men perhaps could not. In a passage worth quoting entirely, Forster detailed how Maurice, rejected by his erstwhile male lover, redirected his sexual needs into public activity: "He joined the Territorials—hitherto he had held off on the ground that the country can only be saved by conscription. He supported the social work even of the Church. He gave up Saturday golf in order to play football with the youths of the College Settlement in South London, and his Wednesday evenings in order to teach arithmetic and boxing to them. The railway carriage felt a little suspicious. Hall [Maurice's surname] had turned serious, what! He cut down his expenses that he might subscribe more largely to charities—to preventive charities: he would not give a halfpenny to rescue work. What with all this and what with his stockbroking, he managed to keep on the go" (*Maurice, A Novel* [New York, 1971], p. 143).

42. For a brilliant and persuasive analysis of the category and concept of respectability, see Peter Bailey, "Will the Real Bill Banks Please Stand Up? Towards a Role Analysis of Mid-Victorian Working Class Respectability," *Journal of Social History*, 12, 3 (Spring 1979). Bailey's model can be usefully applied to the categories "rough" and "rough lad."

43. Rupert Hart-Davis, ed., *The Letters of Oscar Wilde* (New York, 1962), p. 819. For an exceptionally creative treatment of the language of the late-Victorian gay subculture, see Bartlett, *Who Was That Man?*, and on the use of "rough" in particular see p. 90.

44. Paul Fussell, *The Great War and Modern Memory* (London, 1975), especially Chapter 8, "Soldier Boys."

45. Edward Carpenter to C. R. Ashbee, October 9, 1887, Ashbee Papers, Kings College Cambridge.

46. C. R. Ashbee, *The Building of Thelema* (London, 1910), p. 79.

47. Toynbee Hall, Annual Report, 1889.

48. William Smart, *Toynbee Hall, A short account* (London, 1886), p. 18.

49. C. E. B. Russell and Lillian Rigby, *Working Lad's Clubs* (London, 1908), p. 93.

50. Braithwaite, "Boys' Clubs," p. 194.

51. Richard Ellmann, *Oscar Wilde* (New York, 1988), p. 451.

52. Barnett confided to Frederic Harrison, a leading Positivist, his "loneliness in this noisy wilderness of empty voices. . . . The heart of the nation is sick" (Barnett to Harrison, February 13, 1900, Harrison Papers, British Library of Political and Economic Science). For similar expressions of despair about the impact of the Boer War on social reform, see Samuel Barnett to Frank Barnett, November 4, 1899, F/Bar/205 and November 18, 1899, F/Bar/206, Greater London Record Office.

53. See Richard Price, *An Imperial War and the British Working Class* (London, 1972). Price's important study refutes many myths perpetuated by Edwardian commentators about the supposed jingoism of the working class. Price is useful in calling attention to the gulf between middle-class perceptions (fantasies) and the realities of working-class opinion and action.

54. Mrs. Humphry Ward, *The Passmore Edwards Settlement* (March, 1901), p. 11.

55. Lord Meath, "Cadets or Hooligans," Letter to *Times*, December 7, 1900, p. 3.

56. *Times*, December 6, 1900, p. 13.

57. For a good discussion of the events surrounding its publication and its contributors, see Bentley Gilbert's "Introduction" to the reprint of *The Heart of the Empire*.

58. C. F. G. Masterman, "Preface," *The Heart of the Empire* (London, 1901), p. ix. Hereafter all citations will be incorporated directly in the text above.

59. Masterman to Noel Buxton, March 16, 1901, A2/3/2, Masterman Papers.

60. Masterman, *From the Abyss,* p. 71.

61. Ibid., p. 67.

62. On links between adolescence and violent youth behavior, see John Gillis, *Youth and History* (New York, 1981), Chapters 3 and 4; and "The Evolution of Juvenile Delinquency in England, 1890–1913," *Past and Present,* 67 (May, 1975).

63. G. Stanley Hall, *Adolescence* (New York, 1904), pp. xiii, xv.

64. Reginald Bray, "The Children of the Town," in *The Heart of the Empire,* pp. 114–115.

65. Reginald Bray, *The Town Child* (London, 1907), p. 145.

66. Reginald Bray, *Boy Labour and Apprenticeship* (London, 1911), p. 198.

67. Reginald Bray, "The Boy and the Family," in Urwick, ed., *Studies in Boy Life,* p. 77.

68. Bernard M. Allen, *Sir Robert Morant, A Great Public Servant* (London, 1934), p. 126.

69. Stephen Reynolds and Bob and Tom Woolley, *Seems So! A Working-Class View of Politics* (London, 1911), p. 39.

70. Roger Davidson, "Llewellyn-Smith, The Labour Department, and Government Growth, 1886–1909," in Gillian Sutherland, ed., *Studies in the Growth of Nineteenth-Century Government* (Totowa, NJ, 1972), pp. 227–62.

71. For a perceptive and detailed account of the making of unemployment insurance, see Jose Harris, *Unemployment and Politics: A Study in English Social Policy 1886–1914* (Oxford, 1972), especially Chapter 6 on the work of Smith and Beveridge.

72. See Morant's letters to Masterman in 1912, A3/4/16 Masterman Papers, University of Birmingham.

73. Benjamin Kirkman Gray, *Philanthropy and the State or Social Politics,* eds.

Eleanor Kirkman Gray and B. Leigh Hutchins (London, 1908), p. 9. All further citations will be incorporated directly in the text above.

74. Bray, *The Town Child*, p. 67. All further citations will be incorporated directly in the text above.

75. Invalid Children's Aid Association, *Annual Report*, 1909, pp. 13–14.

76. Feminist theorists such as Carole Pateman and Catharine McKinnon have pointed out that the welfare state was and remains inherently, almost definitionally, patriarchal. This deeply pessimistic position may be assailed for its failure to take into account the activities and impact of female activists who sought to create the state in their own image. For a comparative assessment of maternalist politics, see Seth Koven and Sonya Michel, "Womanly Duties: Maternalist Politics and the Origins of Welfare States in France, Germany, Great Britain, and the United States, 1880 to 1920," *American Historical Review*, 95, 4 (October, 1990), pp. 1076–1108.

77. The standard account is Bentley Gilbert, *The Evolution of National Insurance in Great Britain: The Origins of the Welfare State* (London, 1966).

78. *The Observer*, November 19, 1911.

79. On women in the British civil service, see Meta Zimmeck, "The 'New Woman' in the Machinery of Government: A Spanner in the Works?" in Roy MacLeod, ed., *Government and Expertise: Specialists, Administrators and Professionals, 1860–1919* (New York, 1988), pp. 185–202; and "Strategies and Strategems of Women in the Civil Service," *Historical Journal*, 27 (1984), pp. 901–24.

80. Sir Henry Bunbury, ed., *Lloyd George's Ambulance Wagon, Being the Memoirs of William J. Braithwaite, 1911–1912* (London, 1957), p. 80.

81. Ibid., p. 179.

82. Lloyd George to C. F. G. Masterman, September 14, 1912, Masterman Papers, A/3/18/1.

83. The phrase comes from Benedict Anderson, *Imagined Communities: Reflections on the Origin and Spread of Nationalism* (London, 1983).

Part VI

Women, Resistance and the State

Chapter 21

Indian Nationalism, Gandhian "Satyagraha," and Representations of Female Sexuality

Ketu H. Katrak

In India, as in various parts of "the Third World," the struggle for women's emancipation was expediently connected to an anti-colonial, nationalist struggle. After Independence was won, militant women found themselves, typically, back in "normal" subordinate roles and came to recognize the dangers of conflating national liberation with women's liberation. The Independence movement that Gandhi led conforms to this familiar pattern of mobilizing and then subordinating women. But whereas other liberation struggles invited women to fight alongside men, Gandhi enjoined Indian men and women to engage in acts of *passive* resistance which feminized the usually masculinist struggle against the colonizer. Who more than women, used to maneuvering patiently through patriarchal authority, could offer better models of passive resistance?

Yet Gandhi's involvement of women in his "satyagraha" (literally, truth-force) movement—part of his political strategy for national liberation—did not intend to confuse men's and women's roles; in particular, Gandhi did not challenge patriarchal traditions that oppressed women within the home. Furthermore, his specific representations of women and female sexuality, and his symbolizing from Hindu mythology of selected female figures who embodied a nationalist spirit promoted, as I will discuss, a "traditional" ideology wherein female sexuality was legitimately embodied only in marriage, wifehood, motherhood, domesticity—all forms of controlling women's bodies.

Gandhi's nonviolent philosophy evolved from his personal observations of passive resistance from his mother and wife. According to Kumari Jayawardena, "It was suggested that, being used to passive forms of resistance in their daily lives, [women] could more effectively participate in socially organized passive resistance and non-cooperation."[1] Another aspect of nonviolence which Gandhi believed that women optimally embodied was a dual impulse for "obedience and rebellion against authority" primarily within the family and (when mobilized by someone like Gandhi) against the colonial state. Gandhi himself assumed these "female" strengths of nonviolent resistance, and using his personal experience he evolved a political strategy to mobilize women for a nationalist agenda.

Gandhi's literal uses of women's bodies—after all, nearly half the population could not be left out of a nationalist struggle—were mediated throughout by his own personal history and his interpretations of female figures from Indian epics. Gandhi was a man of his time, one who both accepted and challenged certain prevailing notions of masculinity and femininity. Female sexuality was highly problematic for Gandhi himself. His experience of being married at age eleven, tormented by passions which he described as uncontrollable; his questioning of whether one could dedicate oneself to a nationalist cause and simultaneously live a passionate personal life; his vow of sexual abstinence at age thirty-seven—all of these "Gandhi-as-a-man" experiences colored his views on female sexuality. Hence, he could in the same breath acknowledge the privileges of male authority and wish somehow that male authority would become more just and humane towards women within the family. He did not recognize, as feminists do today, that unequal sexual relations within the home are sustained as much by power relations with the larger, patriarchal society as they are by economic systems.

It has often been noted that Gandhi lived his personal life most publicly. Further, as Madhu Kishwar has argued, Gandhi "is one of those few leaders whose practice was at times far ahead of his theory and his stated ideas." For instance, though he insisted on the sexual division of labor, on the home as the major sphere of activity for women, at the same time he "actively created conditions," continues Kishwar, "which could help women break the shackles of domesticity."[2] This, too, forms part of the contradictory Gandhian legacy that I will explore in more detail below.

GANDHI AND FEMALE SEXUALITY: INDIAN "TRADITION" AND MYTHOLOGY

Gandhi's symbolizing and mythologizing of female sexuality was in line with his assertion of an essentialized "national identity" based on symbols such as the "charkha" (spinning-wheel) and "khadi" (home-spun cloth). These national symbols were also strategically gendered through his evocation of mythological figures like Sita, Draupadi, and Savitri which embodied roles for women in the nationalist struggle. His representations of these figures deliberately dehistoricized them. The identification of Sita with Swadeshi (Sita only wore swadeshi, i.e. home-spun cloth) demonstrates how the female body and what it is clothed in can become a symbol for national liberation. Further, since it is "the mother's duty to look after children, to dress them," Gandhi commented, "it is necessary that women should be fired with the spirit of Swadeshi."[3]

Gandhi represented himself as "female," performing "feminine" roles like spinning. His own feminization in this type of political iconography—the image of the "Mahatma" sitting before the "charkha" patiently spinning "khadi"—was effective particularly in mobilizing women and men for satyagraha work. "Khadi" was specifically gendered in Gandhi's following words: "In spinning they [women] have a natural advantage over men . . . spinning is essentially a slow and comparatively silent process. Woman is the embodiment of sacrifice and non-violence."[4] A further contradiction is apparent in Gandhi's response to the charge that he was "wasting the energies of the nation by asking 'able-bodied men to sit for spinning like women'": "It is contrary to experience to say that any vocation is exclusively reserved for one sex only . . . Whilst women naturally cook for the household, organized cooking on a large scale is universally done by men throughout the world."[5]

The arena of female sexuality—fertility/infertility; motherhood; the sexual division of labor—is the site of certain "traditions" most oppressive for women. The key issue of the control of female sexuality has been legitimized, even effectively mystified, under the name of "tradition." Gandhi evoked "tradition" by ahistoricizing its tenets and mythological figures. When we analyze traditions historically and dialectically (focusing, say, on relationships between reproduction and production), we discover the often implicit violence in the many culturally legitimized ways of controlling women's bodies and minds. Gandhi's uses of female sexuality were channelled through his evocations of woman's obedience and nurturance as wife and mother, along with what Gandhi considered a wife's duty to defy her husband for national service. He did not recognize the limits of women's power within the family and the kinds of reprisals they must face for "disobedience."

The belief that women even more than men were the *guardians of tradition*, particularly against a foreign enemy, was used to reinforce the most regressive aspects of tradition. Particularly during nationalist movements, slogans such as "mother land" are glorified to counteract colonialist attitudes. The dangers of reifying "traditions," of treating them as the transcendent emblems of a culture, are felt most negatively by women particularly after Independence when the rationale of justifying tradition against the enemy is no longer needed.

Female sexuality was essentialized through Gandhi's appeals to the "female" virtues: chastity, purity, self-sacrifice, suffering. Gandhi's model for female strength was Draupadi, not the militant Rani of Jhansi who, "dressed like a man" and on horseback, led her troops in a battle against the British in 1857. Draupadi's is the more appropriate, feminine courage which, in the face of imminent dishonor, calls upon Lord Krishna for help. These "female" virtues were an "investment" in his nationalist, nonviolent strategy. "To me," Gandhi stated in 1921, "the female sex is not the weaker sex; it is the nobler of the two: for it is even today the embodiment of sacrifice, silent suffering, humility, faith and knowledge."[6]

The notion of female suffering in the Hindu tradition is dangerously glorified through such use of mythological models. The subconscious hold of socialization patterns inculcated in girls through the popular mythological stories of the ever-suffering Sita as virtuous wife, or the all-sacrificing Savitri who rescues her husband from death are all part of the preparation for suffering in the roles of wives and mothers. Further support for such ideological notions is embedded in popular cultural productions such as dance, drama, and in religious ritual. The dominant message is that of suffering as purifying, even inevitable for a woman.

Sexuality and spirituality were confounded through powerful mythological tales of Rama, of Krishna, where god and lover are merged and where woman's fertility is both feared and revered. But in this very mythologizing of female sexual power lies a deeply oppressive paradox. Male power and male sexuality are legitimate; female sexuality, understood as female power, must be controlled and bounded through social custom, primarily within marriage. Even goddesses were tamed, their power restrained when they were married to strong male gods. A useful analysis of how female power, beneficent and malevolent, has been portrayed in the figure of Kali is presented by Joanna Liddle and Rama Joshi. The myth provides a rationale for the control of female sexuality through men and through marriage:

> The concept of marriage, involving male control of female sexuality, is important for understanding how the mother goddess [in pre-Aryan India] was incorporated into the patriarchal brahmin religion. . . . The story of Kali—India's matriarchal myth—is that she was created to save the gods from their

> more powerful enemies, but having done so, she continued on a rampage of uncontrollable killing, which could only be stopped by her husband Shiva lying down in front of her. In her malevolent aspect she receives blood sacrifice. As Lakshmi she is benevolent, bestower of wealth, progeny and happiness, and passively devoted to her husband. In this aspect she never receives blood sacrifice. The goddess is Lakshmi when she is under the control of the male god. . . . As Susan Wadley suggests, it is marriage and the dominance of the male that transforms the goddess's dangerous power into benevolence.[7]

Ironically enough, the dimension in Hindu mythology that recognizes the spiritual in the physical, often regarding the body as the vehicle to reach spiritual heights (as in Yoga), has dangerous social connotations for women. When sexuality and spirituality merge, women are socialized into subsuming sexuality within a spiritual realm, leaving behind the realms of the physical, of desire, of pleasure.

The inherently contradictory quality of these representations of female sexuality are part of a cultural subconscious for the majority of the population. Gandhi skillfully tuned into these paradoxes—the spiritual in the physical—and evoked these powerful symbols for a nationalist agenda. Our contemporary analyses of Gandhi's views can reveal such contradictions when he stated, for instance, that not every girl is "born to marry." However, the symbols before her were those of ideal wives and mothers. And marriage was necessary only because it set boundaries on sexual activity. Mothering as perhaps the most venerated expression of female sexuality is permitted only within the parameters of Hindu marriage. Although unmarried women had more freedom in Gandhi's eyes than married women, that freedom was to be used for national service, not for personal pleasure. As with unmarried women, widows if they could lead a sexually abstinent life should not remarry but dedicate themselves to the nation's service.

Indeed, according to Gandhi, a woman could only be pure and noble if she renounced sex altogether. This problematic denial of female sexuality, equating sexual abstinence with nobility and service, seems like a projection of Gandhi's personal conflicts between sex and service, between personal passion and public work. As he himself had done, a woman who is "pure and noble" will make the necessary sacrifice—after all, woman's "nature" for Gandhi was supremely suited to sacrifice. Such an analysis could offer only unfair either/or choices to women: be a wife and a sexual being, or remain unmarried and sexually abstinent. Gandhi enjoined the educated woman to remain unmarried, and to abnegate her sexuality so that she could dedicate herself "to work with her rural sisters."

Despite Gandhi's pride in an ancient Indian heritage, when it came to gender issues one discovers subtle points of agreement between Gandhian and nineteenth-century British attitudes. Like other Indian social reformers, Gandhi reinforced British liberal and imperial policies since he did not challenge women's subordinate position in patriarchal family structures, and since he evoked Hindu scripture and mythological figures for political ends. Hence Gandhi's satyagraha movement was not perceived as a threat by either Indian or British patriarchy. Gandhi went further than his British counterparts in assuming "female" tasks like spinning and in validating female participation in a national struggle. Yet it is as if male thinkers, British and Indian, viewing their "woman questions" from different geographical vantage points, arrived at similar conclusions.[8] A Victorian concern with morality feared that women's honor would be unsafe outside the home. Home and hearth assumed an overdetermined reality that women needed both to protect and to be protected in. For Gandhi, that sanctity of the domestic sphere was never questioned or jeopardized in his harnessing of female energies for an anti-colonial struggle. Women were stepping out into a public world *only* for the nationalist cause; thereafter, they would return to their "separate sphere" within the home walls. This was somewhat different from English women leaving their homes to work in factories; their politicizations would have long-term effects and would shake, as Gandhi's agenda did not, unequal sexual arrangments both within the home and outside it. Although Gandhi's movement did give women a chance to participate in a public sphere and to build solidarity, they did not organize to transform and challenge the root of their oppressions within traditional family structures.[9]

Let me give two examples of Gandhi's insightful deployment of tradition for mobilizing women's bodies without upsetting domestic boundaries. In 1921, during one of the first noncooperation acts, he urged women to spin khadi at home, an activity "complementing their household role" and giving them "a sense of mission." This "private" activity was brought in line with the public, economic benefits of khadi to the Indian economy. Such a contribution did not challenge the material or sexual power relations within society. Khadi itself took on an overdetermined reality as embodying "the spirit of nationalism and freedom," as providing a means of livelihood (though unrealistic in competition with textile mills), and (as already pointed out) as specifically gendered.

A significant watershed in women's involvement outside the home was the salt satyagraha—the defiance of British law against salt manufacture. Thousands of women from all classes participated, led by Kasturba (Gandhi's wife), Sarojini Naidu, Kamaladevi Chattopadhyaya and others. In her essay on Gandhi, Kishwar notes that although several women urged Gandhi to let them join him on the famous Dandi march, he refused. The women recognized that they did not wish to duplicate in the public movement the supportive, nurturant role that they played in the home. Vast numbers of women broke the salt laws. As

Kamaladevi Chattopadhyaya recalled, "Thousands of women strode down to the sea like proud warriors. . . . How had they broken their age-old shell of social seclusion and burst into this fierce light of open warfare?"[10] Gandhi had judged that these women were more suited to picket liquor stores and foreign cloth stores. An eye-witness account by Mary Campbell in *The Manchester Guardian* of June 1931 recreates the women's courage vividly:

> I was in Delhi when Mr. Gandhi, on his way back to jail, sent word—"I leave the work of picketing the drink and drug shops to the women of India." I thought he had made a mistake this time, that the Delhi women, so many of whom lived in purdah, could never undertake the task. But to my astonishment out they came, and they picketed all the shops in Delhi, sixteen or seventeen in number. I watched them day after day. They stood there saying nothing but politely salaaming each customer who approached. The same thing happened repeatedly. The man would stop saying: "I beg your pardon sister; I forgot myself in coming here" and went away. That went on for some days until the licencees appealed to the government. The hefty policemen arrived with police vans and warned the women to go away. I thought those delicate sheltered women would give in now; they would never endure being touched by a policeman. But they did, and as fast as one relay was arrested, another took its place. Altogether about sixteen hundred women were imprisoned in Delhi alone. But they had done their work. Though the shops were opened no one went in . . . At last the licencees themselves closed them, and so far as I can hear they are still closed today.[11]

THE GANDHIAN LEGACY FOR INDIAN WOMEN'S MOVEMENTS

Gandhi's legacy for women's movements in India today is a complex, fascinating and debatable area. Certain feminist gains are specifically attributable to Gandhi in his success at involving vast numbers of women in the satyagraha movement. But we need to both acknowledge and problematize the gains and losses of Gandhi's strategies, particularly for contemporary Indian women. The positive legacies of a nonviolent ideology—passive resistance, mass demonstration, appeal to the moral aspects of wrong-doers—are currently used to protest against dowry murderers. The tactic of public humiliation when women "gherao" (surround) the residences of dowry-related murderers is effective in a culture where it still matters what one's neighbors think of one's private conduct.[12]

In terms of women's formal participation in government, the Gandhian influence set "a trend," as Kishwar remarks, "for sponsored, patronised participation of urban, middle class women in the political life of the country."[13] Even today, leadership in women's movements comes from middle-class women.[14] However, at the height of the male-dominated civil disobedience movement, almost all classes of women participated. This tradition of a kind of male patronage was itself an integral part of the Gandhian legacy. As Surest Renjen Bald states,

> In India the leadership of the "women's movement" and the definition of the "women's question" initially came from Western-educated, urban, upper class/caste *men* whose primary concern was to build a strong "modern" India fit for self-government. The "women's question" became defined within the context of the changing goals and strategies of the emerging Indian nation, and the women's movement became an appendage of the nationalist movement. Political independence, therefore, also marked the paternalistic "granting" of gender equality in the Constitution. The patriarchal social system that had remained untouched by the women's movement, however, continued to demand and expect gender hierarchy, thus negating the legal equality embodied in the Constitution.[15]

Given this type of political initiation, the women's movement in India is faced today with a central contradiction, namely a discrepancy between progressive laws and assurances of equality inscribed in the Constitution, along with a sociocultural environment that, in Bald's words, "systematically denies women such equality in society, the family, and the workplace."

In a strategic reversal of the "personal is the political," Gandhi astutely brought the political struggle for freedom right into women's personal lives, extending women's roles from service in the home to service for the nation (initially, from within the home, and later, on the streets). In his nonviolent philosophy, Gandhi interpreted some personal aspects of tradition—e.g., the Indian woman's submissiveness, her ability to suffer silently—as embodying the potential for political resistance necessary for a nationalist struggle. However, one critique of a nonviolent ideology is that it can effectively mask the violence in certain religious and cultural traditions (for instance, Hindu-Muslim conflicts), or the practice of dowry which validates the inferior status of woman-as-property. Such violent configurations were temporarily repressed thanks both to struggle against a foreign enemy and to Gandhi's charismatic personality. In India, the dominance of Hindu religion and ideology was not dealt with, as it needed to be, within Gandhi's mass-based movement which effectively obscured the economic bases underlying religious rivalries. In postcolonial India we find manifestations of a brand of Hindu fundamentalism that is particularly destructive for women—the resurgence, for instance, of practices such as *sati*, or of the most regressive aspects of female subordination as depicted in the vastly popular television rendition of the Indian epic, *The Ramayan.*[16]

Participation in the satyagraha movement certainly gave women a sense of power, but it was a localized power—for a particular historic struggle for independence. Women's public involvement in satyagraha enabled them "to rid themselves," as Nehru put it, "of domestic slavery." But we cannot equate this participation with a transformative politicization that might have resulted in the radical overcoming of women's subordination within the family. Gandhi went as far as "extending" women's roles as wives and mothers, but not in making interventions in patriarchal order or political power. If social customs were challenged at all, they were "in the cause of Swaraj"; and after Swaraj, the gains could easily be repealed. The contradictions in Gandhi's strategies of mobilizing women, the points of convergence and divergence between national liberation and sexual liberation were mystified through typically nationalist appeals—colonialism as the common enemy, and women's "personal" issues as secondary to the national cause. As in other liberation movements, women's roles remained largely supportive rather than central—Gandhi thanked, for example, "the many heroines whose mute work the nation will never know."[17] "Women were lauded as good *satyagrahis* (nonviolent activists), but the real issues that concerned them as women," remarks Jayawardena, "were regarded by the men as of secondary importance."[18]

It is instructive to glance at women's rights movements in the West to consider whether these movements aided or hindered the struggle for women's rights in India. According to Liddle and Joshi, for example, Katherine Mayo's controversial book *Mother India* (1927) "attributed India's subjugation and slave-mentality to the organization of sexuality, and suggested that the abuse of women by Indian men was to blame for India's plight."[19] However, the subordinate position of Indian women is a complex matter and not one solely dictated by male dominance. Liddle and Joshi point out in their discussion of Mayo that the women's movement in India did recognize points of convergence as well as difference between an anti-colonial struggle and a struggle for women's equality, between sexist and imperialist dominations. But Mayo's orientalizing approach focused solely on the most dramatically visible forms of abuse—child marriage, female infanticide, *sati*—heaped upon Indian women by Indian men. She did not discuss at all the colonizer's role in women's oppression. Mayo's book has been certainly influential, and extends even to a recent writer like Mary Daly who describes Mayo's work as "exceptional." As Liddle and Joshi argue, however, neither Mayo nor Daly seem themselves to have had any knowledge of the women's movement in India. Daly discusses male atrocities against women, but she, like Mayo, "does not address the impact on Indian women of British colonialism."[20] It is as if the abuses suffered by Indian women belong in some essentialized, biologistic realm, free of the impact of imperialist and neocolonial forces.

As we dig deeper into our own history, as we discover our own feminist traditions and the contributions of women who have been "hidden from history," we balance our views of the origins of women's struggles in India. While acknowledging Gandhi's success in mobilizing women, we also recognize the significant work of women themselves in the nationalist movement, and the continuing struggles undertaken by Indian women's movements today.[21]

NOTES

1. Kumari Jayawardena, *Feminism and Nationalism in the Third World* (London: Zed Press, 1986), p. 97.

2. Madhu Kishwar, "Gandhi on Women," *Economic and Political Weekly*, 20, 40 (October 5, 1985), p. 1694.

3. Gandhi, *Collected Works* (Ahmedabad: Navajivan Trust, 1982), Vol. XV, p. 291 (Speech at a Women's Meeting, Bombay, May 8, 1919).

4. *Harijan*, December 2, 1931; also in *Collected Works*, LXX, p. 381.

5. *Young India*, June 11, 1925; also in *Collected Works*, XXVII, pp. 219–20.

6. Quoted in Jayawardena, *Feminism and Nationalism*, p. 95.

7. Joanna Liddle and Rama Joshi, eds., *Daughters of Independence: Gender, Caste and Class in India* (London: Zed Press, 1986), pp. 54–55.

8. John Stuart Mill's "The Subjection of Women" (written in 1860 after the death of his wife Harriet Taylor, to whom he attributed many of his ideas) argued, for example, that education and changes in the law would ensure equality between the sexes though each would continue to retain its own "separate sphere" ("The Subjection of Women," in John M. Robson, ed., *Collected Works of John Stuart Mill* [Toronto: University of Toronto Press, 1984], Vol. XXI, pp. 261–340). Mill's views echo those of Gandhi and of nineteenth-century Indian reformers such as Dayananda Saraswati and Sarojini Naidu, whose campaigns for women's education and suffrage were related integrally to the doctrine of "separate spheres."

9. For more on continuities between Gandhian and Victorian ideologies of womanhood, see Sudesh Vaid, "Ideologies on Women in Nineteenth Century Britain, 1850s–70s," *Economic and Political Weekly*, 20, 43 (October 26, 1985), pp. WS 63–67.

Recent revisions of history from the Indian point of view underscore how British liberalism took gender inequality as it existed in Indian culture as both a mark of Indian inferiority and a proof of British superiority. In their essay "Gender and Imperialism in British India" (*Economic and Political Weekly*, 20, 43 [October 26, 1985], pp. WS 72–78), Joanna Liddle and Rama Joshi discuss how the British used gender issues to portray themselves as the liberators of Indian women from barbaric customs like *sati*. Lata Mani's widely cited essay, "Contentious Traditions: The Debate on *Sati* in Colonial India" (in Kumkum Sangari and Sudesh Vaid, eds., *Recasting Women: Essays in Colonial History* [New Delhi: Kali for Women, 1989; rpt. New Brunswick, NJ: Rutgers University Press, 1990]), usefully argues that women were merely the *ground* on which debates about social custom took place.

10. Quoted in Jayawardena, *Feminism and Nationalism*, p. 99.

11. Liddle and Joshi, "Gender and Imperialism in British India," p. WS 76.

12. Despite the Prohibition of Dowry Act (1961), this "tradition" continues with gruesome abuses in recent years. Short news items like the following are common: "Woman burnt to death. A case of suicide has been registered. The police are enquiring into the matter." A growing number of incidents relate how a husband's family, dissatisfied with the amount of dowry brought by the wife, decide to murder her. A "kitchen fire" is staged and the murder is passed off as suicide. The husband is then "free" to remarry and acquire more dowry. Women's groups have mobilized nonviolent demonstrations and insisted that these cases be brought to trial. For more information see Madhu Kishwar and Ruth Vanita, eds., *In Search of Answers: Indian Women's Voices from Manushi* (London: Zed Press, 1984).

13. Kishwar, "Gandhi on Women," p. 1700.

14. A tradition different from middle-class women's participation in government is that of militancy among working-class women. See Gail Omvedt, *We Will Smash This Prison: Indian Women in Struggle* (London: Zed books, 1980).

15. Suresht Renjen Bald, "From Satyartha Prakash to Manushi: An Overview of the Women's Movement in India," *University of Michigan Working Paper*, 23 (April 1983), p. 18.

16. Most recently, since November 1990, the Ayodhya controversy has led to

bloody Hindu-Muslim riots and hundreds of deaths. A fundamentalist Hindu claim asserts a right to build a Hindu temple to Rama at exactly the site where a mosque now stands. One can hardly imagine a more inflammatory demand. As presented at "The Fourth National Conference of Women's Movement(s) in India" (December 27–31, 1990, held in Calicut, Kerala), women and children suffer most severely in these communal riots where religion effectively mystifies political agendas. Several women's groups such as "Jagruti" (Delhi) and "Women's Voice" (Bangalore) have focused their activities around issues of communalism and religious fundamentalism as among the most urgent matters facing women in India right now.

17. *Young India,* May 21, 1931; also in *Collected Works,* XLVI, p. 189.

18. Jawardena, *Feminism and Nationalism,* p. 99.

19. Liddle and Joshi, "Gender and Imperialism," p. WS 72.

20. Ibid., pp. WS 72–73. See Daly's *Gyn/Ecology* (London: The Women's Press, 1978).

21. The Indian women's movement today embraces various women's groups from all over the country, urban and rural, and is a multifaceted, multi-issued reality. The movement, in general, is activist in orientation. At "The Fourth National Conference of Women's Movement(s) in India" (see note 16 above), some 200 different women's groups participated. Nearly 1,800 women from all over India attended, and ten different languages were represented. "Sabala Mahila Sangh" (resettlement "bastis", i.e., communities in and outside Delhi); "Chingari"; "Sewa" (Ahmedabad); "Sahiyar: A Women's Organisation" (Vadodara); "Sarvadana Sangam: Tamil Nadu Women's Movement" (Tiruvannamalai); "Sasvika" (Ajmer); "Stree Jagruti Samiti" (Bangalore)—these were some of the many groups represented at the Conference. Urban-based groups like The Forum Against the Oppressions of Women, The Lawyer's Collective, and Bombay Union of Journalists (Women and Media Committee) deal with issues of rape, inheritance laws, and pornographic publications. These groups publish consciousness-raising pamphlets as and when appropriate. The women's movement also encompasses feminist presses like Kali for Women (Delhi), which has published such significant texts as *Recasting Women* and *Structures of Patriarchy,* among others. Feminist magazines like *Manushi: A Journal of Women and Society* (in English and Hindi), and *Stree Sangarsh* (English) provide a forum for written expression and activist organizing.

Chapter 22

Telling Spaces: Palestinian Women and the Engendering of National Narratives

Mary Layoun

Communities are to be distinguished, not by their falsity/genuineness, but by the style in which they are imagined.

—Benedict Anderson, *Imagined Communities*

. . . we become partners in the common struggle, and not onlookers or mere passive observers. Thus will the inside and outside become one.

—Edward Said, "Intifada and Independence"

We render special tribute to the brave Palestinian woman, guardian of sustenance and life, keeper of our people's perennial flame.

—Palestinian Declaration of Independence (November 15, 1988)

NARRATING INSIDE(S) AND OUTSIDE(S)

The signposts "inside" and "outside" resolutely mark the terrain of Edward Said's "Intifada and Independence,"[1] especially in its conclusion where the essay reaches towards another space and time—or, more properly, towards another time on the same space differently mapped—where the inside and outside can "become one." Very similar signposts mark the "Palestinian Declaration of Independence" and the "Political Communiqué" of the Palestine National Council issued on the 11th of November, 1988.[2] For the latter two documents, the "inside" and "outside" are, most apparently, the space(s) of the Palestinian people "inside" the boundaries of historic Palestine—perhaps especially within the Occupied Territories—and the spaces "outside" of those boundaries for Palestinians in the diaspora. The Palestinian Declaration of Independence, though, necessarily iterates and reiterates a "becoming one" that is postulated as virtually always already in existence. It opens by citing a past of "integral bonds," "everlasting union," and "undying connection" of the Palestinian Arab people with the land of Palestine. This relation is, clearly, both "naturally"—the reference is to being born in Palestine—and historically prior to either the forced construction of "inside" and "outside" or the declaration of independence and statehood itself. The Palestinian Declaration of Independence contrasts an ancient unity of the people and the land of Palestine with a more recent past of denial, injustice, and rupture not only of a people from their land but of a people from their "national life" and "rights." To this account of the natural and historical rights of the Palestinian people are added the legal rights of "self-determination," "sovereignty," and "independence." It is these rights, their subsequent violation, and the resistance of the Palestinian people to their violation that forged the "political embodiment" of the national will in the Palestine Liberation Organization (PLO). This, then, is the framework within which, citing also the crucial impetus of the intifada, the Palestine National Council (PNC), as the executive branch of the PLO, proclaims the independence of the new state of Palestine. The inside and outside are one: "The State of Palestine is the state of Palestinians wherever they are." With this proclamation a new inside is constituted: "The state is for them to enjoy *in it* their collective national and cultural identity, theirs to pursue *in it* a complete equality of rights. *In it* will be safeguarded . . ." (emphasis added). Subsequent to the delineation of this new inside, relations with an outside are referred to—with the Arab world, the League of Arab States, the United Nations, the Non-Aligned Movement, with "all peace-loving states." And in conclusion, the Declaration of Independence salutes the sources of its strength (and its narrative power)—those who have died in the struggle for an independent Palestinian state, those engaged in the intifada, those living in the camps, in exile, in prison, the children, elders, youth. In this context is situated the tribute to the "brave Palestinian woman" quoted as an epigraph above. Interestingly, that praiseworthy tribute to what is in fact the incredible steadfastness and struggle of Palestinian women suggests their position as "guardian" and "keeper" precisely of an "inside" and, arguably perhaps, *from* an "inside"—"of sustenance and life," "of our people's perennial flame."

In contrast, the Political Communiqué of the PNC opens, not with a moment and space prior to the forced construction of an "inside" and an "outside," but precisely in that rift of inside and out. In fact, the past and present of "inside" and "outside" that dominate the first half of the Political Communiqué are in implicit opposition to the second half which offers resolutions and affirmations for a future of specific action. The Political Communiqué, in greater detail and with much more pointed specificity than the Declaration of Independence, calls for renewed and vigorous support from the "inside" and the "outside" for the intifada and reiterates the commitment of the PNC for a "comprehensive settlement of the Arab-Israeli conflict." Toward that end, the Political Communiqué specifies in some detail its relations with a particular "outside"—Israel. The Declaration of Independence mentions this "outside" by name only once—in the phrase "Israel's occupation." It signals that "outside" a second time with the reference to UN resolution 181 that partitioned historic Palestine into two states—one Arab and one Jewish. And, crucially, the Palestinian Declaration of Independence, while including this recognition of the State of Israel in its constitutive text, asserts its own right to statehood based on the same UN resolution. That international document which partitioned Palestine is, equally, the document which legitimates the Palestinian claim to statehood. But the acceptance by the PLO and PNC of UN resolutions 242, 338, 605, 607, and 608 occurs in the context of the Political Communiqué's greater specificity. So too does "the rejection of terrorism in all its forms, including state terrorism," with reference again to specific UN resolutions 42/195 and 40/61. The Political Communiqué then addresses itself to other "outsides"—to relations with Jordan and Lebanon and their peoples—including the thousands of Palestinians living in those countries; it affirms its support for the Iran-Iraq cease fire, for solidarity in the Arab world, for national liberation movements in South Africa and Namibia and throughout the world, and for the struggles of the Israeli peace forces against Israeli extremists. In closing, the PNC Political Communiqué calls on the American people to "strive to put an end to the American policy that denies the Palestinian people's national rights." The "outside" here is clearly not only that of the Palestinian diaspora. And if the "outside" of the Political Communiqué is variously defined, the same is true of the "inside." Certainly the declaration and reality of an independent Palestinian state is the indisputable foundation of the Political Communiqué. But such a state seems to be far more complex in its topography than one in which Palestinians of the "inside" and the "outside" could all be located "inside."

Something like this notion is suggested in the closing lines of Edward Said's eloquent essay. For there, the "inside and outside become one" not necessarily by an ingathering of the same people in the same space and at the same time. Rather, it is the attempt to participate in a "common struggle"—wherever that participation might take place—that reconstitutes the inside and outside as one. That "one" is then by definition collectively maintained and constantly renegotiated from many positions. It is generated precisely in the attempt to negotiate inside and out, in the attempt to link or (momentarily) cross over from one to another. Said remarks these multiple issues or spaces in testifying simultaneously to the brutality and violence of the Israeli military against the Palestinian population, to the active support of the U.S. government for that brutality and the myopic complicity of the Western media, as well as to the losses and suffering and the resistance and determination of the Palestinian people under occupation. His conclusion thus addresses at once the U.S. government and the people of the U.S., whose support and sympathies do not necessarily lie where the government assigns them; the political goals and the "moral and cultural detail" of the Palestinian cause; and "the suffering and the greatness of the Palestinians under Israeli occupation." Clearly, there is more than a single "inside" and single "outside" operative here. The literal "inside" of the Occupied Territories and the "outside" of the diaspora are implicitly far more complex, far more mediated, than geographical boundaries and the spaces they enclose can accommodate. To "become partners in the common struggle, and not onlookers or mere passive observers" predicates a notion of partnership on an "inside" that is neither spatially nor temporally singular or exclusive. That "common struggle," the becoming "one" of inside and outside, could not be sustained on the terms of Said's "Intifada and Independence" simply by drawing lines or building walls. Similarly, both the Palestinian Declaration of Independence and the Political Communiqué are constructed as much on the recognition of the tremendous figurative *and* literal power of a Palestinian state as on the reality of "Palestinians wherever they may be." In that phrase, as in Said's essay as a whole, the spaces of "inside" and "outside" are postulated as complex and multivalent, as differentially "occupied" in their essence and extension.[3]

NARRATING NATIONALISM: OR, WHOSE STORY IS THIS ANYWAY?

Nationalism, for a given time and specific space, constructs and profers a narrative of the "nation" and of its relation to an already existing or potential state. Nationalism lays claim to a privileged narrative perspective on the nation (the "people") and thus justifies its own capacity to narrate its story. From this third-person and often implicitly omniscient perspective, the national narrative seeks to construct its history or to posit a narrative past (usually as continuous and uninterrupted) in an assertion of legitimacy and precedent for the practices of the narrative present. And this narrative of nationalism postulates a narrative future or constructs a telos, presumably one deriving from the structure and content of the narrative—and the nation—itself.

Nationalism, then, is constructed as a narrative. It tells a story by articulating (presumably) linked elements. Not by chance, it also constructs and privileges its own narrative perspective. Narratives of nationalism propose a *grammar* of the nation—the "correct" or orderly use and placement of the constituent elements of the nation. The grammar (or *grammatiki*) of a nation—suggesting *gramme* or line as well as *gramma* or written letter—prescribes, not least of all, the proper and acceptable situation and use of language.

But nationalism also necessarily articulates a rhetoric of the nation. The rhetoric of nationalism-as-narrative persuades and convinces its audience(s)—its implied readers and listeners—of the efficacy and desirability of its terms and of the "natural" relationship between those terms. Its appeal derives not just from the letter and word of truth and order (as "grammar"), but *with* letters and words in the sense of persuasion and likely possibility (as rhetoric). It is from the differences or gaps or contradictions between the grammar of the national narrative and the rhetoric of that same narrative that a certain flexibility or fluidity may be discerned or produced, a momentary space not just for being spoken by the national narrative but, simultaneously, for speaking it—perhaps even differently.

Some more concretely specific sense of this maneuver in the gap between grammatical place and persuasive possibility is suggested by the term frequently used in the last few years by "traditional" Palestinian women to describe their participation in street demonstrations, in confrontations with Israeli soldiers, in organizing and participating in the popular committees of their neighborhoods—"national work" (*'amal al-watani*).[4] The "proper place"—the grammatical position in the narrative—for Palestinian women (and children) is, or at least was, presumably not in the streets confronting soldiers, throwing stones, or staging demonstrations. Their place had been "inside" the home as the nurturing sustainers of life, children, and so forth. But as the oppression in the Territories has become more extreme; as the presumably unassailable "inside" of home increasingly has become the setting for confrontation and for collective punishment exacted by the Israeli military; as the male figures—fathers, sons, husbands, or brothers—who arguably served to mediate the confrontation between home (the "inside") and occupier ("outside") are imprisoned, exiled, killed, or beaten, the problematic vulnerability of the "inside"/home has become apparent.

The "inside" of the home is forcefully revealed to be a privileged construct, every bit as assailable as the "outside" of the streets. And "work" in those streets is now being cast by "women workers," on the one hand, as precisely *national* and, on the other, as a "logical" extension of their narrative positions as nurturers and sustainers of life.[5]

Where Palestinian men, at least initially, were the most direct objects of Israeli reprisals, Palestinian women and children were depicted accordingly—in what is perhaps a "coincidence of interest" between patriarchy and colonialism—as defenseless and passive witnesses or victims. Their place was or is on the "inside," protected by others. Still, in recent years, for Palestinians living in the Occupied Territories especially, it is precisely over that boundary of both patriarchal society and colonial oppression that women and children and men have organized and acted. The grim sight then of a young 12 or 13 year-old boy in Gaza cornered by Israeli soldiers for throwing stones who, realizing that escape is impossible stops running, turns and bares his chest, daring the soldiers to shoot him—and the soldiers obligingly respond with five bullets to his chest[6]—has a certain fearful and tragic "logic." It is one of the outcomes of breaking down the boundaries of old narrative patterns and spaces . . . like the old women who emerge suddenly from a courtyard, encircling the young son of one of their neighbors in an attempt to fend off with pots, insults, and shouting the Israeli soldiers who have come to arrest the boy as a suspected stone-thrower. Their direct and virtually spontaneously agreed upon confrontation with the military, their bruises, broken bones, and missing teeth bear witness to the at least momentary fluidity of their assigned narrative spaces as well as to the quite literal costs of redefining or crossing over into new ones. If the "inside" has elided into the "outside" in such instances, if "home" has become the village streets or camp square, these definitions of inside and outside, of interior/home and exterior/street confrontation have, at least for the moment, shifted. Edward Said, in the essay from which I've quoted, suggests that "perhaps it would be more accurate to say that because of the *intifada*, the role of men was altered from being dominant to being equal."[7] To say this is perhaps inevitably to invoke images of the reconfigurations of national narratives in other instances—Algeria or Sudan, for example—in which women have emerged from the "interior" to which they had been consigned only to "return" in some degree once again.[8] This would appear to be a veritable obsession in certain sweeping discussions of the "Arab" or "Muslim" woman. Still, the possibility of such a potential "strategy of containment" or narrative closure seems relatively clear to women in the Territories. Many express their hope that the momentum of the last 10 to 12 years of grass-roots organizing and of what is now almost three years of the uprising will be maintained "afterwards." Others fear precisely what that continuing momentum might mean for them. Both the desire and the fear attest to the fact that women have organized, participated in, and subtly shaped the "style" in which the Palestinian community conceives of and organizes itself now—even while refusing to defer totally the concerns and organization of women until some future moment.

The proposition of nationalism-as-narrative suggests that we can bring to bear on narratives of nationalism the critical and theoretical insights of analyses of literary narratives with their considerations of narrative voice, time, and space, of emplotment, of closure and strategies of containment. We would do well from this perspective to pay attention to the "narrative voice(s)" who speak these stories, their constructions of time and space, and their postulations of narrative telos. But there are other implications that follow on this recognition of the specific narrative construction of nationalism. If nationalism is articulated as a narrative of the nation and its potential or actual relation to a state, this narrative can be also—within and without its official boundaries—profoundly conflictual in its constructions of narrators, narratees, and narrative characters.

This is not, strictly speaking, solely a "textual" concern: narratives are not only spoken or written but acted out as well.[9] They are internally and externally conflictual whatever their medium. There are no foregone and conclusive master narratives though there are, clearly, dominant or hegemonic narratives (which are, often enough, those *of* the "master"). Internally, narratives (attempt to) contain their constituent elements— actors, actions, story past and present, narrative present, narrative space—within an "orderly" and "naturally" self-justifying framework. But they are also spoken or written or played out from multiple perspectives, not all of which are equal,[10] or equally convincing. Nor do those perspectives account equally for the same array of narrative "facts." Yet, in this context of contestation, I would like to suggest that, in some instances, the very conflict of narrative perspectives, "truths," times, or spaces can undermine and perhaps even alter, or at least prefigure the alteration of, the dominant order of the narrative itself.

My point here is that these analytical and epistemological issues concerning narrative are hardly at odds with practice and agency in the world. I understand the latter not only in terms of the broad screen of historic events but also as the everyday practices of peasants or laborers, of refugees or rural women. For the everyday struggles and choices of ordinary folk, their attempts to come to terms with and sometimes to change the shape of a dominant narrative have too often been minimized by critical consideration. And yet they too—and not just the states or leaders who speak in their names—engage in both theorizing about and acting in the narrative(s) of the nation. While this process should neither be effaced from consideration nor, conversely, treated with nostalgia and overvalorized, there are moments when this everyday experience of parts of the nation/people truly confounds the dominant definition of the national narrative and, sometimes, offers more pragmatic and flexible alternatives to dominant national constructions.

The articulation of these alternatives is based on what I would like provisionally to call narrative (practical) and also narratological (theoretical) competence.[11] The workings of narrative *and* narratological competence are learned, socially shaped, and always partial; they are interjected, articulated, and acted out or practiced in various ways. The competence in question is not simply chosen and "performed" individually from an unlimited array of possibilities but is discursively and practically constructed—and theorized—in speaking, thinking, and acting. Participation in and opposition to established and dominant narratives thus can be considered particular strategies of narrative performance based on both practical and theoretical competences. And it is a story we suspect or know to be lopsided, incomplete, or fictitious that, often as not, forms the basis for an alternative performance which need not postulate the existence of some transcendentally integral narrative or narrator.[12]

NARRATING PALESTINIAN WOMEN: WHO SPEAKS, WHO LISTENS, WHO'S NARRATED?

As a preface to the fiction of the Palestinian novelist and short story writer Sahar Khalifeh as it participates in its own narrative construction of "inside" and "outside," I would like briefly to reiterate some of the nonfictional contexts in which the roles played by Palestinian women in the Occupied Territories are situated. What follows is scarcely a historical account of the Israeli seizure of the Occupied Territories and the character of the military rule that governs the Palestinian population there.[13] But since the everyday realities of occupation are not those most of us live with, it is perhaps too easy to overlook that context. For it is precisely in that context—and not in some imaginary or ideal "outside" terrain—that the "narrative strategies" of Palestinian women stand out most clearly.

So, a brief contextual interjection. Approximately 40% of all Palestinians (ca. 2,000,000) live in historic Palestine: 645,000 in Israel, 938,000 in the West Bank, and 525,000 in Gaza. The Occupied Territories, along with the Golan Heights and the Sinai, were seized by Israel during the 1967 War. Since then the Golan Heights has been annexed; most of the Sinai was returned to Egypt; the West Bank and Gaza Strip remain under Israeli military rule. Since 1967 over 52% of the West Bank and 34% of the Gaza Strip have been confiscated by Israel for military use or settlement by Jewish citizens. The Palestinian population of the Territories, some 1,500,000 people, is increasingly circumscribed both literally and metaphorically into the towns, villages, and refugee camps that remain. If their geographical space has been continually delimited, so too is their movement and growth in every sense of the word. Virtually everything requires a permit from the Occupation authorities—digging a well, enlarging a house or apartment, repairing a damaged home, planting an olive tree or a new tomato crop, opening a day-care center or a health clinic, leaving the Territories, reentering the Territories, bringing money into the Territories, bringing books into the Territories, opening a small shop or factory, marketing produce, altering or augmenting college course offerings, conducting a marriage[14] or funeral ceremony. There are more than 1,500 military regulations governing the daily lives of Palestinians in the Occupied Territories. In addition, there are arbitrary invocations of regulations and restrictions that date back to the British mandate in Palestine. These conditions are not an Israeli response to the intifada; they began with the 1967 Israeli occupation of the West Bank and Gaza. The measures used by the Israeli military in an attempt to suppress the intifada are yet more severe.

Living conditions, even before the intifada, and especially in the refugee camps and some villages, and most particularly in the Gaza Strip, were little short of desperate. For example, the average floor space per person of United Nations-built refugee housing in Gaza is 27 to 35 square feet; the American Correctional Association's recommended floor space per prisoner in the United States is 60 square feet. The infant mortality rate per 1,000 in Gaza is 38.5; in the West Bank, 27.1; for Israeli Arabs, 21.0; for Israeli Jews, 11.6.

Increasingly since 1967, the Palestinians of the Territories have become a cheap labor pool for Israeli factories and industries. And for a number of reasons—including the deportations, beatings, and imprisonment of male heads of households and wage-earners—the percentage of women in this migrant labor force has grown from less than 10% to almost 25% (largely in the last 10 or 12 years). The strictures attached to the mobility of women, more apparent in the villages and camps, but distinct in the towns as well, have of necessity eroded. Not only, then, have women entered the (Israeli) work force but they have also been forced to confront directly—rather than through their husbands, fathers, brothers, or sons—the triple oppression to which they are subject as women, as Palestinians, and as workers. An example of discrimination in the latter category: from 1970 to 1988, deductions from the paychecks of Palestinians from the Territories who work in Israel were $800,000,000; social security benefits paid out to Palestinian workers from those deductions totalled $0. The increasing proletarianization of Palestinian women and men had, before the intifada, created an important expanding market for Israeli products. The average annual net Israeli income (over expenses) in the Occupied Territories is $50,000,000; the annual Israeli expenditure on Palestinians per person in the

Territories is $185. (For purposes of comparison, the annual Israeli expenditure on Israeli citizens per person is $1,350.)[15]

It is not difficult, then, to locate the bases for the tactics and strategies, the counternarrative of the intifada[16]—the selective boycotts of Israeli goods, the refusal to pay taxes to the Israeli government, the work stoppages and limited strikes, the organization and expansion of popular and neighborhood committees[17] to encourage and coordinate more self-sufficient social, political, and economic life in the Territories, the demonstrations in defiance of Israeli injunctions against public gatherings, funerals, and so forth.

In this configuration, both from within the narrative of Palestinian nationalism and as that narrative confronts other conflicting narratives, the active participation (the narrative "performance") of Palestinian women in and their theorizing ("narratological" premises and strategies) of nationalism engenders in particular ways the narrative of Palestinian nationalism. In and against this context Sahar Khalifeh has written two of her more recent novels—*al-Subbar* or *The Cactus*[18] and *'Abad al-shams* or *The Sunflower*[19] (literally, sun-worshipper). In spite of the fact that the former is frequently referred to as Khalifeh's "pre-feminist" work, the narrative construction of *The Cactus* suggests at certain points the contradictions in and of the national narrative even as it attempts to reiterate that very story.

The narrative perspective of *The Cactus* is that of a not-quite omniscient third person whose external account of the novel's characters slips into almost lyric reveries of their inner thoughts or, conversely, into those of the narrator herself. The novel thus "vacillates" between "interior" and "exterior" narration, between an account of a narrative actor from the outside and the revealing of his or her thoughts (or those of the narrator) from within—without any clear grammatical markers of this "slippage."

This narrative slippage is apparent from the opening pages of the book as one of its multiple central characters, Osama, returns via Jordan to his home in Nablus in the West Bank. As Osama rides in a taxi across the Jordan valley, the taxi-driver switches the radio from station to station coming across the Arabic language Israel Broadcasting Service from Jerusalem. The subsequent exchange between them:

—They even speak Arabic, the bastards, as if they were born to it.
—They *were* born to it.

is followed by a third person narration of the silence that ensues and by a description of the scene from the taxi window, presumably from Osama's point of view: he watches "the sun's rays spreading out over the dark hillsides." This scene, however, is then compared to the "stretch marks on women's bellies after they've given birth." The landscape, in a disturbing if familiar enough gesture in the Palestinian context, is metaphorized as a woman's fertile body. But from whom could this observation in particular—of a countryside like a woman's belly after giving birth—come? From the young unmarried man, Osama? This seems unlikely. This is far more likely to be the observation of an (implicitly female) narrator than of Osama. But whatever the source of this simile, the reference that precedes the trope of Palestine-as-woman does not concern Palestinians at all but rather *Israelis* who "speak Arabic as if they were born to it." There is an implicit confounding of ethnic, national, and linguistic boundaries here, however momentary, between Palestinians born from the woman's body as landscape into the Arabic language and Israelis born (from the same woman's body as landscape?) into Arabic as well. It is a confounding of boundaries that is iterated and reiterated throughout the novel. This complex construct of "birthright," language, and identity becomes far more loaded in the context of the virtually explicit suggestion by the novel's Arabic title of the Israeli term "sabra"—an Israeli born in Israel. The Israeli word "sabra" coincides in sound and meaning with the novel's title in Arabic, "subbar"—the "stubborn" and steadfast cactus, the prickly pear full of thorns on the outside but sweet on the inside, a plant "natural," "indigenous," to the land of Palestine/Israel.[20] Here, then, surely notions of the "inside" and "outside" are confounded; a powerfully suggestive crossing over is at work.[21] For if the Palestinian characters of Khalifeh's novel are "subbar," so, at least by extension (or powerful slippage), are the Israelis. The boundaries of "inside" and "outside" and the residents of those spaces are simultaneously (apparently) rigidly designated *and* constantly moving—at least more frequently than exclusionary linguistic, cultural, or national borders might seem to allow. But on what terms, how, and with benefit accruing to whom—with what "style" as Benedict Anderson so aptly puts it—are these boundaries erected and crossed?

But whatever the "citizenship" of the offspring of the landscape as woman's fertile body, the contradictory and ambivalent image of Palestine as the beloved woman for whom the (male) Palestinian longs and to return to whom he struggles is itself explicitly and critically reiterated later in the novel in the person of Zuhdi. A Palestinian worker, he is sent to prison for striking an Israeli fellow-worker and thereby instigating a free-for-all between Palestinians and Israelis on the job. Zuhdi emerges from prison with an altered perspective on his situation, educated by the multinational and intergenerational male community of the prison. As he returns to his wife Saadiyya, he sees her (body) as

> a haven of safety in an occupied land. . . . This treasure is my fortress that no intruder can violate. The fertile land receives the seed and turns it into a profusion of production and consumption.

Ironically, *al-Subbar* on one level is an account of once fertile Palestinian land that is no longer able to nourish seeds or crops, for it has been appropriated for Jewish settlements or the water supply diverted to Israeli farms. The Palestinians who seek work in Israel are precisely one-time landowners like 'Adil and peasants without land or work like Abu Sabir and Shahada. In Khalifeh's *'Abad al-shams*, a sequel of sorts to *al-Subbar*, Saadiyya—now a widow after Zuhdi's death—begins working as a seamstress in an Israeli shirt factory to support her children. She emerges into the "outside" as a worker in Israel. And within her own community, she is forced to yet another "outside" of social ostracization as a woman who ventures across the boundaries of the "respectable." The ironies and contradictions, then, of woman-as-inviolable interior fortress/fertile land resonate throughout both works.

I will mention just one further instance of slippage of narrative spaces, of "insides" and "outsides," in Khalifeh's *The Cactus*. It is one that, like those above, prefigures an alternative organization of narrative characters, an alternative if not an oppositional narrative perspective that suggests a potential retelling of the Palestinian national narrative. That slippage takes place between a Palestinian peasant woman, Umm Sabir—the wife of an unemployed worker whose right hand was mangled in a work-accident in Israel for which, as an "illegal" worker, he will receive no compensation—and the (unnamed) wife of an Israeli military officer. The two women meet at a fruit vendor's shop in the marketplace of the West Bank. Umm Sabir initially seethes with anger and resentment as the Israeli officer, his wife, and daughter approach the fruit vendor to buy the fruit she cannot afford for her own children. She silently curses them for the brutality of the Israeli occupation, for their affluence, for the presumption of the Israeli woman who tries to stop Umm Sabir from striking her son in anger and frustration as he ignores his mother's warning to leave the unaffordable fruit alone. Though saying nothing, Umm Sabir faces the officer and his wife with hostility and barely suppressed anger. As Osama suddenly emerges from a side street and fatally stabs the Israeli officer, the construct in which Umm Sabir and the Israeli family were contained begins to crumble. The officer falls, dying, onto the fruit. His daughter bangs her head against the metal post supporting the shop awning and collapses on the ground. And Umm Sabir's eyes meet those of the Israeli woman:

> Involuntarily something shook the locked depths of Umm Sabir's heart and she softened, answering the woman's silent plea. "God have mercy on you," she murmured.

She takes off her veil and covers the exposed legs of the little girl lying on the ground. As she does so, Umm Sabir thinks first of her own daughters, and then "of all little girls" and, bending over this particular little girl, murmurs: "I'm so sorry for you my daughter." A moment before, at the juncture of initial angry confrontation, of poverty, of violent death, the national boundaries of the "inside" (Palestinian society) and its "outside" (Israeli society) are presumably clear cut and untraversible. And yet, the old peasant woman traverses those multiple boundaries. She ventures at least momentarily beyond the boundaries of a narrative which would cast her as silent if supportive witness to the action of a fellow (male) "insider" against the "outside" enemy. She speaks consolingly to the Israeli woman. She covers the Israeli woman's young daughter with her veil. And she touches the Israeli woman's shoulder, again speaking to her comfortingly. Her initial response to Osama's attack on the Israeli officer—"You're a hero; you've done well"—is recast if not cancelled by her subsequent behavior. Even as 'Adil arrives and urges Umm Sabir to take her son and "go home to your children," she returns to the Israeli woman one last time and strokes her shoulder in consolation before turning away. The juxtaposition of the words and actions of Osama with those of Umm Sabir and later of 'Adil in their interactions with the Israeli officer, woman and child suggest some (utopic) alternative to a very grim narrative present. But there are limitations. Umm Sabir is not afforded narrative license to pursue the implications of her own actions; it is, rather, to 'Adil that this "privilege" accrues. "Despite all the boundaries that divided people," 'Adil speculates that it is possible to "open the horizons of this narrow world." Umm Sabir is allowed no such internal monologue; her thoughts are limited to a third person account of them. And yet it is her actions that precede and even enable 'Adil's realization. It is Umm Sabir who seizes the initiative in a moment of crisis and finds a way across walls and boundaries. It is she who fleetingly suggests a recasting of the dominant narrative demarcation of "inside" and "outside"[22] and of the role of women in those spaces and, at least potentially, of others as well. Still, Umm Sabir's stubborn compassion towards the Israeli woman and her daughter is effectively framed—and arguably contained—between Osama's fierce assault and 'Adil's "masterful" taking control of the situation.

The ambivalence of the image of thorns (*shawka*) as resistance fighters throughout the novel is nowhere more apparent than at this point in the narrative, in this configuration of positions—the violence of Osama; the anger, hostility, and compassion of Umm Sabir; the conciliatory intervention of 'Adil. *The Cactus*, with its constant play on thorns and roses, suggests a well-known poem by the Palestinian-Israeli writer Fouzi al-Asmar entitled "1948" and written in the late 1960s from an Israeli prison.

> When we plant thorns
> in gardens of roses,
> Brother,
> the roses
> go.

The gaps, the telling spaces, in Khalifeh's literary narratives (and in other literal narratives) suggest possible recastings of the narrative which irrevocably opposes roses and thorns, inviolable (and presumably female) "insides" and unapproachable (and presumably male) "outsides." That is surely a story worth hearing. And worth (re)telling.

NOTES

I am grateful to the Graduate School Faculty Research Fund and the Humanities Research Institute at the University of Wisconsin, Madison for their support of the longer project of which this essay is a part.

1. *Social Text*, 22 (Spring 1989), pp. 23–39; reprinted in Zachary Lockman and Joel Beinin, eds., *Intifada: The Palestinian Uprising Against Israeli Occupation* (Boston: South End Press, 1989), pp. 5–22.

2. For the official English translation of the Palestinian Declaration of Independence and the Political Communiqué of the Palestine National Council, see *Journal of Palestine Studies*, 70 (Winter 1989), pp. 213–23. The passages quoted here are from this official translation.

3. This is also apparent in Said's *After the Last Sky: Palestinian Lives* (New York: Pantheon, 1986), in which Jean Mohr's photographs and Said's commentary on them narrate multiple stories that set out—quite literally in the second section entitled "Interiors"—*min al-dakhil*/from the inside. But as Said's narrative indicates, this is a complex and multiple "inside" profoundly mediated and problematized, invoked and told here precisely from the outside—Said's temporal and spatial outside, the outside of Mohr's camera, the "outside" of the first chapter entitled "States." What is "inside" to and from the "outside"? What is "inside" to and from the "inside"? (In one answer to this question, the last pages of "Interiors" tellingly situate, in a particular "private" sense of *al-dakhil*, the "problem" of women, of their "crucial absence.") The obvious and poignant ironies of inside and out throughout *After the Last Sky* are intensified by juxtaposing its inside(s) and outside(s) to those of another virtually "companion" narrative: Kenneth Brown's "Journey through the Labyrinth: A Photographic Essay on Israel/Palestine" (*Studies in Visual Communication*, 8, 2 [Spring 1982], pp. 2–81). Brown's text is based, in fact, on many of the same photographs by Jean Mohr and is situated of course in the same geographical space, signaled by Brown as "Israel/Palestine." In the "silent" exchange

between these two texts, the contradictions of "inside" and the "outside" are painfully evident.

4. For accounts in English of women's organizations in the Occupied Territories, see: Joost Hiltermann, "Women Organize Themselves," *The Guardian*, May 27, 1987; "Women, Resistance, and the Popular Movement," *Palestine Focus*, July–August 1987; "Palestinian Women Organize against Occupation," *Palestine Focus*, January–February 1988; Dr. Shelly Sella, "Palestinian Women in Prison," *Palestine Focus*, March–April 1989; Reena Bernard, "The New Power of Palestinian Women," *Lillith*, 14, 1 (1989); Kris Small, "The Changing Role of Palestinian Women," *AAUG Newsletter*, 22, 1 (August 1989); Rosemary Sayigh, "Palestinian Women: Triple Burden, Single Struggle," *Palestine: Profile of an Occupation*, special issue of *Khamsin* (1989) and "Palestinian Women in the Occupied Territories" in the same issue; Rita Giacaman and Penny Johnson, "Palestinian Women: Building Barricades and Breaking Barriers," in Lockman and Beinin, eds., *Intifada*; Rema Hammami, "Women, the Hijab, and the Intifada," and Joost Hiltermann, "Sustaining Movement, Creating Space: Trade Unions and Women's Committees," *Middle East Reports*, 20, 3/4 (May–August 1990).

5. There are, certainly, limitations to this postulation. But we might do well to consider it a differently gendered reconstruction here of what are called the "public" and the "private" spheres.

6. This and other human rights abuses like it are documented in a monthly bulletin by the DataBase Project on Palestinian Human Rights (Chicago, IL). Al-Haq, the Palestinian human rights organization, also publishes annual reports on conditions in the Occupied Territories.

7. "*Intifada* and Independence," *Intifada*, p. 21.

8. But for a sense of the complexities of this issue, see for example, Sondra Hale, "The Wing of the Patriarch: Sudanese Women and Revolutionary Parties," *MERIP Reports*, 138, special issue on "Women and Politics in the Middle East" (January–February 1986). There has been a great deal written on the roles of women in Algeria—Juliette Minces, "Women in Algeria," in Lois Beck and Nikki Keddie, eds., *Women in the Muslim World* (Cambridge, MA: Harvard University Press, 1978); Fatiha Akeb and Malika Abdelaziz, "Algerian Women Discuss the Need for Social Change," in E. W. Fernea, ed., *Women and the Family in the Middle East: New Voices of Change* (Austin: University of Texas Press, 1982); Fadela M'rabet, *La Femme algerienne* (Paris: Maspero, 1969); Assia Djebar, *Des Femmes d'Alger dans leur appartement* (Paris: Des Femmes, 1980); Marnia Lazreg, "Feminism and Difference: The Perils of Writing as a Woman on Women in Algeria," *Feminist Studies*, 14, 1 (Spring, 1988).

9. Gayl Jones' *Corregidora* is a compelling literary example of this multiplicity of narrative presentation (Boston: Beacon Press, 1986).

10. Jürgen Habermas' postulation, then, of an equalizing and equalized arena—the ideal speech situation—in which discursive communication takes place seems an incredible (if arguably theoretically necessary) utopic construct.

11. For a well-known and arguably a- or prehistorical account of linguistic competence, see Noam Chomsky's *Topics in the Theory of Generative Grammar* (The Hague: Mouton, 1966) or *Language and Mind* (New York: Harcourt, Brace & Janovich, 1972).

12. But see the rather different—and puzzling—appeal to the possibility of "true narrative" in the conclusion to James Clifford's essay "On Ethnographic Authority," in Clifford and George E. Marcus, eds., *Writing Culture: The Politics and Poetics of Ethnography* (Berkeley: University of California Press, 1986).

13. But for a comprehensive account, see Raja Shehadeh, *Occupier's Law: Israel and the West Bank* (Washington, DC: Institute for Palestine Studies, 1985).

14. Michel Khleife's film *Wedding in Galilee* (1987, Belgium/France) is a moving contemplation of the complexities of a village marriage under occupation.

15. For information on the economics of occupation, see: Sara Roy, *The Gaza Strip Survey* (Jerusalem: The West Bank Data Base Project and Jerusalem Post Press, 1986); Fawzi Garaibeh, *The Economies of the West Bank and Gaza Strip* (Boulder, CO: Westview Press, 1985); Meron Benvenisti, *The West Bank Data Project: A Survey of Israeli Policies* (Washington, DC: American Enterprise Institute, 1982); Brian Van Arkadie, *Benefits and Burdens: A Report on the West Bank and Gaza Strip Economies since 1967* (New York: Carnegie Endowment for International Peace, 1977); Eliyahu Kanovsky, *The Economic Impact of the Six-Day War: Israel, the Occupied Territories, Egypt, and Jordan* (New York: Praeger, 1970).

16. See *Journal of Palestinian Studies*, 17, 3 (Spring 1988), pp. 63–65, for the fourteen demands to the Israeli authorities made by Palestinian leaders and spokespeople at a press conference held in Jerusalem on January 14, 1988, a little more than a month after the intifada began.

17. The popular committees organize broader local areas such as towns and villages; the neighborhood committees, as their name indicates, are more localized. These latter include women's committees, health, educational, and agricultural committees,

committees to dispense food stuffs, to visit the families of a neighborhood and attend to their specific concerns, etc.

18. *al-Subbar* (Jerusalem: Galileo Limited, 1976). The English translation is entitled *Wild Thorns* (London: Al-Saqi Books, 1985).

19. *'Abad al-shams* (Beirut: PLO Press, 1980). This novel and a collection of four short stories, *Lam na'ud jawari lakum/We are not your servants* (Beirut: Dar al-Adab, 1988), take a more self-consciously feminist stance.

20. I am grateful to Doris Sommer for pointing out the virtually identical denotive meaning of "sabra" in Hebrew.

21. The title of a recent article by Sahar Khalifeh on her work, its origins and contexts is, interestingly enough, "To change things you have to pass through/go beyond walls" (in *al-Fikr al-demoqrati*, 5 [Winter 1989], 149–56).

22. The insistent and complex resonances of "inside" and "outside" are not only a "poetic" concern of Khalifeh's fiction or Said's essay. As suggested in my earlier discussion of the Palestinian Declaration of Independence and the Political Communiqué, these topoi crucially inform the crises and resolutions of Palestinian nationalism.

Chapter 23

Revolution, Islam and Women: Sexual Politics in Iran and Afghanistan

Valentine M. Moghadam

INTRODUCTION: ISLAMISM, NATIONALISM AND GENDER

The emergence and spread of Islamist movements, and the attendant problem of the position of women, have raised important issues regarding modernization, eurocentrism, universalist values, and cultural specificity.[1] These issues are especially salient in the case of Afghanistan, but tackling them has been complicated by the present epistemological turmoil, by the postmodernist challenge, by the critique of orientalism, and by a variant of orientalism which views Islamism as a more or less permanent feature and "authentic" voice of Muslim societies. How then to interpret the rise of a cross-class, Islamic-populist movement opposed to Western imperialism (Iran), or a tribal- and peasant-based reaction to a "communist" and modernizing regime (Afghanistan)? How to assess the nature of these particular forms of civil society/state contention? How to evaluate the "primitive rebels" of Afghanistan?

What vocabularies are appropriate for the critical analysis of gender in these movements and societies?

Islamist movements raise another set of questions related to concepts of ethnicity, community, and nation-building. Islamist ideologues reject the national boundaries created by colonialism/imperialism which eventuated the dispersion and fragmentation of the Ummah Islam, the "imagined community" of believers.[2] Rebuilding the ummah is mandated by Iran's Islamic Constitution of 1979.[3] And yet, concrete Islamist movements—influenced as they are by twentieth-century discourses and social structures—are also nationalist. In the same Iranian Constitution, the territory of Iran, "national unity," Twelver Shia Islam, and the Persian language are designated in various articles. In this regard Islamist movements are similar to the early Communist movement, which was torn between the international and "permanent revolution" position on the one hand, and the notion of "building socialism in one country," on the other. In Iran, an essential tension over the past decade has played itself out between the proponents of the spread of Islamism throughout the world (the self-styled Trotskyists of Islam), and those who would confine themselves and the country's resources to "building the Islamic Republic in one country," so to speak.[4]

In Afghanistan's case, nationalism has been at best incipient, as the country remains tribal, feudalistic and fragmented along many linguistic and ethnic lines. It also lacks major communications infrastructure and has no railway system. Since the middle of the nineteenth century, various Afghan rulers have sought to unify the country and extend central authority over the tribes, but they have never managed to expand state control with the same success as the Pahlavi rulers next door. The People's Democratic Party of Afghanistan (PDPA), when it came to power in April 1978, sought to further central government control and to establish an "all-Afghan" national identity. This was rejected by mullahs and landlords who counterposed "Islam" to Afghan nationalism. For a while, and especially during the Soviet military intervention, the "Islamic holy war against the infidels" was able to unify the unruly and warring tribes and the Pakistan-based political sects. In the end, however, the central government's construction of an Afghan national identity proved stronger than the "imagined community" of Mujahideen (holy warriors).[5]

A third set of questions raised by Islamism concerns the role of women in Islamist movements, discourses, and programs. Here an interesting dilemma is evinced by Western commentators, who appear torn between their commitment to gender equality, on the one hand, and the presumed right of cultural groups to make their own social and gender arrangements, on the other. Yet upon examination of the separate literatures on Iran and Afghanistan, one sees a double standard at work: the Islamists of Iran are vigorously criticized for their policies on women, whereas the Afghan Mujahideen (the romanticized "primitive rebels"[6]) are not taken to task for what are actually far more reactionary gender practices.

These two cases reveal the structuring effects of gender binarism in periods of social change, in revolutions, and in political movements. Sexual politics are at the center of Islamist movements, which seek the reordering of society and the construction of a new moral and cultural order based on rigid sex roles and the exaltation of the (patriarchal) family. Sexual politics are especially salient in the cases of Iran and Afghanistan, where revolutions took place in the late 1970s. To the typical Afghan Mujahid, self-determination and autonomy (vis à vis the state or the Soviets) are not privileges extended to females. To the Iranian Islamist ideologue, "freedom" and "independence"—slogans of the Revolution—were not to be construed as personal freedoms for women. While Iranian Islamists do not practice purdah (female seclusion) as the Afghans do, the Muslim personal status laws which were strengthened after the Revolution rendered woman's status as that of dependent and minor.

This essay focuses on the vexed but extremely significant issue of the politicization of gender in Iran and Afghanistan. In both countries, the reorganization of state power rearticulated gender rules and gender power, although in divergent ways. These two cases offer contrasting perspectives on the strategic role played by The Woman Question in revolutionary situations and in political contests, and vividly illustrate the sexual politics of contemporary Islamist movements.

ON "REVOLUTION" IN IRAN AND AFGHANISTAN

It is commonly understood that Iran experienced a "social revolution" and Afghanistan a "coup d'état"; that Iran's revolutionary government was "popular" and "representative" (endorsed by 98% of the electorate in the April 1979 referendum) and that Afghanistan's government was and remains a "minority" and "unrepresentative" regime, buttressed by foreign troops.[7] Yet it was the "popular" and "representative" government which passed legislation resulting in a loss of status for women, while the "minority government" next door enacted legislation to raise women's status through changes in family law and policies to encourage female education and employment.

One way of explaining these divergent outcomes is to note that Iran's was an "Islamic revolution" and Afghanistan's a "Marxist-led revolution." This is indeed part of the answer, but the story is more complicated. The Iranian

Revolution was carried out by a populist collectivity, which included liberals, communists, national minorities, and women of all classes. The Revolution included a call for "rights" as well as populist demands, though "Islamic populism" may be identified as the dominant discourse of the revolutionary movement. Following the collapse of the Pahlavi state in February 1979 the coalition dissolved; Islamization was consolidated following a year and half of intense political conflicts. The Iranian Left has since been accused of acquiescing in the Islamist/clerical establishment and not challenging their retrograde agenda for women.[8] The Revolution is in fact an example of how a social revolution does not necessarily guarantee the rights of citizens (or even of participants in the revolutionary collectivity), and of how a nationalist or populist discourse devoid of a specific program for women, minorities, workers, the press, etc., can obfuscate important issues that are subsequently violently fought over. The fate of women (and other tragedies) since 1979 has raised fundamental questions about the Iranian Revolution: was it reactionary, was it "premature," was it in any sense emancipatory, or was it necessarily contradictory?[9]

A social revolution is understood to be one that transforms existing social structures and power relations. It is not clear that such sweeping change has occurred in Iran. Although political, cultural, and ideological changes have been deep, the economic ones have been limited.[10] With regard to Afghanistan, one could argue that what had occurred was a political—as distinct from social and transformative—revolution. It is also worth noting that a number of Third World countries have had self-styled revolutions which came at the heels of a military coup (e.g., Turkey, Egypt, Peru, Iraq) and that what the PDPA attempted in 1978 has been called "revolution from above."[11] The question arises as to why some new states and ruling parties were able to implement their program from above (Nasser, APRA in Peru, the Dastur Party in Tunisia, the Baath Party in Iraq and Syria), while others were not. In the case of Afghanistan, part of the explanation for this failure lies in the unusually rugged nature of its geographic terrain, and in the undeveloped and fragmented character of its social structures.[12] But to a large extent, the Afghan revolution could not proceed because of overwhelming external hostility to the new Government, and active moral and military support for the Islamist opposition.[13]

REVOLUTION, THE STATE AND WOMEN IN IRAN

The literature on Iran is replete with references to the sexual politics of the Revolution and the new regime. Some authors have argued that the revolutionary discourse was explicitly anti-female, that the growing number of educated and employed women "terrified" men who came to regard the modern woman as the manifestation of Westernization and imperialist culture.[14] Much of the early literature on the fate of women following the Iranian Revolution focused on analyses of Islamic texts, on anti-female legislation in the immediate postrevolutionary period, and on the Left's betrayal of the women's movement.[15]

Only three weeks after the collapse of the Pahlavi state and the formation of the revolutionary government, middle-class, educated non-Islamist women encountered the new sexual politics when they devoted International Women's Day (March 8) to a denunciation of clerical calls for the imposition of *hejab* (all-encompassing Islamic dress for women). They were physically attacked by men who called them whores, bourgeois degenerates, un-Islamic, and deculturated. In the Iranian political lexicon the dreaded word for all this is *gharbzadeh*, literally, "struck by the West," sometimes translated as "occidentosis," "euro-mania," or "westoxication": the abnormal state of being unduly attracted to "the West," or simply of being Westernized.[16]

It is necessary to point out that in the 1979–80 period, the women's movement, then quite dynamic, was bifurcated; there were pro-Khomeini and anti-Khomeini women, and even among Islamist women there were different perspectives on women's rights issues, including the veil. Moreover, many women were comfortable with the veil because of male harassment of women in Western dress. During the sixties and seventies, when I was growing up in Tehran, just waiting for a taxi or shopping downtown entailed major battles with men, who variously leered, touched, made sexual remarks or cursed. Women were fair game, and it is understandable that many would want to withdraw to the protective veil when in public. But the legal imposition of *hejab* was not brought about to protect women, and it was certainly not part of any struggle against male sexism: it was about negating female sexuality and therefore protecting men. More profoundly, compulsory veiling signaled the (re)definition of gender rules, and the veiled woman symbolized the moral and cultural transformation of society.

This is spelled out in a booklet entitled *On the Islamic Hijab* by a leading Iranian cleric, Murteza Mutahhari, who was assassinated in May 1979. In the preface by the International Relations Department of the Islamic Propagation Organization, it is argued that Western society "looks at woman merely through the windows of sexual passion and regards woman as a little being who just satisfies sexual desires . . . Therefore, such a way of thinking results in nothing other than the woman becoming a propaganda and commercial commodity in all aspects of Western life, ranging from those in the mass media to streets and shops." Mutahhari himself writes:[17]

> If a boy and a girl study in a separate environment or in an environment where the girl covers her body and wears no make-up, do they not study better? . . . Will men work better in an environment where the streets, offices, factories, etc., are continuously filled with women who are wearing make-up and are not fully dressed, or in an environment where these scenes do not exist?
>
> The truth is that the disgraceful lack of *hijab* in Iran before the Revolution . . . is a product of the corrupt western capitalist societies. It is one of the results of the worship of money and the pursuance of sexual fulfillment that is prevalent amongst western capitalists.

The idea that women had lost their modesty and men had lost their honor during the Pahlavi era was a widespread one. Afrasiabi recounts a conversation he had in early February 1979 with a striking worker named Alimorad, who had just returned from Shahr-e Now (the red-light district in downtown Tehran) which had been destroyed by a fire set by Islamist militants:[18]

> We burnt it all. Cleansed the city, he said.
> And women? I asked.
> Many were incinerated [*jozghaleh shodand*].
> Who are you? Where do you come from? I asked him.
> I am a worker from Rezaieh, married with children.
> What is your business in Tehran?
> To take part in the revolution!
> What is happening in Rezaieh?
> In Rezaieh there is just a movement [*jombesh*], but here there is a revolution.
> Why do you support the revolution?
> Islam, freedom, poverty, *zolm* [oppression], he answered without hesitation.
> What else? I insisted.
> Dignity [*heisiat*].
> Dignity?
> Yes brother. Shah took our dignity. He took man's right from him. My wife is now working. What is left of family when the wife works?
> And what is your expectation of Islam?
> Islam is our dignity. I want to bring bread on my own—to have a wife at home to cook and nurse the children, God and Islam willing.

Such attitudes were behind the early legislation pertaining to women. The 1979 Constitution spelled out the place of Woman in the ideal Islamic society which the new leadership was trying to establish in Iran: within the family, through the "precious foundation of motherhood," rearing committed Muslims. Motherhood and domesticity were described as socially valuable, and the age of consent was lowered to 13. Legislation was enacted to alter gender relations and make them as different as possible from gender norms in the West. In particular, the Islamic Republic emphasized the distinctiveness of male and female roles, a preference for the privatization of female roles (although public activity by women was never barred, and they retained the vote), the desirability of sex segregation in public places, and the necessity of modesty in dress and demeanor and in media images.[19]

REVOLUTION, THE STATE, AND WOMEN IN AFGHANISTAN

In 1978 the Government of Noor Mohammad Taraki, President of the Revolutionary Council and of the new People's Democratic Republic of Afghanistan, initiated a wide-ranging program of change and development. Along with land reform and other measures to wrest power from traditional leaders in Afghan society, the government promulgated Decree No. 7, which aimed at fundamental change in the institution of marriage. A prime concern of the decree, which also motivated other reforms by the Taraki government, was to reduce material indebtedness throughout the country; it was also meant to ensure the equal rights of women with men. In a speech on November 4, 1978, President Taraki said that "through the issuance of Decrees Nos. 6 and 7, the hard-working peasants were freed from the bonds of oppressors and money-lenders, ending the sale of girls for good as hereafter nobody would be entitled to sell any girl or woman in this country."[20]

The first two articles in Decree No. 7 forbid the exchange of a woman in marriage for cash or kind and the payment of other prestations customarily due from a bridegroom on festive occasions; the third article sets an upper limit of three hundred afghanis on the *mahr,* a payment due from groom to bride which is an essential part of the formal Islamic marriage contract. Taraki explained that "We are always taking into consideration and respect the basic principles of Islam. Therefore, we decided that an equivalent of the sum to be paid in advance by the husband to his wife upon the nuptial amounting to ten 'dirhams' [traditional ritual payment] according to *shariat* [Islamic canon law] be converted into local currency which is afs. 300. We also decided that marriageable boys and girls should freely choose their future spouses in line with the rules of *shariat.*"[21] (At the exchange rate of the time, 42 Af=$1; afs. 300 was the equivalent of $7.00. National income per person was $210.)[22] It should be clear from the above statement that the so-called "godless communists" were actually sensitive to Islamic customs.

The legislation aimed to change marriage customs so as to give young women and men independence from their marriage guardians. The ages of first engagement and marriage were raised to sixteen for women and eighteen for men (in contrast to what happened in the Iranian case). The decree further stipulated that no one, including widows, could be compelled to marry against his or her will—this referred to the customary control of a married woman (and the honor she represents) by her husband and his agnates, who retain residual rights in her in the case of her widowhood. The decree also stipulated that no one could be prevented from marrying if she/he so desired.[23]

What motivated this legislation? One concern, as mentioned above, was the alarming level of rural indebtedness. A number of studies cite "excessive expenditure in marriage" as one source of indebtedness: they state that "the heaviest expenses any household has to bear are concerned with marriage," and that the choice of bride, the agreed brideprice, and the time taken to complete a marriage may visibly confirm or indeed increase a household's poverty. Louis Dupree's 1973 study noted that a 1950 law banning "ostentatious life-crises ceremonies prohibits many of the expensive aspects of birth, circumcision, marriage and burial rituals,"[24] while another scholar notes that the marriage law of 1971 was a further attempt to curb the indebtedness arising from the costs of marriages which "are a burden for Afghan society as a whole."[25] An Afghan who devoted his 1976 doctoral dissertation to matrimonial problems in Afghanistan wrote[26]:

> Excessive expenditure in marriage undermines the human dignity of women as it tends to render them into a kind of property of the husband or his family. [It] weakens the financial status of the family and tends to bring or worsen poverty. [It] tends to render the adults highly dependent on family resources; this in turn weakens their position in regard to the exercise of their right of consent in marriage as well as their freedom of choice of a life partner.

The author continues:

> Dependence of the youth on the family resources is enormous even without the stimulus of this additional factor. Marriage becomes largely dependent on the possession of financial means; this leads to intolerable discriminations against the poor. Excessive expenditure in marriage deprives many of the right to marry (e.g., many women); it also leads to late marriages, and often brings about a wide disparity of age between the spouses. Excessive expenditure in marriage constitutes a source of embitterment and conflict during the course of marital life. . . . Costly marriages contribute to the

> continuance of the tradition-bound society and tend to slow down the process of reform. . . . The practice is self-perpetuating.

Another motivation for the decree was the reformers' impatience with the slow pace of change and their desire, in keeping with their modernizing and socialist orientation, to improve the status of women. The PDPA has been accused of trying to impose an alien ideology and praxis, but this is a false argument on several counts. It should be noted that the PDPA reformers were not the first to try to tackle sexual relations. The major Afghan reformer, Amanullah Khan, introduced a family code in 1921 that outlawed child marriage and intermarriage between close kin as contrary to Islamic principles. One scholar writes that in the new code Amanullah reiterated the ruling of his father Abdur Rahman (a previous and unsuccessful reformer) that a widow was to be free of the domination of her husband's family; he placed tight restrictions on wedding expenses, including dowries, and granted wives the right to appeal to the courts if their husbands did not adhere to Quranic tenets regarding marriage. In the fall of 1924, "Afghan girls were given the right to choose their husbands—a measure that incensed the traditionalist elements."[27]

As for the fate of King Amanullah, he was deposed in a 1929 tribal rebellion organized by the British. His successor, Habibullah Ghazi, insisted that to restore the sanctity of Islam and the honor of the nation, women would have to be restored to seclusion under strict male control and that girls' schools, together with all other vestiges of the women's movement, be suspended. For the next thirty years, that is, until 1959, women remained in seclusion and wore the veil.[28]

The PDPA should therefore be seen as part of a tradition of reform, so to speak, that began at least as early as the reform and modern movement of other Muslim countries. For example, the Afghans have their own equivalent of Qassim Amin (the famous North African male feminist): Mahmud Beg Tarzi (1865–1933). Moreover, what the PDPA tried to do was not arbitrary or motivated by an inappropriate ideology (as some have argued); rather, they tried to deal with the same problems that social scientists and previous reformers had recognized. These problems had to do with the chronic indebtedness of the countryside, and the exchange of women—what Monique Wittig has called "the vile and precious merchandise."[29]

THE EXCHANGE OF WOMEN AND THE CONCEPT OF HONOR

In describing customs among the Durrani Pashtuns of north-central Afghanistan, anthropologist Nancy Tapper writes: "The members of the community discuss control of all resources—especially labor, land, and women—in terms of honor."[30] Note that "community" is the community of men. Women are given for brideprice or in compensation for blood, and this "maintains a status hierarchy" among the households. In the exchange system and the differential values given to the various ranked spheres of exchange, men are ranked in the first and highest sphere. Direct exchanges between them include the most honorable and manly of all activities, and these activities are prime expressions of status equality: vengeance and feud, political support and hospitality, and the practice of sanctuary. Women belong to the second sphere; they are often treated exclusively as reproducers and pawns in economic and political exchanges. There is only one proper conversion between the first two spheres: two or more women can be given in compensation for the killing or injury of one man. Mobility and migration patterns also revolve around the brideprice. For example, men from one region will travel to another to find inexpensive brides, while other men will travel elsewhere because they can obtain a higher price for their daughters.[31]

Interethnic hostility among Afghans is well documented.[32] Similarly, Tapper describes Afghan ethnic identity in terms of claims to religiously privileged descent and superiority to all other ethnic groups. Interethnic competition extends to the absolute prohibition on the marriage of Durrani women to men who are of a "lower" ethnic status. After describing these relations and practices, Tapper writes: "Any substantial alteration in the meaning of marriage within these groups (perhaps by the implementation of marriage reforms) could lead to a complete restructuring of ethnic relations."[33] Indeed.

The code of Afghan behaviour among the Pushtuns, who comprise over 50% of the population, has three core elements: hospitality, refuge, and revenge. Other values include equality, respect, pride, bravery, purdah, pursuit of romantic encounters, worship of God, and devoted love for a friend.[34] That these are male values is abundantly evident. Purdah is a key element in the protection of the family's pride and honor. This seclusion from the world outside the family walls (and here wall is used literally, not symbolically) is customarily justified by invoking Quranic prescription and by the notion that women are basically licentious and tempt men. In traditional and tribal arrangements, women are regarded as men's property. Through a combination of tribal, pre-Islamic and Islamic customs, men exercise control over women in two crucial institutions: marriage and property, as illustrated by the institution of brideprice, the Pushtun prohibition of divorce (and this despite the Quranic allowances, primarily to the men), and the taboo of land ownership for women (again contrary to Islamic law and the actual practice in many other Muslim countries). Women are regarded as subordinates dependent on their husbands, as further exemplified by women never asking men their whereabouts or expecting marital fidelity. Women are expected to give all the meat, choicest delicacies, and clothing to their husbands.[35]

Howard-Merriam notes that a woman needs to marry since her standing is maintained primarily through bearing sons. The choice of husband is made by her family with its own concerns for the maintenance of the lineage or for gain and property. The best she can hope for is a handsome and kind cousin or close relative she has known and with whom she has grown up. The worst is an old man from another village whom she has never seen and who is unkind. In either case he is obliged to provide for her materially and, it is to be hoped, father her sons who will endow her with status in her new home. If the husband treats her unbearably she does have recourse to breaking out and returning to her own family or seeking refuge with another family. This weapon is not used often, however, as her natal family has given up rights to her through the customary brideprice at the time of marriage.[36]

Such were the practices that concerned the reformers.

REFORM AND RETRENCHMENT

The emphasis on women's rights on the part of the PDPA reflected: a) their socialist/Marxist ideology, b) their modernizing and egalitarian orientation, c) their social base and origins: urban middle-class professionals educated in the U.S., USSR, and Western and Eastern Europe, and d) the number and position of women within the PDPA. Unlike the Islamic regime in Iran, the PDPA government included a number of women who were a product of the reform movement mentioned above as well as the beneficiaries of education and employment policies. They were eager for more profound change, especially in the forbidden area of family law or personal status. In the words of Anahita Ratebzad, the best known and most influential of the reform-minded PDPA officials: "Privileges which women, by right, must have are equal education, job security, health services, and free time to rear a healthy generation for building the future of this country. . . . Educating and enlightening women is now the subject of close government attention."[37]

In 1978 and 1979 the government launched a "holy war against illiteracy," led by the Democratic Organization of Afghan Women (DOAW), which met with strong rural opposition. PDPA and DOAW attempts to extend literacy to rural girls have been widely criticized for heavy-handedness by most commentators on Afghanistan. Three points regarding this criticism are in order. First, literacy campaigns are common in or following popular revolutions and movements for national or social liberation: the Bolsheviks, Chinese, Cubans, Vietnamese, Angolans, Palestinians, Eritreans, and Nicaraguans all have had extensive literacy campaigns. Second, the PDPA's rationale for pursuing the rural literacy campaign with some zeal was that all previous reformers had made literacy a matter of choice; male guardians had chosen not to allow their females to be educated; thus 99% of all Afghan women were illiterate. It was therefore decided not to allow literacy to remain a matter of (men's) choice, but rather a matter of principle and law. In response, recalcitrant refugees poured into Pakistan in the summer of 1979, giving as their major reason the forceful implementation of the literacy program among their women. In the city of Kandahar, three literacy workers from the DOAW were killed as symbols of the unwanted revolution.[38] A third point is that state coercion to raise the status of women has been undertaken elsewhere, notably Soviet Central Asia and Turkey in the 1920s. And other governments have issued decrees which have been resisted (e.g., emancipation of slaves in the U.S., state-ordered school segregation and forced busing more recently, and the periodic attacks on Mormon polygamous units). This is not to condone the use of force, but to point out that rights, reforms, and revolutions have been effected coercively or attained through struggle.

However, it is true that the Amin period exacerbated the tensions that had already emerged, as he became increasingly authoritarian as well as erratic. A ruthless, ambitious man, deputy prime minister Hafizullah Amin deposed Taraki and had him killed in September 1979; he ruled rather brutally until the Soviet intervention in December 1979.[39] The Soviets were requested several times to intervene militarily. They were reluctant to do so, in part because they did not trust Amin, but no doubt also because the British had such a rough time of it in the late 1800s. When it became clear that not only Amin but the whole PDPA effort was about to collapse in the face of a Mujahideen *jihad* that was supported, financed, and armed by Pakistan, China, the U.S., and the Islamic Republic of Iran, and that calls were being made for the de-Sovietization and re-Islamization of Soviet Central Asia (the Muslim republics), Soviet troops entered in December 1979.[40] The rest is very sad history, for all parties concerned.

In 1980 the PDPA slowed down its reform program and announced its intention to eliminate illiteracy in the cities in seven years and in the provinces in ten. In an interview in 1980, Anahita Ratebzad conceded errors, "in particular the compulsory education of women," to which she added, "the reactionary elements immediately made use of these mistakes to spread discontent among the population."[41] Despite the slowing down of reforms and the legal reinstatement of Islamic family law,[42] the resistance movement spread. The Soviet occupation turned even high school girls against the government, and they engaged in a number of street battles. The most reactionary aspects of Afghan culture, those surrounding concepts of honor, manifested themselves in extreme ways. For example, in Kandahar, two men killed all the women in their families to prevent them from "dishonor."[43] The most fanatic attitudes toward women were brought to the surface, and are rampant among the Mujahideen and within the refugee camps in Peshawar. Among the Mujahideen are many who call for the return of compulsory veiling and gender-segregated education.

HOW THE OTHER HALF EXISTS: WOMEN IN THE REFUGEE CAMPS

Women's separateness and invisibility from the public world outside the home characterize Afghan traditional society. This has been reinforced in the refugee camps in Peshawar, where women's seclusion has been intensified. A 1982 ILO study of Afghan refugees in Peshawar states that

> the influence of both Islam and traditional codes is pervasive and has many ramifications and implications for our work. Likewise, the role and position of women and the division of work in the household among the different Afghan tribes, have defined the limits of what is feasible and acceptable for schemes for women refugees.[44]

In the section on family organization, the report describes

> the practice of female seclusion, belief in the defence of the honor of women, and a well-developed division of labor within the family on the basis of age and sex. The emphasis on manhood and its association with strength is pervasive and we were told in one camp that even old men were expected to remain out of sight along with the women and children. . . . Men assume responsibility for relationships and tasks outside the family compound including purchase and sale of subsistence items from the market (i.e., monetary transactions), agricultural production, house construction, wage labor and maintaining social and political relationships outside the immediate family (including attendance at educational and religious institutions). Where "contact with outsiders" is concerned, there are universal constraints on participation of women. . . . Puberty defines adulthood for women, and early marriage is common.[45]

In the refugee camps in Peshawar, food distribution reflects the secondary status of women and the role women's honor plays: women do not go to the marketplace if there is a male relative in the extended family. As a result, women heading households are not as likely to receive their fair share from the men. Indeed, this is evidenced by incidence of anemia among the adult female population.[46] (Such disparities have not been noted, for example, among refugee populations of Eritreans and Palestinians.)

According to Howard-Merriam, who spoke with women in the Peshawar refugee camps: "As beings set apart and excluded from the public, women are united in their hostility toward men as 'bad, ugly and cruel.'" Women's low level of expectation, the writer continues, stands in contrast to the "men's higher and often unrealistic ones of world conquest . . ."[47] Nonetheless, this same writer can justify the invisibility and isolation of Afghan women as a functional requisite of the resistance. She avers that "the Mujahideen leaders recognize women's importance to the *jihad* (or holy war) with their exhortations to preserve women's honor through the continued practice of seclusion. The reinforcement of this tradition, most Westerners have failed to notice, serves to strengthen the men's will to resist."[48] She continues by arguing that

> *purdah* provides the opportunity for preserving one's own identity and a certain stability in the face of external pressures. . . . Westerners who have been quick to impose their own ethnocentric perceptions should note the value of this seemingly anachronistic custom for a people under siege whose very survival is at stake.

Education for girls is contested terrain. Universal literacy was a priority for the PDPA, and it was precisely female literacy that offended the sensibility of traditionalists. In the early 1980s, according to one expert, "Even the mere mention of education for girls was anathema and those who advocated it were branded as 'traitors' and 'communists.'"[49] Years later, education for girls in the refugee camps in Peshawar, administered by the United Nations High Commissioner for Refugees (UNHCR), remains woefully inadequate. Surprisingly, UN officials have acquiesced to Afghan male resistance to teaching girls.[50] Thus in 1988 104,600 boys were enrolled in UN-run camp schools, as against 7,800 girls. The disproportion is greatest in middle schools and high schools, because most Afghan men consider ten or eleven years the threshold that girls should not cross in education.[51] During the 1980s the UN ran 161 middle schools for boys and two for girls. All four high schools are for boys only. At the primary level, there were 486 boys' schools and 76 for girls. Boys go to school for as long as possible, while girls leave at age ten or eleven to weave carpets. A male Afghan principal is quoted as saying: "I don't think it's bad for women to become doctors [presumably so that women might receive medical treatment], but it's better to weave carpets. They can start earning money from a very young age."[52]

In health care, too, the UNHCR has encountered continued resistance to the extension of services to women. Afghan males do not allow male medical workers to attend women and are reluctant even to allow women to leave their houses or get treatment from female doctors or assistants. Because of the observance of purdah, even infants with developmental problems or disabilities may be overlooked by relief workers and physicians. Medicins Sans Frontiers, a French medical group that was very pro-Mujahideen, eventually expressed exasperation at Afghan male authority. A French woman doctor is quoted as saying, "We have to fight with the men to take women to a hospital when necessary."[53] As a result, Afghan refugee women suffer from ill-health, isolation, boredom, and depression.

In Peshawar, the great majority of the refugees are women, children, and elderly males who cannot participate in guerrilla operations inside Afghanistan. Almost three-quarters of the refugee households are headed by women. The women's immobility is exacerbated by the Pakistan authorities' stipulation that the refugees must remain in the refugee villages to qualify for monthly stipends. So while the men fight their war for Islam, tradition, and honor, the women stagnate in the refugee camps.

In sharp contrast is the situation for women within Afghanistan, especially the cities, where the government has more control. According to the magazine *Afghanistan Today*, there are 440,000 female students in the country's education institutions. The total number of Afghan female professors and teachers is 190 and 11,000 respectively. About 80,000 women are enrolled in literary courses in various institutions and residential areas. Since 1978 the total number of Afghan working women has grown fifty times and has reached 245,000.[54] This is the result of PDPA commitment to equality, the activities of the Women's Council, and women's own political participation. Women were heavily represented at a large party rally I witnessed in early February 1989; some of the women were armed and others were about to undertake military training. One teenaged girl, a member of the Democratic Youth Organization, declared to me that the Saur Revolution "was made for women." Others said that "the women would never allow" a Mujahideen victory. Two women leaders, Massouma Esmaty Wardak and Soraya, insisted that women's rights would not be sacrificed on the altar of national reconciliation, and that the strength of the women's organization would prevent setbacks.[55] In the streets of Kabul, in offices and at the university, one sees Afghan women who are unveiled and wearing make-up. Many of the young women I encountered in early 1989 were rather heavily made-up; I even met a female army officer, stationed at the women's wing of Pol-e Charkhi prison, who was wearing black lace stockings and short high-heeled boots along with her khaki uniform. Tacky? Not at all. This is one way Afghan women confront the politics of gender and identity.

CONCLUDING REMARKS

Since the late 1970s, the women of Iran and Afghanistan have encountered revolution, war, Islamist movements, and intense ideological and cultural pressures. Reformulations of gender went hand-in-hand with (re)constructions of "nation," "state," "community," and "Islam." It is clear from an examination of these two cases that political models and cultural programs are heavily imbued with considerations of gender. Transformations of society entail new concepts of Womanhood, as do struggles over national, ethnic, and religious identity.

This comparative overview of the fate of women following political change in Iran and Afghanistan also suggests that a broad-based and popular social revolution in which women massively participate (Iran) does not entail an enhancement of the status of women. Conversely, a "minority government" (Afghanistan) may institute genuine reform in the direction of women's emancipation. What is key is the program of the revolutionary leadership and of the new state. But while state action is central to understanding women's status, the two cases also point to domestic and international constraints faced by states: war, popular resistance, weak central authority, disagreements within the ruling group, external intervention. Both states have had to modify their original program on women. In Iran, the "domestication" of women is no longer exhorted by the authorities, and women are active in public life, although the ruling on *hejab* has not changed. In Afghanistan, the abolition of the brideprice has been quietly shelved and at any rate ignored by the populace, but the education of girls as government policy continues apace.

It is remarkable that the subversion of a government which was undertaking wide-reaching and progressive social reforms, especially toward the emancipation of women, should have been encouraged (and financed) by the U.S. and China, both ostensibly committed to women's equality. But more dismaying has been the spectacle of Western intellectuals acting as cheerleaders for the Afghan Mujahideen. Attempts to explain away the rather extreme forms of patriarchy existing among the Mujahideen and in tribal community by recourse to a vague cultural relativism are suspect. For one thing, the cultural relativist argument has not been applied to Iran, which has been judged by Western, or universal, standards and norms.[56] For another thing, there is nothing acceptable or "natural" about ethnic, gender, or class oppression.[57] It is entirely appropriate to interrogate cultural practices, political discourses, and social arrangements which occlude important questions about class, property, ethnicity, and gender. Finally, the comparative study of Iran and Afghanistan illustrates the problematical nature of "Islamic gender relations." What needs to be faced squarely is that Islamic canon law, like any other religious law regulating personal and family life, is inimical to women's emancipation and autonomy. Political groups that are keen to bring about liberatory social change but are otherwise silent about women's personal rights are merely engaged in a masquerade.

NOTES

1. See, for example, Guity Nashat, ed., *Women and Revolution in Iran* (Boulder, CO: Westview Press, 1983); Bill Brugger and Kate Hannan, *Modernisation and Revolution* (London: Croom Helm, 1983); Cheryl Benard and Zalmay Khalilzad, *The Government of God: Iran's Islamic Republic* (New York: Columbia University Press, 1984); Edward Said, "Orientalism Revisited," *Merip Middle East Reports*, 18, 1 (January–February 1988); Mona Abaza and Georg Stauth, "Occidental Reason, Orientalism, Islamic Fundamentalism," *International Sociology*, 3, 4 (December 1988); Val Moghadam, "The Critical and Sociological Approach in Middle East Studies," *Critical Sociology*, 17, 1 (Spring 1990); *Race & Class*, special issue on the Iranian Revolution (guest editor, Eqbal Ahmad), 21, 1 (Summer 1979); *Third World Quarterly*, special issue on Islam and Politics, 10, 2 (April 1988). The Salman Rushdie affair has intensified the debate on political Islam: see Malise Ruthven, *A Satanic Affair: Salman Rushdie and the Rage of Islam* (London: Chatto, 1990), and Sadik J. Al-Azm, "The Importance of Being Earnest About Salman Rushdie," forthcoming in *Die Welt Des Islams*.

2. "In Islamic countries, as well as in the countries which are under colonial oppression, the colonizers have expended their greatest efforts throughout this century in the propagation of nationalism as an important principle and a great social value . . . in order to sever the nations' links with Islam. [T]hey were quite aware that Islam, as a principle higher than the principle of nationality, could fuse the Muslim nations with each other and turn them into a united Islamic ummah which would naturally possess extraordinary power" (Masih Muhajeri, *Islamic Revolution: Future Path of the Nations* [Tehran, Jahad-e Sazandegi, November 1982], p. 17).

3. ". . . the Revolution will strive, in concert with other Islamic and popular movements, to prepare the way for the formation of a single world community, in accordance with the Qur'anic verse 'This your nation is a single nation, and I am your Lord, so

worship Me' (21:92), and to assure the continuation of the struggle for the liberation of all deprived and oppressed peoples in the world" (Introduction, *Constitution of the Islamic Republic of Iran*, Tehran, 1979 [English translation by Hamid Algar]).

4. Muhajeri (see note 2 above) denies that "export of the revolution" entails expansionism. It means, rather, the "introduction of the spiritual values and achievements attained in the course of the Islamic revolution" to the exploited nations "to help them liberate themselves from the grip of the exploiters" (175).

5. The Afghan government's nationalities policy is an unprecendented appeal for egalitarian participation of all ethnic and tribal formations. It allows no more special privileges for the Pushtuns in general, and for the Mohammadzai royal clan in particular. This policy of nondiscrimination may have worked to the government's advantage, and could have long-term social benefits. The National Fatherland Front (formed in 1981) includes a number of parties and associations, and is nationalist in orientation. It has fared much better than the Mujahideen alliance. See Ralph Magnus, "The PDPA Regime in Afghanistan: A Soviet Model for the Middle East," in Peter Chelkowski and Robert Pranger, eds., *Ideology and Power in the Middle East* (Durham: Duke University Press, 1988) for discussion of how the PDPA nationalities policy sought to overcome interethnic hostility and hierarchies.

6. The term, of course, derives from Eric Hobsbawm's classic study, *Primitive Rebels* (New York: Norton, 1959). It is surely time that people realized—after Pol Pot, Sendero Luminoso, and the Afghan Mujahideen—how misplaced is this reflexive romanticization of peasant movements.

7. On the Iranian social revolution, see the special issue of *Race & Class* (Summer 1979). On the coup d'état and minority government of Afghanistan, see M. Nazif Shahrani, "Introduction: Marxist 'Revolution' and Islamic Resistance in Afghanistan," in M. Nazif Shahrani and Robert Canfield, eds., *Revolutions and Rebellions in Afghanistan* (Berkeley: University of California, Institute of International Studies, 1984).

8. Azar Tabari and Nahid Yeganeh, eds., *In the Shadow of Islam: The Women's Movement in Iran* (London: Zed, 1982).

9. I have discussed these issues further in the following essays: "Socialism or Anti-imperialism? The Left and Revolution in Iran," *New Left Review*, 166 (November–December 1987); "Populist Revolution and the Islamic State in Iran," in Terry Boswell, ed., *Revolution in the World-System* (Westport, CT: Greenwood Press, 1989); "One Revolution or Two? The Iranian Revolution and the Islamic Republic," in Ralph Miliband,

Leo Panitch, and John Saville, eds., *Socialist Register 1989* (London: Merlin Press, 1989); "Populism, Islam and the State in Iran," *Social Compass*, 36, 4 (December 1989).

10. Hooshang Amirahmadi, *Revolution and Economic Transition: The Iranian Experience* (Albany: SUNY Press, 1990), and "Middle Class Revolutions in the Third World and Iran," in H. Amirahmadi and M. Parvin, eds., *Post-Revolutionary Iran* (Boulder, CO: Westview, 1987); Sohrab Behdad, "The Political Economy of Islamic Planning in Iran," also in *Post-Revolutionary Iran*, and "Winners and Losers of the Iranian Revolution: A Study in Income Distribution," *International Journal of Middle East Studies*, 21, 3 (August 1989).

11. Ellen Kay Trimberger, *Revolution from Above: Military Bureaucrats and Development in Japan, Turkey, Egypt and Peru* (New Brunswick, NJ: Transaction Books, 1978).

12. See Robert Canfield, "Ethnic, Regional and Sectarian Alignments in Afghanistan," in Ali Banuazizi and Myron Weiner, eds., *The State, Religion and Ethnic Politics: Afghanistan, Iran, Pakistan* (Syracuse, NY: Syracuse University Press, 1986).

13. To be sure, civil war, the presence of foreign troops, and persistent external subterfuge are hardly propitious conditions for revolutionary transformation. But inasmuch as two important dimensions of revolutions are changes in class power and the formation of a new state, there has been some transformation in Afghanistan. First, there was a shift of power from the Mohammadzai royal clan to the modern petty-bourgeoisie organized in the PDPA. Second, the traditional rural power structure was disrupted (hence the counterrevolution) by the new state and party. Third, gender relations were an essential part of the program for change, and some progress has been made in the area of women's rights. Fourth, a civil society is emerging with the rise of various associations and "social organizations" independent of the party and government. While the initial revolutionary program could not be fully implemented, the above changes are, in the Afghan context, profound.

14. F. Sanat Carr, "Feminism and Women Intellectuals" (in Persian), *Nazm-e Novin*, 8 (Summer 1987), pp. 56–85. Peter Knauss makes a related case for Algeria, where there existed the perception of emasculation by the French authorities and the *pieds noirs*; see his *The Persistence of Patriarchy: Class, Gender and Ideology in 20th Century Algeria* (Boulder, CO: Westview Press, 1987). Fatima Mernissi raises a similar point in the introduction to *Beyond the Veil: Male-Female Dynamics in Muslim Society*, new edition (Bloomington: University of Indiana Press, 1987).

15. Farah Azhari, *Women of Iran* (Ithaca: Cornell University Press, 1983); Tabari and Yeganeh, eds., *In the Shadow of Islam*; Nashat, ed., *Women and Revolution in Iran.*

16. The term "gharbzadegi" comes from an essay of the same name by the late Iranian populist writer, Jalal Al-e Ahmad.

17. Murteza Mutahhari, *On the Islamic Hijab* (Tehran: Islamic Propagation Organization, 1987).

18. Kaveh Afrasiabi, *The State and Populism in Iran* (unpublished doctoral dissertation, Dept. of Political Science, Boston University, 1987), p. 307.

19. The Iranian Islamists were aware of modern sensibilities. The Introduction to the Constitution mentions women's "active and massive presence in all stages of this great struggle," and states that men and women are equal before the law. (This stated equality is belied by differential treatment before the law, particularly in the area of personal or family law.) Moreover, while they discouraged young mothers from seeking fulltime employment, they did not bar women from the labor market or from elections. All the parliaments since 1979 have had two to four female members. For an elaboration of Iranian women's contradictory positions, see my essays, "Women, Work and Ideology in the Islamic Republic," *International Journal of Middle East Studies*, 20 (May 1988), and "The Reproduction of Gender Inequality in Muslim Societies: A Case Study of Iran in the 1980s," forthcoming in *World Development.*

20. Quoted in Nancy Tapper, "Causes and Consequences of the Abolition of Bride-Price in Afghanistan," in Shahrani and Canfield, eds., *Revolutions and Rebellions in Afghanistan*, pp. 291–305.

21. Ibid., p. 292.

22. The Economist, *The World in Figures 1981.*

23. Tapper, "Causes and Consequences," p. 292.

24. Louis Dupree, *Afghanistan* (Princeton University Press, 1973).

25. Erika Knabe, "Women in the Social Stratification of Afghanistan" (1977), quoted in Tapper, "Causes and Consequences," p. 295.

26. M. H. Kemali, *Matrimonial Problems of Islamic Law in Contemporary Afghani-*

stan (unpublished doctoral dissertation, University of London); cited in Tapper, "Causes and Consequences."

27. Vartan Gregorian, *The Emergence of Modern Afghanistan: Politics of Reform and Modernization 1880–1946* (Stanford: Stanford University Press, 1969 and 1976), p. 244.

28. Ibid.

29. Monique Wittig, cited in Gayle Rubin. "The Traffic in Women: Notes on the 'Political Economy' of Sex," in Rayna R. Reiter, ed., *Toward an Anthropology of Women* (New York: Monthly Review Press, 1975).

30. Tapper, "Causes and Consequences," p. 299. See also the section on "Gender Roles" in Richard Nyrop and Donald Seekins, eds., *Afghanistan: A Country Study* (Foreign Area Studies, American University, Washington, DC, 1986).

31. Tapper, "Causes and Consequences," p. 304.

32. Canfield, "Ethnic, Regional and Sectarian Alignments," p. 89; Nyrop and Seekins, eds., *Afghanistan*, pp. 112–13.

33. Tapper, "Causes and Consequences," p. 304.

34. Kathleen Howard-Merriam, "Afghan Refugee Women and their Struggle for Survival," in Grant Farr and John Merriam, eds., *Afghan Resistance: The Politics of Survival* (Boulder, CO: Westview Press, 1987).

35. Ibid., p. 114.

36. Ibid., p. 314. Catharine A. MacKinnon's dark vision of male domination and forced sex seems an apt description of traditional Afghan gender roles, rather than of the advanced industrial societies to which she refers. See her *Feminism Unmodified: Discourses on Life and Law* (Cambridge, MA: Harvard University Press, 1987).

37. From an editorial in *Kabul Times* (May 28, 1978) quoted in Nancy Hatch Dupree, "Revolutionary Rhetoric and Afghan Women," in Shahrani and Canfield, eds., *Revolutions and Rebellions in Afghanistan*, p. 316.

38. Dupree, "Revolutionary Rhetoric," p. 333.

39. Two studies sympathetic to Hafizullah Amin are Beverly Male, *Revolutionary Afghanistan* (New York: St. Martin's Press, 1982) and Selig Harrison, "Dateline Afghanistan: Exit Through Finland?" *Foreign Policy*, 41 (1980/81). Both authors argue that Amin was basically a nationalist, and that the subsequent label of "CIA agent" by Moscow and Kabul is untrue. Harrison suggests that Amin was desperately trying to make deals with the U.S. and Pakistan so that they would leave his regime and country alone.

40. The best sources on the events of 1978 and 1979 are Raja Anwar, *The Tragedy of Afghanistan* (London: Verso, 1988); Mark Urban, *War in Afghanistan* (New York: St. Martin's Press, 1988); Male, *Revolutionary Afghanistan*; Suzanne Jolicoeur Katsikas, *The Arc of Socialist Revolutions: Angola to Afghanistan* (Cambridge, MA: Schenkman Publishing Com., 1982); David Gibbs, "The Peasant as Counterrevolutionary: The Rural Origins of the Afghan Insurgency," *Studies in Comparative International Development*, 21, 1 (1986), and "Does the USSR Have a 'Grand Strategy'? Reinterpreting the Invasion of Afghanistan," *Journal of Peace Research* (1987); Fred Halliday, "Revolution in Afghanistan," *New Left Review*, 112 (November–December 1978), and "War and Revolution in Afghanistan," *New Left Review*, 119 (January–February 1980); and the many articles by Selig Harrison, particularly in *Foreign Policy*.

41. Quoted in Dupree, "Revolutionary Rhetoric," p. 330.

42. The reinstatement of Islamic family law did not apply to party members. This was first explained to me by a PDPA member and Foreign Ministry official in New York in October 1986. In Kabul in 1989 another official, Farid Mazdak, told me that a longstanding party member had recently been expelled for taking a second wife.

43. Dupree, "Revolutionary Rhetoric," p. 333.

44. ILO, *Tradition and Dynamism Among Afghan Refugees* (Geneva, 1982).

45. Ibid., p. 19.

46. Howard-Merriam, "Afghan Refugee Women," p. 116. Due to its extreme form of patriarchy, Afghanistan has always suffered from an adverse sex ratio, excess female mortality, and sex bias in the provision of food and health. This was confirmed to me by a physician at Indira Gandhi Children's Hospital in Kabul, in February 1989.

47. Ibid., p. 117.

48. Ibid., p. 104.

49. Nancy Hatch Dupree, "The Demography of Afghan Refugees in Pakistan," in H. Malik, ed., *Soviet-American Relations with Pakistan, Iran and Afghanistan* (New York: St. Martin's Press, 1987), p. 383.

50. I have always wondered how the UN could practice cultural relativism in the case of gender relations among Afghan refugees in Peshawar, but preach the Convention on the Elimination of All Forms of Discrimination Against Women. Efforts to obtain answers from various UN officials have yielded unsatisfactory results.

51. Henry Kamm, "Aid to Afghan Refugees, Donors Bend the Rules," *New York Times*, April 2, 1988.

52. Henry Kamm, "Afghan Refugee Women Suffering From Isolation Under Islamic Custom," *New York Times*, March 27, 1988.

53. Ibid.

54. "Leading a New Life", *Afghanistan Today* (Kabul), 6 (November–December 1987).

55. Massuma Esmaty Wardak, formerly president of the Women's Council, is now Minister of Education. Soraya, a founding member of the women's organization and longstanding PDPA member, is president of the Afghan Red Crescent Society [Red Cross]. Other prominent Afghan women are Zahereh Dadmal, director of the Kabul Women's Club, Shafiqeh Razmandeh, vice-president of the Women's Council, and Dr. Soheila, chief surgeon of the Military Hospital, who also holds the rank of General.

56. See references in Notes 1, 8, 15, 19. See also Mahnaz Afkhami, "Iran: A Future in the Past: The 'Prerevolutionary' Women's Movement," in Robin Morgan, ed., *Sisterhood is Global* (New York: Anchor Books, 1984); Haleh Afshar, "Women, State and Ideology in Iran," *Third World Quarterly*, 7, 2 (April 1985).

57. Cultural relativists and communitarians (such as Alisdair MacIntyre) argue for the abandonment of the project of rationally justifying a single norm of flourishing life for and to all human beings, relying instead on norms that are local both in origin and in application. For a critique of this view see Martha Nussbaum, "Non-Relative Virtues: An Aristotelian Approach," WIDER working paper (1987).

Contributors

Henry Abelove took his Ph.D. in history at Yale University. He has taught there, at Brown University, and at Wesleyan University, where he is now Professor of English. He is the co-editor of *Visions of History* (Pantheon, 1984), and the author of *The Evangelist of Desire: John Wesley and the Methodists* (Stanford, 1990).

Julianne Burton is Professor of Literature at the University of California, Santa Cruz. She is the editor of *Cinema and Social Change in Latin America: Conversations with Filmmakers* (Texas, 1986), and the author of *The Social Documentary in Latin America* (Pittsburgh, 1990).

Rhonda Cobham is Assistant Professor of Black Studies and English at Amherst College, where she teaches African and Caribbean literatures and feminist theory. Her work has appeared in *Research in African Literature* and *The Black Scholar,* among other journals and collections.

Lee Edelman, Associate Professor of English at Tufts University, is the author of *Transmemberment of Song: Hart Crane's Anatomies of Rhetoric and Desire* (Stanford, 1987). He has recently completed *Homographesis: Essays in Gay Literary and Cultural Theory* (forthcoming from Routledge).

Marjorie Garber is Professor of English and Director of the Center for Literary and Cultural Studies at Harvard University. She is the author of a number of books and articles on cultural criticism, gender studies, and Shakespeare, including *Shakespeare's Ghost Writers: Literature as Uncanny Causality* (Routledge, 1988), and—most recently—*Vested Interests: Cross-Dressing and Cultural Anxiety* (Routledge, 1991), a study of transvestism in literature and culture.

Sander L. Gilman is the Goldwin Smith Professor of Humane Studies at Cornell University and Professor of the History of Psychiatry at the Cornell Medical College. During the 1990–91 academic year he was the Visiting Historical Scholar at the National Library of Medicine. He is an intellectual and cultural historian who has written and edited over twenty-seven books, most recently *Sexuality: An Illustrated History* (John Wiley and Sons, 1989).

Jonathan Goldberg is the Sir William Osler Professor of English Literature at The Johns Hopkins University. He is co-editor (with Stephen Orgel) of the Oxford Authors *John Milton,* and his most recent book is *Writing Matter: From the Hands of the English Renaissance* (Stanford, 1990). His contribution to the present volume is part of his forthcoming *Sodometries.*

Donna J. Guy is Associate Professor of History and the Director of the Latin American Area Center of the University of Arizona, Tucson. She is the author of a history of the political economy of sugar in Argentina, and of the forthcoming *Sex and Danger in Buenos Aires: Prostitution, Family and Nation in Argentina* (Nebraska).

Geraldine Heng and ***Janadas Devan*** are Lecturers in English at the National University of Singapore. Heng works on medieval and postmedieval romance, and Devan on modernism. They are now collaborating on a study of postcolonial political culture.

Norman S. Holland teaches Hispanic and Latino literatures at Hampshire College. He is completing a manuscript on constructions of masculinity in Spanish-American fiction.

Ann Rosalind Jones is Professor of Comparative Literature at Smith College, and the author of *The Currency of Eros: Women's Love Lyric in Europe, 1540–1620* (Indiana, 1990). ***Peter Stallybrass*** is Professor of English at the University of Pennsylvania, and the co-author (with Allon White) of *The Politics and Poetics of Transgression* (Cornell, 1986).

Ketu H. Katrak is Associate Professor of English at the University of Massachusetts, Amherst. She is the author of *Wole Soyinka and Modern Tragedy: A Study of Dramatic Theory and Practice* (Greenwood, 1986), and co-editor (with Henry Louis Gates, Jr. and James Gibbs) of *Wole Soyinka: A Bibliography of Primary and Secondary Sources* (Greenwood, 1986). Her essays have appeared in *Modern Fiction Studies, The Journal of Commonwealth Literature,* and *Ba Shiru* among other periodicals.

Seth Koven teaches history and women's studies at Villanova University. Now completing *Culture and Poverty: The London Settlement House Movement, 1870 to 1914,* he is also the co-editor of *Gender and the Origins of Welfare States in Western Europe and North America* (both forthcoming from Routledge).

Mary Layoun is Associate Professor of Comparative Literature at the University of Wisconsin, Madison. She is the author of *Travels of a Genre: Ideology and the Modern Novel* (Princeton, 1990), and the editor of *Modernism in Greece? Essays on the Critical and Literary Margins of a Movement* (Pella, 1990). Her essay in this volume forms part of a new book—*Boundary Fixation?*—on cultural responses to nationalisms in crisis.

Valentine M. Moghadam is currently Research Fellow and Coordinator of the Research Programme on Women and Development at the World Institute for Development Economics Research of the United Nations University (Helsinki). She has taught at New York University and Rutgers University, and held a fellowship at the Pembroke Center for Teaching and Research on Women at Brown University. Her work on women and social change has appeared in *International Journal of Middle East Studies, International Sociology, Social Compass, New Left Review, Socialist Register,* and *Monthly Review,* among other journals and collections.

Andrew Parker is Associate Professor of English and Women's and Gender Studies at Amherst College. He is the author of *Re-Marx: Deconstructive Readings in Marxist Theory and Criticism* (forthcoming from Wisconsin), and co-editor (with Sue E. Houchins) of a volume of Selected Papers from the English Institute, *Asymmetries: Problems in the Representation of Race and Sexuality* (forthcoming from Routledge).

Cindy Patton is a critic and activist. She has served as a consultant to the World Health Organization on AIDS-related projects, and has written extensively on AIDS, gender and representation, most recently in *Inventing AIDS* (Routledge, 1990). She is currently working with a research team from the Centers for

Disease Control to produce an ethnography of the effects of AIDS on methadone clients.

Catherine Portuges is Professor of Comparative Literature and Director of the Interdepartmental Program in Film Studies at the University of Massachusetts, Amherst. She has published widely on cinema, psychoanalysis, autobiography and gender, and is the author of the forthcoming *Screen Memories: The Hungarian Cinema of Márta Mészáros* (Indiana).

R. Radhakrishnan teaches critical theory and cultural criticism in the Department of English, University of Massachusetts, Amherst. He is the author of the forthcoming *Theory in an Uneven World* (Basil Blackwell). His essays have appeared in *boundary 2, Cultural Critique, differences, MELUS, Transition,* and other journals and collections.

Mary Russo is Professor of Literature and Critical Theory at Hampshire College. She is the author of the forthcoming *The Female Grotesque* (Routledge), and of many essays in feminist theory and criticism.

Joyce Hope Scott is Assistant Professor of English and African-American Literature at Northeastern University. A former Fulbright Scholar to West Africa, she has published articles on African-American women writers, African-American folktales, and Liberian poetry, and is now completing a critical volume on African-American women writers of the nineteenth and twentieth centuries.

Eve Kosofsky Sedgwick, Professor of English at Duke University, is the author of *Between Men: English Literature and Male Homosocial Desire* (Columbia, 1985), and *Epistemology of the Closet* (California, 1990).

Greta N. Slobin is Associate Professor of Russian Literature at the University of California, Santa Cruz. She is the author of *Remizov's Fictions* (Harriman Institute/Northern Illinois, 1991), and of many articles on modern Slavic literatures and cultures.

Doris Sommer is Professor of Romance Languages at Harvard University. She is the author of *One Master for Another: Populism as Patriarchal Rhetoric in Dominican Novels* (University Presses of America, 1984), and *Foundational Fictions: The National Romances of Latin America* (California, 1991).

Gayatri Chakravorty Spivak is Professor of English and Comparative Literature at Columbia University. She is the author of *In Other Worlds: Essays in*

Cultural Politics (Routledge, 1987), and co-editor (with Ranajit Guha) of *Selected Subaltern Studies* (Oxford, 1988). Many of her recent interviews have been collected in *The Post-Colonial Critic,* ed. Sarah Harasym (Routledge, 1990).

Stephen Tifft is Assistant Professor of English at Williams College. He is completing a book on the status and function of comedy during moments of political crisis, and is editing a volume of essays entitled *Staging Public Outrage.*

Patricia Yaeger is Associate Professor of English at the University of Michigan. She is the author of *Honey-Mad Women: Emancipatory Strategies in Women's Writing* (Columbia, 1989), and co-editor of *Refiguring the Father: New Feminist Readings of Patriarchy* (Southern Illinois, 1990).